The Social History of the People of the Southern Counties of England

George Roberts

bibliolife
old books. new life.

THE

SOCIAL HISTORY

OF

THE PEOPLE OF THE SOUTHERN COUNTIES

OF

ENGLAND

IN PAST CENTURIES;

ILLUSTRATED IN REGARD TO

THEIR HABITS, MUNICIPAL BYE-LAWS, CIVIL PROGRESS, ETC.,

FROM THE RESEARCHES OF

GEORGE ROBERTS,

AUTHOR OF

"THE HISTORY OF LYME REGIS," "LIFE OF THE DUKE OF MONMOUTH," "DICTIONARY OF GEOLOGY," ETC. ETC.

LONDON:
LONGMAN, BROWN, GREEN, LONGMANS, & ROBERTS.
1856.

TO

THE RIGHT HONOURABLE

THOMAS BABINGTON MACAULAY,

&c. &c.

This Work,

INTENDED TO IMPROVE OUR ACQUAINTANCE WITH THE

SOCIAL HISTORY

OF OUR COUNTRY, IN WHICH FIELD HE HAS OBTAINED DISTINCTION;

TO PROVE SUGGESTIVE IN MANY WAYS IN DETERMINING WHETHER THERE ARE OR NOT MANY INESTIMABLE ADVANTAGES ENJOYED BY THE MODERNS OVER THEIR ANCESTORS,

IS, WITH SENTIMENTS OF GRATITUDE AND RESPECT,

DEDICATED

BY

THE AUTHOR.

PREFACE.

THE rare opportunity afforded me of access to archives abounding with new materials for local and general history has furnished employment for the leisure of past years.

Researches commenced in this new field disclosed many particulars of the former condition of our countrymen, the strictness of our borough magistrates, and the general state of provincial civilisation.

These have been made available for the express correction of a very general ignorance of our Social History that prevails.

That great historian Thucydides remarked the existence of the same in Greece; and explains this general weakness of mankind, arising from their receiving alike, without examination, from each other, the reports of past events, even though they may have happened in their own country. And he cites some remarkable examples of incorrect notions possessed by his countrymen, even of affairs of their own time. The same historian concludes with a remark found to be true in every age: — "With so little pains is the investigation of truth pursued by most men, that they rather turn to views already formed."

How many whose attainments in several branches of knowledge are considerable, are totally misinformed about the past. Let us not judge that we have no more concern with this, except as it may furnish us with subjects of momentary interest to beguile a weary hour. No one can meet the present or counsel for the future without turning an attentive retrospect into the former condition and events of his country. The novelist and other writers have created an ideal past, a fanciful conventionality which totally misleads. The object of these pages is to convey a faithful portraiture of bye-gone years, the condition of our countrymen, their manners, and state of progress.

While authenticating our former social condition, the insignificance of our boasted navy and shipping, and of our army, will appear in the clearest light. Our true greatness in the present day then becomes manifest. In another chapter the insecurity of our coasts, owing to pirates, displays a remarkable state of things quite opposed to the opinion of our having always been masters of the seas.

The ignorant of every age and country have shown great unwillingness to admit, and determination, carried even to the use of violence, to oppose novel means by which improvement was to be effected. New plans and manners of doing things have been judged to be wicked. Developments which were matured into what has been now proved to be the greatest of the benefits civilisation has ever conferred, will be found to have been received, not with inquiry, but with clamour and desecration. Potatoes, our most valuable esculent, were branded by some as tending to produce leprosy; and mobs connected that root with a form of religion, and cried, "No potatoes, no popery." Coaches were to cause the ceasing the breeding of hackneys. Spending time in the midst of the refinements of the metropolis was deemed by the learned pedant James I. as very prejudicial to the daughters of our gentry. If they were unmarried, the monarch affirmed they marred their marriages, and if married, they marred their reputations. The use of coal for smelting iron, when the woods began to fail, the ignorant took occasion to assail, and destroyed all the works. Wood was intended, they said, to smelt the metallic ores. But the spirit to resist all change, all progress, was possessed by too many of the higher class, as well as by the ignorant. Good Bishop Latimer preached up archery as a godly art; but the bow has yielded the palm to Lancaster guns and the Minié rifle. Even the leading pure water through pipes into dwelling houses was loudly complained of as an evil, a robbing of the general public. But we need not multiply examples. When the principles of scientific inventions and appliances of all kinds were understood only by a few, novel introductions were often not comprehended at all by the generality of persons. Too many clamoured against the novelty without any consideration of its merits; that it was new was sufficient to engage their opposition and enmity. Now that the meanest objects and materials of the world are made the subjects of analysis and investigation by the greatest minds, what is new begins to be received with some reference to its individual and intrinsic excellence or comparative worth. Mankind would not make progress while they agreed in concluding everything new was not only not good, but positively an abomination.

Even so it obtained with legislation, manners, and many social matters. Their state and bearing yielded to the requirements of this changing world, and the new system become necessary was decried for a time as pregnant with evil.

My illustrations have been sought among the middle and lower classes of borough towns, rather than among those of the metropolis. Royal progresses, and sumptuous entertainments, the doings of the king and the warrior, have been duly recorded in costly tomes, while the inferior condition of the mass of the population, and their poor mode of living, have been totally left out of sight.

What prodigies has not the genius of some men compassed within a few years! They excite, and deservedly so, our admiration, that man, the highest of created beings, has attained to such a pitch of excellence. How many, however, view the results of this progress with widely different feelings. They clearly in their expressions imply, that man is too far in advance of what he should know and practise, and that he is guilty of presumption, and that the Deity views with rival feeling the onward course of invention and science. So was Jupiter reported by the heathens to have been exposed to the aggression of the giants, when Pelion heaped upon Ossa anticipated the prodigies of modern philosophers. Once possessed with this dogma, all advance is viewed as a march to wage war with the divine intelligence. An old farmer said, God made the Old style; man made the New. A Canadian, viewing a steamer ascending a rapid, burst into an exclamation of inquiry, *Est ce que le bon Dieu permettra tout cela?* Are there not many who would arrest the onward progress of man, as not only impious, but as tending to accelerate — and this in the way of punishment — the consummation of all things? They make it to be man's great demerit that he has exalted the divine attribute Mind to a very great degree, and used with wondrous skill the materials of our globe, which, like the living members of the brute creation, were given for his use and convenience, and as an exercise for his intelligence.

Such was the case centuries ago. Old Stow pronounced that some who had indulged in the novelty of his day, — the building of towers to their houses, — had been visited by misfortune, as a punishment for their sinfulness. This consisted in adopting an architectural novelty, and the necessary consequence, the being able to overlook their neighbours.

The warmest friends of the past cannot be blind to the wonderful discoveries of our day. But many of these they assert could well be dispensed with; and they delight in contrasts unfavourable to the new state of things. Love itself, according to them, is become a tame affair, its poetry is turned into prose, and now-a-day forms an episode, rather than the great subject of life. Whereas in bye-gone years treat but of love, and straightways you had to encounter angels, gods, racks, furies, tortures, and to run through all the mazes of metaphorical confusion.

Looking back upon the England of seventy years ago, it seems difficult occasionally to recognise our own country.

My aim has not been directed to the setting the civilisation of one era in contrast, or to array it against that of another. The subject may have induced a belief that this was so, for the remarkable features of the day are occasionally illustrated in juxtaposition.

Many devoid of prejudice have concluded, after due deliberation, that the England of the Tudors, with its common rights, hospitality, and old usages, was a very good England, not exactly that we would bring back if we could, but prosperous and wisely organised by God's good providence, according to the possibilities of the time. Such persons repose much upon the adjustments that society possesses, which are complex, and not to be traced in all their ramifications. Allowing due weight for this working for good, we must arrive at the culminating point after all,—Does the Almighty allow our countrymen to advance in the march of civilisation, using the word in its broadest sense,—in manners and customs, in laws and liberties, in everything that dignifies public and domestic life; or is it that a change only has taken place, and that no real improvement has been effected?

It surely will have been demonstrated in these pages that the whole country presents a wonderful example of amelioration and hope for the future. For wise purposes the Almighty employs his power: his ways are inscrutable.

To discuss why Tudor reigns were less favoured than our beloved Sovereign's, or why the Divine Intelligence did not then effect, through man's instrumentality, the lengths to which material science has since arrived, but chose rather to leave us comparatively dark, would demand of us to anthropomorphise the Divinity and question his justice. Such is not the object of these pages. That the Almighty allows of a state of progress and amelioration, and moreover, that present times possess advantages over the past, is my firm belief. To what extent this is the case falls not within my province to determine. When aiming at conveying a true picture of an earlier England, should I experience the fate, let me adopt the language of Dr. Andrew Borde's distich:—

> After my conscyence I do wryte truly,
> Although that many *men* wyl say that I do lye.

The collection from which this work has been written was commenced many years ago. To enumerate the contributors would savour of ostentation. A genuine love of the subject could alone have carried me through the expense and the toil. Patronage towards carrying on my researches I never experienced. I have met with courtesy which I trust has been reciprocated. May the result be considered satisfactory, and the offering acceptable. Pecuniary consideration is out of the question. The cost of travelling and making researches has been considerable. I have paid for inspection of some of the Records and Wills of my country as if the result were to be my success in an affair of thousands in a court of law, whereas I have only sought knowledge "rich with the spoils of Time."

County historians, many venerable names had not access — without disparagement be it said — to many sources which have yielded to this work. To the plan and design of some of these, my subject, Social History, is quite foreign.

The following list will indicate the sources of much new matter.

Besides my own Collection, I have drawn from the following valuable sources: —

I. The unexplored Archives of the borough of Lyme Regis.

II. The Archives of Weymouth.

III. The Sherren Papers, or part of the Archives of Weymouth, discarded under remarkable circumstances, now the property of Mr. James Sherren, printer and bookseller, Weymouth.

IV. The MSS. Diaries of Walter Yonge, Esq., of Colyton and Axminster, the property of the Author and of the British Museum. The Author's MS. has been since published by the Camden Society.

V. Proceedings in MS. of the Dorset County Sessions between the years 1625 and 1637. Purchased by Mr. Thorpe, and inserted in his Catalogue 1847. [Extracts have been published by Mr. Thomas Hearn, of the Dorset County Chronicle Newspaper, under the signature of "Qui Quondam."*]

VI. Proceedings in MS. before the Magistrates of the borough of Dorchester, from 1654 to 1661. [* As above.]

VII. The History of Castle Combe. Quarto. By

the Right Honourable Poulett Scrope, M.P.; privately published.

VIII. Family Papers; Church Registers, &c.

IX. Collection of the late M. de Gerville, the French Antiquary.

Her Majesty's State Paper Office.

The British Museum Library, Harleian and Cotton MS., &c.

The Bodleian Library.

And other sources, such as County and Borough Histories, &c.

While drawing from these sources, it has been my aim to seek Truth, "Time's daughter." Casual results have not been indicated, I trust, as the intended and legitimate ends; nor occasional abuses as established customs, having no particular school of opinions or politics to serve or advocate.

To enumerate those who have at any time aided in my researches would be just, though an onerous task; but I mention with pleasure the Very Reverend the Dean of Llandaff, J. Davidson, Esq., John Bruce, Esq., the Rev. Dr. Oliver, Sir Frederick Madden, British Museum, R. Lemon, Esq., of H.M. State Paper Office, Mr. James Sherren, Bookseller, Weymouth, J. Waylen, Esq., and some worthies now lost to the world, M. de Gerville of Normandy, and Sir T. H. De-la-Beche.

Many of the woodcuts have been executed by two young ladies, the Misses Eginton, of Perdiswell Cottage, near Worcester, daughters of the late celebrated painter on glass, and sisters of the late Mr. Harvey Eginton, the Elizabethan architect.

Worthing, 1856.

CONTENTS.

THE

SOCIAL HISTORY,

&c. &c.

An Account of Presents made to Great Men, and entertaining them in the West of England on many Occasions, together with the Viands served at Table, &c.; likewise the Manner of their Reception.

JUST as obtains with eastern manners in the present day, so according to established custom in this country, from very early time up to a century or little more ago, no approach to a great man, a magistrate, or courtier was ever made without the oriental accompaniment—a gift. Our early mayors were often suitors for favour, for counsel, for indulgence, and to excuse themselves and their burgesses from accusations brought against them. They were never empty-handed ones.

If a courtier or great country squire was solicited to undertake some troublesome business, a present of some delicacy that abounded perhaps where the applicants came from, or was freely imported thither, might appear to be without objection. A pottle of wine from Gascony, some "broad fish" and "shrimpis" from the south coast, might prove a courteous offering, proper and effective in winning good-will and stimulating the kind patron to energetic exercise of his interest on their behalf. It was not this simple mode of winning favour, but seeking the fountain of justice and diverting the course of its streams, that calls for our animadversion. Presents made to ensure advantages not fairly merited, to exclude the really deserving, are the harbingers and handmaids of corruption. The highest bidder or giver too often gained the desired favour, or even right, that should have been granted without causing the applicant to experience—

"What hell it is in suing long to bide."

The favour of the officers of justice was bought with a a bribe at an early date. In a suit at law preferred by the lord of the manor of Castle Combe in Wiltshire, in 1427, 20*d.* was given to the undersheriff for procuring his friendship.* In a trial of Sir John Fastolf in 1453 there was paid,—

	£	s.	d.
For fee to a clerk to the Justice Yelverton to be attorney for the Lord Fastolf - - - - -	0	1	8
Wine, beer, and pears for a refection to the Judge Yelverton himself - - - - -	0	1	6
Breakfast to the jury after they had delivered their verdict	0	4	7
To the jury for a gift (regardo) for their expenses and labour, as well as to those who were brought as a "tales" *	2	5	0

In the twenty-second year of Edward IV. the mayor and common council of Bristol granted a yearly fee or pension of 40*s.* to Olyver King, the king's secretary, whilst he continued in the office of secretary, and which doubtless was also "for the welfare of the town."

A ready answer may be furnished to one who should inquire how the less opulent, not including those really deficient in means, could win the award of justice against such odds.

The Mayor of Lyme, A. D. 1590, enters for wine and sugar given to Judge Anderson, 3*s.* 4*d.*

In 1605 a calf was given to the sheriff, and two sheep given to the judges at the assizes holden at Marlborough.†

* History of the Manor of Castle Combe, by the Right Hon. Poulett Scrope, M.P.

† Waylen's Hist. of Marlborough.

In 1620 the Mayor of Lyme was directed to ride to the assizes, and there to invite Mr. Sergeant Ashlie to come thither, and to entertain him at the town charge, that his advice may be had touching the charter. It was left to the mayor's discretion what gratuity he would give to the Lord Chief Baron and his men.* When a suit about Pentecostals was about to be tried at the assizes held at Chard in 1621, the corporation sent a purse to the judge, which cost 4*s.*

The renewal of charters was the occasion of much discussion in corporations. The consultation of lawyers and application to courtiers were attended with much expense. Our prudent west-country local legislators found that this system of treating and making presents could not be dispensed with.

	£	*s.*	*d.*
There was paid for entertaining of Sir Francis Ashley from Dorchester assizes - - - - -	1	10	0
Paid more for his horse-meat - - - -	0	10	0
John Newell was paid for 36 yards of fine watered broad dowlas sent to Sir Francis Ashley - -	3	9	0
(Sir F. Ashley's dinner and supper at the mayor's house in 1625 are charged 13*s.* 4*d.*)			
The entertaining the judges by the mayor cost -	15	0	0
For the Lord Chief Baron's horses at Brewer's (Inn) †	1	2	0

While on the subject of bribery, additional facts will confirm us in the opinion that the system was almost universal. Who can have forgotten the disgrace of Sir Francis Bacon, Lord Chancellor of England in 1621? It was currently reported of Sir John Bennett, a judge of the High Commission Court, that he would not only take bribes of both parties, plaintiff and defendant, but often shamefully beg them.‡ Sir Lionel Cranfield, Lord Treasurer, was arrested for taking bribes, two of 500*l.* for the customs, in 1623.‡ The chancellors to the Bishops of Peterborough and Durham were questioned in Parliament, the former for having taken forty bribes!‡

* Corp. Order Book. † Town Accompt Book.
‡ The Diary of Walter Yonge.

It was charged against Richard Tilley, Mayor of Bristol (16 Edward II.), that he required a present from every ship and boat coming to the quay, in addition to what was given to the constable.

The ladies of great officers were infected with the prevailing disorder of their day; and turned their influence into the standard coin of the realm. The Countess of Suffolk, wife of Thomas Howard, Earl of Suffolk, Lord High Treasurer of England, rendered herself very odious by her rapacity in extorting money from all persons who had any business to be dispatched at the Treasury. Both the countess and her husband were confined in the Tower, and fined 30,000*l.* which was reduced to 7000*l.*

Even as with the fashions of a metropolis, so with its vices; when these rage they travel down and spread through the provinces, engage attention, and produce too often by no means bad imitations of the prototype. Fashionable vices are often found to bear a stamp that gives currency to them — the word *metropolitan* ensures a ready adoption. Mrs. Cotton, the lady of the Bishop of Exeter, is reported to have taken in 1610 a fee of 10*l.* from a person "to speak for him."

In 1646 two silver flagons were given to the recorder of Lyme which cost 24*l.*, and two others of like value to Mr. Rose.

When the judges rode the circuit the mayor entertained them on many occasions, as being the head of the corporation, at the town charge.

In 1587 the Mayor of Lyme enters for "The judges' diet, at their being here from the assizes, 30*s.*"

In 1646 the judges were entertained four meals at a cost of 11*l.* 10*s.*, while their hosts paid likewise for their distinguished guests' horse-meat 3*l.* 17*s.* Being upon the subject of the visits (probably by invitation) of the judges, it may be in place to record that their entertainment in 1674–5 cost 15*l.*; in 1676–7 that of my "Lord Jones came to 16*l.* and his men spent at two taverns 4*l.* 10s."

Let me add, for the sake of comparison, that the entertainment of the Dean of Sarum, when he visited his peculiar of Lyme, cost 5*l.* In 1614 the corporation of Exeter paid the mayor of that city 5*l.* towards the great expense he had been at in inviting the judges at the last assizes to dinner.*

Jurymen were openly canvassed and solicited to serve their friends when acting as such. An example of this appears in the case of the Rev. Giles Moore, who wrote the following letter in 1664 to a juryman, with intent to serve a parishioner: —

"Sir, — Because I understand that you are the first and leading man of the jury impannelled for John Wood of this parish, tanner, and my loving friend and neighbour, whose case is to be tried at these assizes, I shall desyre you therefore, as for his owne, so for my sake alsoe, to doe him all lawful favour you may thereon, and to the best of your judgment to serve him therein, whom for your kindnesse therein shewne to him, you will find him no less thankful, than you will find your friend and servant

"GILES MOORE." †

Corruption could require no more effectual process than such personal applications. Each juryman was, by a compromise of principle, to lay up obligation for his future benefit; others were to become corrupt in their turn; and thus a reciprocity of corrupt practices was to be established.

An opinion hastily set up, that bribery was customary and therefore somewhat excusable, is now exploded. Latimer preached against the corruption of receiving bribes in his usually nervous strain: —

"'They all love bribes.' Bribery is a princely kind of thieving. They will be waged by the rich, either to give sentence against the poor: or to put off the poor man's causes. This is the noble theft of princes and of magistrates, — they are bribe-takers. Now-a-days they call them gentle rewards: let them leave their colouring, and call them by their Christian names bribes: *Omnes diligunt munera.* 'All the princes, all the judges, all the priests, all the rulers, are bribers.' What? were all the magistrates in Jerusalem, all bribe-takers? None good? No doubt there were some good." ‡

* Published in Western Times, 1849.

† Sussex Archæol. Coll.

‡ Vol. i p. 123.

And in another sermon we have this anecdote: —

"Cambyses was a great emperor, such another as our master is; he had many lord-deputies, lord-presidents, and lieutenants under him. It is a great while ago since I read the history. It chanced he had under him, in one of his dominiôns, a briber, a gift-taker, a gratifier of rich men; he followed gifts as fast as he that followed the pudding, a hand-maker in his office, to make his son a great man; as the old saying is, 'Happy is the child whose father goeth to the devil.' The cry of the poor widow came to the emperor's ear, and caused him to flay the judge quick, and laid his skin in his chair of judgment, that all judges that should give judgment afterward, should sit in the same skin. Surely it was a goodly sign, a goodly monument, the sign of the judge's skin: I pray God we may once see the sign of the skin in England." *

Justice Hale carried his scruples regarding presents to an extent which exposed him to ridicule from some, and to the imputation of Pharisaical uprightness from others. Thus the Dean and Chapter of Salisbury, having a case to try before him on the Western Circuit, he insisted on being allowed to pay for the six sugar-loaves which, according to long established custom, they presented to him. The acceptance of bribes was common, says Mr. Macaulay †, but never otherwise than as a thing which was disapproved or discountenanced by all good men. The practice of *étrennes* is abolished in France.

See "Madagascar," a poem by Sir William Davenant, quoted by Lord Campbell in his "Life of Lord Keeper Coventry:" —

"Then reconcile the rich for gold-fring'd gloves,
The poor for God's sake, or for sugar-loaves."

The triumphant exposure and punishments of corrupt bribe-takers on a grand scale belongs to the close of the seventeenth century. In 1695 Sir John Trevor, the Speaker of the House of Commons, was compelled to put the question himself that he should be expelled. A bill for securing the right application to poor orphans of freemen of

* Vol. i. p. 130.

† Essay in the Edinburgh Review.

London of funds belonging to them could not be carried without purchasing the support of influential members and of the Speaker himself at a bribe for the latter of 1000 guineas!

Sir Thomas Cook, the governor of the East India Company, paid 167,000*l.* in one year for bribes to members of the House, of which Sir Basil Firebrace took for his share 40,000*l.* Corruption was universal, therefore deemed venial.

These remarks upon bribery and corruption cannot be better wound up than by giving a letter from Thomas Lord Howard, who had been Mayor of Weymouth, to Mr. William Pytt, a diligent promoter of the interests of that borough. The noble writer viewed the system in a business-like way. Before moving in the matter desired, he counted the cost; and formidable did it appear. A great commercial undertaking could not better have been weighed over. The great outlay required to be made was certain: the success doubtful. Without the outlay failure was certain. Thus, at Lyme, to receive 100*l.* for the yearly maintenance of the Cobb, a national work, 68*l.* went in fees and treating!

Thomas Lord Howard to Mr. William Pytt.

1581.

"Mr. Pyt,—I have forborn to write to you and the residue, hoping still to have sent news to your likings; but hereunto I cannot by any means possible bring it to pass, for these many great causes are lets to my labours. First, for doing anything in the Parliament House at the present it was impossible; for when I should have bestowed chargeable sums of money in framing bills, in rewarding them that should speak favourably on them, in gratifying the Speaker and other men of authority, then should I look for a good passage of the bill by reason that Sir Christopher Hatton's countenance and credit would work against it, and surely would overthrow it when it should come to her Majesty's hands; and therefore would I not cast away your money at this time in so [*illegible*] affairs." *

The procuring an annual sum of only 100*l.* for what may

* Sherren Papers.

fairly be called a national purpose occasioned the mayor's accurate rendering of an account for his expenditure and the net proceeds. This detailed matter gains credit for what would hardly be believed, though the scene is laid in the reign of corrupt treating and gift-making.

When we read in Blue Books of returns of sums laid out upon the Cobb of Lyme, we see clearly how deceived the members of the House of Commons have been, except they understood the manner of transacting court business in the Stuart reigns. Sixty-eight per cent. for receiving a sum every farthing of which was greatly wanted! The extortions of Turkish pashas in their little territories of misrule can hardly exceed this example.

A Particular of the Disbursements *of John Ellesdon in the time of his Mayoralty,* 1660, *for the* procuring the Patent *of* 100*l. per Annum, and what was necessary in order thereunto, being for the repairing the Cobb and Sea Walls of Lyme Regis:*—

	£	*s.*	*d.*	£	*s.*	*d.*
Paid for writing the petition to his Majesty -				0	3	0
To a clerk to p'ruse it - - -				0	5	0
For a copy of the old patent - - -	0	12	4			
For new writing and examining - -	0	6	7			
				0	18	11
To Sir Richard Brown for the order of council at two several times - - -				4	0	0
To his clerk at two several times - -				1	0	0
To Mr. Attorney General 5*l.* and to his clerk 40*s.* - - - - - -				7	0	0
To Sir Edward Nicholas for his Maty's. hand twice on the warrant - - -				10	0	0
To his clerk, for each time, 20*s.* - -				2	0	0
To the Signet Office - - - -	4	16	8			
To the Privy Seal Office the like - -	4	16	8			
To the Patent Office - - - -	4	7	6			
To the Hanaper Office - - -	1	18	4			
For a box to put the patent in - -	0	0	8			
				15	19	10
Carry forward -				£41	6	9

	£	s.	d.
Brought forward - -	41	6	9
For a *treatment* on Mr. Hyde and friends, where was also Mr. Yonge and Mr. Strode - - -	8	10	0
Given to several clerks for expedition - -	6	10	0
To my Lord Chancellor's servants - - -	0	7	6
For post of letters - - - - -	0	2	3
For my charges, 34 days at 6*s.* 8*d.* per diem - -	11	6	8
	£68	3	2

Forty years from this date the deduction was forty-seven per cent., then twenty-six, and at last 7*l.*

The magnates of the country were the objects of great attention and worship. When treating of the intercourse between them and our mayors, the mention of the presents made to them will draw forth some remarks illustrative of the times.

Mr. John Tudbold, Mayor of Lyme in 1545, enters: —

"*Item*, paid for a bowe and sheffe of arrows to Mr. Strangways, 5*s.* 4*d.*"

Who will cavil at any mention of our early national weapon, so soon to be disused? At the words bow and arrows who does not appear to be carried back into antiquity in real earnest? Can we not fancy the practising at the butts by our townsmen habited like beef-eaters?

"A potell of wine that Henry Cranley did bear to Mr. Wadham [of Catherston] for to have a copy of the seizing of our harness [armour], 6*d.*"

The above wine must have been of the best kind, perhaps of sack, as it bore so high a price. Some wine is charged only 4*d.* per gallon in 1549.

The Mayors of Lyme had a rich store for the gourmands at their country seats in the *shrimpis*—the word prawn not being then in use. These delicacies were sold at 4*d.* per hundred. Some were sent as a present by John Hassard, Mayor of Lyme in 1550–51, who enters a charge of 4*s.* 7*d.*

"for a venyson sent at Whitsuntide." This was most probably for the great feast, the Cobb Ale.*

Some crabs given to Mr. Poulett were charged from 2*d.* to 4*d.* each.

In 1557 Sanders Davy was paid for himself and two horses to carry broad-fish, now called flat-fish, to my Lord St. John, 2*s.* 2*d.* The 2 cwt. of fish cost 1*l.*, or 10*s.* per cwt.

At this date flat- or ground-fish were taken with baited hooks set along a ground-line called a trot. The trawl-net had not, I believe, been invented. The trawl-net, or trawl, that was first introduced, was not judged to be hurtful. Whenever it may have been first used, it continued without interruption to the year 1631. Afterwards a net of the same name was in use which it was declared destroyed the fry. In 1635 this trawl-net was no longer allowed. Whether the trawl-net of the present century is the same, and when, if so, it was again allowed, are points which I cannot determine.

Whether it was difficult at all times to know what to give, or that some did not from circumstances require the same reception as others, we find that money was presented.

John Hassard, mayor in 1550-1,—

"Paid to my Lord Poulett's parson, to welcome him to town, 6*d.*"

In another entry: —

"Master Polett's clarke" received 5*d.*

There is mention of *Lord Thomas Poulett* at this date. The two entries refer to the same individual. The head of the ancient Poulett family of Hinton St. George, near Crewkerne, about eighteen miles from Lyme, was LORD of the paramount MANOR of Marshwood, and exercised manorial rights in the parish of Lyme. Sir Amias Poulett, when governor of the island of Jersey in 1576, made presents of red-legged partridges to several great men, who much co-

* The fine puddings of Widow Cornwallis, presented to Henry VIII., procured her a fair house and divers tenements of some dissolved priory, as Stow records.

veted that variety of the partridge. The Lord Chamberlain received some March 19.; the Earl of Leicester two dozen, as did also the Lord Admiral. Sir Amias Poulett refers to a great catch of porpoises, then accounted a delicacy. See in the Harleian MS. No. 279. fol. 14., a receipt for making "a pudding of porpoise." In 1491 a large porpoise was sent from Yarmouth as a present to the Earl of Oxford. The fish continued for many years to be prized as a delicacy. Salted porpoise, lampreys, sardines, and stock-fish are all mentioned as articles of food at Southampton in the reign of Edward III. A penny in twelve was paid in Elizabeth's reign at Newcastle as market-dues upon the sale of porpoise and seal, when cut up and sold in pieces. Of every porpoise and seal the head, fins, and numbles were taken in addition.

In 1553 a sugar-loaf was presented to Mr. Waldron of Bovey House which weighed 7 lbs., at 1*s.* 1*d.* per lb.* (7*s.* 7*d.*)

The late Lord Rolle married the last of that branch of the Waldron family. The house remains about ten miles west of Lyme. The sugar-loaf was charged at a high rate, considering the greater value of money in Queen Mary's reign. This article began to be highly prized. The sugar-cane, which had been grown from the year 1148 in Sicily, had been imported into Madeira A. D. 1419. About the year 1503 the art of refining sugar, before called "blanch powdre," was discovered by a Venetian; before which the juice, when selected instead of honey for sweetening, was used as it came from the cane. Only twenty-seven years from this date, in 1526, it was imported from St. Lucar in Spain by Bristol merchants. Let not the present of the Mayor of Lyme be considered as a cheap article produced in abundance in the islands of the West Indies. The sugar-cane was not imported thither into Barbadoes from the Brazils till the year 1641. How surprising the result of official inquiries in the year 1853 into the consumption of sugar! It

* MS. Letter, Hinton House.

amounted to 7,523,187 cwts., or 30 lbs. each individual of the United Kingdom.

Mr. Morys the mayor was paid for a *dinner,* when Mr. Yonge, the ancestor of the baronets of that name, of Axminster and Colyton, and Mr. Wadham, the barrister of Catherston above Charmouth, were at Lyme, 16*s.* 2*d.*; and for wine with the same, 1*s.* 9*d.*

The mayors entertained the illustrious visitors, travellers, and judges, and carefully entered the particular price of each article of food. These civic worthies had the great yron brooche, *i. e.* spit, and the town pewter for any feast; and were doubtless bound to invite the brethren or council to join the festive board. It is only of late years, since the building of the Mansion House in London, that the lord mayors ceased to entertain at their private houses.

The smallest sums expended in the town's behalf are faithfully recorded. Such entries set before us a picture of manners true to the life. How very difficult it was in the reigns of the Tudors to learn what was stirring at critical periods! How embarrassed the leading men of boroughs must have often felt at a time when mistakes endangered personal security and brought punishment from the court! In 1552 Mr. Tudboll had the sum of 5*d.* paid him "for to drink with Mr. H. Wadham" of Catherston "*to hear news* of the proclamation."

How delightful must have been the meeting at the festive board with great men, courtiers, and consequently gentlemen of high station, who knew personally or from friends what was passing in the world! Can anything be paralleled with this in England in the present century? Newspapers diffuse knowledge throughout the land. No circle lives on for days, even weeks, in ignorance of the state of affairs. The wandering *boccough,* or beggar of Ireland, only twenty years ago carried the news to western farms on the projecting promontories of that island, and was a welcome guest. A great man will ever be a desirable guest in a remote provincial town: his manners and station, his knowledge of the latest news, ensure a warm reception; but nothing can make up for the loss of exclusive knowledge and superiority which his equals possessed in the Tudor reigns. Happy meetings were doubtless those when "the jentell meyn weyr entertained." The fare was not to be despised, for we know what the viands were, for reasons before stated. Do we find cause to suspect these were spoilt in the dressing? Rather say of the good Mayors of Lyme,—

> "A cook they hadden with them for the nones,
> To boil the chickens, and the marie bones,
> And poudre marchant tart, and gallingale.
> Well could he know a draught of London ale.
> He coulde roaste, and sethe, and boil and frie,
> Maken mortrewès, and well bake a pie."
>
> CHAUCER.

When entertaining and even feasting great men, did not the mayors sometimes remember at their festive board how courtiers had brought into the west a death-warrant for their civic host, and, the tables cleared, execution had mercilessly followed? Take for example the case of the Mayor of Bodmin, who was thus treated after a dinner at which he had done the honours. This was after the western rebellion about religion in the reign of Edward VI.

The town-feasts, like other matters of which proofs may be adduced, were by comparison humble in the early reigns, such as that of Henry VIII. and his successors. We will quote as an example a venison feast in Edward the Sixth's reign, at Lyme Regis. "Mr. Strangways and Sir Giles Strangways are recorded as kind donors of a 'doe' and 'venyson.' These gentlemen were ancestors of the present Earl of Ilchester of Melbury House near Sherborne, and Abbotsbury Castle."

In an account about 1551 appear particulars of

The COSTS *done upon Mr. Strangways.*

	s.	d.
(The venyson was a present.)		
Baking of the venyson - - - - -	- 1	0
Item, more for a capon - - - - -	- 0	9
" " *jelly* in one entry (*reward* for the venyson)	- 0	8
Carry forward - -	- 2	5

		s.	*d.*
Brought forward	- -	- 2	5
Item, to Mistress Prat for a capon and 6 chicken and motton, and a potell of wine	- - - -	- 3	6
Item, for bread, ale, and beer, and victual of our ladies		- 1	8
Item, for ii. gallons and a potell	- - -	- 1	8
Item, for a potell of sack *	- - -	- 0	6
Total	-	- 9	9

So much occasionally as 3*s.* 7*d.* have been paid for "one that brought a doe from Mr. Strangways;" more than one third of the expense of the whole feast.

The ladies partook, but was this not apart from the company of their civic partners? Why or how could a separate account have been entered for the ladies, had they been at the general table?

Mistress Prat kept a tavern in Lyme. A barrel of olives given to the Mayor of Poole in 1561 cost 8*s.* 6*d.* Saffron was a choice present also.

Pepper and ginger are mentioned in the archives of Southampton in the reign of Edward III.:—

"The saucers dealt in sauces, herbs, and vegetables.
The spicers, besides spices and condiments, sold medicinal drugs."

The wine, ale, and beer appear to have cost about one third of the whole charge, when the viands were purchased sometimes one eighth. This is unlike what obtains in our west country now. The wine at a festive board at a tavern costs more than twice as much as the viands generally, too often more than three times. A civic feast in former days yielded nothing to the revenue; now every gallon of wine furnishes 6*s.* to the country at large for the purposes of government. No music is the subject of an entry. Ten years after this money was paid to the minstrels at the mayor's house when Mr. Wadham was there.

Sir Philip Sidney presented her Majesty Queen Elizabeth with a smock of cambric, the sleeves and collar wrought round with black silk and edged with a small *bone-lace.*

* Wine continued to be sold dearer. Malvesy or Malmsey, in the reign of Henry IV., used to sell 140 gallons for 50*s.* or 53*s.* 4*d.*; by the time of Richard III. the price was 5*l.* 6*s.* 8*d.*

Some routes included towns fated to be put to great charge when the monarchs of England passed either way, to whom a purse of money had to be presented. Swans, with a profusion of other dainties, were served to three dukes at Shrewsbury in 1535, at a cost of *5l.* 18*s.* 2*d.*

Some choice wine, together with sugar, the latter occasionally in very small quantities, suitable it may be to the costly nature of the article, was occasionally presented to great men: thus in 1551 "a potell of sack and *half a pound* of sugar were given to my Lord St. John and the rest of the justices at a cost of 1*s.* 6*d.*" John Hassard charges 2*s.* 2*d.* for wine given to my Lord of Bedford in 1557. The same nobleman was entertained in 1569 at a cost of 3*l.* 9*s.* The business which took him round our west coast was important, and it was a great point with our citizens along the coast to keep him in a temper to view their exertions and occasional privations with a favourable eye.

It is gratifying to perceive proofs of kindly and courteous intercourse between the country gentry and the merchants or tradesmen of the boroughs in a century when great barriers existed around the landed gentry.

The Poulett family lived at Hinton St. George, near Crewkerne. The squire, sometimes a knight, the head of that house, imported his wine from Gascony at Lyme. When the little craft with her expected cargo arrived, the squire rode over, and "my Lady Poulett came to town" with him.

A banquet was furnished my Lady Poulett which cost the town 7*s.* 6*d.* The "shrimpis" and the choice wine were approved of. A kindly feeling was promoted. The burghers directed that no toll should be demanded for the great man's horses between the Cobb-gate and the Cobb, whither these were driven to convey away the wine. Till a settlement was afterwards come to, there were rights along the shore exercised by the Poulett family as lords paramount of the manor of Marshwood, the former property of the Mandeville who accompanied William the Conqueror.

Sir (Amias?) Poulett sent to the mayor and his brother a venison, the charge *for eating* of which was 8*s.* This, rejecting the technical phrase, means the expense of what was set on table with the venison.

The complimentary treatment and presenting wine and sugar in small quantities—for how could much have been carried on horseback?—to great men whose stay was brief was not a costly affair. Occasionally, from whatever cause the departure from usual custom arose, perhaps sickness, or to procure greater convenience, mine host furnished refreshment, and sent in his reckoning to the mayor:—

	s.	*d.*
In 1577 a potell of wine was presented to Lord Mountjoy at a cost of - - - - - -	1	4
And again wine - - - - - - -	10	0
In 1587 wine and sugar to my Lord Zouch - -	2	6

The importance of any business in question may almost be learned from the activity displayed and the value of the presents. The Cobb Act was in agitation in 1585. This was a weighty affair, all important to the welfare of the town of Lyme, which depends so much upon the harbour called the Cobb.

The heavy matters Lord Howard saw in prospect when he wrote to the Mayor of Weymouth about important town business that had to be forwarded, were realised at Lyme. The givers of gifts were not indifferent to the duties before them. A STURGEON was dispatched to the Speaker of the Parliament House for his provision in Lent. The sergeants of the House had sugar presented to them at the same time. The door-keepers of the court at Greenwich, each perhaps like any other Cerberus, required a sop of sugar to be thrown to them. This Madeira sweet, potent as any medicated ball, lulled each to friendly quiet, or lured them to active intercession. The messenger that rode upon this errand may be compared to the Amphrysian prophetess in his treatment of the before-mentioned janitor:—

"Cui vates, horrere videns jam colla colubris,
Melle soporatam, et medicatis frugibus offam
Objicit. Ille, fame rabidâ, tria guttura pandens,
Corripit objectam, atque immania terga resolvit
Fusus humi, totoque ingens extenditur antro.
Occupat Æneas aditum, custode sepulto."—VIRGIL.

The chamber of Exeter agreed, 10th January, 1610, that, on behalf of that city, its burgesses of Parliament should present the *Speaker* of the Parliament, in token of their good will, with a hogshead of Malaga wine, or a hogshead of claret, whichever they thought best in their discretion, together with one *baked salmon-pie,* and Mr. Receiver to be allowed the charge thereof.

The Recorder of Exeter, Mr. Sergeant Hale, received yearly for life, from a grant made A. D. 1600, eight *salmons* of the river of Exe, which was it appears the like number that was allowed to the mayor of that city for the time being. In 1612 every member of the common council that had served the office of mayor was to receive two salmons from the farmer of the fishery, who was to be allowed 3*s*. 4*d*. for each.*

From some entries about a Town or Cobb bill for Lyme we learn that the doorkeeper of the council had his fee.

The corslet was made clean at Lyme in 1587, at a cost of 2*s*. 6*d*. Morren wore the same at Bridport 2 days, 1*s*. 4*d*. Another entry exhibits the policy by which both the corslet and the wearer might find favour in the eyes of those in authority—"Paid for *shrimps* to the captains, 9*d*."

Doubtless, after eating two hundred prawns, the captains judged Morren's corslet glittered brighter in the sun: spots and defects waxed smaller or entirely disappeared.

The judges' diet, at their being at Lyme from the assizes in 1587, is entered as having cost 30*s*.

My Lord Norris came along the shores of the western coast in the spring of 1588, when the great Spanish Armada was expected. This was Sir John Norris, the lieutenant, and his company, who were entertained at supper and wine by the Mayor of Lyme, April 19. 1588, at a cost of 4*l*. 6*s*. 4*d*.

The worthies of a borough sometimes rode to the houses of the landed gentry. They carried a present with them. Thus in 1590 the Mayor of Lyme enters:—

* Published first in the Western Times, 1849.

	s.	d.
Paid for wine we carried with us to Mr. Pollet - -	3	6
Again wine and sugar for Mr. Pollet - -	3	4
Paid for horse-hire and for the serjeant to ride to Mr. Waldron's and for a loaf of sugar, and for CONSERVES given there to Mr. Poppel - - - -	21	1

These sweets called conserves begin to figure in presents.

In 1593 Sir George Trenchard had a box of marmalade and six ORANGES* presented by the Mayor of Lyme, at a cost of 7*s*. Sir Matthew Arundel was entertained, but the cost was only 3*s*. 4*d*.

This worthy lived at Chideock Castle, five miles east of Lyme. He only lunched or partook of a banquet.

The chamber of Exeter, about 1610, used to vote sugar-loaves to Mr. Canon Bodley and Mr. Canon Leach, in token of their approbation of their pains taken in the morning lecture at St. Peter's.

There must, when giving presents becomes a system, be a change as of fashions to be worn. Wine and sugar began to be obsolete. The entries figure in much grander style.

Mr Ellesdon, Mayor of Lyme in 1595, enters: "Given to Sir George Trenchard a fair box of marmalade gilted, a barrel of conserves, orange and LEMONS and POTATES, 22*s*. 10*d*."

The sweet potato, or Spanish potato (*Convolvulus Batatas*), was known in this country before the common potato, which received its name from its resemblance to the Batata.

This plant was introduced into England by Sir Francis Drake and Sir John Hawkins in the middle of the sixteenth century. The roots were about the clôse of the reign of Elizabeth imported in considerable quantities from Spain and the Canaries; and were used as a confection rather than as a nourishing vegetable.

* The first oranges and the first earthen plates were brought from Spain in the reign of Edward I.

Mr. Ellesdon, Mayor's Accomp. 1595.

	s.	*d.*
Given to Sir George Trenchard a fair box of marmelades gilted; a barrel of conserves, orange, and lemonds, and POTATES - - - - - - -	22	10
1595, given to my Lord Marquis (of Winchester) a box of marmelade gilted, containing 7¼ lb. at 2*s.*; a barrel of conserves, containing 4 lb. at 13*d.* the lb.; 4 lb. dry conserves at 2*s.* the lb.; ORANGES AND LEMONS at 6*s.* the HUNDRED - - - - - - -	32	10
Carriage of the same, and the serjeant's charges - -	21	3

On this occasion no ordinary messenger rode with the present to my Lord Marquis, but the sergeant had the choice sweets confided to his care. We have seen what a really expensive thing communication with parts not very distant was: upwards of sixty-four per cent. was added to the original cost for mere expenses of sending a messenger with the sweets.

A letter is extant from Sir Francis Walsingham to a correspondent in the Weymouth corporation, anxiously pressing for the purchase of a quantity of conserves. These western ports must have been the places where these delicacies could be procured. Great men found them very desirable for presents to courtiers and their equals. In 1581 all persons in Scotland, not being dukes, earls, &c., possessed of at least 2000*l.* of yearly rent, that is, of 250*l.* sterling, were prohibited from the use of confections, foreign drugs, and costly spices, which were wont to be lavishly used at weddings, christenings, and other banquets by persons of low estate.

A slight digression may be excused while upon the subject of presents. Officers of rank sufficient to require their presence at the court of a native prince in our Indian possessions, have, according to oriental use, to make a present; and they, by a reciprocity nicely adjusted by an eastern, receive a present in return. Some had laid themselves out to make great profit by this system, till the abuse caused the Company to take the matter into their own hands. The resident has a store from which he furnishes each officer with a strictly suitable present, and into which is carefully put away whatever article has been given in return.

Towns in the road liable to be traversed by royalty had demands made upon the corporations, under certain circumstances, and claims to be considered under other cases, which merit notice.

The harbinger had 1*l.*, the trumpeter 10*s.* and 22*s.*, the macebearer 10*s.*, and the swordbearer 11*s.*

When these sums were paid at Marlborough in the year 1618, there was an entry, for the future guidance of the mayor, to this effect, that these gifts were *by consent* all given out of courtesy only, for that there is nothing due unto any such of his Majesty's servants, unless the king go through the town in state, and then only, as they themselves affirm, are their fees belonging unto them of right by patent.*

The king's brewers and bakers had faggots furnished them at a cost of 10*s.* 9*d.* in 1623. In 1677 paid for herbs and beer when the queen went to Bath, 15*s.*; and in 1687, for rushes when the king came, 30*s.* Presented to the king, 50*l.**

The passing of the royal family and court was viewed as a great misfortune.

The entertaining Lord and Lady Hertford and their followers at Marlborough in 1617 cost 30*l.* 7*s.* 4*d.*

Having treated of the reception of great men at dinner, let us see what a dinner for the company, that is, the corporation, was when they were without illustrious guests—such as is charged at about 16*s.* There was paid for an *accounting dinner,* or one given after making up the Cobb accounts at Lyme in 1608, clearly at a tavern:—

	£	s.	d.
Item, for a chine of beef - - - -	0	3	4
More for a rib of beef - - - - -	0	2	0
Carried forward -	£0	5	4

* Waylen's History of Marlborough.

		£	s.	d.
	Brought forward -	- 0	5	4
More for a piece of boiled beef and CABBAGE	-	- 0	1	4
"	leg of mutton - - -	- 0	1	4
"	loin of mutton and bruse (broth) -	- 0	1	8
"	capon - - - -	- 0	1	6
"	couple of wigeons - - -	- 0	1	4
"	fruit and cheese - - -	- 0	1	0
"	fire - - - - -	- 0	0	4
"	bread and beer - - -	- 0	3	4
		£ 0	17	2
"	potell of Malaga wine - -	- 0	2	0
"	" " claret " - - -	- 0	1	4
"	pint of Canary " - - -	- 0	0	5
"	quart of claret " - - -	- 0	0	8
		0	4	5
	Total amount - -	£ 1	1	7

CABBAGE was, half a century after this, introduced into Scotland by Cromwell's soldiers. It was deemed worthy of mention here. Did Sir Anthony Ashley of Wimborne St. Giles introduce the cabbage, a vegetable unknown to our countrymen, or did the specimen at his feet on his tomb indicate that he introduced that variety? Hudson Turner states that the cabbage tribe was known in the middle ages.

In 1623 Nicholas Somers's wife was paid for a dinner for the company, *i. e.* the whole corporation of Lyme, 16*s.* 8*d.* (N. B. This was about the sum each member of the town council had to pay for his dinner at the Cups' Hotel, in the same town, in 1846.)

The same year Mr. John Drake and his company came for a burgess's place in the room of Mr. Robert Hassard, deceased. Their entertainment cost 16*s.*

This is strikingly in contrast with some feasts resulting from elections in this century, given in the same town, when about 500*l.* were spent.

The frugality of receptions, when business had to be discussed, was very great. Sir Walter Erle and his brother, who had been very active about procuring ordnance for the government for Lyme, dined with the mayor in 1625 at a cost of 6*s.* 8*d.*

Afterwards, the same year, Sir Walter Erle and his brother and their men were entertained at two meals, when they came to receive instructions for the Parliament, 1*l.*

A larger party, consisting of Sir Walter Erle, Sir Richard Strode, Mr. Recorder and others, were entertained, 27th July, 1630, by the mayor, who charged 1*l.* 13*s.* 8*d.*

The great feast of Lyme does not come within the bounds of this article. It was paid for by those who partook, and was not an entertainment given by the town.

The entertainments, made up from presents and contributions of friendly gentry, render nugatory any attempts to ascertain the real cost.

While on the subject of homely and other feasts given or paid for, it will be appropriate to show the bill of fare in the west for two receptions of royalty in 1625.

King Charles I., when riding into the west to Plymouth, stopped to dine at Ford House near Teignmouth, 15th September, and again on his return, 24th September.

The king lay the 14th September at Hinton House, the seat of Mr. Poulett (soon after created Lord Poulett), while the Duke of Buckingham, the Earl of Holland, the Earl of Derby, Sir Robert Killigrew, and many other gentlemen lay at Ash House, the seat of the Drake family, at Musbury, between Axminster and Colyton, near the coast road from Dorchester to Exeter.

The Earl of Essex and the Earl of Arundel passed westward soon after, all being on their way to review the fleet and land forces at Plymouth under orders for sea.

Ford House was the seat of Sir Richard Reynell, a learned and eminent lawyer of the Middle Temple.

His Majesty returned to Ford House 24th September.

A great proportion of the viands were sent in, as it was termed, for the king and great lords' entertainment.

There were at the —

FIRST ENTERTAINMENT.

A buck and a side of venison from Mr. Reynell of Ogwell.
A buck from Mr. Poulett of Hinton House.

Fish.

3 dories,
2 mullets,
2 gurnets,
25 peels,
2 salmons,
8½ pair soles.

Game and Fowls.

140 partridges,
7 pheasants,
61 chickens,
46 capons,
10 ducks,
14 pullets,
6 geese,
71 turkeys,
28 pigeons,
1 pea-hen,
2 mallards,
2 green plovers,
8 plovers,
1 gull,
36 larks,
38 rabbits,
1 hare,

Besides mutton, veal, lamb, and
6 artichokes.

Whole expense of what was purchased, 28*l.* 13*s.* 5*d.*

SECOND ENTERTAINMENT.

A buck from Sir Amias Poulett.
A doe from Mr. Luff of Torre.
A hunted teague (a doe of one year old) from Dr. Clifford.
A mutton, killed and dressed, from Mr. Beard.

Fish.

160 mullets,
42 whitings,
4 salmons,
7 peels,
7 dories,
21 plaice,
26 soles,
48 lobsters,
550 pilchards, &c.

Game and Fowls.

69 partridges,
5 pheasants,
12 pullets,
14 capons,
112 chickens,
4 ducks,
6 geese,
30 sea-larks,
11 curlews,
258 larks,
1 heath-poult,
2 nynnets,
6 sea-pyes,
1 stone-curlew,
4 teals,
3 pea-hens,
2 gulls.

Substantials.

6 oxen and kine,
5 muttons,
2½ veals.

Several entries of ribs of beef, quarters of mutton, chines, tongues, a side of lamb, and a Westphalia gammon.

Liquors.

2 hogsheads of beer,

1 barrel Canary wine,

35 quarts white wine.

Whole expense, *55l. 5s.* *

The visits of royalty made to private individuals when on a tedious journey to execute a necessary public duty, might well have passed with universal approbation. The travelling and the feasting brought no addition to taxation, while many great men gratified themselves and neighbours with a feast in this monarchical country of which the king partook in person.

The gentlemen of the country party must have been greatly dissatisfied with the state of affairs. An incident will prove the existence of this feeling.

Mr. Pyne, a country squire, having a company of guests at his table at his seat at Curry Malet, talked very irreverently of the king, saying to one who had boasted of having seen the king at Mr. Poulett's at Hinton House, "Then hast thou seen as unwise a king as ever was; for he is carried as a man would carry a child with an apple. As for meeting him at Mr. Poulett's, that is nothing, for I might have had him at my house; he is to be carried any whither. Before God he is no more fit to be king than Kirkwright." This Kirkwright was a well-known simpleton.

For these words the government wished that Mr. Pyne should be hanged, drawn and quartered. Chief-Justice Richardson said, though the words were as wicked as might be, they did not amount to treason. This saved Mr. Pyne.†

Mr. Hugh Pyne the counsellor, Mr. Jo. Symes, and some others of Somersetshire were soon after put out of the commission of the peace. In 1627 Mr. Hugh Pyne was committed for saying the king was stripped and governed by a company of upstarts.‡

* Lysons' Devon, from Chapple's Collections.

† Lord Campbell's Lives of the Chief-Justices of England, vol. i. p. 391. Life of Richardson.

‡ Diary of Walter Yonge. Camden Society. Edited by Geo. Roberts.

About the close of James I.'s reign presents continued to be made. In 1621 the Mayor of Lyme sent, on the part of the town, a sugar-loaf weighing 15 lb., and oranges and lemons, to Lord Poulett, 1*l.* In 1625 a pottle of Canary wine to Sir Thomas Fooke, Sir Walter Erle, and the Lord Treasurer's steward, 2*s.* each. In 1631 one hundred oranges and lemons to my Lord Poulett, 14*s.* 4*d.* In 1631 sent to Salisbury to the Doctor, *i. e.* the prebendary Dr. Roger Bates, 6 lb. conserves and a little sugar-loaf, 15*s.* 10*d.* — 1*l.* 7*s.* 10*d.*

The gentry who met at Charmouth in 1665, to settle some differences between the town of Lyme and the hundred, were entertained on each occasion at an expense of 2*l.* 7*s.* 4*d.*, 7*l.* 6*s.* and 6*l.* 15*s.*

Sir John Strode, of Parnham, had a present sent to him of wine, and the carriage, 7*l.* 6*s.*

A dinner for the corporation in 1672 cost for—

	£	s.	d.
3 peck of flour - - -	- 0	3	0
12 quarts of Canary - -	- 1	4	0
11 quarts of white and claret -	- 0	11	0
Mutton and lamb - -	- 0	6	0
Dressing and other charge -	- 0	10	0
Rose-water, sugar, and salt -	- 0	0	9
	£2	4	9

The Lord Chief-Justice and his colleague were entertained at Lyme in 1674–75 at a cost of 15*l.* A bill for shell-fish enables us to ascertain the prices paid in Charles II.'s reign for these delicacies. Mr. Walter Tucker, mayor, paid for the judges, for—

	£	s.	d.
30 lobsters - - -	- 1	10	0
6 crabs - - - -	- 0	6	0
100 scallops - - -	- 0	5	0
300 oysters - - -	- 0	4	0
50 oranges - - -	- 0	2	0
	£2	7	0

	£	s.	d.
For wine - - - -	0	6	6
" beer - - - - -	0	5	0
" fire - - - - -	0	1	6
" horsemeat - - - -	0	5	6
" oats - - - - -	0	10	8
" 3 pocket of beans - - -	0	4	0
	£1	13	0

The judges on the circuit had so many presents of venison, fruit, wine, &c., that these half kept their table. These presents were discontinued after the year 1784, when so much was subscribed for the defence of the nation then expecting invasion. Till the passing of the Municipal Reform Act the corporation of Gloucester always sent each judge in spring a salmon and a house lamb, and in summer a salmon and a whole sheep. The corporation of Oxford still continue their present to each judge of white kid gloves, edged with gold lace and ornamented with gold tassels.*

	£	s.	d.
In 1676-7 Mr. Robert Cawley, mayor, entertained my Lord Jones, as he styled the judge, at an expence of - - - - - - -	16	14	2
Thomasin Davy †, keeper of a tavern, entertained the judge's men - - - - - -	0	9	4
Bowdidge do. - - -	4	1	0
	£21	4	6

Soon after the Duke of Monmouth had marched out of Lyme, the "Suadadoes" frigate captured the duke's "Pink" and "Dogger."

	£	s.	d.
Captain Trevanion was entertained at a cost of -	1	7	0
Captain Dyer was honored by a treat - - -	0	7	0
Sixty men, who landed 29 June, 1685, from the frigate, and whose services were likely to be required, had three loaves of bread, and three cheeses - - -	0	10	0
Beer from Goody Collier - - - -	1	3	0
A gratuity among them in cash - - -	1	15	0

* Notes and Queries, No. 319.

† Her pigs ran at large in the streets; but being found to have prejudiced the graves, they were presented by a jury.

When the "Bloody Assize" was in progress Judge Jeffreys and his four attendant judges partook of a dinner extraordinary for its expense. The mayor had long to contend with the objectors to his accounts. Mr. Gregory Alford wrote, at the end of his mayoralty, that this dinner had cost him more than 40*l.* Gammons, wine, and a sturgeon had been omitted.

As the subject leads to mention of the articles of food for entertainment the following may be deemed not irrelevant:—

The bill for attendance at the Dorchester Assizes in 1686 of Mr. John Bragge, the town-clerk of Lyme, presents this novelty—the article COFFEE is charged 2*d.* This may have been drunk at a coffee-house. Coffee was introduced from Turkey in 1650.

An advertisement in the Mercurius Politicus, Sept. 30. 1658, instructs how "That excellent and by all physitians approved *China* drink, called by the Chineans Tcha, by other nations, *tay* alias *tee*, is sold at the Sultana's Head Coffee-house, in Sweeting's-rents, by the Royal Exchange, *London.*—"

There was a "cophee-house" in St. Michael's-alley, Cornhill, about 1657.* Tea, coffee, and chocolate were placed under the excise. There was no tax upon these commodities when imported, but when made into drink, as tea was, at 8*d.* a gallon, and sold at these houses.

In Charles II.'s reign great men travelling into the west were honoured by a TREAT, and not always *entertained* at dinner. The latter often required a delay beyond what was convenient to the host and his guest. The treat was given at a tavern. The junket was a treat given *al fresco* in the country.

The Earl of Stamford highly commended the *great treat* the town of Lyme had given him after the Oxford Parliament.

In 1699 the treating the Duke of Bolton and his attendants at the "Three Cups," Lyme, cost 1*l.* 5*s.* 3*d.*; besides this honour, the guns were fired twice, 13*s.* 3*d.*

* Quarterly Review, 1854. Eccleston.

In 1702 the Earl of Rochester's entertainment cost 4*l.* 12*s.*; firing the guns, 5*s.*

In 1703 there was spent in treating the Barons of the Exchequer and Judge of Assize, 1*l.* 9*s.* 3*d.*

In 1708–9 for the gentlemen appointed to survey and report the condition of the Cobb to S. Butler, a tavern-keeper, 7*l.* 7*s.* 11*d.*

The practice of purchasing wine from a wine merchant to be drunk at a feast held at a tavern now obtained: Nathaniel Gundry was paid for wine on the above entertainment of the government officers, 1*l.* The gallon of sack required for the mayor's feast under the will of Thomas Tudbold, and paid for out of the Tudbold rents, cost, in 1687, six shillings.

In 1734–5, entertaining the Bishop of Bristol, 10*l.*

That the great who happened to be at Lyme and the corporation should feast at a tavern about this time need not surprise us, when we learn that the town pewter had been sold; and thus the mayor was deprived of the means of furnishing out his table as of old: 24 platters, 6 pie plates, 2 pasty plates, 72 trencher plates, weighing 411 lbs. at 7*d.* per lb. fetched 11*l.* 19*s.* 8*d.*

The principal cause, however, which worked the change, was the low state of the town of Lyme, like that of Weymouth, owing to the altered circumstances of trade, and the different class of individuals that filled the civic chair. Many lived in houses where the great spit and the town pewter would not have been in place. A change from the private residence to a tavern became indispensable.

At Marlborough, when that town flourished, by the LIII. law of the borough, made in 1627, this evil was provided against in the following language by some prescient local lawmaker: "If a mayor neglect to occupy a reasonable house during his term of office, he shall be fined 50*l.* in addition to losing his fee, and be disfranchised in the room of another more fit man."* This was good against the meanness of a miserly mayor; but inefficient where a town

* Waylen's History of Marlborough.

was in such a declining condition that no residents able to feast their municipal brethren could be found.

In the years 1680 and 1703 a cook and a barber received their freedom at Youghal, county Cork, in Ireland, on condition that they would respectively dress the mayor's feast and shave the corporation gratis![*]

Little tavern accounts may enlighten us as to the varying manners of the age. Some bills prove that the progress had not been towards refinement. At a feast, 5th November, 1737 (say for twenty persons), at a tavern there is charged for —

	£	s.	d.
Ordinaries - - - - - -	1	10	0
Wine - - - - - - -	2	6	0
Beer, CIDER, and ale - - - - -	0	8	10
Candles and tobacco - - - - -	0	3	6
Beer, gunners, and drummers - - - -	0	3	4
For firing - - - - - -	0	1	6
Sugar, lemons, and glasses - - - -	0	14	0
Wine after the bill delivered - - - -	0	6	0
Beer, firing, and tobacco - - - -	0	1	10
	£5	15	0

Sherry wine, in a commercial point of view, dates from about this time.

No bill for feast or treat at any place, of all examined for this article, was found to have any mention of CIDER as used at table, and charged for with beer and ale before this one.

In 1746–7 appear two novelties in the bill of a corporation dinner — a dish of lobsters and *prons* (prawns), previously called shrimps, 3*s.*, and a bowl of PUNCH (large) 5*s.* A bottle of wine, 2*s.*, only was used. Beer, ale, and cider, 10*s.* 4*d.*; a foreign ham, 12*s.*; an English ham, 7*s.* The gunners, beer, and wood for the bonfire made the bill amount to 7*l.* 14*s.* 6*d.*

It is a proof of sense in our old corporation heads that they were anxious to obtain the advice of clever professional men respecting the sea-works. When Kane William Hor-

[*] Notes and Queries, April 1. 1854.

neck, Esq., was engaged in making anew the harbour at the mouth of the River Brit, called Bridport Harbour, he was invited over and consulted.

	£	s.	d.
A treat was given to Mr. W. K. Horneck in 1744 at the "Three Cups," which cost - - - -	1	11	6
A messenger to Bidport to ascertain about the time for ordering the treat - - - - -	0	1	0
Chickens and *spring-grass* to young Mr. Horneck -	0	6	6

The honour of the freedom of Lyme Regis was conferred upon this civil engineer in 1744.

When the town of Lyme was reduced to its lowest state, a desire to honour remarkable occasions and striking events by a feast at some one of the two principal inns was made manifest. In 1760–1 no less than 40*l.* were expended in celebrating the King of Prussia's beating Count Daun, the taking of Belleisle, Pondicherry, &c., and in providing the boys with furze and wood for a bonfire.

In many boroughs no notice is taken of great persons, and feasting is discontinued for the best of reasons, because the funds are in a low state. Conviviality is believed to have been productive of union in a borough and in a parish. If there is but little for a feast now and then, there can be no funds for grand entertainments of great men, their attendants, and horsemeat.

The mention of the town broche or spit recalls to mind that indispensable prime-mover of the same with its savoury charge, the turnspit dog, a breed now rarely seen. Without his friendly or compulsory labours the due progress of dinner was arrested as much as if the millstream were diverted from its course, or the steam-engine of a mill had exploded. Some seventy years ago cooks and their underlings were seen running about the city of Wells with great inquiries each for her truant. Some one just arrived from the country had seen a frolicsome young midshipman giving fifty turnspit dogs an excursion upon the neighbouring Mendip hill. The spits could not be turned, and the necessity of the case prompted each cook to provide other viands as a substitute.

The improved jack caused the breeding of turnspits to be discontinued.

Having treated of the presents made, and viands served up to great men, let the manner of their coming, and the style in which they were met and welcomed be deemed worthy of some slight notice. This will present a contrast with the manners of the present day.

In order to give an idea of an ordinary reception of a great man, the following picture has been drawn from a digest of many instances recorded:—

Where great men rode through the country honours were expected to be paid by towns to them, and there was seldom occasion of complaint, so fond boroughs would seem to have been of maintaining a character for making such a display. The highways, properly lanes, were mended. The great man's time of arrival on horseback having been ascertained, some seven or eight hundred horsemen rode out to accompany him to town; but three or four hundred formed an especial escort, and these wore white waistcoats, and had rods or wands in their hands. Musicians tooted as they marched.

The mayor and principal corporators presented wine and sugar. Some of the principal inhabitants proffered all their houses contained, and had wood from their premises carried out to make a bonfire in honour of the great man. While this was burning the townsmen stood round, and the best drank the health of the honoured visitor: the lower in station were treated with beer.

The above picture is one of peaceful tribute by the whole town of respect and the highest honour. When in Charles II.'s reign towns were divided, the bonfire-scene assumed a different aspect. In the midst of this joyous festivity of complimenting and drinking of healths, a determined party came to disturb the quiet and harmony and to quench the bonfire. This interruption would at all times call forth the fiercest elements of discord; but, to excite a greater ferment, the foremost carried vessels not applied in domestic economy to any but undignified uses, and selected these purposely in order to produce a *casus belli;* whereupon a fearful riot at once ensued.

If the great man went to church, a path was swept all the way; a voluntary was played on the organ when he entered; and the sermon with the whole service was like a reception as we may fancy in a Roman basilica. When all went off pleasantly, eulogium and panegyric were the only sentiments heard; to assist in which Scripture was ransacked and dextrously wrested. When there was opposition, an unfriendly preacher assailed the great man, and perhaps drove him from the church with his immediate friends. The rioters stayed to curse the preacher with the bitterest imprecations, and to accompany him home with these and dreadful threats.

Supper was a favourite meal for the assembling of the great man's friends. Inferior partisans, distinguished for great zeal, and even daring, were introduced after the cloth was removed, and words of encouragement were addressed. The Duke of Monmouth's stereotyped phrase was, "Thou art an honest fellow: thou deservest encouragement." The great man generally hunted, and also rode round the bowling-green, the place of resort for many years, which was full for the occasion. The Quakers were fond of presentations, and spoke with their hats on language of adulation, though not couched in the usual strain. "We are all for thee" is a phrase that could not be exceeded in clearness of expression, though the sentiment might have been extended into the domain of hyperbole. The latter figure was too often used when the time was truly "a drunken and a roaring one."

Vails to Servants.

VAILS given to servants, vestiges of the ancient *largesses,* made the visiting at great men's houses a very expensive affair.

Bishop Hoadly visited the Duke of Marlborough at Blenheim, together with Sir Richard Steele. On going away, they had to pass through an army of laced coats and ruffles in the hall, and as the bishop was preparing the usual fees, "I have not enough" cried his companion, and, much to the episcopal discomposure, proceeded to address the footmen; told them he had been much struck by the good taste with which he had seen them applauding in the right place at some theatricals up-stairs, and invited them all gratis to Drury Lane Theatre, to whatever play they might like to bespeak.

A colonel of engineers relates an anecdote of his grandfather, a man of engaging manners, who was a resident of the city of Hereford, and who was invited frequently to dine at the palace with the bishop. When taking his departure at night for his own house, the servants used to assist him, each having contrived to present some article of his dress, hat, coat, stick, gloves. On one occasion this officer having an old pair of gloves, and disgusted at the thought of the money he had already given to the domestics, made a present of the gloves to the bearer of them. Having repeatedly refused the bishop's invitation, his lordship fancied there had been some cause of affront; so he asked the reason of so many refusals. With great candour, the invited guest said he could not afford to eat so costly a dinner. The good bishop was startled, and, upon asking for an explanation, was told what the average cost was of dining at the palace and doing as others did. The bishop was forcibly struck at this, and could then account for the absence of others. He at once took measures to remedy the evil.

When vails were given the servant inquired as much about his proposed master's doings and habits as the master now does into those of the servant that offers. This is said to be the case in some parts of the sister kingdom. "Pray sir," said James, a deceased gentleman's butler, to a rich master in want of a servant, "how often do you entertain, and how many do you invite at a time?" The gentleman said, "Once a week; I see eight friends at dinner." "Then, sir, I am afraid your place will not suit me: I should not like to engage where there is not company twice a week.'

Certainly the man was right, if his wages were little in consequence of vails, to be sure that these were likely to be adequate or remunerative.

In giving vails to the servants it must be apparent that there ought to be some graduated rule observed in the distribution, as the recipients, however deserving, filled various offices, not equal in point of degree or estimation. And such was carefully observed by a Sussex gentleman, Mr. Timothy Burrell. His ratio for the distribution of 3*l.* 0*s.* 9*d.* is appended. With a round of visitors behaving with equal generosity throughout the year the sum each domestic received would have compensated for low wages which were given at the close of the seventeenth century. Can we expect that all servants were exempt from the ordinary feelings of humanity? no; we must allow to them their share of the common weakness of mankind. They lavished beyond all doubt an extra share of attention upon those who were very liberal, and must too often have made a distinction to the prejudice of those who had not given with the same bountiful hand. This made a great house furnish a comparison with an inn.

	£	s.	d.		£	s.	d.
Mr. Johnson -	0	10	9	Brought forward -	2	5	9
Chambermaid -	0	10	0	Under-cook - -	0	2	6
Cook - -	0	10	0	Boy - - -	0	2	6
Coachman - -	0	5	0	Under-gardener -	0	2	6
Butler - -	0	5	0	Nurse - -	0	2	6
Chief gardener -	0	5	0	&c. &c.			
Carried forward	£ 2	5	9	Total, -	£ 3	0	9

Mr. Burrell enters on one occasion 10*s.* 6*d.* to the servants of a relation's family without specifying how it was to be shared.

The honoured person upon whom certain court distinctions have been conferred is still called upon to pay certain fees, in which the servants of the royal household receive in stated portions their ancient largess or vails.

The early Visits of Stage-players.

EVERY supreme civil functionary of borough towns in the south of England had much to enter in his accounts, owing to the visits of the earliest perambulatory stage-players. The mayors were mixed up with the performance, the locality and the licence. We shall learn how intimately the borough magistrates were obliged to enter into the circumstances of the scenic exhibition, to which many of them were little adapted by previous taste or education.

The date of the first visit of a company of stage-players to the west—whether earlier than Henry VIII.'s reign or not—has not been ascertained.

The visit of my Lord Admiral's players to Lyme Regis proved a memorable event in the year 1547.

These performers played at Richard Leonard's house; clearly an inn or public house. The Mayor Thomas Ellesdon used an expression which will require some remark.

This worthy ordered that 1*s.* should be paid *towards these players.*

The entertainment must have been well attended; for the town had to bear a light burden by comparison with that on other occasions.

The travelling party occasionally fixed the sum which they demanded for their performance.

A collection was made, or entrance money paid, as in the case of the Duttons in the year 1593, when 7*s.* 6*d.* was gathered, and the deficiency, 12*s.* 6*d.*, was made up by the town. This amount was doubtless much grudged, as the performance began to be odious to a party.

Some companies of stage-players demanded more than others, as being retainers of noble personages, while others were more humble in their demands, being, as Percy supposes, only strollers. The Duttons received at Lyme 1*l.* The players of great men, or "Lordis players" had 10*s.* given to the company by the Earl of Northumberland in

1512.* These were retainers or menial servants of particular noblemen, who protected them in the exercise of their profession. Many occasionally turned strollers.

Though it is usually believed that no female performers were found, or were allowed to act in the reign of Queen Elizabeth, yet it is a fact that there was an exception. We read of the "unchaste, shameless, and unnatural tumbling of the Italian women." †

They played early in the afternoon. There were penny benches. There was little aid derived from the *mise en scène*. None of the many adjuncts of the modern country theatre could have been available. The party walked from town to town, and perhaps, as in the metropolis, acted their parts in the inn-yards or in a barn, if the weather proved inclement.

Besides the penny benches, there were seats for which *2d.*, *3d.*, and even *6d.* were paid in James I.'s time for admission. Tobacco, wine, and beer made play-going expensive. The audience at a play, as at church, smoked.

The popular drama preceding Shakspeare was low, tentative, inartificial, yet amusing.

All with our early dramatists was of purpose and forethought, and they gave to the English language a literature which is a marvel among nations.‡

The first true English comedy is Ralph Roister Doister, written by Nicholas Udall, master at Eton, printed at least in 1551. The next is Gammer Gurton's Needle, about 1575, composed by John Still, afterwards Bishop of Bath and Wells.

Players were licensed by Queen Elizabeth and James I. The licence of James I. to William Shakspeare himself and the players his fellows authorised them "to use and exercise the art and faculty of playing comedies, tragedies, histories, interludes, morals, pastorals, stage-plays and such like."

A few entries from the archives of Lyme are appended.

* Regulations of the Household of Algernon Percy, the Earl of Northumberland. Lond. 8vo.

† See Archæologia for 1855.

‡ Athenæum, No. 1432.

The poppit players visited the town in 1569, and the Queen's jester received 3*s.* 4*d.* the same year. In 1567 Sir Thomas Neville's and my Lord of Worcester's players had each 2*s.* 2*d.*

In 1569,—

		s.	*d.*
Lord Mountjoy's players	-	1	6
The Queen's	-	5	8
My Lord of Exeter's	-	2	6

In 1577,—

			s.	*d.*
My Lord of Leicester's players,	17 Oct.	-	7	0
Mountjoy's,	13 Dec.	-	2	6
Certain players,	20 April	-	4	0
Lord Suffolk's players,	6 Sept.	-	3	0

In 1589,—

		s.	*d.*
The Queen's tumblers	-	6	6
Queen's players	-	10	0
Lord Sherborne's	-	2	8
Lord Essex's	-	2	6

The distance from the metropolis caused some of the mandates of authority to be tardily obeyed and the doings of more important corporations to be imitated after some interval of time.

We may instance the case of Bonner, Bishop of London, who in the year 1542 (33 Henry VIII.) issued a proclamation to the clergy of his diocese prohibiting all manner of common plays, games, or interludes to be played, set forth, or declared *within their churches or chapels.*

What a curious scene must Lyme have presented in 1558! The Queen's Majesty's players had arrived and proceeded to play their piece in the parish church. The corporation contributed 4*s.* 5*d.* We may suppose that money was taken at the doors by some official of the mayor, who ascertained the deficiency to be as above.

Was the performance on this occasion very offensive to the authorities, or to the town generally? There is no trace of any expression to that effect. At this date the decided disapprobation of many against such performances in the sacred edifice may not have been pronounced in this country town. Probably the players presumed upon their licence from the Queen's Majesty, and the mayor and his brethren did not venture to come into collision with them.

The time was near at hand when many entertained a perfect horror of the profanation of the church fabric.

Speaking of the minister, Cartwright the Puritan, in allusion to the church service, writes, "He posteth it over as fast as he can galloppe; for eyther he hath two places to serve, or else there are some games to be playde in the afternoon, as lying for the whetstone, hethenishe dauncing for the ring, a beare or a bull to be baited, or else a jackanapes to ride on horsebacke, or an interlude to be plaide; and if no place else can be gotten, this interlude must be *playde in the church.*" *

There is an entry in the church register of Syston in Leicestershire in 1602 of 12*d.* paid to Lord Morley's players, because they should not play in the church.

We learn that at Leyden in 1608 the authorities of the city allowed W. Pedel, a comedian, to exhibit various beautiful and chaste performances with his body, without using any words, in the church of the Bagynhoff, provided he cease during the preaching of God's word, and that the poor orphans there have half the profits.†

At the present time, in the United States of America, where there is a town of recent growth which has not been able to raise a hall for the purposes of lectures, the church is used for the delivery of such a means towards knowledge.‡

In New Zealand travelling parties go to the churches and make them answer the purpose of eastern caravansaries.

The players continued their perambulations; but at length their visits were very disagreeable to some of the ruling

* Admonition to Parliament, by Thos. Cartwright, A D. 1572.

† Minutes of the Council of Leyden, 18th Nov. 1608. — Notes and Queries, Jan. 29. 1853.

‡ Old England and New England, &c., by Alfred Bunn.

bodies, who, like the Wickliffite reformers, took part against the stage.

It was in 1575 that the Lord Mayor and aldermen expelled the players from the City, when the Blackfriars' Theatre was built.

Provincial municipal bodies began to discountenance popular, scenic, and other exhibitions. It was determined at Leicester, in 1582, that no fee or reward should be given by the body towards any bear-wards, bear-baitings, players, plays, interludes, or games, nor any players to be allowed to play at the town-hall. The authorities still hesitated to interfere with those who came with a special licence for dramatic performances, granted by the Queen or the lords of the Privy Council. Though they did not venture to forbid any performance in such a case, they so contrived matters that the injurious effects arising from it should be circumscribed, —they determined that the acting should be witnessed by the mayor and his brethren *only*. They considered themselves play-proof.

In 1586 the Mayor of Leicester provided Lord Worcester's players, eleven in number, with a dinner as an inducement to proceed without playing. They notwithstanding afterwards asked to play at their inn, and were told "the mayor willed them not to play at this present Friday, for that the time was not convenient." They, however, said they would play, and went through the town with drum and trumpets. They afterwards submitted themselves for their injurious expressions to the mayor, begged him not to write against them to their master, and had permission to play; so that they told their audience the mayor allowed them to do so, and they were sorry for the words that had passed.*

The feeling in the west of England against stage-plays ran very high, and terrible stories were circulated against such in order to deter persons from attending the performance.

* Shakspeare Society's Papers, vol. iv., communicated by Mr. Halliwell.

A volume printed in 1585 * has a written account of "certain players of the migratory kind, who were acting at Exeter upon the stage the tragical story of Dr. Faustus the conjuror. As a certain nomber of devils kept every one his circle there, and as Faustus wás busie in his magicall invocations, on a sudden they were all dasht (put out, alarmed), every one hearkening other in the eare, for they were all persuaded there was one devell too many amongst them; and so after a little pause desired the people to pardon them, they could go no farther with this matter: the people also understanding the thing as it was, every man hastened to be first out of dores. The players (as I heard it), contrarye to their custom, spending the night in reading and in prayers got them out of the town the next morning."

Many were the stories fabricated with pious intention to effect what was conceived to be a good object.

Walter Yonge, Esq., of Colyton, records in 1607, from persons at Lyme, who had come out of France, how at Lyons a terrible thunder-storm had burst upon a theatre, where the representation of the Last Judgment Day was begun to be shown, and had killed the greatest part of the people present. That magistrate's abhorrence of all scenic exhibitions, stage-plays, interludes, masques, mixed dancing, &c., was so great, as to lead him to believe that "they tended to the high provocation of God's wrath." †

Many of the corporations having adopted the opinions of the Puritan party in the reign of James I., they did not hesitate to lay out their money in order to save their borough from the profanation of a performance.

15th November, 1621, certain players licensed under the King's Privy Signet arrived at Exeter. Mr. Receiver was ordered to pay them the sum of 40*s.* as a gratuity, and not to be suffered to play.

A few examples from Lyme will further illustrate the practice of that day.

* See Gentleman's Magazine, Sept. 1850.

† Diary of W. Yonge, Camden Society.

	s.	d.
1621. Given to the players not to play here - -	6	8
1623. Given to John Jones, who had a license to show feats of activity, to depart the town by consent of the company (*i. e. the corporation*) - - - - -	2	0
1624. Given to the Lady Elizabeth's players to depart the town without playing - - - - -	5	0
1633. Given unto stage-players for sending them out of the town - - - - - - -	5	0

Intemperate views with respect to religious opinions are to be expected at this date. Men ran into extremes, and in nothing more so than with respect to stage-plays.

Ignatius Jourdan, twice the representative of Exeter in Parliament, and who laboured for a bill to punish adultery, had great influence in that city. He prevailed upon Valentine Carey to speak to James I. respecting these plays and sports, upon which he entertained a strong opinion. King James at once declared he "would hang the fellow." Carey had much to do to pacify the king, who considered he was interfered with.*

Archbishop Williams, the Lord Keeper, although supposed to favour the Puritans, incurred, writes Lord Campbell, great scandal with that sect by encouraging stage-plays. He used to have the players down from London to Buckden. The Midsummer Night's Dream was exhibited there on Sunday, 27th September, 1631; and some write that on that very day an episcopal ordination was held, so that the play was for the amusement of the young priests. Bishop Hacket asserts that Archbishop Williams did no more in recreating himself with diversions than he had seen Archbishop Bancroft do at Lambeth. King James's Book of Sports, commanding all good Christians and churchmen to play at football and other such games every Sunday afternoon was read during the morning service in every church and chapel in the kingdom.

A case brought before the Michaelmas sessions at Bridport, in 1630, proves the matured hostility between the Puritan party and any travelling showmen.

* Communicated by the Rev. Dr. Oliver.

The complaint made set forth that William Sands the elder, John Sands, and William Sands the younger, and about nine others, wander up and down the country with certain blasphemous shows and sights, which they exercise by way of *puppet-playing:* and are now, as the constables of Beaminster and other inhabitants state, come to that town; and have set up their shows of puppet playing and feats not only in the day-time, but late in the night, to the great disturbance of the townsmen there. The attraction must have been great, for the complainants state they cannot keep their children and servants in their houses by reason they frequent the said shows and sights late in the night in a disorderly manner.

These travelling show-people commenced their performances in the evening after the agricultural and clothing population had left their work, in which they are imitated by their successors in various lines.

The preacher of Beaminster, a character distinct from the minister of the parish, who probably had no licence, assailed Sands and his show in the Sunday's sermon. The discourse ended, Sands and two of his company pursued the preacher from the church to his house, entered it, and "there challenged him for his sermon, and gave him threatening speeches." That this was allowed by the population proves that the great majority favoured the showman.

The constable reported a brawl between Sands and a townsman; upon which the court, considering the great dearth of corn and other victuals, and the extremity likely to come on the poor by reason of the said dearth, and also two several proclamations, by which his Majesty commands the law to be enforced against such wanderers, ordered Sands to remove on the following Monday, and to depart out of the county, and if found again in the county to be taken before a magistrate and committed to the next assizes.*

How the travelling parties fared after the Restoration has

Mr. T. Hearn, "Qui Quondam."

been treated of by the writer * whose valuable contributions have been already acknowledged.

"The natural consequence and reaction of the excessive austerity and rigidity that prevailed was manifested in the extreme laxity in regard to Sabbath observances, and in the customary use of offensive language, into which the people rushed immediately after the Restoration, and the traces of which are not even yet obliterated from national manners; as also in the eagerness with which they resorted to the amusements of all kinds which, after having been long forbidden, were now sanctioned and encouraged by official authority and royal example. Recreations were promptly provided for the people, and itinerant exhibitions of every description were speedily to be found traversing the country, offering the temptations of mirth and novelty. Dorchester of course was not unvisited by the conductors of these undertakings.

"On the 6th of October, 1660, it is recorded that William Darrant came 'to this towne to shew the dauncing of divers creatures on ropes and dogs, pretending a licence from General Munck.' A copy of the licence is given, purporting to be under the Royal Signet, authorising Darrant to show publicly throughout the realm 'a morin, ape, monkyes, and other foraigne creatures;' and dated 'at our pallace at Westminster ye 27 day of March, in ye 13 [12] yeare of our reigne.'

"After the Restoration rope dancing and tumbling were very favourite amusements amongst all classes of the peeple. One of the most celebrated of the rope dancers and managers of tumbling companies about this time was Jacob Hall, of whom an account is given in Grainger's Biographical History. He and his company were occasionally engaged 'to express the height of their activity in tumbling and the like' before the sovereign, in the Lord Mayor's pageants in London.

"A somewhat similar application was made on the 9th of November following, when Richard Arris desired leave to show puppet-plays under a licence from the master of the revels, authorising him to 'make shew of a puppet-shew called Patient Grizell, with music and six servants.' This licence is dated on the 15th June, 1660.

* Mr. T. Hearn, the "Qui Quondam" of the Dorset County Chronicle, from MS.

"And on the 8th February following there was another application to 'make shew of a shew called Crispin and Crispianus,' under a similar licence.

"These puppet-shows,—plays performed by means of small wooden figures, of which Punch is now the last lingering representative,—or, as they were anciently termed, 'motions,' were very favourite spectacles with our ancestors. They are of very early origin, and in the times of the Papacy were exhibited by the priests and monks, and were confined to religious subjects, being nearly allied to the 'mysteries' and 'pageants,' notices of which so frequently occur, and the history of which is so full of curious interest. During the rule of the Commonwealth they were strictly forbidden, together with all other dramatic representations and amusements; but, as is here seen, they sprang again into active existence immediately after the Restoration, under the countenance and authority of the master of the revels,—an office created by Henry VIII., and at this time filled by John Herbert, and afterwards bestowed upon Charles Killigrew. Both the touching and sad story of 'the patient Griselda,' and the tale of the two brethren of 'the gentle craft,' were especially favourite 'motions' with the public. The municipal authorities of Dorchester, however, appear to have sturdily retained much of their accustomed severity of tone, and all these applications were refused; and in one instance we meet with the following quaint allegation of motive:—

"'May 17. 1661.—Richard Pavey of London of St. Giles in the fields coming to town this day to shew a motion of the witches of the north is told that we have noe waste mony for such idle things and is denied to shew here att his perill.'

"On the 5th of June, 1661, occurs the following notice of one of the ancient mountebanks, a class who became extinct only since the commencement of the present century; itinerant quacks, who combined the attractions of tumbling and merry-andrewism with the dispensing of medicines, powders, pills, and potions, sure specifics for the cure of tooth-ache, ague, colic, fever, and all the natural ills, that flesh is heir to:—

"'This day Richard Amyas desired Mr. Mayor's licence to sett up a stage to shew feats of activity and to sell druggs under culler of a licence from ye master of y^{e} revells.'"

The power vested in the hands of magistrates was sometimes stretched beyond all bounds.

A company of vagrant showmen were taken up by the constables at Lewes in 1694, and conveyed to a ship for the sea-service.

Ship of War of the 15th Century. (Harl. MS.)

Early Shipping and Maritime Affairs.

POPULAR ignorance is perhaps displayed upon no subject more than upon that of the state of the early maritime power and resources of our country. Visit our sea-ports in the British Channel, and listen to what the inhabitants delight in telling of the former condition of their trade, the size of the shipping, and, more than all, the foreign ports with which intercourse was maintained. At the words Barbadoes, Guinea, Barbary, Newfoundland, and the Straits it is concluded that the interests of the port have declined. This is not surprising, as none but large vessels now trade thither.

When it is objected that the depth of water was insufficient, we are told the sand has collected; but, under any circumstances, there was indisputably a brisk foreign trade carried on at many ports where there is none in the present day. The halo of antiquity being thrown around the ships of the Plantagenets and Tudors, they loom large through the mist.

When were there not vessels on either coast of the British Channel? Cæsar found 220 assembled, high out of the water compared with his own craft, all of oak, sails of prepared skins, anchors fastened to iron chains in part, if not altogether for cables. We may perhaps compare these to modern stout French fishing-luggers. They were gathered from Britain and the Gallic coasts, and could stand a knocking-about. The wicker-boats, talked of as navigated by northern heroes, would have disappeared before a channel off-shore wind during a summer night. Who can gravely assert that our climate has experienced any change?

In Richard I.'s expedition to the Crusade in the year 1190-1 there were 13 dromons, 250 ships of the second class, and 53 galleys, accompanied by a vast number of barques and other vessels used as transports.

The siege of Calais, like a certain recent modern siege, was a great operation. There were 733 ships carrying 14,956 mariners, or 20 to each ship.

We read of	Bayonne	furnishing	15	ships,	495	mariners.
	Spain	"	7	"	148	"
	Ireland	"	1	"	25	"
	Flanders	"	14	"	133	"
	Guelderland	"	1	"	24	"

The king had 15 ships called "his own," manned by 419 mariners.

As to the names of the several classes of vessels there is some confusion. Dromons were so named from their speed. Carracks were large vessels, as were Grand Niefs. What shall we say of busses and barges but that they were inferior in class? Vissers were flat-bottomed, for the transport of horses. Ballingers were for a light draught of water.

Henry III. had a great ship of 80 tons called the "Queen." John Blanchbouilly had a license to trade with this ship of the royal navy, if we may use such an expression, paying a rent of 50 marks.*

Rudders were first in use about the reign of Edward III. Fire-pence were the sum of 2*d.* paid by each vessel when beacons were maintained by the Cinque Ports. Fire-beacons were established on the south coast A.D. 1325 from a fear of the French and of Queen Isabella.

Ships in the fleet of Edward III. (A.D. 1373) were not more than two or three in number that measured 200 tons; most of them were from 40 to 100 tons each.†

Our subject lies with the shipping of the ports of the Channel individually and in detail, so that many points upon which error exists may be cleared up. General history wants much aid from the local pioneer: he brings the accurate knowledge the former needs.

Another source of error should be pointed out, which is a parallel with that of descanting only upon the scenes of grandeur witnessed in royal and lordly halls, entirely overlooking and confounding all the transactions of private life. This is the dwelling upon the shipping of William Cannynge, the famous merchant of Bristol, and that of this city generally.

Cannynge's Mark.

Bristol was a very great emporium, that furnishes no just comparison with the majority of our sea-ports. William of Worcester tells us of the ships there in his time, about A.D. 1480. William Cannynge, who founded the church of St. Mary Redcliffe, where his tomb appears, had ten ships built at his expense, which measured 2930 tons. One is said to

* Sussex Archæol.

† Weale's Papers on Engineering.

have been of 900 tons, others of 400 and 500 each. These were marvels, but not most probably of English build. The large ships in use are supposed to have been purchased of the Venetians, Hanseatics and the Genoese.* When John Taverner of Hull built a ship as large as a carrack in the year 1449, no such vessel had been constructed before in England.

Henry V. had built some dromons, or large ships of war,

A Ship of War, A.D. 1588.

at Southampton, as is said, such as the world had never seen before.†

Besides Cannynge's ships, there were at Bristol the

	Tons.
Mary Grace - - - -	300
Le - - - - -	360
George - - - - -	200
Kateryn - - - -	180
Mary Bryd - - -	100

* Anderson's History of Commerce.

† Pictorial History of England.

	Tons.
Cristofer - - - -	90
Mary Shernman - - - -	54
Leonard - - - - -	50
Mary of Bristowe - - -	

Thomas Strange and others had some ships likewise.

The value of shipping per ton about this date was, 1*l.* 10*s.* or 2*l.*

A small Craft.

Accurate investigation of the details of borough history has enabled us to attain some definite estimate of the im-

A trading Vessel.

portant terms SHIP and MERCHANT. We now style a three-masted vessel having square sails on each mast a *ship;* and a trader in an extensive way of business a *merchant.* In the Tudor reigns every kind of craft was set down under the general term of *ship,* as every dealer or tradesman was

A Merchant Ship.

under that of *merchant.* This has mislead many. There can be no fair comparison between the ship and merchant of Queen Elizabeth's and her present Majesty's reign. *Shipping* and *trading community,* or inhabitants that were engaged in trade, and some of these in a very small way, would be the modern equivalents.

This point is dwelt upon, as much of the erroneous account about former greatness, as sea-ports and places of trade, has arisen from a misconception of these terms. Let these be wrongly interpreted, then accounts of sea-port towns under the Tudor sovereigns, their "ships" and "many rich merchants," sound very grandly. Nineteen ships and fifty-four merchants at Lyme, A.D. 1578, are an example of this use of words. Every detail is given in "an assessment towards the charge of the Q(ueen's) ship" at *5d.* in the pound.* This was the odious grievance known as ship-money.

"The ships throughout the realm as they were found in

* Archives of Lyme Regis.

1568 by the vice-admirals of the counties, and certified to the Lord Admiral and Lords of the Council," is the subject of a MS.*

How valuable are these old returns in all their formality towards the undeceiving us as to early naval grandeur.

The "sayles of topemen," referred to at this period are sail of ships carrying topmen, that is cross-bowmen and engineers, who were placed in the battlemented tops, where their services were very marked in battle.

It is interesting to compare the returns.

	Topmen.
Poole, 2 ships of 100 tons a-piece - -	- 10
Lyme, 1 " " " - - -	- 12
Hampton Water and Portsmouth - -	- 10
Plymouth, 8 ships from 400 to 110 tons - -	- 20
Dartmouth, 4 " 400 to 100 " - -	- 20
Falmouth - - - - -	- 4
Weymouth - - - - -	- 8
Bridgwater - - - - -	- 6
Salcombe - - - - -	- 6.
Lynn, in Norfolk, 2 hulks of 100 tons a-piece -	- 8

Martin Frobisher sailed 8th June, 1567, to discover the north-west passage, with two barques of 25 tons each.

Ships of Lyme Regis, A. D. 1578, *from an Assessment in the Archives.*

	Tons.		Tons.
The Golden Ryall	- 110	Brought forward	- 564
Jonas -	- 60	The Demon -	- 30
Swallow -	- 60	Gallant -	- 27
Dove -	- 58	Lion - -	- 22
Flower de Luce	- 60	Edward -	- 18
Bravo -	- 32	John Pley -	- 16
Sweepstake -	- 56	Elizabeth -	- 12
Minion -	- 48	Mayflower -	- 14
Angel -	- 40	Robert -	- 12
Primrose -	- 40	John of Lulford	- 8
Carry forward	- 564	Ships 19, tons	- 724

* Harleian MS. 168—249.

The ships and ballingers of Poole were about this date (1574) twenty in number.

In the year 1575 there were only 135 ships in England above 100 tons; and only 656 vessels between 40 and 100 tons.

The navy contained twenty-three ships, most of which should properly be called vessels.

Sir Francis Drake had sailed the year before with five vessels, the largest not being of 100 tons, for the circumnavigation of the globe. Sir Humphry Gilbert explored the coast of America in the "Squirrel" of 10 tons.

It was the small size of the craft navigated by the earliest and truly heroic discoverers that caused storms to be deemed so formidable. Early accounts of storms that drove the ships out of their course, and threatened all with loss of life, &c., have given rise to an opinion that seas were more tempestuous in former centuries than they now are. The solution of such an inquiry is to be sought for in the small size of the vessels employed.

Maritime matters are somewhat different to what obtained when the "Mary Rose" sunk in 1545, carried her stone shot. Our armaments proudly rule, and every craftsman is called into requisition to furnish something to that extreme aggregation of human industry—a modern ship, except a stonemason.

Much is to be learnt from A Remembrance for Sir Françis Walsingham for the Town of Lyme Regis, A. D. 1586.

"The number of ships, masters, and mariners belonging to and using the pier and town there.

"There are belonging to the said pier and kept going in voyages in the trade of merchandise by the merchants of the town and country thereabout, 23 barques and pinnaces.

"There is belonging and dwelling in the town there, of able and skilful mariners, besides masters of ships able to take charge, 108 mariners.

"There are able masters to take charge of ships, 18 masters.

"There are dwelling within four miles of the said town of

Lyme, which are kept going in voyages by the shipping of Lyme, 80 mariners.

"So there is maintained and kept going in voyages by the shipping there, within the town and without, 206 mariners." *

Besides the information to be derived from this document in other respects, the data which it affords to estimate the value and importance of Lyme in relation to the country at large, are very valuable.

In Bree's work it appears that the number of ships had declined since the reign of Edward III. He gives the number of ships, as they were then styled, in 1589.

	Above 100 tons.	Under 100 and above 80.	Under 80.
Dorset	9	1	51
Devon	7	3	109
London	62	23	44
All England	-	-	- - 180

In Thompson's Illustrations of the History of England the seamen of this country, in 1582, were computed at 14,295, and the vessels at 1232, only 217 being above 80 tons. Then it appears that about this time Lyme had a 53rd part of the number of *shipping* of all England, and with Charmouth, and a few parishes round, a 69th part of the *seamen*. Even London, that present mighty mart, had not six times as many vessels! Previous to 1613 there were not more than 10 vessels of 200 tons belonging to the port of London. By the year 1640 the number of seamen in England was tripled; and in 1831 England and Scotland had 22,000 merchant vessels.

In 1591 a survey of the vessels belonging to Poole was taken by order of the queen, which furnishes additional confirmation of the smallness of the ships.† These would now be set down as small vessels. Only three very small craft, of the whole shipping of the only port of Dorsetshire,

* Harleian MS. vol. 368 fol. 124.

† Sydenham's History of Poole.

POOLE, were unarmed. A whole volume could contain nothing more conclusive as to the insecurity of the seas.

The Ships of Poole A. D. 1591, *with the Tonnage and the Ordnance.**

Name	Tonnage.	Fowler.	Saker	Mynion	Falcon.
The Castle of Comfort - -	70	- -	2	2	2
Grace of God - -	50	- -	- -	1	6
St.tts Bonaventor - -	60	1	- -	3	2
Sea Flower - - -	50	- -	- -	4	2
Sea Bright - - -	60	- -	- -	- -	2
Angel - - - -	55	2	- -	- -	2
Lion - - - -	60	- -	- -	4	4
Eagle - - - -	50	- -	- -	- -	3
Edward - - -	40	- -	- -	- -	5
William and John -	45	- -	- -	- -	4
Primrose - - -	30	- -	- -	- -	2
May Flower - - -	30	- -	- -	- -	1
Barque Lambert - -	24	- -	- -	- -	1
Margaret of —— - -	26	- -	- -	- -	1
Marygold - - -	20	- -	- -	- -	1
Hopewell - - -	18				
(*Defaced*) - - -	24				
Carvel - - - -	25	- -	- -	- -	2
Peter - - - -	14				
Sithe - - - -	25	- -	- -	- -	2
New Barque - -	40	- -	- -	- -	4
	816	3	2	14	46

Insecurity may not have been the sole cause why so many pieces of ordnance were mounted in the small vessels of Poole. The pieces borne by each craft are carefully noted, and the reasons are assigned why this was done, and why a similar survey of other ports would be beneficial. There was a custom of selling good and serviceable ships to foreign countries, and also ordnance; so that ships set out upon a voyage with ten or twenty pieces of ordnance, and returned with only half that number, the others having been sold to foreigners; by which our enemies were strengthened.†

A place where small vessels, or luggers, were to be found in any number, whether for trade or fishing, was dignified in Tudor reigns with terms that are apt to mislead, and which

* Sydenham's History of Poole. † Ibid.

The Great Harry.

have misled. In Borde's Book of Knowledge, published about 1542, among the "more noble havens" is Brighton, a fishing town only, and other inconsiderable sea-ports. A lugger of seventeen tons is not in the present day classed as a vessel, but as small craft. At certain seasons such craft are hauled up upon the beach, and at great labour, which has to be repeated in the launching. This might take place anywhere, but the presence of these craft does not establish a harbour.

The year 1588 brought the exciting news of the coming of the Spanish Armada. In April, General Sir John Norris, Sir Henry Ashley, Kt., and George Trenchard, Esq., accompanied by other justices, rode from Weymouth to Lyme, to view and make a report—enter the view as it was termed —of the state of the sea-coast. As this worshipful party proceeded they called to consult with them the most skilful seamen, both for information, and generally respecting the Armada and the nature of the bays along the coast, as to

A Galley, A. D. 1588.

the facilities they might afford for the landing of the enemy's forces.

Supper and wine were furnished at Lyme "to my Lord Norris, the lieutenant and the rest of the company, 19 April, 1588, at a cost to the town of 4*l.* 6*s.* 4*d.*" The mayor and his brethren partook of the repast. It was a stirring occasion. English loyalty was called forth in an unexampled degree. Should we muse upon the alarm of the time, let us not forget an interesting fact, that General Sir John Norris used to say, he wondered he could see no man in the kingdom afraid but himself. Viscount Wimbledon, who relates this anecdote on a subsequent breaking out of war, makes this reflection, "the danger of all is, that a people not used to a war believeth that no enemy dare venture upon them; which may make them neglect it the more, for that their ignorance doth blind them." * We cannot help concluding that Sir John Norris's experience of the valiant overmuch, was at table over the pottle of sack. The beacons and preparations must have greatly alarmed the country.

Sir John Norris, taking a comprehensive military survey of the country, did not overlook the great earthworks near the borders of Dorset, Somerset, and Devon. Had the worthy general taken a different view, many of our fine

* Park's ed. of Noble Authors, vol. ii. p. 309.

British remains, afterwards occupied by the Romans, might have been so altered as to have lost their interest. As it happened, the following conclusion was adopted: "Old intrenched camps in the country could be strengthened, but to little purpose, as they are not placed in situations to stop an enemy." * Fancy a Maiden Castle, a Pilsdon Hill, or a Hembury Fort surrounded by Spanish chivalry and held by our county muster men!

Sixty men were ordered at Blanford to be sent to Lyme by Mr. Strangways, furnished, "twenty shot, twenty bows, the rest bylles." By *shot* we are to understand men provided with fire-arms. In the same MS. there is an order for "shott to be horsed to watch the coast." Thus armed, riding officers were anticipated in the sixteenth century.† These hoblers or light horsemen were to fire the beacons, which had been erected in profusion upon the summits of the coast-hills. Understanding men were to be appointed to this service; for on previous occasions men of another stamp had fired them when there was no enemy, and had alarmed the country without occasion!

On the approach of the enemy the whole force was, according to Sir John Norris's advice, to assemble at Weymouth, except such as was appointed for the guard of particular places.

The whole of the English navy at the time of the ever-memorable Spanish Armada in 1588 consisted of only twenty-three ships, some of which would now be called vessels.

		Tons.		11		Tons.
There was	1 of	1000	There was	1 of		350
	2	900		1		330
	2	800		1		300
	2	600		1		200
	2	500		8	from	120
	2	400		—	to	50
	11		In all	23		

* Sir John Norris, his Account of the State of Dorsetshire, its Fortifications, &c., anno 1588. Lansdown MSS. 113. No. 37.

† Harleian MS. 3324. No. 6.

The largest ship carried only 40 guns. Before the end of Queen Elizabeth's reign the ships of the navy numbered only forty-two.

Contrast our shipping with that of the great Italian maritime republic in her flourishing condition: —

Venice had 3000 vessels;
17,000 seamen;
300 ships, carrying 8000 seamen;
45 galleys, 250 men each.*

The hiring an auxiliary force to join the Royal Navy, the pay and authentic information will prove interesting. It is amusing to learn the smallness of the tonnage.

Among the merchant craft, or coasters that formed part of the gallant fleets that served under the Lord Admiral and the Lord Henry Seymour, on the seas against the Spanish forces, collected 13th December, 1588 †, were —

Tons.		Master.	Men.
60	The Revenge of Lyme - -	Richard Bedscodge,	30.
90	Jacob - - -	- -	40.
60	Thomas Bonadventure -	- -	30.

Among those vessels with Sir Francis Drake were —

Tons.		Master.	Men.
60	The Elizabeth Drake - -	Thomas Seelye,	30.
140	Bean - - -	John Yonge, Gent.	60.

This Thomas Seelye was probably a relative, if not the father of the gallant man Thomay Ceely, who as governor defended Lyme Regis in 1644. John Yonge was a gallant gentleman of a good family, whose two mansions were in Colyton and Axminster.

With the Lord Admiral † were —

15 ships, from 800 to 600 tons.
27 " 400 to 20 "

With Sir Francis Drake —

33 ships, from 400 to 30 tons.

* Libel of English Policy. Macpherson, Pictorial Hist. of England.
† Harleian MS. 168.

Weymouth sent—

	Tons.	
The Galleon	100	
Catherine	60	
Heath Hen	60	
Golden Lion, or the Royal	120	volunteered.
Sutton, a bark	70	volunteered.
Expedition	70	volunteered.

The cost of employing merchant shipping was as follows: the charge, at per ton per week, was 6*d.* victual per day, each man 4*d.*

	£
The Revenge of Lyme, 2 months' wages for 30 men,	42
Jacob " 2 " 50	70
Tonnage of the two ships, being 160 tons	32
Victualling " 2 months	112
Thomas Bonaventure of Lyme, 30 men 6 weeks,	31
One month's victual	21
Tonnage of the same, 60 tons	9
	£317

Pay of each —

	£	s.	d.
Lieutenant, per mensem	15	0	0
Naval surgeon	1	10	0
Pilot	2	0	0
Trumpeter	1	5	0
Halberdier	1	0	0
A sailor	0	14	0

Thus have many particulars respecting the approach of the Spanish Armada been presented to those who can estimate the excitement of that day.

At this heroic period our annals bear mention of men who were a compound of many valuable qualities. Officers at sea in the naval service of their country directing mercantile adventures in undiscovered regions with great ability and profound skill in seamanship; acute merchants who could command their own vessels against the common enemy, and engage the foe when met with. These duties are now separated; and most persons could not venture out of their line, the naval officer to conduct a mercantile expedition; the merchant to take the command of his own ship at sea and fight her too! It was not so in the reign of Queen Elizabeth.

To exhibit the class of men that made the reign of Elizabeth so justly famous, let us consider the individual whose martial conduct has been already alluded to.

John Yonge, Gent. figured as a man of mind, of courage as a merchant and as a warrior. This ancestor of a line of baronets was a merchant who resided in his mansion in Axminster, and that in Colyton, south-east Devon. He gallantly joined his country's armament in the "Bear" of 140 tons and 60 men. He presented a Discourse for a Bancke of Money, &c. to Queen Elizabeth, and was a leading merchant in the first regular trade to Africa, being associated with several others in a patent granted by that queen, 3rd May, 1588, for a trade to the Rivers Senegal and Gambia. In one of the old Cobb account books is mentioned the sailing of the "Bark YONGE for Barbary." Much of the trade was probably carried on from Lyme. Arms were granted to John Yonge in 1583. The Massachusetts Bay Company commenced with certain grants of land made by the council for New England to six gentlemen of Dorsetshire; Sir Henry Rosewell, Sir John Yonge, Thomas Southcoat, John Humphrey, John Endicott, and Samuel Whetcomb. The settlers were not separatists from the church. Some of the merchant adventurers, first known by their title of the brotherhood or fraternity or guild of St. Thomas à Becket, resided at Lyme, and vessels traded to the Senegal and Gambia.

Some of these incidents are adduced to furnish proof how erroneously these facts have been received by many of those who have chanced to peruse them. Foreign voyages, foreign trade, and shipping have been interpreted to mean what these matters do in the present century. Large ships, and consequently ports with adequate depth of water, were supposed to have been available. Such was not the case.

The men who made these foreign voyages in small craft were venturesome, and partook of the excitement of their age caused by the great discoveries of new lands. There are bold spirits who would now-a-day not shrink from any similar voyages; but the pecuniary loss would be great and certain. These early adventurers reaped enormous profits, which are no longer to be earned.

Maritime matters were not developed otherwise than by a slow process. The over-timid, the slow to alter their course a jot from the beaten track, anticipated evils as likely to spring from every change. The history of expected evils that were to arise out of improvements would be a striking one.

Henry VIII. founded the Trinity House for the ordering of beacons, lighthouses, buoys, &c. These were, however, sparingly used. Dungenness Lighthouse was built in the reign of James I. One Reading took out a patent for lighthouses, which drew attention to these safeguards, about the year 1679. We may be struck with the reception of a plan for the extension of these night-guides that assure the doubting seafaring mariner. The merchants of Liverpool we know, and doubtless those of other ports, judged lighthouses to be likely to prove of no benefit to our mariners, but a hurt rather. These novelties, it was believed, would expose mariners to more danger if they *trust* to them, and, besides this, prove a very great and unnecessary burden and charge to them.

The Diary of Walter Yonge, M. P., contains many entries exemplifying the wretched state of the navy in the reign of Charles I. There were great complaints about the bad, even the stinking victuals, and the riotous visits of sailors, in parties of 250, to the house of the Duke of Buckingham to demand their pay, which course was generally successful. It must be confessed that such a party of *duns* was formidable; and, moreover, the London apprentices were expected from time to time to be about to join these ill-used men, who had been obliged to journey far away from their proper element, and clamour in order to obtain their due. Sailors were sometimes necessitated to part with their tickets for their pay at forty per cent. discount.

Could the old seamen have viewed our crews seated upon a spar, placed for the purpose, forty at a time, having their pigtails dressed each by the man behind him, they might have formed an unfavourable opinion of their habits.

A proclamation, sent out in 1674, prohibits merchant vessels from using the Union Jack, so that they could not be distinguished from men-of-war.

Barges were used till 1780 for keeping merchandise afloat, that could not be landed for want of room, when the Brunswick Dock at Blackwall was constructed.

Is the Royal Navy to furnish an exception to the progress of universal improvement? Has not every observer who has the slightest opportunity remarked a surprising moral change in the right direction in that service?

The Royal Navy accounts itself a profession from the reign of Henry VII.; but its highest honours have only been realised of late years, since ships have belonged to the crown and have been exclusively commanded by naval officers and not by soldiers. The great improvement consists in the dying out of the Trunnion school, who made oaths to appear to be necessary accompaniments of exertion and operations on sea water. Cruel and unjust floggings and treatment came to be thought indispensable if discipline was to be preserved. Ships are now maintained in the finest order, and the crews are treated as human beings and subjected to a reasoning discipline, having their duties which must be performed, and their rights which are engaged to be preserved, and which are ensured to the smallest particular. Punishments are now for the offender, and are a safeguard to the many steady men who delight in order.

Officers of the Royal Navy leave all trafficking at foreign ports in any kind of goods to the merchant or trader. It is useless to offer to officers boxes of watches got up for the foreign market. One port may be preferable to another from the greater safety of its anchorage, but not because the captain and officers can get rid of their several adventures.

A captain of a frigate within a few years has been known to purchase slaves in the West India market, have them entered as able seamen, compel the artificers to teach them a trade; so that when the ship returned each was sold at a high rate as a valuable piece of property. The worst, however, has to be told. Upon sailing from Portsmouth, some of the best men were sent away upon duty in a ship's boat, in order that they might be returned "run," by which they lost pay and clothes, but made room for the negroes lately kidnapped, who were entered, though they did no work for the ship, as able seamen! We have all heard of a naval officer who had his pocket picked at a Westminster election, and who openly professed his vow, which he rigidly performed, of flogging every Londoner that joined his ship for this act. This, it is said, was no idle vow!

The croakings about effeminacy and decline of naval excellence have proved vain. The doings of our naval force, abroad and on shore, in this war with Russia, have realised all that could be asked for in discipline, daring, and endurance.

When the havens of our coasts were few in number they were viewed with a feeling approaching to veneration. This is not surprising. In many parts a friendly haven was "a succour for shiplets" caught by a storm against certain destruction had no port existed.

The construction of havens was really a work of Christian mercy, for they saved life where human means had in great storms proved unavailing. The consideration about the preservation of property and their utility were left out of the question, the preservation of the lives of the poor mariners was alone considered. This prompted bishops to stimulate congregations to contribute to the construction of fresh havens and the repair of existing works as a Christian duty; and briefs were issued and carried about England upon the score of general beneficence and humanity towards the tempest-tost mariner.

An example of one of the early briefs is here furnished. It was granted by King Henry VIII. for the collecting money for the Cobb, 23rd June, 1545.

"To all true Cristen people to whom the present wrighting shall come to see, rede, or here, we John Tanner al Mopaige* mayor of the town of Lyme Regis, in the county of Dorset, and the burgesses of the same, sendeth greeting in our Lord God everlasting. *And* whereas upon sute made by us, the forsayd mayor and burgesses unto the Kings most Royal Majesty, for succour and suffultation of the intollerable charge that all the inhabitants of the said town of Lyme dailie doth sustain and be at in defending the violent tempestuos flowing and reflowing of the mayne see upon the said town and port there, in such wise that the inhabitants of the same be not of theymselves hable to do, unless the charatable devotion of good and well disposed people be thereunto extended. *The kynges* grace of his bountiful goodnes, graciously considering the occasion of our pore sute and supplicacion, moved in pitie, zeal, and heartie affection towards the relieving and comforting of us, his poore subjects, in our great necessitie, hath graunted unto us his gracious licence under the great seale for the terme of one yere, to send into divers shires of this his reyelme of England, our lawfull proctoures and messengers to collect and gather the devocion of well disposed people towards the socouring and helping of us in our great and intolerable charge. *Know ye* that we have appointed Henry Drake and Nicholas Somer, of South Brent, to erogate and distribute," &c.

The tempest-tost mariner in Tudor and earlier reigns had no friendly shore upon which he might save his cargo in case he lost his ship. The shipwreck season was the coast season of harvest to the inhabitants of those parts. The mariner's misfortune was their occasion of plunder and profit. A bad season to the wrecker was one when the tranquil sea had delivered over less than the wonted share of spoil. The sea-coast pirates only plundered the unfortunate; and no one doubted his title to everything that he could lay hands upon in the general scramble. The dead bodies often lay neglected while wine was being drunk and large packages rifled.

False pilots and lights belong to old times. By one of the laws of Oleron the captain who discovered the treachery of

* This worthy had two names, like many others about this time.

† Archives of Lyme.

a pilot might take him to the lee side of the ship and decapitate him. Such a law implies that the crime was well developed and practised.

How is the length of time spent in voyages at this period to be considered in reference to our knowledge of the time required to perform the same, whether more or less distant? how could the owners of vessels make any profit when such intervals of time elapsed between the going and returning? add to this the greater comparative cost of building and rigging each craft; and more than all the smallness of the tonnage. The answer lies in the great per-centage returned from vessels upon their value. This appears almost incredible in the history of early voyages to the East; but the freight per ton on our coasts was enormous. In 1616 the price of freight from Guernsey to Lyme was no less than 55*s.* per ton. In 1852 the same would be not more than about 5*s.*; or, considering the relative value of money, one-sixteenth only of what it was. Hence we have an insight into the high price of many articles, and consequently the smallness of their general consumption throughout the whole breadth of the land.

Many small vessels were probably laid up during the winter season, and those afloat were not rashly exposed to danger. The little communication between Jersey and this country may be learnt from the following anecdote: —

Sir Amias Poulett, then governor of Jersey, wrote to the Lord Chamberlain in 1576 (March 19th), stating that the partridges, the red-legged kind, which he wanted, had been procured; but that his servant had lain by the water's side for ten weeks without being able to pass. Sir Amias sent two dozen partridges at this time to the Lord Admiral and to the Earl of Leicester.*

Early times abounded with superstition, and sailors have had ascribed to them that they possess this weakness in more than ordinary degree.

Among the great naval officers of Elizabeth's reign must be ranked Sir George Summers, the discoverer of the

* MS. at Hinton House.

Bermudas, often called the Summers Islands from that circumstance. Here is a representation given of what the descendants of Sir George Summers call the "Summers

The Summers Magnet, or Loadstone.

magnet, or loadstone." It is in the possession of Peter Franklin Bellamy, Esq., surgeon, second son of Dr. Bellamy of Plymouth. These gentlemen say the tradition in the family is that the ancient admiral before going to sea used to touch his needle with it. The stone is dark-coloured, the precise geological formation doubtful. The curious stone with armature of iron was probably a talisman. A naval historian lately lost to us has thrown light upon the subject of a compass.

"The loadstone was termed in Edward III.'s reign the 'sail-stone' or 'adamante,' and the compass itself 'sailing needles and dial.' In 1345 a 'sailing-pier' or stone was supplied to the 'Plenty' of Hull; and in June, 1338, 'two sailing needles and a dial' formed part of the stores of the barge 'Mary' of the Tower. But the most remarkable entries are in the accounts of the clerk of the king's ship the 'George' in 1345. After stating that he had purchased, at Sluys in Flanders, sixteen 'horologies,' probably hour-glasses, twelve of which cost 9*s*., and paid for repairing 'deverse instruments pertaining to a ship,' it is said, that he had spent six shillings for 'twelve stones called adamants, or sail-stones.' Chaucer mentions a 'compass,' but it is doubtful whether he meant a mariner's compass, —

'Round was the shape in manere of a compas,
Ful of degrees the hight of sixty pas.'

"He says elsewhere that vessels are steered at night by t e pole-star: —

'For they were cleen in despeyr, because they myghte not se
The loder, whereby these shipmen ther cours take eche one.'"*

To elucidate the hardship of ship-money, it is here added, that in the expedition to Cadiz in 1596-7,—

"Weymouth, Lyme and all other the ports of Dorset were to furnish 2 ships.
Plymouth 2 and Dartmouth 2 ships."

Soldiers must have suffered great inconvenience on board ship from overcrowding. The "Black Lion" of Lyme, a vessel of not more than 110 tons, carried 20 mariners and 100 soldiers.†

Such was the beginning of our naval greatness: its growth was not of a day. We can afford to be amused at the small size of the craft, for our ships are now vast. The military armament cannot appear altogether contemptible, for on board were real men of valour. What a martial, patriotic spirit led John Yonge, Bart. (elsewhere mentioned), and Thomas Seelye to sail against the Armada!

The State of our South-western Coasts when infested with PIRATES, *early* NAVAL EXPEDITIONS, *Warfare waged by some of our Seaports against each other, &c.*

Ὦ ξεῖνοι, τίνες ἐστέ; πόθεν πλεῖθ' ὑγρὰ κέλευθα;
Ἤ τι κατὰ πρῆξιν, ἦ μαψιδίως ἀλάλησθε,
Οἷά τε ληϊστῆρες ὑπεὶρ ἅλα; τοί γ' ἀλόωνται
Ψυχὰς παρθέμενοι, κακὸν ἀλλοδαποῖσι φέροντες.
Od. v. 71.

"And whence your race? on what adventure, say,
Thus far you wander through the watery way?
Relate, if business, or the thirst of gain,
Engage your journey o'er the pathless main;
Where savage pirates seek, through seas unknown,
The lives of others, venturous of their own."
POPE'S *Homer's Odyssey*.

* Sir N. H. Nicolas, History of the Royal Navy, vol. ii.

† Harleian MS. 253. p. 51.

We are not about to picture Greek pirates in deep bays amidst foaming rocks stealthily returning to their hiding-place after having plundered some defenceless and, perhaps, crippled merchant vessel; much less are our pages devoted to what passed in very remote times—those by general consent treated of as dark or fabulous, with names to which no biographer has devoted himself. The scene of our acted drama is the south-western coast of England, the Bristol Channel, and well-known localities. The epoch is hardly more remote than two centuries; the parties who figure are honest worthies, members of families, whose descendants still live on in our western parts; and the marauders, if not all of them intimately known, earned a bad name in their day and are here treated of not as myths, but as realities substantially placed with due reference to time and space without any touch of romance.

The subject demands a full exposition of details of names of persons and places. Without this who could credit the narrative of doings on the coasts of our western counties herein contained?

The pirates and rovers we treat of will be shown not to have been stealthy intruders into the Channel, withdrawing as furtively as they came, but bold cruisers, requiring the power of the supreme government to put them down. Sea robbers were masters of the Channel or narrow seas at times in the reigns of Mary, Elizabeth, James I. and Charles I. At a period of greatness in Roman history much the same state of things occurred. Greatness and absolute dominion ashore had not procured for that people the mastery at sea. The evil being insupportable, the cure was entrusted to Pompey, who gave to the Romans what they had not enjoyed before, the uninterrupted possession of the Mediterranean.

According to Thucydides, Minos, who began to reign A.C. 1431, was the most ancient of those who acquired a navy. This early conqueror and ruler of the Cyclades, the islands of the Archipelago, found that pirates interfered with the collecting of his revenues.

The great historian quoted above asserts that the Grecians

in old time, and those of the barbarians who lived on the continent, and all those who inhabited islands, so soon as they were accustomed to cross over to one another in ships, and so became sea-faring people, turned to piracy under the conduct of their most powerful men with a view both to their own gain and to maintenance for the needy; and falling upon towns that were unfortified they rifled them, and made most of their livelihood by this means, as this employment did not involve any disgrace, but rather brought with it even somewhat of glory.

Thucydides describes the ancient state of the coasts of Greece in language that would be suitable to a picture in olden time of the coasts of England. The old towns of both countries, owing to the long continuance of piracy, were built farther off from the sea, or inland. The later towns were built on the sea-shores and on isthmuses, surrounded by walls for protection.

. And was not this the case in England? The first church, the parent church of many towns, is from the sea. Towns that quite eclipse the original village exist, but are much more recent. Thus, for example, see Wyke, the parent of Weymouth; Sutton Poyntz, of Melcombe; Littleham, of Exmouth; Broadwater, of Worthing; Tor, of Torquay; Brixham, of Brixham-quay, for shortness Brixham. See Bridport, Abbotsbury with its monastery, and Charmouth, placed back from the sea. Our old Cinque-Port and sea-side towns were walled, and they needed that protection.

Of all the social calamities of modern historical times the incursions of the Barbary pirates was, perhaps, one of the greatest, as it is one of the most forgotten. In Corsica the traveller can even now trace the results of that long-continued plague. Population has been driven even from the healthy parts of the coasts, and the hamlets, closely packed for self-defence, stand high and conspicuous on the slopes of the mountains, in sight of the little watch-towers on the shore, &c.*

* Edinburgh Review, 1855.

Endless is the confusion that exists respecting the word PIRATE. This is applied in a very loose manner to foreigners carrying on war against their enemies; to marauders and enemies whose warfare was somewhat irregular; to privateers; and to the genuine pirate, who is a sea-robber — a dishonest man who goes to sea ready to plunder whatever craft he chances to meet with. The buccaneers of the seventeenth century only plundered the Spaniards; but, like poachers, their occupation tempted them to be become thieves when a good opportunity offered.

Privateers, whom the government in the present war refuse to sanction, make war it is true on their private account, and go forth in their own private vessels to cruise against the enemy; but they had the sanction of authority. Letters of marque, or a licence to cruise against the enemies of their country, were granted by the executive.

Our subject leads us to treat of genuine sea-robbers who infested the British Channel, and whose exploits, unless circumstantially related, would appear fabulous. These pirates were thorough-going seamen, thoroughly lawless and infamous several of them in their transactions with one another. Among men of different nations our countrymen obtained notoriety. Scaliger has affirmed of us that none make better pirates than the English (nulli melius piraticam exercent quam Angli).

Teignmouth was burnt by a French pirate in 1340.* Yvan de Galles, or Evans the Welshman, who landed in Guernsey A.D. 1372, in the reign of Edward III., was in the service of France; Pero Nino, who burnt Poole in 1406, was from Spain; Philpot, an eminent citizen in the reign of Richard II., hired a thousand men, and sent them to sea, where they captured fifteen Spanish vessels with their prizes. The first was a Welshman in the service of a nation then our enemy; Pero Nino may, perhaps, be styled an enemy warring against us in an irregular manner †; while Philpot resembled the privateer of recent wars. Colin Dolphin, of evil fame for his exploits in the Bristol Channel, may be

* Stow's Annals.

† A filibuster.

fairly called pirate: and as such was treated by Sir Edward Stradling, the bold owner of St. Donyatt's Castle, who hanged him. When the Baron of Rosmital set out from Poole to Guernsey upon his travels * through France and Spain, his party of Bohemians were attacked and captured by pirates, who, however, after detaining them half a day, and having learned the rank of their prisoners, and how many powerful kings and princes were their protectors, allowed them to continue their voyage. Such, at all events, was the ambassador's view of the case; which, if a true one, makes us deem that pirates in their robberies prescribed to themselves some bounds.

The marauding expeditions in the time of the Plantagenets, and landings upon the coast to sack towns and burn property, attended with horrible ravages, resemble those generally assigned to pirates. But Southampton was sacked by distinguished admirals of their day; Bocca Negra, or in French *Barbe Noire* or Black Beard of Froissart; Sir Hugh Quieret; and Sir Peter Behuchet. They commanded the French, Spanish, and Genoese fleets at Sluys. Though we detest such brutal warfare, we cannot deny them the title of regular commanders. They were in no sense pirates. They conducted warfare according to the fashion—for war has its fashions—of the time.

Tarring and Broadwater are about a mile inland from Worthing in Sussex, and lie east and west about the same distance. Tarring, though in the reign of Henry VI. a place of repute, had no market, but procured a charter for one about the year 1452. The reasons assigned by the men of Tarring for their requiring a market savour doubtless of exaggeration. Notwithstanding, no men could have indulged in such language, had not the coasts presented incessantly scenes of violence, caused by the incursions of lawless enemies. They represent, that while at Broadwater market, they had "dyvers times ben taken prisoners and byn slayn,

* Translated by Isidore Hye. Ghent, 1847.

as well the men as the women, childer, maidenes, wives, and doters therein beying and beleyving" by their enemies.*

The warfare upon the seas in the fourteenth and fifteenth centuries was dreadful. As carried on by commanders of different nations against their enemies, it may have assumed the character of piracy as defined by modern rules. Still we cannot view the exploits of the dreaded Arripay against the Spaniards as anything more than irregular English daring against foreigners.

This Dorset worthy—in plain English, Harry Paye of Poole—was a daring naval hero in the fleet of the Cinque Ports with their admiral Lord Berkeley. When commanding the fleet of these ports, once so important, that every naval matter appeared to emanate from them, the French had proofs of his prowess, and likewise Owen Glendower in his revolt in Wales. The Spanish historians record in bitter language his visits to the coasts of Castile, carrying off ships and barques, and the most holy crucifix of those parts of Finisterra, which he burnt, as well as Gijon, making prisoners and taking ransoms, scouring the coasts of Flanders, and such deeds of naval daring. He brought home from the coasts of Bretagne, after one expedition, 120 prizes, laden with iron, Rochelle salt, and oil.

The monarchs of Spain and France agreed to unite their forces to withstand these attacks. Forty ships were equipped at Santander, and three galleys; the latter under the command of the celebrated Pero Nino, of great fame in the Mediterranean, who became Conde de Buelna. At Rochelle two shallops, having French archers and arbalisters on board, and two French galleys, commanded by a courtier who had been brought up with Charles VI., and who had fallen into disgrace, Mosen (Monsieur) Charles de Sabasil.

The crews of the galleys, which had sailed without the ships, upon arriving upon our coast landed and plundered, according to the fashion of the time. Pero Nino having learnt that he was near Poole, the abode of his countrymen's

* See Cartwright's Rape of Bramber; Warter's Parochial Fragments

dread enemy Arripay, boldly determined to avenge himself. In 1405 Ferdinando Nino landed with the Spanish force at Poole, the French commander deeming the enterprise too rash. The Spaniards carried off arms and sea-stores, and fired a storehouse, when the Poole men collected against the invaders, holding doors before them as pavaises to protect them against the crossbow shot. Pero Nino, finding matters were becoming critical, landed, as did the French, to the cry of "Santiago;" when at length the brave townsmen retreated, leaving among the slain a brother of Arripay. The invading Spaniards and Frenchmen went on board and proceeded on to Southampton.

Lymington, which had been made a port in the reign of Henry I., furnished in the twenty-ninth year of Edward I.'s reign 9 ships and 159 men towards the fleet for the protection of the south coast.

The dread of a foreign enemy continued for years to be so great, that we can comprehend how Sir John Lyster, the Lord Chief Justice, cautioned the famous Thomas Hancock, in the reign of Edward VI., against preaching at Southampton. He may have done this without having really adduced a ridiculous or insufficient reason against the exercise of his acknowledged powers in that way. The Lord Chief Justice foresaw a division would be produced, owing to the preacher's gospel-preaching against the mass. He feared the divided town would afford a *gap* for the enemy to come in. A predilection for the old form of worship probably suggested to the judge the adducing some reason for silencing its great assailant; still we cannot believe that sheer nonsense was uttered; but, on the contrary, that he had recourse to an argument current at that epoch, and which we learn proved to be of weight with the mayor of that town.

The plundering enemy, called pirates in an ancient account of Brighton, caused a loss of 30,000*l.* to the fishermen of that town.

Having learnt what the coast warfare between foreign enemies and our English countrymen was, the next step leads to the hostilities carried on between our countrymen who inhabited different towns upon the coast upon some real or pretended wrongs inflicted. No warfare between different races could be more decided. Men fought to the death in their quarrel, whatever the cause was. Many sea-port towns deemed themselves to be too distant from the supreme government to expect aid therefrom; so they addressed themselves to remedy any evils they had to complain of to avenge their own wrongs. Hence, when the country was at peace, perhaps, with foreign powers, civil war was urged between town and town. Let us take for an example the case of Lyme and Dartmouth, two seaports of West Dorset and South Devon.

Towards the close of the reign of Henry III. a great feud existed between the inhabitants of these towns. The cause is not known. Tradition is silent.

"Many enormous transgressions" had been perpetrated, when a fight at sea ensued, in which conflict blows, wounds, and homicides resulted. The king anticipated great disturbance in these parts, unless a stop was put to this petty warfare. A writ of inquiry was directed to Martin Littilbor', John de Aure, and Simon de Grindham. The sheriffs of each county were directed to summon witnesses and arrest the guilty.*

The master fishermen of the Channel luggers found it, as they now do, the best course to visit the Norfolk coast to fish. They required to dry their nets ashore, and this at Yarmouth was the main cause of a ferocious quarrel between the men of Yarmouth and the sailors of the Cinque Ports. When Edward I.'s navy was lying at Helvoet Sluys, in the presence of an enemy, the crews of the Cinque-Port vessels attacked the Yarmouth men, when twenty-five ships of Yarmouth were burnt. King Edward III. was obliged to prohibit any communication at sea between the rival vessels of Yarmouth and the Cinque Ports, until he should have composed their quarrels.

It is scarcely credible, were not these matters of history so

* Patent Rolls in the Tower, 49 Henry III. m. 17.

well attested, that regular safe-conducts were granted by the king Edward I. to some vessels of the Cinque Ports requiring to visit Yarmouth, as if it were an enemy's port.*

Camden, describing the town of Yarmouth, records, that about the year 1340 the citizens walled that town round; and "in a short time became so rich and powerful, that they often engaged their neighbours the Lestoffenses, or men of Lowestoff, in sea-fights, with great slaughter on both sides," having a peculiar spite against them.

Great privileges had been bestowed upon the Cinque Ports, in accordance with the spirit of too many of the enactments of ancient times, by encroachments upon the privileges and even common rights of others. The western mariners suffered from this favour shown to the Cinque Ports. This sense of wrong done them in favour of others, who had become odious to them, led to violence. The exercise of unjust privileges, as these were deemed, led to resistance, while the others enforced their rights, and disputes and bloodshed arose.

The authority of the king was required. Edward II. in the year 1321 issued a writ to Edmund Earl of Kent, constable of Dover Castle, setting forth that he had understood that great dissension and dispute existed between the barons of the Cinque Ports and the men and mariners of the western parts of the towns of Poole, Weymouth, Melcombe, Lyme, and Southampton, and other towns of the ports adjacent, and are now anew sprung up, which have led to murders, depredations, and burnings of ships (*homicidia, depredaciones et combustiones navium*), and very many other injuries.

The king ordered public proclamation to be made in each of these parts that no man do injury to men, mariners, or ships of the aforesaid ports. Six barons were to attend at Westminster and lay their complaints.†

We remain uninformed as to the precise causes of this

* Sussex Archæol.

† Rymer's Fœdera, vol. ii. p. i., p. 456.

lawless state of the English Channel, which equalled that of real warfare with foreign enemies. Bad government was in this reign the fertile source of domestic evils. Trifling matters could hardly have roused such angry spirits in several towns at once, and set them in array against other towns of their own country. The western ports had enjoyed privileges, and could not brook to see them taken away or rendered valueless or nugatory by a wanton or corrupt grant to some favourite of the hour.

In the year 1342 the principal inhabitants of Yarmouth were fined 1000 marks for committing trespasses and other unwarrantable acts on the sea-coast. This famous seaport and Hull sent out marauders against London and Bristol. The seamen of Fowey in Cornwall, known as the Fowey Gallants, carried on a system of plunder on the coast of Normandy. Being suspected of piracy in the reign of Edward IV., their vessels were taken from them and given to their rivals of Dartmouth; a reverse of fortune from which the town never recovered.

We need feel no surprise that the men engaged in such local feuds became lawless when opportunity offered. Without any navy to keep them in check, the captains could do what pleased them so soon as they were fairly at sea. They could with ease cruize about the Channel without being observed, as the number of vessels was then so inconsiderable. Men took to the sea to rob, as men ashore begin poaching, and proceed to acts of thieving and burglary when opportunities offer and there is no police to keep them in check.

Having dismissed that part of the subject that embraces early invasions conducted in the fashion of the time, but which are now deemed irregular or even piratical, and those violent feuds between towns on our coast which led to deeds that national warfare claims as its own, we proceed to treat of REAL PIRACY.

By this and pirates is meant nothing less than actual robbers upon the seas,—dishonest men, who, without any warrant, sailed to secure plunder from any vessel they might fall in with, foreign or of their own country. Some perhaps confined themselves to plundering vessels of foreign powers, as certain robbers seem to prescribe a particular field of action ashore; and many spared no English vessel, having abjured their country and adopted another land as their own. There were pirates, or robber-cruizers, who were foreigners, and who had a kind of predilection for English craft.

Incidents will be adduced that serve as proofs of the state of the English Channel.

William Morfote, who represented Winchelsea in Parliament in 1428, was a privateer with a hundred men under him. He found it necessary to obtain the king's pardon in 1435, by the advice of Parliament, there being a legal difficulty about his having broken prison at Dover Castle.

Two merchants of Sherborne in Dorsetshire were robbed of their cargo, worth 80*l.*, A.D. 1322, by Robert de Battayle. This transaction did not lose him the good opinion of his townsmen, who chose him Mayor of Winchelsea a few years later.*

Columbus, before he found a patroness in Isabella of Spain, sent his brother Bartholomew to our Henry VII. in 1488.

In his passage to England Bartholomew was captured by pirates, plundered of everything, and made a slave. After some time he made his escape, and reached this country; but in such a state of destitution, that he was obliged to apply himself to drawing sea-charts for a livelihood, and for the means of procuring himself decent clothes, before he could appear in the royal presence.

King Henry so far listened to his proposals as to desire him to bring his brother to England; and he was on his way to Spain for that purpose when, on reaching Paris, he learned that Columbus had already set out on his voyage under the patronage of the Spanish court.

How would this adventure figure in the history of events that might have happened? What would have resulted to the fortunes of England, for good or harm, if the brother of

* Contribution of W. H. Blauw, Esq., to the Sussex Archæol., vol. iv. p. 111.

Columbus had succeeded in reaching these shores unmolested by pirates?

The famous Cardan was at Dover in 1531, on his return to the Continent. Contrary winds had detained him; but he sailed at last at short notice, "the ship being in a hurry to depart through fear of pirates."

King Edward VI. issued a proclamation, A.D. Oct. 1548, against sundry lewd and evil-disposed persons who had become pirates and had robbed the king's own merchants and others the subjects of friendly powers. They had taken sailors and others out of ships, and had compelled them to serve against their will. Their names follow, and the reward offered for each, quick or dead. John Thompson, 1000 crowns; Richard Cole, 600; Thomas Freeman, 400; David Poore, 300; Morrice Kelly, Richard Eyre, Patrick King, Thomas Outlawe, and Michael James, each 300 crowns reward.

In a report of the prisoners in the Tower, Oct. 22. 1549*, is a highly illustrative account of Richard Coole of Minehead, in the north of Somerset. He had been a pirate for one year, and had taken divers prizes. At last he sued the Lord Deputy of Ireland, Mr. Bellingham, in five petitions to be allowed to come in and submit to the king's mercy. The Lord Deputy employed him; and sent him to a castle in Straugham in Ireland, which the Scots had taken from the owner and occupied it. The pirate, now engaged in the cause of right, of lawful government and order, recovered the castle, and reinstated the owner. The Lord Deputy next engaged the successful pirate against one Savage, a rebel whom his servants were about to attack, promising as a reward to sue for his pardon. It is presumed his services were successful. He surrendered voluntarily at the Isle of Man and had been in prison to the time stated. The answer was that he was to be examined, and the admiral's officers were to decide upon his case.

* Sir F. Tytler's England under the Reigns of Edward VI. and Mary, vol. i. p. 271., from the State Paper Office.

In a book of the Admiralty Court of Poole, commencing A. D. 1550, among directions for the jurors, appears:—

"Also you shall inquyere of all piratts that robbyth uppon the sea any of the king's leadge people, or any other w'ch are in leage and amyty with the kinge of this realme. If you know any such, you shall present ther names, as also the ownners, masters, victuallers, mayntaynners, comforters, abettors and recevers, as also what manner of goods or marchandizes is so robbyd." *

The bailiff of Seaford (24 Elizabeth) charged all in court to declare at their peril, "those who did foyster, ayde, vitell, maynteyne, or succor any theves or pyrates." †

It is mentioned in the poem "The Libel of English Policy," that the inhabitants of St. Malo were accustomed to roam the seas as pirates, little regarding the authority of their duke. They made descents upon the east part of England, plundering the country, and exacting contributions or ransoms from the towns.

In 1557 the lords of the Privy Council, among whom were the Earls of Sussex, Winchester, Rutland, Pembroke, Anth, Mountague, &c., addressed a letter ‡ to our western ports, desiring the mayors to use vigilance for defence of the towns and coasts against the enemy. From this year dates the first visit of the Earl of Bedford to the south-western coast. John Hassard, Mayor of Lyme, charged in his account 2*s.* 2*d.* for wine given to that nobleman. Again in 1569 the charge for entertaining my Lord of Bedford was 3*l.* 9*s.*; a very large sum, which no doubt included the expenses of the suite and keep of their horses. The Earl of Bedford's visits to Lyme were upon important business, as will be shown. He was a commissioner appointed by her Majesty's letters patent for the authorising certain persons to be sent to the seas for the taking of PIRATES HAUNTING THE COASTS, or, in the words of the INSTRUCTIONS *for the*

* Sydenham's History of Poole.

† Sussex Archæol.

‡ MS. lately sold at Mr. Thorpe's, London.

*direction of the commissioners**, "for the apprehension, suppressing, and removing such pirates as do haunt or infest the sea-coasts within the precincts of their commission."

Whenever the commissioners had understanding of any such pirates they were to confer with the officers and merchants residing in our ports that authority might be given to some honest (*i. e.* honourable) persons to arm forth some vessels to the seas to apprehend or chase away the same with some speed. They were to consider in a secret manner how the thing may be done, and, what intimately affected the men of the west, to settle how contribution was to be made of the merchants and inhabitants thereabouts for the charges requisite.

Such impositions as these upon a particular locality, which ought to have been borne by the state at large, were felt to be a cruel injustice, as they really were.

The great attention paid to the procuring proper persons, and the care to provide against their turning out sea-robbers or pirates themselves, is very striking.

The commissioners were to choose suitable persons, who would attempt nothing for private lucre. They were directed to take bonds of the persons themselves who sent out the vessels, and sureties of the captain and mate of the ship, to behave and demean themselves honestly, and neither rob, spoil, nor evil entreat any the good subjects of her Majesty or other princes being in good peace or amity. These officers were to do their best endeavour to capture the pirates, and not by any kind of collusion, agreement, or compact to suffer them to depart. They were not to remain at sea, but for the capture of the pirates haunting the coasts, and were not to sail again unless provided with a new commission. When pirates were captured they were to be landed at the nearest port, presented to the vice-admiral or the commissioner, and then sent to the common gaol for trial. The piratical vessel, and all she contained, was to be brought

* Harleian MS. 168. A collection of state matters in the hand of Mr. R. Starkey.

into port and valued upon the oaths of four skilful and expert persons of those parts. The inventory was to remain till it could be found what belonged to the pirates, and what was the plunder taken from others. But lest this arrangement should create disappointment, it was enjoined upon the commissioners to inform the parties interested, as a matter certainly determined, that in the distribution of the ships and property taken from the pirates "no charge shall more sooner be considered, allowed of, and paid than of those that have borne the burden of setting forth the ships; and the reward of such as have adventured themselves in that service to be paid of the proper goods of the pirates."

The cruisers after pirates were not to board or molest trading or fishing vessels, and they were to take such a number of men as was needful, so as not to hazard her Majesty's good subjects in a doubtful service.

Though the above instructions may date from the year 1578, they have been inserted here as being appropriate in elucidating and introducing the subject.

Henry Palmer, Esq., was appointed captain of her Majesty's ships sent forth for the clearing of the seas and apprehension of pirates, 19th March, 1576.

Her Majesty understood by the grievous and sundry complaints made by her subjects of the great spoil by them daily sustained at the hands of such as now of late have sore infested the narrow seas, as not only not her own said subjects, but also no foreign merchants can in anywise occupy their honest and lawful trades of merchandise. Pitying therefore greatly the case of many of her subjects who by those spoils have been utterly undone, and weighing besides how dishonourable it is to her Majesty to suffer those seas of which she and her predecessors have been accounted to have always held supreme sovereignty, to be by such lewd persons haunted, besides the great abatement of her customs as well outwards as inwards, thought it most necessary to set out certain of her ships, whereof she committeth to their discretion for the clearing of the seas and the apprehension of the said malefactors.

Captain Palmer was to arrest ships armed for war — not trading — between Yarmouth and the Isle of Wight, and not to molest the Dutch.

The lords of the Privy Council, 6th August, 1576, addressed William Holstocke, Esq., a captain appointed to serve at the seas for apprehending of sea rovers.

Captain Holstocke was informed that men of Flushing, pretending to be in foreign service, caused daily complaints to be made. Her Majesty was determined to scour and cleanse the seas. Captain Holstocke, in his command of the "Lion," the "Swiftsure," and the "Dreadnought," was to join the "Archat," the "Foresight," and the "Handmaid," under the orders of Captain Palmer, and these ships were to form a fleet. The lords of the council informed him that at Torbay, or about the coast, were thirteen ships of Flushing, which not only daily spoiled and robbed her Majesty's subjects, but infested and troubled all others that traded upon the coast, whereby men were put in fear in those parts to make any voyage on the seas.

The fleet was first to sail to Torbay and take the Flushingers peaceably; if not so, by force.*

Queen Elizabeth sent out in 1575 a proclamation against people keeping on the seas armed vessels to commit robberies.

In 1577 the lords of the Privy Council wrote to the Mayor of Poole respecting a French ship upon which an embargo was laid, and pirates.†

With such a state of affairs existing the coming of a great courtier with intelligence and powers to act, after consultation with our western borough magnates, must have been hailed as a great event. What excitement at this time can equal it? William Jurden, Mayor of Lyme, duly impressed with the greatness of the occasion, made some preparation for the event. He enters in his account, 13th January, 1577–8.

"*Item*, for the mending of Colway Lane, 13 Jan., against the coming of my Lord of Bedford, 3*s.* 4*d.*"

* Harleian MS. 168. † MS. Letters on sale at Mr. Thorpe's.

Entertainment suitable to his lordship's rank was furnished; so that by the 16th January there was entered "for charge, at my Lord of Bedford's being here," no less a sum than 10*l.* 6*s.* 8*d.*

There was soon occasion for further steps to be taken; so the mayor and Mr. Ellesdon rode with a servant, 18th April, to Exeter to my Lord of Bedford, at a charge of 8*s.*

The lords of the council now instructed William George, Esq., 17th June, 1578, to take as captain the command of her Majesty's ship the "Foresight," and sail from the Thames into the narrow seas in the west of England towards Plymouth, particularly to take two special pirates named Hamilton and Twittie. Captain George was to inform the Earl of Bedford of his coming upon the coast, and follow directions for the pursuit of the aforesaid pirates or any other, and to inquire what pirates or avowed enemies are upon the coast of Brittany, Normandy, or other places towards Spain or Portugal.

The "Foresight" had not arrived at Lyme by July 23rd, when the mayor enters in his account:—

> "*Item,* for charge of myself, Mr. Ellesdon, and Richard Carpenter [a lawyer, who became, at the incorporation of the town, town clerk] to ride to my Lord of Bedford about the coming of the Queen's ship, 13*s.* 4*d.*"

Great was the satisfaction at the protection about to be afforded to our townsmen in their commerce, which lawless hands interrupted; but in Queen Elizabeth's reign such good was of a mixed nature,—the townsmen of Lyme had to pay for the benefit about to be reaped, as if it was not for England generally, but for Lyme, or Dorset, or Devon individually considered.

The mayor adds further:—

> "*Item,* to my Lord of Bedford of the money received of Mr. Ellesdon for the fine of the mill, 30*l.*"

At this time Captain Winter was sent to sea upon her Majesty's service; and directed to look after one La Roche, a Frenchman who was fitting out ships, and conferred with James Fitzmorris, an Irishman.

We read as appropriate to the matter before us, that Cardinal de Lorraine, when Mary, Queen of Scots, set out from France to Scotland in 1561, was in fear for the safety of many valuables his niece took with her, as Queen Elizabeth had fitted out a fleet under the pretext of clearing the North Seas from *pirates.*

Queen Elizabeth had three ships in the North Seas in 1561 to preserve the fishermen from *pirates.**

In the year 1570 a great contest arose between the Bishop of Chichester and the Lord High Admiral respecting the right to the wreck of a pirate's ship.

Certain Flemings, pirates, were complained of for being in the narrow seas and assailing the King of Spain's subjects. It appears clear that the goods and merchandise captured was sold to our countrymen in the bays and creeks along our coasts.

About the year 1577, when France sent 150 ships to Newfoundland to fish for cod, Spain 100, Portugal 50, and England only 15, as they mostly fished off Iceland, these early fisherman were a prey to pirates. The English ships were the best; and beat off the pirates, taking from those they had protected a boat-load of salt, or other present of that nature, which it had been of old a custom to make for this service.

A notorious pirate, one Thomas Purser, infested the south-western coast. On the 5th February, 1582–3, he made a "very insolent and rebellious attempt" on the Dorsetshire coast. He drew near Weymouth harbour, and attacked many ships, both English and French, riding in the road at anchor. This pirate took a ship of Rochelle of 60 tons; and in his attempt to carry another near was interrupted by the stout townsmen of Weymouth and Melcombe, who came to the rescue. They killed seven of the pirate's crew, hurt and maimed several others, and compelled him to

* Miss Strickland's Life of Mary, Queen of Scots.

sheer off. Purser dealt out threats of vengeance by spoil and fire upon the ships and town that had so resisted him.

The Weymouth men now feared for their town, which was not sufficiently protected. They asked assistance from the county for their own protection, and that of the country round, towards bringing and planting some ordnance, procuring powder and shot, and towards the maintenance of the whole, after having erected a small bulwark upon the seaside.

The lords of the council seconded their request, and a letter signed Burleigh, Leicester, Walsingham, Christopher Hatton, &c., was sent to the sheriff and justices of Dorset for a contribution towards the above object, having learnt all the particulars from the Mayor of Weymouth, February 10.

	£
The estimate for 8 pieces of ordnance was - -	80
powder and shot - - -	40
carriages, wheels, sponges, &c. - -	20
Expense of the bulwarks and platforms, 2 in Weymouth, 2 in Melcomb, and powder-houses -	60
	* £200

As thieves upon land must find receivers of the stolen goods, so it is with pirates. The cheapness of the articles they wish to dispose of proves too great a temptation to the dishonest, and thus piracy was supported, and too often perhaps rewarded.

The Mayor of Weymouth examined, January 9. 1583-4, four persons, John Hunt, Richard Bownell, Henry Higgens and William Bond. These men, upon being sworn, confessed that they went aboard one Thomas Purser the pirate's vessel the day before, that is, January 8., then riding in Portland Road, in Richard Bownell's boat, having been sent aboard by John Wade with a letter written in French.

John Wade's name occurs as a merchant or tradesman of Weymouth. The nature of his business with the pirate will appear from the answer of the latter. His breast still burning with vengeance for his defeat, he said openly, if he could

* Sherren Papers.

take any shipping of Weymouth any day these six months he would surely set them on fire. John Hunt affirmed that a letter produced which follows here was in the handwriting of the pirate.

"Mr. Wade,—I have received a letter in French from you, and having no man aboard that can read it, so by this bearer I understand it is to buy the ship*, which willingly I would sell her, with all the goods that is in her, saving six barrels herrings. The price that he shall give for ship and goods is 100*l.*, otherways he shall see her to make a beaune fyer (bonfire); moreover, he shall bring 1000 byskey (biscuit), 2 ton of beer, in part of payment of the money. Thus I rest, yours to command,

"THOMAS PURSER."

As there are various kinds of morality in practice in the world, so doubtless there was one kind in respect of dealing with pirates. Perhaps it was allowed under that code to buy vessels and cargoes taken from traders of another nation. Wade was at Weymouth in 1587. Men of no morals we may readily believe bought bargains at every opportunity, and sent off a boat whenever a pirate came along the coast. Neither highwaymen by land nor pirates by sea could exist long if all the world were unfriendly. They must have had many to co-operate with; many who felt indifferent or even well disposed towards them.

Valentine Dale and David Lewis, doctors of civil law, were specially consulted touching *aiders of pirates.* Nicholas Herbert, Esq., John Thomas Bener, and William Richards had been examined at Cardiff touching the lodging, victualling and buying the goods of pirates.†

A commission was issued by the Crown, 20 Eliz. 22nd January, 1578 which had become absolutely necessary. In it was recited that divers ill-disposed persons had of late in sundry vessels and ships frequented the seas upon the coasts of this realm, robbing and spoiling honest quiet merchants and others; which pirates were victualled and furnished

* The "Angel" of Rochelle. Sherren Papers.

† Harleian MS. 168.

by persons residing near or within the havens, creeks, or landing-places of the realm, taking the stolen goods of the pirates in exchange. Under this commission were appointed the Mayor of Poole, William Marquis of Winchester, Thomas Viscount Howard of Bindon, Sir Henry Ashley, Sir Matthew Arundell, Sir John Horsey, Sir John Yonge, the Recorder of Poole, George Trenchard, and William Hussey, Esquires, commissioners to prevent such enormities being used in the havens, creeks, and landing-places of the town of Poole; with power to choose honest, discreet, and trusty persons dwelling within or near every of the said havens, creeks, and landing-places of the town of Poole, for the prevention of such practices, to repair once every month to such havens, &c., to ascertain how the deputies performed their duties, and to issue precepts to the sheriff to impannel juries to try offenders.

A French pirate, as it was conjectured, went to sea upon a cruise between Guernsey and Dorsetshire, having twelve men. They boarded a small barque of Poole on her return from Guernsey within one league of Swanage, taking canvas to the value of 12 marks and 6*l.* in money. The authorities of Poole declared that the trade with Guernsey could not be maintained unless piracy was put down. They applied for a license to set forth a barque or two well manned at their own charge against these pests of the Channel.

This must have been in 1583, for a commission was issued, August 8. 1583, giving power to some of the Poole magnates to set forth ships against the pirates and rovers and to try them; and the Mayor of Poole was ordered by Lord Burghley and the lords of the council to fit out a ship against the pirates infesting the coast in 1584.* Lyme and other ports near the scene of these lawless visitations prepared to make head against their special foes the pirates.

Who knows of the victory of the Weymouth men and capture of the pirate Sprage? or who would have known it but for complaints to the ministry about the transaction?

* MS. Letter on sale at Mr. Thorpe's, London.

In August, 1584, a ship of Chichester stood into Portland Road for shelter. The same bad weather must have caused the pirate Sprage, together with a prize, to run into the same anchorage. Being known, the men of Weymouth sent a merchant aboard the Chichester ship, desiring, but not commanding, the captain to join a ship and pinnace of the town in the apprehension of Sprage. Great expedition was required, as it was stated, lest secret information might be furnished of the intended operations against the pirate—another intimation of the understanding that existed between these desperate characters and many people ashore.

Powder and every requisite having been furnished, the Chichester men began to repent of their having entered upon this undertaking [*here the MS. is indistinct*]. The whole ship's company at one time refused to sail; they changed their minds, got under weigh, and anchored near the pirate, discharging a few shot without doing any damage. The Weymouth men boarded the pirate and carried her. The Weymouth pinnace having three or four of the Chichester men aboard her besides her own crew, boarded the pirate's prize. So soon as the Weymouth men had carried the prize the others came aboard and helped themselves to many articles, which were begrudged.

The Chichester men complained to Sir Francis Walsingham, and pretended they were the principals in capturing the pirates. This occasioned a full narrative of the whole transaction to be made, of which we have availed ourselves.

A defeat of the lawless was procured farther west in 1586, or at least in the year of Mr. Ellesdon's mayoralty at Lyme. Nothing more is known of the affair than appears in the following account.* How daring these marauders must have been for the captains of certain French vessels then on the coast, or sheltered in the Cobb of Lyme, to have joined in the expenses of an outfit against common robbers! Do we not see herein the benefits of centralisation? Did the west of England fully enjoy what we can really call civilisation at this epoch?

* Loose sheet among the Archives of Lyme.

Money disbursed about the PIRATES as followeth: —

	£	s.	d.
First, paid for the use of eleven horses and eight men, to carry the prisoners to Dorchester - -		28	2
Item, paid for the prisoners' meat and drink during the time they were here - - - -		2	6
Item, for the watchmen to watch the prisoners - -		0	12
Item, paid for 2 mayling cords to bind the prisoners -		1	2
Item, paid to the gaoler of Dorchester for receiving [ten in number, at 4*d.* each] the prisoners - -		3	4
Item, paid for Mr. Hardes charges, dinner and supper, and for his horse-meat for 2 days, and to take the examinations and to make the mittimus - -		14	6
Item, for 60 pound of gunpowder and the shot -	3	10	0
Item, paid for one *hogshead of beer* for the mariners to carry to the sea, and one dozen and half of bread		14	10
[The Lyme mariners, who cruised after the pirates.]			
Item, paid to two men of Birpott [Bridport], which did help conduct the prisoners to Dorchester -		2	0
Sum total - - -	£6	17	6
Whereof received of the French men and of Sidmouth men - - - - - -	3	16	8
So rest unpaid of this bill - -	£3	10	0

[Here is an error of 10*s.* Certain Frenchmen and Sidmouth-men made common cause, and defrayed part of the cost of the expedition and committal of the pirates.]

The dreaded Spaniards did not land in the west after 1595, when they disembarked at Mousehole near Penzance. Our townsmen the same year captured more *pirates.* William Ellesdon, mayor, charges for the hire of a horse to carry Robert Williams and three pirates to Dorchester gaol.

	s.	d.
Paid to three men to carry four prisoners to Dorchester gaol - - - - - - - -	7	6
for cord to pinion the prisoners - - -	0	3
the jailer to receive the prisoners - - -	0	8
to the same prisoners to drink by the way - -	0	4

	s.	*d.*
Witness to Dorchester, each - - - -	2	0
Meat and drink for four days in the town prison - -	2	3

In 1597 France and England were mutually complaining and quarreling about the violence and injury committed by the pirates of either nation.

Our western mayors not only contended with pirates but had to exercise their authority to restrain parties from setting out upon irregular warfare or actual piracy. A pinnace of Weymouth, called the "Gift," was arrested by the mayor in July, 1587, as she was bound to sea in "warlike sort." Edwards, one of the crew, waited upon Lord Winchester, the Lord Lieutenant of the county, and showed him a licence from the Lord Admiral; upon which the mayor was directed to allow this vessel to sail upon her privateering cruise. No vessel was to sail without a licence.

The Mayor of Weymouth was directed at this time to make diligent search about the town for a notable pirate, Thomas Davers, alias Puterell or Putteirs. Weymouth and Melcombe petitioned for forts in 1587.

A pirate, one of a body whose leader was named Laynton Atkinson, took a barque belonging to John Ward of Weymouth, and carried her to Swanage. There 40 packs of canvas, worth 100*l.*, belonging to John Mounsell, were taken out. The Mayor of Weymouth adds that, if there is not good information that summer about the presence of the pirates, "no man will be able to travel;" which means, it is to be presumed, that the Channel will be impassable to merchant shipping.*

Of the 21 craft that composed the shipping of Poole, the only port technically so styled of Dorset, in 1591 but three, varying from 24 to 14 tons each, were without ordnance, either fowlers, sakers, mynions, or falcons!

These statements convey an idea of the state of the Channel and of some of the transactions. Much is lost or buried perhaps amidst archives or old papers. There was a pirate hanging at this time at Studland, an eyesore to his

* Pitt, the Mayor's Letter—loose sheet, no date. Sherren Papers.

living fellows, who landed and cut down the gallows.* The capture of pirates was referred to as a very common occurrence in certain articles drawn up to avoid contentions between the Mayor of Weymouth and the officers of the Lord High Admiral. It was a pirate, Captain Fleminge, who first saw and gave warning of the approach of the Spanish Armada.

There was a mania for lawless roving inthis reign, and, we may add, lawless dealing. Warrants came to our mayors in 1593 from the Lord Admiral to seize a carvel which belonged to Thomas Alworthy and Thomas Ware of Bristol. The crew carried her off and sold her. The purchasers changed her name to that of the "Tobacco-pipe," and sent her to sea as a privateer. She had captured a rich cargo of hides.

The pirates were occasionally worsted, and suffered the punishment due to their crimes. We may learn this from a quarto pamphlet, entitled "The Lives, Apprehension, Arraignments and Executions of the Nineteen Pirates, Captains Harris, Jennings, Lancaster, Downes, Halse, and others."†

We learn from a proclamation in 1603 that the offenders named had done violence principally upon the Venetians, Captain Thomas Tomkins, Gent., Edmond Bonham, mariner, Walter Janverin, ditto, and divers other English pirates.

In a proclamation, November 12. 1604, Captain William Hull of the "Talbot" of Topsham, Philip Ward of the "Thomasine" of Dartmouth, Christopher Newman, Edward Follet, Henry Burt, and others are named, who in 1602 had spoiled La Serene of Cloud in France, and murdered divers of the Frenchmen.

Again, on June 13. 1606, there was a proclamation against pirates who had committed in the course of their piracy murder and robbery against foreigners in the Mediterranean. There was Captain Richard Giffard or Gifford of the ship or

* Pitt, the Mayor's Letter — loose sheet, no date. Sherren Papers.

† This was marked in Thorpe's Catalogue 3*l.* 13*s.* 6*d.*

fly-boat the "Fortune," Richard Lux of the "Hopewell," William Mellon, Humphry Rastoll, Thomas Better, Robert Gyles, John Thomas, John Burrage, Baldwin Barber, Henry Radcliffe, John Banister, William Smith.

A proclamation of 1608 was sent out against pirates and John Ward. It directs that no munitions of war should be imported into Algiers and Tunis to the pirates there.

There is some mention of *Dunkerks,* or frigates, from the well-known port of that name, in 1603, which is not explained.

"Town Accompt Book.

"Mr. Harvey received of Mr. John Vyney [a receiver of Cobb duties], about the Dunkerks, 5*l.*"

King James I. in his patent, August 28. 1610, refers to the sufferings of the men of Lyme, which will confirm the view taken of the losses caused by the unruly characters who took possession of our sea. He proceeds thus: "And forasmuch as the inhabitants of the said town are of late much impoverished by PYRATES on the sea and otherwise,—now know ye, that we, tendering the good of our said town, and of other our loving subjects, which in distress of weather or of PYRATES, or upon other occasion, may be presumed by reason of the said harbour commonly called the Cobb, &c., do grant twenty pounds by the year for twenty-one years."

About the end of March, 1627, Sir William Courtenay experienced the great insecurity of property in the then actual state of the British Channel. He possessed a castellated mansion, Ilton Castle near Salcombe, in the most southerly part of Devon, not far from the Start Point, which was built by Sir John Chiverston in 1335, who had a grant from the crown for that purpose. It came to the Courtenays by marriage; and is now, though but small remains exist, the property of the Earl of Devon. Certain pirates, writes Walter Yonge in his Diary *, came up in boats from Salcombe, and carried off much of Sir W. Courtenay's pewter-plate and household stuff, and fled the same way they came, without being ap-

* Diary of Walter Yonge, published by the Camden Society. Edited by George Roberts.

prehended. This circumstance has been nowhere recorded except in the above Diary.

Pirates occasioned entries in the churchwardens' books. The evil was understood, and charity was not withheld. Take for example an entry made at Broad Blunsdon: "Paid to one that was burnt in Ireland by pirates."

The second period in the history of piracy upon our western coast has now to be treated of. The comparatively ignoble names of Coole and Purser find no mention in this division of the subject; others more aristocratic usurp their place. Much of the history would appear to belong to fable, were it not mixed up with well-known names of persons and places. Our country truly appears disgraced by the transactions that are here recorded from archives of borough seaports, where the scenes were enacted.

The possession of our Channel by Algerine, Tunisian and Salee, Turks, or Mahometan corsairs, is sufficiently startling. Such was the fact; some explanation is, however, demanded, in order to show how such a miserable state of things was produced. Fashionable it was at one time to take to the road; popular, if not strictly fashionable, it was to turn Turk and lead the life of a corsair.

A great antiquary in his genealogical labours has recently thrown great light upon this subject, when explaining the common report that Ralph Verney had gone into Africa and "turned Turk." *

The death of Muley Hamet, Emperor of Morocco, was followed by a war of succession; his three sons disputed the right, and a considerable body of Englishmen volunteered. One of the claimants, Muley Sidan, had 200 Englishmen under the command of one of the Giffards, of which few were left alive after a great battle.

Elizabeth had employed many English as privateers against the Spaniard. After the war many were loth to lead an inactive life. They had their commissions revoked, and were

* John Bruce, Esq., editor of the "Verney Papers." Published by the Camden Society.

proclaimed pirates. The public looked upon them as gallant fellows; the merchants gave them underhand support; and even the authorities in maritime towns connived at the sale of their plunder. In spite of proclamations, during the first five years after the accession of James I. there were continual complaints. This lawless way of life even became popular. Many Englishmen furnished themselves with good ships and scoured the seas, but little careful whom they might plunder.

The ports of England were shut against them. They went where they were welcome, to the ports of Tunis, Algiers, and the coast of Barbary. Thither they resorted for occasional shelter, and thither English traders followed on purpose to barter and traffic with them. There was Captain Richard Giffard, of the ship or fly-boat the "Fortune," a dread name in those days. Their chief was Captain John Ward, one Bishop, Sir Francis Verney, Glanville, and others. Mr. Bruce continues his information, and tells us that Sir Francis Verney adopted the costume of the country. The Genoese, the Florentines, and the Spaniards all suffered. In 1612 James I. attempted to show what kindness might effect. Many came home upon the proffer of pardon for life and goods; the greater number still adhered to their wild and desperate life. How they scoured the English and St. George's Channel, leading the Barbary corsairs to plunder property and make captives of our fellow-countrymen, will be shown in detail.

The Algerines landed in Ireland in 1627, killed 50 persons, and carried off about 400 into slavery. One vessel captured by them was worth 260,000*l.* They made purchases of stores and provisions they wanted in the western parts of Ireland by Baltimore, and in 1631 carried off 100 captives from that town. They landed their poor captives at Rochelle, and marched them in chains to Marseilles. Twenty-six children are said to have been carried off at one time from Cornwall. In 1633 Lord Wentworth, appointed lord deputy of Ireland, named noted pirate vessels off the coast of Ireland and their captures. Persons in their wills used to leave sums of money for redeeming well-known captives from bondage in Algiers and other places. Entries were made in borough accounts of expenditure under this head; *e. g.*,—

"Lyme Regis Town Accompt Book, 1623.

"*Item*, paid unto Mr. Nicholas Leate the 19 Sep. 1823, 19*l* 10*s*. whereof was disbursed by the company's consent for Ellize Raphe and his son, and Richard Showers and his son, for redeeming them out of Algier, 4*l*. 10*s*."

The fear inspired by these maurauders was general, and natural enough to those who possessed intelligence. We find the dread of pirates was carried into the business of life. The course of human affairs was affected by it. R. Eburne, of Henstridge in Somerset, wrote a work in the year 1634, entitled "A plain Pathway to Plantations." The writer, a man of great depth, recommends Newfoundland for eight reasons. The second reason is, "Because it was most out of the way of *pirates*."

An entry at Lyme in 1627 doubtless refers to pirates:—

"Paid Morren for beating the drum and watching all night, 6*d*."

The speech of Mr. Dannet Burgess for Yarmouth in the House in 1601 upon the violence of the Dunkirk and Nieuport privateers is very exciting.

The speaker asked how it was that such a number of her Majesty's subjects be spoiled, robbed, beaten, wounded, themselves taken, used with such extreme torture, racked, carried away, imprisoned, ransomed, fined, and some executed, and all this time no wars?

"I dare boldly say it," he concluded, "they have done England more hurt since they begun than all France, either in the time of Henry VIII., Edward VI., or Queen Mary.*

After these statements of the existence of so great an evil generally bearing upon the kingdom at large, let us turn to its particular application to the western counties.

* Sir Simonds d'Ewes's Journal of Proceedings in Parliament in the Reign of Elizabeth.

The mayors wrote letters to each other, inviting all the seaports to combine. A name frequently occurs in archives, that of Mr. John Crewkerne, a solicitor who had been town-clerk of Lyme Regis in 1619. He resigned that office upon some misunderstanding as to the "duties necessary to be performed." This lawyer lived in 1636 at Exeter. He was of a good family of Childehay House near Crewkerne; and was entrusted with the direction of the important business now treated of. The paper is entitled "A Copy of the Instructions given to Mr. John Crewkerne for Solicitation of the Lords of the Councell and Petitioning His Majesty for Redress against the Pirates, 23 July, 1636."*

23rd July 1636. — From Plymouth, it is advertised, that fifteen sail of Turks were upon this coast, and had done much mischief. The losses sustained from this source, as set forth by letters from Plymouth, were as follows†: —

"The 'Dorothy' of Dartmouth, of 80 tons, taken near Scilly about a month since.

A collier of Axmouth coming with culm was chased by the Turks, and very hardly escaped.

The 'Swan' of Topsham set upon by two great Turkish men-of-war near Scilly, and (the crew) were obliged to run ashore in order to save themselves.

Divers fishermen to the number of 40 were taken.

The 'Lark' of Topsham, of the burthen of 80 tons, having 15 men and a boy, was lately taken, and the master slain.

The 'Patience' of Topsham was taken two days after her setting out on her voyage to Newfoundland.

The 'Rose-garden,' a barque of Topsham coming from Morlaix, and having aboard her near one hundred fardels of white ware belonging to the merchants of Exeter and other places, and the barque, goods, and seamen carried away by them.

There are five Turks in the Severn, where they weekly take either English or Irish, and a great number of their ships in the Channel, upon the coast of France and Biscay, whereby it is come to pass that our mariners will no longer go to sea, nor from port to port; yea the fisherman dare not put to sea

* Sherren Papers. † Ibid.

to take fish for the country. If timely prevention be not used the Newfoundland fleet must of necessity suffer by them in an extraordinary manner.

The annoyances are principally by the pirates of Salee, which is a place of little strength, and they might easily be kept in if some few ships were employed to lye upon that coast."

His Majesty was therefore to be petitioned to have some ships always stationed off the bar-foot of Salee to blockade the harbour and capture the prizes as they may be brought home; that a convenient number of nimble (fast-sailing) ships may always be kept upon the Irish and this coast, which may be victualled here and there without going for that purpose to London or Portsmouth; that a commission may be granted to any of his Majesty's subjects to take Turks and other pirates and dispose of them and their goods, giving his Majesty his fifteenths.*

· It is desired that in such ships as shall be sent to Salee *seamen* may be appointed by his Majesty to be commanders.

The glaring inconsistency, as it is now universally admitted, of sending officers of the army, not seamen, to command at sea, was then the common practice. It is interesting to view our western advance in civilisation beyond that of the government,—to read the same practical advice tendered to the executive upon a great naval matter. Boroughs in the west are now far behind the government in intelligence.

The harbour of Salee, famed for its rovers, has been silted up by the deposit of mud.

The following additional information was forwarded:—

"Since the above was written a ship was taken by the Turkish pirates within three leagues of Dartmouth; 5000*l.* loss was sustained by Exeter besides the loss of the ship and the seamen. They were likely to have sustained a far greater loss in three ships coming from St. Maloes and Morlaix, but which ships escaped, being near the shore. The merchants of the port towns are utterly disheartened, nor can they get seamen; who say 'they had rather starve at home than be brought under the tyrannous and Moorish subjection of those Mahometans.'" †

* Sherren Papers. † Ibid.

Mr. Adam Bennet, Mayor of Exeter, then the metropolis of the west and a place of considerable trade, sent Mr. John Crewkerne to the other mayors to cause them to unite with Exeter and bear a part of the expenses.

The petition eventually drawn up was from Exeter, Plymouth, Barnstaple, Dartmouth in Devonshire, Weymouth, Melcombe Regis, Lyme Regis, and others the members of those parts in Dorsetshire.

The petition dwelt upon Salee having become powerful in addition to Algiers and Tunis.

The King answered that he had written to the Earl of Northumberland to provide against such damages.

Mr. John Crewkerne reported progress in a letter September 3. 1636; and describes the effect produced upon the king by the several petitions entrusted to him. At their delivery the king, striking his hand upon his breast, said, that whilst he had breath in his body he would do his utmost endeavour to advance so necessary and consequential a business; and that he was resolved to take such a course, as that within these twelve months not a Turkish ship should be able to put out of their harbours.

This active agent adds in a postscript: "The fleet are ordered to come down, and will be with you the first fair wind."*

The corporation of Exeter were agitating, September 21. 1636, the question of sending Mr. J. Crewkerne again to the council and supplying him with 40*l.*

It was proposed to procure a commission dormant for the city of Exeter and all other western ports, to set forth a ship against Turks and pirates which shall be in the Channel, and to press men if they cannot procure volunteers.† Having no more borough extracts to give, one from a biography of Lord Strafford will prove appropriate, as confirmation of the substance of the foregoing:—

"Among the redeeming qualities of Lord Strafford is included his having secured the sea from piracies, so that only one ship

* Sherren Papers. † Ibid.

was lost on his first going to Ireland, and no more all his time; whereas every year before not only several ships and goods were lost by robbery at sea, but also Turkish men-of-war usually landed and took prey of men to be made slaves."*

Read Macaulay's description of the British Channel in 1689, how it was abandoned to French rovers. Our traders hired Dutch privateers to protect them, and found this more advantageous than to obtain the convoy of a man-of-war, so immense were the bribes required to procure this.

An annual gift of a few hundred pounds was paid to the Emperor of Morocco for the protection of British trade and the liberation of British captives, till about the year 1690. The American government made a treaty with the Dey of Algiers in 1792, and paid 5000*l.* annually.

If the ancients are arrayed against the moderns, let us be no blind partisans. Let fair truth prevail. Acting upon this view, a statement is given, extracted from a petition to the Admiralty from the Mayor and Bailiffs of Weymouth so late as 1780.

Privateers, English-built, and chiefly manned with English and Irish smugglers, who are perfectly acquainted with the coast, by showing English colours and hailing in English, have frequently eluded the vigilance of his Majesty's ships. One Matthew Langrish, of Weymouth, master of the "Union," of Weymouth, sailed 27th October from the Downs with provisions for his Majesty's service at Plymouth, under convoy of his Majesty's cutter "Viper." When about six miles from Portland he was captured by a cutter under English colours, which had just before passed the convoy. During the four days that Langrish was kept aboard the cutter privateer she captured four English vessels between Portland and the Lizard. She was called the "Civility," and was commanded by one Bennet, an Englishman, having a second captain, Connor, *alias* Bachelor, an Irishman; and the major part of her crew consisting of

* See a Biography of Lord Strafford.

British and Irish, with a French commission aboard. Privateering leads to what is near to piracy.

The privateers of St. Malo have earned a great name for boldness: they were much complained of at the beginning of the eighteenth century, and came close off our western ports.

The Mayor of Lyme, Mr. Nathaniel Butler, charges, A.D. 1704-5, the sum of 1*s.* 8*d.*, which he gave two men to drink when two privateers were in sight. Mr. Nicholas Newel in 1705-6 gave the man who watched 3*s.* The same mayor paid Mr. Hart to pay the men for watching when a privateer lay off the town, 16*s.* There is a charge for Robert Puckett's horse-hire and expenses to Weymouth, when a French privateer took a boat off the town, 9*s.* There was given beer to the sergeants and others when the guns were fired at a French privateer, and putting small arms into the chest. Another of similar entries will enable us to understand how troublesome these fast-sailing and fast-rowing craft were long before steam was introduced.

1704, Gave the *young men* to drink when two privateers were in sight, 1*s.* 6*d.*

The town-drum was beat in 1706, and the gun fired at two privateers. No less than eighteen pieces of artillery were sent down to Lyme, with shot, ladles, &c.

The arming of Towns. — Introduction of Ordnance. — Musters. — Illegal Games.

OTHER than purely municipal matters and the quiet government of our towns obtrude themselves upon the notice of him who would record their annals before there existed a standing military force or army, and when centralisation had not attained its present importance. Our south-western boroughs on the coast had not only to govern, but to defend themselves, as frontier towns, against the enemy. The mayor for his year had to superintend all kinds of military duties, which were very complicated before the weapons of the earliest ages had yielded to the arms of modern times; in a word, ere bows and arrows were disused, owing to the introduction of great guns, or cannon, fired with gunpowder, and the smaller arms, musketry, &c. The mayor was captain of the soldiers, but appointed some one under him to discipline and lead them. A mayor unwilling to be troubled with the office turned the matter over to the lieutenants of the county, who put in a captain.*

That Lyme was fortified seaward, according to the system of the middle ages, at an early period, cannot be doubted. There was, indeed, great occasion for protection against a roving, plundering, and destroying enemy and pirates, such as our coast so often suffered from. At what precise time the coast towns were fortified, in the modern acceptation of the word, having walls upon which cannon were mounted, is uncertain. The archives of Lyme Regis (excepting some charters, &c.) do not extend back so far; in some towns they are lost. The subject is of high interest.

Many towns were fenced in with walls before the invention of gunpowder. In 1262 Henry III. made a murage grant; that is, for the walling in (or repairing, as was the case in this instance,) of Chichester. In 1266 a similar grant was made for walling in the town of Lewes. A cart-load of iron paid 1*d.*; a horse-load of iron, ¼*d.*; a cart-load of corn, ½*d.*; a cart of sea-fish, 4*d.*; 1000 herrings, 1*d.*; a load of brushwood, ¼*d.*; a tumbrel of squirrels, ½*d.* Thus the protection of property was effected by a tax upon the industrious classes and on even the lowest of the population.† This walling in of a town by way of protection is not the fortifying a town in the acceptation attached to it when gunpowder was invented.

Many towns were not entirely surrounded by walls until the time of Edward I. Many border towns were imperfectly protected by fortifications before the fourteenth century.

* Foolscap sheet in the corporation archives of Lyme.

† See Horsfield's Histories of Lewes and Sussex.

Southampton was enclosed by walls in the reign of Edward III., as a deed in the archives attests.

The mayor and burgesses of Poole were about to wall, entrench, and fortify that town and port in the eleventh year of Henry VI., 1433, being a town inhabited, as the king's letters patent have it, by a multitude of people. The king gave licence for the same; and ordered that Melcombe should be no longer a port, but a creek, owing to its being weak and insufficient, from the scarcity of people there.

Bristol was fortified, in the modern acceptation of the word, in the reign of Henry VI. That important city was not left to the mere strength of walls and towers, but had the means of keeping at a distance enemies assembled to assail it.

There was 20 cwt. of gunpowder in store at Bristol in the reign of Henry VI. The sum of 40*l.* was to be laid out there for the purchase of certain guns and "other stuff," for the defence of the town.

A dozen brazen guns were to be made, shooting "peletts as grete as a Parys balle or lesse, and every gonne with iiij chambers."

Without reference to the invention and introduction of modern artillery, we may not sufficiently estimate the merit due to our borough worthies in regard to their choice of new arms, and laying aside the former implements of destruction. A few lines will show us the several dates of the introduction of the weapons of modern warfare.

Bombards were invented about the time of Edward III.;

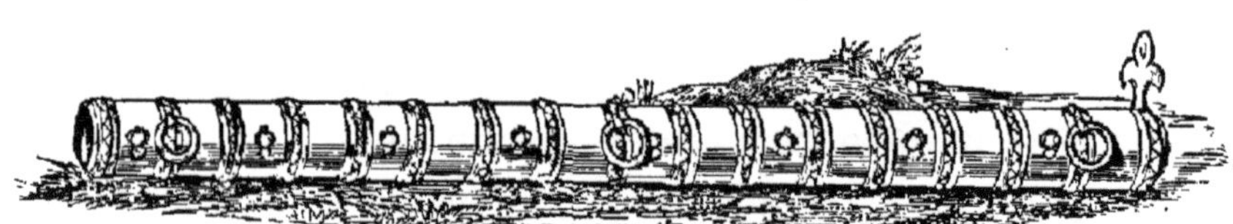

Old English Cannon, formerly in the Tower of London.

they were bars of iron hooped together. Cannon was a name given from the chamber to admit the *can,* or canister.

The first cannon used in England was at the siege of Berwick in 1405. Whether cannon was used at Crecy is very doubtful.

The ship which carried Philippa, sister of Henry IV., Queen of Denmark, Sweden, and Norway, to her home, A.D. 1406, had two guns, 40 lbs. of powder, and forty *stones* for guns.*

In 1512 brass ordnance was first founded by an Englishman.

Gunpowder was manufactured in England in 1412, but not perhaps in large quantity.†

The first Englishman who made artillery of font metal in England was John Owen, who in 1535 began to make brass ordnance, as cannons, culverins, and such like, in Sussex. The first cannon of cast iron made in England was at Bucksteed in Sussex, the iron country at that time, in 1543.‡

In 1573 there was a piece of ordnance at Edinburgh three yards long and more, unstocked, which "shoteth a stone bygger than a greate peny lof." This loaf was then very large.§

It was enacted, 4 Henry VIII., 1513, that good and substantial bulwarks, brayes, walls, and ditches were to be made whenever the justices and sheriffs (not officers skilled in war) shall think needful. Such bulwarks were to be erected in the lands of any persons without any manner of payment to them (the many benefited at the unfair cost of the few), and earth to be dug gratis!

St. Catherine's Fort at Fowey was erected by the townspeople in the reign of Henry VIII.

The same king erected block-houses in particular spots, such as at Brownsea Island, at the entrance of Poole Harbour, in 1547, and furnished a whole culverin, a demi-culverin, sakers, a portpiece with two chambers, a slinge with

* Ellis's Original Letters.

† Weale's Quarterly Papers on Engineering, vol. v.

‡ Stow's Annals.

§ Ellis's Letters.

two chambers, a serpentine with two chambers, ladles, sponges, powder, and shot.

The charge of maintaining the fort fell upon the town of Poole. In the 4th of Elizabeth the town procured by petition fresh cannon. Lyme Regis was most likely provided with great guns by the king. At what time is unknown. The fort called the Gun Cliffe was a well-known locality in the reign of Henry IV., but only as *Le Cliffe.* There were no guns for years afterwards.

It was in 1544 that the townsmen of Lyme beat off the French vessels that made an assault upon the town, when King Harry had made the voyage to Boulogne. This they did at their own charge. It is not surprising that our principal men took great pride in the "town gonnes." William Tudbold, in 1551, left 20*s.* to the "mainteynance of the same." John Hassard, mayor, charges in his accounts the same year one penny for two men "dressing the goones at Christmas." A penny was the customary Christmas gift or box to the gunners.

> "Robert Willyams had paid to him to 'chute the gones on May-day, iiij*d.*'"

In all our borough sea-ports the maintenance of the guns and the due *shooting* the same at stated seasons, and when great men, "the jentlemen, bethe in town," was a considerable burden. The mayor and his brethren were glad of an opportunity to relieve themselves and barter a share in the immunities possessed by their borough for gunpowder. William Pytte, merchant, of Weymouth, wished to enjoy the advantages to be acquired at Poole. He agreed to reside at Poole upon the death of his mother; and was made a free burgess in 1583, upon payment of 2 cwt. of good corn powder yearly, and for his absence, 20*s.* a year.

The bill for Melcombe to be fortified was read the first time February 9. 1558-9.*

After escaping now from the violence of an enemy by

* Sir Simonds d'Ewes Journal of the Proceedings of Parliament.

means of artillery, we should be led to reward the men who served the guns, and that arm would ever find honourable mention made of it by our grateful tongues. In Edward VI.'s reign, however, the guns were a novelty. We trust the men who served them were well rewarded; but a feeling bordering upon veneration was at that time felt for the very guns themselves. A raging enemy had been kept from landing, and all the evils of former invasions, too well handed down to them by their parents, averted. The old man about to die reviewed his past career, and piously set about the just disposal of his worldly goods. He judged that when he should be under the sod more enemies might come along the coast and harass those he had left behind, who were very dear to him. King and country were much to him; but his dear borough was more. He needed no prompter to remind him of "the toun gonnes," and associated them in his mind as being a terror to enemies that would harm those he loved so well.

A proclamation, 3rd August, 1542, limited the price of weapons as follows. Persons were empowered to enter into men's houses, as a forfeiture of 10*l.* was laid upon those who exceeded the price.

	s.	*d.*
Bow, best sort	3	4
" second	2	6
" third	2	0
Sheaf of livery arrows	5	0
Leaden case	0	6
Girdle	0	2
Sheaf of arrows, 8 or 9 inch the feather	2	4
Gross of bowstring	3	4
Demy lance, with cuirasse, vambrace, potren headpiece, with a beaver	45	0
Demy launce, called a Collyn cliff, ready made and headed	2	8
Arming sword for a horseman	2	8
Pair of gauntlets with joints	2	8
Almayn ryvett, best sort	7	6
" second	6	8
Javelin, best sort	1	2

	s.	d.
Javelin, second - - - -	0	10
Fighting bill ready helved - - -	1	0
Flemish halberd, best sort - - -	1	8
" second - - -	1	4

The yeomen of the guard of Henry VII. were armed half with bows and arrows, half with harquebusses. Some mention is made in a coming page of a drawing representing the march of an army, in which armour and artillery appear, with the callyver and long bow. Charges for bows and arrows and guns appear mixed up in the same accounts. John Tudbold, Mayor of Lyme in 1545, paid for "a bowe and sheffe of arrows, a present to Mr. Strangways, 5*s.* 4*d.*" In the same account is a charge for sending a man to Weymouth about gunpowder, 1*s.* 6*d.* In 1545 was also paid to "Wm. Deane for a molde to cast the pellets in for the basys, 10*d.*" A rate in the corporation archives, in the reign of Henry VIII., is labelled "The bill for the gon powder."

A piece of ordnance, or in other words, a great gun or cannon, was purchased in London for the town by Roger Garland, mayor 1550, when 10*s.* earnest money was paid. It is a singular fact, that the piece of ordnance was carried from London to Taunton, at the great charge of 43*s.* 2*d.*; the further charge from Taunton to Lyme was 8*s.*

This interesting fact clearly proves that at this date a cannon could only have been conveyed into the west of England by way of Taunton, the present route to Lyme from London; whether this arose from the want of bridges in Dorset, Wilts, &c. The expense incurred was very considerable.

In 1557, John Hassard, mayor, charges —

	s.	d.
2 yards of canvas to make bags to put gunpowder in, and for the marking - - - -	1	10
35 lb. of big shot for the ordnance at 2*d.* the lb. -	5	10

Gunpowder was made on the Continent.

The maintenance of the town guns, in a word, the garrisoning Lyme by the corporation, was an expensive matter.

In 1597 the Town Accompt Book shows a heavy expenditure for a small borough. There is under one head alone —

	£	s.	d.
274 lb. of powder - - - -	14	14	0
One barrel - - - -	9	5	1

Among the "town stuff" to be used in case of need or war's alarms was this formidable array: six bows; two black bills, and two daggers.* The next year, 1560, witnessed the addition of a pair of corslets complete. An act was passed, 33 Henry VIII. cap. 9., that all persons under sixty years of age were to have bows and arrows. Aliens were not to practice archery.†

The town of Lyme and coast of the south-west of England was for many years, at the close of Elizabeth's reign, a frontier country towards an enemy greater by comparison than Napoleon in modern times. Directly opposite West Dorset lay St. Maloes, full of shipping, and Brittany, then in the hands of the Spaniards. The hatred of our Dorset and Devon countrymen was then almost entirely directed against Spaniards. Philip of Spain had a navy of 140 galleys, which interrupted the wine trade between England and Gascony. While England had not one single battalion in constant pay, Philip had a standing army of 50,000 excellent troops. With these he had usurped Portugal, made conquests in the East Indies, and was a dangerous neighbour to Guernsey and Jersey. Hence the expressions of alarm and indignation at the Spanish nation, which was then looked upon as the natural enemy of England. Our townsmen, who witnessed the conflict between their countrymen and their townsmen too, in their own town's ships or vessels, and the proud Spanish Armada, in sight of Lyme, though without spy-glasses, which had not been invented at that time, had their animosity keenly excited against the Spaniard. Their reluctance to march inland to distant musters can be readily accounted for, as they left their town exposed to the enemy.

* Town Accompt Book, A.D. 1559.

† Ten bow-staves had to be imported for every butt of malmsey wine imported by an act of 1 Richard II. cap. 2.

Certain gallant active and forward citizens having had experience both abroad and at home, voluntarily exercised themselves when the Spanish Armada was expected, and trained others for the ready use of war. These 300 merchants Stow speaks of met every Tuesday.

The following lines of Mr. T. B. Macaulay breathe the spirit of excitement that men felt at the lighting of the beacons, so bountifully distributed upon our coast hills: —

"For swift to east and swift to west the warning radiance spread —
High on St. Michael's Mount it shone — it shone on Beachy Head.
Far o'er the deep the Spaniard saw, along each southern shire,
Cape beyond cape, in endless range, those twinkling points of fire."

Beacon upon a Coast Hill.

The beacons set up in 1588 were partly of wood, and consequently temporary. These are not to be confounded with the beacons *built* in Charles II.'s reign.

There are in parish books charges in 1665–6 and 1678 for "carrying warrants about building the beacons."

A beacon built upon Trinity Hill, near Axminster, in 1678, cost 22*l.*; which sum was defrayed by the foregoing and some other parishes. The erection of these stone structures is due to the plots and alarms which distinguished that reign, and which appearing to be indefinite as to time, a permanent provision was made for alarming the counties, and not a temporary one, as in the remarkable example of a Spanish invasion.

The dread of a foreign enemy was very great, and an alarm in Mr. Ellesdon's mayoralty in 1595 gave rise to a highly illustrative entry: —

> "*Item,* paid for the carriage of a letter to Mr. Drake [of Ashe House, in the parish of Musbury] to give him advertisement of the Spanish ships, and to cause his parishioners to come hither to help us, 4*d.*"

A bulwark, or fort, was constructed at the Cobb (where at that time were no houses), by a spot called "Birch Door." Rods, stakes, and seams of turves are charged for by William Brooke.

The forts of many ancient maps, and bird's-eye-view maps and drawings, are, like the church towers and castles of those Tudor illustrations, purely conventional. The ordinary type is a round tower, with two guns or more run out from the first story; with one or two guns, or more, mounted on the flat roof *en barbette.* Some, as if for variety, have a parapet embattled, others not.

Leland speaks of a similar earth or mud fort at Portsmouth.* Such constructions came into vogue from the

* He alludes to "a mudde walle armed with tymbre, whereon be great peaces of yron and brasse ordinanns. This peace of walle having a diche without it."

absence of splinters or pieces of stone when struck by shot. Some details will explain what was done at the Gun Cliff, Lyme, in 1595.

	s.	d.
Item, paid for three seams of straw for the *mud wall* at the Clyffe, and for horse hier to carry the same straw	2	0
Item, paid to five workmen for the making up of the mud wall at the cliff, for four days, at 8*d*. the day, and one at 10*d*. the day - - - -	14	10
Item, paid for 2 horses, for two days, to tread the mortar - - - - -	2	0
Five labourers to make mortar and 2 horses to tread -	4	0

This *mortar* is the soft earth mixed with chopped straw, such as in Devonshire obtains the name of *cobb*.

The Dorsetshire MUSTERS of the sixteenth century, and VIEW OF ARMOUR AND WEAPONS, are rendered doubly interesting from the transition state of offensive arms, and the clear exposition of the nature of the force that alone existed to protect the country from invasion, and what means they possessed for so doing. Extracts from the MUSTER PAPERS, or MUSTER BOOKS, in the archives of Lyme, will exhibit much information of the chivalrous marchings and display of weapons, and too often the "faulty" state of the same when the justices and great men visited the borough.

The first entry is a charge in 1558 —

	s.	d.
For a muster bill - - - -	1	6
Riding to Hinton [St. George, the seat of the Poulett family], to certify Mr. Poulett of the muster - -	0	6
Horse-hire to Hinton - - - -	0	6
Man's trouble - - - - -	0	6

The following abstract of weapons, &c., has partly appeared in the Author's Introduction to the Yonge Diary, and has been made from a muster paper six feet long, entitled "A View of Armour and Weapons taken at Lyme Regis, the 6th April, in the 15th year of the reign of Elizabeth, &c., by the mayor and his brethren of the said town, as well of all the householders, their sons, journeymen, and prentices, as also of all sojourners remaining within the said town by vertue of a warrant directed from the Lord Howard Viscount Byndon, William Lord St. John, with other justices of peace within the said county of Dorset."

No. of Men.	Offensive and Defensive Weapons each possessed.
11	had bows and sheaf of arrows, a steel cap and a bill, and a sword and dagger. Some had either a corselet, a currion and a murrion, "more" (*i. e.* in addition), a callyver and murrion, some a currion, a murrion, and a skull.
3	bows and 12 arrows each.
14	bills.*
9	pikes.
1	a bill and a pike.
1	a bill and steel cap.
6	sword and dagger.
3	sword, dagger, and pike.
3	curryons.
1	skull and a pike.
6	harquebuss and murrion.
2	harquebusses.

Two callyvers and 9 corslets were supplementary arms.

The following is an estimate of the charge for the buying of eight pieces of ordnance, and the mounting and planting of them with powder and shot convenient for the same at Weymouth about the year 1582-3:—

* "The very beadsmen learn to bend their bows
Of double fatal yew against thy state;
Yea, distaff women manage rusty *bills*."
Shakspeare's Richard III.

Eight pieces of ordnance —	£
4 demy culverins, 5 sacres } 16,000 lbs. at 5*l.* the 1000 lb. - -	80
2 cwt. of powder, at 5*l.* the cwt. - - -	30
2000 shot, 10*s.* cwt. - - - -	10
8 carriages and wheels, with ladles and sponges and other necessaries - - - - -	20
	£140

Charge of the bulwark and platform, 2 in Weymouth, 2 in Melcombe, with 2 houses for the keeping dry the said ordnance - - - - - - £60

The prices of the above and other armour were set down: —

	s.	*d.*		*s.*	*d.*
Corslet - -	30	0	A harquebuss - -	8	0
Callyver - -	20	0	A currion - -	16	0
A pike - -	2	0	A murrion - -	8	0
Bow and sheaf of arrows in 1545 - -	5	4	Head piece and lining	7	0
			Head piece - -	4	0
A sword - -	6	0	Pair of drum-heads -	4	0
A sword girdle -	1	2	Mould.		
Barrel of gunpowder, £6	19	0	Flask and touchbox.		
20 bullets - -	0	2	Girdle.		

The classification of the 186 men was not determined by the weapons any one may have brought; for among the pikemen were men who had only a bill and no pike. They were classed as follows: —

30 pikemen.
16 archers.
49 harquebussers.
4 gunners for great ordnance.
1 the "drome" (a drummer).
17 billmen.
8 old men not serviceable.

Some sojourners, journeymen, and apprentices had no arms, but were classed thus: —

* A loose sheet amongst the Sherren papers.

11 pikemen.
27 harquebussers.
4 archers.
18 billmen.

In 1580 an account of the want of such armour as the justices found lacking in Lyme Regis was taken: —

18 men with callyvers, harquebusses, and currions wanted something or other: many wanted several things.
2 archers: one wanted a bow, dagger, and scabbard; the other wanted a skull.
3 corslets: one wanted a sword and dagger; second, was faulty in all; the third, all untrimmed.
3 pikes: all faulty in all.
21 able bodied men were without weapons.
19 archers, calliver men, &c. were "not at home."
21 men of Stockland are entered on this muster paper as having appeared at the same time: 21 are complained of as being harquebussers without their harquebuss; and archers without a bow.

In 1587 in a muster paper appears a list of those who mustered, arranged under the head of the weapon they wielded, opposite the names of those townsmen who furnished the weapon. Here and there the names of townsmen appear who served and furnished their own weapon. To distinguish those who serve from the substitutes they are called "soldiers." *The Troop* in 1590 consisted of eight principal residents, who furnished their own weapons, and are distinguished from the *Trayns*, as a *corps d'élite.*

On the 12th March, 1587, several magistrates gave notice that they were about to proceed along the coast from Weymouth to Lyme, to view those places that were dangerous in respect of the facilities they afforded for the landing of an enemy. The mayors were to attend and bring those persons skilled in fortification. Some remarks upon this have been furnished in another place.

The warlike entries in the town accounts in 1595, on the occasion of some of the town soldiers being pressed for

Boulogne, exhibit a mixture of the ancient and modern arms.

	s.	*d.*
Given to the souldiers pressed for Bullayn - -	1	0
Item, for making clean of a corslett, sword, and dagger to be sent for Bullen - - - - - -	1	0
Item, paid for a pike for the corslett that was sent to Bullen - - - - - - - -	3	0
Item, paid for a horse to carry the harness, and for his charges that carried the corslett and rest of the furniture to Bridport - - - - - -	1	4
Item, paid Varland for a *mould* to cast the shot for the great ordnance - - - - - -	0	2
Half a hundred of Saker shot - - - -	6	8
Powder to the value of 25*l.* was now provided.		
Item, paid for a *staff* to carry the ensign on - -	1	0
„ two pounds of *lead* to put into the ensign staff, and for a *spear* and a *ring* for the same staff - - - -	1	8

Captain George Summers, afterwards Admiral Sir George Summers, marshalled the force of the town, consisting of 126 men, in May, 1598, when Sir Edmund Uvedall, knight, viewed them.

The corslets were 4; musquets 48; callyvers 45; men that bore only pikes 29.

Weymouth and Melcombe had 187, Poole 106 men, armed as above.*

In 1599 the bows and arrows finally disappeared from the muster rolls.† The musket gained ground; no more, perhaps, by its value, than by the special recommendation of the deputy lieutenants, 18th April, 1596, signed Sir Matthew Arundel, Sir George Trenchard, and Sir Ralph Horsey, "to encrease armour and weapon, especially corslet and musket." Nichols writes, that at Leicester, the queen, in 1598, ordered the bows and arrows to be refused and supplied with muskets.

* Certificate of the forces of Dorset, Harleian MS. 3324.

† Five archers out of 145 men mustered in 1591.

The following is an abstract of weapons at two several dates:—

	A.D. 1591.	A.D. 1599.
Corslets	5	*
Callivers	26	49
Pikes	6	6
Halberds	10	6
Bills	8	7
Bows	2	0
Sword and dagger	1	0
Able men without arms	49	Musketeers 65
	107	169

It is a curious fact that Kurds, armed with bows and arrows, were lately with Omer Pacha at Varna.

The Lyme muster men were summoned, 20th July, 1598, to appear at Bridport by eight o'clock in the morning, by Sir William Poulett, John Yonge, and Robert Williams, justices. The Marquess of Winchester, from Basing House, directed the deputy lieutenants of Dorset not to muster the Lyme men in any foreign shire, as they are upon the sea-coast, and had been very forward in furnishing themselves with armour and weapons; to have to march many miles in our own country, when the terrors of the enemy were so rife, and every step led away from the locality the foe would first visit, became the subject of special complaint. The train men occasionally mustered about 1577 at Dorchester, Beaminster, and Bridport. Permission to muster at Lyme was afterwards obtained; but not permanently, for our townsmen were again required to leave the town unprotected, and march to distant musters.

In 1623 Sir John Brown laboured to obtain a removal of this evil, and Mr. Hugh Pyne, a counsellor, of Cathanger, Somersetshire, was paid 3*l.* 14*s.* for the pains he and his men had taken to free the townsmen from going out of town to muster.

* Perhaps the musketeers were supposed to possess a corslet.

We have spoken of the affection displayed by the good townsmen towards the "town guns," that is, the guns actually belonging to the borough. Their love for the guns was probably diminished when the pieces of ordnance were lent to boroughs on the coast by the crown.

The crown probably — it may be the townsmen themselves — deemed the sea-side batteries inefficient, and so pieces of artillery that were serviceable were lent.

This first occurred at Lyme in 1625, when five pieces of ordnance were delivered to Sir Walter Erle. This fact is recorded by an entry of the payment of certain fees, which, in keeping with the times, amounted to 12*l.* A bond was sent up to the king as security for the ordnance so lent.

With our improved modern views, how strange does it appear that the defence of a tract of the country at large should have been left to the burgesses of a little town upon the coast. The whole country was interested in the repulse of a proud foreign enemy, and should have borne equally its share of the burden. However, this injustice was corrected in part in 1625.

The charges at Lyme on this occasion were: —

	£	*s.*	*d.*
Five pieces of ordnance delivered to Sir Walter Erle and sent down. The fees	12	0	0
A bond sent up to the king, as security for the ordnance, in a box, charged	0	0	1
Powder and match	0	2	6
Two axles for the brass piece and for two tomkyns and other necessaries	0	5	0
Six pounds of shot	0	1	9
Freight of the ordnance from London	3	15	0

It is to be remarked that the next year, viz. 1626, some ordnance was conveyed from London to Lyme by land, by what route is not known, the charge for which was 26*l.* 6*s.* 7*d.*

The military preparations along the coast continued. At

Lyme the borough prepared for what must be deemed a little war. There is an entry of—

	£	s.	d.
The two drummers at the muster - - -	0	1	4
Two men bearing the *town* musquets - - -	0	1	0
To a cutler for making clean the arms - -	0	0	6
To Robert Sweet for one day's service with the flute -	0	0	4
The town ensign cost in 1628, with 3*s.* for lines -	5	0	0

In 1627 great activity was manifested at Lyme and at other parts of the coast. In the Yonge Diary, p. 106., is stated, "There being difference between this state and France, we began a fortification at Seaton for the defence of that place [six miles west of Lyme] against *pirates and other enemies.*" The magistrates of that neighbourhood, Sir Edmund Prideaux, Sir William Pole, Mr. John Drake, Mr. Fry, and Mr. Walter Yonge, granted warrants for the hundreds near, and even rather distant ones, to send some thirty, others twenty men, for a week, or else pay for men at the rate of 8*d.* a day for each man. Thus was thrown up upon Seaton beach the great mound of earth, which cost 24*l.*, now called the "Burrow," by corruption for the "Barrow." A fort was constructed on the summit. No one knew in 1845 how it came there; which proves how tradition often fails to perpetuate the recollection of really important transactions.

	£	s.	d.
1627, Baronet Seymour [perhaps Sir Edward Seymour, who was to have his companies of trained soldiers, like other gentlemen named, ready to march for Plymouth, in 1622, at an hour's warning] gave towards the fort at Lyme - - - - - -	5	0	0
Several persons, Mr. Anthony Ellesden gave 30*s.*, Mr. William Davy, 20*s.*, &c., to the building of the fort [I believe the "Stoning, or Stone Fort," west of the sea, front of the town, towards the Cobb] - -	3	17	8
Dinner to Sir Walter Erle when he came hither about the fort - - - - - - -	0	6	8

When a country had to be defended by the walls of a

borough, which had to be erected and maintained by the burgesses themselves, technicalities about rating, and the rights of certain residents, produced the effect that will ever occur where the respective obligations of each individual are not accurately defined. Whatever reasons predominated, some persons persisted in refusing, while the contributions of others amounted to 3*l.* 18*s.* 8*d.* in subscriptions, ranging from 2*s.* to 30*s.* each.

The parties who refused were not allowed to remain quietly. An entry in 1628 will show this: —

	s.	*d.*
Paid to Mr. Richard Harvey, that he paid in London to solicit the Lord Suffolk to get an order to compel them to pay towards the building of the fort - -	3	5

The butts were at Millgreen. William Whetcomb gathered 7*s.* 4*d.* to make the butts in 1555. Again, in 1557, 12*s.* are charged for the cutting of turfs, and carrying them home, and for making the butts.

In 1569, May 2nd, a jury at the court of hustings presented, as a grievance, "that there is to much *bowling* and to little *shoting*."

There was doubtless some alarm of enemies, for the same jury expressed their anxiety for the safety of the town, by precepting the mayor: "*Item*, that Mr. Maior do cause our ordnance to be in a readiness and placed, and also to see all such powder as hath been lent out to be had in by Whitsunday next, or be fined 40*s.*" * In the following year, 1570, it was ordered that Mr. Mayor do cause to be mended the butts at the Millgreen, upon pain of 10*s.* Complaint is again made, in 1571, that "to much unlawful games are used and no bowes exercised." The mayor, in 1578, was directed by the court leet, under pain of 10*s.*, to see that every man have and exercise artillery (*i. e.* bows and arrows) according to the statute: in which particular all were found faulty in 1581. At Castle Combe many

* The corporations of boroughs on the coast lent gunpowder to each other.

were fined, in 1576, 6*s.* 8*d.* each for not exercising bows and arrows. The fine was reduced to 12*d.* each. The constables were to search every month to see if the people had bows and arrows. Every one, from seventeen to sixty, was to procure bows and arrows.*

The unlawful games in the reign of Edward IV. were dice, "coyts," and even football. They were doubtless objectionable, not of themselves, but for their consequences, as will be shown in allusion to a later reign.

In 1542 (33 Henry VIII. cap. xi.) the bowyers, fletchers, stringers, and arrow-head makers, finding their occupation affected by the introduction of other arms, procured an "Acte for Mayntenance of Artyllerie and debarring of unlawful Games, such as Logating in the Fields, Slide-shrift, otherwise Shovegrote. No one was to keep a common house or place of bowling, coyting, cloyshe cayles, half-bowle, tennys, dysing, table or carding, or any other manner of game prohibited." This is a good specimen of class-legislation. Our countrymen adopted a better kind of arms; those who continued to make a decidedly inferior kind procured the enactment of laws which aimed at doing away with most of the sports with which men recreated themselves, hoping by such an exclusive system to drive men to archery, so little was liberty understood in the reign of the Tudors. Only a few years from this date religious feeling prompted to a suppression of all games and sports: such a feeling did not enter into the question at this time.

The admirer of the game of cricket will desire to learn something about its introduction. It does not figure among the unlawful games, for it was first mentioned only about the year 1719.†

Stow exclaimed "our bows are turned into bowls." And before him Bishop Latimer, in one of his sermons preached before Edward VI., indulged in indignant reclamations against the disuse of archery. Historic recollections gave to the use

* Hist. of C. Combe, by G. P. Scrope, Esq.

† Timbs's Cur. of London.

of the bow and arrow in his eye so very great importance, that the good bishop eulogises it as a gift of God for us to excell all nations withall. The art of shooting he styles "God's instrument whereby He hath given us the victory against our enemies." Without noticing the "músquet," the bishop desired the lords, even as they loved the honour and glory of God, and intended to remove his indignation, to send forth some sharp proclamation to the justices of peace, because they did not perform their duty. He desired the lords to charge the justices upon their allegiance that this singular benefit of God be practised and not turned into bowling, glossing, and dicing within the towns. After an account of his father's teaching him to shoot, and the increase of his bows and arrows according to his strength, the bishop winds up with this sentence: "It is a godly art, a wholesome kind of exercise, and much commended in physic."

The clergy of this reign, wiser in one respect than the good bishop, leave our gallant men in the field to the use of the Minié rifle and Colt's revolvers, if they do with their professional skill determine that with these they can act with greater effect offensively and defensively.

By a statute made 33 Henry VIII. it was enacted "that none under the age of seventeen should shoot with a bow of yew, except his parents were worth 10*l.* per annum in lands, or 40 marks in goods; and for every bow made of yew, the bowyer not inhabiting London or the suburbs should make four, and the inhabitant there two, bows of other wood." *

The constables of Lyme in 1577 made this presentment, "that sometimes there be divers merchants and other honest (*i. e.* honourable) men that doth bowl as followeth:—

Richard Baret,	Richard Davey,
John Jurden,	Nicholas Hassard,
William Semons (?),	with others.
John Bellamy,	

Some persons used the butts on the Sabbath day, which

* See Notes and Queries, Sept. 20. 1851.

caused a presentment in 1581, as being contrary to a statute. It was added on the file of presentments, "*Item*, for artillery so many Sundays."

Bowling was the great offence in the eye of the authorities. Thirty bowlers were presented in 1596.

On 2nd October, 1598, were presented, upon the evidence of the constables, Peter Brown and others, who were players at tables on 26th May. Each was fined 12*d.**

John Gosse, the last man who mustered with "bow and arrow," was presented for playing *ad tabulas* — at tables.

John Somers, John Thornton, and others were similarly fined as players at cards.*

In 1602 no mechanic at Castle Combe was to play at unlawful games unless he could spend 40*s.* a year.†

There were presented as bowlers Richard Lamberton, ‖ William Davy, Anthony Moone, Robert Bragg, John Vyney, Thomas Kelke, William Ellesdon, jun., Thomas Clarke, John Herridge, Nicholas Perrat, Thomas Diggens, Robert Amarsh, ‖ Silvester Jurdeyn, Nicholas Daye, Robert Breholt, Andrew Davy, Nicholas Holcomb, Robert Davy, sen., John Spering, Philip Stansby, Ynes Winter's servants, John Sprake's servant, and Robert Barnes, jun.

Each was fined 12*d.*: they were "common bowlers." Those with ‖ before their names were actually on the jury, whose names are appended.‡

Robert Barnes.	Thomas Pears.
James Hill.	Thomas Whitford.
Richard Roze.	William Legg.
William Jurdeyn.	Henry Palmer.
George Pley.	Robert Collens.
Walter Tucker.	Phillip Harvey.
Silvester Jurdon.	William Ellesdon.
William Davy.	William Hill.
John Kerridge.	

Richard Sommers and Thomas Clarke, who were pre-

* In 1600 such offenders were fined 6*s.* 8*d.*

† Hist. of C. Combe, by G. P. Scrope, Esq.

‡ The bowlers in 1600 were fined 6*s.* 8*d.*, according to the statute.

sented at the same time for fighting and drawing blood, were fined 9*d.* each.

In 1567, at Castle Combe, butchers' shops were of all other places the special resort of gamblers, who made the meat before them the stake for which they played. Butchers who allowed this were to be fined 6*s.* 8*d.*

Having shown that what detracted from archery was exposed to punishment under statutes made to support and encourage the same, it should be added that the butts at Lyme, being out of order, furnished matter for a presentment in 1601. They were repaired in 1633 at the cost of 1*l.*

Bows and arrows appear no more in the muster papers after the year 1599.

The exact time when long bows were disused is unknown; but in 1621 it was moved in Parliament to repeal some regulations, as "guns be now the service of the state, and long bows obsolete." Arrows were shot by the English at the isle of Rhé in 1621.*

Bows and arrows are much lauded in a proclamation sent forth in 1633 for their service, by which great victories were gotten in ancient times; and then the praise turns from victories to their use, by the exercise of shooting to preserve health, strength, and agility, and by which we avoid idleness, unlawful disports, and such like enormities. The train bands were at this time to learn an exercise invented by an ancient archer, William Neade, who used the pike and bow together. The same veteran invented a new quiver for the arrows. He had begun to teach the service to the Artillery Company of London.

The author has a drawing of the march of horsemen in complete armour, both man and horse; footmen with callyvers or harquebusses fired with a slow match or cord, artillery on wheels drawn by horses, and companies of archers armed with the long bow. This drawing is from a MS. of about the time of Henry VIII.

There is an entry of a presentment of a jury at Lyme in 1648, which will be judged to be more extraordinary as that

* Weale's Quarterly Papers on Engineering.

town stood a dreadful siege in 1644 for seven weeks, and was defended by Admiral Blake against Prince Maurice. To crown all, we give a presentment of the court leet, 8th May, 1660: —

"And that there are no butts within the parish of Lyme Regis, and there have been none here by the space of 3 months last past, for which the inhabitants of the said parish have forfeited the penalty in the statute mentioned, viz. 20*s*. And nevertheless it is ordered that the inhabitants of the said parish shall make and set up butts there before next court, under the further pain of 20*s*."

In the reign of Charles II. some attempts were made by the nobility to revive archery.

The arms that the Duke of Monmouth brought for his rebellion in 1685 were partly offensive partly defensive. Backs and breasts were stored at the Town Hall, and were captured by the captain of the frigate that was in pursuit of the duke. These do not appear to have been valued. Defensive armour was just going out of use.

The Royal Scots guard, commanded by the Earl of Orkney, had not at Anne's accession adopted the use of firearms; they wore heavy steel caps, and used bows and arrows, with broadswords and targets.

The Behaviour of Soldiers upon the March and in Quarters.

We can hardly realise the fact of a country being taxed to make good the wanton spoil and damage committed by soldiers, our own countrymen, marching through in time of peace. Such was however the case.

Richard Chafin, of Sherborne, informed the magistrates at the Easter sessions, 1629, that at the last removal of his Majesty's soldiers out of the county of Devon towards London, he had two horses (being all he had, and of more value than his estate besides) taken from him [*i. e.* impressed], and employed for the removal of the said soldiers and their armour from Sherborne; and one of these horses was by the soldiers killed outright, the other spoilt, and by their means long kept from him [taken away towards London to be sold, though ultimately recovered], to his damage of five pounds at the least, for which he is without remedy. Humbly moved to commiserate his case and afford him some relief out of the treasury of the county, the court ordered the treasurer of the western division to pay Richard Chafin for the loss and damage which he had sustained in his horses.

As the troops marched through the country in 1588, the year of the Spanish Armada, they sold their arms as they went, falsely alleging that they had received no pay and were obliged to do so. See the proclamation sent forth by the queen denying the truth of the soldiers' statement.

The soldiers sometimes enacted a bloody tragedy. The Wellington murder is a terrible example. One hundred and sixty soldiers, lately pressed in the county of Devon, were on their march towards the north, at the town of Wellington in Somersetshire. There they murdered one of their officers, Lieut. Compton Eyres, and dragged his body about the streets. Having thus brutally behaved themselves, they disbanded. A proclamation was issued in 1640, calling upon the authorities to seize these men and naming several of them.

At the beginning of the Diary of Walter Yonge, Esq., of Colyton, the writer states that the plagues of England are noted by figures in the margin. In recording the coming down to Plymouth of 10,000 soldiers in 1625, the writer forgot not to draw a rose in the margin, marking soldiers as one of the greatest plagues of the country. During their stay all kinds of violence abounded. Under modern discipline the people of an invaded country suffer less than did the counties formerly at the hands of their own countrymen in arms. The Lyme men knew the sad inconvenience of this, and used means to avert the evil, which the accounts partially disclose. We find an entry in 1625: "Given to the ensign of the soldiers for avoiding the town, 1*l.* 0*s.* 4*d.*" At the same date the town clerk was sent to come to an understanding with the officers fifteen miles from the borough,

"To Mr. Carpenter, for his journey to Beaminster, for avoiding the soldiers, 3*s.* 6*d.*" "Mr. John Seward, for his journey to Dorchester about the soldiers, 5*s.*" In 1626 an entry appears thus: "Given to Capt. Gylpen for passing his soldiers by the town, and for entertaining of himself and his wife and five soldiers, 1*l.* 7*s.* 11*d.*"

In 1627 the sum of 2*l.* 7*s.* 7*d.* had been paid at Lyme for expenses incurred by the marching of some soldiers through the town. This is followed by another entry: "*Item*, more than could be collected towards hose, shoes, and shirts, and conduct money, and horse for them to Bridport, 8*s.* 2*d.*" Again the same year, "Coat and conduct money for the soldiers, 30*s.*"

The "setting forth" soldiers to Guernsey in 1593 occasioned charges to be incurred for which a rate was levied upon Lyme, amounting to 6*l.* 10*s.* 6*d.* Some paid 5*s.* 5*d.*, others only 3*d.* and 2*d.*

Mr. Ellesdon, the Mayor of Lyme, charges 7*l.* 7*s.* 6*d.* about setting forth the expedition to Cales (Cadiz) in 1597. There is another entry for the same, 10*l.* 15*s.* 0*d.*

These are the matters which caused towns to wish the wars were over, and spread dissatisfaction with the conduct of the affairs of the country.

Well might our forefathers declaim against a standing army. How different was the behaviour of the soldiery in the Stuart reigns to that which characterises them in the present century! When soldiers were in the country we read of outrages and disorders. After Monmouth's rebellion some soldiers of Lord Cornbury and Lord Churchill's troops of dragoons broke into a house at Colyton, and stole bone-lace worth 325*l.* There were disorders at Bideford, and Lord Weymouth wrote that his neighbours at Frome and Warminster were in dreadful apprehensions. The licence was shameful. The conduct of Trelawney's regiment in Shaftesbury and Sarum was atrocious. Captain Wolseley encouraged his soldiers to toss the Mayor of Scarborough in a blanket, and said he would make him know that the military power was above the civil. Thomas Coad, in his Memoir, records how a party of soldiers found him at an ale-house wounded, and how brutally they treated him in order to extort money for the payment of their debauch.

Complaints were made to the House of Commons in 1695, that some military men did not pay their quarters at Royston, alleging that their own pay was in arrear. This affair was of great importance, as it led to an inquiry into corrupt practices, which were universal through all the departments of government. The secretary of the Treasury was proved to have taken 200*l.* for procuring or expediting the payment of arrears due to a regiment. Col. Kirke, of western fame, had a regiment on the books which was by a fiction marching about Ireland; but it had no bone and muscle,—it existed only on paper. With such plunder — for pay was drawn for officers and men — handsome hush-money could be well afforded to procure freedom from exposure at the hands of officials who knew of the wickedness.

Wounded Veterans pensioned by the Counties.

Instead of old, worn-out men, who had fought their country's battles for years, being supported from the finances of the country at large in whose cause they had bled, counties were left to provide for their natives as if the war had been for the interest of a particular county.

In 1634 Lord Viscount of Valentia certified the good conduct in the wars of William Nicholls, who had become decrepit. The Court thereupon ordered 3*l.* a year to be paid by the treasurer of the county of Dorset, in quarterly payments, with a quarter's pay in hand. Thus the county of Dorset was taxed to pension a man who had served the country at large. If it happened that many men of any particular county went to the wars, the burdens of the county might have been increased to a great degree. Hence officials would in some cases be led from pecuniary motives to discourage the going to the wars, lest a pension might be required to be furnished.

Nath. Herne, of Netherbury, had 40*s.* a year granted him for his services and wounds.*

Pilgrimage to St. Jago de Compostella.

Ship of the Time of Richard II. (Harl. MS.)

"Than longeth folk to go on pilgrimages,
And palmers for to seken strange strondes
To serve halwes couthe in sondry londes."

CHAUCER.

THE rush of great numbers of persons from the country to our sea-port towns in the fifteenth century, in order to take ship as pilgrims to the holy shrine of St. Jago de Compostella, partook of the character of a mania, which possesses a nation in some form or another from time to time, in religious as well as in temporal matters.

This special rage, however, for the pilgrimage to Spain, at

* MS. Book of Dorset Sessions. Mr. Hearn, "Qui Quondam."

one epoch, must not be allowed to call off our attention from a much earlier period.

Pilgrimages to St. Jago were established in the time of Richard I., who, when on his way through France, stopped, like another Hercules, to punish evil doers. Lord William, of the castle of Chisy, was a marauder who spoiled pilgrims on their way to St. Jago. The lion-hearted monarch took the castle and hanged the offender on the spot.*

The Cinque Ports in 1243 loudly complained to the king that the French were masters of the Channel. Not only was fishing interrupted, but the carrying pilgrims to St. Jago was entirely prevented. This trade the shipmasters declared had brought them much profit, as well as the carrying pilgrims to Canterbury by water from distant counties.†

Valorous Crusaders and peaceful pilgrims to the Holy Sepulchre at Jerusalem were held in especial honour. Danger from enemies, men of other nations, mere marauders, and from the infidels themselves, the perils of the distant voyage, arising from storms and rocks, and the great expense made such a pilgrimage to all a serious and to most persons an impossible undertaking.

With a view to meet the exigencies of the time the Pope decided that a pilgrimage to the shrine of St. Jago de Compostella, the capital of Gallicia, in the north-west corner of Spain, should be of equal virtue with a voyage to Jerusalem. Here was an inducement to the religious devotee, to those who had money, leisure, or were under a vow, to benefit their soul at a quarter-peril and a quarter-cost! The offer was a splendid one. It proved irresistible.

The bodies of St. James, the patron saint of Spain, and those of two of his disciples, Athanasius and Theodorus, were to be adored in a subterranean altar.

A series of religious ceremonies had to be performed at this Mecca of Spain; which the Baron of Rosmital duly entered upon at his visit in the year 1466, an account of which is now extant.

Our English pilgrims landed, and had a journey of thirty-

* Hoveden.

† M. Paris.

five miles to perform before arriving at the shrine. The exciting effect of the usual processions was increased by a military display, which gratified the pilgrims generally, and quieted the fears of the less resolute. An armed escort, ostensibly to guard the devotees from the Moslems, gave a semblance of oriental warfare and perils to the undertaking, which might otherwise have appeared tame and insipid. Probably many viewed the whole as a miserable substitute for a pilgrimage to Jerusalem, and rejoiced at anything which savoured of alarms from infidels, and as requiring the protection of the knights of a military order.

These redoubtable knights formed the military order of St. Jago, who undertook to protect the pilgrims on their way to the shrine of their patron saint from the violence of the Moslems. All the pilgrims were not able to do battle in their own defence; for whole families formed themselves into large parties, like caravans over the desert, and wended their way to their Mecca, carrying the young and infant children with them, transported with the resistless spirit of the time. Each party must have unsettled every locality through which they passed. Their chants — their banners — the blessings of the priests — their taking an oath before the mayors of the seaports—the crowds of spectators—their distant voyage, if going — their mirth and satisfaction and merry songs, if shrived and returning,—must have proved irresistible. Some Religious were jealous of St. Jago; and we find Charles V. procuring for the Abbey of Mont St. Michel from the Pope permission to grant indulgences to induce the faithful to make pilgrimages to that abbey, and to present donations, because it was *consacré au prince des anges, et de ce qu'il a été honoré de miracles éclatans.**

Parties on their pilgrimage to Spain must have roughed it on the voyage and journey, as all travellers had to do in that day. The vessels that conveyed them were very small. No doubt the pilgrims made of the hold upon the ballast a hall for meals and a dormitory.

* Dr. Hairby's Mont St. Michel.

In the year 1428 eleven towns sent 926 pilgrims: 122 went from Weymouth, and 90 from Dartmouth. In the year 1433 the numbers had increased to 2480.

The names of owners and masters of vessels who received, from the year 1413 (1 Henry V.) to 1456 (34 Henry VI.), licences to transport pilgrims to St. Jago de Compostella are given in Rymer's Fœdera.

The vessels are named bargeæ, crairerae, balingeræ, and naves. Who shall distinguish these?

There are inserted in the list the names of some great men who went to the Holy Land, in order to prove that it was possible to do so at that date, and that the shorter voyage was with few exceptions the only one made for forty-three years.

The seaports from Yorkshire to Somerset furnished the vessels for this brisk summer trade. The Cobb, or harbour of Lyme Regis, had been destroyed.

Some vessels received a pilgrim for every ton of measurement besides the crew, others were not so crowded.

A.D. 1413. Edward, the son of the Earl of Devon, appears first in the list of those who obtained a license to take the number of 40 pilgrims, in the Margaret of Plymouth, a bargea.

		Pilgrims.	
	Richard Stonard	—	Edward of Fowey *
	Rich. Hill	40	Leonard of Weymouth.
	J. Joy	50	Helen of Ipswich.
	J. Russel of Fowey	50	Mary of Penzance
1415.	Rich. Nicholl	80	A balinger, called Leonard of Weymouth.
1423.	John Gower	60	

1426. William Bowes Miles had licence to go to the Holy Land with his servants. This worthy was probably not satisfied with the compromise of going to St. Jago.

Henry, Bishop of Winchester, had licence to go beyond sea with such attendants as shall appear necessary to pay his vow which he made to perform certain pilgrimages, as he said.

		Pilgrims.	
1428.	Thos. Buk	40	Thomas of Dartmouth.
	J. Filip	120	Holy Ghost of Weymouth.
	Wm. Pollard	40	Mary of Plymouth.

* Called a navis. The pilgrims might be shipped at Fowey or Falmouth.

		Pilgrims.	
A.D. 1428.	Rob. Boner	60	Falcon of Yarmouth.
	Thos. Asteley	20	Mary of Ipswich.
	Thos. Fysh	100	St. John of Bristol.
	Nich. James	140	Mary of Cley.
	Hugo Dere, Rob. Shadde } masters	140	George of London.
	Wm. Coton, Jordan Sprynge, John Monke } owners	100	Mary of Bristol.
	Thos. Adam	50	Mary of Fowey.
	Rich. Davy	30	Mary of Exeter.
	John Stanbury	50	Trinity of Dartmouth.
	John Davy	80	Nicholas of Poole.

1431. John Bishop of Bangor, 7 persons, 8 horses and harness, to visit the Holy Sepulchre, in performance of a vow.

		Pilgrims.	
1433.	John Nicoll, owner	50	Cok John of Fowey.

12 Henry VI. So that the pilgrims are laymen, and the mayor takes a corporal oath from each that he will do nothing prejudicial to the king.

		Pilgrims.	
1434.	J Heddon	40	St. James of Kingswear.
	Roger Broke	60	St. John of Portsmouth.
	J. Williamson	40	Michael of St. Michael's Mount.
	J. Lye	40	Anthony of Dartmouth.
	Rich. Pette, Wm. Wenard, J. Cole } owners	50	Margaret of Topsham.
	T. Jaudrell	60	Mary of Landhelp.
	Roger Cule	40	Trinity of Bideford.
	Thos. Marshall	30	Catharine of Hull.
	Henry Hawkin	30	Mary of Brixham.
	J. Woderoufe	80	Christopher of Bristol.
	R. Walter	60	Peter of Dartmouth.
	J. Bigbrook	100	Mary of Southampton.
	Rich. Noble	60	Mary of Blakeney.
	William Truwe	60	Garland of Cromer.
	John Burdon	40	Trinity of Wells.
	John Slug	60	Thomas of Saltash.
	Rich. Lindesay	30	John of Teignmouth.
	John Godyng	30	Thomas of Dartmouth.
	John Lysard	40	Catherine of Dartmouth.
	Hugo Dene, J. Ryffawe } owners; Robert Shedde, master	80	Gabriel of London.

		Pilgrims.	
A.D. 1434.	Rob. Porter	60	Trinity of Winchelsea.
	Thos. Gerard	60	Julian of Fowey.
	J. Nicholl	80	Michael of Penzance.
	J. Kydeston	50	Bartholomew of Landhelp.
	Thos. Crouch	60	George of London.
	Wm. Heustas	30	Nicholas of Weymouth.
	Wm. Weston	60	Trinity of Bristol.
	John Papenham	80	Mary of Bristol.
	Roger Kyng	40	Catherine of Minehead.
	John Gerard	40	Trinity of Exmouth.
	J. Gobbe	40	Nicholas of Barnstaple.
	J. Colman	30	Lawrence of Dartmouth.
	Rich. Russel	20	Peter of Great Yarmouth.
	John Deken, owner / Nich. Holswell, mastr.	60	Christopher of Ipswich.
	Rob. Bowen	70	Bernard of Poole.
	Rob. Gregory	20	The Ghost of Bishop's Lynn.
	Thos. Andrew	60	Bartholomew of Harwich.
	Rob. Selby	30	Helen of Colchester.
	Wm. Sutton	50	Nicholas of Sandwich.
	John Mower	60	Michael of Poole.

1435. The Earl of Oxford had a licence to go to the Holy Land, and take 100*l.* with him.

1445. 23 Henry VI. At the request of Philip Courtenay, knight.

	Pilgrims.	
John Godyng	200	Trinity of Courtenay.
John Lysard	50	Anthony of Dartmouth.
Rob. Stormy	200	St. Anne.
John Shipley, owner / Thos. Hygges, master	60	St. Catherine of Plymouth.
Thos. Colbere	140	Mary Carew of Dartmouth.
Wm. Wakelyn	120	Margaret of Wells.
Rob. Philip	80	Mary of Cromer.
John Mower	30	Mary of Lymington.
John Staube	40	James of Landhelp.
John Gerard	140	Nicholas of Dartmouth.
Thos. Kestall	50	Trinity of Falmouth.
John Herchin	100	Mary of Courtenay.
Daniel Cosyn	60	Michael of Penzance.
John Stappilhyll	40	George of Payton.
Henry May	120	Mary of Bristol.
Nicholas Wandre, and / Roger Amys *		Nicholas. / Christopher of Saltash.

* One of them to take in 100 pilgrims.

A.D. 1445. The Earl of Oxford had built The Jesus of Orwell. This craft was licensed to take as many as would go.

	Pilgrims.	
John Fyke - - -	50 -	James of Weymouth.
— Hugo - - -	30 -	Motyn of Fowey.
— Langakre - -	60 -	Little John of Sandwych.
— Hastyng - -	28 -	Grace Dieu.
Thos. Vathy - -	40 -	Margaret of Mountsbay.
— White - - -	40 -	Mary of Falmouth.
John Gurdeler, master of a crairera - -	30 -	Peter of Exeter.
David Selby - -	40 -	Catherine of Plymouth.
J. Stobbe - - -	40 -	James of Landhelp.
Rich. Felawe - -	(12 ?)	
John Burton - -	12 -	Bartholomew of Orwell Haven.
Walter Fylpot - -	100 -	Catherine of Bristol.

1446. Reginald West, miles to the Holy Land.

1448. Lord Scales, having been preserved for 30 years in the wars, desires to pay a vow in the Holy Land.

		Pilgrims.	
1451.	Rich. Skilman - -	30 -	Mary of Southwold.
	Simon Hagun - -	60 -	Trinity of Wyneton.
	Rich. Arnald - -	60 -	Mary of Cromer.
	J. Waynflete - -	30 -	Christopher of Southwold.
	W. Humfrey - -	80 -	Trinity of Orwell.
	W. Bourchier - -	40 -	Trinity Fitz Waryn of Barnstaple.
	J. Pygot - - -	30 -	Catherine of Bishop's Lynn.
	J. Paten - - -	100 -	Margaret of Blakeney.
	W. Cobbe - - -	24 -	Mary of Pembroke.
	R. Burgony - -	40 -	Nicholas of Wells.
	R. Stormy - - -	100 -	Catherine of Boston.
1455.	34 Hen. VII.		
	Peter Gytton, 47 tons	50 -	Herring of Lymington.
1456.	Jno. Marshal, 80 tons	50 -	Jesus of Brixham.
	John Weston - - John Towcker	60 -	Trinity of Dartmouth.

The pilgrims now took an oath before leaving not to divulge the secrets of the realm.

	Pilgrims.	
Philip Alene, 100 tons	30 -	Mary of Dartmouth.
Thos. Calbot, 100 tons	100 -	Mary Calbot of Lynn.
Vincent Pyttesdon, 100 tons - - -	30 -	Mary Flower of Plymouth.
Simon Farncombe -	80 -	Helen of Winchelsea.
John Cade, 50 tons -	20 -	John of Dartmouth.

		Pilgrims.		
A.D. 1456.	Thos. Tregyn, 140 tons	100	-	Mary of Fowey
	James, Earl of Wiltshire, his ship, with 30 attendants	-	-	James of Weymouth.
	Rob. Sturmy, merchant	60	-	Catherine Sturmy of Bristol.
	Thos Clement - -	60	-	Mary of Landhelp.
	John Merchant - -	40	-	Mary of Stonehouse.
	Wm. Brown - -	80	-	Edward of Blakeney
	Wm. George, 200 tons	80	-	Andrew of Plymouth.

Going on pilgrimage was one of the characteristic features of the fifteenth century — an age of superstition; which in this instance blended jollity with pomp and religious ceremonial. A short sea-voyage with such gay parties to a shrine so famous, whose virtues were so lauded, in the fine weather season, too, must have held out irresistible charms. The pilgrims were a motley group. With some doubtless religious performances, for with a few the soul's good had some weight; animal enjoyment and novelty entirely prevailed with others, to the exclusion of all spiritual considerations.

Thorpe the Lollard told the archbishop that whosoever were to examine twenty of the pilgrims of his day he would not find the man or woman that knew scarcely a commandment of God, nor can say their Paternoster and Ave Maria, nor their Credo readily in any manner of language. The reason he affirmed why many men and women go hither and thither on pilgrimage was more for the health of their bodies than of their souls.

A scallop-shell marked the person who had made the pilgrimage to St. Jago de Compostella; as a palm did the pilgrim to Jerusalem; and a leaden ampulla, or bottle filled with the diluted blood of St. Thomas à Becket, suspended from the neck, him who had been to Canterbury.

The two great shrines of Europe, St. Jago de Compostella and Loretto, have been visited by a body of armed pilgrims in this century who were their own knights.

Marshal Ney, in 1809, advanced upon St. Jago, and seized upon the treasures, which only amounted to 40,000*l.*;

of which the marshal reserved one-half to pay his troops. The gold statue of St. James was found to be only of brass gilt; and the diamond eyes only imitation stones.

Loretto dared to show some resistance to Bonaparte, who gave it up to his soldiers for a pillage of twenty-four hours.

Pilgrimages were wont to be imposed as punishments. The consistorial court of the Bishop of Rochester sentenced one Agnes Sharpe to make a pilgrimage to the Rood at Bloxley, and to carry in procession, on five Lord's days, a lighted taper, which she was to offer to the image of the Blessed Virgin, for having voluntarily changed the name of her son at confirmation to Edward, who had been christened Henry.*

If the representation of the old pilgrimages exhibited in the merry excursions to St. Jago de Compostella had become by comparison contemptible and a degenerate display, so did the summer or early autumn pilgrimages to Mont St. Michel, when compared with the trips to Spain.

These pilgrimages, continued to the era of our Commonwealth and later, present a curious compound. Family pride, religious observance, military display, jollity, an aping reality and for it substituting a farce,—all are exhibited in a detailed account, here abridged, of an excursion made to Mont St. Michel in the autumn of 1654.

Few such pictures of manners exist as that conveyed in the following account of a journey to Mont St. Michel by the Brotherhood or Guild of the Church of St. Peter of Caen, with twenty-two ecclesiastics, and many inhabitants of the other parishes, of which Monsieur Pierre de Rosirignan, eldest son of Monsieur de Chambay, governor of the town and castle of Caen, was the captain.†

The distance traversed by this party is about seventy-

* See Edinburgh Review, April, 1855.

† See the Appendix to a Journal of a Residence in Normandy, by J. Augustus St. John, Esq., in Constable's Miscellany, p. 289., from an ancient and rare book of travels: Caen, "Chaud le Blanc."

five miles in a direct line, while the pilgrims to Spain had thirty-five miles only of land journey.

The pilgrimages to St. Michael's Mount had genuine earlier ones for their prototype. Not possessing a diary of any original excursion to Spain, we must content ourselves with the imitation afforded in the time of our Commonwealth. There will be abundant room to observe the many and remarkable features of such a strange jumble of opposite qualities of the mind and the state of society.

"Learn how on Sunday, the 6th day of September, 1654, the standard-bearer of our captain and the pilgrims went to meet him at the barrier of the château of Caen. Then they proceeded in order to the church of St. Peter. On the way to which the Lord of St. Martin, a doctor in theology, who having been invited to that pilgrimage by the brotherhood, and by other considerable persons, went to meet them, and conducted them to the said church, where the VENI CREATOR was sung. Then the ecclesiastics marched before the captain; who, preceded by the trumpeters of his father and of the town, marched covered with a coat richly stuffed with a gilded gorget, his sword at his side and his pike on his shoulder. Then marched a number of pilgrims, four and four; and then was carried a beautiful large flag, on which was painted a pyx, Saint Michel, the arms of our King (of the pilgrims chosen for this excursion), of his Highness of Longueville, of this town, and of our captain. Seven drummers, with red campaign coats ornamented with silver lace, given by our captain, kept continually beating.

"The Lord of Menil, our major, assisted by six sergeants, each with a white scarf, likewise a present from our captain, sword by their side and halberd in their hand, led the company in such fine order, that at each step every one ran to see them.

"At Hoyers an ample repast was given by the Lord of La Linette, lieutenant of a company in the Castle of Caen. The entertainment was agreeable; for, besides the pleasure of hearing the drums and trumpets, our captain had a chariot of six horses, which carried excellent wine, venison pasties, and other provisions, to which the Sieur la Montagne, *maître d'hôtel* of M. de Chambray, had added all that he could find in the hotels, which he visited early.*

"Monday, the 7th of September, we set out from La Blanche Maison, and went to sleep at Villedieu, which is almost six leagues distant. Our quarter-masters always arrived the first; they made presents to the principal minister of the church where we wished to say our prayers; they reserved places at the hotels, and, if there were not enough to lodge us, they sent us among the citizens, conformably with the permission which our captain had from his Highness of Longueville. The inhabitants of Villedieu came to meet us, so very impatient were they to see so fine a company, composed of almost two hundred persons. Having arrived, we entered the church, which is a commandry of Malta. They sent an officer of the said church to meet us, and a priest received us at the door. The music was sung by our twelve musicians, led by the Sieur Guilbert, who everywhere received great praise for it. We set out in order from Villedieu, and went to Avranches; on the way to which town, some one having said that the Lord of St. Martin had just seen the Mount St. Michel, immediately our captain and all the company cried out, 'Long live the King!' caused the drums to be beaten, and trumpets to sound, and they all drank to the health of the King; then our captain gave him one of the trumpeters and two sergeants, and permitted him to have the drums beat, and order all things the rest of the journey. The King thanked him and the company for having made him 'king.'†

* The extent and luxury of pilgrimages in early times almost exceed belief. Nine hundred camels were employed merely in bearing the wardrobe of one of the caliphs, and others carried snow with them to cool their sherbet. —BRODERIP's *Note Book of a Naturalist*.

† From Avranches to the mount is a distance of thirteen miles. St. Benoist in his Chronicle writes —

"De St. Michel l'angle des ceux,
Sos ciel n'en eust nul leu si bel."

"A quarter of a league from Avranches we halted to form in good order, and it was judged proper that the King, who was clad in a short cassock of taffety, and carried a cane in his hand, should ride into the town on one of his horses, and that he should be preceded by the said trumpeter, and be accompanied by two sergeants.

"On the way one of the attendants of M. de Canisy came to salute our captain on his part, and to beg him to make use of his house, and that they should fire the cannons at his arrival, as they had done when the company approached the town. Our King mounted a horse; conducted us to the cathedral, where they were singing the office of the Nones; afterwards he begged that the vespers may not be continued as usual, but that they would allow the music to be sung, which was immediately granted.

"Our own musical performance over, we took some refreshments at the hotel, but lightly, on account of the strong desire which every one experienced to arrive at the mount; and it was amusing to see every one go on the shore the best manner he could. The King there chanted the litanies of the Virgin, and saluted St. Michel in invocating that saint; then he took one of the pistols from a cavalier, which he fired opposite the mount, and bid the company advance. On arriving there they fired from the guard many musket-shots, and the soldiers formed themselves into a lane.

"The next day, the 9th of September, they rose early, impatient to see the church, although they were told the evening before that no one is permitted to enter till after seven o'clock. Every one was charmed in considering such a beautiful and vast church, built on the top of a rock, with a very spacious abbey, governed by thirty reformed Benedictines. Before entering it our captain presented a crown of silver to the King, who thanked him, and immediately caused the drums to beat; and we marched from the foot of the mount as far as the church. Many had left their knives at the hotels, for fear that the guards at the gate would take them away as usual; but, on consideration of M. de Chambay, they searched nobody, and even permitted our captain and his officers to wear their sword, which is very seldom granted, for fear least any should seize the place; moreover, they fired, on our arrival from the castle, all the cannons; and our King having entered the church, he chanted three times *Sancte Michaël, ora pro nobis!*

"The company said the responses with much devotion. He said afterwards the night prayer, and prepared to say the mass, which was chanted in music, as that at the parish of St. Peter's of Caen; then the company continued in their devotions. He went away thence to see the relicks, which are in very great number, and very precious. On coming out some monks led us in parties to see their abbey, where they provided breakfast for the King, for our Captain, and for a great many of our company."

Among other wonders of the abbey the narrator mentioned the cisterns for collecting rain water. He continues: — "They share it with the pilgrims and the inhabitants of the place, who are almost all hotel-keepers, or sellers of chaplets and shells. As we left the mount they fired the cannons, and the officers payed great civilities to our captain. Having returned to Avranches, where we arrived in good order, Mon. de Canisy came to look for our captain at the hotel; invited him and our king to sup at his house, where they invited the nobility of the town to a well-served table, and where they drank to the health of Monsieur the Governour of Caen, amidst the roar of all the cannon of the place."

Judge from the above example how completely our south-coast towns must have been disturbed by the arrival of foreign and homeward-bound pilgrims. Fancy the scallop shells worn for ornaments — in fact, as pilgrims' medals; the children, wives, and sweethearts hastening to receive the little presents in shell-work and chaplets.

The pilgrimage to Mont St. Michel was performed, as clearly appears, in style. Honours like the venison pasties and the wine attended the guild wherever they went.

Unlike the eastern pilgrimages, no vultures followed, — no bleached bones of men and beasts marked the route that had been taken.

To the latest day of their lives all remembered so festive a week. Not every party could have enjoyed so much pomp and circumstance as the one recorded here. The question obtrudes itself "Did the party believe this excursion was efficacious for the soul?" We believe "Not so" would be the answer.

Nothing is recorded of the accommodation for the sleeping of numerous pilgrims, as at Canterbury, in the dormitory, of a hundred beds. At some of the great fairs in Normandy, held in places distant from towns, booths or tents, with a great number of beds, are set up. Persons arriving at the fair order their bed, and at the ringing of a bell all retire at the same time, and rise at the same hour in the morning. Pilgrims doubtless were accommodated in numbers together in some such way.

Numbers now assemble from the neighbouring country at St. Jago to celebrate the festival of their patron saint St. James, July 25. Fireworks and processions attract, in the absence of other, the former inducements. When the Spaniard speaks of what we call a picnic — the setting out into the country well provided with a good store of eatables — he uses the word *romeria;* that does a double duty, expresses picnicing and pilgrimage, as exchangeable terms. Persons of high family are still anxious for their admission to the order of St. Jago; but as pilgrims no longer require protection, they take the honourable distinction as a proof of their high descent. Thus does age cause nearly everything to depart from its early use and application.

The Importance of the Office of early Mayors.

"Each many a year
The helm of this town's government did steer," &c.
Epitaph of the Ellesdons.

EACH mayor and his brethren formed in reality a board of guardians, a board of health, of trade, and a provincial legislature. Did they not manage the poor, regulate about what caused sickness and the treatment of the diseased, settle prices of commodities, define what number of attorneys should practise, and prescribe how trade should be carried on and how it should be fettered, and fix punishments for new offences?

Their bye-laws, if not wise, were so accounted, and were in accordance with the progress of social economy. They were alive to the presence of new domestic evils, and proceeded to correct them by Precepts and Orders. The pursuivant that brought a proclamation furnished the local legislators with work, as did also the bad character who displayed some manifestations of a new or disused vice.

It was not only against positive acts that bye-laws were framed, but indications of moral error occasioned the passing of these to meet the threatened outbreak. We now punish for acts, but do not presume to conclude what is the true indication of a design to do wrong, should opportunity offer; and many mean actions are left to the contempt and scorn which they deservedly bring upon the perpetrators. Our predecessors, the authorities of Castle Combe, in the fifteenth century, fined a man 4*d.* for lying about with *intention* to ravish women. They likewise presented eavesdroppers, or listeners at windows; a mean class, whose character would, after proof of such a habit, be now left to the ridicule of being compared to that of "Paul Pry."*

All persons not members of a borough were accounted aliens or foreigners. These were impeded in trading at every step, and were treated much as if they owned allegiance to some foreign king. Their dues were higher, their

* Hist. by Right Hon. P Scrope.

facilities less, and they could only buy after freemen had viewed the merchandise and declined to purchase. Persons who for a consideration passed off the wares of out-of-town traders as their own in order to evade these exactions were heavily fined: their offence was styled "colouring foreigners' goods." When freemen were contumacious in respect of the laws of their borough they were suspended, and lost their freedom and the privileges and immunities it secured. Thus did the inhabitants of a borough repay themselves for the expenses and the responsibilities they incurred. It was but fair that the legislators, the entertainers of great men, the providers of ordnance and gunpowder, the payers of rates to send burgesses to the Parliament, should have some return beyond inhabitants of the country, who had no such burdens. Each borough was truly an *imperium in imperio.* Like other institutions, boroughs have played their part, and have been modified so as to have lost much of their former character. The central government has eased the mayors from many of their duties. They are no longer legislators, directors of the defences of their borough, and we know not what besides. The performance of these duties, however, is provided for in a way suited to the state of civilisation that now obtains. Old mayors had duties for which no directions had been prescribed; they were left to their own judgment, like a Turkish cadi, and much ready ability and conduct was often demanded from them, and that not in vain.

The state intermeddled with everything. Nothing was left to the prudence and self-government of the people. Such is not the case now-a-day. Still matters are conducted in an improved manner that indicates constant progress. Mr. Macaulay treats of this, and asserts that it has not resulted by the intermeddling of the state, but by the prudence and energy of the people which has carried England forward in civilisation; and to the same prudence and energy we look forward with comfort and hope: "Our rulers will best promote the improvement of the nation by strictly confining themselves to their own legitimate duties, by leaving capital to find its most lucrative course; commodities their fair price; industry and intelligence their natural punishment, by maintaining peace, by defending property, by diminishing the price of law, and observing strict economy in every department of the state. Let the government do this: the people will assuredly do the rest."

May the political economist find in the following pages material for inferences from the economic experience of early reigns. Nothing was then left to self-government.

The mayors were excusable. They carried out the orders and laws of the state, and had, from the multiplicity and variety of duties, a prominence that causes us to view them as very remarkable men.

A Litigious Person punished.

THE jurisdiction of the county magistrates, either assumed, or which of right belonged to them, gave them a power, that was at times exercised in the correction of gross abuses and acknowledged social evils, that no law can be made to reach; whereas they addressed themselves to the offence, and adjudged summarily. Take, for instance, the case of a litigious dweller and oppressor of the inhabitants of Piddletrenthide. We learn from it, that the people looked to the magistrates to relieve them from the most out-of-the-way instances of personal annoyance, oppression, or social disturbance. We will illustrate this from the business of the Sherborne Easter sessions, 1650.

"Divers credible persons, inhabitants of Piddletrenthide and others, upon oath complained of many great extortions and intolerable abuses by colour of law, practised by one John Bryne of the same place; whereby he had drawn many to great expenses in law, upon frivolous suits of no value, and such whereupon he had received satisfaction at the least twelve years before his suit commenced, and to the utter undoing of others, whom (for fear of going to prison at his suit) he hath caused to enter into bond for payment of debt, long since discharged, to the general vexation of all his neighbours and others that ever had any manner of dealing with him by buying, selling, renting, or otherwise, sometimes making justice a pretext for his unsufferable exactions."

The picture of the offender is repulsive. His career was arrested in a manner calculated to have made the magistracy very popular, for the court ordered that John Bryne be committed to the county gaol, there to remain without bail or mainprize by the space of three months, and from thence till he shall put in two sufficient sureties, good subsidy men, that will be bound in fifty pounds a-piece, and he himself in a hundred pounds, to the king's Majesty's own use, upon condition that he shall in time to come well behave himself towards the king and all his liege people. But in case that he give full satisfaction to all such persons as he hath unjustly wronged, and that now have complained against him, then upon putting in of security this court doth think fit he be discharged of his imprisonment.*

A Discontented Politician suffers.

A PROOF of religious feeling in favour of a party, and the danger of rash spouting on political matters, are given in an entry made at the Michaelmas quarter sessions held at Beaminster, A.D. 1625.

"It is ordered by this court that John Barton, for using manie contemptuous wordes against the king's proclamation concerninge Jesuits and Recusants (and selling ale without a license), in saying he wished halfe of them hanged which procured the saide proclamation, is committed to the House of Correction untill he hath receaved his punishment by whipping, and then to be delivered to the keeper to remaine three days, and for such further time until he shall pay the penalties according to the statute. Henrie Mamford enformeth." †

William Stone and John Lane the elder, of Castleton near Sherborne, were proved in 1629 to have spoken and

* Mr. T. Hearn, "Qui Quondam." † Ibid

uttered contemptuous and scandalous speeches of his Majesty, his laws, and the Courts of Parliament. They were bound over to appear at the next assizes and answer for their conduct." *

A Railer punished.

POVERTY in 1631, as in every age, gave confidence to some who had nothing to lose in the indulgence in great license of language. One Robert Hancocke, *alias* Randell of Maiden Newton, being by reason of his poverty unable to satisfy the law, indulged in railing upon the governors, officers, and others, his neighbours, in such an open, foul, common, and usual manner as was insufferable. Dr. Whatcombe admonished him in vain. This man was to be committed to the House of Correction at Dorchester for a month, where the keeper was to receive him and set him on work, and give him such due correction as the quality of his offences shall deserve. Submission to Dr. Whatcombe was to procure his enlargement sooner.†

The Magistracy coerce and protect the Clergy.

THE functions now exercised by the Ecclesiastical Courts were many of them performed by the county magistracy, and in boroughs by the mayor and his brethren.

At Blandford Christmas Sessions in 1627, a warrant was issued against Thomas Bartlett, clerk, for sowing sedition between William Hopkins and his wife, and for the like between —— Rake and his wife. The offending minister stood charged with prosecuting a suit against one Lucas, and also for refusing to baptize his child, and further for "challenging the field" of Mr. Martin, Lucas, and Fudge, and for that he standeth indicted this present sessions upon two several bills, viz., one for ale-house haunting, and the other for drunkenness.

Brawling in church fell within the same jurisdiction.

* Mr. T. Hearn, "Qui Quondam." † Ibid.

At Sherborne Sessions in 1631, a minister sought and found relief by informing of divers misdemeanors, disturbances, and uncivil behaviour, offered and used towards Samuel Norrington, clerk, both in time of his prayer before sermon, and also at the time of service in the parish church of Charmouth, by Mary Limbry, the wife of Edward Limbry, of Charmouth, sailor, and Joan her daughter. The Court desired Henry Drake and Roger Gollop, Esq. to call the parties before them, and to examine into the misdemeanors alleged; and if these were found to be true, then to proceed against the parties according to the form of the Statute.*

It was the wife and daughter of Stephen Limbry who shut up that mariner in his bed-room, and there kept him, when he ought to have, according to agreement, transported Charles II. to France after the battle of Worcester.

Neighbouring Counties are restricted in their Intercourse by Magistrates, as if they were of separate Realms.

MANKIND is but too ready to create a secondary kind of caste on every soil; not exactly to separate into right-hand and left-hand castes in western lands, this institution being Oriental, but to exclude others upon trifling distinctions, and to form cliques and parties.

This was formerly the case in a remarkable degree in England; but thanks to increased intercourse, our countrymen are becoming more like members of one great family.

Some twenty years ago, in the middle of a broiling summer's day, some persons were taking refreshment in a front room of the "Hunter's Lodge Inn," situated on the turnpike road two miles on the eastern side of Axminster, a mile from the boundary line of Dorsetshire. They perceived a man running as if for a wager, much distressed by his speed and the heat of the day. As he came up to them he touched a chord to which their feelings responded. At the words, "Race Gem'men, Devon 'gainst Dorset," a seat was placed, refreshments bountifully afforded; and "Devon," restored, addressed himself to his course like one who was piqued for

* Mr. T. Hearn, "Qui Quondam."

the honour of his county. The party soon saw "Dorset" coming up with an attendant, both greatly distressed. Bets were offered for "Devon;" when the party were soon addressed to their mortification, and inquiries made for the thief they, the constables of the neighbouring town, were pursuing, as he had been seen robbing a gentleman's garden! However, the refreshment afforded the thief enabled him to escape. Like many others, to serve his ends he used party words to excite an interest for an unworthy object, with what success we have seen.

Having first asked pardon for this illustrative anecdote and digression, let us observe that bye-laws of borough worthies and of county justices were long framed, as if men outside the bounds of boroughs and counties were foreigners, and too often were treated as hostile, as those whom it was a duty to exclude from what was beneficial, and frequently as though deserving the most annoying restrictions.

Every page of the history of boroughs displays this. Restrictions as to the commercial intercourse between "Devon" and "Dorset," or that of counties, existed, and are not so well known.

No grain could be transported for sale from the county in which it had been raised without a special license, in which the exact quantity and description of grain to be removed was specified. Dorsetshire butter, which retains its reputation, could not be sent to our countrymen residing in other counties who wanted some of it except in defined quantities, and by parties duly licensed at the Quarter Sessions for that purpose.

Such a license as the following is most valuable to sceptics who might question the possibility of such a state of things having ever obtained. This entry, made at the Michaelmas Session held at Bridport in 1631, will carry conviction with it:—

"For as much as a letter hath been directed unto this Court from the maior of the cittie of Exon, therein praying that this Court would license one Humfrey Perry, of that citie, to buy butter within this county for the provision of the same: this Court doth therefore give way that a license be granted unto the said Humfrey Perry, for the weekly buying in this countie two horse-loade of butter, and to carry the same unto the said citie for the provision of the same."

It is amusing to read how powerful an effect the eloquent letter of the Mayor of Exeter produced. The authorities "gave way," and the "outside barbarians," as the natives of the Dorset "inside flowery land" might then have styled them, had their two pack-horses with butter in their dorsers. The good people of Exeter can now in four hours get what the metropolis has that is good without troubling the mayor to intercede for them, or being pestered about a license.*

Regulation of the Number of Attorneys-at-law, Practice, &c.

ATTORNEYS-AT-LAW, now in so many cases the richest inhabitants of country towns, and who have obtained in very many boroughs a position above the numerous householders that form the constituency, were no exception to the general rule. They were regulated by the mayor and his brethren, the merchants or principal traders as to their numbers and manner of practising their profession, not dissimilar to the handicraftsmen, the fullers, the shoemakers, and others of like trades. The latter were subject to the operation of corporation bye-laws that were really a tyranny, and so were the attorneys.

In 1455, their numbers having increased, and a lachrymose account being given of their practices and the effects produced, most prejudicially, upon the people, a statute provided that there should be six common attorneys in Norfolk, six in Suffolk, and two in Norwich, to be elected and admitted by two of the judges. So in Dorset their numbers were judged to be disproportionate. In the year 1594 Thomas Densloe, Richard Ellyot, and all other attorneys practising in the Hustings Court of Lyme, except *three*, were, for certain good causes, which moved the mayor and his brethren, dis-

* Mr. T. Hearn, from Sessions Book.

missed from their attorneyships. The three attorneys were obliged to take an oath to observe all lawful orders about the practice of the Court of Hastings. They did this before George Wadham, Recorder.

That this expulsion or exclusion was more than a forensic entry in the court books of Lyme—mere words, and nothing enforced after the hour when the order was passed—is clear from the history of the borough. Mr. Thomas Densloe set up a school; his scholars were the subjects of a presentment in the year 1597. He submitted to the decree of the borough magnates, and inculcated the rudiments of Latin grammar, expecting perhaps the happy day when he might again plead in bar, or have to make entries salutary and sanitary in Latin, which, if "bad, did not quash indictments" (*Faux Latin ne quashera inditement*).

The orders passed for the lucky trio who were allowed to continue to practice were stringent.

No attorney was to advise his client to bring in any demurrer touching any action for debt or detinue, being but of 20*s*. or under. If above 20*s*., the attorney or party shall inform the court of the insufficiency of the declaration or plea, and pray to have the defaults amended before further proceedings. If this be refused, then the party may enter his demurrer.

And likewise, in actions of trespass, breach of covenant, if but of 20*s*. or under, the attorney shall not advise a demurrer.

Also, not advise the removal of causes begun and depending which may be lawfully tried and determined in the same court.

Also, not to take more than the ordinary and accustomed fees, except for journeys.

Also, not to plead any foreign plea in bar in any plaint, action, or suit, but such plea as the attorney shall swear that the matter or averment is true and above 20*s*.

The county magistrates undertook the settling matters of etiquette or rule between counsellors and attorneys.

Attorneys and solicitors were, by an order made in 1626,

not permitted to plead at the Dorset Sessions if there were any counsellors present that could be retained. This was represented to be in compliance with the ancient order, and as obtained in other countries; also for the encouragement of counsellors attending, and honour of the court.*

These matters would now be left to their own correction. If eight attorneys were to commence practice where three were only needed, five would be found to move elsewhither. The population, too, ought to learn to refrain from litigation, except in cases actually requiring it, as they would from strong drink, too expensive luxuries, or ruinous pleasures. In a word, self-government was a power not confided in. Modern legislation understands this much better.

The Tumbrel, Pillory, Cucking-Stool, and other Borough Instruments of Punishment, &c.

> "These mounted in a *chair curule*,
> Which moderns call a *cucking-stool*,
> And o'er the waves in triumph ride
> Like Dukes of Venice, who are said
> The Adriatic Sea to wed," &c.
>
> *Hudibras.*

BOROUGH towns were like some little independent states that acknowledge a sovereign ruler, but which, upon the whole, manage their own affairs, provide for their own internal government by local legislation, and settle a code of laws for the punishment of offenders in various ways.

Often do we hear in boroughs of lax discipline, of a daring population that defy authority, and disturb the quiet of "our street," while comparisons are instituted with that good old time when offences could not be perpetrated with impunity, and when troublesome townspeople were made to know themselves by the administration of sound discipline. Town clerks made their learned entries of these doings, and recorded the use of *pilarum sive Collistrigium, cippos*, &c.

* "Qui Quondám," Dorset Session MS.

The jury at borough court leets, till of late, persevered in their presentments for the renewal of the practice of punishing forestallers or regraters; and they desired a return to the borough punishments, which many believed, together with the other case before mentioned, would restore our little societies to a state bordering upon that of Elysium.

The borough codes of laws assigned punishments for offences against the well being and order of the little *imperium in imperio.*

Travelling thirty miles to a county town was quite a labour to the honest members of society. Offenders could not be taken to the county gaol, as now-a-day, with facility; so "grete murtherers, arrant theveș, and other grete mysdoers of many shires, as of Sussex, sometymes for ferry distance, and charge, and jiapardie of conveyance ben suffered to escape."

It was necessary that offenders should be punished for all but great crimes in their borough, or not at all. Laws for the good government of boroughs were in use under innumerable heads, and the penalty and punishment for neglect of them were appended.

Much might be written upon the effect produced by borough penal legislation, as compared with that resulting from the system of centralisation. Formerly townsmen witnessed the punishment of offenders with their own eyes. As they viewed the disgrace or discipline, each realised the result of offending conduct, and the observer knew he might make the culprit's lot his own by following a like course. A greater effect was produced upon the spectators than the sentencing to imprisonment with discipline in a gaol at a distance. Herein consists the great difference between ancient and modern punishment.

The system was marked; the borough magnates aspired to rule by fear, not because they were cruel or specially delighted in inspiring fear, but from a belief that such was the proper course, that such was necessary, indeed indispensable. No class doubted it. The townsmen called for the instruments of punishment, and thought there was no safety, no quiet without these. The judges that rode round to the assizes inspired fear. How tame a county assize appears in comparison with those in the reign of Elizabeth. Many assizes now pass without any execution. In Somersetshire alone, in 1596, forty persons were executed, thirty-five burned in the hand, and thirty-seven severely whipped!

Thirteen prisoners, men and women, were conveyed to the gallows at Worcester about 1787 in four carts, not one of whom had committed murder. Eighty-five of the *chauffeurs* were executed at Chartres in France about the same time, which fact is adduced as a proof what scenes the gallows presented when the legislature determined to check crime by investing punishment with as many appalling features as possible. The result was unsatisfactory. Offenders were not deterred, but crime increased.

When borough towns were the seats of local legislation, and the scene of trials and punishment, the instruments used for the several sentences of the dread mayors and the other principal men were necessarily provided. The decay of these implements, or their destruction, have caused entries without which these pages could not have been written.

The TUMBREL of Lyme Regis was out of repair in

A Tumbrel at Wootton-Bassett in 1760, date 1668. (From the Wiltshire Archæol. Mag.)

1581. This was that low-rolling cart or carriage (in law Latin, *tumberella*) used as a punishment of disgrace and infamy. Millers, when they stole corn, were chastised by the tumbrel. Persons were sometimes fastened with an iron chain to a tumbrel, and conveyed bareheaded with din and cry through the principal streets of towns.

"*Court of Hustings Book*, 1581. (*Lyme.*)

"The jury present that the tumbrell be repaired and maintained from time to time according to the statute."

In 1583, Mr. Mayor was to provide a tumbrel before All Saints Day, under a penalty of 10*s.*

If the foregoing instrument of punishment was needed for one class of offenders, we shall find that evils existed that immediately called for other machines deemed necessary to abate such, whatever they might prove to be. A learned town-clerk of Lyme, in 1592, thus enters, as was customary, in Latin in the Hustings' Book, what had been given him in plain English :—

"*Item* præsentant uxorem Thomæ Lacy unam SCOLD."

Translated thus: "They likewise present the wife of Thomas Lacy to be a scold."

By another entry further information is to be gleaned : —

"*Item,* we find that William Welsh, his wife, and his daughter Elizabeth Purden, are *common scolders,* one with the other, to the disturbance of their neighbours."

A "wrangler from house to house," in 1596, found a place in a presentment in the court of Hustings' Book. Whether such publicity produced any amendment in the party is doubtful. To be written down in a great book by a scrivener in one's true character must have been viewed as a stigma. A goodwife Pupe for "mis-using her tunge to the hurt of here naybors" was presented.

The peace had to be maintained; therefore irritating expressions which led to angry answers and jangling discussions were matter for a jury, who acted upon the legal saying, "that the greater the truth the greater the libel." The jury of Seaford found Thomas Woman's wife saucy. This good wife perhaps experienced the "stool, the dread of every scolding quean," for a criticism upon the commodities another woman sold. She said, "her beans and pease were spillde" (spoiled). How just a remark if these articles were not good for food, and how easily refutable the assertion if they really were so.

A proclamation had been issued in 1547 by Henry VIII., "that all women should not meet together to babble and talk, and that all men should keep their wives in their houses." The conduits and dipping places in running streams were the places of constant resort of the gossips.

After a presentment at the manorial Court of Seaborough, near Crewkerne, in 1486, two women were fined a penny each as *common scolds*. At the same time an order was made that the *tenants* of the manor should not *scold* their wives under pain of forfeiting their tenements and cottages. Not fifty years afterwards an order was made that tenants' *wives* should not scold under pain of 6*s*., one-half to go to the repairs of the chapel, and the other half to the lord of the manor.*

In the parish book of Axminster is an item (1675): "For a warrant to ly against the scoulds, 1*s*." The evil must have become no longer endurable.†

The long church porch of Lyme contained one part of the dreaded CUCKING-STOOL, ready for the correction of certain

A Cucking-Stool or Treduchet, near Worthing, about 1776.

"No brawling wives — no furious wenches —
No fire so hot but water quenches."

WEST.

* Pulman's Book of the Axe. † Ibid.

offenders. Sundry entries are here given to prove that this branch of borough discipline was not neglected.

Cucking is a corruption of *coquine*, so that cucking-stool is that for troublesome, noisy women.

In 1608, a woman was ordered to leave the town of Southampton, who had been guilty of slander, and when a few days later it was discovered that she had not gone away and had repeated the offence, she was condemned to be set in a cage with a paper before her.*

Scolds used to be punished at Leicester by the mayor on a cuckstool before their doors, and then carried to the four gates of the town.†

Town Accompt Book of Lyme.

		s.	*d.*
1631.	For bringing the cucking-stool out of the church -	0	6
1633.	For amending the cucking-stool - - -	0	6
1653.	Paid for a piece of timber for a cucking-stool and six boards - - - - - -	16	2
1657.	For timber to make a cucking-stool - -	12	0
1658.	For making a cucking-stool, George Baker -	5	8
	See *Court of Hustings' Book.*		
1685.	30th April. *Item*, we present the corporation for not repairing the cucking-stool - - -	6	8
	Therefore it is ordered that it be repaired within one month *subpœna.*		
	[There was soon employment for greater severities this year.]		

Bound Book of Presentments.

1724. The corporation was presented for not keeping up a ducking-stool as it was formerly allowed by the informations of several persons. [Everything was now in decay in the town.]

Kingston-upon-Thames.

1572.	The making of the cucking-stool - -	8	0
	Iron work for the same - - -	3	0
	Timber for the same - - - -	7	6
	Three brasses for the same, and three wheels -	4	10
		£1 3	4

* Archæological Institute. † Nichol's Hist. of Leicester.

At Marlborough *, in 1625, a man had for his help at the cucking of Joan Neal, 4*d*.

Gravesend.

		s.	d.
1636.	The porters for ducking of Goodwife Campion	- 2	0
	Two porters for laying up the ducking-stool	- 0	8

The cucking-stool was used by the pond in many village greens as commonly, about one hundred years ago or little more, as stocks now are. By the sea the quay offered a convenient spot. The barbican at Plymouth was the locality, doubtless terrible to offenders, however careless of committing their wordy scolding nuisance. Two pounds were paid for a cucking-stool at Leicester in 1768. Since that it has been placed at the door of a notorious scold as a warning. Upon admission to the House of Correction at Liverpool, a woman had to undergo the severity of the ducking-stool till a little before the year 1803, when Mr. James Neild wrote to Dr. Lettsom. The pump in the men's court was the whipping-post for females, which discipline continued, though not weekly.

See the law case of Hannah Saxby in an interesting article, "Wiltshire Archæol. Mag." Vol. I.

In 1629 Beaminster was without the necessary and customary implements of borough discipline stocks, ducking-stool, and pillory. Peter Hoskins, farmer of the manor, was ordered to procure all these in three months, under pain of five pounds.

Edith Coplyn, of Stoke Abbot, had a feud with another labourer's wife. If she misdemeaned herself, she was to be taken before a magistrate, who was by the Court desired to give her the punishment of the ducking-stool or some other like punishment.

One husband at Bristol brought an action against Edmund Mountjoy, whose year of civic supremacy was then out for having had his wife ducked for a scold. Evans, in his His-

* Waylen's History.

tory, mentions the circumstance. Ducange may be consulted for this practice under the word *superundatio.*

Cucking-Stool.

Lord Holt, the judge, said of a woman whose case was before him, that cucking her would rather harden than cure her, and that if she were once ducked she would scold on all the days of her life.

At Preston, in the "Book of Customs of the Manor," fraudulent tradespeople and insolvent burgesses occasionally underwent the cooling operation.

Our American brethren have found that in running bebeyond the sea, the Scold family have accompanied them. The grand juries of Philadelphia from 1717 to 1720, in good set terms, deplored the absence of a ducking-stool for scolding women, and the necessity that existed for that *public convenience.* So late as the year 1824, a woman was convicted of being a common scold, in the Court of Quarter Sessions of Philadelphia county, and sentenced to be placed in a cucking or ducking-stool, and plunged three times into the water; but the Supreme Court of Pennsylvania, upon the removal of the case by writ of error, decided that this punishment was obsolete, and contrary to the spirit of the age.*

Baretti, the Italian lexicographer, journeyed from London to Exeter in a six-inside coach, in four days, in 1760. He records the seeing the ducking-stool over the water by Honiton, where they dipped those old women suspected of being witches. There, if they sunk, their fate was decided; if they swam, they were supposed to have been clearly proved to be witches.

Some half century after this, the writer of these pages being at the same town, a man led forth his wife with a halter round her neck, and sold her for eighteenpence. The purchaser led off his bargain, and it was said by the bystanders that he was the man most likely, or whom they

* Notes and Queries, 1854, March 11.

expected, would buy the woman. Bakers who gave out bread short of weight were subjected to the ducking-stool so late as the great Howard's time, about the year 1775.

Such was the punishment of weavers in the reign of Charles I., who did not return cloth of honest weight, according to what had been given out.

This ancient implement of punishment was used for those who dressed meat a second time.

Hashed meat (*carnes recalefactæ*) was cooked as a snare for tender consciences of fasting monks, who persuaded themselves that in that form it ceased to be meat. This relaxation of discipline was condemned by the constitution of Gregory IX., given to the monks of St. Benoit. In a journey of Edward I., A.D. 1299, Damele, the cook, for rewarming his meat, was fined 3*s.* 4*d.**

The BRANK, for taming shrews, was preferred to the cucking-stool in some counties, and was used there for

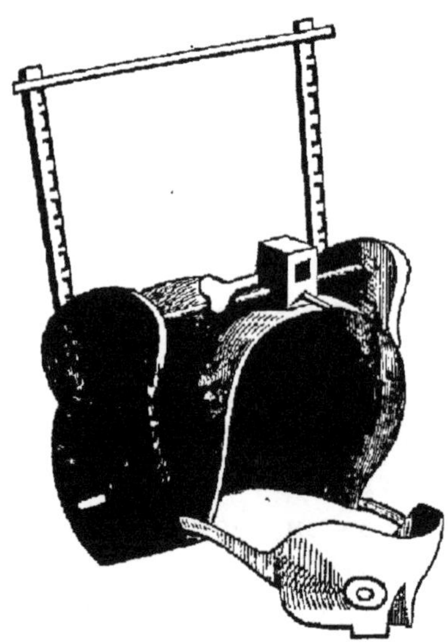

A Brank, or Scold's Bridle. From that in the Guildhall, Worcester. (From Stanley's Guide to that City.)

the same purpose. The brank was in favour in the northern counties, and in Worcestershire, though there were

* Royal Journeys in Sussex, by W. H. Blauw, Esq.

notwithstanding some of the other instruments of punishment used, called in that county gum-stools.

The brank was put over the head, and was fastened with a padlock. There are entries at Worcester about mending the "scould's bridle and cords for the same."

The cucking-stool not only endangered the health of the party, but also gave the tongue liberty 'twixt every dip. The brank was put over the head, and was fastened with a padlock.*

There is a representation of Robert Sharp, an officer of the corporation of Newcastle, leading Ann Bidlestone through the streets, with the branks or gossip's bridle on, in "the Local Historian's Table Book of Northumberland," &c. † In the church of Walton-on-Thames, in Warrington Museum, and in the Guildhall, Worcester, are branks.‡

The CAGE, or PILLORY, having been neglected, the jury made this presentment in 1584: "That Mr. Mayor do cause the cage, or pillory, to be set up in good order before the feast of St. John Baptist, upon pain of 10*s.*"

The pillory was coloured in 1650, at a cost of 4*s.*

The mayor and corporation having been presented again, in 1694, for not repairing the pillory, Mr. Samuel Courtenay, mayor, paid for boards about the shambles and pillory, in 1699, 1*l.* 15*s.* 8*d.*

In 1724 the constables were presented for not discharging their duty respecting the pillory and stocks; which presentment doubtless referred to the subjecting offenders to due discipline by means of these machines.

The *Stocks.* William Tudbold, mayor, paid to John Cogan for making of the (strap?) of iron, and for two staples and nails for the stocks, in 1551, 17*s.* 6*d.*

There are other entries for repairs at Lyme.

Wood stealers, or, as they were styled, hedge-tearers, were, about 1584, set in the stocks two days in the open

* Stanley's Worcester Guide.

† Vol. i. p. 283. See Brand's Hist. of Newcastle, vol. ii. p. 292.

‡ See the Transactions of the Historic Society.

street, with the wood stolen before them, as a punishment for a second offence.

Let no one view the pillory as an instrument for the punishment of offenders under the direction of the magistrate, whose judgment results from a deliberate estimate of the nature of the offence.

A longer or shorter continuance in a constrained exposed position was assigned to each. Such would be a very incorrect view.

The magistrate sentenced to the pillory, and some official assisted; but the populace administered, and regulated the punishment.

Some sentenced to stand found the punishment easy, or a very triumph of popularity, while others were frightfully lacerated, and almost killed with brick-bats and all kinds of missiles. The magistrates and the populace often took opposite views of the guilt of the party pilloried. The populace were practically either joint administrators of the law with the magistrates, carrying the punishment further than was ever contemplated, or else parties to nullify completely the sentence.

Titus Oates is made to express fears for his person in a ballad: —

> "See the rabble all round me in battle array,
> Against my wood castle their batteries play;
> With turnip granadoes the storm is begun."

A knife, like a pruning-knife, was sometimes in request to cut off the culprit's ears; scissors to slit his nostrils, and a hot iron to sear the wounds.

How numerous are the *laudatores temporis acti* those who commend the preceding age. How few, probably, who are so have carefully scanned the whole bearing of any subject, the good and prejudicial — that which still remains available, and that which is obsolete. This brief remark was occasioned by a presentment of the constables of Lyme so late as 1752. Doubtless sincere in their estimate of what in their judgment would prove a panacea for the lax discipline they had to witness and deplore, still we must judge them to have been men behind their age.

"1752. A pare of stocks wanting in the borough.
A pilary wanting.
Stocks, pillory, and cucking-stool all wanting and necessary, and ought to be erected next court leet.
Giles Davie, Edward Godfrey, J. Kerby."

Lest any reader of this history might suppose that these formidable machines were set up as objects to deter our townsmen and women from committing the offences to which each was appropriated, and not so much for actual use, some specific information is submitted.

There is an entry in the archives of Weymouth respecting the pillory, which does not appear to be readily understood. Some little history connected with election matters requires to be explained.

An inhabitant of Weymouth (A.D. 1727) having addressed Mr. Isaac Harvey respecting election matters, and having read a printed letter or handbill, the same person added, that if the corporation durst repair the pillory he would get upon it and read that letter, and would preach half an hour to the people, and then come down and burn the pillory.

Whipping.

"*Gloucester.* My masters of St. Albans have you not beadles in your town, and things called whips?

"*Mayor.* Yes, my lord, if it please your grace."

SHAKSPEARE.

NOT only was a tumbrel needed, to which the offender was secured, but a particular coat had to be provided for the operation.

Mr. Ellesdon, Mayor of Lyme, in 1595, paid for —

	s.	d.
Four yards of canvas to make a coat to whip the rogues in	3	0
Making the same - - - - -	0	6

	s.	d.
Whipping of three of the ship boys for stealing of Mr. Hassard's salmon fish in the Cobb - - -	1	0

(N.B.—Salmon was plentiful in the west at this epoch.)

The charge of fourpence made for whipping a boy continued for many years the same. The whipping of a woman who was a stranger was little more costly; but the inflicting such a punishment upon a townswoman was remunerated at a higher rate, as may well be supposed, from a consideration of several circumstances. To take a violent, noisy woman from her chamber, tie madam to the tumbrel and whip her round the town, was an undertaking that demanded assistance and protection to the official or hireling that wielded the thong. In the Town Accompt Book are found such entries as those which are given in illustration:—

	s.	d.
1625. For whipping William Wynter's boy - -	0	4
,, Agnes Abbott twice - -	2	4
1644. Paid two soldiers to attend the whipping of a woman - - - - - - -	2	6
Paid to whipping four women - - -	4	0

To visit a gaol the morning the women were whipped was the practice of some men about town. They discussed the courage of the poor wretches, and it was deemed highly entertaining.

It sometimes happened, just as might have been expected in a small town, no townsman could be found willing for some fourteenpence to incur the violence and resentment of the person whipped and his friends by undertaking the office. Other parishes had to be visited in order to find some bold executor of the law.

The constable's charge in 1657:—

	s.	d.
Paid Edward Norwood going to Wooton and Uplyme to get a man to whip Emanuel Lincoln - - -	0	6
Paid Edward Norwood going to Charmouth to conduct E. Lincoln thither - - - - - -	0	3
Paid a man to whip the said E. Lincoln - - -	1	0

Are we not to understand that though a man of another parish was found willing to whip the offender, yet that he did not come into the borough to carry out the sentence, but would do so if the delinquent was sent to him, which was done? Let us take another whipping-bill, and see if this is not a correct view of the case.

	s.	d.
1657. Paid Robert Milley's wife for going to Wooton [three miles] to get a man to whip two prisoners -	0	4
Paid a man for whipping them - - - -	2	0
Conducting them to that tithing - - - -	1	0

At Lewes a goodwife earned her shilling for whipping offenders so late as 1718.

The Lyme constable's accounts for many years about the year 1662 were principally made up of charges for whipping and rending on men and women. For execution of this sentence upon strangers the difficulty in finding an official was not great. See a bill for 1662.

	s.	d.
Paid towards the whipping of the cutpurse woman -	0	6
Paid the Barbadoes boy for whipping a strange woman -	0	6

The female culprits had not only to suffer from the sentence, but from the most odious vice which is incident to human nature, a delight in misery merely as misery. This led such as Judge Jeffreys to scare them into fits by dilating on all the details of what they were to suffer.

Thus, when ordering an unlucky adventuress to be whipped at the cart's tail, "Hangman," he would exclaim, writes a great living authority *, "I charge you to pay particular attention to this lady. Scourge her soundly, man! Scourge her till the blood runs down! It is Christmas, a cold time for madam to strip in! See that you warm her shoulders thoroughly!"

In the Court of Hustings Book, 1578, it was ordered that the constables do suffer no vagabonds which wander about

* Macaulay.

without lawful authority to go unpunished upon pain of 6*s*. 8*d*.

The preparing false briefs was a common occupation.

In 1661 there were incurred for expenses in prosecuting those who had false briefs and sending them to gaol, 4*l*. 15*s*. 11*d*.

How summarily such persons were occasionally treated appears in the Hustings Book, May 14. 1679, and 1688.

John Handson, of the parish of Newington in Southwark, in the county of Surrey, and Margaret his wife, were both there openly whipped for wandering rogues, and were assigned to pass from parish to parish the next straightway to Newington aforesaid, where the said John Handson confessed he last dwelt, to be there in sixteen days.

1688. Andrew Campbell and Walter Scott, two pretended Scotchmen, with a counterfeit and false pass, whipped for sturdy vagrant rogues, and sent on to the next tithing.

Dinah Page for having obtained goods under false pretences was sentenced at Marlborough to one month's imprisonment, and to be publicly whipped on a market-day in 1807.*

There was a *Dark House* in the borough of Lyme which may be styled a dungeon. Hedge-tearers were numerous before the introduction of coals, and wrought much mischief. Persons found with wood had two days and a night in the *Dark House*, and during that time to have brown bread, which would perhaps be worthy the name of *black* bread, and water.

The Stocks were not the instrument of punishment and disgrace only for those who offended in the vicinity of the church, their use was more extended; inhabitants whose conduct was presented by the constables as highly immoral were sentenced to the disgrace of the stocks and to the smart of a whipping besides.†

* Waylen's Hist. of Marlborough.

† In the archives of Weymouth there is a presentment by the constables, that on 16th September, 1621, John Bascombe and Amy Pushman, the wife of William Pushman, were taken fast-locked in a chamber in the

The stocks are remarkable for the punishment inflicted upon Cardinal Wolsey, when incumbent of Lymington near Yeovil, by the direction of Sir Amias Poulett. This strict moralist seeing that the minister of the parish was then in liquor, it being fair time, had him set in the stocks.*

Should any suppose that this mode of punishment was only for the low in station, and that it was only the humble who were subjected to this and similar modes of discipline, the above and following statements will undeceive him.

The scholars and residents in the colleges of Cambridge were by a decree of the vice-chancellor and heads of houses forbidden to bathe in 1571 in any river, pool, or pond, by day or night. Offenders, undergraduates, were to be punished with RODS; graduates were to be set in the STOCKS the whole day in the common hall of their college and pay a fine of 10*s*.

The following instrument might be in request now-a-day. The "drunkard's cloak" was a cask with a hole at the top, through which the drunkard's head protruded, and one on each side for either hand. The legs were free for the offender to perambulate with the instrument of punishment about him.†

Were not valuable possessions taxed? and was not the rightful possession of stocks and whipping-posts deemed to be such by lords of manors? Undoubtedly. They were held to be proofs and signs of manorial property, and tests of its genuine character. Hence taxes were paid upon the manorial implements of punishment, the stocks, whipping-post, &c., by the too often proud possessor, the lord of the manor.

The precise object of these immediate pages was an

night, either doing naughty, or altogether suspicious of doing naughty; and, therefore, by order of the court, punished by whipping and setting in the stocks. The male offender was living in Weymouth some years after.

* See Lord Campbell's Lives of the Chancellors for the affair, and for Wolsey's revenge.

† J. Brand's Hist. of Newcastle, vol. ii. p. 192.

enumeration of the instruments used for the due carrying out of borough punishment — the weapons of a borough police. Borough legislature is much too large a topic to be wholly embraced under this head. It has its due proportion of space assigned to it, when the orders, precepts, rules and laws for brewers, tipplers, bakers, foreigners, &c., are under consideration. The use of the stocks as a punishment of offenders against conventional morality during the Protectorate brings the following particulars within our scope: —

"The affectation of extreme attention to outward observances of decorum, and the assumption of a saintly demeanour, were not confined to the excessive enforcement of a regard for the Sabbath, but were displayed also in a minute attention to verbal conversation and the phraseology of the period; and the laws for the due observance of a decent and moral demeanour in this respect were frequently applied to an extreme that would be ridiculous in this day of certainly advanced refinement.

"Few sittings of the justices of Dorchester took place during the term comprised between 1654 and the Restoration, at which they had not to adjudicate upon some charge of swearing, of which the most frequent and obnoxious instances are, 'By the name of God;' the fines imposed varying in amount, but being chiefly 5*s*. In one instance 'a gentleman not named' for swearing such an oath was convicted in the fine of 'a noble;' and '*Mr.* Robert Lawrence, *Esqr.*' is fined 10*s*. for a similar oath. We see here, that if the law was no respecter of persons, those who administered it paid some attention to titular distinction.

"It is to be regretted that even the fair sex were sometimes amenable to punishment for this offence; to wit, on the 13th March, 1656, 'Charitie Rabats was set in y[e] stocks for hir cursinge.'

"There are several instances in which such expressions as 'Plague take you' were visited with the penalty for cursing. On one occasion an information was laid against a lad who, whilst playing at fives with a companion, 'cursed and said "Plague take him," meaning y[e] baule.' It is well that Gray wrote some years later, or he surely would have been visited for his magnificent ode, commencing —

"'Ruin seize thee! ruthless king!'"

"But the judicial functionaries of the day took cognisance not only of cursing, but of other foul and intemperate language. Such expressions as 'rogue,' 'base rogue,' 'thief,' 'foul toad,' and other verbal unpleasantries, were regarded as offences of sufficient magnitude to be brought before the notice of the bench. These things frequently arose out of the political hostilities of the time, as we meet with such epithets as 'crop-eared rogue' and 'cavalier knave.' One Matthew Pouncy, for abusing the mayor, the recorder, and all the rest of the bench, as 'knaves and roags,' was bound to appear at the Quarter Session to answer the charge.

"The interference of the justices in these minor matters of social decorum and the properties of demeanour, was also manifested in their constituting themselves as arbitrators in cases of private scandal. On the 26th of February, 1657, Charles Gardiner was informed against for using, regarding two of his neighbours, 'words tending much scandoll to them boath.' And, even beyond this, it appears, by the following extraordinary entry, that the court of justice was occasionally converted into a very court of love, Venus and Cupid being displaced to make room for Mr. Mayor and Mr. Bayliffe Stansbie.

"'The 12th of Septem., 1656. — This daye Alice Hill vppon examination is found to keepe company with Phillip Bartlett in vnseasonable time, and saith shee will not forsak him vnlesse hee will forsak her. Shee is ordered not to keepe him company againe without leav.' All honour to Alice Hill! 'Faithful found among the faithless,' she was a pattern for her sex. Faithful as fair, what cared she for Mr. Mayor or Mr. Bayliffe? Strong in the deep affection for her dear Philip, firm in the loyalty of her love, she defied the might of judicial authority in the very spirit of the old couplet: —

"'If you love me as I love you,
No 'bench' shall cut our loves in two.'"

This appeared in the "Dorset County Chronicle," under the title of "Dorchester in the Seventeenth Century," Nov. 4. 1844. Mr. Hearn was the author; since become an emigrant to Australia.

Upon information being furnished of immorality being practised the magistrates were not slow to act.

At the Dorset sessions in 1626 the court was informed that one Eleanor Martin, the wife of Thomas Martin, of Burton, is a woman of ill name and fame, and suspected to live very incontinently with one John Patie, of the same place, tailor.

Eleanor Martin was forthwith committed to the House of Correction, there to remain at the pleasure of the court, and a warrant was issued against John Patie for his personal appearance at the next sessions. It was further ordered, that if the said Eleanor Martin shall again frequent the company of the said John Patie, the said order was to be a sufficient warrant for the constables of the hundred of Sherborne forthwith, upon such her suspected society with the said John Patie, to apprehend and convey her to the House of Correction. This case gave their worships trouble at several sessions; for, notwithstanding the prohibitions, the parties continued their familiarity in a suspicious manner.

The court ordered that if at any time Patie should be seen or known to be in the company of, or to frequent the house of Eleanor Martin, he was, upon complaint before a justice, to be sent to the House of Correction, and likewise Eleanor Martin. The proper guardian of his wife's honour it seems was not vigilant, so it was ordered that if Thomas Martin, the husband, did at any time give any, or connive at such meeting, he was to be sent to the House of Correction, there to remain till further order therein.

This threat of visiting any one — in this case a husband — for neglecting the performance of a social duty, exhibits great interference with the private concerns of families, but at the same time much superintending concern for the good government of the members of the community. This branch of the exercise of authority has ceased: magistrates only administer the written law. These worthy men bore a resemblance to the Roman censors; and what would now be deemed to be tyranny was in Charles's reign judged to be a vindication of offended morals and religion.

William Steevens, of Swanage, for having frequented the company of Christian, the wife of Edward Coles, "in a very suspicious manner," had lain in gaol for the space of three quarters of a year, or thereabouts. His liberation had been effected after promise and hope of reformation; but he relapsed into his former habits of suspicious visits to Goodwife Coles, and was again consigned to gaol.

We hear nothing of the informers. Were they jealous or hostile towards the accused? What a field for private malice did this system lay open? *

The crime of sheep-stealing was visited by the magistrates at the sessions for Dorset with the punishment of branding the offender on the left hand with the letter F (felon) and liberating him.

The extreme punishment, death, was inflicted at sessions. Thus, at the January sessions held at Blandford in 1631, Maria Ryves, *alias* Collins, and Walter Sampson, were sentenced to be hanged. At the January sessions in 1635, held at the same town, Robert Keat, and at the Easter sessions of the same year, held at Sherborne, Nicholas Grant, were left for execution. The offences are not specified.

At the Michaelmas sessions held at Bridport the following entry occurs: —

"*Elizabetha Johnson, alias Stevens, pro vagrant tanq. vagabund. incorrigibil. suspend. per collu. usque dm. mortua sit.*"

If either the incorrigible vagrant or the sheep-stealer were to be hanged, the latter now-a-day would suffer. In 1635, however, one got off with branding, the other was doomed to the gallows.†

* Mr. T. Hearn, "Qui Quondam." † Ibid.

Some boroughs possessed privileges which they set great value upon. Judge Jeffreys in his terrible charge at Bristol refers to the dignity of that great emporium, saying, "This city it seems claims the right of hanging and drawing." The right-hand quarter of a rebel was sent to the city or borough in highest honour. Should we not now hesitate to advance claims which would procure such distinction?

The dreadful scenes which followed the last business of a county assize did not prevent a festive beginning of the same. On the commission day at each county town was held an assize ball. The judges attended in black silk gowns with band and two-curl bob-wig. They did not dance, but usually played at whist.*

A County Gaol in the Reign of Charles the First.

PRISON discipline has become one of the standard topics of the day. The great turn their thoughts to the lowest members in the social scale, and proper necessaries are provided for those whose incarceration is the result of crime. Though immured, the guilty are not considered to have forfeited all claims to compassion or regard. All hope for the future is not lost on entering the prison house, for much is done to amend the criminals. Their punishment is proportioned to their crime. The only question lies between them and the offended law; nothing besides intervenes. The officials carry out, not as principals, but subordinates, the sentence. This makes imprisonment a very simple matter compared with what it long continued to be, till indeed that sainted visitor, the revered Howard, rapped at the prison doors, and mankind shuddered at his accounts of what passed within the walls.

In any mention of the county gaol of Dorsetshire in Charles the First's reign it should be clearly understood that a great change had taken place. Between the years 1630 and 1637 such abuses had crept in, that the

* Notes and Queries, No 319.

governor or keeper Thomas Devenish was dismissed, or, it may more properly be said, was discontinued, or not allowed to agree any longer with the under-sheriff to hold the former post.

Of the gaol at Dorchester, before the correction of the abuses referred to, we know nothing. We may fairly infer that it may be received as a type of such houses. Compared with what gaols are in the nineteenth century, every one of such places was a Pandemonium. Want of proper and necessary diet, neglect of a proper supply of water, bad ventilation and drainage, occasioned the dreadful gaol fever and a tainted atmosphere, in which the smallpox revelled. These destroyed throughout the realm, so late as 1773, more than all the public executions; and these were fed by 160 different offences.

The judges of assize caused to be issued under their own direction certain orders, which are here given as an example of embodied gaol reform of the reign of Charles I. The claims of society, the due regulation of the house and its inmates, were at that era deemed to have been amply provided for. Perhaps the reform was viewed as a final one; probably may have been judged to be too sweeping. It has proved, however, a small anticipation of that which a truly great character effected 140 years after throughout the land.

Orders for the better Government of the Gaol and Mainprize of Dorchester.

"1. By this rule the building formerly used as a House of Correction within the precincts of the gaol is directed to be set apart for the employment of poor prisoners, as well debtors as felons, that shall be willing and able to get their livings by labours; and that the gaoler shall at his own charge provide such tools and materials as every able man desiring work and duly performing his labour shall and may have fourpence at the least for every day's work; and every woman and other person above the age of fourteen and under the age of eighteen years may and shall have threepence at the least for every day's work. And if they deserve more, to have so much more for their labour respectively, as they shall deserve," &c. &c.

Workhouses and houses of correction are mentioned with little distinction. Such were permitted to be erected at Blandford, Shaftesbury, Cranbourne, and other places in the county. The Marquis of Winchester, the Lord Lieutenant of Dorset, directed mayors, &c., to levy their proportion due toward the expense of a House of Correction for Dorset, A.D. 1583. The gaol inmates, the starving debtor, and equally starving felon associated in their Gehenna were set to work; so that the place became a great workshop for the benefit of the governor, who reaped the profits. The masters or governors had power to put fetters or gyves upon those set to work and labour, and to whip them moderately.*

It has been frequently affirmed that the pauper is too often cared for and provided for less than the prisoner. At this date a pauper past labour had 4*d.* a week assigned for a *week's* maintenance, which, upon complaint, was raised to 6*d.* per week. This is the sum directed to be paid for a *day's* labour of a prisoner; but the latter was perhaps understood to be an artisan or skilled labourer.

In the celebrated act 43 Elizabeth, 1601, the foundation of our present system of poor laws, a test was instituted, and by which it was ordered that such persons (*i. e.* able-bodied applicants) were to receive relief only on condition that they should work for it. The act of 1607 authorised the building "houses of correction," in which implements and machinery were provided for all such as were able to work.

These "houses of correction" were, as their name implies, so much of the nature of penal establishments that an act was passed in 1723 for the correction of workhouses.

The gaol of Dorchester appears to have been applied to

* Hearn's Dorset Sessions.

the reception of, 1. felons, 2. debtors, and 3. paupers, a mixture of the prison and union, or poorhouse.

"2. Also, that every sheriff from henceforth shall and may freely choose whom he please to be his gaoler (which is desired to be a free choice, without taking any recompense for that office)." Then follows a provision for allowing the sheriff the free use of the whole gaol, and directing that the gaoler shall enter into a bond of 200*l.* to the treasurers of the county for the due performance of his office, &c.

Every sheriff had his right confirmed of appointing his gaoler, who might be styled the farmer of the gaol, or head of the working parties, the letter-out of the rooms, vender of eatables and drinkables, and extortioner general. Females often took or undertook the management of gaols. Some of the largest gaols were in Howard's time in the hands of females. The under-sheriff usually received 40*l.* a year for his opportunities from a gaoler. Are we to wonder that the renter addressed himself in earnest to repay himself for his outlay, and remunerate himself for his services and labours? *

Beds were never thought of for prisoners. Often there was no straw. When the window-tax had become a great fact, gaolers who paid the taxes looked to their interests. Howard found the debtor's ward at Gloucester without any windows; a part of the plaster wall was broken through to let in light.†

In Ludgate Prison, enlarged by Dame Agnes Foster between 1454 and 1463, a copper plate had recorded:—

> "So that for lodging and water prisoners here nought pay,
> As their keepers shall all answere at dreadful doomesday."

The gaoler was really a very important personage. Imprisonment now wholly depends on the judges and magistrates. In 1630 another party had authority. Some prisoners against whom the grand jury found no bill,— some whose prosecutors did not appear against them,— after having

* Noted felons were shown at 2*d.* a head.

† Hepworth Dixon's Life of Howard.

been confined for months, were dragged back to gaol, and locked up till they should pay sundry fees to the gaoler. These fees were the cause of imprisonment, apart from crime or debt.

"3. That the gaoler shall take allowance of a penny a day in bread for no more prisoners under his charge than the law doth require; and that the same poor prisoners shall have their full allowance in Ranged bread after the rate of twelve to the dozen, according to the assize" (*i. e.* price, &c. fixed by the magistrates at that date).

"4. Also that the gaoler for such bread as he shall serve to the rest of the prisoners under his charge shall not take above a penny profit to himself upon every dozen, which shall be made according to the assize.

"5. Also that no gaoler shall make or brew any beer within the house of the gaol or precincts thereof that he serveth the prisoners withal, but shall take it from some brewhouse in the town, the best beer, after the rate of 12*s.* the hogshead, whereof he shall utter and sell to the prisoners an ale quart for a penny; and the small beer at six shillings, wherof he shall sell to the prisoners two quarts for a penny, according to the statute; which rates shall be uttered by the justices as they shall see cause."

These regulations are similar to those appointed for tipplers or alehouse-keepers.

"6. That all the lodging chambers which were built for the mainprize shall be converted to that use, and no gaoler shall take above 4*d.* a week of any one prisoner that lieth or lodgeth in any one of those chambers for his lodgings, nor above 6*d.* a week of any one that lieth or lodgeth in the rendezvous chambers."

We shall find that a poor clergyman named Russell, who lay in gaol for debt, had a small sum allowed by the magistrates for his religious exercises, and besides a further sum of 3*l.* 6*s.* 8*d.* for his chamber. We may suppose how little acceptable the religious duties performed by a gaoler, as by order 7., would prove.

"7. Also that the keeper or his deputy shall read one

chapter and Common Prayer every day, morning and evening, unto as many within his charge as may conveniently be assembled to hear him.

"8. For swearing and cursing, every prisoner so offending to be punished according to the law.

"9. Also that no common tippling house for townsmen or strangers, nor playing at fives, bowles, or other unlawful games, shall be kept or allowed within the gaol or precincts.

"10. Also for such prisoners as shall detect any that shall intend to make an escape, or shall discover any dangerous places or persons, for the better safety of the inhabitants of the county, to have favour, and to be well lodged, and his service commended at the assize or sessions where he shall be tried.

"11. Also that the gaoler shall keep a ledger book of all prisoners committed to his charge; and by whom they were committed, how punished, and when and by whom discharged, and at every sessions to be ready to give his accompt therein.

"12. Also that the said house of the gaol and mainprize, being first well repaired by the county, shall be kept in due and orderly reparations, and the chambers and sinks thereof to be kept scoured and free from offence, by the keeper or his servants, and so left well repaired, scoured, and cleansed at the end of the year, when the possession thereof shall be required.

"13. That the fee of 20*s.*, heretofore exacted by the keeper upon every commitment to the gaol for felony, or for want of bail, or for the first week's lodging and diet, shall be no more taken by the keeper, nor by any other or greater fees than the law doth allow, as namely, not above 6*s.* 8*d.* for a common commitment in court, nor above 13*s.* 4*d.* upon the delivery of any other criminal offender after his trial.

"14. Also that at every Easter sessions yearly the treasurers of the county shall be nominated and appointed to be supervisors of the gaol for the year following, and shall at the least four times in the year visit the gaol, and certify the breach of any of the orders aforesaid if cause require."

The set religious duties performed in the Dorset gaol were comprised as already shown, in the reading the chapter and Common Prayer by the keeper or his deputy as by the 7th order for the regulation of the same. However, in 1628, a minister, Mr. John Russell, having become a prisoner for debt in the sheriff's ward, the opportunity was seized by the magistrates of procuring regular religious instruction. As the law then stood, many years might elapse and find the debtor still pining in hopeless captivity. Mr. Russell was allowed a yearly sum of 6*l.* 13*s.* 4*d.* for public and private religious exercises, and a chamber toward his better maintenance and relief. Now, as the governor Devenish let out everything, the treasurer was empowered to pay the chief functionary 3*l.* 6*s.* 8*d.* yearly for the minister's chamber.

Two years subsequently the sheriff's ward was cut off from all communication with the other parts of the building. Mr. Russell still lay in gaol, and was by this alteration in the prison shut out from performing his duties; perhaps more so by the voluntary and acceptable services of William Benn, clerk parson of All Saints, Dorchester, who now had the 10*l.* assigned to him which had been before paid for the services of Mr. Russell.

We ought not to expect more than the acknowledged state of advancement and progress of the particular time. The Dorset worthies had doubtless cleansed their Augean stable of much that was bad. The era was not late enough for us to expect the setting in play any reformatory plans. The fallen prisoner lay without the benefit of any system to raise him, to rescue and protect him from his own antecedents.

We have nothing about the care of those who were "sick and in prison" at Dorchester. A few years elapsed, and Mary Blake, the schoolmistress of the "Taunton Maids," sank amidst the felons, with many others of the unfortunate Monmouth followers and idol worshippers, a victim of small-pox. According to general accounts of such places, each was a lazar-house of every loathsome and infectious pestilence.

The poor afflicted lady died in the felons' quarters, then the nurseries of every crime.

At Exeter in 1775 there was an infirmary, and a surgeon who, hardly will it be credited, was *by contract* excused from attending any prisoner sick of the gaol fever! As well might our gallant defenders contract to serve, except when there happened any serious warfare. A female gaoler at Exeter paid 22*l.* to J. Dennis Rolle, Esq., as a grantee from the duchy of Lancaster for the felons' gaol, though this gentleman possessed an estate granted for the purpose of enabling that very prison to be upheld in a state of *security and conveniency.* Two sailors, who had been fined 1*s.* each, had 1*l.* 15*s.* 8*d.* each to pay for prison fees; which not being able to do, they were detained.

At length the venerated Howard called attention to the gaol system. No gaoler could be found who received a salary; all lived by fees. No precedent could be found for charging a county with the expenses of a salary to a respectable keeper. Till a bill passed for abolishing gaolers' fees, about 1773, no true reform could be hoped for.

Whether the effect of much that has been done has been to render the condition of criminals undergoing what is supposed to be punishment, in many respects more comfortable, if not actually more desirable, than that of the poor but honest labourer, is beside our present subject.

Rewards offered to the Prosecutors of Offenders.

THAT self-interest is the mainspring of human action must have been well understood by the Dorset magistrates in 1639. They show by their proceedings great wisdom in remedying the evil set forth. To toil without any hope of reward has ever proved fatal to exertion; to hold out certain gains acts as a sure stimulus to work success in the desired arena.

At a general sessions of the peace held at Blandford in 1639 (13 Charles I.) the magistrates set forth that sundry good laws and statutes are not put in execution as they ought to be, because the doing thereof is chargeable and the prosecutors receive no reward for their pains and trouble.

The court, for the encouragement of prosecutors of offenders, with the consent of Francis Gape, gent., deputy-clerk of the peace of Dorset, agreed that no fee should be taken henceforward from prosecutors, and that every prosecutor shall receive from a sixth to an eighth part at the least of every fine or penalty hereinafter mentioned:—

Offences.	Fines. s.	d.
Of any innkeeper or alehousekeeper that sells not a quart of his best beer and two quarts of his ordinary beer for 1*d.*	20	0
Unlicensed alehousekeeper	20	0
Suffering a townsman or other to tipple in an inn or alehouse	10	0
For drunkenness	5	0
For tippling (ten groats)	3	4
Barrel of beer sold by a brewer to an unlicensed alehousekeeper (a noble)	6	8
Keeping unlawful games	6	8
Using unlawful games	6	8
Neglect of constable or tythingman to search monthly after unlawful games and gamesters	40	0
Where a constable or tythingman willingly suffers a rogue to pass unpunished	20	0
A person opposing the punishing of a rogue	100	0
Giving alms to a vagabond, and not sending or bringing him to the officer to be punished	10	0
The overseers of the poor neglecting to meet monthly to confer about the better relief of the poor, and for neglecting to set the poor to work, and for neglecting to place out apprentices, or for any other neglect of their office	20	0
For opposing and hindering the setting the poor to work	100	0

And of all other sums of money which by any other laws or statutes are given and limited to the poor people.*

There was formerly a county marshal, who was so useful

* Mr. T. Hearn, "Qui Quondam."

in Dorsetshire about 1632 in the searching out and apprehending rogues and vagrants, that twenty or thirty shillings were voted to him for his good service.*

There was a standing order of vestry at Liverpool to prosecute all robbers, shoplifters, and housebreakers at the parish expense, when discovered. In 1760 the state of that town required some steps to be taken.†

The Treatment of Under-Tenants or Incomers.—The Regulating the Population by restraining them from Marriage.—Each Cottage to have Land attached.

When, in the course of events, the religion of the land was changed, and the poor had no longer the same clergy and religious houses to look to in distress, public officers in the several towns and parishes undertook the distribution of the funds committed to them by voluntary sympathy for the relief of destitution. In 1572 an act was passed for a compulsory assessment for the poor.

This must have produced an immense effect upon communities. The inhabitants of boroughs now comprehended that they might be taxed, in a way not experienced before, to a great extent; and that the remedy against this evil was in their own hands.

They determined to regulate the numbers of those who resided and those who were employed in their borough, in order to provide for their own due protection against being burdened; as modern times have furnished examples of, when half the rental has been known to be sacrificed to the maintenance of the poor.

Absolute in the exercise of the power reposed in them, the borough magnates turned out those whom they judged likely to become chargeable, and made orders and bye-laws for this object. Viewed apart in court and hustings books much savours of cruelty; but let the whole be viewed in connec-

* Mr. T. Hearn, "Qui Quondam."

† Historical Society of Lancashire and Cheshire.

tion with the subject, and then a fear of ill consequences, and a desire to protect themselves after the manner of the time from a pauper population, will be apparent. Do not inhabitants of parishes and towns in the present day decline to employ those who will by such means gain a settlement, and be likely to lessen the value of property when they and their families have become chargeable to the parish?

A few entries will suffice to show the summary manner in which these under-tenants, incomers, or lodgers, as we now style them, were treated.

The lodging of strangers was among the evils complained of at Brighton about the year 1580. The townsmen little dreamed of future inroads of visitors of all classes and either sex who would not stop for this inquiry.

"No under-tenants or incomers were to be admitted at Brighton till the oppynion of the conestable and churchwardens had been first set down in writing, that such under-tenant was thought to be of sufficient ability to maintain himself or family without burthening the town."

A.D. 1592, Andrew Ham of Lyme was directed to remove his sister from his house, — subpœnâ 40*s.*

William Martin to remove Anne Dolman, 5*s.*

It was finally ordered in 1584 that no person do take in any under-tenant into his house at any time without Mr. Mayor's licence, under pain of 10*s.*; and this sum was raised in 1594 to 40*s.*

At Leicester the mayor chose two discreet persons to search their ward every month to discover under-tenants.

When a trespasser within the precincts was detected the process for expelling him was simple.

Henry Webb, the new tailor at Lyme, had a day given him, in 1595, by which day he was to depart the town.

"The jury made a presentment in 1597 that one Clattey had received into his house a man and his wife; and William Skorch harboureth his wife's sister, a maisterless maid; and Joan Peter, a maisterless maid, a wrangler from house to house, and a common tale-teller.

"Also they present that Edward Borough keepeth a young child in his house, which is not to be harboured, and

Poynter doth the like; and Wm. Crewe keepeth his mother in his house, which is not to be harboured, and Poynter doth the like; and that John Domett likewise harboureth his wife's sister; and Mary, Mrs. Barret's servant, is not removed, being often warned and commanded to depart the town. George Hoop harboureth Thomas Tucker; and that Mary Cooke, a maid maisterless, being a common picker and filcher, is harboured by Thomas Lacy."

Ideo quilibet eorum in misericordiâ. So each is fined; And that Christian Clattey, a maisterless drab, be presently removed; and that Wm. Goldsmith's daughter and children do the like.

1598. Also they present that Mr. Robert Hassard hath taken in an under-tenant contrary to the order, 12*d.*

In another place, "All these to be presently avoided."

To no purpose did the head of a family secure a good servant if the authorities feared future inconvenience as likely to arise from that quarter.

The seaport town Rye was surrounded for miles by forest in Tudor reigns. A man who resided there, practising the calling or profession of a "husbandman," was ordered to depart the town, "the place not being fit for such an artificer."* It may be well asked how did such forced removals terminate? The answer is, in poverty, grief, and death!

The following entries from Lyme further illustrate the subject:—

"The jury present, A. D. 1592, Eleanor Ellyot, widow, for not having turned away her maid servant as she had been ordered to do. To be done by next holyday, under pain of 5*s.*"

"*Item,* presentant qd. Ellinor Ellyot, vidua, non removit a servicio suo servam famulam suam sicut ad ultimam ei precipiebatur."

"1597. *Item,* that Mr. Mayor do cause all those persons all ready come in (according to the words of the order, without the condiscent of the mayor and his brethren) to be presently voided, upon pain to forfeit for any of them not so to be put away, 40*s.*"

* Horsfield's Sussex.

In all our borough towns there was precaution taken against the being burdened with families under the poor act. In 1617 an inmate at Weymouth was ordered to be removed, or else the landlord to give a bond that the party should not become chargeable. In 1647 John Wall, merchant, of the same borough, was fined 20*l.* for taking in one Henry Tizer, with his wife and children, likely to be chargeable, and would not send them away.

In Norfolk, to prevent the necessity of strangers being taken in to lodge, a tenement for an inn was provided by the corporation at Norwich.* These strangers were doubtless useful, so they were admitted and placed under *surveillance.*

Some men preferred jobbing about as casual labourers. The jury of Seaford presented for the offence, viz., "living at their own hands." The parties were ordered to get into service within a fortnight. 14 Charles I.

In 1614 Batten the dyer had not removed out of the town, as he was enjoined the last law-day, and therefore he was amerced 40*s.* Several others were amerced 3*l.* for not having removed their inmates.

So late as 1697 several foreigners, *i. e.* strangers or incomers, were presented for residing at Lyme. No undertenants at Castle Combe were to be taken in in Charles I.'s reign without giving security that they should not become chargeable. The practice of most boroughs coincided on this point. By the 13 & 14 Charles II. a stranger that rented a tenement of 10*l.* a year, or could give security against his becoming burdensome, could not be removed within forty days of his arrival by the magistrates upon complaint of the parish officers.

The persecution of needy persons likely to become chargeable to a parish, and of those who harboured any one, led to some persons actually wanting a habitation and to acts of great inhumanity, even to danger of perishing from exposure to the weather while compelled to sleep in open fields and under hedges. So determined were the inha-

* Blomfield's Norfolk.

bitants of towns and parishioners of country places to protect themselves, — often perhaps a clique were alive to their own interests, — that much injustice, and doubtless cruelty, resulted. A humane or public-spirited clergyman, who had patronised a poor, perhaps useful family, appears to have been severely taxed.

"Beaminster, Mich. Quar. Sessions, A. D. 1625.

"It is ordered by this court that Mr. Jefferies, parson of Beere Hackett, within this county of Dorset, clerk, shall, within one month next, give securitie to the overseers of the poore of the said parish of Beere Hackett, to defend them in time to come against anie charge or burthen which maie arise or be, by reason that he hath received into the said parish one Christopher Sprage, a man of no worth [*i. e.* having no property], with seaven children and three apprentices, verie likely to be chargeable to the parish; which, if he shall refuse to do, that then the said overseers shall have power, by vertue of this order, to rate the said Mr. Jefferies to the poor at ii*s.* or ii*s.* vi*d.* per week more than his ordinary rate, and so to continue untill he shall remove them out of the said parish." *

Corporators thought they knew what the constitution of a town should be as to the elements of which it was composed.

The common, as it seems to us, right of moving into any town where a prospect opens for our labours, was not formerly enjoyed without certain payments for liberty or licence to set up one's calling. In a curious survey among the archives of Weymouth is given "the names of such tradesmen and artificers as have liberty for them, their children, and apprentices, to use only their trade within this town, being no freemen within the same, 1617."

We have here the proportion the corporation thought fit of the several tradesmen. The surgeons (barbers without doubt) are placed with the mechanics.

14 tailors.	5 weavers.
4 caps (cappers).	6 joiners.
14 ship carpenters.	6 bakers.

* Mr. T. Hearn, "Qui Quondam." MS. Book of the Dorset Sessions.

7 shoemakers.	7 tanners.
2 blacksmiths.	1 chapman.
2 surgeons.	1 brazier.
1 wheeler.	4 helliers.
9 butchers.	

In spite of all this care to exclude strangers, it is evident that the civic authorities might meet with disappointment as to the number of the poor, from too many couples of townspeople marrying and having families. This difficulty was not insurmountable in the Stuart reigns.

At Yarmouth the corporation undertook to regulate the increase or decrease of the population to the wants of their town, anticipating, like Malthus, a possible supply beyond the demand; and those enactments for the nation at large which that gentleman's followers prophesy will one day be positively required. In 1625 an order was made that no poor people should be married unless they should first procure the handwriting of the alderman and chief constable of the ward wherein they lived, for that purpose!

Craftsmen or operatives about to set out from their own parish to look for work in other parts procured a document signed and sealed by well-known parish officers and parishioners. This set forth, in scrivener's language, the intention and object of the party in leaving home, prayed good treatment, &c. What rendered the formal document so serviceable was, that those whose signatures were attached acknowledged the parishioner as their own, and not leaving it doubtful if he were not creeping into a town under pretence of seeking work, but in reality to obtain a settlement.

The following extract will explain the decision of the court respecting the old law enjoining cottages having land around them for the inmates; a provision intended to secure the neighbourhood from a great increase of parishioners, and from the depredations of cottagers without gardens or land to cultivate. The quantity of land assigned would now be judged too great for labourers, and rather as likely to convert them into small farmers. In 1627 Roger Crocker, of Fontmill, was convicted for erecting a cottage within the manor of Fontmill "without having four acres of land continually to be occupied with the same. This court doth therefore order that the said Roger Crocker shall forthwith, upon sight hereof, remove Jolliffe Toogood and his family (whom the said Roger hath permitted to inhabit therein) out of the said house, and hereafter not to suffer him or any other person or persons whatever to inhabit in the same."

In some other similar infractions of the law the parties are peremptorily ordered to pull down the cottages so erected.*

The Shoemakers faulty in respect of their Leather.

In 1597, there were complaints of the leather being badly dressed, and so not wearing well when made into shoes. The jury of Lyme presented the shoemakers as "faulty," in not causing their leather to be well curried; upon which they were fined 12*d.* each. Again the same year, 6*d.* each; and the following year the curriers were fined 20*d.* each.

Cordwainers or shoemakers often used the mystery of tanners and curriers; hence the justice of amercing them for using badly-dressed leather.

Tanners used to keep hides in the tan-pit a year or fifteen months; but it was a subject of complaint in 1548, that hides were then tanned in three weeks or six weeks. An act was passed requiring tanners to keep hides nine months in the pit.

Some mention of Apprentices.

The inhabitants of borough towns, besides advantages over country persons arising from privileges and from associating in a community, had an importance assigned them by the legislature. Their burghers and craftsmen could not lower their calling by the associating with them persons inferior in station to themselves, as some low professional men

* Mr. T. Hearn, "Qui Quondam." MS. Book of Dorset Sessions.

now often do. They were restrained by an act of Parliament passed in 1405 from receiving the child of any man or woman out of the borough as apprentice to any craft, unless the parent had 20*s.* a year in land. This was repealed in the reign of Henry VII.*

Those who followed a handicraft business as masters were subject to many regulations in respect of their apprentices. Great restriction, as to the class and residence of those whose sons were to be received as apprentices once existed. The laws upon this point were relaxed before the reign of Elizabeth.

Borough laws, which indeed comprehended all subjects, did not, in the matter of apprentices, furnish an exception. Many orders and regulations exist, which prove that much good sense and good feeling were employed to procure a fair arrangement between master and apprentice. Apprentices were to be taught the use of the bow. While the richest persons in the west buy salmon as a delicacy at a high price, so that it is an expensive luxury, our town worthies carefully legislated, and no doubt it was requisite, that apprentices should not eat salmon more than three times a week for dinner when it was sold at 1*d.* a pound. Our rivers then abounded with salmon. This fish was brought to Lyme by the boat-load in the reign of Elizabeth. Some hard masters had no doubt given their apprentices salmon, when a glut in the market, till they were surfeited, and the hardship was much complained of. Apprentices were not to keep fighting-cocks for the first seven years of their time, nor hunting-dogs. They were to wear no long or short wigs above 15*s.* in value, and no point-lace.

Some lines of business were judged to require a longer apprenticeship than others. For instance, an apprentice to a glover was bound for seven years. He was to be clad in every particular and well fed, have 12*d.* a year, and clothes for working-days and holy-days.†

In 1608 John Damon of Weymouth, shipwright, took W.

* Blomefield's Norfolk.

† Lyme Hustings Book, A.D. 1592.

Moatyer apprentice for ten years. He was to find him meat, drink, linen, woollen hose, shoes, and all other things necessary; and at the end of the term of ten years to allow him four suits of apparel, linen and woollen, to pay him 20*s.*, and to allow and deliver him his axe, an adze, an auger, a caulking-iron, a mallet, a clarshammer, a church-clummer, and a gimlet.*

An orphan was apprenticed at Marlborough, in the reign of Charles I., to a maker of bone-lace, for eight years.† This must have been soon after the introduction of the art of making that new article.

Apprentices were associated with the masters and their families, and not, as in the present day, apprentices in name; but knowing nothing of their master's household. The sending out apprentices to glean was an abuse which the farmer groaned under. How this primitive custom came to be perverted will appear under its appropriate head.

Town apprentices were to be preferred by an order made at Lyme in 1618: "No artificer or trader within the town is to take any apprentice from out of the town if there be any one fit in the town to serve him, unless he first have the leave and goodwill of the mayor and capital burgesses. Any one violating this order shall not open his shop windows any more within the town."

In the year 1660 Thomas Newton of Lyme, having ventured upon what the borough legislators had forbidden, became the subject of a presentment. He kept a tailor's trade in the town without serving an apprenticeship there; a thing not allowed.

Parties of Irish wander about.

IRISH tramps infested our counties in 1629, and prove to have been types of those parties who lately roamed about here after the great potato famine and fever.

* Sherren Papers.

† Waylen's Hist. of that town.

Some of the latter peaceably progressed in family parties till, meeting other parties of their countrymen, angry words, unnecessarily used, led to attacks upon each other and an indiscriminate knocking down of unoffending wayfarers.

Treolan Mac Brean and divers other Irish people were taken in the town of Sherborne wandering, as dangerous persons; for, as it appeared by the oath of Mr. Richard Reives, they had offered violence to divers upon the highway. It was also manifest that their pass was forged and Sir Ralph Freeman's hand counterfeited. The court adjudged that as many of the party as were able to undergo punishment should be openly whipped at a cart's tail, and be sent by a pass from parish to parish the nearest way to Minehead (Mynyard); where they were to take shipping and to be transported into Ireland, from whence they came.*

A proclamation of the year 1634, for the speedy sending away of Irish beggars into their own country, is a proof of the evils that were occasioned from this source. Parish account books have many entries of money given to a "company of Irish people," to "Irish men," &c., from 1632 to 1648. The disbanding of the Irish army in 1630 occasioned many of the complaints about the Irish.

A Jury recommend a Censorship.

THE grand jury of Bristol, in the year 1681, recommended that no printed or written news or pamphlet be suffered to be read in any coffee-house or tippling-house in that city, except such as has been first shown to Mr. Mayor or the alderman of the ward for the time being where such coffee-house is situate.

Sundry coffee-houses had been noticed, which were described in this strong language. They were said to be commonly frequented, as well on Lord's days as other days, by many schismatical and seditious sectaries and other dis-

* Mr. T. Hearn, "Qui Quondam."

loyal persons, where, for their encouragement in tippling, they were usually entertained with false news, lying and scandalous libels and pamphlets, tending to the reproach and dishonour of the established religion and of his Majesty's government, and divers of his great officers and ministers of state.

We learn from this recommendation, that restrictions upon the liberty of the subject did not always emanate from kings and ruling powers, but from the governed themselves. A state must be prepared for liberty as well as for other developments which civilisation gives rise to in the course of time.

Abuses into which Gleaners of Corn fell.

THE gleaners in the field that has yielded its abundant harvest often present a beautiful picture to the sensitive mind. They often appear as if brought upon the scene to make it complete, like figures in a *tableau vivant*. We can fancy another Boaz befriending another Ruth. This privilege of gleaning, which has suggested these remarks, has, however, been greatly abused, like too many other privileges. In Charles I.'s reign the magistrates of Dorset, at Easter sessions, in 1635, found their interference necessary.

Their order displays in its recital how human interest operates in creating a complete perversion of the use of worthy objects. Some of these abuses are very striking. People, under pretence of gleaning, refused to work at harvest work for hire; some, who engaged to reap corn by the task, secretly agreed with others to glean after them, and took money of them to neglect to gather the corn together; others would not forbear to glean until the winter corn was mowed together and the summer corn made into rick; others walked abroad in the night, and carried sheets and great cloths to put the corn in which they stole; and if the constables offered to lay hands upon any of these wrongdoers, they were threatened with an action at law. The order continues:—

"Wherefore the court, being desirous to reform those abuses, and, to the end that offenders in that kind may receive punishment, constables, &c., be directed and defended in their just doing, the honest and painful husbandman comforted and encouraged, and aged, weak, and infirm poor restored to and maintained in their just and lawful right of gleaning, doth in the first place declare that those gleanings do not belong nor ought to be gathered but by those who have not wherewithal to receive and maintain themselves; and that masters neither should nor ought to send their servants and apprentices to glean corn to make a private gain or commodity thereby, in defrauding the impotent poor; and doth admonish the constables to keep the watches duly set, especially in harvest time, and that with able and sufficient men, and not with boys or lewd persons; and doth further declare and order that such as have not corn nor other especial occasion to be in the fields, and shall be found there in night time, are night-walkers, and may and ought to be apprehended and imprisoned until they find sureties for their good behaviour. And that in harvest time the constables of every township may and ought to cause all such persons as be meet to labour to serve by the day, according to the rate set down for wages, upon pain to him that shall refuse of two days' imprisonment and one night in the stocks; and the constable to forfeit forty shillings for not executing his office," &c., &c.

The sending of apprentices by masters to glean was a gross case of perversion of the original purpose of such an act. A rural police is clearly fore-shadowed by the worthy magistrates.*

The Prices of Articles of Food, &c.

THROUGHOUT these pages the actual prices of many articles have been quoted.

Most persons speak of the good old times as one of

* Mr. T. Hearn, "Qui Quondam," Sessions Book in MS.

universal cheapness. "Our cathedrals," say they, "cost a mere trifle, and we may see the table in some chapter-houses upon which the master-builder paid his masons each a penny a day:" and they might have added that building materials were equally low in price. Still the cathedrals were costly structures, and much more so than they would prove to be in the present day. The value of money was very different. A pound of the precious metals procured in the reigns of the Plantagenets fifteen or twenty times what it now would: and yet it was a dear time, even much dearer, than the present; for the pound was hard to be earned, rents were low, and money surprisingly scarce.

When the Archbishop of Canterbury chose to visit his lands at Tarring, Sussex, about A.D. 1277, the prices of articles to be supplied by his tenant were settled by agreement; and they appear very low.

	s.	*d.*
A bushel of wheat - - -	0	$2\frac{1}{4}$
" oats - - -	0	1
Carcass of beef - - -	1	4
Yearling hog - - -	0	8
4 gallons of beer - - -	0	1
2 good hens - - - -	0	1
5 score eggs* - - -	0	1

The exact comparative value of money is not known. Was it worth at this date fifteen or twenty times its present value? Perhaps so, or even more. In the archives of Lyme is a small parchment deed, by which a tenant under the mayor of a croft and curtilage of the king's demesne in 1338, judging himself over-rated, had his rent reduced from 16*d.* to 12*d.* a year. The difference of 4*d.* a year was sufficient to cause a deed to be drawn, and the form to be gone through in full hustings court, as now-a-day for large amounts.

When the knights of Cornwall pulled up to bait, on their ride to Parliament, in the reign of Edward II., it may seem

* Cartwright's Rape of Bramber.

very little for these worthies to pay 2*d.*; but then it should be known that each received but 2*s.* 6*d.* for his whole day's travelling expenses, knight and horse.*

According to the erroneous system of ancient fiscal policy, every article in a household was liable to be rated, and a proportionate part of that value had to be paid in money. This led our ancestors to dispense with every article nearly, except the necessary and indispensable household stuff.

Convenience, comfort, luxury, ornament, found no one ready to entertain them: these would have been the cause of intolerable charges, and yielded, as would be found to be the case at any era, to circumstances.

Roger the dyer, of Colchester†, lived when the most minute taxation on record, that of the year 1300, was made.

He had in his several apartments but few articles for luxury or convenience. The inventory gives us an insight into the internal economy of a house in the reign of Edward I.

Roger the dyer (there were then no surnames) had,—

	s.	*d.*
In his Treasury or Cupboard.		
1 silver buckle, price - -	0	18
1 cup of mazer (maple) - -	0	18
In his Chamber.		
2 gowns - - - -	20	0
2 beds - - -	half a mark	
1 napkin and 1 towel - -	2	0
In his House.		
1 ewer with a bason - -	0	14
Andiron - - - -	0	8
In his Kitchen.		
1 brass pot - - - -	0	20
1 brass skillet - - -	0	6
1 brass pipkin - - -	0	8
1 trivet - - - -	0	4

* Mr. P. Collier. † Morant's History.

In his Brewhouse.	s.	d.
1 quarter of oats - - -	2	0
Wood ashes - -	half a mark	
Great fat (vat) for dying - -	2	6
Item.		
1 cow - - - -	5	0
Calf - - - -	2	0
2 pigs (each 12*d.*) - - -	2	0
1 sow - - - -	0	15
Billet wood and faggots for firing -	1 mark	
Sum - - - -	71	5
Fifteenth of the above which had to be paid - - - -	4	9

What a low state of domestic civilisation does this pourtray. The taxgatherers took nearly the value of the dyer's cow for one contribution. This man kept some animals to run in his little croft or upon the common. We may readily account for the riots that ensued when the great infringed upon the rights of common which the poor had enjoyed. The effects of vicious legislation can be traced in many points of view. The dyeing vat, the implement of the man's art, was not spared under this taxation. Any new or improved vat would have been set down at a higher value, and the poor artificer would have been taxed for having made progress towards the better discharge of the duties of his craft. Extend this view to every trade, and we shall find it trammelled. Roger had no materials used in the dyeing art in his house. May he not have anticipated the visit of the taxgatherer, and so used up or secreted his stock? His fuel was perhaps necessarily in store, and he had accordingly to pay 13*s.* 4*d.* England could not improve under such a system. Let us ask if legislators have not learned to be wiser. We are, by a return, enabled to ascertain what was a CONSIDERABLE MAN in the reign of Henry VI. 1433. Four commissioners were empowered at that date to summon and tender an oath to persons of *quality* to keep the peace, both themselves and retainers.

John Crogg and Thomas Tinham, of Lyme, Dorset, were placed on the list as considerable men, who were able to dispense 12*l.* per annum. Let those, who have judged that some error exists as to the low prices of early reigns, be assured that nothing but such low prices could have availed for any one to live upon such an income.*

A great authority writes that 1400*l.*, so late as the reign of Henry VIII., would be equivalent to 8000*l.* in the reign of Queen Victoria. The price of every commodity was soon raised, as the resources of new countries, particularly of Peru, opened out. Rents rose, and the stipendiary bedesman, poor scholars, and that class, could not live upon the salary which amply sufficed only a century before.

The "commons" allowed to the choristers at Winchester in the reign of Henry VIII. was charged 8*d.*, and that at Eton 10*d.* a week. There was a suit of livery allowed to each at Christmas. This may appear quite insufficient for maintenance. Let us see how prices were fixed by authority in a country town, Marlborough, in 1524†: —

Hucksters were to sell —	*d.*
A bushel of oatmeal for - -	12
A quart " - -	0½
12 eggs - - - -	1
6 eggs - - - -	0½
Chandlers to sell 12 lb. of candles -	15
" " 1 lb. " -	1¼

In 1545 the wages of a superior mechanic and a sawyer were 4*d.* a day; his meat and drink, in addition, were given him, and they were set down at 3*d.*

Valuation of the horses and oxen, the property of the last Lord Delawarr of Offington, Sussex, A.D. 1554 —

	£	*s.*	*d.*
The best horse - - -	5	0	0
Two others, each - - -	4	0	0

* Archives of Lyme. † Waylen's Hist. of Marlborough.

	£	s.	d.
Other horses, each - -	2	0	0
Some horses, each - -	0	8	0
A working ox - - -	1	8	4
A fatting ox - - -	1	4	4
A sheep - - - -	0	2	0*

Prices doubled themselves in Queen Elizabeth's reign.

The charges and prices of builders' work in 1564, the prices at the same place in 1850, and the comparative prices, taking into account the altered value of money, are set down. (*Archives of Lyme.*)

	Price A.D. 1564.		Price A.D. 1850.			Comparative Price.		
	s.	d.	£	s.	d.	£	s.	d.
A sack of lime - -	1	0	0	1	8	0	4	0
Hundred of lathes - -	0	10	0	1	3	0	3	4
Lath-nails per thousand -	1	8	0	0	8	0	7	8
(Nails of every kind were dear.)								
Healm stones per hundred - Elsewhere called healing stones (used by helliers). Were these slates?	0	7	0	2	6	0	2	4
Crease, each - -	0	2	0	0	7	0	0	8
Artificers' work, per diem -	0	6	0	3	0	0	3	6
Meat and drink - -	0	$4\frac{1}{2}$						
Boy - - - -	0	3	0	0	0	0	1	0
Lead (A.D. 1551) per cwt. -	8	11	1	9	3	1	15	8
A wheelbarrow - -	1	0	0	12	6	0	4	0
Lock for the Council-house door - - -	0	8	0	0	0	0	2	8

Many a page of old diaries and chronicles truly is occupied with the inclemencies, remarkable features, sometimes with the benignity of the seasons. The readers of such entries, led away by the perusal of what was almost ordi-

* Parry's Sussex.

nary, though couched in terrifying language, whenever eclipses and thunderstorms gave employment to the chronicler's pen, have been induced to believe that the vicissitudes of the seasons were in latter centuries greater than they now are.

Conclusions have been hastily drawn that the weather was once very different, and the sea more tempestuous. Let it not be forgotten that vessels were, by comparison, mere boats; and agriculture was on quite a different footing to what it now is. Particular seasons, that now produce no very serious inconvenience to the agriculturist beyond the greater consumption of hay, were attended with great loss to the farmer, who was exposed to the greatest trial in order to subsist his cattle, when long continued frosts and a late spring had produced an unusual backwardness of vegetation. It was not till 1657 that Bligh, in his "Improver Improved," pointed out the advantage of growing CLOVER; and Sir Richard Weston enlightened our countrymen by an account of the cultivation of TURNIPS in Flanders, by which cattle might be fattened in winter.

HAY sold in the late spring of 1643, at 8*l.* 14*s.* per ton, nearly the value of three fat bullocks. What was the value of hay in our present money? May we not conclude that it was at least 17*l.* a ton. The charge for the run of a horse in salt-grass, or pasture occasionally overflowed by the sea, as Seaton marsh, was about three times more than that of the present day.

The fluctuation in the price of wheat must have exposed our ancestors to the extremes of famine and plenty at intervals of only a few months. It appears almost difficult to realise such changes in our day. An effort may be made by the aid of the following table. It will be seen that wheat was sometimes ten times higher than at others.

A. D.	Wheat	Rye.	Barley.	Oats.
	s d.	s. d	s d.	s. d.
At Weymouth, 1586.	3 6 8 0	6 0	2 4 5 4	*
At Barnstaple, in August, 1587	10 0	2 8	2 3	1 6
at Christmas	2 8		2 2	
1588 1590 1591 1592 1593 1594	from 2 8 to 6 8	1 6 to 3 0	1 6 to 3 0	†
1595	9 0			
1596	10 0 12 0 15 0	7 6	6 0	2 4‡
Standard, 1597	9 0	6 0	5 0	5 0§
In July	18 0 20 0	14 0 - -	13 0 15 0	4 0
1598	8 0	6 0	6 0	1 10
1599	4 0	- -	2 6	
1601	5 4			
1602	8 8			
1604	6 8			
1621	2 8 2 6 2 0	1 3	1 3	
1622	6 8			
1637	4 6	4 0		

* Rye was purchased, and sold at a cheaper rate to the poor. Ships laden with corn, bound to Spain, were arrested and carried into Weymouth, that the cargoes might alleviate the distress in the south-west.

† In 1588 best beef sold at 1*d*. per lb. By the year 1591 provisions had become very dear. Pease and beans, in their cods, sold at 12*s*. a bushel. On Whitsunday, for a heifer that had newly calved, 6*l*. 6*s*. 8*d*., *i. e.* 19 nobles.

‡ The Earl of Bath, by order from the council, fixed at Barnstaple a standard price, beyond which no one was to sell corn. This was considered an inadequate price; therefore, of course, no one brought corn to the market. It could not be procured for money. In order to prevent starvation, corn was sent for from Dantzic. — *Account-book of a Town-Clerk of Barnstaple* v. *Lysons.* No MALT was allowed to be made.

§ The agriculturist complained of the low prices. Land fell from 20 to 16 or 17 years' purchase. The poor, who would have been glad a few years before of the coarsest rye bread, traversed the market to find out the finer wheats. — *Sir Symonds D'Ewes.*

PRICES IN THE REIGN OF CHARLES II., A.D. 1655.*

	£	s.	d.
Wheat, per bushel	0	3	3
Oats	0	1	10
Malt	0	3	0
Peas	0	3	9
Tares	0	1	0
Beef, per lb.	0	0	2¼
Butter	0	0	6
Suffolk cheese	0	0	4
Hops, per lb.	0	1	6
2 doz. wheatears	0	1	0
A pheasant	0	2	0
A worthy turkey	0	5	0
Pullet	0	1	0
Duck	0	0	6
Ordinary at an archdiaconal visitation	0	3	0
Coachman (coat and breeches)	6	0	0
Received in lieu of the livery	2	0	0
Footman half the wages of coachman.			
Yearly man servant's wages	5 3	0 0	0 0
Woman cook and chambermaid	3 2	0 10	0 0
Worker in a garden a day	0	1	0
Broad cloth, a yard	0	23	0
Grey woollen stockings	0	3	0
worsted stockings	0	6	4
Walking boots	0	12	0
Shoes	0	4	0
Black Shag hat	1	2	0
Knitting pair worsted stockings	0	2	6
Spinning a lb. wool	0	0	7
Carding a lb. wool	0	0	1
6 doz. beechen trenchers, some square, some round	0	4	0
Saddle, with stirrups, &c., and best Dutch bridle	1	6	0
New horse-pillion for a lady	0	8	0

* Sussex Archæol. Rev. Giles Moore's Diary.

Trees for a Garden in the Reign of Charles II.

	s.	d.
Apricock tree - - -	1	8
Orange tree - - - -	0	8
Pair royal Windsor pear tree -	1	8
2 Kentish pippins - - -	2	4
2 Flanders cherries - - -	2	6
26 *roots of* Provence *roses* - -	5	6
8 young apple trees - - -	7	0
A mulberry tree - - -	4	0
peach - - - -	2	6
medlar - - - -	1	0
2 dozen tulips - - -	3	0

Potatoes, the root which has produced upon mankind and to the politician such immense effects of late years, were sold in 1613 at 2*s.* the lb. Then they were a luxury, and so continued till ninety years ago, when in 1765 Lord Sheffield bought some, and soon after farmers began to plant them in the fields. This novelty experienced the usual fate, viz., that of exciting prejudice against it. At an election at Lewes, potatoes shared with popery the indignation of the people, and "No popery! No potatoes!" was the popular cry. One Moore, an Irishman, planted the first field of potatoes in Devon, at Poltimore, where he resided. A few farmers about Chard, in Somersetshire, followed this example about 1784. Potatoes excited so much prejudice in France, from a belief they would bring back leprosy once more, that the growing crop required to be watched for protection. So late as 1816, the cook of a large establishment at Valognes, Normandy, did not know how to dress a present of that root sent from Guernsey.

Cranes could live here when "England was merry England;" now, alas! they cannot. The wicked gentry are the cause. By draining the marshes and swamps they have added fine land for the use of man; but the interest of the cranes has been overlooked. Their feeding ground is taken from them. We strew no rushes as our ancestors did, and why? — because they do not grow in the well-drained lands.

Ignorance is a humiliating excuse, at the best, for being insensible to great blessings we daily receive; still it is better than wilful indifference. What is the case with our feeling in respect of the great blessing salt proves to us? We speak of the monasteries having salt-pans upon the coast, and of salt water, as if it contained nothing but salt and water, while many chemical ingredients enter into its composition. From these salt-pans all that essential condiment, salt, was obtained; but the Lord Abbots used a very inferior article to what the poor man now does, and perhaps not so wholesome, though certain pans were dignified with fine names. That of Otteham, in Sussex, was called "the golden salt-pan." Before salt mines and rock-salt were known and worked, those in Staffordshire, &c. being discovered in 1670, the quality was inferior, the price at times much higher. Lymington was the last of the places where sea water was evaporated. In 1703, Lymington salt-pan salt sold at 7*s.* a bushel. The duty alone was 5*s.* a bushel, and afterwards this was raised to 15*s.* per bushel, or, in other words, a duty of thirty times the cost of the article.

Let money be of what value it may, whether it could purchase ten times or twenty times what it now can, we must come to this point, what facility was there for earning money? Suppose a bushel of wheat to be the commodity in question, — how long was a man in earning money to purchase it? What rent was paid for land to enable a gentleman to purchase commodities?

In Tudor reigns fish occasionally rose so as to equal in price that of the present day. Taking into account the comparative value of money, this was a famine price.

The division of labour was not complete, as civilisation was not sufficiently advanced. This state is incompatible with low prices. Cathedrals, well-built houses, clothes, ships, freights, food, generally speaking, cost more by comparison than they now do. The CHEAPNESS and the

PLENTY of the olden time are delusions. The good living we read of was such for the rich; but the poor knew not the white bread, the butchers' meat, some of the cheap vegetables, the cheap coal fire, the resident medical man, and many other of God's blessings permitted to be worked out for the use of man.

We desire to say, finally, of prices, that the value of money cannot be found with accuracy for all periods of our history. In quoting prices, likewise, great allowance must be made for locality, season, fashion, and many other circumstances.

The price of every article of food and general consumption, about the year 1700, was nearly *one-third* that of 1854. Rents, mechanics' charges, schooling, were very low, we may almost venture to say, proportionately low. Clothing, however, was not so cheap in proportion. Tea was about nine or ten shillings a pound.

Some estates in Dorset that now let for 400*l.* a year, about the year 1749 let for 70*l.* a year.

The wages of the agricultural labourer at Bow, near Exeter, in 1749, were, when wheat sold from 2*s.* 10*d.* to 4*s.* a bushel,

	s.	*d.*
Man, per diem	1	0
Woman ,,	0	6
Threshing wheat, per bushel	0	4
,, barley, ,,	0	1¼
Cutting wheat, per acre	4	0
Man's day's work at harvest	1	6
Beef and mutton, the best joints, a lb.	0	2½
Cheese, per cwt	11 17	0 0
Peas, a peck	0	10
Butter in May, a lb.	0	4
,, December	0	6

With such wages and such prices the labouring man fared well. From this date prices of every article kept rising, but the labourer's *wages* remained stationary. It follows that every year witnessed a deterioration in his condition. To add to this, the agricultural labourer's habits were unfavourable. He drank to excess at wake, revel, wrestling-match, and every occasion of wonted festivity.

The first Price Current was published in 1634. In the assize or assessment of prices to be paid for articles of food, it was understood to be that paid in a market. If sold in a shop, not at market time, or on a market day, an additional price was allowed.

Suppose that the exact equivalent of money in every reign could be found, is there not also its value and estimation in the social scale to be still considered? In the year 1553 a proclamation was sent out licensing merchants and others passing with license beyond the seas to carry four pounds in coin with them to defray their expenses!*

We may learn what fortune caused a man to be thought very rich at a later date. This recalls to recollection the estimate of what a very rich man possessed years before, and in 1838 made by a clerk at Liege. A few years had made a great difference.

One Argentine or Argenton, of Dorset, was called Golden Argentine because his buckles which he wore in his shoes and boots, and the taggs of his [points] and his lace, were commonly all of gold. He was also called Duke of Bellmore, because he lived under Bellmore Hill.

The income which caused so much reputation was about 500*l.* per annum from land, and he was also esteemed a great moneyed man having, as some supposed, above 6000*l.* in his purse.

He kept some three or four men with their cloaks lined through with silk, and their feathers in their caps.

His wealth was judged to be so considerable in those days as to prove a hindrance to a quiet death.†

* Procl. Soc. Antiquaries. † Notes and Queries. H. F. Sheppard.

The Profit made by coining Corporation and Tradesmen's Tokens.

It is, perhaps, generally known that a little beyond two centuries since a great want of small coin was experienced, upon which retail tradesmen caused tokens to be struck and issued in tin and lead.

Some projectors issued copper farthings with the king's stamp, having a patent for this; they made an ounce of copper, not worth quite a penny, do the work of twenty-

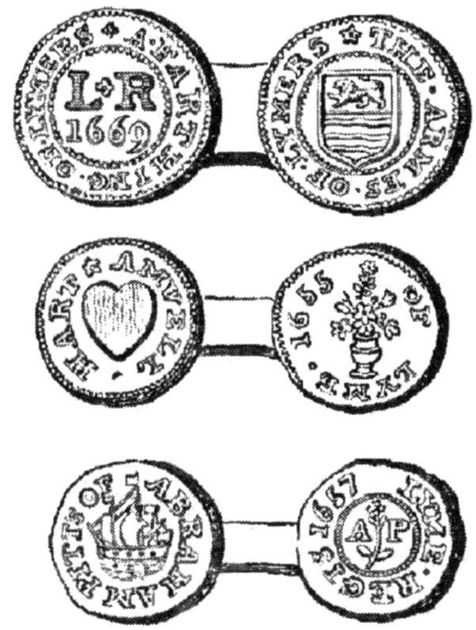

Specimens of a Town and Tradesmen's Tokens.

pence in tokens. The patent was disannulled, and the tokens were left upon the subjects' hands. Some were pilloried for having issued tokens without a patent. There were token makers and public farthing token offices in London. There was great cheating about taking the farthings back that had single rings. Before 1644, when a pamphlet was published, entitled "A Remedy against the Loss of the Subject by Farthing Tokens, discovering the Great Abuse of them heretofore, &c.," there was 100,000*l.* out in farthings among the poor.

Separate works have been devoted to the illustration of

the curious devices of London and provincial tradesmen stamped upon the tokens now forming interesting collections, such as Mr. Beaufoy's, lately presented to the Corporation of London, &c. Our business lies with the pecuniary benefit or loss attending the issuing this money.

The corporation of Lyme ordered a barrel of town farthings in 1669, fifteen years after the first tradesman of the borough, Amyell Hart, had issued his token, and a second barrel six months after. Both barrels of farthings cost 45*l.* 8*s.* 3*d.* A profit of 8*l.* is acknowledged to have been realised, or 17½ per cent. in the mayor's account.

The corporation of Poole exceeded this rate of profit. They laid out 10*l.*, and realised just cent. per cent.*

In spite of old experience, upon a scarcity of halfpence in Ireland in 1724, one Wood obtained a patent for coining halfpence and farthings to the amount of 108,000*l.* So much alloy was used that the whole were worth not 8000*l.* The patent was revoked after the publication of Dean Swift's *Drapier's Letters.* When the tokens, farthings, or mites were not legal coin, the loss *mostly* fell upon the poor.

An idle Woman falsely charging a Man with having promised her Marriage is Punished.

To conduct which inflicts wrong and pain upon any member of society there is assigned, in many instances, a due punishment. The aggrieved party has, it is true, a remedy prescribed by law, but practically certain classes of society cannot avail themselves of it, owing to want of means; they are, in a word, debarred from the possibility of availing themselves of any benefit which the law seems so fairly to hold out.

The magistrates at Sessions in Charles the First's reign could and did address themselves to questions arising between parties moving in humble life, very important to them, and who could now-a-day in vain seek redress in the same

* Sydenham's History.

quarter. A modern Bridget might continue to charge men with a breach of promise of marriage without legal measures being available against her. This was not so in 1626. Her case was considered, her injurious conduct and mode of life were duly estimated, with what result we shall learn.

"Forasmuch as it hath appeared unto this Court that Bridget Howsley of Langton, spinster, liveth idly and lewdly at home, not betaking herself to any honest course of life, and hath lately falsely and scandalously accused one [left blank in the original] of Honiton, in Devon, challenging a promise of marriage from him, which tended much to his disgrace, and that she is a continual brawler and sower of strife and debate between her neighbours, inhabitants of Langton aforesaid, this Court doth therefore think fit and order that the said Bridget Howsley be forthwith committed to the House of Correction, there to be set on work and remain for the space of six whole months, and from thenceforth until she shall find very good sureties for her appearance at the next Sessions, after the said six months shall be expired, or until she shall procure a master that will take her into service." *

The fixing by the Magistrates the Wages of Artificers and Servants, with a full Table of the Rates for the several Classes.

AFTER the mortality occasioned by the great plague of the reign of Edward III., the numbers of hired labourers being sadly reduced, the value of labour was much increased. The poor workpeople, no longer *villains* or slaves of their lords, wished to be better paid for their labour. This was not in those days allowed them. The legislature fixed with precision the rates at which they should work, by the famous Statute of Labourers, A.D. 1352.

The ruler who should at this present time attempt to fix with precision by edict the price or value of labour, which must be ever changing, would be thought deserving a place in Bedlam.

* Mr. T. Hearn, "Qui Quondam."

The master or employer now bargains with his servant or workman as to wages for the labour to be performed, the time, the manner, and all the circumstances. If the conditions suit, the two agree; if not, each goes his way; there is no compulsion. Each is free to take his own interest for his guide.

This was not so formerly. The party desirous of becoming the employer was not allowed to give what he was willing; the party wishing to hire himself could not take what he was willing to receive, unless these wages or rate of service agreed with the rates fixed once a year by the magistrates. A list of these rates is given, by which the extensive application of the system will be perceived, and the contrast the present system affords may be appreciated.

Should it be remarked that the present system of letting the rate of wages alone works well, and that in an earlier state of society the opposite system was equally well suited to the times, a view which is not unfrequently taken, be it known that there is much to be considered in the case. The two states of society are not such that a parallel can be hastily drawn. The question goes deeper than to the relative value of money at the two several eras. Some would too readily conclude that both parties were satisfied under either system; that men learn to accommodate themselves to the customs and manners of the times. If this were really so, there would be no melioration, all would go on as before. Wordly wisdom would not be required to remedy any great evils of society, which in truth there are, the offspring of every era and phase of human life.

Be assured the fixing by the higher orders what the lower class should receive for their services was a system of class legislation, and began to be viewed as such. That there was an under current of party feeling is undoubted. A regard to this helps to the understanding an occurrence at Wells at the first outbreak of the war between King Charles I. and the Parliament.

The first act of the Crown that enabled the country to realise the presence of civil commotion was the setting the commission of array in force. The Marquess of Hertford and Lord Poulett were at Wells in September 1642. There must have been a question raised, amidst much excited feeling, about the remuneration assigned to a yeoman. It may be fairly concluded that complaint was made of the rate fixed by the magistrates in this particular, and Lord Poulett found a determined expression of feeling against the unequal and unfair treatment of one class. This active cavalier, in his speech at Wells, was induced to defend the system and enter upon particulars. After much excitement (it is recorded) Lord Poulett, "with many imprecations, oaths, and execrations, cavalier-like (in the height of fury)," said that "it was not fit for any yeoman to have allowed him from his own labours any more than the poor moitie of ten pounds a year; and when the power should be totally on their side, they shall be compelled to live at that low allowance, notwithstanding their estates are gotten with a great deal of labour and industry." Upon this the people attempted to lay violent hands upon him, but a regiment passing at the time most opportunely saved him.*

The wages of master mechanics, or tradesmen, skilled workmen, artificers, journeymen, or operatives, and of agricultural labourers, were fixed annually at the Dorset Easter Sessions; they did not much vary from year to year; those given are for the year 1633.

Let this list dispel the idea that the working labourer or servant only had the amount of his labour fixed by authority; the master was treated in the same manner.

The difference in the amount of wages assigned to the mere agricultural labourer, and the artificer or skilled workman, is less than would be found to be the case in the present day. The wages within brackets are those of the Statute of Labourers for the year 1444, when it was allowed that "such as deserve less shall take less."

I. No servant of any clothier, woollen-weaver, tucker, cloth-worker, sheerman, dyer, hosier, shoemaker, tanner,

* State Collection of Pamphlets, Brit. Mus. 113. 69.

pewterer, baker, brewer, glover, cutler, smith, farrier, currier, sadler, spurrier, turner, cooper, hatmaker, feltmakers, bowyer, fletcher, arrowhead maker, butcher, cook, or miller, able to have the leading and government of the rest of the servants retained in the same art or mystery that he is of, for the whole year, shall not take for his wages above 3*l.*, and for his livery 10*s.*, meat and drink.

II. No other servant retained in any of the same sciences, crafts, arts, or mysteries, for the whole year, shall not take for the same year above 50*s.* for his wages; and for his livery, 6*s.* 8*d.*; meat and drink.

III. No bailiff of husbandry shall take above 3*l.* 10*s.* by the year; and for his livery, 13*s.* 4*d.* [23*s.* 4*d.*; clothing, 5*s.*]

IV. No chief hind, carter, ploughman, or shepherd shall take above 2*l.* 13*s.* 4*d.*; and for his livery, 13*s.* 4*d.*; meat and drink.

V. No common servant of husbandry above the age of twenty years shall take above 40*s.* by the year; and for his livery, 6*s.* 8*d.* [20*s.*; clothing, 4*s.*]

VI. No man servant from the age of sixteen years and upwards, and under the age of twenty years, shall take above 20*s.* by the year; and for his livery, 6*s.* 8*d.*

VII. No man servant under the age of sixteen years shall take any wages, but convenient clothes, meat, drink, and other necessaries. [Boy under fourteen years, 6*s.*; clothing, 3*s.*]

VIII. No woman servant under the age of sixteen years, unmarried, shall take any wages, but only meat, drink, and other necessaries, as shall be agreed on between them, their master and mistress. [Woman servant, 10*s.*; clothing, 4*s.*]

IX. No day labourers in harvest shall take for their wages, the man for reaping of corn, above 6*d.*, for mowing of corn and grass, above 6*d.* the day; the woman for reaping of corn 4*d.*, and for making of hay 3*d.*, meat and drink, and not above. [Mower 4*d.*, with meat and drink; 6*d.* without; reaper, 3*d.* to 5*d.*; woman, 2½*d.* to 4½*d.*]

X. No day labourer at husbandry shall take, from Allhallowtide to the 25th of March, above 3*d.* the day, with meat and drink; and from the 25th of March to Allhallowtide, 4*d.* the day, with meat and drink, and not above. [2*d.* to 3½*d.*]

XI. A master-mason, a master-carpenter, a master-joiner, a master-plumber, a master-thatcher, every one of them to take, with meat and drink, 6*d.*, and without meat and drink, 12*d.*, and not above. [Mason, 4*d.*; master-carpenter, 5½*d.*; master-tiler, 3*d.* to 4½*d.*]

XII. A master ship-carpenter from Candlemas to Michaelmas shall not take above 12*d.* the day, with meat and drink, and 20*d.* the day without meat and drink.

XIII. A master ship-carpenter, called a hewer, shall not take above 12*d.* the day, without meat and drink, and 6*d.* with meat and drink; and from Michaelmas till Candlemas, a shipwright by the day shall not take above 20*d.*, without meat and drink, and 10*d.* with meat and drink; and the hewer not above 10*d.* without meat and drink, and 5*d.* with meat and drink.

XIV. None shall be accompted a master workman in any of the occupations aforesaid but such as have good skill of the work, and shall have working under them one or two journeymen, and one apprentice at the least.

XV. Every other carpenter, mason, rough-layer, bricklayer, tiler, slater, plumber, glover, tailor, painter, joiner, plasterer, lime-burner, brick-burner, tile-burner, cooper, tinker, every of them, shall not take by the day above 5*d.*, with meat and drink, and without meat and drink 10*d.*, and not above. Every apprentice to take by the day, with meat and drink, 3*d.*, and without meat and drink 6*d.* A pair of sawyers to take by the day, with meat and drink, 8*d.*, and without meat and drink 16*d.*, or else to take for every hundred sawing of boards and planks 20*d.*, and of housing timber 2*s.*, and not above.

XVI. No artificers under the age of sixteen years shall receive any wages, but meat and drink.

XVII. Every artificer and workman aforesaid to find himself tools for the work and art of his science.

XVIII. If any man will put his work to task, to give his

workman 4*d.* by the day for meat and drink, and not above the wages above-limited by the day; and every woman working by the day to have 3*d.* for her meat and drink, over and above the wages above limited by the day: the choice whether he will have them by the day, and find them meat and drink, or else to task at the rates aforesaid.

XIX. For reaping an acre of wheat to task, 2*s.* 6*d.*; and for mowing an acre of hay at task, 12*d.*, and not above.

XX. No person shall take, for making an acre of hay to task, above 12*d.*

XXI. No person or persons shall take, for threshing of a quarter of barley to task, above 8*d.*; and for a quarter of beans and oats to task, above 6*d.*

XXII. No person or persons shall take, for threshing a quarter of wheat or rye, above 6*d.*

XXIII. That no woman servant unmarried, from the age of eighteen years and upwards to four-and-twenty, shall take above 25*s.* per annum; and for her vesture or garment, 5*s.*; and from four-and-twenty and upwards, not above 26*s.* 8*d.*, and for her livery 6*s.* 8*d.**

Purchasing Corn of great Men. — Famine Prices.

THE exchange of presents, sugar-loaves and conserves, to be returned in venison, between great men and the corporation worthies of our borough towns, did not entirely originate in mere civilities. The pleasing intercourse had a stronger bond to unite the parties. Profitable dealings brought the two ranks together; and the connection with the merchants of the boroughs must have proved very useful to the great landed proprietors, in the sale of the superabundant produce of their estates.

It is worthy of remark how individuals clang to their order, and acted in concert, particularly where those of another class were concerned.

The following letter from Thomas Lord Howard, after-

* Mr. T. Hearn, "Qui Quondam." Dorset Sessions, MS.

wards third Lord Bindon, Mayor of Weymouth, to the corporation of Melcombe, is a curious example of several points alluded to. The great man employed his influence in favour of one borough before that of another with which he had no connection.

Sir Amias Poulett, of Hinton House, who is referred to, had been the keeper of Mary Queen of Scots, and had honourably discharged his trust, when some proposition was made by Sir Francis Walsingham, the Secretary of State, about obtaining information through his servant. This worthy was governor of the Isle of Jersey, and ancestor of the present Earl Poulett.

The period offered, viz. seven years, for the agreement brought on the time of want and high prices, which prevailed about the years 1586 and 1587.

"A. D. 1581.

"Thomas Howard, Mayor of Weymouth, to his loving friends of Melcomb.*

"I understand, by Sir Thomas Leyton, that the merchants of Lyme hath written very earnestly to him to buy his wheat, and offered him 2*s.* a quarter ready money; but under 3*s.* he saith he will not sell it; but at my desire, if it shall like any of you to have it, you shall pay half your money by our Lady-day, the other half at Midsummer. And so from hence shortly if you lust he will bargain with you, by my request, for five or seven years, at such prices as Sir Ames Powlett selleth, and will give you the quarter-day of payment, beginning at Michaelmas with a third portion, so with like portion to pay quarterly."

An immediate answer to this was desired.

The prices at Weymouth, at one period of the year 1586, were the following: —

	Per Bushel.	
	s.	*d.*
Wheat cried at	3	8
Barley	2	4
Malt	2	6
Wet fish, per cwt.	16	0
Dry fish	9	0†

* Sherren Papers. † Ibid.

The arrest of outward-bound vessels with corn falls under another head. It proves how great the scarcity was. The month when the above prices were cried at Weymouth does not appear. In the West of England, in August of this year 1586, wheat sold at 10*s.* a bushel! Are we to be surprised at plagues sweeping off the attenuated population?

An Act to restrain the excessive use of malt passed in 1597, which empowered justices in Quarter Sessions to suppress the making of malt, and restrain the number of maltsters.

Mode of relieving great Want and Scarcity in the Reign of Queen Elizabeth.

THE study of antiquity may be at one era less cultivated than at another, when it may attain to the just name of a mania. However this may be, mankind, while civilisation is retained, will ever delight in learning what their ancestors did in periods remarkable for striking incidents. They may not always desire to know of precedents for imitation, but may seek for facts that will furnish a good subject for comment, perhaps for censure, often for glorification of the present day; while the admirers of everything by-gone will continue, to the end of the chapter, to see in the past superiority over the passing age.

There was great distress, owing to a scarcity of food, about the year 1587. It was greatly felt in the south-western parts. The means adopted to alleviate the distress claim our attention.

In 1587, rye, an article of food much in request, was sold to the poor at a reduced price. Every kind of provisions was then at a famine price. The Mayor of Lyme enters in his accompt:—

Item, that was lost upon 10 peck of rye that was sold to the poor, 4*s.* 6*d.*

In the early summer of 1587, three English ships, meaning, very probably, vessels, arrested and brought into

Portland roads certain hulks or vessels of burthen laden with provisions and other goods, as these were in their course bound to Spain. The Mayor of Weymouth, George Trenchard, Esq., wrote letters setting forth how much the sale of the corn and other victuals would relieve the want and scarcity that prevailed in his part of the country.

The following great men, R. Leycester, F. Walsingham, Chr. Hatton, C. Howard, Hunsdon, and Ant. Ashley, wrote to the Mayor of Weymouth, approving of his discretion. They directed that the foreigners so detained should be told that by the law of nations such an arrest, under the circumstances of the case, was legal, and that they might be compelled to sell their victuals; still, if they were unwilling to do so, the mayor was to allow them to depart.*

What the parties determined upon doing is not known. How soon would similar treatment of foreigners on their voyage to other countries produce war in this century.

During the late famine in Ireland there were cases of robbers going off and boarding vessels at the mouth of the Shannon, which were bound to other towns than their own. This arrest of vessels on the high sea by force to procure food, where the parties deemed it was wanted, drew forth great exclamations at so unheard of (?) a crime. Is there anything new under the sun? True it is that many novelties, as they are called, are proved to have prototypes.

The Hiring of Preachers. — Early Sermons. — Brawls and Legal Proceedings that ensued. — The Progress of the Reformation in the Country.

THE great moral and spiritual agent, preaching, which has produced such mighty effects in the Christian world within the last three centuries, was scarcely known before the Reformation. Religious instruction then began to flow in a copious stream from books, and the untiring eloquence of many who exercised their gift in the pulpit.

This valued means for the extension of each hearer's reli-

* Sherren Papers. Letter 2d June, 1587.

gious knowledge did not quietly and without interruption obtain a firm footing at once when the Reformation had been accomplished. The favourers of the old worship engaged in bitter contests with their opponents, those of the new

Preaching at St. Paul's Cross.

learning. While many hung, as if charmed, upon the preacher, others raged at his words, and longed to catch him in some breach of any law or proclamation that prescribed punishment for the offence.

How such matters were conducted in our provincial boroughs will be the subject of these pages. To other historians be the task of recording the proceedings of Courts, the acts of the illustrious, and the scene as laid in the Palace. Court manners and the doings of the nobility there have been aped by the nation at large in every era; but too great was the distinction between royal manners and expenditure for much that has been drawn from them as applicable to humble country life to be correct. A universal desire for preaching at length extended over city and province. It was the craving of the age. Local particulars will set forth the state of the country, and how the service was conducted in our parish churches at the time when 1*s.* 6*d.* was paid at St. Margaret's, Westminster, for the mending the pews broken by the crowding of persons to hear Dr. Latimer.*

So early as the year 1546, a noted preacher, Thomas Hancock, was nominated by the Crown perpetual curate of Poole, in Dorset. Much will be said of the great effects he produced in that and adjoining counties in succeeding reigns; for soon after his appointment in the reign of Henry VIII., he was strictly inhibited from preaching.

Corporations gratified the want of the day. Thus at Lyme Regis, in 1549, there is an entry: —

> *Item*, paid for a dyner when that the prysse preached here, 4*s.* 8*d.*

The worthies of the borough superadded the benefit of the preacher's conversation to that of his pulpit discourse. This priest had been, perhaps, a member of one of the dissolved religious houses on the borders of Dorset, Devon, or Somerset — some gifted man, too well known in his day for it to be required that his name should be set down in the entry, just as another, styled "the prysse," went about to practise the healing art.

The Court of Augmentation granted pensions to the monks of the several abbeys. The fourteen monks of Ford Abbey, at its dissolution, received pensions varying from 8*l.* to 5*l.* each per annum. The abbot, Thomas Charde or Tybbes, had 80*l.* a year, and forty wain-loads of fire wood.

If the priest before mentioned had been a member of a religious house, he must have become a preacher of the gospel. The principal men or council of Lyme Regis had shown themselves so remarkable in their religious zeal for the new learning, that they were accounted, as they set forth afterwards in a petition, "heretics for their religion." Queen

* J. Nichols.

Mary withdrew an allowance of 20*l.* a year, pressed the Cobb workmen, and removed them for the repairs of Dover harbour, which was accounted a great injury to the borough. The inhabitants of Poole are entitled to the honour of being the first Protestants of these parts; though divisions ensued. They fell from their profession. Lyme is proved to have aspired to the same distinction from having sent for the preacher, through whom the former town had embraced God's word.

The scarcity and slackness of preachers was so great, that some of the king's chaplains were appointed to ride circuit about the kingdom to preach to the people.

In 1552, Robert Taverner, educated at Benet College, Cambridge, and Ch. Ch. Oxon, a layman obtained a special license to preach in any part of the king's dominions. He preached before the Court wearing a velvet bonnet, or round cap, a damask gown, and a chain of gold about his neck. In like manner did other laymen preach.*

Preaching began to be called in aid of the Government, who, perceiving the grand opportunity for reaching the ears of the subjects, set preachers, by a special order, to the task of correcting the grievance or special sin of the day. This appeared to the king and council in 1551 to be — Covetousness. The bishops in their own persons, and by their preachers, were to assail this vice, which was thought to be leading men to monopolise corn, promote enclosures, tearing away the substance of the church, the universities, and even the hospitals.†

The pulpit's aid was called in at Edinburgh, in unison with the Court of Session, to denounce the popular pantomime of the southern outlaw, Robin Hood, which, with the May games, had been banished.

Just in the same way the Mayor of Lyme and his council, the principal men before incorporation, when special occurrences, some great act of sin had disturbed the minds

* M. Wacott, M.A., "Notes and Queries," Oct. 27. 1855.

† Tytler's Edward VI., vol. i. p. 425.

of those in his little borough, sent for a preacher to assail the startling crime, or fashionable vice, at the critical time for doing so.

Mr. William Tudbold, mayor, paid in 1551, "at Mystres Pratt's house upon Mr. Godwyne, xvi*d*."

We have here, perhaps, the name of "the priest" before alluded to, and the bare cost of his dinner, without hire or travelling expenses, at a tavern.*

When R. Hunt was mayor, in 1558, John Chylds lost his life at the hands of Henry Chylds, doubtless a relative, perhaps a brother. This man was bound with a cord, set on horseback, and conveyed to Dorchester. This mention of the crime will enable us to understand the following entry:—

> *Item*, paid to Mr. Handkocke for his sermon that he made in the church by the advice of Mr. Perrot [or Barret] Mr. Raffe, and Mr. Morrys (principal men) with others, 8*s*.

Mr. Hancock the famous preacher's services were duly estimated. He had been an exile for religion during Mary's reign. His eloquence was bespoke, upon the remarkable occasion before described, for the pulpit; his dinner was gladdened by a friendly act, the subject of another entry:—

> *Item*, for a potell of wine and a quart of sack that we gave him at Mr. Holcome's at his dinner, 12*d*.

Mr. Holcomb was a merchant who served the office of mayor the next year: he entertained the preacher on this occasion. When mayor, he paid for a preacher's dinner 6*s*. 6*d*. It should be added that the borough worthies par-

* An able preacher was much valued by comparison likewise with too many others. About the year 1550, the curates appointed by the laity were both ignorant and scandalous in their lives. The people called them "asseheads," "dodipots," and "lacklatins." Strype makes the rustics complain of one that "he slubbereth up the service, and cannot read the *humbles*" (*i. e.* homilies). Tytler's Edward VI., &c., vol. i. 320.

took of the same, and enjoyed the conversation of one in whose religious opinions they placed implicit confidence.

In giving a narrative of the career of Thomas Hancock, from the Annals, Memorials, and Life of Cranmer, by Strype, in which recent information is embodied, the state of religious opinion in the south of England will be fully set forth. Many things in local histories become intelligible after this memoir, or as he has it, "his relations of himself from the last year of King Henry VIII."

The energetic and diligent preacher, Thomas Hancock, was born at Christ Church, Twinham, in the county of Southampton. After having preached the gospel, and declaimed against papal abuses in the diocese of two bigoted bishops, Gardiner and Capon, of Winchester and Salisbury, he was suspended by Dr. Raynold, Chancellor to Bishop Gardiner, upon pretence of a breach of the Six Articles; because he had taught out of the ix. Hebrews — "That our Saviour entered once into the Holy Place, by the which he obtained unto us everlasting redemption; that he once suffered, and that his body was once offered, to take away the sins of many people, and that one oblation sufficed for the sins of the whole world." Strype remarks, that though all this was mere Scripture, they found it to contradict their notions.

Archbishop Cranmer licensed Mr. Hancock in 1547, being struck with his diligence and merits as a preacher of the gospel. In the first year of Edward the Sixth's reign, many zealous preachers of the gospel, without staying for public orders, earnestly set forth the evangelical doctrine. Many of the laity in the borough towns now more openly took a decided part in favour of the new learning.

Hancock having obtained his license, which every preacher was required to do, or he could only read the prayers, preached in the parish church of his native place, from the 16th chap. of St. John — "*The Holy Ghost shall reprove the world of sin, of righteousness, &c., because I go to the Father.*"

How curious a picture does Strype present us with.

Churches were the scenes of the greatest excitement on many occasions, and the passions of earnest, even furious partisans, broke out and found vent in paroxysms of frantic actions and bitter taunts. How happy our time when those who cannot think the same sit apart, and the worship of the whole community proceeds without any drawback, save the lukewarmness of those assembled.

On the occasion of this sermon in the parish church of Christ Church, Twinham, behold three conspicuous characters: 1. the preacher, Thomas Hancock, in the pulpit, holding forth with great earnestness; 2. the vicar of the parish, Mr. Smith, sitting in his chair before the pulpit, attending to the sermon; 3. the priest performing mass.

As we view the parties, can we hope they will remain without a collision, or railing, or great uproar? Our experience forbids us to look for a quiet termination of the service.

The preacher, Thomas Hancock, declared unto the people the reasons why they made an idol of the host, and were committing most horrible idolatry. The vicar, after this pointed address, could no longer restrain himself, but addressed the preacher in these words: — "Mr. Hancock, you have done well until now; and now have you played an ill cow's part, which, when she hath given a good mess of milk, overthroweth all with her foot, and so all is lost;" and with these words he rushed out of the church.

When we learn what sermons were in the early part of the reign of Edward VI., and who composed the congregation, we are led to admire the daring spirit of Thomas Hancock, whose labours terminated not with the discourse. The pulpit vacated, the bar of justice had to be entered. Gospel difficulties mastered, legal subtleties had to be encountered. He who would expound exposed himself to storms, and the attacks of furious assailants.

Hancock preached in St. Thomas's Church, Salisbury, at this time. Dr. Oking, chancellor to Bishop Capon, and Dr. Steward, chancellor to Bishop Gardiner, were present. His text was from xv. Matthew, 13.: "Every plant which my heavenly Father hath not planted shall be rooted up." The preacher inveighed against superstitious ceremonies, and against the idol at the altar. He called those who kneeled before it horrible idolaters. Whereat the doctors and certain of the clergy went out of the church; which, Hancock perceiving, he charged them with not being "of God, because they refused to hear the word of God."

The Mayor of Salisbury, Mr. Thomas Chaffen, came to the preacher after the sermon,—set on, as was judged, by some of the clergy,—and laid to his charge the having disregarded and behaved contrary to a proclamation sent forth by the Protector, "That no nick-names should be given to the Sacrament, such as Round Robin or Jack in the Box." Hancock excused himself by saying, that what he spake against was no sacrament, but an idol. The mayor would have committed him but for six honest men being bound for his appearance.

At the assizes Sir Michael Lyster, the lord chief justice, desired Hancock to procure sureties. The bishop being then on the bench, the preacher requested him, that forasmuch as his trouble was for the word of God, he and his chaplain would be bound for him. The chief justice reproved him and said, if the bishop would be his surety he would not take him. A draper named Dymoke, having asked what the bond was, the judge replied 100*l.* This favourer of the preacher spoke again to this effect, that a hundred would be bound for him; another exclaimed that a thousand would. Upon this his lordship addressed Hancock in these words: "See what an uproar you make among the people." A conversation ensued between the judge and Dymoke. The latter owned that Hancock had no command over himself in the pulpit, and he thought would forfeit the bond; but this enthusiastic supporter of the preacher, in the face of exasperated authorities, exclaimed: "It would never grieve them to forfeit 20*l.* apiece in such a quarrel." Ten sureties were bound in 10*l.* each, and Hancock in 90*l.*

The legal forms having been complied with, Hancock rode to my Lord of Somerset at Sion, who caused the lord-treasurer, Lord Burghley, to write to the lord chief justice to have the bond discharged.

The intrepid preacher was at Southampton with the lord chief justice, in order to deliver this letter, when the bell rang for the sermon. His lordship asked him if he intended to preach, which he answered in the affirmative. The judge bade him remember that Southampton was a haven-town, and that if he preached there such doctrine as he preached at Salisbury the town would be divided, and so there would be a gap for the enemy to come in.

After a long and angry discussion, in which the lord chief justice said that Hancock should not preach, and that there was one in the Tower (meaning Bishop Gardiner) that he would believe before four hundred such as he, the mayor and his brethren having been sent for, at last a Mr. Gryffeth was brought, who preached.

The lord chief justice attended, and had no great cause to compliment himself upon the change, for the preacher challenged him openly with suffering images in the church, the idol hanging in a string over the altar, and the people honouring the idol contrary to law, with much other good doctrine, to Hancock's delight, who was a hearer. His sureties were discharged.

A change took place at Poole. Hancock offered a prayer for the town. Many fell from their professions, and divisions had ensued.

Hancock preaching there in the routine of duty in July 1, 1 Edward VI., against idolatry and covetousness from 1 Timothy vi., and against the mass which the priest was then performing, he addressed himself to the passing service, and spoke against the real presence. A scene ensued too frequent in that day.

An aged merchant very rich, Thomas Whyte, who was at the head of the Papists, rose from his seat and left the church, saying, "Come from him, good people; he came from the Devil, and teacheth unto you devilish doctrine." John Nothrel, *alias* John Spicer, following him, said, "It shall be God when thou shalt be but a knave."

The same year on the feast day of All Saints, White and Nothrel, with Thomas Haviland, another influential merchant of Poole, came into church to the priest, commanding him to say DIRIGE for all souls. Hancock commanded the priest the contrary. These merchants said they would make the latter say it. He answered, "Not while they lived." They all three upon this called Hancock knave, and his wife, strumpet.* Some of them threatened — and too intelligibly so in those sad times — what they would cause him to do at the place of execution.†

The mayor, Mr. Morgan Reed, thrust Mr. Hancock into the quire and pulled the door fast, commanding them to keep the peace. The mayor had much ado to quiet the hurly burly, till he got most of them out of the church, and was himself called a knave for his protection of the preacher. Hancock again had recourse to my Lord Somerset, who referred him to Cecil, afterwards Lord Burghley, from whom he procured another letter, which enabled him to preach in quiet in Poole to the end of the reign of Edward VI.

To preach faithfully (by which is meant according to the real sentiments of the preacher) at St. Paul's cross was often attended with danger. The celebrated Gilbert Bourne, in the first year of Queen Mary's reign, had the temerity to defame Edward VI. and exalt Bishop Bonner; but for the interference of Bradford and Rogers, the subsequent martyrs, the preacher would have been torn to pieces. The one caught the dagger which was thrown at him, and the other assisted him to escape into St. Paul's school.‡

Towards the end of Edward the Sixth's reign, Hancock had to consider with his friends a matter strikingly in unison with the spirit of the time.

The wife of one Woocock of Poole gave out that there was a voice which followed her which sounded these words always in her ears: "He whom the King best trusts shall deceive him, and work treason against him." After having

* It was declared lawful for the clergy to marry, 4th Nov. 1547.

† Viz. to draw his guts after him.

‡ J. Bruce, Esq., Archæologia.

a good while continued to report this, Sir William Barkley, who married the Lord Treasurer Winchester's daughter, sent her up to London to the Council with two of his servants. She was not long there; but returned with her purse full of money, and without having made any communication to the Duke of Somerset, whom it seemed most to concern, he being the person the king most trusted.

After her return the woman was more active than before in circulating the report, and even went for that very purpose to Wimborne.

Some persons of discernment thought the whole looked like a plot against the Protector Somerset, and two merchants of Poole begged Mr. Hancock to inform the Duke, then at Sion, of the words. He complied with the request. The Duke remarked, "Ah! sirrah, this is strange." This conversation took place only three weeks before the Duke's arrest. Strype believed Gardiner, Bishop of Winchester, to have been at the bottom of this plot. The Protector was beheaded 22nd January, 1552.

When Mary ascended the throne, we may expect to learn that the two parties in the church at Poole had violent contentions. Some were for setting up an altar in the church, while others opposed this.

Hancock read Queen Mary's proclamation, and interpreted it to his parishioners. Whyte the merchant and his party erected an altar, and procured a French chaplain, one Sir Bryse, but the altar was pulled down. The rood or image over the altar at Poole was brent, *i. e.* burned. In Devonshire some roods were sold for exportation to Spain and Portugal, perhaps France, by thrifty churchwardens.

In 1538 the image of Walsingham, with those of Ipswich, Worcester, Welsdon, and many others, were all brought up to London, and burnt at Chelsea.

Whyte, who had an altar at his house, was threatened with a hand-gun if the bell was rung out of the window, so violent were the two parties. Hancock's opponents went to church to try to catch him in some proscribed doctrine. Some of his accounts of occurrences—for at such an era sermons contained historical and political matter as well as doctrine — gave offence, and he was obliged to fly to Normandy, whence he did not return for two years. It was after his return that Mr. Thomas Hancock was procured to preach at Lyme. This favourite preacher, and, if I may so style him, the Luther of the south-west of England, was paid in 1582 the sum of 13*s.* 4*d.* This sum was doubtless for his journey and dinner, of which the principal men partook. It was more than others had received. Robert Davy, Mayor of Lyme, in 1569, charges for "a precher that did preche here, 12*d.*" Preachers received at this time about 5*s.*

In the archives of Weymouth is an order dated 1653, that two ordinaries be provided weekly at some public house for the lecturers.

There are entries in the parish books of Minchinhampton of many charges, with the prices affixed (Archæol., J. Bruce, Esq.): —

		£	*s.*	*d.*
A. D. 1554.	An Antiphonarium cost - -	0	16	4
	A skin of leather to cover the volumes	0	1	0
	A porthose - - - -	0	1	3
	A rood - - - - -	0	20	0
	A tabernacle - - - -	0	12	0
	A Pyx - - - - -	0	3	10
	Wax, per lb. - - - -	0	1	0
	Glass, for a window, per foot - -	0	0	9
A. D. 1560.	A Bible, besides carriage - -	0	12	6
1561.	A paraphrase of Erasmus - -	0	8	0
	This was ordered by authority to be set up for the instruction of the people in the church.			
1563.	The second book of Homilies - -	0	3	6
	1st tome of Homilies - - -	0	1	3
	Oil was used with bread in baptism at Minchinhampton in 1569.			
1555.	Making of the sepulchre - -	0	1	0
	Watching the same - - -	0	1	0
	Points, pins, and packthread - -	0	0	2

		£	s.	d.
1556.	A surplice	0	3	4
	Making two small surplices	0	0	3
1558.	Mending the best surplice	0	0	2
1568.	A bundle of rushes for a marriage, in 1568, cost in London	0	0	4
	Strawing herbs	0	0	3
1615.	Washing the surplice	0	0	4
1620.	Holland for the surplice and making	0	35	10
1592.	Breaking up the church for an interment	0	6	8
1613.	A weathercock	1	0	0
1618.	Pulpit cushion	0	7	2
1620.	Bell metal, per cwt.	5	6	0
1636.	The book of canons	0	1	2
1660.	An hour glass	0 0	0 0	8 4

Charges were incurred in some parishes for "mossing the church;" we presume, strewing it with moss for the festive season.

In a parish book at Broad Blunsdon, in North Wiltshire, the sum of 3*s.* 6*d.* for this purpose is entered in 1616; 19*s.* 6*d.* in 1633, and 4*s.* 6*d.* to the same workman, a slater, for two days and a quarter for himself and his boy "in gathering moss for the church." In 1647 no less than 1*l.* 8*s.* was paid.

Hogling money was a customary payment made by the sheep farmers for their hoglings or hoggets, that is, their sheep of the second year. This payment was not continued, writes Mr. John Bruce, after 1595.

When pews were constructed, about James the First's reign, the green baize was found to harbour insects, which gave rise to charges "for salting the fleas." Quarrels about the occupancy and right to pews soon began.

The particular information available for an account of the contests in our boroughs that took place a few years after the Reformation, has been communicated in the few foregoing pages. When all became Protestants, other struggles ensued of a different kind. The Puritan contended with his fellow churchman upon the lawfulness of many matters in daily life. This subject is not intended to be discussed at present.

Matters were not always in the church as they now are in the day of its exaltation. Ministers and preachers were distinct characters. The ordinary minister, beneficed or not, was not allowed to take the higher office of preaching without a license from the bishop of the diocese, that he was "a sufficient or convenient preacher." Without a license the minister was only allowed to read plainly and aptly (without glossing or adding) the Homilies (49th Canon). If beneficed, when the living allowed it, he had to procure, once a month, the services of a licensed preacher (46th Canon). The people, not respecting the "unpreaching ministers," as inferiors in ability, refused to have their children baptized by them, or to receive the sacrament at their hands. The 57th Canon threatens such with excommunication, and ministers who baptized children belonging to another parish with suspension.

The 54th Canon, sent forth A.D. 1603, menaced all licensed ministers with loss of license if they did not conform to the laws, ordinances, &c. of the church. So soon as 1606, ministers had their licenses recalled for the purpose of having new ones issued, which would be withdrawn from those who were deemed to have been imbued with Geneva doctrine. In Cornwall there was not a single minister capable of preaching a sermon.

A plan has been proposed in this century for creating an inferior order of clergy in the Church of England. A review of the past will show us what their reception would have been. Our ancestors craved "a learned ministry."

So far back as the beginning of the year 1641, commissioners were ordered by the House of Commons to visit the various counties in England, and investigate certain alleged abuses and innovations. Amongst other complaints which reached the House was one of the refusal of many incumbents to preach a sermon themselves every Lord's Day, or to admit another minister to their pulpits, although the parishioners were willing to maintain him. A committee, called "The Committee of Preaching Ministers," was appointed to send ministers where they were required, and to provide for their maintenance.*

We have shown the earnest desire to hear sermons, and how and at what cost a preacher was procured. The writer has had an opportunity of witnessing, only some ten years since, the effect produced by an occasional preacher. The Abbé Guyon, a Missionaire sent out to preach in the churches of Brittany and Normandy, held forth at Dinan, and denounced dancing with such effect that only one French lady could be found to subscribe to the season balls. Had preaching been customary in the Romish church, this Abbé would surely have failed in his high-flown invectives. The novelty and the fashion that attended the preacher inspired a *fureur* that would have hailed a crusade. Forewarned of what awaited them at St. Malo, the lovers and husbands raised an *emeute* so violent that the ruling powers saved the Abbé by sending him off in disguise.

In Dec. 1614, Walter Yonge, Esq. records, in his Diary, that the ministers of the diocese were called before the Bishop of Exeter, who read letters from the Archbishop directed to correct the besetting fault of the time — a running after fine preachers. Every minister was to exhort his parishioners to continue together on the Sabbath day, and not to wander to other preachers who had better gifts than their own pastors, but to content themselves with the word of God read, and Homilies. 2. All to kneel at the receiving of the sacrament. 3. To declare to their parishioners that it is not necessary to have the word preached at the sacraments.†

We learn from the distrust in the mind of the admirer of Mr. Thomas Hancock, as to his being able to restrain himself when excited in the midst of his sermon, that he preached *extempore*.

There is much confused statement about this practice. This preacher, doubtless, introduced much matter that was

* Somersetshire Sequestrations, a Paper by John Batten, Esq.: Somerset Archæol. Soc.

† Note to Yonge's Diary, p. 9.

never considered beforehand, so that it was truly the offspring of the moment.

Sermons before the Reformation were uncommon, and were, after that signal epoch, restrained in number by authority, and the refusal of licenses to preachers. The practice was to write out and *learn* the sermon, whether in Latin or English, by memory, and then deliver it. Dr. Westphaling preached before Queen Elizabeth at such an unreasonable length, that her Majesty sent to him "to make an end of his discourse without delay." Being called to account for his presumption in having gone on half an hour more, the divine excused himself by stating that he found it impossible to omit any part in order to shorten it, lest he should put himself so entirely out of cue that he should forget the rest, and so be brought to shame before the University and the Court.* Bishop Patrick's objection to being made king's chaplain in 1671 was "the finding it very difficult to get a sermon without a book."

The practice of reading sermons in the pulpit, without the labour of having learnt them, which was thereby saved, appeared so objectionable to Charles II., that the Duke of Monmouth, as Chancellor of the University of Cambridge, was directed to interfere. It was designated as a "supine and slothful way of preaching," that took beginning with the disorders of the late times. The names of those offenders who should continue this practice, and wear their hair or perriwigs of unbecoming length, were to be signified to his Majesty.

The impassioned addresses of Hancock and the long sermons of Hugh Peters never were learnt by heart. They preached too often, and the hour-glass was too often turned, for this to have been the case. Peters, on one occasion, told his hearers they were good fellows, and he would "have one glass more" with them.

Communicants after the Reformation seem to have made

* Life of Duke of Monmouth, vol. i. 40. Miss A. Strickland's Life of Queen Elizabeth, p. 271.

an offertory donation only at Easter. From about the year 1604 the offertory money began to be collected at Minchinhampton on every occasion of receiving the Lord's Supper. In the fifteenth century a scrivener made the churchwardens' accounts in Latin, amusing as a witty story to a scholar.

Till the year 1635, the churchwardens of Minchinhampton and others employed some persons to write and cast their account. Transcripts of the parish register were generally made by the schoolmaster.

A scrivener was employed likewise to make the "Book of Vermin," those creatures which churchwardens paid persons for having destroyed. "Foxehead, xij*d.*," and in some parts 2*d.*, is a frequent entry. Otter's head, xij*d.*, a Gray's head, *i. e.* a badger, xiiij*d.* Many whoops' heads, *i. e.* bullfinches, 1*s.* 6*d.*

Churchwardens likewise provided "silk strings and ribbands" for the poor children that had the king's evil.

A clergyman in the reign of Charles II. who supplied the place of another for a Sunday received ten shillings.

The funeral sermon followed the decease of every person in decent circumstances. Ten shillings was the sum paid to the clergyman for writing and delivering it. An old story is told of a widow who, inquiring what was the cost of a funeral sermon, learnt that some were 10*s.*; one at 7*s.* 6*d.* no one would know to be a funeral sermon, but there would not be a dry eye in the church if the guinea one was preached.

The mournful discourse, prepared, if not newly composed for the rich friends who assembled to attend the parish church the Sunday after a funeral, was deemed deserving of a higher remuneration. Two guineas were paid for such a performance. More than this amount was often laid out in comfits at the funeral; about a century and a half before a priest had 6*d.* for singing mass at a burial.

Among the varied information the centenarian, Mrs. Bartlett, lately gave at Exeter to a Poor Law Commissioner, was the practice of her early days in that city to beat the bounds, and fight with gads in the presence of the clergy. The discontinuance of the fighting part of this annual custom was a source of satisfaction to her. We see how, when intercourse between counties was so limited, practices continued which had been denounced centuries before. Traces of ancient customs and religious rites may be discovered, when diligently ferreted out, which have continued from the middle ages, just as ancient Catholic rites were continued, on, somewhat modified from the heathen age. The "beating the parish bounds," and the fighting with gads by crowds, in which were the clergy up to the lifetime of one now able to describe the scene; the drinking and Saturnalian festivity, conducted under the name of a social duty, were the allowed remains, or Protestant continuation, of the ancient Rogation PROCESSIONS. In some large parishes it took three days to beat the bounds.*

To the solemn service of Rogation, *processions* were early added by the Western church. Though at first there was no harm, many abuses followed in the train of *parochial* perambulations.

In the *Inquisitiones* of the Archdeacon of Lincoln, A.D. 1223, it is inquired if there is any *fighting* in the course of the procession with the banner of the mother church, &c. "30. *An alicubi leventur arietes, vel fiant scottali* [compotations] *vel decertetur in præundo cum vexillo matricis ecclesiæ.*"

How many spectators, and of those who so lately took part in the scene, did not know how ancient a custom they were perpetuating.†

Boys were *bumped,* and put to considerable pain in the operation, in order to impress a recollection of the locality upon the *memory* — a faculty which, by the way, a quack doctor undertook to recruit by means of a pill which he vended for that purpose. A western esquire, named Drew, of Wooton House, Dorset, tried the effect of kindness upon the same mental faculty. When about to plant a number of beech trees, he distributed currant buns to young children. Eighty-five years after the scene was as vivid as

* Mr. E. Chadwick.

† See Dansey's Horæ Decanicæ Rurales.

any *cruelty* could have ensured. The aged saw in their mind's eye each hedge row, the squire and madame, the great basket loaded with buns, and those children who rejoiced to partake of the treat. They remembered the taste of the cakes.

Music in the Service of our Churches soon after the Reformation. — Choristers. — Organs, &c.

HAVING dwelt at length upon the feuds which the change in religious opinions gave rise to, and the brawls that ensued — a necessary consequence — in our parish churches, let us now turn to the exercise of sweet harmony. Not but that a great difference of opinion existed upon this subject.

The "principal men" of Lyme, that is, the influential members of the council soon after the Reformation, which they espoused very warmly, directed much attention to the service of the church, particularly to the vocal and instrumental part, besides that of preaching.

The Mayor of Lyme, John Hassard, in 1550-51, records proofs of his care of the choristers by his entries: —

	s.	d.
Item, paid for iii yerds and half of kersey to make hoses* for iii laddys which singeth in church - -	5	10
Item, paid for ij pere of says for ij of them - -	1	5

These were not, it appears, boys of the town: —

Item, delivered to the lad that sang in the quire, when he departed - - - - - -	0	12

When William Tudbold was mayor in 1651: —

Item more paid to John Abatt for dyeing of the boyes cotts - - - - - -	1	8
Item more for making of them - - - -	1	4

* The first pair of knit worsted stockings was seen by William Rider, says Stow, near the foot of London Bridge in 1569, in the hands of an Italian merchant. He borrowed them for a time, and caused others to be made like them. The Earl of Pembroke wore the first in England.— *Weale's Quarterly Papers on Engineering*, vol. v.

Richard Buckford, mayor, in 1562, made several entries, testifying his care of those who assisted in giving solemnity to divine service:—

	s.	d.
Item, for a quayre of paper for that lad that singeth in the quire - - - - - -	0	3
Hoosecloth, do. - - - - - -	2	6
Making of the hooses - - - - -	0	6
Pair of shoes for the said lad - - - -	0	7
Alex Davey in part payment of the lads board that singeth in the quire* - - - - - -	1	0

In 1569 Robert Davey entered:—

Paid to Hugh of Bristowe for playing in the church and at my house - - - - -	1	5

Thus, when a good performer travelled round the country, he was engaged to add to the solemnity of the services of the church.

There is nothing to show that the singing lads were in Lyme church by compulsion. If any press-gang had laid violent hands upon them, such treatment is not mentioned.

The famous Thomas Tusser, the younger son of a gentleman, was destined by his father, from his having such a good voice, to follow music. He was sent to the collegiate chapel of Wallingford to be instructed in choral singing. The severity of the discipline made him in after years exclaim:—

"What touzed ears, like baited bears!
What bobbed lips, what jerks, what nips!
What bread how stale, what penny ale!"†

His singing powers being known, Tusser was literally

* The choristers at Winchester, in the time of Henry VIII., received for their commons eightpence per week; those of Eton tenpence a week. Cloth sufficient for a suit was allowed each at Christmas.

† More severity is used in Germany towards the learners of music than of any other branch of instruction; hence a saying, "he hates as a youth hates Handel."

pressed for the choir of St. Paul's, which exercise of despotic power he refers to in the following lines: —

> "Then for my voice I must (no choice)
> Away of force, like posting horse,
> For sundry men had placards then
> Such child to take."

Writs or placards used to be issued, encouraging the officers to whom they were directed to impress the male children of poor persons in order to their being instructed in music for public worship

Organs were not mute in all our country parish churches. Much mention is to be found of them about the middle of the sixteenth century. These were not the "great organ," but "regals," or "a pair of organs," played upon the knees of the performer, such as may be seen in a painting of St. Cecilia. The virgin with rapturous look holds a double organ, or pair of organs, in her lap,

> "And whiles that the organs made melodie
> To God alone thus in her harte sang she."

Regals are mentioned in the Roman de la Rose, written about the year 1300. These were the single regals.* There were two instruments, that is, two pair of organs at Poole, when the famous Thomas Hancock was appointed to the ministry of that town. The "horgons" were duly repaired at Minchinhampton in anticipation of the Easter service. They were somewhat costly. A pair for St. Michael's Church, York, cost in 1536, 8*l.*

One Robartt lived at Crewkerne about the time of the Reformation, who was an "orgyn-maker," and let out organs to churches by the year. He was paid by John Hassard, Mayor of Lyme, in 1550-51, his year's rent, 11*s.* There are many entries respecting the orgyn-makers coming "for to see the orgyns," 2*s.* and 2*s.* 4*d.*, and this for a journey of fourteen miles.

* See Sir J. Hawkins's Hist. of Music, vol. ii. 448. Carter's Ancient Sculpture, vol. ii. p. 12.

There was an officer in the lists of the establishment of the Royal Chapels, called "Tuner of the Regals." Queen Elizabeth paid her tuner 10*l.* a year. Robartts' instrument in Lyme Church was in the hands of an adept, whose services were appreciated, as we may learn from the following entry: —

"1552. The mayor and his brethren grant to John Coke 5*l.* yearly, in consideration of the good service that he hath performed in the church of King's Lyme from time to time, in singing and playing at organs, and which the said John Coke was to continue during his life in the best manner he could, as God had endued him to do."

How long Robartt and Coke continued to exercise their honest calling is not known. They promoted devotion till opinions gained ground, which made to many their concord worse than any discord could be. Their instruments, their sounds of sweetest accent, were deemed unholy.

The protestation of the clergy of the Lower House, within the province of Canterbury, contained these sentiments: — "That synging and saying of mass, matins, or even song, is but roring, howling, whisteling, mummying, conjuryng, and jogelyng, and the playing at the organys a foolish vanity."

Great houses had their pair of organs. Those of Lord De la Warr, of Offington House, near Worthing, were valued at 3*l.* in 1554, but cost more when new. A pair cost about the value of two good horses, or five working oxen.

From the beginning of the reign of Elizabeth dates the first singing of psalms after the Geneva fashion, that is, all the congregation singing together. Psalm-singing such as this, and heresy, were synonymous. The cathedral service was held in abhorrence by many within and without the pale of the Church. The Puritans allowed of the "people's joining with one voice in a plain tune, but not of tossing the psalms from one side to the other, with intermingling of organs." * They desired to reform church music, which they deemed to be not edifying, being so full of art; but they wished to leave a solemn music unmolested.

In respect of church music, both art and charity have been dragged away by the humour of the time.

Bishop Copleston writes of the wisdom of the Reformed Church, which, instead of rejecting this auxiliary, music, and confining its province to the singing of psalms and hymns by the whole congregation, as was the wish of the Puritans, and as is the practice of nearly all the Reformed Churches of the continent, has wisely retained both vocal and instrumental music.

All organs were removed from churches by an ordinance dated 1644. The earliest Dissenters felt called upon to agitate at their provincial periodical meetings or convocations, the difficult subject of instrumental music in private life. At a Baptist convocation held at Bridgewater in 1655, the question was proposed, "whether a beleeven man or woman, being head of a family, in this day of the gospell, may keepe in his or her house an instrument, or instruments of musicke, playing on them, or admitting others to play thereon?"

The answer was: "It is the duty of saints to abstaine from all appearance of evil, and not to make pensioners for the flesh to fulfil the lusts thereof, to redeem the time, and to do all they do to the glory of God; and though we cannot conclude the use of such instruments to be unlawful, yet we desire the saints to be very cautious lest they transgress the aforesaid rules in the use of it, and do which may not be of good report, and so give offence to their tender brethren." †

Oliver Cromwell, in 1656–7, prohibited all persons called fiddlers or minstrels from playing, fiddling, or making music in any inn, ale-house, or tavern, &c. If they proffered themselves or offered to make music, they were to be adjudged to be rogues, vagabonds, and sturdy vagabonds, and were to be proceeded against as such.

* See Neal's Hist. of the Puritans.

† Church Book of the Baptist Chapel, Lyme Regis.

William Taswell, A. M., rector of Wooton-under-Edge, Gloucestershire, preached and published a sermon in 1742 upon "the Usefulness of Sacred Music," 1 Chron. vv. 16 to 42. Many in that county doubtless entertained scruples.

Dissenters in the west of England generally retained their great objection to instrumental music to this century. Now organs are in general use; and all the female children of a certain position in life learn the piano.

At a chapel in New England, United States, in 1799, it was voted, amid much opposition, to procure a bass viol. This was precisely a counterpart of what has occurred in the dissenting places of worship in this country. Music has triumphed. The pitch-pipe has yielded to musical instruments and the organ.

So late as this century an aged member of an Independent congregation refused a tenant for her house, a lady who kept a school. She dreaded music and the possibility of "young Herodiasses being brought up under her roof."

The last quarter of a century has seen the termination of the grand and miscellaneous performances of a choir in our parish churches provided with fiddle, clarionet, and every kind, we may almost affirm, of musical instruments. The incumbents were hardly aware what a task they had taken in hand when they meddled with these important personages. They hardly succeeded in many parishes till the leaders had died off. The "church singers," who played anthems, with selections "from Handel, but mostly composed by themselves," had a position in their parish. They had an admiring congregation. Their afternoon anthem was the theme of conversation at the church hatch before the service, and of inquiry and critical disquisition after. "And did John," would one ask, "keep to his time?" "Samuel was crowding very fitly till his string broked." This was said after a performance difficult in all the categories in which difficulty — close up even to impossibility — may be found. And there was, I was about to say, a finale, but it seemed endless; it was a concluding portion, and a long one, of the anthem. Mary began an introductory recapitulation in which she was ably followed of the words, the subject of the composition, the master-piece of one or of many, if the choir lent a helping hand. It happened that Mary had to manage three full syllables, and all the cadences, and trills, and quavers connected therewith, as a solo. Then followed, through all the turns of the same intricate piece, Thomas, of tenor voice, who evolved his music, but did not advance to any elucidation of the subject of his concluding effort. He only dwelt upon the same three syllables, at which the good minister was seen to smile and become restless, particularly when Jonathan took on with deep bass voice, accompanied by the tones he drew from his bass viol. He, as best suited a bass singer, slowly repeated the syllables that Mary and Thomas had produced in so many ways, and with such a series of intonations, OUR — GREAT — SAL —. May some who tittered at this canonization of, as it were, a female saint, be forgiven. Had they waited a few minutes the grand union of all the performers in loud chorus would have enlightened them to the fact that the last syllable was only the first of one of three ending in VATION, which would be loudly repeated by the whole choir till they appeared fairly tired out.

One word more about John Coke the organ player. He made himself useful to the mayor, when there were no Poors Laws, in carrying out charitable objects.

In 1553 John Coke found (*i.e.* provided with all necessaries) the poor children and the clerk.*

Many men in orders were at this unsettled period in indigent circumstances. Some gave their time to practice *leechcraft;* others were glad to earn a subsistence by other means. This was the case with "Our Lady Clerk" at Lyme, who had lived perhaps in comfort in "Our Lady House" in Comb Street, and had been at the head of the fraternity of our Lady of Mount Carmel, a religious house elsewhere treated of. After the dissolution of religious houses, Mr. John Tudbold, in 1545, employed him as follows:—

"*Item,* more send to Mr. Wadham (of Catherston) by our Lady

* Town Accompt Book of Lyme.

Clarke, when that he did go to him to fet (fetch) a copy of the seasing of our harness, a potell of sack, 6*d*."

Item, more paid our Lady Clarke to go to Mr. Wadham's to wryte a copy of the seasyng of our harnys for his labor and the wryting of yt, 4*d*.

The ancestor of the present Earl Poulett employed a useful emissary who was in orders. There was a sum of fivepence paid in 1545 to "Master Polott's clarke," by the Mayor of Lyme.

The Sabbath Day.—Punishments for Non-Observance of it exhibited in Absence from Church, &c., and Profanation of it in various Ways, &c.—Caps to be worn on Sundays, &c.

Any consideration of the observance of the Sabbath day in reference to our moral obligations to that generally, or to any particular form of worship, is quite apart from the object of these pages. The manner in which the Sabbath was, or ought to be kept holy, falls under the decision of the theologian. The antiquary furnishes matter for reflection upon the past, by which, if wisely conducted, the present and the future may be improved. Nothing can make us so considerate towards our fellow men as to enlarge our views of mankind by looking at the by-gone generations who lived under a totally different state of society. If anything can produce toleration in an individual mind, this will.

In the reigns of Edward VI. and Queen Elizabeth municipal authorities were found, who began to move in enforcing, by local enactments and penalties, the observance of the Sabbath day. This holy day was desecrated in the West of England in various ways. Those who agreed with the Puritan party laboured to procure the making of orders, the issuing precepts, and the settling of penalties against the non-observance of the Sabbath. Hence in some measure the contests in our country towns between the two parties, who viewed this matter in so different a light. These were violent and rancorous.

Some tradesmen, one might conclude, did not regard the Sabbath at all.

So early as about the year 1550, the juries in the Admiralty Court of Poole had their attention called to this subject. They were by an entry bidden to their duty in these words:—

"Also you shall inquyere if any use to fyshe the Sundayes or suffer any engynnes to lye in the sea the Sundayes to take fish withall."

In the Custom Book of Brighton, 1580, a penalty was fixed for any one who should drive for herrings on any Saturday night or Sunday till evening prayer be done.

Shameless, open desecration of the house of God was visited with punishment soon after the Reformation.

A shoemaker and merchant of Yarmouth were fined 2*s.* each for merchandizing, bargaining, and selling a last of white herrings in the church in the time of divine service, November 2.*

In 1581 an order was made at Lyme to this effect:—

Item, that no tuckers do sig or wash any cloths upon the Sabbath-day upon pain of 3*s.* 4*d.*

Item, that no artificers do open their shop windows [and in another order] nor labour upon the Sabbath-day, upon pain of 3*s.* 4*d.*

The individuals who were carrying out their religious views in 1581, did not excuse even those who were exercising with the bow.

Some persons were presented "for practicing at the butts on the Sabbath day, as being contrary to a statute." On a file of presentments the label is this: "Artillery (*i.e.* practiced with bow and arrow) for Sundays."

In the next reign the rulers at Exeter laid a fine of 3*s.* 4*d.* upon every person who was polled, barbed, and trimmed on the Sabbath.

* History of Norfolk.

These precepts and orders had, it is probable, to experience the opposition of the majority. Lyme was torn in the early years of James I. by religious feuds respecting "profane abuses." In 1610 the jury presented the constables "for suffering unlawful games to be played at Beaufront (a locality at Lyme so called where a great feast was held), as well the Sabbath day as the week days." This was doubtless the proceeding of the party that seconded the former vicar, whose license had been withdrawn, against those who strove to perpetuate the celebration of a noted local festivity.

There were presentments made at Castle Combe in 1611, an epoch remarkable for activity in such matters,—of those who were habitual card-players and players of shrift groat on Sundays.*

The Protestants of Poole were very zealous under their famous minister, Mr. Thomas Hancock. In a letter from the Mayor of Poole and three others the feeling respecting the observance of the Sabbath day and the religion of their neighbours is strikingly displayed. The writers of this letter to Sir Francis Ashley, the vice-admiral of Dorset, dated 4th February, 1586–7, speak of James Mounsey of London, the farmer of the mines of Brownsea, as one whose religion they doubted, for they had not seen him at church since he had been there. He was probably a Romanist or an Infidel. They add, "He hath a brother a very bad fellow, and of an odious religion, who serveth the Brownsea mines under him. He persuadeth the workmen there to labour the Sabbath day, and to rest the Saturday, which he saith is the Sunday."†

Dissent was unknown. All the population, except those of the old form of religion, had the parish church for worship. The terrors of the law, and of bye-laws in boroughs, were directed entirely to correct and punish those who neglected attendance at divine worship from indifference, idleness, or a want of religious principle within them. It

* Scrope's History of Castle Combe.

† Sydenham's History of Poole, 386.

was not, as in after years, in Charles the Second's reign, to persecute a party who espoused another form of worship. Absence from divine worship, and that alone, caused parties to be the object of presentments and of fines.

Jane Scrope, a member of that ancient family, was presented at the Manorial Court of Castle Combe, in 1596, for not having been at any church.

In 1597, the jury at the court in Lyme presented that John Crandley and Henry Davy do not keep their church at the time of divine service, and are therefore amerced 12*d.* each.

Several others were presented, in 1599, "for having been absent from God's divine service for six Sundays, at 12*d.* each time." — Again, " absent eight Sundays, eight shillings each."

At Castle Combe, in 1594, an order was made that all butchers should shut their shop windows before the chiming of the second bell for morning prayers, under the pain of v*s.*

At Lyme, in 1599, beer was not to be sold during the time of divine service.

Three persons were presented at Weymouth, in 1623, as having been at Sandsfoot Castle, therefore absent from evening service, and fined xii*d.* each.

Archbishop Arundel endeavoured to put down the holding of fairs in churchyards on Sundays; in a word, keeping the ancient wakes there. Barber surgeons were not to keep open their shops on that day.

As enjoined by King James's Book of Sports, published in the sixteenth year of his reign, A.D. 1618, the people (at least those who did not abstain from going to church, and had attended the service) after divine service might indulge in lawful recreation, such as dancing, archery, leaping, vaulting, or any other such harmless recreation, May games, Whitsun ales, morris-dances, and May-poles, and other sports therewith used, so as the same be had in due and convenient time, without impediment or neglect of divine service. The unlawful games for Sundays were bear- and bull-baitings, interludes, and, at all times in the meaner sort of people by law prohibited, bowling. Plays were acted in the first regular theatre only on Sundays.

The king feared the deterioration of the people for want of warlike exercises, and from an opinion that no honest mirth or recreation is lawful or tolerable in the Protestant religion.

The west of England was, generally speaking, shocked at the publication of the "Book of Sports."

Ignatius Jordan, a native of Lyme, who had become a great merchant of Exeter, petitioned King James through the bishop for the observance of the Lord's Day. This interference drew forth the anger of the king, who declared he would hang the fellow.

A writer *, referring to a record of proceedings at the Dorset County Sessions, and one of proceedings before the magistrates of the borough of Dorchester, from 1654 to 1661, sensibly remarks, "that sources of this description for illustrating the social peculiarities of other times have not met with that attention they merit. The municipal archives of the kingdom — those obscure and mouldering hoards of tawny paper and yellow parchment concealed in the chests of the various incorporated towns — comprise very extensive and copious stores for ascertaining and illustrating the state of society at different periods, and the transitions of popular habits and customs. The relative manners and ordinary occupations of the community, the peculiarities that distinguish particular times, the influence of national events upon social manners and upon local practices, — all these things are here developed and faithfully pictured, together with much matter of an individual and personal character."

These sources are much more fertile in this respect than might at first sight be supposed; and the casual and incidental notices in which these social lineaments are pourtrayed are the more interesting and important, because

* Mr. Hearn's MS. Book of Proceedings before the Magistrates of Dorchester.

they may be relied upon as apart from all historical partisanship or social theory.

In the examination of such records we become better acquainted with the habits, the manners, the daily occupations, and the social and personal peculiarities of our predecessors.

These proceedings before the Dorchester justices teem, during the earlier portion, with indications of the fanatic spirit which prevailed in those times, and which appears, in our criminal courts, to have been particularly developed in attempts to enforce the extreme observance of the Sabbath, in the punishment of swearing and the use of other intemperate language, and in severe visitations for tippling and any indulgence in mirthful propensities. Entries for offences under these heads are numberless: a few may be cited. Thus, for the general neglect of divine worship, under date of Jan. 22rd, 1656, it is entered that

"Phillip Hulett was questioned for misdemenors as for neglectinge to heare the word on the Lords daye divers times," &c. He was leniently dealt with for the nonce, being discharged, but with a menace that "upon the next complaynt he is ordered to bee sent to Bridwell to bee put to worke."

Again, "Ffebruary 7th, 1658. — Samuel Cole, being convicted for absenting himselfe from the publique ordinances vpon the sabboth day, was demanded 2*s.* 6*d.* for his default, and for want of money was sett by the heeles."

"9th ditto. Katherine Bartlett, widow, vpon her owne confession did absent herselfe from Church the last Lord's day, contrary to the Law, in the morning; was ordered to pay 2*s.* 6*d.*, and in default of paying shee was ordered to be sett in stocks."

Five days after, viz. Feb. 14., it is noted that

"John Samwayes, by his own confession, hath not bin at Church these five weekes, and having not monny to satisfy the law, was ordered to be stocked for his sayd offence." And Jan. 17th, 1658, three delinquents at once "paid halfe a crowne apiece for neglecting to come to the publike worship yesterday in the afternoon."

Travelling on the Sunday, and other breaches of the Sabbath, were visited with severity.

On the 1st of April, 1657, proceedings are taken against Thomas Pouncye, on the charge that he "did travaile upon the Lord's day a horseback towards Charmister in ye afternoone." And on the same day information is laid against Robert Fooks for "riding in the cross lanes above Broadclose towards Charmister, and soe towards Som'ton, as hee (the informant) thinks." So strict was the surveillance in this respect, that one unfortunate wight is proceeded against for "travailing vpon the Lord's day at three of the clock in morning, who was taken by the watch."

Even a rural stroll in the neighbourhood on a summer Sunday evening was deserving of condign punishment in the eyes of the sturdy Puritans of the time. On the 9th of July, 1655, informations were laid against no fewer than ten individuals for walking abroad on the Sabbath, including "Thomas Standish and his wife, for walking in Frome Lane in sermon time." On another occasion a pair of "swetehartes" were convicted of a similar offence; a course of proceeding that would be provocative of a rebellion in the present times. On another day an unhappy lad is "ordered to be whipt by his master" for riding on a gate at West Mills on a Sunday afternoon. Whipping and stocking appear to be the punishments more frequently awarded for this description of offence. The following entry is curious, as showing a mode of recreation prevalent at the time, and the cost of such an entertainment: —

"May 19. 1656. — Mathew Traske being quested for goeing to Charmester esterdaye, being the Lords daye, sath that hee ded goe to Charmester emedyately after dener, and came home agayne a letell after the sermon wase done at trentie, it beinge the parish in which hee leveth. Further hee saith that there went with him Edward White, Josef Foye, Mary Foye, Thomas James, Edward Wingate, George Toogood; and further hee saith that Josef Foye, Mary Foye, and Josefe Foy's sweteharte eate milke and creme in a rome by themselves; and the said Traske, White, James, Wingate, and Toogood eate milcke and creme in another rome by themselves, and further saith that they spente there 2*d.* a pece in melcke and creme." The record goes on to state that "this examt. was stockt 3 owers for said offence."

There are many instances of parties going from parish to parish to hear sermons as in these more advanced times, when it is made a matter of fashion to "sit under" some popular preacher. A remarkable change, however, has taken place in this respect. At the present time the practice is observed by the more Puritanical professors; whilst, at the period treated of, it was the looser members of the community who were addicted to this impropriety, seeking, under colour of attending a place of worship, opportunities for gossiping and holiday keeping; inducements, perhaps, not altogether uninfluential with those who are now so prone to stray from their own parishes on Sundays. On the 13th of June, 1655, Thomas Hopkins and Richard Hopkins are fined 1*s.* each for going to Stinsford Church on the afternoon of the preceding Sunday. On the 5th of May,

"Charles Gardner confesseth that he traveled vpon Saboth day the 27th of April, 1656, to Fossen (Forston), as he pretends, to heare a sermon, and is convickted to pay 10*s.*"

May 19, in the same year, Thomas James was put in the stocks three hours for attending to hear Mr. Bartlett preach in Charminster Church. How would the sermon-hunters of the present day approve of this practice of "setting by the heeles"?

The laws against trading on the Lord's Day were also enforced with like severity. In addition to proceedings against butchers, bakers, and chandlers, for supplying provisions on Sunday, is the following record of a somewhat extreme case: —

"January 11, 1655-6. — The information of Andrew Hobbs vppon oath, who saith that on Saboth day the 30th of December, at two of the clocke in the morninge, Richard Abbott was at worke in his shopp at his trade of a taylor;

and beinge told by this examt. it was time to leve of, beinge the Saboth daye in the morninge, the said Abbott notwithstanding continued in his work, and this examt. cominge to him againe a quarter of an ower after, founde him still at worke."

On the 28th of the same month Charity James was fined five shillings for carrying coals and stones to his kiln on the Sabbath.

Tippling on the Sunday was also severely punished. On the 23rd of July, 1655, Nicholas Day, Thomas Churchill, John Pride, Leonard Gawler, John Reynolds, and Hugh Eastmond, were severally fined 10*s.*, a penalty of considerable amount in those times, being equal to at least 40*s.* at the present day.

Children also are convicted of playing at juvenile amusements on the same day. Amongst the games mentioned, are "spur point," and "nine stones." The first of these is probably the same as "blow point," an ancient childish game of which a few incidental notices are to be found, but no description that I am aware of. Marmion in his Antiquity, 4to., 1641, Act 1., says, "I have heard of a nobleman that has been drunk with a tinker, and of a magnifico that has plaid at blow point." And in the comedy of Lingua, 1617, Act 3. sc. 2., Oramnestes introduces Memory as telling "how he plaid at blow point with Jupiter when he was in his side coats." The "nine stones" mentioned is, doubtless, the sport of "nine men's morris," or "merrils," which was played on a sort of chessboard cut in the ground, and nine small stones for each player. It was very similar to the "tit-tat-to" played by schoolboys on their slates at the present day. Frequent references to "nine men's morris" occur in ancient writers.

Proceedings were also taken on several occasions against women for hanging out clothes to dry on the Sunday, the general fine for which offence appears to have been 5*s.*"

The churchwardens received the conviction money for having profaned the Lord's Day, which they gave away in small sums to the suffering poor.

In 1682 the churchwardens of Lyme were presented for not giving an account of those that absent themselves from divine service. The juries did this office for the churchwardens in some future presentments, whether it was that the churchwardens were remiss, or that the juries were inflamed against dissent. This is set apart from other matter, because the fine was imposed to punish the following a *particular form* of religious worship, and not for total neglect of public religious ordinances altogether.

How the Legislature caused the sabbath day to be often mentioned in respect of caps and hats may prove interesting.

Hats and felts were invented in France in the year 1449, in the reign of Charles VII., and were, like other novelties (though fashion was here not the only recommendation), introduced into England, and were approved of by our countrymen.

Caps, if personified, may be said to have long won the day in the contest with all competitors for the favour of the Legislature. Hats, bonnets, and caps were considered to be faithfully made when they were wrought, fulled, and thicked by men's strength, that is, with hands and feet. Alas! about 1482 they began to be fulled and thicked in fulling mills. An Act prohibited this, which was revived in 1552. In the year 1566, it was enacted that no foreign material was to be used in the making caps.

Though in 1512 no wrought caps or hats of felt were allowed to be imported, in 1530 a change ensued, and outlandish or felt hats were then admitted.

Hats in the reign of Elizabeth began to be made of various substances. Stubbes, greatly shocked, no doubt, at the new vanity, writes that some were made of silk, some of velvet, some of taffetie, some of sarcenet, some of wool, and which is more curious, some of a certain kind of fine haire; these they call *bever hattes* of xx., xxx., or xl. shillings price!!

Hats became fashionable; and the cappers, or makers of caps, worn before the introduction of hats, suffered accordingly in their trade.

These matters were not allowed in the reign of Queen

Elizabeth to find their level; nor was a man, either old or young, able to decide upon what was best for his health, or most becoming for his person, without meeting with some interference. A great contest would have to be settled, not according to its merits, but as either of the parties succeeded in obtaining the more powerful court favour.

The cappers of England won the field in the year 1571 (13 Eliz. c. 19.), and procured a statute to be passed in favour of those who "used the art of making woollen caps." It was enacted that every person above the age of six years (except maidens, ladies, peers, &c.) should wear upon the sabbath and holy days upon their head one capp of woll knyt, thicked, and dressed in England by some of the trade of cappers, under the penalty of 3*s*. 4*d*. per day. One half of this fine was to go to the mayor or justice, the other half to the poor.

At a Court Leet at Lyme in 1578, and a Court of Hustings the same year, it was directed, "that Mr. Mayor do appoint a surveyor to take notice and present such as wear hats and no caps upon the sabbath day or holy days, according to the statute, upon pain of 10*s*." A presentment was accordingly made of many offenders at 3*s*. 4*d*. each, styled offensores contra statut' p piliis. John Gosse, jun., a name connected with the last display of bow and arrows and the post, was among the number fined. The Act was repealed by 39 Eliz.

Lest there might be any one thing over which civic authorities did not impose some law or some restriction as it might be supposed, we find women's dress engaging the attention of the chief magistrate of a city.

The Mayor of Chester, Henry Gee, in order to distinguish between married and unmarried women, ordered that no unmarried women should wear white or other coloured caps, and no woman to wear any hat unless she rides or goes abroad into the country (except sick or aged persons) on pain of 3*s*. 4*d*. *

* Lyson's Cheshire.

All recipients of relief at Eastbourne, in 1674, were compelled by the vestry to wear a badge upon the right side of their upper garment.

Are we to believe that these personal restrictions were punctually obeyed? Could the authorities enforce such matters?

At Birmingham, about the year 1775, the vestry passed an order that each person receiving relief should wear a badge. A number of these were cast for the purpose. The day arrived. An old woman, the first, was brought before the board, who told her what the order was, and gave her her badge of disgrace. She courtesied, and expressed her readiness to do as they commanded without delay. Pulling up her gown, she pinned it on her petticoat; then, letting fall her gown, the badge was invisible, and thus the plan was frustrated, to the great annoyance of the parish law makers.

The companies, guilds, or brotherhoods of tradesmen in France were antagonistic like the cappers and hatters, and engaged in ceaseless and acrimonious disputes with each other as to the precise limits of their respective functions. To determine these knotty questions, the tavern-keepers went to law with the bakers, and the fruiterers with the grocers; and a protracted contest before courts was necessary to determine the precise point at which the appropriate office of the shoemaker gave place to that of the cobbler. The tailors commenced, in 1530, an action against the old-clothes-men, which expired in the year 1776, in the 246th year of its age. And thus also, in the year 1509, the poulterers commenced a suit against the rôtisseurs, to determine whether, within their privilege of selling rôtis, the defendants were entitled to sell roasted game and poultry. The Palais de Justice decided, in 1628, that is, in the 120th year of the discussion, that no rôtisseur might supply the meat required at any marriage or other festival, unless it were celebrated under his own roof, but that within those domestic precincts he might sell to any customer "trois plats de viande bouillie, et trois de fricassée.*

* Sir J. Stephen's Lectures on the History of France, vol. ii. p 375.

Collection of Money made for Geneva.

THE interest felt in every thing relating to Geneva, on the part of our western countrymen and townsmen for many years, was very deep. The *first collection* for Geneva in 1582 took place in consequence of a letter from the bishop who had received a letter from the Council recommending it to be made for that foreign city. Geneva had suffered, 29 Jan. 1582, from an attack of the young Duke of Savoy, instigated, as the Council asserted, by the Pope.

Eighteen persons of Lyme subscribed 3*l.* 3*s.* 6*d.* Each gave not less than 1*s.*, not more than 10*s.* Mr. Simon Norrington, minister of the parish, received for the Chancellor of Dorset; and the *second collection,* amounting to 1*l.* 10*s.* 10*d.*, was paid to Sir John Horsey, Kt., and George Trenchard, Esq., by virtue of their precept to the mayor.*

Fish Diet, Licenses to eat Meat in Lent, &c.

OUR legislators in Tudor reigns contrived many of what we may term *Politic Laws,* and the correction of a particular evil was aimed at by a somewhat tortuous process, and one liable to be greatly misinterpreted.

Though the population of England was so small in the 16th century by comparison with that of the present census, still the produce of the land was also very inconsiderable, and the ruling powers became anxious to secure a supply of food. The "preserving the navy," which meant the fishermen and seafaring men of this country, by keeping these in full employment so that they might be ready upon an emergency to serve the State, was likewise an object that began to be considered with attention, owing to the posture of Continental affairs.

* See List in the Archives.

Our present Parliament would address themselves, if required, directly to the object aimed at, "Feeding the population," and "Encouraging fishermen and the breeding up of seafaring men." The process did not use to be so simple.

In the early part of Queen Elizabeth's reign a marked desire was displayed for the encouragement of the fisheries, as Strype records, and the great question of the expediency of a more extensive fish diet was settled by the higher powers. Thereupon, in 1564, legislation for that purpose commenced; and though the Protestant form of religion had been fully re-established, the ancient FISH DAYS were restored, and that compulsorily.

These were defined to be every Friday, Saturday, Embering days, other days called Vigils, the days of Lent or any other days, commonly repealed fish days; but Wednesdays were added in an Act passed this year at the instigation of Cecil, who was a great promoter of this line of policy.

As may readily be expected, warm partisans of the discarded religion rejoiced in this turn of affairs, and ascribed the enactments and proclamations to a sounder view of man's obligations which the Reformation had interfered with. The Protestants viewed the return to fish days with dislike, as tending to Popery. The Queen's ministers clearly saw how these opinions, turning upon religion only, would interfere with their method of securing the object aimed at, so it was declared that "those who said the eating of fish and abstaining from meat was of any necessity for the saving of the soul of man, such persons were to be punished as the spreaders of false news."

Notwithstanding this rousing religious partisanship by a particular policy, a result that would seem to have been inevitable from the peculiar position of civil and religious affairs, the plans were persevered in.

First came the State enactments; then in due course followed the municipal orders throughout the country about killing and eating flesh.

Persons eating meat on fish days were to pay for the first

offence 10*s.*, for a second offence 20*s.*, and to suffer imprisonment. The fine was before the end of the reign so high as 3*l.*

Various causes had operated in Tudor reigns, as of late years, to favour or depress the trade of fishing. This occupation is not exempt from the fluctuations of wages, prices, local advantages, and improvements or ruin of works that render our harbours accessible, or work their final decline. When we read in local histories of the rise or decline of fishing, we must not conclude too hastily that fish were not to be taken, or that fishermen had given up that occupation. Thus we read that the Vicar of Eastbourne received, for tithes of fish, 20*l.*; but that in 1603 these produced but 20*s.* A more favourable locality perhaps very near, or many other circumstances, may have caused the fishermen of Eastbourne to remove. Just as in the present war, there are no fishermen to be found for the usual number of fishing-boats and vessels in the West of England. Great numbers left the occupation for the merchant service at seaports, where the wages were 3*l.* 10*s.* a month. When the Allies have made peace, men in numbers will return to fishing; but there is fear, should the war continue long, that the marks for choosing the good ground and avoiding the rough or rocky ground will not be perpetuated. Boys from the Union Houses might be sent fishing, and instructed by those fishermen who still continue trawling.

Abstinence, as is set forth in a proclamation, occasioned the *saving* and *increase* of flesh. The two Universities and Winchester were exempted from the observance of this Act, by which the food of the country was to be eked out. The people at large looked on with great ill humour, owing to these exemptions, and their "being much addicted to flesh-meats." Some feigned excuses, pretending that the proclamations were issued so near Lent that they could not make a convenient provision of fish; "others undutifully pretended that they ought not to be restrained of their liberty." These were not listened to: they could not be allowed to eat what they liked, and so disappoint "the great benefit that wise men apprehended to be by spreading much fish in the realm." * If butchers killed no meat in Lent, then fishermen, it was asserted, would go to sea with better encouragement. The confounding Lent with other seasons was called by Elizabeth's successor "an evil, an enemy to the plenty of our kingdom." † Strype tells us that Queen Elizabeth's subjects were very unwilling to comply, and exhibited "a licentious and carnal disorder."

In the archives of Weymouth, A.D. 1568–9, is an entry:—"Paid horse-hire to go to Dorchester to sett the proclamation for the eating of flesh, vi*d*." ‡

The books of corporations contain many casual scraps of information about the time when the law in this particular was enforced.

No flesh was to be killed in Lent; none was to be dressed by any innkeeper. Privy search was to be made in order to discover if this was done. Licenses were to be granted for the eating flesh to certain persons in a certain state of health. All these persons who had a license to eat flesh were to notify the same to the alderman.

We read of the Queen's almoner sending to the Mayor of Leicester, in 1589, for the fines and forfeitures of persons for killing and eating flesh in Lent, to be disposed of by him as Queen's alms. §

Recognizances were taken for brewers, tiplers, and for abstinence from flesh during Lent, and other times, in "the use of those things which were prohibited, and are to serve for a supply for the whole year following."

Persons had begun to make special choice of Friday nights for suppers and entertainments in the reign of James I., and of the fish days for riot and excess. Innholders were not to dress any supper on Friday nights, either in Lent or out of Lent.

An office for granting licenses to eat flesh in any part of

* Proclamation.

† Fry's Complete Treatise on Artificial Fish Breeding.

‡ Sherren Papers.

§ Nichol's Leicester.

England was opened in St. Paul's Churchyard, and advertised in the public papers so late as 1663.*

The law required that parties, who supplied persons who had procured a license to eat flesh, or the shipping, should themselves be licensed.

Nicholas Hunt was licensed at Weymouth, 1607, to kill flesh within the town in the time of Lent, and to utter and sell the same, either beef or pork, only to those who were licensed to eat flesh during Lent, or for provision of shipping to the seas, according to the laws and statutes of the realm. This butcher entered into recognizances with two sureties of 100 shillings each.†

The form of a license to eat meat, granted on the eve of the Restoration by the Puritan minister of Colyton, was entered by him in the book of burials for that parish: —

"Having been certified by two approved physicians of the necessity of Sir John Yonge's eating flesh, upon which, having granted him a former licence (so far as in me was), the same distemper still continuing, as is certified by one of the said physicians, and Sir John Yonge's having the same, I do (as much as in me is) give the said Sir John Yonge licence to eat flesh during the said necessity. In witness whereof, I have subscribed my name the 9th of March, 1660.

"Jno. Wilkins, Vicar.
"John, younger son of John Wilkins, one of the churchwardens." ‡

The operation of laws can but be learned by local entries, of which a few are here selected.

In St. Giles's, London, are parish entries of fines for those who had offended.

A.D. 1646. Mr. Hooker paid a fine of 2*s.* 6*d.* for having brewed on a fast day.

Fair-men travelling on a fast day were fined 1*s.*

1652. Mr. Huxley and Mr. Morris, who were riding out of town during sermon time on a fast day, 11*s.*

After the Restoration in 1663, at a meeting of the corpo-

* Wilson's Life of Defoe. † Sherren Papers.

‡ See the Yonge Diary, Camden Soc., ed. by George Roberts.

ration of Weymouth, it was ordered that John Eborne, George Parry, &c. were not to dress, sell, or utter any flesh during the time of the present Lent.

When the desire of the "wise men" to extend the fish diet began to be carried into effect, fish was considered to be very dear.

In 1563, green or fresh herrings were so scarce, that at Yarmouth, the great mart, they sold at an unusually high rate.

	£	s.	d.
In 1563, a last, *i. e.* 80 bushels, sold for - -	9	0	0
1569, " " - -	8	0	0
(the same price as a ton of lime.)			
1586, wet fish (cod) per cwt. - - -	0	16	0
dry fish " - - -	0	9	0
1611, a last of Windsor herrings - - -	15	5	0
1855, a last at Worthing only about - -	12	0	0

King James sagaciously surmised that this kind of legislation was setting up the fishmonger against the dealer in flesh, and that fishmongers might raise their prices, which they did not fail of course to do, when we consider all the machinery used to create a demand for the article, Fish, in which they dealt. They were enjoined to sell their fish at moderate and usual prices (though the demand was raised to such an extent), and the justices were to see this was attended to, A.D. 1623.*

To these enlightened men, who think profoundly how legislation ought to be carried out for the benefit of all, and not to cause a conflict of classes, and to prejudice or exalt one class at the expense of the other, the above account may prove suggestive.

Ponds and all waters that could be made available for the breeding of fish were formerly of great, and, as it would sometimes appear, of exaggerated value. In Catholic times there was a great demand for fish in Lent and on fast days.

* Proclamation.

Lent is the season when little sea fish can be taken in the best of seasons; hence the attention paid to the stocking of fish ponds with the fresh water tribes of fish.

About three centuries have elapsed since the first mooting of the question about fish diet. Some persons now advocate the abstinence from flesh and fish, and recommend others to become converts to their mode of dieting themselves. The Court quietly, like the Legislature, partake of the prize ox, and the Greenwich dinners upon the little fish known as white bait. The British are allowed to eat what they like, and no licenses are required, no recognizances taken. What is best for the human sustenance is left for mankind to determine and select from a lengthy catalogue of articles furnished by God's good providence. The choice of food is a matter of opinion. Borough magistrates no longer spend their time in punishing those who became law-breakers, by eating what they like, and which suits them best. Tastes do not agree. The persons devoted to a different diet try to convert others to their opinion. Much argument, but no law, is had recourse to. When Dr. Delany, the Dean of Downe, published, in 1734, his tract, "The Doctrine of Abstinence from Blood Defended," the meat-eaters were especially satirical against that renowned founder of an universal Peace Society.*

Early Account of Gipsies.

THE lanes and commons of old England were in ancient time without the occupants, which are now deemed to be their appropriate ones, sheltered under tents and the tilts of carts. No encampments of a foreign race sent forth their parties to the neighbouring towns to be stared at for their strange features and novel mode of life.

* Fry's Treatise on Fish Breeding.

Our object is to illustrate the time when parties of gipsies were first seen in this country roving about in their accustomed way, and the impression they created upon our ancestors. These were surprised at the appearance in numbers of a foreign race, speaking a strange tongue, which the lower orders even now take to be a slang dialect invented by them to assist in communicating with each other when planning or carrying out their frauds.

That individuals have discovered Hindústani words among our wanderers of the country downs and heaths is a known fact. Many believe such instances, however, to be exceptional, and account for the circumstance in various ways.

Recent researches into eastern antiquities have enabled Sir Henry Rawlinson to ascertain the date of the migration of the gipsies from India towards the west. In the fourth century they proceeded to Beloochistan; from thence they reached Susiana, and in the sixth century they occupied the Chaldean marshes; from whence they were moved to the Cilician gates, and continued to inhabit North Syria till the Greek emperors moved them to Iconium. In the thirteenth century they had reached the Bosphorus, and they were first heard of in Europe in the fourteenth century. Their arrival in Moldavia occurred in 1428, where they number 130,000, and are badly treated and sold. Consul Gardner, who has described them, says*, "they call themselves by the Egyptian appellation 'Pharaon.' Everywhere their dialect corresponds with the Hindústani, and in Aleppo they may be conversed with in that language without difficulty."

An entry in the parish register of baptisms at Lyme will prove that this people had reached the south-western parts of England in Queen Mary's reign: —

"Feb. 14, 1558. Joan, the daughter of an Egyptian, born at Charmouth, the quarters theyre being fixed."

The minister deemed the occurrence sufficiently remark-

* Meeting Geographical Soc. Feb. 25. 1856.

able for him to add some information beyond the mere baptismal entry, and not surprisingly so, as he had administered the rites of his church to one of a foreign race that had made their appearance in England not fifty years before.

Would that ministers recorded remarkable occurrences more frequently.

Samuel Rid, in his "Art of Juggling or Legerdemain*," speaks of what he was informed of and could gather of the performers in this line, and states that "this kind of people beganne to gather ahead as the first here about the southern parts of England only about the year 1512."

What he wrote of their characteristics will serve for comparison with their descendants of the present day. We might receive it as a portraiture of a modern group round their camp fire in one of our southern shires.

"Certain Egyptians banished their country, belike not for their good conditions, arrived here in England, who, for quaint tricks and devices not known here at that time among us, were esteemed and held in great admiration, insomuch that many of our English *loyterers* joined them, and in time learned their craftie cozening. The speech which they used was the right Egyptian language, with whom our Englishmen conversing at last learned their language. These people continuing about the country, and practising their cozening art, purchased themselves great credit among the country people, and got much by palmistry and telling of fortunes, insomuch they pitifully cozened poor country girls both of money, silver spoons, and the best of their apparel, or any goods they could make."

The same writer speaks of Giles Hather and one Calot, the king and queen of the gipsies, who rode through the country on horseback, and, in strange attire, had a pretty train after them.

The gipsies early incurred the imputation which has clung to them up to recent years—of carrying off children. In Wellington church, Somerset, is the effigy of Judge Popham, who tried Guy Faux and his fellow conspirators of the Gun-

* Lond., 1612, 4to.

powder Plot. The tradition is that he was recovered from gipsies who had carried him off, and that his wanderings with them, continued as they were for several years, restored his delicate constitution to a healthy state.

In some counties this people did not find favour, and this, too, when very little ceremony was used in dealing with those who were not in good odour. Five of these people, some of them bearing north country names, as Featherstone and Fenwicke, were hanged in one day at Durham simply because they were Egyptians!* Gipsies were to forfeit all their goods and chattels, and to leave the kingdom within fifteen days after command to do so, on pain of imprisonment.

The gipsies continue to be what they were when they first landed. They frequent fairs and assizes. The gallery of the Court at the Lent Assizes, Dorchester, in 1855, was in great part filled with that strange people, for whom a cold shower of rain had made shelter desirable. Fortune-telling still brings in from towns no small gains, and will do so while superstition lingers.†

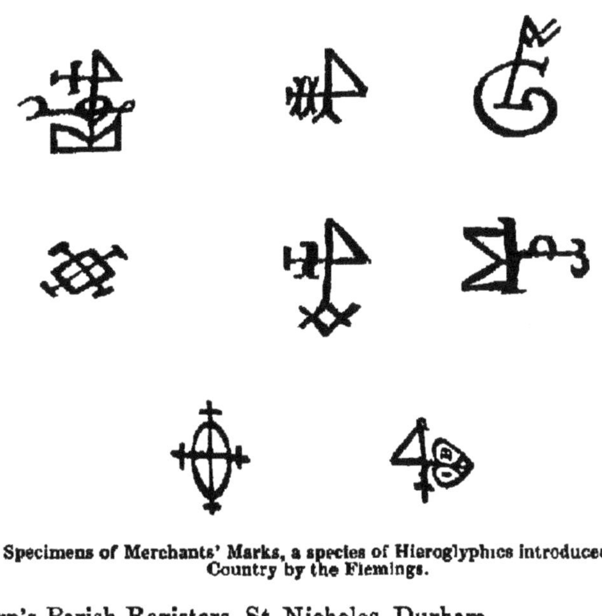

A few Specimens of Merchants' Marks, a species of Hieroglyphics introduced into this Country by the Flemings.

* Burn's Parish Registers, St. Nicholas, Durham.

† See Notes and Queries, April 6. 1855, for an article and reference to Hoyland's work on Gipsies.

Medical Practice. — Care of the Sick and of the Poor by the Mayors.

How can the account of any period be complete as a picture of the time without full mention of the condition of the poor members of society, and their bearing and relative position to the class above them? When we hear of the poor of former reigns living in comparative comfort, possessed of rights of common, protected from abject want owing to the absence of that competition which an increased population occasions, we are apt to conclude, being led away by the erroneous description, that the real comforts of the lower orders have gone on decreasing. Just as the meanest member of civilised society surpasses in the enjoyment of comfort the highest child of barbarism, so in many particulars does the lowest inhabitants of a borough in Dorsetshire possess advantages which were not enjoyed by the better classes in the reign of Queen Elizabeth. To establish this proposition, some entries shall be given with others that may appear pertinent.

Besides the great sufferings of the poor from the scarcity of wood, before coal was introduced into Dorset, we may add the absence of a regular system of provision for their necessities by Poors' Laws.

When John Garland was Mayor of Lyme in 1569, that officer recorded his care of the afflicted poor in various ways: —

	s.	*d.*
Item, gave to Elizabeth Harris first in her sykness, and to John Porcher, being both syke - - -		xii
Item more to Elizabeth Harris the 16th January -		xii
Item to her when she went to Lechecraft with her -	ii	vi

Thus it appears that the leech or medical practitioner did not reside in Lyme. We find shall that this personage was a priest who journeyed from his residence to Lyme to see the patient. Thus Lyme was without a medical practitioner. What a deprivation would this now be thought to be! A patient that required attention was in these days set on horseback and taken to be boarded near this medical priest, and this, too, when so ill as to require attendance.

Item, for the coming first of the prist for his paynes - ii*s*.

Here we have the cost of a medical practitioner's advice and his journey. Where did he reside? Perhaps the priest-doctor had been a dispossessed inmate of some neighbouring monastery. Newenham and Ford Abbeys had witnessed very possibly the effect of his exercise of medical skill. He was one who

> "knew
> The virtues of all herbs of mount or vale,
> Or greenwood shade or quiet brooklet's bed."
>
> SOUTHEY'S *Madoc*.

In a subsequent entry we find—

Item, to her agayne when she came home and returned, xii*d*.

The priest did not board the patients. She had her "tables," that is, her board, found in the very house or near the priest, and the Mayor of Lyme paid for the same as follows:—

Item more payd for her tables for four weeks - v*s*. iiij*d*.
Thus board for a sick person at per week was 1*s*. 4*d*.

The advice given to poor Elizabeth Harris was charged and entered separately:—

Item more for lechecraft first - - iii*s*. iiij*d*.
Item more to Bowden's daughter to fetch salve for her - xii*d*.

This charge would warrant a belief that the priest lived as far off as Ford Abbey, a distance of ten miles, or even Crewkerne, still further.

The same mayor dispatched another afflicted townswoman named Alice Berret, who furnished matter for another entry: —

Item, paid the prist for lechecraft and for her tables, *xs.*

Mr. Robert Davy, Mayor of Lyme, in 1569, took care of a Fleming who had been hurt in some fray.

Item, paid to William Merchant [most probably a barber who practised surgery] for healing the Fleming's head, and three days his meat and drink, 20*d.*

The clergy and the Jews were the leading men of the medical profession during the 10th and 11th centuries. From 1131 down to 1163 the Popes took occasion to thunder against practising ecclesiastics. A chief justice about the year 1223 recommended to the Bishop of Chichester one Master Thomas, an army surgeon, as one who knew how to cure wounds, a science particularly needed in the siege of castles. Barbers assisted in baths, shaved, and applied ointments. Henry V., at Agincourt with 30,000 men, had one surgeon and fifteen assistants. During the reign of Henry VIII. there were twelve surgeons in London. In 1512 physicians and surgeons had to be approved of by the Bishop of London or the Dean of St. Paul's.*

Females were everywhere to be met with practising the healing art.

The tooth-drawer's, now the dentist's art, is not of recent date. Sir John Blagrave, in the reign of Queen Elizabeth, had all his teeth drawn, and afterwards had a set of ivory teeth in again.† Otter, in Ben Johnson's "Silent Woman," says all her teeth were made in the Black Friars.

Eccleston quotes Guy de Cauliac, who published a system of surgery in 1363 for the classes into which surgeons might be divided, and their style of practice: —

* We believe the Archbishop of Canterbury has the privilege of granting a license to one medical man each year to practise as a physician.

† Ashmole's Museum, Notes and Queries.

I. Follow Roger and Roland and the four masters, and apply poultices to all wounds and abscesses.

II. Follow Brunus and Theodoric, and in the same cases use wine only.

III. Follow Saliceto and Lanfranc, and treat wounds with ointments and soft plasters.

IV. Germans who attend the armies and promiscuously use charms, potions, oil, and wool.

V. Old women and ignorant people, who have recourse to the saints in all cases.

Down to the time of William Estouteville, the Cardinal Legate and Archbishop of Rouen, who reformed the University of Paris, 1452, a mist of superstitious awe still hung over the "clerks in physic," or professors of medicine, none of whom were permitted to marry.*

The midwife was, like the physician and the surgeon, an important person in the eye of the church, and was not allowed to exercise her office until she had been duly examined and licensed to do so by the bishop or ordinary, or his chancellor or commissary.

The midwife baptized children in case of great necessity. The child so baptized was afterwards brought to church for inquiry to be made about it, but was not re-baptized.

In a license granted by Thomas Exton, Kt., Doctor of Laws, Commissary-General of the Dean of St. Paul's, London, in 1675, to Anne Voule, she is declared, upon the examination of able, cunning, and expert women, to occupy and exercise the office of midwife. Anne Voule was not to forsake the poor woman to go to the rich, and in no wise to exercise any manner of witchcraft, charms, sorcery, invocation, or other prayers, than such as may stand with God's laws and the king's. She was not to connive at or allow any baptizing by any mass or Latin service. A century before a midwife had to make oath that she would use pure and clean water only, and not any rose or damask water, or that made of any confection.

* G. M., Notes and Queries.

At bishops' visitations the form of summoning all physicians, surgeons, and midwives, to show by what authority they practise and exercise their several offices, is still adhered to, though now but a vain form.*

Mrs. D'Ewes, the mother of Sir Symonds D'Ewes, was attended in her confinement at Coxden Hall, near Axminster, about the beginning of the seventeenth century, by a midwife whose head being on one side from deformity, her appearance greatly terrified the lady. Sir Symonds D'Ewes suffered in his right eye all his life from her want of skill. When Mrs. D'Ewes set out with the infant for London, and arrived in one day at Dorchester, the shocks sustained, owing to the road and the particular build of the vehicle, were so great, that the infant son and heir cried so violently all the way that he ruptured himself, and was left behind at that town under the care of Mrs. Margaret Waltham, a female practitioner.

While medical practice was in its unimproved state, agreements for the cure of diseases for a specified sum were very general, as among quack doctors to the present time. With some this mode of proceeding has great charms. To agree to give a certain sum is a test of the patient's faith in the skill of his medical attendant. At the January sessions, 1634, held at Blandford, it was represented that one Agnes Hoble, of Toller Porcorum, widow, was languishing with a dangerous and deadly disease, for the cure of which the sum of 12*l.* was demanded; the Court ordered the churchwardens and overseers forthwith to levy a rate upon the whole parish to raise the sum of 8*l.*, which they are directed to pay "to the partie that shall undertake the said cure, taking from him good caution for performance thereof."

The magistrates of Dorset had not yet withdrawn their countenance from female practitioners. Grace Greetch, wife of Richard Greetch of Stockwood, set forth, in a petition to the magistrates, that she had endeavoured to cure Bridget Parker of that place of a disease she had. This woman

* Sussex Archæol.

quack must have taken her patient into her house — a customary thing — where she died; for she alludes to having been at charge for her burial.

Sir John Strode, Knt., had ordered the overseers of the poor to pay her eighteen shillings for the medical care and burial expenses, which they refused to do. The Court made out an order for the overseers to pay the money, or to be bound over to the next sessions to answer their contempt.*

Remarkable individuals have belonged to every profession. To receive them and their sayings and doings as ordinary persons is a great error. We must exercise due discretion to select an ordinary type, or the acts arising from a distempered brain may pass current for the manners of the age.

Dr. Andrew Borde, a native of Sussex, and long a practitioner at Winchester in the reign of Henry VIII., to whom he was physician, did and said many strange, witty things, which were exclusively his own as an individual. Much curious matter can be gleaned from his history, that exhibits the manners of his time and class. Learned, travelled, meddling with astronomical prognostications, which are fairly supposed to have been for the purposes of astrology, living in celibacy, drinking water three times a week, wearing a hair shirt next his skin, and having his burial-sheet at the foot of his bed — are so many notes for his biographer. The age in which he lived has affected every particular, as well as his mode of increasing his practice. In the absence of a newspaper or other medium for advertising, Dr. Andrew Borde frequented fairs, markets, and places of public resort, where, like the Italian quack doctor of the present day, he harangued the assembled crowd. His eloquence, like that of his modern compeers, abounded with wit. It must have been remarkable, for his imitators were numerous, and had, like the physician from his Christian appellation, the name of *Merry Andrews*, now generally applied to itinerant eques-

* Mr. T. Hearn, "Qui Quondam."

trian performers, whose jocose humour is specially exercised in dialogue with Merryman, the chief joker.

The portrait of a Dorset physician, an A. M., residing at Bridport in the reign of James I., will serve to indicate a change in manners. Doctor Grey was a little desperate doctor commonly wearing a pistol about his neck. As most of the gentlemen of the shire that were young and sociable were adopted his sons, we cannot hesitate to ascribe conviviality as being a characteristic of this medical practitioner, or, as appears on his tomb at Swyre, 1612, "Professor of Medicine." When a sheriff's officer, disguised as a pedlar, once served him with a process, he seized him, drew a great run-dagger, and brake his head in two or three places.

Dr. Grey was famed for a point of practice much thought of in those days, — the predicting how long the patient would last, or, as is elsewhere expressed, having a "judgment good to discern how near men were to their ends." He used to pronounce beforehand at what time the patient would begin to talk lightly, and when lie still, and when depart. This he did, among others, to a famous character of Dorset called Golden Argentine, from his riches and display. When the sheriff was at Dorchester with sixty men, this desperate doctor came, protected by twenty of his adopted sons, true roysterers no doubt, and those the lustiest young gentlemen, and of the best sort and rank, and drank before the Sheriff, who had some writ out against him, bade who dare to touch him; and so after a while blew *his horn* — a singular appendage for a physician, and came away.*

All physicians did not rely solely upon their intimate knowledge of the nature of man — as their name implies, — but dealt in the mysterious occult workings of the Almighty as veiled in the system of the universe, to be disclosed by the deep science of astrology. Drugs might work to the desired end, and the physician not see how the result was likely to obtain. Hence the adept consulted the stars as to

* Common Place Book. Communicated by H. Fleetwood Sheppard, Esq. to Notes and Queries, April 7. 1855.

whether a cure was to be, or was permitted to be effected. He treated himself as an agent of limited powers, and cast a patient's nativity to discover if those powers and skill were permitted to be crowned with success. It is probable that many patients would have despised a practitioner who looked only to his Herbal and store of drugs, and neglected Capricornus and Ursa Major. How could the unlearned fail to be awed by a language or jargon so profound and diffuse, that a dictionary of the technical terms, by James Wilson, sold for 14*s.*? Many may have practised astrology in self-defence; some with an eye to fortune. Let Dr. John Case, a native of Lyme, who became a noted London practitioner of physic and astrology, serve as an example of this class. He possessed the magical utensils of the famous Lilly, so that he was looked upon as his successor. Granger records of him that he would sometimes expose these articles used by Lilly in derision to his intimate friends, and particularly the dark chamber and pictures whereby that famous conjurer used to impose upon persons under pretence of showing them persons who were absent. Dr. Case had that worldly wisdom which led a man to accommodate himself to the opinions and habits of the time.

Over his door in London was a distich which is said to have procured him more solid advantage than Dryden obtained by all his works: —

"Within this place
Lives Dr. Case."

His poetic vein was in request to furnish an inscription for his pill-boxes: —

"Here's fourteen pills for thirteen pence
Enough in any man's own conscience."

The practice of astrology in physic had long been customary; but in the time of the Commonwealth the *lawfulness* of this union had been questioned. The subject was submitted to a meeting of Baptist ministers at Bridgewater in the year 1656. A decided answer was not given, from the great difficulty of the question; but great caution was recommended, and it was stated that several brethren, who knew and practised the same, "formerly had left the practice thereof, upon the account of evil work they saw in the same."

How interesting has proved the chit-chat visit of many a fashionable physician in the present day. Ailments and the *on dits* of his *coterie* are his staple commodity. How greatly dull by comparison with Dr. Case's stock of subjects. Our physician, selected here to illustrate the manners of Charles II.'s reign, was the author of the "Angelical Guide," showing men and women their lot and chance in this elementary life, in four books 8vo. Granger writes, "it is one of the most profound astrological pieces that the world ever saw. The diagrams would probably have puzzled Euclid, though he had studied astrology."

We need feel no surprise that this physician was successful. Having realised a good fortune, he was still living in the reign of Queen Anne, and placed over the arms upon his carriage this line, containing an allusion to his good fortune: —

"The case is altered."

Bloodletting, considered to be necessary for every one in health or not, at spring and fall, was an operation performed by the country surgeons on the labourers on a Sunday morning, at a charge of 6*d.* each. Bleeding in bed by a barber was, in the reign of Charles II., sometimes charged, for a lady, so high as 10*s.*, and for a gentlemen, 1*s.* and 2*s.* 6*d.* The operator perhaps barboured the patient at an additional charge. Barbouring by the year was charged 16*s.* Superstition had marked certain days in each month as dangerous for bloodletting, which were called *parlous* days. In July, the 1st, 7th, 13th, 12th, 25th, and 20th were of the above kind.

As the whole population had recourse to bloodletting twice a year, bleeders or barbers were in constant demand.

From the time of Plutarch they have had the character of being before other men in the collection and circulation of intelligence, and this in every country. When the good town of Shrewsbury was desirous to maintain its honour in 1535, as three dukes were said to be likely to pass through it, a reward of 2*s.* 4*d.* was given to R. Clarke, barber, riding to know perfectly of the coming of the great personages.

When our ancestors were likely to be infected, or their feelings shocked by the presence of loathsome disease, a preventive or precautionary line of policy was sometimes had recourse to by our ancient mayors for their townsmen's good. Thus, John Garland, Mayor of Lyme in 1569, accounts: —

Item, gave to a toker (*i.e.* a tucker or fuller) who had the leprosy, to rid him - - - - - -	iiij*s.*

Tradition was, perhaps, still busy with the horrors of that loathsome disease which had raged so furiously in this country, and which had occasioned a leper's hospital to be founded in the West, now Broad Street.

Being on the subject of the poor and afflicted, a few brief entries not foreign to it are appended: —

	s.	*d.*
Three yards of cloth to make a shroud (there was no coffin used for the poor, only a winding sheet)* -	iii	iii
Making the grave for a child born dead - -		iii
Shroud for this child - - - - - -		vi
Grave for Thomas King - - - - -		v

John Davye, Mayor of Lyme, 1589–90.

	£	*s.*	*d.*
Item more given to the poor people in the almeshouses and other at Christmas tyde and at Ester, as by a nowtt (note) doth appear - - - - -	2	0	3
Pd. unto Henry Palmer for the keeping of a sick Scottishman in his house, 3*s.*, and a porsyvant -		4	2
Pd. to widow Cadwell for houseroom and sending Jonne Gill, and for a shroud to Long John, with other charge - - - - - -		15	0
Gave the young woman that died in the almshouse -		0	10

* The burial of a poor young man at Lichfield in a coffin in 1632 is recorded as a strange occurrence.

	s.	d.
Pd. for clothes given Wayers Basterd - -	5	2
More for the keeping of the Basterd from the week before Easter to a fortnight after Michaelmas, at six pence per week, which is xxij weeks at 6 pence -	13	0
Paid goodwife Cram for the keeping of the basterd, and 16*d.* for a whittle - - - -	6	0

Similar duties are now delegated to overseers. These little matters then occupied the attention of the highest local authority, the mayor, who gave in 1569

	£	s.	d.
To the poor this year - - -	6	8	0

There were at this time many small charity properties which had been given to the mayor for the poor, who often must have been, as my researches show, greatly distressed.

In 1587 rye was in use, and an instance occurs of this article of food being sold to the poor by the mayor at a reduced price, when every article of food was at a famine price: —

Item, that was lost upon 10 peck of rye that was sold to the poor, iiij*s.* vi*d.*

Fagots and money to the amount of 22*s.* 10*d.* were given to the poor at Christmas.

Every Friday four poor men received, in the reign of Queen Mary, each one penny (that was enough for the maintenance of each for the day), the income arising from the property left by John Tudbold to the poor.

Thomas Ellesdon and John Holcomb were wardens of these lands.

The London physicians of note in the reign of James I. were better paid than those of the present day. Dr. Giffard and Dr. Baskervill visited Paul D'Ewes, Esq., the father of Sir Symonds D'Ewes, twice a day during his illness in Chancery Lane, and received at each visit 20*s.* each.

A medical man rode twenty-five miles to see the Rev. Giles Moore, in Sussex, about 1665, and received each time

12*s.* A physician came the same distance, and charged 1*l.* Another physician came and stayed two days, who was paid 1*l.* 10*s.*

In 1602 two surgeons, who "searched a corpse suspected to be of the plague," were paid 6*s.* 8*d.**

A medical bill about the time of Charles I. is given as a curiosity: —

Goodman Hoor ows per—

	s.	*d.*
p a purgative potion - -	01	00
It p 2 purges more - - -	2	06
Sum - -	3	6

For salere and ointment (sum defaced),
Paid 5*s.* for William Hore, by consent.

SAMUEL LACY.

A purge for a young lady at school at Richmond is charged 1*s.* 6*d.* in 1646.

If in 1590 we find a good mayor of Lyme paying 1*s.* 6*d.* to those that did watch by day, for fear of the sickness, for four days, we also learn in 1724 that a reward was given for information; thus: —

Paid two messengers from Halstock to give notice the small pox was there, 5*s.*

The mayor had at times to provide for distant journeys to enable the afflicted to find a cure which was denied them nearer home.

In 1665 Robert Vickery had given him to help him to Ireland to obtain cure of his lameness, 10*s.*

When so much medicine was given under mysterious names, some quacks by their nostrums acquired a prodigious fame. This poor man was on his way to some wonderful practitioner, and the authorities approved of his voyage and assisted him.

Quack doctors were the first advertisers in newspapers in

* Nichols.

1652. Some of these were princely in their equipage, and had certificates hanging about of cures effected upon eastern monarchs.

A century ago a medical man in the cathedral cities put on his full dress before paying his visit to the bishop.

The gold-headed cane carried by physicians was long viewed as containing some safeguard against infection, which the members of the medical profession are supposed now-a-day to possess as a great secret among themselves.

Any account of medical practice in this part of England would be imperfect without an allusion to the contract entered into by the medical man of the Exeter county gaol at the time Howard visited that city. This individual had a clause in the contract to exonerate him from attendance and services when the gaol fever should rage. Is not this equivalent to a soldier agreeing to serve, but stipulating that he should have a complete exemption in case of real war?

Medical accounts used to be settled on fair-day; a practice which has continued in some country towns.

Old women, in respect of midwifery and acquaintance with herbs, have retained some credit in the rural districts to the present time.

In the fondness for simples, enmity against other now preferred medicines was engendered.

"For salves the country parson's wife seeks not the city, but prefers her garden and fields before all outlandish gums."

The last professed herbalist's shop has not long ceased to exist in Holborn, London.

It was the celebrated Dorset worthy and learned physician Dr. Thomas Sydenham, of the reign of Charles II., who introduced, amidst great opposition, the cool treatment in small pox, and administered, in some diseases, laudanum and bark in attacks of ague.

How can we sufficiently estimate the value of Dr. Jenner's discovery, by which that dreadful scourge, the small pox, is exterminated! How much does private history contain of small pox and its ravages, the flight from it, and incidents arising from this!

Before the introduction of turnips, potatoes, &c., the scurvy was very often felt by even the better classes. There were cases of that affection, at the time the potato disease raged, from want of vegetables.

Scurvy grass, which cost by the peck 1*d.*, and diet drinks, so high as 13*s.* 6*d.*, appear in diaries and account books.

The power of herbs against the pestilence or plague itself was declared to be sufficient when these were administered in a drink. The patient was to take: —

Vedervoy	-	Featherfew.
Matfelon	-	Black knapweed, *Jacea nigra.*
Mogworte	-	Mugwort, wormwood, *Artemisia vulgaris.*
Solyge	-	(Difficult to identify.)
Scabyos	-	Devil's-bit, *Scabiosa succina.*
Avense	-	Bennet, *Geum urbanum.*

These were to be mixed in equal proportions, washed, and bruised with stale ale, and six spoonfuls taken at a time. If taken in time we are assured "hyt chal distroye the coroppcion and safe the man or the woman."*

The mania for sea-water bathing, sea air, and for mineral waters has been treated of under the head of the "Decay of Mercantile Coast Towns."

The modern practice of medicine, and the elegant exhibition of drugs from every part of the world which our drug warehouses present, force us to conclude that we now enjoy advantages over those whose maladies had to be assailed by practitioners armed only with simples.

Our common garden herbs possess undoubtedly valuable properties. These it was the common practice of the herbalist leech to exaggerate. Take the case of the sage plant, whose reputation enthusiasts had raised. It was good against infection, and had such special properties, that, though it was not asserted that immortality would result from its use, it

* Bury MS., published by the Bury and West Suffolk Archæological Institute.

was demanded why any one should die that had sage in his garden: —

> "Cur moriatur homo, cui salvia crescit in horto?"

Truth compelled the disappointing answer: —

> "Contra vim mortis non est medicamen in hortis." *

It has been somewhere beautifully said that "the reappearance of exploded errors, both in natural and moral science, is one of the least satisfactory phenomena observable in the history of our race."

Happening to be where a young female had behaved in a way that indicated an aberration of reason, a grave old man, not redolent of modern civilisation, recommended by all means this person should have a sound whipping. He desired the old trial and test of insanity to be resorted to as was the practice in the days of Henry VIII., when the stump of a tree set up for such a purpose was called "the tree of truth." Let the reader read the biography of Sir Thomas More, in Lord Campbell's Lives of the Chancellors. Were stripes really believed to be a cure for madness, according to the notion of the time, or were they intended to cure feigned madness?

Thus we see vestiges of old medical opinions and practice still remaining in the land, which we meet with from time to time in remote corners. The bustard is extinct in southern England, but ignorance still holds its ground.

Churchwardens provided "silk strings" and "rib bond" for the poor children of either sex that had the king's evil, at a cost, about the year 1664, of *5d.* and *7d.* each; sometimes the charge was *9d.* The strings for the poor of the parish of Minchinhampton and for "ribbon," in 1688, amounted to 1*l.* 5*s.*; in 1689, to 7*s.* 4*d.*; in 1690, to 4*s.* 8*d.* Mr. Bruce writes that the entries for ribbons continued up to 1736. For touching for the king's evil see the Life of the Duke of Monmouth, &c.

* Notes and Queries, Dec. 2. 1854.

For superstitious treatment of disease at Uffculm, in East Devon, see a communication of a resident esquire in 1855. It is a practice there to carry a child fasting on Sunday morning into three parishes, which, according to popular belief, is of great service in hooping-cough.

For a sore mouth the eighth psalm is read seven times for three successive mornings over the patient.*

Medicines of the patent kind were sold at stationers', or by the side on the same shelf with stationery at grocers' and mercers' shops combined. Chemists and druggists' shops in small towns date from the first quarter of the present century. These are substitutes for apothecaries' shops. Few medical practitioners in the country now keep an open shop, or sell anything except to a patient.

Physicians and general medical practitioners have risen in public estimation, and are much advanced in relative position of late years. The professional man a century ago was not treated with much real respect by gentlemen of landed estate. Dr. Thomas Bill received 12*l.* 10*s.* per quarter as one of the physicians to Henry VIII. Physicians received in James I.'s reign a guinea for each visit, though there were two in a day. The guinea was comparatively worth much more than it now is. Reverting to the respect paid to professional persons, it may be remarked that an articled clerk who accompanied his master to a great squire's house dined in the housekeeper's room.

To conclude this subject, let me add, that most carefully prepared returns of health, duration of life, and such matters confute individuals who, till lately, without contradiction, went on denouncing modern civilisation for the physical weakness which it entails. The contrary is the fact.

The hot beverages did not bring in nervous diseases; for the case books of Sir Theodore Mayerne, physician to James I., prove that half the ladies mentioned were treated for "melancholia" or "hypochondria." †

* Notes and Queries.

† Athenæum, V. Sternberg.

Sanitary Measures, the Neglect and Observance of.—Dung-Mixens in the Streets, &c.— The Streets straitened by sundry Erections.

Our ancestors were in many particulars very attentive to certain sanitary precautionary measures. Again, in other matters they appear most negligent. This was strikingly evinced in respect of the collecting matter for manuring their little fields and gardens, which they did in a dung-mixen near the door of their dwelling-house. Others sometimes were induced to complain of this practice, which led to presentments of juries; but it is not in every case that the dread of disease alone operated. The obstruction of the highway, and the dislike of particular individuals to a contiguous offensively-smelling heap perhaps led to the institution of complaint and recourse to presentments. We shall see that some felt aggrieved at the encroachment of neighbours and the too great proximity of another's mixen.

Whether the disposition to produce a sound state of sanitary matters increased or diminished in past centuries is a question of interest. Some would at once assign all attention to sanitary laws as the offspring of modern times. The truth is, that in the time of the Plantagenets the health of the community was more thought of than in that of the Stuarts.

In the year 1472 King Edward IV. in a proclamation enjoined the execution of divers statutes made against the casting of filth, dung, and other *noyous* things into the River Thames, and into the rivers flowing by other cities and borough towns of this realm.

The injurious effects upon the human frame of noisome smells and emanations from open drains were acknowledged in some towns. The covering over of the gutters and drains on the quay of Yarmouth in 1610 is recorded as a work deserving notice.

The centres of some of the best squares of London now adorned with gardens were places in which heaps of filth and rubbish were laid.

The corruption of the King's Ditch at Cambridge was judged to be the secondary cause of plague, the corruption of the air being the primary cause. This ditch was, however, left to be cleared out when the first hard frost should set in. It did its work during the autumn.*

There are entries which might mislead us as to the state of the streets had we no other evidence. Thus in 1604 Robert Thornton was paid for making clean of the street at Lyme weekly for the year 4*s.* An order would seem to embrace everything that could be desired in the case.

"1632. Every inhabitant shall every Saturday, before night, cleanse the street over against his dwelling-house, so far as his house extendeth; and shall remove the soil, dung, and other filth that shall be there gathered, so as the streets may be kept clean and in a decent and comely manner, upon pain of forfeiture of 12*d.*, to be levied by way of distress by the serjeants."†

Our further inquiries lead to proof that these sweepings went to augment the dung-mixens in the course of formation in the streets, which were complained of when the site caused obstruction or annoyance to some individual — not otherwise. When Mary Bartlett, aged 105, conversed with Mr. Edwin Chadwick, this aged serge-maker clearly described this state of the streets of Exeter about 1760–80. They were filthy and unscavenged.

In 1613 a jury presented R. Gale for having made a dunghill close by the house of Joseph Alford to the hurt of the king's subjects.‡

> "*Item*, p'nt 9*d.* R. Gale erexit quoddam sterquilinium juxta domum Joseph Alford ad nocumentum populi dmi. Regis."

Gregory Alford, a leading character personally known to Charles II., made, after his return to Lyme at the Restora-

* Cambridge Transactions. Bohn, 1855.

† Corporation Order Book of Lyme.

‡ Court of Hustings Book.

tion, a dung-mixen before his house in the street to the annoyance of others, and was ordered to remove the same. In 1669 Sarah Ellesdon, one of that family to whom Charles II. looked for assistance in escaping from Charmouth after the Battle of Worcester, with three others, was presented for making a dung-mixen in the street at the church hatch, which was to be removed under pain of *5s.*

In 1675 Humphry Limbry and two others had notice from the Court of Hustings to remove each a dunghill made before his door in the street in a month's time, under a fine of 3*s.* 4*d.* John Wesley, an ancestor of the celebrated Wesley, was on the jury. John Drake was ordered to remove a dunghill which he had made before his shop in the middle of Broad Street.

Little attention was paid to these orders of the court. The same nuisances were committed as if the presentments were necessary for a jury to make by virtue of office, while the compliance with the order was optional.

Three noisome dunghills in the middle of Broad Street are complained of in 1677. In 1684 several dunghills between Mr. Spicer's and Stile Lane were to be removed in two months, or a fine of 6*s.* 6*d.* to be imposed. Many more were presented at a court baron in 1685.

A dunghill against the cockmoil, or prison, was presented in 1749. The practice of forming such in different streets was not discontinued.

Noisome dunghills were complained of as such in some cases where the stench was intolerable. Thus, at Castle Combe, in 1417, one on which the entrails of the animals killed by the inhabitants of the street were thrown, was ordered to be removed. It was, however, more the obstruction of the thoroughfare than anticipated evils to men's health that prompted complaints.

In 1590 the inhabitants of the west street of Castle Combe were enjoined to remove a collection of filth at a certain man's house, and to lay no more there *within X foot of the way.**

* G. P. Scrope, Esq., History.

Great cities were no exceptions to the general presence of dunghills. When royal personages were about to make a formal entry into a place, suitable preparations were ordered. Dunghills were deemed obstructions and unseemly. Queen Elizabeth being expected at Worcester in August, 1575, the Council Chamber ordered that every person having any "*donghills*, or myskins and tymber within the liberties, shall cause the same to be carried away within ten days next, and so shall keep clean their soyles, and *pave* the same with all convenient spede to a certain point, and beyond this to a certain point the soyles or foot ways unpaved were to be covered with *gravel*."

May we not say that the clearing of the streets from obstructions had as much to do with the order as any sanitary reasons? The timber and dunghills would have obstructed the procession.*

Lyme had its scavenger. This worthy, John Lock, carefully collected the dirt, and made a dunghill in the middle of Broad Street, the principal street of the town. For this he was complained of in a presentment in 1753, and in 1756 he and his sons had made five dunghills in so many streets.

Lest any reader should suppose that this disregard of the preservation of health, and of a decent appearance of the principal streets, was confined to one town, we add the following: —

The spot at Weymouth, or more properly, Melcombe Regis, now called the Parade, was that chosen for the throwing all the rubbish of the place, and bore the name of the *Mixen*.†

The pigs belonging to Thomasin Davie, keeper of a public-house, wandered about the streets of Lyme, which was, perhaps, a not unusual circumstance; but they *prejudiced the graves*, which caused a presentment in 1677. The pigs at Brighton caused an order that no hog was to go

* Hist. of Worcester.

† Ellis's Hist. of Weymouth.

unringed on the Steyne, where the nets lie, under a penalty of 8*d.*

One who chanced to enter Lyme, Weymouth, and the generality of our towns when the streets were studded with dung-mixens, and covered with impurities, might have quoted these lines from Dante's "Inferno:"—

> "Needful it is that our descent be slow
> Until the senses somewhat are inured
> To this foul blast, and it shall case to vex."*

That harm might arise from decomposing animal and vegetable matter was an opinion firmly entertained, but never fully acted upon till pestilence stalked abroad. There was no provision against the coming of epidemics. When they were firmly seated, then sanitary measures were enforced. The following routine was practised:— All dogs and cats seen at large were to be killed; pigs were to be kept from wandering; and no carrion or manure was to be deposited in the streets.† The leaving dead animals about only a little way from dwellings was a common practice, and everywhere occasioned presentments.

The decaying bodies of traitors suspended upon gibbets at no great elevation from the ground in the confined street of small country towns were productive of disease. To view the change produced upon the body of a once honoured friend or pastor must have had a very depressing effect upon those who espoused the cause for which the gibbetted man had suffered extreme punishment. Those who had opposed the dead victims could not have rejoiced in the stench that filled and oppressed their street. In a sanitary point of view, the authorities punished all alike when ordering the the suspension of the victims of rebellion.

The quarters of the Monmouth men executed at Lyme Regis in the autumn of 1685 fell down upon the ground,

* Pollock's Translation of Dante, Canto XI.

† See Waylen's Hist of Marlborough.

a prey to the numerous dogs kept before the dog tax in the May following. The mayor, May 11th, 1686, enters: —

To mone pd. for beare at Geo. Alford's for the men that set up the rebells quarters that were fallen, 1*s*.

The absence of the necessary, as they are now deemed, convenience to houses, was felt to be a public nuisance when numbers were congregated. Mr. Thomas Denslowe's scholars and the grammar school-boys, in 1597, offended to an extent such as to draw forth a presentment of the jury that decency might be preserved. The entries are contained in the foot-note below.*

The town of Newcastle was much in the same state at the outbreak of the cholera there.

In 1617 the authorities of Weymouth addressed themselves to the great evil that arose from children "filthing the streets." For each offence a child above seven years of age was to be fined sixpence, and the child's master or parent to be made to pay. This offence was transferred in 1654 to the churchyard. An order in the archives exists against making it "a place of convenience."

Mrs. Mary Bartlett, of Exeter, aged 105, described how annoying it was to walk the unscavenged, narrow, dark, and filthy streets; how dangerous to pass through them at night, for fear of being befouled by what was thrown out of

* 1597. *Item*, that henceforth Thomas Densloe's scholars do not use to go into the cleves to dung there, to the annoyance of those that go that way, nor the way that leadeth into the cleves, upon pain of 3*s*. 4*d*.

Item, that henceforth the schoolmaster which teacheth grammar do not let his scholars to filth the churchyard, nor going into Silvester Jurdeyn's cleves, upon pain of 3*s*. 4*d*.

1598. Children not to *be filthy* in or make the streets a convenience.

At Castle Combe, in 1590, offenders in this way in the churchyard were to pay for every time xii*d*. Children, whose parents are mentioned by name, not to do as above. The parents not to suffer them to do so in the streets, and the way towards the Mill Green.

There was a public convenience on the Gun Cliff in 1645. Five shillings are charged for nails to mend the "house of office in the Cliff."

the windows, and during rain by the water-spouts from the unguttered houses.*

Private convenience was too often consulted to the disregard of the public good, even to the straitening of the streets. Though these were, as now appears, so very narrow, stones were set up to answer the purpose of tables or stools for housewives to stand their tubs upon in order to wash out of doors and in the public street. Attention having been directed to this evil, it was ordered in 1597 that Phelps, the mason, and others that had set up any stones to wash upon, do presently remove them upon pain of 3*s*. 4*d*.

This was not the whole extent of the encroachments now being made in our time. One Mark Barnes was fined 2*s*. 6*d*. in 1599 for having set out a bulk or stall (which was an open projecting shop) for the straitening of the street; such had no glass windows. Several persons were presented this same year for having made seats before their doors without any agreement with the mayor. These were stone seats, a permanent evil; still it was agreed that 4*d*. should be paid for each for the use of the town. The liberty or license taken in erecting such things would seem to be the evil the authorities restrained, and not the straitening the thoroughfare. Ask permission and pay the money, all else seemed disregarded. In 1615 a bench in advance of a shop window was presented, and an order made that in future 2*d*. should be paid.

One way of obstructing the streets and making a great litter in the highway was the "winnowing of corn." This practice was denounced in 1562. The entry is curious:—

(*Court of Hustings Book*, marked 3., 20 April, 1562.)

Curia legalis cum vis franc pleg.

Item, ordinatum est quod Johannes Hassard nec aliquis alius habitans infra villam de Lyme Rs non *purgaverint grana sua a pulvere* in Regia via ante domos suas decetero subpena cuilct delinquenti forisfac per quotet temp sic invent quin solid.

* Communication to Mr. E. Chadwick.

This specimen of an entry at a court leet with view of Frank Pledge, decries, under a penalty of *5s.*, the winnowing corn in the king's highway before men's houses.

The following order was made that another evil might be corrected: —

1671. Divers persons having put up posts, erected porches, and built bulks, and other things, by permission of one or more lords of the manor (*i. e.* members of the corporation) in future the mayor and six others must consent.

Mr. Solomon Andrew was presented in 1695 for having set up a new upping stock at his new house in Church Street.

The care shown in shutting up persons suspected of being infected has been treated of elsewhere. Messengers were paid for bringing tidings of the presence of infectious diseases in the neighbourhood, and even within a circuit of twenty miles. The ale-tasters performed their office that the sellers of drink might only send out such as was good for man's body. In various ways the care of our mayors was manifested for the health of the community.

An entry of the date of 1551 proves that the beach was sometimes driven up so as to close the mouth of the river, as it is in modern times. The accumulated water and filth then becoming very offensive, the mayor had a passage for the river dug through the beach, with a due regard to sanitary measures.

1551. *Item*, paid to Colman and to Prechyll to dig away the chesil beach) of the bodyll (Buddle), 8*d.*

The fearful visitations of disease, whether devastating plague, or *stoupe gallante*, the sweating sickness of the Tudor reigns, impressed fear upon all classes, and gave some individuals of the better sort an impression that cleanliness was a preservative against these evils. Some nobles were before the age in enlightened views upon sanitary matters. Those who would fain connect cleanliness with godliness, and who advocated the removal of noisome collections of matter, found in too many unwilling ears. Like many improvers, their wisdom was accounted impertinent folly. Thomas Howard, afterwards the third Lord Bindon, once Mayor of Weymouth, wrote in 1581 to William Pyt, his correspondent in the corporation.

"I ernst to find the town clene, and all the annoyance behind the town removed according to promise."[*]

The Court of Hustings at Lyme had made sanitary orders respecting the casting filth upon the beach at the Cobb gate, where the tide might carry the same away. These orders were by some disregarded, and probably ridiculed. The offenders figure in a presentment at the Hustings Court, A. D. 1580.

Item, presentant quod Thomas Hiat et Philippus Haroy jecerunt fimum infra le full sea mark contra ordinem in eâ predictâ editum. Ideo quilibet eorum in misericordiâ, iij*s*. iiij*d*.

Also they present Thomas Hiat et Philip Haroy for having thrown filth within the full sea mark, contrary to the order in the aforesaid particular set forth. So each is amerced 3*s*. 4*d*.

The bodies of deceased friends were not subject to any uniform law respecting their interment. Sir Symonds D'Ewes kept his grandfather's corpse at Coxden for fourteen days. His own father's body was despatched from London towards Suffolk the third day after his decease. Mr. Boldero, his friend, a lawyer, was buried the day after his death, as was an old servant of the family. Of two children, each was interred the day after his decease. Mr. John Drake, of Ash House, in Musbury, near Axminster, who died the 11th of April, 1628, was buried privately the same night. Mr. Willoughby, of Pehembury, Devon, who died aged eighty-six, was buried one week after.†

It may be said with truth that the interval between death

* Sherren Papers.

† Diary of Walter Yonge, Esq., p. 112.

and burial was much shorter in those days than at present, seldom exceeding two or three days.

Funerals were, in Devonshire parishes, usually fixed for Sunday. The deceased was laid at the beginning of the afternoon service in the middle of the centre aisle, and was left there to the close, when the obsequies were performed. In the heats of summer the inconvenience of this practice, owing to the length of time since the decease took place, was felt to be very great. At times the congregation suffered in a sensible degree from a practice of the worst example.

Precautions against the Spread of Sickness.

WERE this heading of our subject read in a recent newspaper, our thoughts would revert to the removal of nuisances, covering of drains, and other similar modes of guarding against infection by lessening the extent of the nidus in which disease delights to revel. Such, however, is not the nature of the precautionary measures adopted in the Tudor reigns, which we have in view.

We intend to exhibit the course pursued, not when disease might be expected, but when it had arrived in full force, in order to prevent it from spreading.

The sweating sickness, the plague, and other great forms of the visitation of disease, entered our towns. Our magnates treated them like unruly characters, and endeavoured to shut them up, to imprison them wherever they were found, and set watchmen to guard the locality in which they had seated themselves by night and day.

When the plague visited the Universities, those who did not set off shut themselves up in the colleges, allowing no one to have intercourse with them. The plague was believed to be greatly dependent upon the moon, and that the change of that satellite made appear who was infected or not.*

* Cambridge University Transactions during the Puritan Controversies of the sixteenth and seventeenth centuries

Families could not be shut up without some care being taken of their having food for their subsistence during the period of their incarceration. Hence there were entries in borough archives about expenses incurred in carrying out this system.

In the year 1590, there was paid at Lyme to "those that did watch by day for fear of the sickness, for four days 1*s.* 6*d.*" The watchmen were to prevent intercourse with infected parts and persons.

There is an entry in 1645 of money paid for the constables' bill for relieving thirty-two poor persons shut up upon suspicion of infection, 10*l.* 0*s.* 7*d.** This *shutting up* of so many may have often proved a very cruel proceeding. Occasionally charges were made for the support of infected people who were shut up in other contiguous parishes. The mayor, 7th Aug. 1593, "delivered," as he entered it "to the constables of Whitchurch, 20*s.* for the infected people, whereof I (he enters) could collect but 14*s.* 6*d.*, so the rest to the town account."

Are we to suppose that all, either the incarcerated or their friends without, were obedient to the orders and special directions of corporations? No; some were contumacious and rebellious, so that recourse to violent measures was necessary.

When any infectious disease broke out, the authorities were empowered, by an Act passed in the reign of James I., to shut up the sick; and the watchmen or guards were protected from any proceedings against them, owing to violence used in keeping them closely confined. Discipline had to be administered, when the persons so watched proved troublesome. At Great Staughton, Huntingdonshire, the constables, so late as the year 1710, charged thus in their accounts: "Pd. Thomas Hawkins for whipping two people that had the small pox, 8*d.*;" and in 1714, "Pd. for watching, victuals, and drink for Mary Mitchell, 2*s.* 6*d.* Pd. for whipping her, 4*d.*"

* Town Accompt Book.

Individuals in good circumstances would not always readily obey borough mandates.

At Lewes, in 1710, a Mr. Holmwood occasioned a charge of 12*s.* for several men to watch to prevent him from bringing his son up in the town with the small pox.

Parties running away from the plague without a clean bill of health were advertised in the newspapers, and the parish in the country in which they were supposed to have secreted themselves.

We must not confound the watching or sitting up with an individual sick person with this public exercise of caution towards other towns. The mayor ministered to the wants of the afflicted like an overseer now-a-day. Mr. William Ellesdon, Mayor of Lyme, in his accompt 1595, enters —

> *Item*, paid to Goodford's daughter for watching two nights with Hill the hellyer, 6*d.*

Friendly parishes sent persons round upon the outbreak of disease. "These prophets of ills" were rewarded as was really just: "Paid two messengers from Halstock to give notice the Small Pox was there, 5*s.*"*

In 1602 a surgeon was paid for "searching a corpse suspected to be of the plague, 3*s.* 4*d.*" This is equivalent to "making a *post mortem* examination."

The plague being once declared, all dogs, swine, cats, and tame pigeons seen at large were killed, as it was believed these animals spread infection.†

The dog, be it remembered, was sacrificed in Etruria to Apollo in times of pestilence.

The flocking to court of persons to be touched for the king's evil was checked.

Nosegays were placed in courts of justice, not for ornament, but as preservatives against the pest.

The number of dogs killed in Westminster was surprising. Before the tax on dogs, persons kept dogs in great numbers.

* Archives of Lyme.

† Waylen's History of Marlborough.

Windows facing houses suspected of containing infection were to be kept closed.

Fires were to be made in movable pans in churches. Bonfires were lighted in the streets. At Leicester the following bye-law was made, which may indeed be styled a despotism:—"Any one having been visited with the plague who for two months presumes to go among those that are clean, to forfeit 5*l.*, or lose his freedom and be banished for ever out of the town without any redemption."*

The presence of the plague being declared, the inhabitants of towns took flight. Herein they deemed their safety to lie. In certain "Constitutions" or laws framed at Lyme in the year 1570, we may learn the habit of flying from the seat of the dreadful pestilences of early times, which desolated England.

A freeman was to lose his valuable franchise if absent a year from the borough, *plague time excepted.*

The same fear which prompted flight to some, suggested danger to those among whom they arrived. Intercourse with the fugitives was avoided. Corporations and counties, little *imperia in imperio,* acted up to the spirit of their own bye-laws. We learn that in the "Great Plague," the Gloucestershire men would not suffer the Bristol men to have any access to them, as Stow writes, nor into their county by any means. "Plague stones" still exist, upon upon which deposits of provisions were made for those shut out from intercourse with society from fear of infection. Archives abound with entries touching the shutting up towns against strangers in plague time.

When the plague raged in 1593, a proclamation prohibited the holding of Bartholomew Fair, London, in the usual manner, as people from every part of the realm attended it, and might carry the sickness to all parts. As the wholesale trade was so important, that was allowed; while the retail trade was suppressed, as if the wholesale clothiers would

* Nichol's History of Leicester.

not have been as surely a medium of infection as the retail dealers.

Among the preservatives against the plague by Francis Herring, Doctor in Physic, 4to. London, 1665, is recommended the frequent opening of the pipes from the New River to cleanse the channels of every street, the cleaning out of all ditches, and the ringing of bells often, and the discharge of great ordnance to purify the air.

If the Londoners interfered with the country traders, it will be found that the country in return was not slow to legislate for traders coming from the metropolis.

When the plague raged at a distance, such as in London or any other great town, fear suggested a *cordon sanitaire*, a barrier to all coming from that way. Magistrates in Charles the First's reign acted upon this fear, and endeavoured to shut up the inhabitants of the infected place for all practical purposes; for they would not allow any such to be received and sheltered from weather, or have entertainment, or even refreshment furnished them.

This must always have proved ineffectual. Relatives could not mercilessly turn the traveller from their door, but were ready to incur some risk; and the landlord could not bear to close his doors against a roystering party of carriers, whose revelling had often brought him much profit, and who would resent his slavish obedience to the magistrates' order, and draw down upon him the hostility of the whole fraternity.

In the following case the *agreement* appears to have made all the difference in the amount of the offence. The magistrates of the Michaelmas Sessions, 1636, held at Bridport, adopt all the terms of the agreement, and would have led in the faction of Dorset against London.

"Forasmuch as information hath been given unto this Court that an agreement was lately made by the inhabitants of Blandford Forum, in this county, that (in regard of the great danger of the infection of the plague, by carrying goods, and travelling of passengers from London and other places infected) no carrier, with horse, cart, or waggon, or other passenger or traveller, on horse or foot, that should come from London or any other place infected, should be suffered to lodge or abide within that town or parish; and for that purpose a good and sufficient watch and ward should be kept by the inhabitants of that parish; which agreement was confirmed by Sir Francis Tulford, Knt., and Gerrard Wood, Doctor of Divinity, two of his Majesty's justices of the peace for this county. Notwithstanding which agreement and confirmation, Thomas Stowell of the warnership of Pymperne, within the parish (but without the borough) of Blandford aforesaid, innkeeper, hath divers times entertained carriers, travellers, and others that came from London, and doth give out that he will continue to do so, which this Court conceiveth to be done in contempt, and to be very dangerous to the said town of Blandford, and to the country adjoining; and doth therefore order that the constables or other officers of the warnership of Pymperne shall forthwith, upon sight of this order, convene the said Thomas Stowell before some one of his Majesty's justices of the peace of this county, who is desired to cause the said Stowell to enter into good security to appear at the next sessions, &c."

[And in default, he is ordered to be committed to the county gaol.] *

Weyhill and many other great fairs were not allowed to be held the year of the plague, 1665, as the King's proclamation sets forth.

During the raging of the great plague of London in 1665, it was agreed "at Weymouth to watch to keep out people infected with the plague." There is an entry at Lyme the same year:—"Paid several watchmen, put on by Mr. John Ellesdon, upon neglect of others, and in observance of his Majesty's strict order about the quarantine, 1*l*."

The terror inspired by the plague, whatever that disease may really have been, was very great. Seventy years ago no one could have been found bold enough to have dug a grave in one knoll in Lyme churchyard where those had been buried who had died of the plague. It was believed

* Mr. T. Hearn, "Qui Quondam."

that the earth was deeply tainted with infection, and could not be disturbed without imminent risk to human life.*

In 1604 the plague, which destroyed above 3000 weekly in London, reached Exeter. In 1613 it raged many weeks at Axminster, and carried off great numbers of the inhabitants. In 1625 the plague was at Bridport, and in 1627 raged in other parts of Dorset.

The magistrates of Dorset relieved parties who were greatly distressed after the visitation by the plague.

Hugh Densloe of Allington, a part of Bridport, glover, had become miserably poor, owing to that town having been visited with the plague. Since that visitation a flood had carried away his house, — his whole property. The magistrates signed an order upon the deputy treasurer of the county for 40*s.*†

The *modus operandi* adopted upon extraordinary occasions by the magistrates was such as would puzzle the most sagacious to conjecture now-a-days.

After the plague that raged in the West had passed away, by the time of the Midsummer Sessions, held at Shaftesbury in 1629, one Symon Furnell, a poor labouring man, was an applicant for relief. He was owner of a house near Shaston, late in the possession of one Richard Street, who, and all his family, died therein of the plague. No one had tenanted the house since, not because no person could be found to do so, but because no one was permitted by the magistrates to occupy it. The poor owner of the house was distressed, this having furnished the greatest part of his maintenance; so he prayed the assistance of the Court, as he could not, by reason of his poverty, suffer the house to be any longer without a tenant.

The magistrates entered upon this difficult piece of jurisprudence,— the allowing the poor man to have some benefit from the use of his own, and still to preserve the inhabitants from an outbreak of plague.

* See Macaulay.

† Dorset Sessions, MS. "Qui Quondam."

In more recent times, when human life has been required to be jeopardised for the benefit of mankind, a person under sentence of death has been selected, and life, and even rewards, were offered. This mode of proceeding had not suggested itself to the worthy justices. They ordered that the inhabitants of the borough of Shaston and the liberty of Alincester should procure some person to go into the said house, and to carry out such stuff as shall be found therein, and cause the same to be burned, and then, "the said party shall be shut up within the said house by the space of one month next after, and he to be maintained indifferently between them!" *

At the Michaelmas Sessions held at Dorchester, 1625, an order was made for the collection of 40*l.* weekly within the divisions of Dorchester, Sherborne, and Bridport, towards the relief and sustentation of the sick and distressed people of the borough of Bridport, now visited with the infection of the plague." Allington, a parish adjoining Bridport, was to participate.

In 1627 a rate was levied on the surrounding parishes for the relief of Shaftesbury, the parishes of Gillingham and Motcombe, and the liberty of Alincester, under a similar visitation. The Court recites that the sickness doth still continue in Shaston, very dangerous, and that the inhabitants thereof are much impoverished thereby;" in consequence of which the Court ordered the divisions of Blandford and Sherborne do contribute to their relief.†

* Mr. T. Hearn, "Qui Quondam."

† Ibid.

The Great Plague of the Reign of Edward III.

"*Rex Ballivis de Lym, &c., salutem.*

"*Quia non modica pars populi regni nostri Angliæ in præsenti pestilentiâ est defuncta,*" *&c.*

"Because a considerable part of our population of the kingdom of England is dead of the present plague," &c.

RYMER's *Fœdera.*

WHAT locality can be the peculiar site claiming as its own subject the "Great Plague of Edward III?" None surely can be designated when all the whole world suffered.

To treat of this stupendous visitation at any length would be foreign to these pages. The object aimed at is some such mention of the particular facts that may establish a complete realisation of the great plague as having raged in the West of England.

While engaged in the perusal of the general history of so great a scourge in the East, Sicily, Germany, and other countries, we may read of its visiting the coasts of Dorset, and thence spreading inland without feeling much local interest concentrated upon our own part of the world.

Modern visitation of fell disease travelling from the East, sparing those only as it were from caprice, and driven from its victim by no art nor device of the physician, gives an additional interest to the consideration of former pestilence, particularly as to whether God in his providence has been pleased to visit us with a heavier hand than heretofore. The reign of Edward III., in spite of astrology and much ignorance of physical causes and phenomena, is not so remote as to be beyond historic times. The marvellous and the fabulous can be sifted, and the solid facts be preserved.

The "Great Plague" of England and the "Black Death" of Northern Europe appeared in the East in 1346, and was brought from the Levant to the great towns of Italy in 1348. It crossed the Alps that year, when, after spreading over

France and Spain, it appeared on the sea coast of Dorset in 1349. Hence the pestilence was communicated to Devon and other parts of the kingdom at a season of great prosperity.

One mile south of Axminster stood the stately abbey of Newenham, whose annals have been lately published.* During the administration of this Cistercian community by Abbot Walter De la Houe, the most fatal pestilence recorded in the history of mankind visited the house.

Twenty monks, three lay brethren, and eighty-eight secular persons of both sexes, who lived within the walls, were carried off by its violence, to the great loss of the house (ad magnu' dampnu' hui' doms'), leaving of the members of the convent only the abbot and two monks surviving!

In the history of Castle Combe are these references to the plague:—

> A tempore pestilentiæ tenementum ruinosum et decassum.
> Pestilentia prima et magna, 31 May ad 29 Sept. 1349.†

The duration of the plague is set down as being generally of five months. In some parts nearly half the population is said to have been cut off. The city of Bristol suffered so that grass grew several inches high in High Street and Broad Street. The Gloucestershire men, from fear, would not suffer the Bristol men to have any access to them nor their county by any means, having recourse to what in modern times has been named a *cordon sanitaire.* This was deemed a hardship, for the inhabitants of towns, judging safety to lie in avoiding the crowded haunts of men, were induced to fly into the country.

The Sarum registers from August 8, 1348, to Lady Day 1349, contain the admission of seventy incumbents. A chaplain could hardly be had to serve a church under ten marks, or ten pounds per annum, whereas one might have

* By J. Davidson, Esq.

† Hon. Poulett Scrope's History of C. Combe.

been had at two pounds with his diet, and men would hardly accept of a vicarage at twenty marks per annum.

Let Fabyan, Walsingham, Cantacuzenus, and other historians be consulted as to the origin, progress, and their account of the nature of the disease, which quite puzzled the astrologers. What has been communicated of the ravages of the disease at Newenham Abbey will gain credit for Walsingham's assertion, that in some parts scarce a tenth part of the people remained alive; that in many towns all the inhabitants died besides those who fled, and that houses fell down and were never rebuilt. In London 50,000 perished; Avignon, then the residence of the Pope, was nearly depopulated.

In the East a bleeding at the nose preceded the pestilential attack, and certain death. At Florence a swelling in the groin or arm-pits larger than an egg marked the disease, which, without fever in most cases, terminated fatally without benefit from medical skill on the third day. Boccacio attributes the plague to something corrupt in the air, while the history of the time is replete with accounts of curious atmospheric phenomena, of comets, meteors, fiery beams, and other coruscations.

The disease fell upon the brute creation, while great numbers of animals perished from inattention, their owners having died.

The mere disease, however dreadful, is but a part of the evils of such a time. These were found to be famine, &c., and a raising of their wages by the labouring population. A statute was passed for the old rate of wages, which was disregarded. Abbots, friars, and other great men were fined for disobedience in this particular. The subject is, however, left for the general reader.

We cannot refrain from exhibiting a proof how completely man in every relation of life is influenced and affected by the atmosphere, the phenomena, the medium in which his lot is cast. Great natural disturbances on the surface of our planet are felt through numerous ramifications. So many of the clergy fell victims to the great plague, that for want of learned masters *English* began to be used in schools in the teaching of young persons instead of French.

Remarks upon Domestic Architecture, Materials, Price, &c.

In the south-west of England, where the red marl abounded, mud houses, or mud mixed with chopped straw, called cob, were constructed upon a stone foundation. In other parts a stone foundation carried up of the same material was succeeded by a wooden framework with mud between, and the whole whitewashed.

In towns few houses were built of stone. The expense was so much greater than was incurred for those of wood or timber framework, as oak was very cheap. The latter were to be found in Bristol and most of our country towns. The stories projected, so that the upper rooms were the longest; and in narrow streets persons could almost shake hands out of the topmost windows. The plasterers filled up the space between the framework. The souterrain or cellar had no groined roof, as in the more costly buildings of cities; it was entered from the street by steep steps which encroached upon the roadway. Low doors and a trap secured the entrance. The shop was on the ground floor, with stalls or bulkheads (a word often contracted into *bulks*) open to the street, in which were no glass windows—another reason why our ancestors hailed the return of summer. The framework of the Vicarage of Lyme, destroyed in the siege of 1644, was rebuilt at a cost of 12*l.*

When houses were constructed of wooden framework, we can understand why aldermen were provided with a proper hook and cord. In case of fire these were used to pull down the wooden framework buildings in flames.

Norway planks were known in England, doubtless, by the 12th century; but in small boroughs oak timber was, I may say, solely used for the construction of houses, and also of floors. In ordinary residences there was no ceiling. The under side of the planking of the floors was whitewashed, and this was the ceiling, so to speak, of the lower room. A ceiling to rooms raised the character of the house.

The plaster was spread upon reeds as well as upon laths, and was mainly composed in the towns near the greensand formation of *Fox mould* sand or earth. Near Lyme people dug pits close to the king's highway, which were very dangerous, and the material thrown about made the way almost impassable. Presentments of juries followed which tried the Latin of the town clerk; *i.e.*:

Item, presentant quod Thomas Case de Hole effodit terram rubram Anglice *Fox mould* in Regia alta via ducente vers' *Three-legged Cross.*

Chimneys were rare in the country towns in the reign of Queen Elizabeth. Leland had expressed some wonder at a chimney in Bolton Castle. Fire-places and chimneys were built very often of plaster only. Some allusion to this subject has been made elsewhere.

The burning of limestone in a kiln was not practised. Neither coal nor culm was used for the purpose. A skilful lime-burner used wood and frith upon the hills to calcine a mass of stone, very ingeniously disposed so that all should feel an equal degree of heat. Lime-burning was a trade—an art. Very little lime was used.

The Somersetshire churches have been famed. They were constructed of an inferior oolite from Hamden Hill, commonly called Ham-hill, near Crewkerne. Beer-stone for interiors, a freestone where the chalk and greensand pass insensibly the one into the other, was much used. Portland, Purbeck, and Petworth quarries were early known; but the expense of conveying the material to a distance, except for churches and great houses, kept the use of it within very narrow limits. Caen-stone was imported, as its excellence justified. The use of stucco as a protection to buildings constructed of perishable stone is very recent.

Healing or healm stones, indurated flags used by helliers for covering roofs, were from well-known localities, such as Horsham, where the quarries are said to be worked out. Slates may occasionally be meant; they were, however, generally called slatt-stones.

The fashion of building towers about the middle and close of the fifteenth century extended into the country. A merchant named Borough built a goodly one in the Butter market of Lyme. The merchants in the towns had their merchandize stored in their own residences, the country not being so secure as to warrant storehouses being away from the owner's own eye. The tower was at the entrance, and had to do with the security of the building, as we may suppose. A portcullis let down at night shut out the public from the inner court.

There was a great fondness for these towers, which honest Stow viewed and felt offended at. He judged some afflictions into which the possessors had fallen to have been judgments sent for their desire to overlook their neighbours. Thus in almost every instance we find a novel introduction, however useful and harmless, to have been designated by one class or the other as positively sinful.

Oak Timber in the West of England, the Price, Labour about it, &c.—Notice of the wooden-framed Houses, Healing-stones, &c.

In the reign of Henry VIII., and for many years after, oak timber was that principally in demand, as fir timber from the Baltic was very sparingly imported. The roofs of churches in many instances display a lavish expenditure of oak timber. It was much used for piers and sea defences; the great consumption about Lyme Regis was for the construction of the Cobb and the sea defences of the town against the inroads of the stormy element. Oaks set upright in rows round great rocks had been the mode of constructing the harbour from the reign of Edward I.

The value of oak timber was very inconsiderable. More must have grown on the borders of Dorset and Devon than could well have been used in that vicinity. The vessels then in use were small craft. The material required for them was trifling, and cost, like the beams for the roofs of churches, a small sum.

Some years after, in 1614, when Mr. Brooke tendered a bill against extravagance in apparel, he observed that "women carry manors and thousands of oak trees on their necks."*

A brief illustration of this subject from ancient accompts of mayors in 1545 is here offered. May not the page of history be changed or even enlivened by our sturdy oaks?

Many at first inexplicable entries appear in the reign of Edward VI., about the mayor and his brethren "going to the wood," and of their expenses "in the wood." In 1652 the sum of 3*s.* 4*d.* is charged for "engrossing the indenture of the wood called Chickeradge, between Mr. Pole and the Town." This was the ancestor of Sir John Pole of Shute House, near Axminster, the proprietor of a locality on the north side of the road between Hunter's Lodge Inn and Lambart's Castle, in the parish of Hawkchurch, now called Chackeridge. The mayor used to meet Mr. Pole at the wood, and buy okys (oaks) from him.

Many localities on the hills around Lyme were at this time covered with oak timber, such as Trinity Hill, &c., where the soil is either bare or lately planted with firs.

A separate heading in the mayor, John Tudboll's account

* The Progress of Machinery and Manufactures in Great Britain: Weale's Quarterly Papers in Engineering, vol. v.

for 1545, directs to the following details of the prices for timber and wages. It stands as follows:—

Buying of the town okis * —

Wages { hewing in the wood / sawing / setting by the sea-side } 4*d.* a day.

Meat and drink in addition, 3*d.*

I, John Tudboll and John Daye, bought of

			s.	*d.*
John Long	xx okis for		6	8
Hary Danyell	xx „		12	6
Hary Cranly	ii „		1	6
John Abbot	iv „		2	0
Robert Cok	vi „		5	0
Tho. Lov'gis	ii „		1	6
Richard Lassy	vi „		1	6
An oke of John Days †			0	8
Sum of all these okis aforesaid, 56, which cost 30*s.*				
The which did make, one with another, with (pieces?) that I had in the wood besides, 56 load.				
The cost of every carydge of the said okis, without meat and drink			1	4
The carydge of the whole amounteth to, without meat and drink		£3	14	8
Item, more for meat and drink to the said carriers for the said okis			16	8
Thomas Dare and Jesse did carry of the aforesaid okis 30 okis, and the men of Musbury did carry the rest.				
The which okis cost at the fyrst, with the carriage, meat and drink in all		£6	16	0
(*i. e.* 2*s.* 5*d.* each oak, showing that the expense of carriage, meat, and drink was nearly four times more than the original cost.)				
In 1546 ‡ Rusley was paid for 2 oaks			4	0

* Mayor's Accompts, 1545.

† The initials of this worthy are carved on the column opposite the south door of Lyme Church.

‡ A sack of lime, in 1546, cost 5*d.*

	s.	d.
In 1547, hauling a load of oaks from Wooton (3 miles, and very steep hill) - - - - - -	1	8
In 1551, the carriage of oaks is charged as follows:—		
Carriage of 3 oaks from Hawkchurch, and meat and drink - - - - - - -	9	0
Paid to Robert Pynny for bringing home of 2 oaks from Hawkchurch - - - - - - -	2	10
A. D. 1744. 5 oak trees bought of J. Tucker, Esq., of Nash, cost the corporation - - - £7	14	0

In 1849 a load of oak timber was worth 1*l.* to 1*l.* 15*s.*, according to locality.

The celebrated Round Table at Windsor was made about the year 1356. The Prior of Merton sold from his wood near Reading fifty-two oaks for 26*l.* 13*s.* 4*d.*, or at the rate of 10*s.* 3*d.* each.

In 1394, forty-two oaks in the park of Combe sold for 9*l.* 19*s.* 1*d.*, or 4*s.* 8$\frac{3}{4}$*d.* each; while 467 maples brought 19*l.* 13*s.*, or 10*d.* each.

In 1458 one great elm tree there sold for 20*s.* Cotham Wood, belonging to the manor, was let to farm according to the practice of that and later eras.*

In the reign of Edward VI., 200 large trees, "grossos arbores," near Drogheda in Ireland, were valued at 16*l.*, *i. e.* 1*s.* 7*d.* each.†

Most of the houses in narrow streets were constructed of oak framework, oak beams, and oak flooring. The latter was laid lengthways, and not across the floor joists, as in the present day. There was no ceiling to the under rooms. The beam, joists, and flooring were whitewashed. Oak wainscoting, tables, chests, and furniture were universal. Much of this has been bought up and made its appearance as an ingredient in modern fittings up of rooms after the old style. Very little lime was used. Oak came much cheaper than Ashlar stone.

Laths were not in use. The daubers, afterwards plas-

* J. P. Scrope, M.P., Hist. of Castle Combe.

† From the ancient records of the Irish Exchequer. Notes and Queries, communicated by James F. Ferguson.

terers, spread their mortar upon spear grass. Healing stones, or, as they began to be called, slatt-stones, wer sparingly imported from Cornwall for the houses intende to be stone-healed, of which there were few, as thatch wa very general.

Early Civil Engineering, particularly in respect of Marine Constructions.

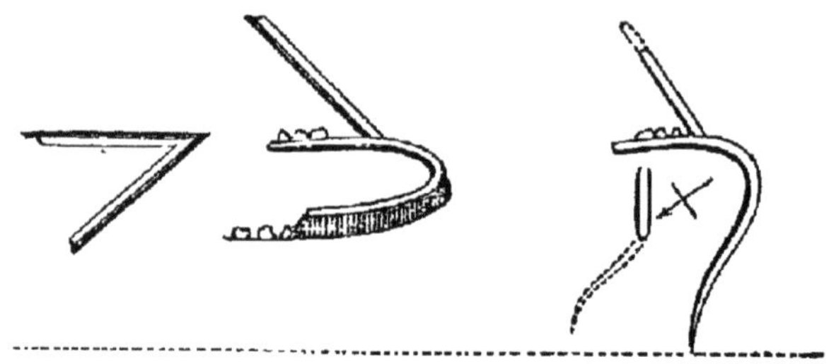

The Cobb, or ancient Harbour of Lyme Regis, about A.D. 1588 and 1856.

At what epoch could it be said there existed no civil or royal engineer? The genus is not of recent growth, though many of the appliances are so. When such men as the free-masons flourished, and were executing their immortal works, was there not ability of the highest kind available? The genius that could plan and construct a cathedral would not shrink from a marine work, though in practice a stranger to the tempest lashed sea coast. The theoretical was in Plantagenet reigns blended with the local and practical. On many occasions we have instances of the summoning of those who had local knowledge,— sailors, clothiers, persons skilled in fortification, to communicate with great men.

If the civil engineers of Great Britain want an ancient appellation, let them adopt that of the reign of Edward I., *Prodeshommes des plus sachantz.* Four of these, viz. civil engineers, were to be sent to that king, who were most clever and sufficient in the laying out and planning a New Town, who were to be all ready to go whither they might be ordered.

The subject leads to the laying out and founding the borough of Lyme Regis. This was a BASTIDE, *Ville Neuve* or *Ville Franche* of Dorset, as much as those ancient towns so called in the once English possessions in France.

On this occasion the want of local knowledge, excusable as there had been no respectable inhabitants, and especially the ignorance of the action of land springs and high tides upon the land, here composed of the superior Blue Lias, was fatal.

The town was destroyed by the joint action of a storm and the slipping of the land. Practical geology was a branch of human knowledge quite unknown.

After such a lesson as that afforded by the destruction of the town in the last year of the reign of Edward III., we may readily believe great attention began to be paid to the protection of the sea front, and the construction of the harbour.

John Hudcresfield was, we may fairly suppose, an engineer for marine constructions. He obtained a grant from King Richard II., A.D. 1389, for making a harbour at the mouth of the Brit, two miles below Bridport, for which he was to have a toll of one halfpenny on every horseload of goods imported or exported. In 1444 a new port was constructed a short distance from the former haven. The name of the second engineer is unknown, unless it be found in the Dom Book of Bridport.

That a favourable view of the projected work should be taken by the bishop was highly important. In this undertaking the Bishop of Sarum looked upon the affair as so likely to prove beneficial, that he granted an indulgence for building and repairing a new port, to be called Bridport Haven, for the preservation of merchants and mariners.* Bishops were then, it is probable, in close relations with architects, the civil engineers of the day.

From a remote period the mode of constructing marine

* Reg. Aiscott, quoted in the last edition of Hutchins.

works such as was displayed in the Cobb, the name of the harbour at Lyme Regis, was the same as that pursued in the reign of Elizabeth. It was built, viz. Le Pier, Le Key, or Le Cobb, *de maëremio et petris,* of timber and of rocks.

These rocks abounded westward of the town as debris of the greensand cliffs of hills which are outliers of the Blackdown range of hills; they lay upon the shore, and were floated to the sea-work by means of vats or casks. These were dropped in their site, and then oaks were "squatted" or let in on either side, thus: —

Ancient manner of constructing piers.

Rocks are floated by modern engineers, and placed in front of some sea-works at Banff, in Scotland.

These *cockle* rocks — a local term — and oaks were employed to "enforce a harbour in the main sea, and for the groynes or jetties, as well as the defences of the town from the ravages of the sea." There were no sea walls. If any "grave, skilful mason had given in his opinion that nothing but stone could secure the dominion," he had not been attended to, for the carpenter was followed, who said, "'Twas better by far to defend it with oak." The Cobb and sea front must have presented a very different appearance, when such numbers of dark brown trees were in sight, to what it does when other material of a light colour has been substituted. Oak trees were in abundance in West Dorset and South-east Devon. Age and the "artes" worms so affected the sea-works, the wooden walls of Lyme, that about the reign of James I. or Charles I. stone began to be substituted.

The fame of the workmen employed at the Cobb of Lyme induced the men of Hastings, A.D. 1595, to send for a party of them to build a pier of huge rocks piled edgelong without timber. (Queen Mary had caused these men to be pressed for building Dover pier.) The next winter overthrew this work. Another gang, with a master-workman, was again sent for in 1597, when timber in cross dogs, braces, and bars was used. The work was thirty feet high, "bewtyfull to behold, huge, invincible, and unremoveable in judgment of all beholders," who contributed, as did the whole shire, to the work. On All Saints' Day a storm upon a spring tide scattered the whole. The entry in the archives is full of advice to posterity, not to build without a mighty frame of timber, the want of which caused the downfall.

Blue lias stone, now so valuable for burning into hydraulic lime, resists very badly the effects of the weather, particularly frost. Where so great an extent of ledges, dry at low water, is found, it is not surprising that the quality of the material differs in some degree. Some of the hardest and most durable kind had doubtless been tried in our marine works, but was not found to answer.

West of Lyme, near the present famous landslip of Dowlands and Bindon, are found boulders of green sandstone of the greensand formation lower in the course of stratification than the cockle or yellow sandstone previously spoken of. These masses are locally called *cow-stones*, a translation of *Les vaches noires*, by which similar masses are designated on the coast of France, near Dives, from their supposed resemblance to *black cows* on the beach.

This material began to be used for the Cobb as a superstructure upon the cockle rock foundation outside the oak stumps that the "artes" or age had spared. The casing was of cow-stone laid without mortar, and filled in with rubble. When the work at any part became weak, or showed symptoms of falling, it was taken down and rebuilt. Oak wedges made out of the former outer defence often saved the weak part from falling. Modern science explodes this method of laying a foundation of rock not accurately squared off for a superstructure to rest on. The water flowing into the masonry at the base often blows up the mass so imposed. The masonry was, in technical phraseology, said to be "dry," as no mortar was used. Agricultural lime from the white and blue lias beds at Uplyme, one mile inland, was burnt centuries ago with furze and frith; no architectural lime, though the best material in the world was at hand, was made. There was no coal brought into Dorset for burning lime in any quantities. Lime was first burnt with fern instead of wood by Mr. Timothy Burrell of Sussex, as recorded by Dr. Ray, about the years 1680 or 1690. Cow-stone was moderately durable. When squared, it assumed in time a rounded form.

Cow-stone Casing resting on Rocks.

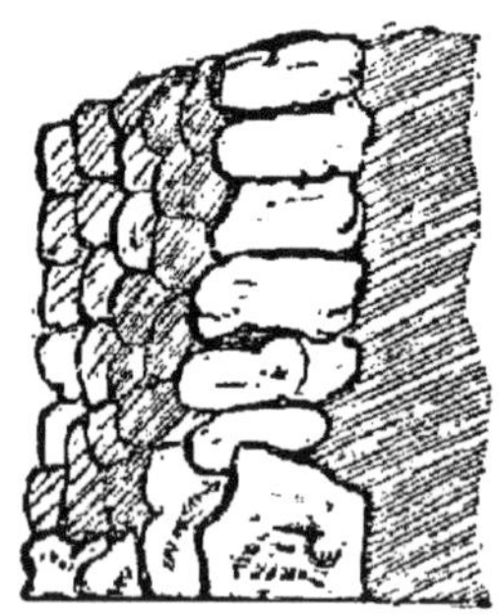

Side View of a weathered Cow-stone Wall.

This mode of construction was very faulty. It continued, however, for some two centuries, when the outer pier having been destroyed, the new mode was introduced.

Portland capstone casing of solid materials, well worked, arises from a deep foundation, and is filled with solid masonry of cow-stone. The blocks of Portland capstone (that above the Portland stone of commerce for architectural purposes) are worked to a fine joint, and are united by oak dovetails, and secured to the blocks below by iron bolts. Thus the whole forms one solid mass. There are at intervals of a few feet cross-courses of Portland stone.

Marine constructions such as this must necessarily be very

costly, compared with the expense of a dry wall of squared cow-stone collected three miles to the westward, without any payment having to be made for the latter, as there is a royal charter granting the same. Notwithstanding, the economy of the new method is much greater. Once built, the work will remain, we may believe, for centuries, while the old plan led to outlays every year, either in taking down parts that threatened to fall, or which had been breached by the sea.

The several ground-plans of so ancient a work "enforced in the main sea," as a petition describes it, may prove interesting in connection with this account of marine architecture, if for no other reasons, at least that it still exists, whereas the fury of the elements has destroyed every other similar work. (See the head of this article.)

Canynge's Mark.

The Subject extended to the transporting Rocks from the Shore of West Dorset and E. Devon, by Means of Casks, Butts, Vats, or Tuns.

So early as Queen Elizabeth's reign, in 1585, the men of Lyme complain that they have to fetch the cockle rocks two miles further than before, having used all that lay on the shore near the Cobb; and that all things were become dearer than they used to be.

Doubtless great casks were used in very early reigns to

float home the rocks, and which are mentioned as the town vats, butts, casks, or tuns.

	£	s.	d.
Rich. Wright, Mayor of Lyme in 1617, charges for 24 butts and their charge in London - - -	6	16	0
Freight down - - - - -	7	5	6
Item, of Mr. Evans of Exon for the great vats -	15	4	0

Mr. Rob. Bragg, mayor in 1619 enters thus:—

Paid for hammers and nails for mending the cobb casks	0	5	0
In 1643 one Minson bought 12 casks at Bristol -	6	4	6

London, Exeter, and Bristol supplied what we may presume no cooper in these parts was skilful enough to construct.

Carts for drawing great stones to the sea-works were made at Lyme in 1661; these would now be called *stone-carriages*. The present carts would have been, at the before-mentioned date, called *ploughs*.

In 1663-4 Walter Tucker, mayor, enters:—

	£	s.	d
Paid for a boat to carry Capt. Alford and myself to the west land to look after the workmen (there being no cockle except at a distance) - - - -	0	3	0
Mr. Nath. Butler, mayor in 1690, received from Mr. Courtenay, a townsman, who was building some wall not of the old sea defences, for damage done to the town tuns lent him - - - -	6	18	2

A few entries will throw light upon the subject:—

A. D.	£	s.	d.
1699. J. Morris and J. Rendall, coopers, for hoops and work about the cobb tuns - - -	2	5	6
1707. Saving the tuns in the great storm - -	0	2	4
1707–8. Nine men's labour placing the great rock -	0	4	6
1709. Two coopers' notes about the tuns - -	9	14	0

		£	s.	d.
1715.	Lathy and Denning bringing a large rock by agreement - - - - - -	2	0	0
	Lathy and Seaward for bringing 43 bendings of stones and rocks for the cobb, each bending being three carriages of four large casks - - - - -	43	0	0
1729.	Four new tuns - - - -	4	0	0
	34 doz. hoops, and setting them - -	15	16	0
	Cooperage - - - - - -	2	8	0
	2 men three days to put them into water -	0	15	0
1769.	J. Fudge and others for bringing 4 large rocks at the Cobb gate, at 1*l.* 7*s.* per rock -	5	8	0
	Chains for the tuns - - - - -	3	0	3
1769.	Rich. Churchill Davie, the cooper, tuns and trimming - - - - -	11	2	9
	There are many entries about this date, amounting to about - - - -	48	0	0

The rocks at the mouth of the river, to prevent the channel from being deepened, were floated thither about this date.

The corporation of Lyme found casks, boat, and chains. The workmen charged by the bending of three carriages of four large casks each at 20*s.* each bending. If forced to unbend by bad weather, they were allowed 6*s.* a bending. Some rocks weighed from 7 to 10 tons.

The bringing in of a Supply of Water into Towns; the Pitching and Paving of the Streets, with Details of the Efforts made from the Reign of Henry VIII. to effect Local Improvements in the above Particulars.

If it be true that Rome was not built in a day, it is equally so that neither were the towns of this country expanded into their present growth and condition, replete with so many conveniences, without the fostering aid of time, thought, labour, and development, sometimes slow, at other epochs more accelerated, as circumstances favoured or not.

A needlewoman, upon the point of signing an agreement to emigrate to some part of Australia, refused to go when she found there were no shops. "She could not imagine a place," she said, "without shops; she could not bring it to her mind." Can we realise the state of our country towns before an era of improvements broke upon them? We think not.

About the era of the Reformation came one of social development, of progress which obscure country towns felt. There were doubtless some remarkable exceptions.

The city of Worcester was first paved by Bishop Gifford, as we learn, so early as the year 1281, which means that the streets were pitched or laid with stone. Nearly three centuries after that city had no foot pavement, as we now understand the word; for when Queen Elizabeth visited it the soyles or unpaved ground in front of the houses were to be *gravelled* beyond certain limits, and within those limits to be *paved.*

Even the model city London, the metropolis, the emporium, the residence of the Court, occasioned the first act in the Statute Book for paving a highway between the Strand Cross and Charing Cross, A.D. 1533, though the first general statute did not pass till the year 1555.

The Act recites that the streets were "very foul, and full of pits and sloughs, very perilous and noyous as well for the king's subjects on horseback as on foot." When the sovereign went to Parliament, fagots were thrown into the ruts in King's Street.*

How interesting to witness the well directed efforts of men evidenced in distant and distinct movements! Some latent energy appears to have slumbered, and it breaks forth almost simultaneously. Happily it is one of progress, as peaceful intercourse must be.

* Timbs' Cur. of London.

Of the towns of England feeling this movement, let us instance that of Lyme. The mayoralty of John Hassard is rendered memorable by the "Paving," *i. e.* pitching the West Street, now known as Broad Street, and the "Getting in of the Water." Paving in the modern acceptation, then styled "setting of broad stonys," was also had recourse to.

The promoters of this useful measure caused the town to be extended on the healthy slope of a hill, whereas before it was confined to a comb or valley. This street and its extension forms the best part of Lyme.

The effect of some novel introductions may be problematical, and require experience before we can pronounce decidedly in their favour; but the forebodings resorted to in many other cases are truly of a nature to create a hearty laugh at the habitual "prophets of ill." About the same date umbrellas and smooth pavements at the sides of the streets made their appearance. Some gentlemen abjured both, and never availed themselves of either; they saw what was decidedly effeminate in both these novelties. Men whose feet were never tried by rough pitching must degenerate by becoming effeminated, they affirmed, as would those be who never got wet through; so they in self protection walked on the round rugged flint pitching, and streamed with rain.

If cleanliness be next to godliness, we must rejoice that some clever person pointed out how a supply of running water might be procured, and this, too, where no funds existed for a costly aqueduct or any similar work.

A small provincial town was to be blessed with a running stream of water. And what did the inhabitants before this improvement? Let those who believe our ancestors could have done very well without many of our modern introductions reflect upon the toil, the labour, the inconvenience that all must have felt before the reign of Edward VI. The townsmen of Lyme had to fetch water from a greater or less distance. Some in the West Street, now Broad Street, had a right to go peaceably to an *accustomable well,* which one William Long, in 1586, interrupted them in doing. Our ancestors in every part of the realm were badly supplied with water. In their household expenses charges for fetching water from a distance enter largely. In the household roll of Eleanor, Countess of Leicester, A.D. 1265, appears an entry for carrying water to the establishment when the Countess was at Dover. *In aqua deferenda ad opus comitissæ,* 14*d.**

The conveying water by buckets or in pitchers from a river or well a quarter or half a mile from the residence is a laborious task. In the reign of Edward III. the inhabitants of the city of York found it useful to employ *Water-leders* or water carriers to bring them pure water from the Ouse and other sources. So it was till recently at Shaftesbury in Dorsetshire, and continues so in that semi-barbarious city Madrid.

Leaden pipes conveyed spring water to London city from Tyburn in 1236; and in 1285 the first great conduit of lead was begun there. In 1442 Henry VI. granted to John Hatherley, Mayor, license to take up 200 fother of lead. The pipes from Highbury brought in the water in 1483. We may learn how much was thought of this useful work by the fact that the Lord Mayor, Aldermen, and many worshipful persons used to ride and *view* the conduit heads at Tyburn; and after dinner there, somewhat different from recent sportsmen, they hunted a fox.

The water-works at London Bridge were established in 1512. In 1534, two-fifteenths were granted by the Common Council for defraying the expense of bringing water from Hackney to Aldgate to a conduit. But Peter Morris did not bring his supply of water to the highest parts of London till the year 1569, and Sir Hugh Middleton's far-famed New River was only rendered available in 1618, that is, a space of sixty-eight years after the introduction of a stream of pure

* See the Roll in the publication of the Camden Society.

water into the western parts of the town of Lyme in Dorset.

Leland furnishes us with information respecting a memorable improvement in a country town some little time before the date of our step forward in the right direction.

"Parson Edmundes (Dr. John Edmund inducted 1496) of late dayes perceyving the great lak of water at Petworth, causid chiefly a great spring, the hedde whereof is about a mile from the toune, to be brought in lede to Petworth, part of the water cumming to the manor place, part to the parsonage, the residue to ii or iii places yn the streate of the toune." *

In 1582 Peter Maurice, the German engineer, had a lease granted him by the city of London of one arch at the north end of the bridge as a place for fixing his engine to supply the city with water.

The movement became almost universal. The want of a good supply of fresh water caused Mr. Thomas Barfoote, Mayor of Melcombe Regis, and the inhabitants, to write a letter to Francis Howard and his lady to obtain their consent, 9th Sept. 1593. They desired to erect one conduit or more in the common called "South Down," in their manor of Sutton Poyntz. He and his lady permitted the same, and in their letter styled it "a godly enterprise."

The town conduit was the great place for gossiping. When many came for water, some had to wait, and the town news was discussed.

A loose paper, headed "Getting in of the Water and Paving the West Street, John Hassard, Mayor, 1550," contains a list of the subscribers' names, and the sums given. These vary from 4*d.* to 8*l.*, the average of small contributions being about 2*s.* 6*d.*

The amount of subscriptions was 29*l.* 2*s.* 4*d.* This was 11*l.* short of the expense, which came to 41*l.* 18*s.* 11*d.* for the charge of getting in of the water from St. Andrew's Well, and equalling or levelling of the street and

* Leland, edit. Hearne, vol. vi. p. 30.

paving of the same, and also making of the gutters and wall.

The items of charge were: —

	£	s.	d.
Equalling of the street - - - - -	2	0	0
Wages, $6\frac{1}{2}$*d.* a day, without meat - - -			
$5\frac{1}{4}$*d.* a day for meat - - - -	0	0	$11\frac{3}{4}$
A labourer for his work altogether - -			
A man and 2 horses, a day - - - -		1	2
Two ploughs (*i. e.* carts) to carry away stones -		1	8
Meat and drink besides - - - -		0	4
520 yards of paving (*i. e.* in modern language *pitching*), at $1\frac{1}{4}$*d.* - - - - -	3	5	0
Setting of brode stonys (*i. e.* in modern language *paving*), 2*d.* a yard.			
A sack of lime - - - - - -		0 0	8 6
A pair of pots, 2 panyers and 3 scoops - -		1	5

Extended arrangements for promoting the comfort, health, or luxury of mankind, are necessarily found to demand more or less attention to obviate new and before unheard of, indeed never contemplated evils.

It was found at Lyme that a new officer was required, a water bailiff. Robert Lerstock was appointed at a Court of a View of Frank Pledge, in 1596, to that office (probably there was one from the first) to make clean the water-courses and lakes for the pot water running into the town. In 1769 there were two officials, one for the east, the other for the west pot water. The former had been presented for neglect of duty.

The water ran into the town by an open channel in the middle of the street, above the town cistern, to the time of some persons lately deceased. There was so little travelling that the packhorses did not much foul the water.

Even as uncivilised man is not in a state to receive, because he does not comprehend, and therefore cannot appreciate and benefit from liberty, which is to him only an occasion for licentiousness, so it is with the advancing steps of civilisation. The proper use of the running water was so little regarded by the filthy and lazy, that all would have lost the benefits of the wholesome cleansing stream had not authority stepped forward with powerful hand. We may learn, from the history of the fresh water of towns, how sad a picture would our communities present if there were no ruling powers. The good, the pure, would be the victims of the impure and disorderly.

Before running water is mentioned as a blessing enjoyed by the inhabitants of Leicester, the corporation were obliged to order, A.D. 1467, that no woman do wash clothes or other corruption in the common wells.

An order of the court of Lyme, A.D. 1608, has it, that none do wash their books in the street under a penalty of 6*s.* 8*d.*, a large sum for a poor person to pay. Thus was the pure running water defiled by parties taking out their books, or family linen requiring to be washed, into the street.

Sir John Falstaff pictures his position in a buck, or book-basket, into which he was

> "Ramm'd with foul shirts and smocks, socks, foul stockings, and greasy napkins, that, Master Brook, there was the rankest compound of villainous smells that ever offended nostril."
>
> *Merry Wives of Windsor*, Act. iii. Scene vii.

Shakspeare again uses the words —

> "She washes bucks here at home."
>
> *Henry VII.*, Act. iv. Scene x. ii.

The dipping places were called *pills* — perhaps a corruption of *pools*; and the running water, the *shute* lake.

Widow Tilman was to no more wash her maulkin in the pot water, under a penalty of 3*s.* 4*d.* for each offence. This woman with her maulkin, or wool oven-brush, fouled all the town water below her residence.

By Charles the Second's reign houses began to have pipes conveyed into their interior. This was viewed with an evil eye; so much so, indeed, that the corporation was presented at a court leet, in 1682, for suffering so many water-pipes to draw away the water, to the detriment of the adjacent neighbours.

The whole of the town water was leased to James Hooper, plumber, of Lyme, for one hundred years, at a yearly rent of 10*l*., 28 Oct. 1706, who was to lay down pipes, and supply the inhabitants at a reasonable rate, which is now about 15*s*. each house.

Lest an investigation of the practices of antiquity should lead to pride on national or local grounds, or as being moderns, that we have shaken off the night that obscured the past, an occasion is here taken to mention that these boasted recent improvements are not all new. Sir H. Rawlinson has deciphered an inscription upon a great slab found on the banks of the Euphrates. Among other similar matters, the introduction of water into Babylon, and such particulars in detail, are recorded. The moderns have indeed been anticipated.

The Paucity of many Articles of great Convenience in daily Life.

THE fascinating pictures of early convivial scenes like many other vistas of the past, viewed through Time's telescope, mislead the modern many. Still they are true pictures. Allowed; but they are features of the past, taken from kings, dukes, and the powerful. The many gaze with admiration, and apply in their mind's eye the splendour of royal and lordly halls to the dwellings of the humbler classes of burgesses and inhabitants of small country towns. Cloth of gold and costly silks were early used, but not by the middle classes, if there was really such a class. This topic might be pursued to a great length. The utility would be what ought to be the object of all inquiry — the elucidation of truth. Instead of pining and whining over the decline of hospitality, the disuse of what are called the good old customs, if we pursue the subject we shall discover how comfortless the past was by comparison with the present; that the days of Good Queen Bess were bonny for the great, but miserable for the smaller folk. Many of our notions of the past were erroneous. Present but the reality and the delusion under which we have laboured becomes manifest.

In the fancied good times a hundred little conveniences were wanting, which are now indispensable. Treen trenchers were not so good as pewter platters. These were scarce, or Sir Lawrence, Vicar of Lyme, would not have left some to be let out for the use of the poor. Simples had not the efficacy of our mineral and foreign drugs, that attack disease at once in its strongholds, and soon obtain, if there be not a speedy death, a joyful victory. But let reality be our aim. Learn what value was once attached to what are reckoned very common articles now-a-days.

An able antiquary has furnished additional confirmation of these views.*

On the suppression of the order of the Temple in 1309, a survey was taken of their houses, from which it appears that at their chief mansion, the New Temple in London, the brethren all slept in a common dormitory, the master only having separate lodgings; a state of things scarcely reconcilable with the statement of those writers, among whom Sir Walter Scott is pre-eminent, who attribute great wealth and luxury to the order.

The fact is, however, that it has been too much and too long the custom to view the manners and habits of remote times through a medium highly tinged with the results and conveniences of modern life, and, therefore, they have been seen under a false aspect; it is only by looking carefully into the day schedules of the household effects of our remote ancestors, and taking the number of their pots and pans,

* Architecture of the Middle Ages.

their beds and tables, and other domestic goods, that we can be enabled to judge how meanly they were lodged, and how far from luxurious their daily mode of life must necessarily have been.

Read the will of Isabel Fossyn, or Fauchin, of Lyme.* It savours of another age. Who can dwell upon the legacies therein recorded without feeling great interest in the several particulars, and the articles so generously bequeathed? These things were regarded as treasures, and as such were bequeathed to the beloved and the deserving.

Will of Isabel Fossyn.

Archives of Lyme Regis, 1508.

In dei nõie, Amen. The 10th day of August, the yer of our Lord, M. S. VIII., and yn the yere of Kynge Henry the VII. 23th Issabell Fossyn wydow of Lyme Regis, yn the county of Dorset, hold of mynde and fresse of memory, make my testament yn thys maner: fyrste, y bygueve my soole to Almygthy God; my body to be byryd yn our lady chapell of Lyme forseyd; also y geve to the repacyone of the cathedrall churche of Sar, iiij*d.*; and to the stoore of the church of Uplyme, vi*s.* viii*d.*; and to the repacyon of the Cobbe of Lyme, vi*s.* viii*d.*; to my curat for my forgetyng tethys, ii*s.*; also y will that the last wyll of John Fossyn, my hoosband, be well and trwly pformed accordyng to the tenõ and effecte of hys testament; also y geve to Emott Lewys of Axmynster my best blew gowne, an apron, and a thredon kercheff; to John Morook a brasyn pott †, a panne, a payre of schetys, a bord cloth, xii yerdys of lyncloth, a lytyll cofer, and xx*s.*; also to Johañe Crewe a vylett cortell, a vylett tryppe goune, my best mantell, and a lytell federbedd ‡; and y

* The last of the Fauchins resided in Guernsey, and has died within the last twenty-five years. The property went to T. Andros, Esq., whose heir was one of the jurats, now deceased.

† Kitchen utensils in a former age were not only deemed worthy of being bequeathed with all due solemnity, but were sometimes included in royal inventories. The inventory of the jewels of Edward III. gives a list of his Majesty's frying pans, gridirons, spits, &c., as j patella ferri pro friaturâ, iiij broch ferri magni.—*Domestic Architecture*, Parker.

‡ There were very few beds or bedrooms either in town or country houses. Beds were esteemed very valuable.

geve to the same Johñe and to the heyres of hyre body, lawfully bygetyn, my burgage yn the which John Coppe now dwellyth yn for ev[9]more. But for defaut of yssew of hyre body lawfully bygetyn y give the forseyd burgage to the mayre of Lyme and hys successors for ev[9]more to pỹ for the soolys of John Fossyn and Isabell hys wyffe yn the frat[9]nie of oũ lady of Lyme forseyd. The resydew of all my goodys y geve to my ij sonnys Phylyppe Lyllyng and John Lylling, and make them my executors, that they well and trwly pforme thes pmysses, and the remayne to dispose to theyre mynde, part to them to lyve by, and parte for the welth of my soole; so all the lest (?) wey y wyll they kepe an obett honestly yerly, w[t]yn the church of Lyme forseyd dwryg

vi*s*. viii*d*.* vi*s*. viii*d*.

theyre lyvys, and I ordeyne John Borow, Willyaz Dare, and

iij*s*. iiij*d*.

Willyaz Tyttbyry supvisors of thys my testament they to see my laste wyll to be well and truly pformed, and to have for ther labor as it ys entlynyd yn thys wrytyng on theyre heddys. Wyttnys, John Borouth, notary public, Ric Cleffe, John Brit w[t] oder moo.

Inspect the archives of boroughs about the beginning of the sixteenth century. On how small a scale was everything conducted. How poor most men must have been. Everything did not stand in due ratio to each other. The comparative value of money has not been accurately assigned; and though many things were tolerable taken in reference to men and manners of the time, much misery had to be endured in various ways.

What has been remarked of the citing examples of manners and living from lordly halls will apply with equal effect to boroughs and their civic splendour. For truthful pictures we have drawn too much from London, Chester, Bristol, and such eminently famous cities.

Turn we now to an annual accompt of a small borough.

* The merchant spoken of by Leland, who built the house in the butter market, with a goodly tower at the entrance.

The Accompt of John Dey, *late Mayor of King's Lyme for* 1549, *taken by* Roger Garland, *his Successor.*—(*Town Accompt Book.*)

Received:

	£	s.	d.
First received for the town rent - - -	9	3	$0\frac{1}{2}$
Item, of the porters - - - - -	1	0	0
{ of John Gay for his standing in the shambles		13	4
of Balston - - - - - -		10	0
of White, 5*s.*, Loome, 5*s.*, Hodder, 6*s.* 8*d.*, Sprake, 6*s.* 8*d.*, Woodcock, 5*s.* - -	1	8	4
Sum - - -	12	14	$8\frac{1}{2}$

Allowed:

	£	s.	d.
First allowed for the mayor's fee - - -	2	0	0
Item, steward's fee - - - - -	1	0	0
recorder's fee - - - - -		13	4
butler for the Exchequer - - -			8
town clerk's fee - - - -		13	4
gathering of the town rent - - -		6	8
serjeant's fee - - - - -	1	0	0
keeping of the pound - - - -			4
looking to the Cob - - - -		1	8
Sum - -	5	16	0

For further illustration take a catalogue or list of the Town Stuff of a borough. Many of the articles were prized beyond any present value assigned to them. The conveyance had been comparatively costly.

Town Accompt Book, 1550.

Here ensueth such stuff *as Roger Garland, late Mayor of King's Lyme, hath delyvered unto John Hassard, nowe Mayor there, the 3rd Day of November, in the Fourth Yere of the Reigne of our Soveraigne Lord Edward the Sixth, by the Grace of God of England, Fraunce, and Yrland, King, &c.*

First, iiij water bushels, three of theym with bands of yron and oone with owte.

Item, oone strik and a yron to strick potts.

Item, a payer of balannce.
xxviij pound of brasen weighte and oone pound of small weights.
xj pies of leden waights conteyning xxij.
a boke for assise of bread.*
two yrons to mark w[t] all.
the scale of the mayor's office.
two hookes of yron w[h] chaynes.
a case of counters.

Stuff delyvered to Thoms Battyn and Nicholas Hassard, Receivers for this yere following.

First, a crane, a shever of brasse w[h] a pyn of yron.
Item, two shyvers of wood, and a cock of brasse, and yron pyn.
two pickesses.
iiij barres of yron.
two barowes.
a sledge of yron.

At the beginning of Queen Elizabeth's reign, A.D. 1560, the Town Stuff was increased by many articles:—

Item, two pecks of land measure.
two cabonets of Jersey measure.
three hanging locks for the prisons [padlock].
a pynt pot of pewter.
three ale quarts of timber and iiij gillis.
a payor of Allmon rivets complete.†
(6 bows, 2 black billis, 2 dagars.
Whistle of silver for Cobb ale, 2 barrels of gunpowder.)
A payor of Shereman's sheres that John Denyng did give.
a payor of manakells of yron.
Ten cartuches of canvas.
oone symyn of yron [symmyne].

Additional articles in 1562:—

Pair of corslets complete.
A great brooche [spit] of yron.‡

* This book was used to contain entries of the price of bread fixed by the Mayor at a sessions or assize.

† Alman ryvets; a light kind of armour because riveted after the old Almayne fashion.

‡ For the feasts then kept at Mayors' houses, or for the Cobb ale.

It is not always easy to realise the state and extent of accommodation our country towns afforded before the introduction of railways, and the making of roads as a substitute for the narrow lanes which alone had been the channel of communication. What advantages did not every one forego by not having ready access and speedy communication with his fellow man some leagues off? The division of labour was not realised to any great extent. This cannot happen except where the means of intercourse are cheap and rapid.

Orders for various articles might be sent to many cities, but nothing would be returned.

When William of Wickham was building Windsor Castle, Adam de Hartyngdon had the control of the works. He was obliged to have all the metal work executed on the spot, and forges and furnaces were built for the smiths and plumbers. No supply of coal could be had in the metropolis, so the king's master of the works bought a cargo at the pit's mouth in Durham.*

Let us compare the executing work in Dorset in 1609, as by an entry in the Lyme Cobb Accompt Book:—

Paid to Mr. Hill for iron, and delivered it to Guppy to make nails for the Cobb boat, 9*s.* 6*d.*

Thus we learn that the blacksmith had to turn nailer for the occasion, and we may infer what had to be repeated in many branches of artificers' trades. Hence, what delay, expense, imperfection, and general inconvenience must have been occasioned. We need not be surprised that the conveniences of life were few. A just and proper division of labour did not then obtain.

While on the subject of a boat for the Cobb or harbour, let us add that there was purchased, in 1617,

	£	*s.*	*d.*
A new town boat - - -	7	0	0
A cwt. of pitch to careen the same -		8	0

* Turner's Domestic Architecture.

These charges were greatly in advance of what would be paid in the present day.

To the question, what was barbarism? a reply was made: A time when bows and arrows were hung up in men's houses, and querns (or small hand-mills) were used, many hundreds of years ago. These articles have, however, been retained at a period much less remote. Bows and arrows were the later.

At Castle Combe, so late as 1556, no tenants of the manor were to keep in their houses any mill called *quyrnez*, that is, *querns*, because they ought to grind at the lord's mill under a forfeit of xx*s*.*

Thus, in the heart of our West of England, did old customs and practices linger beyond the dawn of modern civilisation.

Ships were small; carts and carriages rare; clothing dear; many vegetables unknown. The shops were open to the streets, and not glazed; books were scarce, and very dear. Hundreds of articles, each a great convenience, saving of time, and promoters of elegance and neatness, had never been heard of. The shank bones of sheep were formerly used for skates.

Country shopkeepers not only keep large and miscellaneous stocks of goods, but they can speedily procure anything from the metropolis and other great towns at the price the same articles sell for where they are made. So great was the charge for conveyance before turnpike roads and railroads that many articles were sold according to the distance from their place of manufacture, and some were virtually from the same cause excluded. Very many articles shopkeepers did not keep; such were only to be procured as fair time came round.

Iron wire was first drawn in the Forest of Dean about the year 1565, and sail-cloth was not made in England till about the year 1591.

Country houses were generally without ceilings. Plaster

* G. P. Scrope, Esq., M. P., History of Castle Combe.

of Paris was brought to Southampton in the reign of Edward III., but we may state it was only used for the houses of the great. A ceiling with an ornament was a rare thing in country towns in the reign of Queen Elizabeth. The flooring of the upper story had its lower part white-washed; this is now hid by the ceiling.

Introduction of Luxuries.—Chimneys.—Pewter, &c.

THE investigator of antiquity stumbles at every step upon proofs of the great deficiency of the necessaries and conveniences of life in Tudor reigns. Articles now common amongst the lowest cottagers were scarce to a degree, and artificers must have been few in number, even taking into account the small population. When John Mores, Mayor of Lyme in 1562, resigned his office to Robert Davie, his successor, that worthy handed over, among the few articles that constituted the *Town Stuff*,—

> Three ale quarts of tymber (! !) and 4 gills.
> A pint pot of pewter.

The introduction of vessels of pewter in the place of treene (*i. e.* wooden) ones, particularly platters and silver and tin spoons as substitutes for wooden articles, is noticed by the chronicler Holinshed as remarkable proofs of the progress of what he calls "luxury." In the village where he lived were old men dwelling, who remembered when a man would hardly find four pieces of pewter in a good farmer's house. The prices of things in Elizabeth's reign were doubled. There began to be a vast influx of the precious metals from Mexico and Peru.

While on the subject of pewter at this period, a curious charitable bequest claims special attention.

Twenty-four pewter platters were given by Sir Lawrence,

i. e. Mr. Lawrence, Vicar of Lyme, to be lent yearly for the profit of the poor.*

This Sir Lawrence appears with Ellesdon as patrons of the living. We are not to understand that these platters were lent to the poor who used wooden trenchers, but were lent out perhaps for the *Cobb Ale*, a great feast, and other feasts, and the money paid was appropriated to the use of the poor.

A pewter platter taken in distress about this date was valued at 1*s.*; a tynnen quart, 10*d.*; a square tynnen pot, 6*d.*

The time was not distant when (if not now) there was the "Town Pewter," for the mayor's use and that of the company, who, in the language of the chronicler, found "the means to obtain or achieve such furniture as heretofore has been impossible."

We learn from many sources how scanty were the articles of domestic furniture, and how few of the appliances that add to the convenience of mankind had been introduced, On considering this we are ready to exclaim: —

"Sardanapalus had not then arrived
To teach what might in chamber-gear be done."
POLLOCK'S *Dante*, Canto xv.

The conveniences of life are first named "luxuries;" then, when firmly established, "necessaries." So it was in the time of "good Queen Bess." Many, like our good chronicler, viewed the introduction of novelties with aversion. He conversed with the old men, who remembered when there were only about two or three chimneys in a town, except in some religious house, manor place, or great parsonage. Each made a fire against the reredosse in the hall, where he dressed his meat and dined. In a bird's-eye view of the coast and towns in the Cotton Library, intended to show where the beacons were placed at the time of the expected coming of the Armada, towns, villages, forts,

* Town Accompt Book, p. 21.

and castles are purely conventional. The houses of the towns have no chimneys, but there is one house intended to represent the manor, squire's house, or parsonage, which has that novelty. The chimney marks the artist's idea of a great house. The old men, sympathising with Holinshed, went on to compare the great amendment in lodging. They had slept full oft on straw pallettes covered only with a sheet under coverlettes made of dog-swaine or hop harlots, and a good round log under their heads instead of a bolster. Pillows were thought meet only for women in childbed. As for servants, if they had any sheet it was above them, to keep them from the pricking straws that ran oft through the canvas, and raised their hardened hides. The old men bewailed the effects of the change. The introduction of chimneys had brought rheums, catarrhs, and poses, while, before pillows, heads did never ache! The improved mode of building had, according to their views, done much harm; for when houses were built of willow, the men were of oak, and when oak began to be used then were the men of willow. Thus will the enemies of improvement deceive themselves in anticipations, and in the realities when the changes have been effected. Stage coaches were to cause the extinction of hackney horses; guano was to produce universal disease, and when the cholera came it was attributed to that fertiliser, though miles distant from where any had been applied to the soil.

Should we omit, among luxuries, the *sedan* chairs introduced by Sir Samuel Duncombe in 1634, and which were used at once by the Duke of Buckingham, who has had the credit of introducing them?

The Cobb Ale of Lyme Regis. — The Puritan's Triumph over it. — Church Ales, &c.

> Mynstrellys had giftes of golde,
> Eight full days this fest was holde.

THE great festivity that claims this page could alone belong to Dorsetshire. No other county is known to have had a harbour by the name of COBB; while that had two, one at Swanage, the other at Lyme Regis, the only one remaining. Constructed during the reigns of the Plantagenets, its name is no longer to be derived with certainty. Its importance to the town and to the country at the back, including portions of several counties, was very great.

The ALE requires some remarks, though it was no

> "Marshalled feast
> Served up in hall with sewers and seneschalls."
>
> *Par. Lost.*

Scattered and unintelligible allusions to our great feast had been met with. Till 1848 no records allowed me to connect a narrative of this celebration, and I never conversed with an individual who had any knowledge or traditional account of so important an affair. In many places there are entries upon parish books, traditions well preserved, and here and there slight remains of Church Ales, Whitsun Ales, Clerk Ales, Leet Ales, Midsummer Ales, Lamb Ales, Bride Ales, and Scot Ales. Those who have known some obscure parish clerk "brew a peck o'malt" at Easter or Whitsuntide, which he sold with an Easter cake or bun to the mechanics of his vicinity, to enable them to keep the season, which they are scrupulous to do, saw only a shadow of an ALE. Such festive celebrations never survived the death-blow dwelt by the Puritans.

Beer was for the morning and evening draught, before tea was known; *ale* furnished the festive board, not for aid to a meal, but for indulgence.

An *ale* meant, four or five centuries ago, some good

malt liquor, brewed to be drunk in good fellowship by neighbours of the same parish; but as good drinking is said to require good eating, so an *ale* came to mean a *feast*,— a Church or Whitsun Ale, a Church or Whitsun Feast.

There were DRINKINGS in Lent, to which private persons and parishes contributed. There is much virtue in a name; though, like Whitsun Ales, these were allowed in King James's Book of Sunday Sports, while there was a canon against the drinkings.

These feasts were the prototypes of our great Cobb Ale. Justice to the rude and more enlightened forefathers of our hamlets and towns demands that the objects of the ancient *ales*, when strictly such, and after they became occasions for good eating as well as good drinking, should be explained.

Ales and fancy bazaars, or fancy-fairs, have precisely the same object, however paradoxical this may appear. A good end both had in view. This was the motive power. Now-a-day a parish school is without a residence for the teachers; an organ is wanted, or there is some opportunity for the respected middle classes and gentry to contribute to the furthering of what is good, and the cause of good for future years. While all approve and are provided with means, why do not all at once contribute? The manners of the day recoil from such a summary proceeding. The virtuous end justifies, and custom sanctions, a more circuitous course, while pleasure allies herself with innocent occupation, industry, and no little excitement. On some day of smiling summer, articles more varied than ever ship's Manifest disclosed are exposed for sale. There is no public eating and drinking, though much private hospitality. All are dressed in their best. Waverers are fixed, introductions take place, and bargains prove to have been made of more kinds than one. In a word, the good end in view has been compassed in a manner that the most rigid moralist cannot find fault with. This picture represents the present manners and mode of proceeding of the nineteenth century.

Let me now turn to an *Ale*, and entreat a charitable perusal of early manners and customs, which "Time marks, with change," so that a due allowance may be made for the institution, and the possible perversion or abuses that may have crept in.

The ancient church or Whitsun ales, like the recent meetings of gay people just described, had a good object in view. The repair of the church fabric, the occasional maintaining of orphans, the benefit of the common fund for the relief of the poor as at Castle Combe, &c.*, could have been provided for by pecuniary assessment or individual contribution; but such a method of proceeding yielded to one more accordant with the spirit of the age. The end was approved of; it was to be attained through the profits made out of festivity.

Before church-rates were established, there were voluntary assessments given of every man's good will towards the repairs of the church. In 1568, at the church of the Holy Trinity, Minories, London, 8*l.* 15*s.* 2*d.* were collected; the highest contribution was 2*l.*, the lowest 1*s.* 6*d.*†

The churchwardens brewed some ale, employing the most skilful parishioner as the real operator. As the ale — soon to become a feast — was annual, we must expect, as was the case, to hear of "the church chyttel," *i. e.* kettle, "the parish chettle or furnace," "the parish crock," and "the parish panne" for brewing the drink.‡

The apparatus now called the *batterie de cuisine* occasioned entries in accounts of the church stuff. In 1603, at Minchinhampton, the pewter for the church ale cost 26*s.* 6*d.*; the best pan, 24*s.*; the two broches (spits) and the pair of racks, 20*s.* 4*d.*; the furnace and the other pan, 55*s.* 3*d.*; for the pot, x*s.* A form at the same time is charged xii*d.*§

The church-house was mossed at Minchinhampton, in

* G. P. Scrope's History. The year 1490.

† Notes and Queries, No. 319.

‡ See Notes and Queries, Feb. 3. 1853, for mention of these in the churchwardens' accounts at Chudleigh, and 1*s.* 2*d.* for "the lone of the parish panne."

§ J. Bruce, Esq., Archæologia, vol. xxxv. p. 409.

1611, at a cost of 12*s.* 8*d.* Perhaps there were no rushes, or else moss was preferred.

At Tarring, near Worthing, Sussex, the church ale was holden without interruption from early times till the year 1548, the second year of the reign of Edward VI., when the parish, having lost 7*s.* 6*d.* by that festival, it was laid aside till 1559, when it regained its attractions, and was attended with profit.*

In 1515, 1*l.* 7*s.* profit was made.
1525. Making 4 quarters of malt for the cheyrche was charged 2*s.*
1534. *Item*, for Gode's goude for our bruying, 1*d.*

Now the worthy parishioners began to eat as well as drink: —

	s.	*d.*
4 cawvys are charged - -	13	9
2 wethers - - - -	4	1
2½ lams - - - -	2	7

In 1562 some worthies of Tarring feared, perhaps, that the feast would not remunerate; so we read: —

	£	*s.*	*d.*
1562. Received of devocion money to the ayll -		2	11
" cheyrche ayll - - -	11	1	11
" in weyt 2 quarters 1 bush., 1 peck.			
" in malt, 3 quarters 3 bushels.			

The two last entries record presents or devotion.

There is added by the same authority † —

Charges laid out by the Wardens.

	d.		*s.*	*d.*
Hoppes - - -	4	1 capyn and 4 lovys of		
Lygke of motton - -	4	breyd - -	2	0
2 Cawvys hedes - -	2	The cook, for his		
Quarterne of peper - -	10	wagys - -	2	0

* Topography of the Rape of Bramber, by the Rev. Edmund Cartwright, M.A. Fol. Vol. ii. London, 1830.

† Ibid.

	£	s.	d.		s.	d.
Nuns of cloys and mays - -			8	Wm. Pott, for his wagys - -	2	0
Saufrone - -			2	Edward Stacy -	1	0
Half a motone -		2	4	3 women for their wages - -	1	0
Vinegyr - -			4	The mynsteryllēs -	6	8
5 bushel of malt -		6	8	2 loydes of feyrs -	4	0
4 sheype - -	1	1	4	The drome pleyr -	1	0
4 calvys - -	1	5	7			
8 lams and one calf more - -	1	9	0			

At Broad Blundon, in North Wilts, the Whitsun feast gained 4*l.* 14*s.* profit.*

We have above full details of the cost of a rural parish festivity drawn from the locality itself. Another author states that two persons were chosen previously to the meeting of the Whitsun or Church ale, to be lord and lady of the ale, who dress as suitably as they can to the characters they assume. A large empty barn, or some such building, was provided for the lord's hall, and fitted up with seats to accommodate the company.†

Here they assemble to dance and regale in the best manner their circumstances and the place will afford; and each young fellow treats his girl with a ribbon or favour. The lord and lady honour the hall with their presence, attended by the steward, sword-bearer, purse-bearer, and mace-bearer, with their several badges or ensigns of office. They have likewise a train-bearer or page, and a fool or jester, drest in a party-coloured jacket, whose ribaldry and gesticulation contribute not a little to the entertainment of some part of the company. The lord's music, consisting of a pipe and tabor, is employed to conduct the dance.‡

No one was permitted at Castle Combe to brew so long as any of the church ale remained unsold.§

* MS. in the possession of J. Y. Akerman, Esq.

† Douce.

‡ See the drawing of a Whitsun ale jug, Illustrated London News, 2nd June, 1849.

§ G. P. Scrope's History. See Carter's Specimens of Ancient Sculpture.

The ales certainly originated from the wakes. Elverton and Okebrook, in Derbyshire, agreed to brew some ales, and bound themselves to attend each other's ales. Every husband and his wife were to pay twopence.

The festivities of a church ale were so associated with the fabric itself, that several pieces of sculpture at Cirencester and Chalk commemorate these merrymakings, in which music held an important place.

Grotesque Figures from the Porch of Chalk Church, Kent, illustrating the merry scenes of a Church Ale.

Philip Stubs thus breaks out, in moderate terms for him, against this popular vice and immorality of the time:—

"In certain townes!" (says he) "where drunken Bacchus bears swaie against Christmass and Easter, Whitsunday, or some other time, the church wardens, for so they call them, of every parish, with the consent of the whole parish, provide half a score or twentie quarters of mault, whereof some they buy of the church stocke, and some is given to them of the parishioners themselves, every one conferring somewhat, according to his ability; which mault being made into very strong ale, or beer, is set to sale, either in the church or in some other place assigned to that purpose. Then, when this nippitatum, this huffe-cappe as they call it, this nectar of life, is set abroach, well is he that can get the soonest to it, and spends the most at it, for he is counted the godliest man of all the rest, and most in God's favour, because it is spent upon his church forsoothe. If all be true which they say, they bestow that money which is got thereby for the repaire of their churches and chappels; they buy bookes for the service, cupps for the celebration of the sacrament, surplesses for Sir John [*i. e.* the minister], and such other necessaries," &c.

A poet, referring to the Puritans, writes: —

"These teach that dancing is a Jezabel,
And Barley-break the ready way to hell;
The Morrice idols, WHITSUN ALES, can be
But prophane relics of a jubilee.
These in a zeal t'expresse how much they do
The organs hate, have silenced bagpipes too;
And harmless May-poles all are railed upon,
As if they were the towers of Babylon."

RANDOLPH.

The return of Whitsuntide and warm weather inspired our countrymen in former times, and stimulated them to festivity. They had escaped a cheerless, and then a *coal*-less winter, without the comforts that disarm that season now-a-day of its terrors. To the poor, winter was a season of suffering, and to the rich it was one of denial, and often of suffering. A consideration of the former state of things must make us grateful. A consideration of this subject will remove any surprise at the joyous welcome with which summer was hailed. Each person was ready to exclaim with the poet, —

"With greater light Heaven's temples opened shine;
Morns smiling rise, evens blushing to decline,

Clouds dappled glister, boist'rous winds are calm.
Soft zephyrs do the fields with sighs embalm;
In silent calms the sea hath hush'd his roars,
And with enamoured curls doth kiss the shores."

DRUMMOND.

The purchase of a store of onions and carrots comprises all the duties of a house-keeper at some fairs in October, in lieu of what was formerly so important. The salting in, or saving animal food or flesh, was undertaken at this time. Much was covered with pig's lard, hence the word *larder*. Fresh meat was taken leave of till the following April or May, and salted food supplied its place. Indigestible and unwholesome to some constitutions, scurvy and cutaneous eruptions often relieved, says a writer*, while they gave warning of a disordered state in the stomachs and the blood of thousands of all ranks, nay, even of the opulent, because their appetites were more gratified in quantity than by quality. This made fresh vegetable food of great consequence in Spring and early Summer, and much edible herbage bore the general name of salads; thus we find their alterative value recited by Chaucer: —

" After that they went about
Gathering pleasant salads, which they made ete
For to refresh all grete, unkindly hete."

Frequent were the cases of attacks of great heat from the effects of diet. Water-cress was cried about the streets as

" Fine spring water-grass, fit for lad or lass."

It is a famous anti-scorbutic. All such were once doubly valuable when there were no turnips, and the severity of winter had cut off all the cabbage tribe.

Cabbages had been first introduced out of Holland scarce a hundred years, writes Evelyn, before his time by Sir Anthony Ashley, of Wimborne, St. Giles's, in Dorsetshire,

* Dowden, " Walks after Wild Flowers."

who first planted them. They were introduced into Scotland by the soldiers of Cromwell.

After these preliminary remarks let us now consider the Cobb Ale, the great festivity of Lyme, which probably dates from the destruction of the harbour in the year 1376.

No accompts exist before the time of Henry VIII., in which mention of it can be found. The first entries are those of Thomas Ellesdon, mayor, 1547, in this style:—

"*Item*, more I made of Cobb ale, 3*l.* 6*s.* 4*d.*"

All particulars of the festivity when it was only an ale, if ever such, and not a feast, are wanting.

When bishops preached sermons and encouraged good Christians to give at the church doors, to help maintain the Cobb, we must view with complacency the institution by which a fund was yearly raised for that express purpose. In the Cobb, the weather-beaten mariner found safety; and it enabled a large tract of country to export and import merchandise, when no other harbour within a great distance existed. The dues in some of these ancient harbours continued what they were originally, though the price of everything was so much raised, and the value of money kept declining. The early dues had become inadequate to the maintenance of this marine work. How preferable in every way was the plan of a convivial meeting to support the Cobb to that of England at large, adopted at this very period for a precisely similar purpose. The harbours and havens of England on the whole line of coast were out of repair. The only mode adopted for procuring money for their repair was by Lottery. The first on record in England was drawn in 1569. The prizes were partly in money, and partly in silver plate, and the profits went to the harbours. There were 400,000 lots, the drawing of which kept the people in a state of excitement for four months.*

The managers of the Lyme feast were dignified with the title of "Wardens of the Cobb Ale." The mayor's accompt

* Characters and Chronicles of the Stock Exchange, by John Francis.

book records, in 1555, the receipt of the sum, considerable at that date, of 16*l.* 15*s.* 3¼*d.*, from Thomas Dare and Alex. Davye, then officers with the above title. The practice was to choose the wardens yearly at the Guildhall, then situated in the Millhill or pit by the mill. Doubtless the choice fell upon individuals who were not likely, by their mismanagement, to mar the festive occasion. The proceeds of the Cobb Ale were duly carried to account. When money was wanted in 1591 for renewing the fee farm from the Queen by a new grant, Mr. Robert Hassard and Mr. Bydgood, who had both served the office of mayor, lent for the purpose respectively some 20*l.* out of the Cobb Ale money, which was repaid to the Cobb account.

Would that some contemporary had described the gaiety of the time. My labours in gleaning would have been spared.

The mayor for the time being was Lord of the Cobb Ale, and in comely and befitting ornament was not wanting. William Barret, some time mayor, had generously contributed to the dignity of the feast, by a present to the mayor of a WHISTLE with a CHAIN OF SILVER for this occasion. The form of this is lost. John Holcombe, mayor in 1559, acknowledges the receipt of these articles in his accompts, and sets them down as weighing eleven ounces. Spanish and Portuguese officers on board the great Carracks of this time are spoken of as wearing great whistles. The rude elements probably no more required a shrill and searching sound than did the din and uproar of so many revellers in the COBB HALL. Such was the name of the hall appropriated to the feast, and we may fairly add to the revels and the dancing.

> "Merry it is in halle to hear the harpe
> The minstrelles synge, the jogelours carpe."

An originator of jokes and witty dialogue was wanted to enliven the feast where so many guests sat so long around the festive board. None but large towns could keep a fool, who, by the way, it need scarcely be said was no fool, but a zany or merriman, whose business it was to prepare the jests that seemed to come, as many must needs have done, *impromptu.*

Many a private individual may now be found, on the occasion of great festive meetings, to set the tables in a roar by the exercise of a wit that takes with all. Ever and anon comes forth some ready joke that straightway produces the desired effect, and without being conscious of it the witty talker becomes a substitute for the mottled gentleman of ancient times.

The musical department being in 1595 incomplete, Mr. Vyney was paid for a basse horne for the Cobbe (Ale), 1*s.* 6*d.*

> "They had menstrelles of moche honours,
> Fydelers, sytolyrs, and trompeters,
> And else it were unright."

William Barrett's example was followed by Richard Barrett, who demised to the mayor and burgesses, in 1579, all that part of his house called the Cobb Kitchen in the tenure of John Cogan, in the corner between John Davey's house and the Cobb Hall there. The mayor and burgesses were to hold and enjoy the same Cobb Kitchen, with the commodities thereunto belonging, once every year at the feast of Pentecost for and during the whole time, and so long as the Cobb Ale and feast, for and to the Cobb use, shall continue and endure, so it exceed not twenty days, paying yearly 5*s.**

From an "account of the charges of John Roze,"† the

* Wedding feasts lasted a fortnight. That of Miss Moore, at the Blackfriars', London (Archæol.), is a notable example. Of the immense quantity of all kinds of victuals consumed, much was presented by friends, such as swans, cygnets, &c.; but this lady had been courted by Toby Matthew, who became an archbishop.

Indenture in the archives between John Seward, mayor, and R. Barrett, merchant. There was a *Church House* at Minchinhampton, where the feast was holden. The profit to the church generally amounted to from 3*l.* to 5*l.* per annum. After some occasional intermissions, the church ale was finally discontinued from 1589.—J. Bruce, Esq. Archæol.

† John Roze complained against Mr. Robert Hassard of a misde-

receiver, "which I have (he writes) laid out for the COBB HOUSE the 9th April 1601," much is to be learned.*

	s.	d.
Paid for 4 potels of wine with a banket (banquet or dessert)	4	0
grinding of the malt, the sum of - -	9	0
a present sent unto Mr. Fugemes - -	2	2
[Here the practice of giving a sprat to catch a mackarel is illustrated. Mr. Fugemes, in return for the present of shrimps, fish, or conserves, gave 15s.]		
4 hundred ½ of venison - - - -	10	6
[Was not this sum given to the gamekeepers or those who brought the venison?]		

Deer stealing was so common at this date that all the cooks' shops in London were supplied with stolen venison. Great men doubtless sent this as a present.

	£	s.	d.
Stivens to brew - - - - -		7	6
2 ton of casks and the hooping - - -	1	6	6
A bushel ½ of wheat to brew - - - -		5	0
George Rocquey's wife - - - -		10	0
38 lbs. of hops, at 8d. per pound - - -	1	5	0
Staigge to help to brew - - - -		3	11
88 bushels of malt, whereof 40 bushels were 8 gl. 2d., and the other 8 gl. amounteth - - -	11	18	0
25 lb. of butter - - - - -		5	3

This was a great dainty. Melted fat or lard was used where we now use butter.

	s.	d.
The crock to brew the ale [loan of it is presumed] -	2	0

meanour in the Star Chamber. The latter was to clear himself, but he compounded with John Roze.

Robert Hassard had been suspended, and was a professed favourer and upholder of John Geare, an unbeneficed preacher, who had been the cause of great factions and divisions.

N. B.—J. Roze was mayor 1611.

* Loose foolscap sheet in the search of 1843 trampled upon on the floor, and a duplicate half sheet.

The "Church House" is spoken of in the History of Castle Combe, by W. P. Scrope, Esq., M.P.

	£	s.	d.
Spent at Waffort (Wayford, near Crewkerne) in the purchase of commodities - - - - -	2	2	0
Shrimps and 21 chickens - - - - -		6	6
Goode and Niscon that went to begging - -			4

[A begging. This begging through the neighbouring towns and villages in London, and even at St. Maloes, was systematic.]

No shame is here expressed, any more than would be by one of a mendicant order who made begging an occupation in due exercise of his duty. The ultimate object of the feast, viz., the succour of the embayed and tempest-tost mariner, was a noble one.

	s.	d.
½ hundred of faggots - - - - - -	4	2

Wood was burnt for cooking the viands. As yet no coal was in use along our coast, still it was mostly applied to heat furnaces. Its noxious vapours were firmly believed in; so no cooking, much less the delicacies of a great feast, were exposed to the abominations of coal fire.

	£	s.	d.
Calfshenge and other victuals - - -	1	2	2
4 capons - - - - - - -		3	4
Richard Pamer - - - - - -		13	0
George Rocquay [and his wife were the chief cooks]*	1	0	0

"At dressur also he shall stonde
And sett forth mete dressed with honde
Ye spicery and store with hym shall dwelle
And mony thynges also as I noght telle."

	£	s.	d.
Lace for 7 doz. bread - - - - -		7	0
Candles, and for burch (wood) - - - -		5	6
Wood and (obliterated) - - - - -	2	3	6
Lace for victuals that he did buy - - -		16	0
Clatey for cakes - - - - - -		7	8
Wine - - - - - - - -	2	16	4

* There was a great brooche of iron (a spit) among the Town Stuff in 1562, handed by the mayor to his successor.

	s.	d.
2 Venice glasses and 8 other glasses - - -	4	0
One spong [see further on] - - - -	6	0
12 Coupes (cups) and bacon - - - -	9	0
Beef - - - - - - -	2	6
Unto Smalling back again - - - . -	5	0
Unto Bery back again - - - -	2	6
Paid at Burport (Bridport) when we went to bagging	4	3
John Piters for his cellar - - - -	6	8
Victuals - - - - - -	11	2
A platter that was (stolen?), and for vinegar - -	3	2
Powder and for hiring of horses - - -	10	0
[Powder for firing the town guns.]		
Westover - - - - - - -	8	6
John Davy to brew in his brewhouse - - -	10	0
Sum - - £33	19	1

The warden, Mr. John Roze, next accounts for his receipts, 12 June, 1601:—

	£	s.	d.
Received of Mr. Fugemes - - - - -		15	0
„ When we went to Brancon (Branscombe) and Beer and Colyton and Burport (Bridport) - - - - -	3	4	0
„ Axminster - - - -		8	0
„ Charmuthe (Charmouth) - - -		7	1
„ of the Handmaye (the "Handmaid," a vessel so named) - - - -		11	2
„ of those that went not with us at Waffort		8	0
„ of my wife and of George Rocquay's wife		5	0
„ in Wisson (Winsham) in Axmue (Axmouth) and other places - -	1	0	0
[The duplicate sheet had received of my wife Bagg in Opplam (Uplyme), 2*s.* 6*d.*]			
„ of the Londoners and of Mr. Brown -		18	0
Received the Tusdaye - - - -	16	0	0
„ Wansdaye - - - -	6	7	0
„ Thirsdaye - - - -	2	19	0
„ Frydaye - - - -	2	15	0
„ Saterdaye - - -	1	10	0

	£	s.	d.
Received the Sundaye - -	8	16	0
„ Tusday - - - - -	4	10	0
„ Fryday - - - - -	3	4	0
Received of Thomas Whee for a hogshead of beer, and paid him for his spices, &c. - - -		17	0
Received of Tinscons and Colson by me, John Roze	£55	19	1

We cannot learn how long the feasting or dinner lasted on each day. There was in those ancient festivities no precipitancy. Many hours, perhaps, saw no termination to the consumption of the good cheer, which the enchantments of vocal and instrumental music and jesting made to appear short.

A word or two about spoons, knives, and forks used at this date.

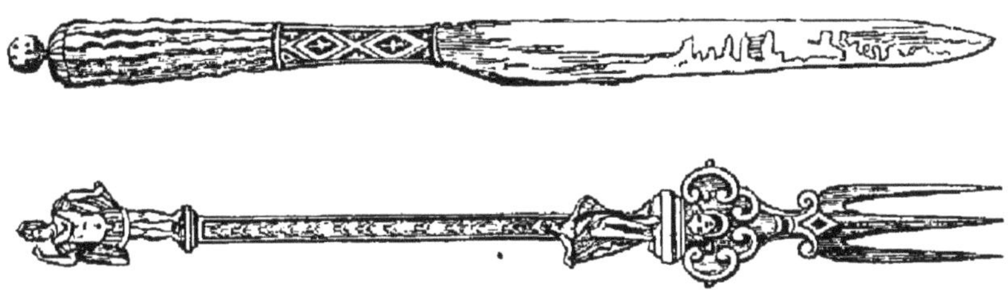

Girdle Knife and Fork.

Common spoons were made of horn. Knives were imported from St. Maloes in 1553, and cost from 2*d.* to 4*d.* each. They were first made in England in 1563. None are referred to as being purchased or in use at this feast. Forks are not mentioned. Silver forks came into fashion for invalids about the year 1680. Forks are said to be an Italian invention. Old Tom Coryate, whatever kind it may have been, introduced this "neatnesse" into Somersetshire about the year 1600, and was therefrom called *furcifer* by his friends. Alexander Barclay thus describes the previous

English mode of eating, which sounds very *ventaish*, although worse mannered: —

> "If the dish be pleasant, eyther flesche or fische,
> Ten hands at once swarm in the dishe." *

We ornament the knuckle of a ham with paper. This used to be placed for cleanliness, as each person took it when he helped himself.

In 1816, at the College of Valognes, in the department of La Manche, Normandy, dinner was served without there being any knives, except carving knives, placed at table. There was a fork for each pupil.

A clasp knife was taken from the pocket of each person, opened, and placed by his plate. After dinner many might be seen inserting the blade in the ground to clean it. Salt, in pieces about half the size of a pea, was served, and those at table taking a portion rolled their tumbler upon it to triturate it. Potatoes were such novelties that the cook did not know how to cook them.

There is no charge for vegetables. The cabbage tribe, some believe, was known early. How comes it that a cabbage appears at the feet of the monumental effigy of Sir Anthony Ashley, of Dorsetshire? Could his heir have ordered a cabbage to be sculptured without its full significance being intended? We think not.

Cider is not mentioned.

Thus the sum cleared for the benefit of the Cobb was no less than 20*l.* Upon the duplicate half-sheet it is mentioned that on Tuesday the sum of 16*l.* was taken at the Cobb House. The feast lasted eight days. The first day brought the greatest income; the following Sunday must have the next day in gaiety. There was received at St. Maloes, 1*l.*; at Morlaix in Brittany, 17*s.* 6*d.*; a gilten spoon was charged 10*d.*; the charger, 6*l.* 15*s.*

The contributors to the ale at Morlaix, London, and other places, were directly interested in the feast; for the outlay

* Ford's Gatherings from Spain.

upon the Cobb, which was for their safety and convenience, depended in some degree upon the profits realised on the occasion.

Andrew Davy and James Estmond, wardens of the Cobb Ale, made a return, in 1604, of a profit of 16*l.* 10*s.*

A Cavalier in Buff. A Puritan.

The Puritan party gained great influence at Lyme and in many other corporations. The companies of players were paid to go on to the next town without playing, for scenic representations came to be treated as horrors. Eight days' festivity, music, and mixed dancing, that is, the dancing together of the two sexes, must have raised a ferment. We must expect that the Cobb Ale would be assailed. The religious feuds in the corporation had proceeded to a great height in 1612; Mr. John Geare, the Vicar, having preached puritanically, had his license withdrawn; the Court had now taken part against the Geneva doctrines. Mr. Geare, now styled "an unbeneficed preacher" by his enemies, now procured an act, *i. e.* a lawsuit against the mayor and his brethren, and the Cobb wardens, *i. e.* the wardens of the Ale, for the using of profane and religious abuses. He was favoured by Robert Hassard, Gent. The opposite or Court party agreed that the action should be defended at the Town charge. They charged Mr. Robert Hassard with misdemeanours wilfully committed in his mayoralty, and laid the matter before the Star Chamber; and he was accordingly dismissed from his rule and place of magistrate. Some honourable person interceded, and Robert Hassard was restored, provided that he cleared himself by a judicial hearing in the Star Chamber, which he neglected to do. For this, and being a professed favourer of John Geare, he was expelled. John Viney was suspended for the latter cause, and was deemed unworthy of his place till, by some worthy fruits of his conformity and amendment, the Mayor, &c. be moved to alter or change the order."

The attack upon our great feast began so early as 1610, when the jury presented the constables for suffering unlawful games to be played at Beaufront, as well the Sabbath day as the week days. Such was the troubled state of the borough a type of others, till the Puritan party gained the ascendancy.

The Puritans were determined assailants. Thus writes the enemy of them:—

"Rather than fail, they will defy
That which they love most tenderly,
Quarrel with minc'd pies, and disparage
Their best and dearest friend, *plum-porridge*.
Fat *pig* and *goose* itself oppose,
And blaspheme *custard* through the nose."

BUTLER'S *Hudibras*.

Difference of opinion and religious animosity, in 1614, gave occasion for an entry of an order to restrain those of the corporation who probably carried on their wordy contentions in as nervous a style as this municipal enactment displays:—

It is this day ordered, enacted, and agreed by the mayor,

recorder, and his brethren the capital burgesses, that if any one chosen into the said company shall break out into any brawling, unusual, undecent, foul, lewd, or disgraceful speeches, either by comparison, obrayding, disdayning, scorning, misnaming, or abusing one another, or otherwise misdemeyne himself in proud, insolent, or scornful gesture or fashion of behaviour not fitting for the civil government of the place, he shall forfeit, for the first offence, 6*s.* 8*d.* for the poor; 2d offence, 13*s.* 4*d.*; 3d offence, dismissal.

Richard Harvy, merchant, collector of the customs, was sworn and admitted to the freedom of the town (gratis), and without any fine only in regard he vouchsafed to take the wardenship of the Cobb Ale for the benefit of the Cobb upon him, 30th May, 1610. In this entry we may, perhaps, see proof of the difficulty that began to be felt in procuring a Warden of the Ale. A reward, a distinction, had to be offered as an inducement for him to take office.

To undertake the management of such a feast was no light matter. It furnished subject matter for conversation the rest of the years.

Documentary evidence is wanting as to the precise date and the manner in which the celebration of the Cobb Ale ceased. It had its origin from an early date, perhaps from the first difficulties experienced in repairing the Cobb, and was a noted feast. It was a great fact. Let us not glean for little circumstances as to excesses or abuses. They doubtless existed, for who can use the gauds of life at all times in moderation? The Whistle and the Chain are unknown. The mayor sits unadorned on his bench, and is not called upon in his year of office to be Lord of the Cobb Ale. The cessation of so much annual jollity made many a townsman exclaim, in the words of the poet:—

> "O days to be desired! Age happy thrice
> If you your heaven-sent good could duly prize!
> But we, half palsy-sick, think never right
> Of what we hold, till it be from our sight.
> Prize only summer's sweet and musk'd breath.
> When armed winters threaten us with death;

In pallid sickness do esteem of health.
And by sad poverty discern of wealth.
I see an age, when, after some few years
And revolutions of the slow paced spheres,
These days shall be 'bove other far esteemed,
And like Augustus' palmy reign be deem'd."

DRUMMOND.

The Introduction of Coal into Domestic Use. — Wood Stealing, Local Laws and Punishments of Pollers of Trees, Hedge-tearers, &c.

"The grim ore
Is from its prison brought and sent abroad,
The frozen hours to cheer, to minister
To needful sustenance and polished arts."

JAGO'S *Edge-hill.*

HOWEVER hard to be believed, yet true it is that when some of our beautiful fabrics, the cathedral churches, had been completed, and our countrymen viewed them in their grand proportion and finish, unscathed as they were by time's rough hand, our southern population were ignorant of the now common article COAL. Some knew no more of that substance than the Spaniards living on the shores of the Parana, who, having heard from one of our countrymen that the British burned black earth for fuel, treated the statement as a fiction. A naval captain of a steamer*, in his recent ascent of that river, kindly furnished, by the present of a basket of coal, a refutation of the calumny upon the Englishman. This was not the only case in which the internal produce of our land deceived a stranger, if indeed he did not purposely describe what he had witnessed in enigmatical language.

Œneas Silvius, who afterwards assumed the purple under

* Mackinnon.

the name of Pius the Second, visited this country about the middle of the 15th century. He relates that he saw in Scotland poor people in rags begging at the churches, and receiving for alms *pieces of stone*, with which they went away contented. This was pit COAL. The Germans call it *stein* or *stone* coal. The two things were confounded.

To revert again to the use of coal away from the coal field. The time at length arrived in England when for certain purposes coal began to be used at some distance from the coal field, for furnaces, owing to the increasing price of wood, which smiths, brewers, and great consumers of fuel felt. Towards the close of the 13th century, the metropolis was supplied for the use of such trades from Newcastle; hence the name *Sea Coal*, because transported by sea, and to distinguish it from another article called *coal*. There is a street called Sea Coal Lane, by the Old Bailey, London.

One of the early uses of coal was for being dug into the earth to serve as land-marks, or boundaries, the substance being imperishable.

Coal, as an article of fuel for general purposes, was not thought of. Its use was special. The opinion formed of it as fuel was altogether unfavourable. An idea prevailed that its fumes corrupted the air, and exerted an injurious effect upon health.

For some purpose or another ten shillings' worth of coal was consumed at the coronation of Edward II., which was entered in the accounts as *carboun de meer pris al paleys al coronement.*

In 1325 a vessel from Pontoise carried corn to Newcastle, and took back coal.

At the mention of Newcastle and coal we might readily suppose that no explanation was here necessary. The case, however, is not so. The coal dug at the coal field by Newcastle formerly would not burn without wood, as the Northumberland House book shows, which proves that the miners had not then found means to win the deep strata known as the MAIN COAL.

The consumption of coal in London by the year 1306

was enough, it was deemed, to prove injurious; so the king was petitioned to stop the consumption of the noxious article in the city. King Edward I., by royal proclamation, prohibited the burning of coal under severe penalties. As wood began to be scarce, the royal command was disregarded, so that a commission was appointed for the purpose of ascertaining what persons used sea-coal, with power to punish by fine for the first offence, and afterwards by the demolition of the offending furnace.

Experience soon taught the great value of coal, and many persisted in employing it. This occasioned the passing of a law that made the burning of coal within the city to be a capital offence. One man was actually executed in the reign of Edward I. for the commission of this crime.

Lest it might be judged that it was only at a distance from the coal countries that ideas of the injurious or even noxious effects of the fumes of the fuel in question were entertained, it should be known that so late as the year 1349, in the religious house at Whalley in the very neighbourhood of the coal fields, peat and wood were alone employed. In the reign of Edward III. two *colliers* are mentioned in the archives of York, but the inference that they sold pit-coal is not supported.

The good monks, like the ladies, believed their complexions would be injured by entering a room where coal was burning. We need not wonder that persons would not eat meat which had been roasted at a coal fire. They anticipated some injury from so doing.

When the fire used to be lighted in the centre of the hall, coal was not so fit for the place, before chimneys were introduced, as wood.*

Coal.

Sir William Petty, who established Kenmare, co. Kerry, in 1670, found it a gainful speculation, when wood became

* See the Quarterly Review, No. CXCI.

dear in Sussex, to send iron ore to be smelted by means of the oak and arbutus of that country; thus spoiling the picturesque, and confining the wolves to a narrower range.

The Weald, which means the wooded district, is a tract extending from Kent to Hampshire, a distance of about 120 miles, by 30 miles in breadth. This, which the Romans named Anderida Sylva, was, according to Asserius, a great forest anterior to the conquest.

This weald, "Great Andradsweld" of Drayton, was the great iron country—the region of furnaces, castings of cannon of the earliest and improved pattern, all by means of wood in the form of charcoal, when fossil coal was not only not used, but was not judged to be ever available for iron furnaces.

A husbandman was expelled the town of Rye, in 1591, that place not being fit for such an artificer, the country all round for miles being a forest. Hammer Wood, Cinder Hill, Furnace Place, &c., are local names. The balustrades of St. Paul's, which cost 11,000*l.*, were from Sussex iron works.

The first cannon was cast in Sussex in 1535. In after years bonds were taken in 1000*l.* from the owners of the charcoal furnaces, that none should be sold till a license for the sale or issue of the ordnance had been procured. Fears were entertained that the enemy would purchase them.

Sir Anthony Shirley procured 100 pieces of cannon for the King of Spain. He served that monarch, who granted him a pension. There were two reasons for his engaging in this affair. He obliged his employer, and benefited his father Sir Thomas Shirley, a great manufacturer of iron in Sussex. Thus was patriotism wont, as now-a-day, to wither under the baneful shade of private interests. Enemies of our state can at all times find sellers of saltpetre and arms.—Spanish iron was largely used in the 14th century for the anchors of the English navy. In 1336, 11*s.* per cent. was paid for a great anchor, weighing 1100 lbs. when manufactured. The cost was 6*l.* 6*s.* 6*d.**

Just as the western woollen manufacturing district has furnished terms which have been transplanted to the north, the cotton counties of recent fame, so the iron country of former centuries, the Weald of Sussex, had terms in use which are now no longer heard nor understood there, except in the newer application of them instituted in the north, and in respect of an entirely different substance.†

The *coal* or cole of Sussex and of the greater part of England was Charcoal. A *collier* was one who burned wood into charcoal. The *coal wains* of Sussex were the carts that conveyed charcoal from the woods. Men were paid for *coaling*, that is, burning wood for a store of charcoal. The Rev. Giles Moore, in his diary, enters, "Luxford who coaled for me 15 cord, of which I had 8 coal wains full of coals, of which I sold to Thomas Young 3 loads for 2*l.* 11*s.* 0*d.* I paid Luxford for coaling the said pit 1*l.* 11*s.* 6*d.*" Thus the cost of burning fifteen cord of wood into charcoal is here recorded: the writer continues, "I had of Edward Snell for 12 bushel of my coals laid up 3*s.*" *Smaller* and *bigger coals* are terms often met with in reference to smelting. The "musical *small coal* man" of the last century did not sell pit-coal or sea-coal, but charcoal, faggots, and wood split up for lighting fires.‡ A *woodmonger* was a seller of wood.

A full explanation of this part of the subject will prevent much confusion and mistake in respect of the early mention of coals, colliers, and such terms now in use for another article.

Sussex was taxed annually at a considerable quantity of *coals, i. e.* charcoal, which was sent to the king's palaces. The king's purveyor, in 1615, demanded 400 loads for the following year, which was reduced to 250 bundles. In 1627 Lewes was assessed 58*s.* towards the provision of coal (charcoal) for the king's household.

* Issue Roll, W. N. 579, Sussex Arch.

† Sussex Archæol. Coll. ‡ Ibid.

So early as the year 1563 is an item of 40*s.* in the constable's account of Lewes about preferring a bill for the preservation of great timber. Wood was becoming scarce in many parts, and the want of it, as there was no sea coal for general use, was much felt. Tusser, like many other writers, took occasion to complain of some great evils of his time. He notes the reckless consumption of wood for fuel, and its immediate bad consequences:—

> "Some burneth a lode at a tyme in his hall,
> Some never leave burning till burnt they have all,
> Some, making of havock without any wit,
> Make many poore soules without fier to sit."

The iron furnaces near the downs by Brighton had caused timber and wood to be so scarce and dear that from 3*s.* 4*d.* a ton it had risen to 13*s.* 4*d.*; from 2*s.* 6*d.* a load of wood to 7*s.*; and from 6*s.* 8*d.* a load of coal, *i. e.* charcoal, to 14*s.*; from 2*s.* 6*d.* the hundred billot or tale wood to 8*s.*; and ship board from 16*s.* the hundred to 50*s.* the hundred.

The Duke of Richmond has a pair of metal curfews to cover a wood fire.

It is recorded that 12 acres of timber were worth in Sussex, in 1223, 2*l.* 13*s.* 4*d.* per acre.*

Old Fuller felt the scarcity of wood to be a growing evil. He was not one given to despair of the future, and writes, it is to be hoped that a way be found out to char the sea-coal in such a manner as to render it useful in the making of iron. The great iron-masters of the United Kingdom will smile at the hope here expressed. The years that have since elapsed enable us very fully to confirm the sound sense of the same writer contained in the following expression:—"All things are not found out in one age, as if reserved for future discovery, and that perchance may be easy for the next, which seems impossible for this generation." Lord Dudley discovered that coal was equally efficient as wood for the reduction of iron ore, and procured a patent, which was allowed to stand

* Sussex Archæol.

in 1623, when so many others were abolished. A deluded mob destroyed his works.

Glass, owing to the quantity of charcoal easily to be procured in Sussex, was manufactured at Chidingford in the reign of Henry VIII. In 1557 a poet writes:—

"As for glass makers, they be scant in this land;
Yet one there is, as I do understand;
And in Sussex now is his habitation,
At Chedingford he works of his habitation.*

James I. forbade the melting of glass with timber, or wood, or fuel made of the same.

Drayton, in his "Polyolbion," puts a complaint into the mouth of the Sussex forests, who personate the daughters of the Weald district upon their altered condition and reduced extent, owing to the iron works.

They bitterly exclaim:—

"These iron times breed none that mind posterity."

And in despair continue:—

"'Tis but in vain to tell what we before have been,
Or changes of the world that we in time have seen;
When not devising how to spend our wealth with waste,
We to the savage swine let fall our larding mast.
But now, alas! ourselves we have not to sustain,
Nor can our tops suffice to shield our roots from rain;
Jove's oak, the warlike ash, vein'd elm, the softer beech,
Short hazel, maple plain, light asp, the bending wych,
Tough holly, and smooth birch, must altogether burn,
What should the builder serve supplies the forger's turn;
When under public good base private gain takes hold,
And we, poor woful woods, to ruin lastly sold."

Song xvii.

The Romans found it necessary to restrain, by sumptuary

* T. Charnock's Breviary of Philosophy, quoted by Allen, Hist. of Surrey and Sussex.

laws, the expense of funerals and great consumption of wood in burning the bodies of the dead.

When forests are properly managed, it is, writes Tegoborski, sufficient for the wants of the country if they cover a fifth part of the surface.

In Russia the woods exceed in extent the superficies of the Austrian empire, and four times that of France. Still, as the winters are long, the trees of slow growth, and the people wasteful of fuel, a large proportion is wanted, and the empire is in many districts insufficiently wooded. So great is the demand for wood fuel in the absence of coal!

When was sea-coal or mineral coal first brought to the ports of the south of England?—is a question which may be asked. The solution of this has not been without difficulty.

Though in a list of customs duties at Poole in Dorset, A.D. 1341, "a quarter of coals" is set down as paying a farthing (the same as was paid for a salmon), we are not to suppose that sea-coal is designated. James Blount, Lord Mountjoy, had property at Poole, where he boiled alum in 1564. The fires were fed with turf, proving that sea-coal was not in general use there at that date.

In a carefully drawn up table of rates of customs payable at Lyme, dated 1490, there is no mention of such an article as coal.

John Tudbold, a beneficent merchant of that town, in his will dated A.D. 1548, gave his wood to the poor; but there is nothing said about a fuel named coal.

Searching among the dusty Cobb accompt books of Lyme Regis, there is found, that "The Grace of God" entered the Cobb from Bristol with *cole* July 19. 1569, and her dues amounted to 3*s.* 4*d.*

There was at this time a vessel belonging to the port of Poole*, of this name, of 50 tons burden. Her whole cargo was not needed, so a part was delivered, as was customary, and

* Sydenham's Hist. of Poole.

the craft proceeded to some other port with the remainder of this Welch pit coal. Soon after a vessel from Yarmouth brought some chaldrons of north country pit-coals. The first instance of a vessel being styled a *collier* is that of one which on her voyage, laden with culm, a variety of Welch coal, bound to Axmouth (*i. e.* Exmouth), was chased by Turkish pirates in the channel.

The port of Yarmouth had great comparative importance in the Tudor reigns. When the great plague raged there in 1579, the alderman and sheriffs of Newcastle forbad the inhabitants to come thither for coals. Though this may have interfered with some traders, such a refusal had not the effects which a similar exclusion would create now-a-day.

But a great change was about to take place. In a description of England, in Holinshed's Chronicles, A. D. 1584, it is stated that sea-coal "beginnith to grow from the forge into the kitchen and the hall of most towns that lie about the coast;" and that if the waste of wood continues, the discredited mineral will be good merchandise, even in the city of London.

It is a curious fact that coals were not used in any quantity in localities near the coal field. It is recorded at Worcester that the first barge load of coals was brought to that city in 1570.*

In 1577, wood and money, no coal, were distributed amongst the poor of Lyme, to the amount of 1*l.* 3*s.* 4*d.*; 280 faggots, distributed in 1587, cost 13*s.* 4*d.*

At this date the consumption of coal in the West of England was very inconsiderable. It was, perhaps, only used for furnaces, and not for domestic purposes generally. The artful lime-burner plied his trade for years without using coal. He required all his skill in order to thoroughly roast his well-arranged mass.

Coal was destined to be used in greater quantities than it had been. In the last year of Queen Elizabeth's reign we

* Stanley's Guide.

find the grantee of the Lord High Admiral relinquishing his claim to measure salt, grain, and *coals* in the Cobb of Lyme. In 1644, the *coal bushel* was repaired; and one Cook charges, in 1645, for measuring 100 bushels of coal, 5*s*.

So late as the close of Charles II.'s reign, only 10,000 tons of iron were produced; now, 1854, more than twelve million tons. 350,000 tons of coal were brought to the metropolis in Charles II.'s reign; four million at the present time.* The price of wood in the reign of Elizabeth must have risen greatly. The east gate of Exeter having been taken down in the year 1511, it was agreed to sell *six acres* of the *wood* at Duryard, to meet the expense of rebuilding the same. The sum realised was 28*l*.†

The number of collieries worked in 1855 amounted to 2397.

The surprising collection of proclamations possessed by the Royal Antiquarian Society furnishes the following prices of fuel in London in the year 1632: —

	s.	*d.*
A sack, 4 bushels, of the best old charcoals - -	i	ij
,, middle sort do. - -		x
,, smallest do. - -		viij
A sack containing 4 bushels of the best and largest small coales - - - - -	vi	
1000 best Kentish billets of the true assize at the water side - - -	xvi	
Essex - - - - -	xviij	
Western - - - - -	xiiij	
Kentish faggots - - - -	vij	
Essex ,, - - - -	vi	
Western ,, - - - -	vi	

There is nothing about sea-coal, but of the wares in which the famous musical small-coal man dealt. This person, Thomas Britton, dwelt in an obscure street, Aylesbury Street, Clerkenwell, with a ladder to mount to his crowded concert room. At his meetings Pepusch and Handel played

* Macaulay's Hist. † Archives of Exeter.

the harpsichord; and the highest nobility and most elegant ladies were but too happy to attend. The Earl of Mornington was a visitor; his son became the great Duke of Wellington.

By the year 1624 the coal trade had become of sufficient importance to make it an object of attraction to the fraudulent, who delight in new fields for their wickedness. A proclamation was issued at this date to survey the sea-coals of Newcastle, Sunderland, and Blythe, in order to prevent the deceit and abuses arising from the mingling black earth, slate, stone, and other unfueable stuff amongst the good coals.* Sailors aboard of coal vessels bound to London were not to be impressed into the navy, about 1665,—a proof that coals were in demand.

Prejudices founded in error must always yield to increasing intelligence. Our ancestors at length abandoned their fanciful ideas about coal towards the beginning of the 17th century; and our neighbours on the other side of the channel adopted and retained them to our day.

It is not more than a quarter of a century ago that an ambassador at Paris issued cards for a large party, and found to his dismay that only gentlemen attended, the ladies having absented themselves on learning that his lordship warmed his house by means of English coal. This may be paralleled with the idea that potatoes would create leprosy.

Coal can now be fetched from the vessel's side by farmers not too distant, and found to be cheaper than firing cut from their own under cliffs. Wood is become very dear in France, so that the poor of Normandy and Britany suffer greatly in severe winters. Women take their work into the cowsheds in order to partake of the warmth of the beasts. At Paris the courts of justice, the theatres, and the cafés are crowded by those who fly from a cold home, or a room warmed at a great cost. Without economy, 25*s.* a week may be spent in wood by the occupier of a sitting-room! The late J. Stein, Esq., of Chalmington House, Dorset, employed 500 Irish

* Proclamations, Society of Antiquaries, Feb. 16. 230.

near Limerick, in digging peat for his distillery in that city; but he told the author that he could have purchased coals with equal economy. The turning so many out of employ restrained that gentleman.

Apropos of fuel. Nicholas de Yhonge, of Flanders, astonished the citizens of York by his introduction of the domestic bellows in the reign of Edward III. The bellows of the Minster organ had been there probably from the time of the Anglo-Saxons.*

The scarcity of fuel before coal began to be regularly supplied to the inhabitants of the south-western parts was severely felt. Warmth in an inclement season, and more than that, fuel for culinary purposes, must have stimulated the poor to sally out into the fields and supply in an illegal manner their necessities. We are not to understand, in the beautiful language of Goldsmith, that each woman went

"To pick her wintry fagot from the thorn."

There were the regular *wood-stealers*, *hedge-tearers*, or spoilers of hedges, and to crown all, the *pollers of trees*.

Ranulph Hocket was appointed in 1578, besides his office of piggerd, "to have and take all the wood from the hedge-tearers that they shall bring into the Comb Street from over Gosling's Bridge, and therewith to take their ropes and hooks." Fifteen common wood-stealers and spoilers of hedges were presented by name in 1597. The number is sufficient to account for great devastation in the neighbourhood, and these trespassers and spoilers acted in defiance of an order in the Court of Hustings' Book, Lyme, 1584, p. 279., as follows: —

"*Hedge tearing or breaking.* — Persons found with *wood* to have two days and one night in the *dark house*, and during that time to have brown bread and water.

"*Second offence.* To be set in the stocks two days in the open street, with the wood stolen before them, and one night in the dark house, with brown bread and water.

* Phil. Society of Yorkshire, 1855.

"*Third offence.* To be whipped about the town, as such persons ought to be who commit peckery and petty larceny.

"*Fourth offence.*" (Page torn out.)

It is a true remark that bye-laws had become practical despotisms, which Bacon observes it was the endeavour and policy of Henry VII. to keep within reasonable bounds.*

A precept from the manor of Castle Combe in 1557, against harbouring a hedge-tearer, proves that this habit prevailed extensively.

Præceptum est quod nullus infra dominium istud hospitat Elenam Otes, neque aliam personam in dominiis suis quæ frangit sepes vel spoliat boscum sub pœna foris faciendi domino, x*s.* In the same manor, in 1586, it was ordered that the tenants shall put away those under them that stelithe wood, breke hedges, or are common scolders, under a penalty of 6*s.* 8*d.*

The destructive effects of tree-polling were witnessed in some parishes in South-east Devon at the decline of smuggling. The "helps," that is, those who were hired to run a cargo, being seldom employed, and not having given up night work for honest labour, were poor and lawless. Many a good-sized ash tree that figured in the landscape lost its poll or head in the night, and the stump alone remained.

Security against Fire. — Chimneys, Mantels, &c.

BEFORE civilisation attains a very high state of advancement, some precautionary matters fall to the province of individual members of a community. These are very apt to be neglected. As it advances, these cares are removed from individuals, and become the business of the State, the borough, or other authorities, who give their special attention to them.

* Weale's Papers on Engineering.

Who now troubles himself about the general security of the buildings of a town against fire? No one, except some individual who may be either more fearful than his fellow-townsmen, or has some special occasion of alarm, owing to the well-known bad condition of the house of some careless neighbour. The agents of the many excellent institutions, the insurance companies against fire, examine the fabric of each house offered for insurance, watch over the general safety, and so relieve the community at large from what was formerly every man's duty. So, when the sovereignty of the law among our Anglo-Saxon brethren is established in their once wild districts, *Lynching*, or the executing the laws by private individuals, or society at large, ceases; and judges legally constituted assume the duties of their office, and spare quiet members of the community their often necessary and harassing agitation.

Our page refers to the time when there were only two or three chimneys in a town, and when these necessary parts of a house began to be general. No insurance companies existed; hence the care and scrutiny of individuals, who, either as members of the jury, or by their information of jurymen, caused *precepts*, and *orders*, and *presentments* about MANTELS, dangerous mantels, &c., to be inserted so abundantly in our Court of Hustings' Books.

A mantel, sometimes entered as *caminus sive mantella, mantella caminata*, so often presented by our court leet and other juries, was a projecting fire-place (hence mantel-piece) which had sometimes a great deal of wood in it, while the rest was mud or plaster. When this became ruinous from neglect, there was great danger of fire; and the houses themselves, except the basement, were of wood and plaster. Neighbours trembled, and acted upon their fears in a way here deemed worthy of being set forth:—

"3 Elizabeth, 1561, at Lyme. "It was commanded to John Somer to amend his mantalle, payne of v shillings."

Around the spacious cupola, over the French and Italian

fire-places, is a ledge to which are affixed pegs, on which the postilions straightway proceeded to hang their wet cloaks to dry. We call the stone or wooden shelf over our fire-places *mantel-pieces*, or *mantel-shelves*: but we no longer hang our mantles upon them to dry. In some of the old palaces of Rome, the *mantel-pieces* are applied to the similar original purpose.*

The hole to allow the escape of the smoke at the back of the projecting fire-place was often so placed that there was great danger. There is no end in some archives to the list of "mantles presented."

Corporations made bye-laws for the general safety. Thus at Marlborough, in 1577, runs one:—

> "Whoso kindles fires in dangerous places, or without chimneys, after warning given, shall forfeit 20*s*., or be imprisoned."†

In 1581, a chimney at Lyme being in a dangerous state as to fire, the Court directed,—

> "*Item*, that the tenants of George Hooper do make no more fire in his house until the chimney be repaired, upon payment of 5*s*."

The very next year a similar order was given to an individual, who perhaps, judging his premises to be secure, and not dangerous, disregarded the mandate:—

> "Richard Bowden, of Lyme, was fined, in 1582, 4*d*., and the next law day, 6*d*., for making a fire before his chimney was repaired, as ordered at the last court day."

The constables had directions in all the boroughs to observe the state of the fire-places. By a bye-law at Castle Combe, upon default pointed out, those who did not amend were to pay x*s*.‡ In the same little borough, "no one was to enter a stable or barn with a candle, under pain of x*s*. No one to

* Notes and Queries, Aug. 19. 1854. Signature, D. W. S.

† Waylen's Hist. of Marlborough, p. 119.

‡ Hist. of Castle Combe, by the Rt. Hon. Poulett Scrope.

carry fire in the street unless protected from the violence of the wind, under pain of x*s*." A lantern would have secured the party requiring to be lighted from a fine.

Thus necessary was it deemed to exercise a strict discipline in borough towns over the insecurity of buildings, and so prevent a conflagration. The precise remedy was sometimes defined. One townsman of Lyme, in 1581, received an order that he "do plaister his mantell." In 1599, we find,—

"Also it is precepted unto William Swain, that he doth plaister his cockloft over the kitchen where he dwelleth, sub-pœnâ 10*s*."

With a view to good in the arrangement of domestic architecture, Silvester Jordan was precepted to alter the hanging of his door before Robert Brooke's house, upon pain of 20*s*.

Private ovens are proverbially the cause of fire in farm houses. A *focale* or oven was presented as out of repair in 1582. I believe there was no public bakehouse in this reign. In Penrith, a town of 7000 to 8000 inhabitants, there was no public baker in 1841, if there is one now. Rob. Holden, who had a public bakehouse at Lyme in 1669, was presented at the court leet to amend his dangerous oven where Edward Staple lives, to the endangering the setting the town on fire.

Londoners, as a precaution against fire, were compelled to whitewash the thatches of their houses.*

There are towns in which the bye-laws positively forbad, two centuries ago, the use of thatch for new houses. Thus at Marlborough, in 1622, no house was to be built without being covered with tile or slate.†

In Norwich, a fine of 5*l.* was received in 1640 for having covered a house with reed. The walls round the pest-house were built with the money.‡ At Castle Combe, in 1674, no customary tenant to remove tiles and replace with thatch, under pain of 39*s.* 11*d.*

* Turner's Domestic Architecture. † Waylen's Hist. of M.

‡ Blomefield's Norfolk.

The whole mass of borough legislation respecting fire-places or mantels, ovens, &c., is rendered useless by the establishment of fire insurances, and the operation of their rules.

A brief mention of a practice not altogether foreign to the subject may, perhaps, be excused.

At Douglas, in the Isle of Man, there is a simultaneous burning out of the chimneys of the town after a fall of rain. A gentleman writes, in May 1852, from Douglas, that a stranger would think the town was in flames, while it was only the clearing off the accumulated soot.

Steven Kent, of Pimperne, blacksmith, was presented in 1631 for an improper use of his forge, by which there was danger of a firing his neighbours' houses. Nothing was said about a chimney; so we may fairly conclude his forge had not that useful, and, for safety, necessary appendage. The complaint states that Kent made fires, not only for the use of his trade, which would have been safe, but also for the dressing his necessaries for his family, and for washing, and such like businesses. Whereby the inhabitants of that parish have been often endangered to have their houses set on fire by the use of frith and wood for the fire in an improper place, without any, or else an insufficient chimney. The Court ordered that Kent should be bound over to answer for the same at the next sessions, and directs "that he shall not make any fire in time to come in the said forge, save only with *sea-coal,* and that for the necessary use of his trade only, or be committed to the county gaol if he do not obey this order."

Before these sessions were over, the Court was applied to against widow Gay, of Wimborne Minster, dwelling in the heart and middle of that town. Her case is a good specimen of the evils of early times, and a great drawback to the comfort and safety of the neighbourhood it must have been.

Widow Gaye, in the heart of Wimborne, carried on a very thriving trade as a tipler, and brewed her own beer and ale. The situation probably required a draft, and a somewhat elevated exit for the smoke; so Widow Gaye had erected a FLUE, or CHIMNEY of TIMBER, as others in so many instances had mantels of wood. This, or some part of the said house, by the nature of its construction and materials, had taken fire, and very likely to have adventured the whole town. Widow Gaye was to be prevented from henceforth selling beer or ale, or from tipling or brewing in the said house; and the constables of the town of Wimborne were to bring her before some justice of the peace, to give bond not to tipple any more, nor to brew for her own use in the said flue, until it be amended and adjudged by the constables to be sufficient for her own use.*

Before Fire Insurance was known and practised, great fires produced much misery. Grants were wont to be made from the county purse in relief of the sufferers.

Five sufferers from a fire at Wimborne Minster, in 1634, petitioned the magistrates, who granted a sum of ten pounds, to be divided among the parties as Sir Walter Erle, Knight, and Thomas Hooper, Esq., should think fit.

A far heavier calamity called forth the sympathy of the Court shortly afterwards. A fire broke out at Bere Regis, which in the space of four hours consumed houses and corn to the value of 7,000*l.*, leaving 306 persons utterly destitute. The sum of 50*l.* was granted from the county fund, and the justices authenticated the facts set forth in a petition to the King, praying him to grant letters for a general collection in aid of the town.†

The Phœnix was the first fire office established, in 1682. There were used in towns squirts, or syringes for extinguishing fire, which did not exceed two or three feet in length. These yielded to the Fire Engine, with leathern pipes, which was patented in 1676. Water-tight, seamless hose was made in Bethnal Green about 1720. About this date —

* Mr. T. Hearn, Qui Quondam. † Ibid.

	£	s.	d.
A fire engine and pipe for Lyme cost - - -	6	0	0
A square pipe, 23 feet long - - - -	1	18	0
12 leather fire buckets - - - -	2	3	3

A Fire Engine was considered an appropriate present for an aspirant to a borough. At Lewes, in 1726, T. Pelham, Esq., gave one, and having been chosen representative in 1731, he presented a second.

The Clothing Trade of the West of England,—a kind of Clothiers' Parliament.

THE West of England was once a manufacturing district, —the seat of the clothing trade. It is generally supposed that some great natural advantage determines the choice of locality for such matters. The contiguity of coal, iron, &c. is presumed to be the leading motive in such a choice at present. In former centuries this had little to do with the clothing trade. The factory system had not been introduced, and the matter was conducted on a very simple plan.

A farmer's partner—the goodman's wife, or goodwife—kept servant maids for the kine, no more than for a department of the clothing business. The wool was washed and dried by these, then spun with a distaff, the old accompaniment of a rustic building. The woollen thread was now an article for market, where the clothiers held a divided sway with the growers of produce for human food.

Parties bought woollen thread, and employed weavers to weave the same into cloth at their own shops, outhouses, or places that would receive a loom, in bye corners of lanes and backlets.

This work done, the employer of the weavers, who perhaps kept many at work, had for sale pieces of undyed and undressed cloth.

Let it be distinctly understood, that no buildings existed of any size where many processes were carried on by one party or firm.

The pieces of undyed and undressed cloth were now sent to foreigners, principally the Flemings, who finished them off, realising a profit of 500,000*l.* a-year by so doing. The pieces of finished cloth were then exported for sale in Spain and Portugal by the Flemings, or Dutch, who had purchased them to finish them off, and were then sold as Flemish bays. The Norman peasantry wore our kerseys.

Alderman Cockayne practised an art which he had learnt or invented — that of dyeing and dressing cloths. James I. granted, in the year 1608, this improver an exclusive right to dye and dress cloths, and prohibited the exportation of undyed cloths. This called into action the States of Holland and the German cities, which prohibited the importation of English-dyed cloths. As the cloth finished in Holland was better and cheaper than Alderman Cockayne's, he could only sell his at home, where the patent proved so offensive that it was annulled in 1615.

English clothiers adopted a new method, that of dyeing the wool before weaving it. A Dutchman taught how a fine scarlet dye might be procured about 1635, when the art of fixing colours produced from logwood was also acquired, and the act for prohibiting the use of logwood was repealed in 1660. The brilliant and permanent scarlet dye, for which the waters of Chalford, in Gloucestershire, became celebrated even to China, was a great discovery.

The early legislators had great dislike to dealers purchasing wool who were not going to make it up into cloth. They would have no wool staplers about 1464.

A weaver who did not return cloth of honest weight, according to the wool given out to him, was set in the pillory or cucking-stool. 3 Henry VIII. c. b.

A law of 1551 provided that all weavers of broad cloth should serve an apprenticeship of seven years.

The nomenclature of our early trade may not be known to many. The names familiar to the initiated are given; but no description of the several properties or qualities of each is attempted, from want of information. There were serges, broadcloths, Medley and Dorset kerseys, Dorsetshire dozens, single bays, Bristol, Bridgwater, and Taunton COTTONS, a woollen article that gave a name to a very important substance and manufacture that has sprung into notice with a world-wide fame.

There were weavers, walkers, fullers, fulling-mill men, shearmen, dyers, forcers of wool, carders and sorters of wool, and spinners; carders and spullars of yarn.

In addition to colours now in general use, such as scarlet and blue, there were others designated as tawny, russet, marble grey, puke or dark grey, sadnew colour, asewer, watchett, sheep's colour, lion colour, motley or iron grey, friar's grey, crane colour, and old medley colour.*

In 1621 the price of everything except corn was at a very low rate. The poor tradesmen of the western parts, that is, men of the trade of the country, which was clothing, could find but little work, so that many offered to work for meat and drink only. The merchants who bought of the weavers could not dispose of the cloths they had purchased.†

In Exeter, the centre of the manufacturing trade, there were 300 poor weavers about the streets craving relief by begging. The justices met at the Assizes, 12th of March, to consider of some course for finding work for the poor men, and to prevent an insurrection.

In London the merchants, for so those who bought and dealt in cloth were styled, were enjoined to buy a quantity of cloths weekly at Blackwell Hall. Legislation affecting one class was adopted instead of a course that might have remedied the evil, or allowed it to fall more equally. It is stated as a penal condition, that if they did not buy as directed they should be disfranchised of their liberties and freedom as (cloth) merchants in London.

In 1622 the sheriffs in the west were directed to call

* See Statute 4 & 5 Phil. and Mary, c. 5.

† Purchased as a market house for cloth in 1397.

before them all clothiers, out of which two of the most efficient of every county were to be sent to London before certain commissioners appointed to inquire into the cause of the deadness of trade, and to settle a course to revive the trade of clothing beyond the seas; which two clothiers so sent should deliver their opinions of the causes and reasons of the deadness of trade before the said commissioners, so that some course may be taken for some redress therein.*

The High Sheriff of Dorset called the clothiers together, who selected John Gardner and Richard Downe, two of their calling, to journey to London as their representatives. These two champions of the clothiers experienced a pitiful, but too customary a fate. Their services having been rendered, and the manner of performing them never having been questioned, oblivion stole over the minds of the many who had stimulated them to aspire to the honour and ride to this *quasi*-parliament.

In this employment they made two journeys to London, and spent above two months in the prosecution of the business to their great charge, travail, hindrance, and expense, amounting to one hundred marks, and were robbed on their return homewards.

It had been promised by the other clothiers that their charges and expenses should be repaid, and that they should be fully satisfied; but after four years they had received no recompense, nor a penny of contribution for their expense and loss. Hereupon they petitioned the Honourable Privy Council, who referred the matter to the magistrates at the Dorset sessions. These thought fit, and ordered John Gould the elder, Richard Blachford, Dennis Bond, and Joseph Pratie, all of Dorchester, being four clothiers of that county, to call before them all such clothiers as they conceive are liable to the contribution in question, and to make an equal and indifferent rate for raising the sum required.†

The commissioners appointed to inquire were to consider

* Yonge, Diary.

† Mr. T. Hearn, Qui Quondam.

if it were not behoveful to put in execution the laws still in force, which obliged merchant strangers to lay out the proceeds of the merchandise imported by them on the native commodities of the realm.

The merchants of that great manufacturing city, Exeter, exported till the latter part of the 18th century serges and cloths to Italy.

Before the factory system was introduced, which annihilated the former mode of cloth-making, the little towns of Devon had busy markets and fairs. There was a bustle at the times when these were held, and the clack of the weaver's shuttle was heard in all directions. The next generation that had the large factory building, the water-wheel at work, and capital employed, saw the unequal contest with the North of England, to which our cloth trade has nearly all passed, Frome, &c. being exceptions.

"A walker" in the time of Edward III. meant a fuller. The fulling of cloth was performed by walking over it, as is now practised in the remote Isle of Sky.

The treasurers for the county of Dorset had been, before the year 1632, either Knights or Esquires. The rule was broken through at this epoch, and worthies of the cloth trade, &c. were elected. Israel Sherley, of Blandford Forum, woollendraper, and Josias Cuth, of Sherborne, linendraper, were the next year succeeded by John Hill, of Dorchester, merchant, and Richard Ryves, of Shaftesbury, merchant.

It is important to have one class emerging from an inferior position to a higher grade, and eventually to a participation in honours. Such changes cannot happen without great causes being at work in the framework of society.*

A gentleman who lived in the country usually kept a few sheep. He had his own wool carded, and then spun and wove into cloth for his domestic purposes. The gentleman who records the following charges must have been very economic in his arrangements: —

* Mr. T. Hearn, "Qui Quondam."

	s.	d.
13 lbs. of wool combed came to - -	3	4
21 yds. of cloth wove - - -	11	0
Scouring and fulling - - -	7	0*

Before this subject is dismissed, let a few observations be introduced respecting an important scheme of the time of the Commonwealth. The sending about of sale goods, partially worked, to fair and market, there to be purchased by those who undertook some more advanced process, whether of dyeing, setting, or such like, proved very expensive and inconvenient. This was, however, indispensable, as each clothier had his limits, beyond which he could not go. In the North, at Leeds, Huddersfield, and other places, are vast Cloth Halls, where cloth goods, more or less advanced, are exposed on certain days to purchasers. In that part of the kingdom the factory system for clothing has not fully obtained, and could not well be carried on without such great marts.

In the year 1657 a scheme was in agitation to build a DRAPERY HALL over the shambles in Broad Street, Lyme Regis. This would have been a type of the great buildings in the North, where such a great amount of business is done. But trade was not left without shackles and gyves. Restrictions and exclusion, distinctions between freeman and out of town man or foreigner, as he was called, had not been removed or worn out.

The time had not arrived for freemen of a borough to surrender their privileges, or for legislators to compel them to do so; and clothiers would not of course travel to the enchanted ground of a borough where a code of bye-laws existed up to that time unalterable, which made against them in every particular.

Thus Dorsetshire lost the benefit of the scheme.

* Sussex Archæol. Burrell's Diary.

Smuggling or Contraband Trade.

BOLD, venturous spirits, fond of excitement, and, moreover, tempted by a chance of realising great profits, after a brief period of exertion and risk, have ever been found ready to engage in *Smuggling*. In time of peace, the whole of the south coast of England may appear to the casual observer equally suited as a starting point for the contraband dealer. He buys the commodities required at some French port; whence, upon taking his departure, he enters upon the perilous adventures of stormy nights, surf-bound coast, vigilant officers, treacherous confederates, and many mishaps arising from unforeseen causes. When war closes the ports of France, then the coast opposite the Channel Islands, Guernsey, and Alderney, is more especially the seat of smuggling, as the east coast from its proximity to Holland.

Before smuggling had received its death-blow, parts of Dorset and Devon were as much concerned with smuggling as some counties with any particular trade. The population of whole villages supported themselves by such an unlawful occupation. Who was there that deemed the purchase of contraband articles sinful or improper? The best of the residents of sea-side towns made no scruple of buying anything the dealer of smuggled goods had for sale. Well might old Rattenbury, the bold smuggler, when boasting at a trial that he had brought up his son very carefully, say in answer to a question, if he had taught him the commandment, "Thou shalt not smuggle," that he did not see any harm in a little free trade. His superiors did not set him a good example. *Free Trade* did not bear its present occupation, but was an euphemism for contraband dealing, a disregard of fiscal laws. In 1735, when there was a duty of 1*l.* a gallon upon rum, that spirit, as well as brandy and wine, were landed on our south-west coast. The Custom House officers had riding officers, tidesmen, and boatmen upon the look out, who made seizures sometimes in consequence of information, at others by sweeping at the bottom of the sea, where a raft of tubs containing rum, brandy, &c. was supposed to be sunk.

It is not on every occasion that the dryness of fiscal matters can be enlivened by the labours of the poet. The late Rev. W. Crowe, in his much admired poem entitled "Lewesdon Hill," a lofty eminence of West Dorset, thus apostrophises Burton Cliff, east of Bridport harbour, and gives a beautiful and true picture of the coast as it was:—

"From hostile shores returning, glad I look
On native scenes again; and first salute
Thee, Burton, and thy lofty cliff, where oft
The nightly blaze is kindled; further seen
Than erst was that love-tended cresset, hung
Beside the Hellespont: yet not like that
Inviting to the hospitable arms
Of beauty and youth, but lighted up, the sign
Of danger, and of ambush'd foes to warn
The stealth-approaching vessel, homeward bound
From Havre or the Norman isles, with freight
Of wines and hotter drinks, the trash of France
Forbidden merchandise. Such fraud to quell
Many a light skiff and well appointed sloop
Lies hovering near the coast, or hid behind
Some curved promontory, in hope to seize
These contraband: vain hope! on that high shore
Station'd, th' associates of their lawless trade
Keep watch, and to their fellows off at sea
Give the known signal; they with fearful haste
Observant, put about the ship, and plunge
Into concealing darkness. As a fox
That from the cry of hounds and hunters' din
Runs crafty down the wind, and steals away
Forth from his cover, hopeful so t'elude
The not yet following pack,—if chance the shout
Of eager or unpractised boy betray
His meditated flight, back he retires
To shelter him in the thick wood: so these
Retiring, ply to south, and shun the land
Too perilous to approach: and oft at sea

Secure (or ever nigh the guarded coast
They venture) to the trackless deep they trust
Their forfeitable cargo, rundlets small
Together link'd upon their cable's length,
And to the shelving bottom sunk and fixt
By stony weights ; till happier hours arrive
To land it on the vacant beach unrisk'd."

The lighting fires upon the hills along the coast as signals to the returning smuggler has become a punishable offence under an Act of Parliament. The poet would now miss this feature in the western landscape.

The great changes wrought in the laws that refer to smuggling were important to the interests of great numbers of persons of property who risked money in such ventures. As the laws in force were evaded with the adroitness too generally displayed in such matters, others were framed that had in their turn to be remodelled, or which became a dead letter.

All the cutters which cruized after smugglers were not the property of the Crown. Some belonged to private individuals, who fitted them out to capture smugglers and their crews, as privateers do an enemy. This was a speculation depending upon the success of the vessels so fitted out. Capt. Lisle of Lyme, afterwards of Weymouth, the son of an officer of customs at Lyme, owned several of those cruizers.

The fast sailing and fast rowing luggers were in great request for the voyage across the channel. Then came some enactments, and these were no longer permitted to be used. Small sailing vessels were licensed, and two bondsmen were required in a good sum of money. If the craft had not a sliding bowsprit, only that fixed one called a steaved bowsprit, no bond was required. Owners that intended to send their craft "across," *i. e.*, over to France, steaved their bowsprit, and so, as it were, proclaimed their speedy intention. All the Beer fishing luggers, known as Beer boats, went smuggling. Caught in a gale, they have been known to make their tubs into a raft, throw them overboard, and drift to leeward. The sea broke upon the floating tubs of spirits, and the open boat lived through the storm.

The poet says nothing of tobacco. This was an important branch of the illicit trade. The store of captured tobacco was occasionally so great in the Lyme Custom House that it was burnt in a lime kiln, which was situated where the first warehouse on the Cobb now stands. The kiln was actually filled with tobacco, and each of the assembled bye-standers had an opportunity of stuffing his pockets full. At length the fire was applied, and the flavour could be sniffed at a great distance to leeward by the hardy mariner, who deplored such a waste of this cherished commodity. Tobacco-stalks and fibres have also been smuggled for the being ground into snuff.

Smuggled spirits may well be styled "the trash of France." The article is a very inferior one, and is believed to be mainly derived from distillation from potatoes. In France the price was about half-a-crown a gallon, which the retail dealer here sold at fourteen shillings. The kegs held six, but the greater number only four gallons. These were slung across the shoulders of the *helps*, as those men who went down to the shore to run a cargo were called. At certain points strings of pack horses carried the cargo inland, or their substitute, light carts, where the improved roads admitted of their use.

The law's changes within a few brief years respecting smuggling would occupy much space. At one time, so late as about the year 1780, smugglers were allowed a latitude that will be scarcely credited. Nothing could be seized above high-water mark; so that pipes of wine have actually been landed close to the Custom House at Lyme, then at the bottom of the town, and allowed to remain on the beach and Cobb-gate leading to the Custom House! Vessels used to come along ashore; when, if no officer of the customs — the only one who made captures — was there, the goods were landed. If there was any interruption, the craft went elsewhere, and landed, or returned again to the same spot. At one time some vessels of about 100 tons were employed, called tonnagers. The papers were made out as if from Cherburg to Ostend. One of these was boarded off the Cobb, and found to be full of wine, and her papers were inspected. The next day she entered the Cobb without a single pipe of wine. Mr. Raymond, the collector of customs, seized her, as he said she could not have gone to Ostend and back in one night. The smugglers contested the matter in a trial at Dorchester. The evidence was complete to prove that the vessel was laden with wine one day, and the next was empty. The smugglers pleaded their having thrown overboard the cargo, to prevent the vessel from sinking. The judge having questioned one of the custom-house officers who boarded the vessel as to her condition at the time, the man, who had been bribed, answered, that he said to another officer, "Let us be off, or we shall share the fate of poor Admiral Kempenfelt." This saved the smugglers.

Some who were deeply engaged in smuggling ventures used to go round the country after the manner of mercantile travellers, and ask gentlemen what they would "give to have a pipe or hogshead of wine put into their cellars?" The price being agreed upon, it was only a question of conveyance. In a store at Bridport harbour, there were hundreds of pipes of wine at a time, not seizable as the law then stood.

A smuggler named Gulliver kept forty or fifty men constantly employed, who wore a kind of livery, powdered hair, and smock frocks, from which they obtained the name of the "white wigs." These men kept together, and would not allow a few officers to take what they were carrying, when the law was altered, and seizures were made from other weaker parties. Gulliver amassed a large fortune, and lived to a good old age. He employed lawyers to arrange his affairs so that all who should take any benefit from his fortune should bear the name of Gulliver. If not impressed, like the ancients, with a desire of posthumous fame, this worthy dreaded posthumous determination to be silent as to the founder of the fortune. Till of late years a chamber, open towards the sea at the mouth of the river Lyme, was in existence, where the "white wigs" took refreshment, and remained in waiting till their services were required. This was not one hundred yards from the former custom house. One party of smugglers, with their convoy of spirit, fought with officers in the streets of London, and were victors. Let no reader understand that Gulliver's men were assailants, or ferocious in any encounter. The smugglers of the south-western coast have ever been remarkable for their quiet manner of pursuing their illicit calling. There never has been a series of violence and bloodshed such as has disgraced so often the south-eastern coast.

A great blow has been dealt to smuggling by the establishment of the Preventive Service. The whole coast is patrolled, and cutters cruize, so as to make smuggling a very unprofitable affair. The rich have disconnected themselves from it entirely. For a time the "goods" were brought over in French bottoms. A large new boat was launched, and Englishmen rowed to land, where the boat was sure to be sacrificed if the spirits were run without interruption. None but naval lieutenants are now admitted into the Preventive Service, under the inspecting naval commanders. Rewards for captures depend upon the strength of the spirit so seized; and the scale is altered if the men are captured as well as the goods.

A man convicted of smuggling playing cards, tobacco, spirits, &c., if a seafaring man, used to be sent to serve for five years in a man-of-war on a foreign station, receiving pay however. Now, each offender pays a fine of 100*l.*, or is committed for six calendar months. Women and children coming over in the passage-vessels, decked out with tobacco bustles, pay not exceeding 5*l.*, if the weight is under 5 lbs., at the determination of the magistrate; but if the weight is above 5 lbs., a fine of 100*l.* or imprisonment for six months must be imposed.

After all these terrors and means to crush smuggling, the great cheapness of British gin, the fear on the part of the consumer of being fined, and of being at the mercy of any informer, now that smuggling is in such very low hands, and an increased sense of moral duty to the state, combine in a great degree to keep down the illicit trade in spirits, which would continue to a greater extent did these not exist.

The Lace Trade, its Origin, early Introduction into West Dorset and South-east Devon; with Particulars of the making Bone, Lyme, Pill, i. e. *Pillow, or Honiton Lace.*

"In tenui labor." — VIRG.

A FOREIGN land claims the invention of a light beautiful fabric, everywhere known as lace. But the time of its introduction into West Dorset and South-east Devon has not been ascertained.

The several appellations of our lace require some explanation, and have puzzled strangers. The same light fabric is spoken of as bone, Lyme, pill or pillow, and Honiton lace. It is sometimes designated as real or hand-made lace.

From the bobbins upon which the thread is wound, having been made of *bone* before the general introduction of some of the hard foreign woods, the article was called BONE lace, as it was *pill* or *pillow* lace, from the globe-shaped cushion upon which it was fashioned. From the circumstance of the dealers, who visited the metropolis and the great towns, residing at Lyme and Honiton, their bone lace was extensively known as Lyme lace, and Honiton lace, though much of it had not been made in either town.

Our lace was not wove. It had neither warp nor woof, but was rather, writes Beckman, knit after the manner of nets, filets, or stockings. The pattern is stuck upon a slip of parchment, and fastened to the globe-shaped cushion. The thread is wound upon the requisite number of spindles called bobbins, and these are thrown over and under each other various ways, so that the threads twine round pins stuck in the holes of the pattern, and by this means produce that multiplicity of eyes or openings which give to the lace the desired figures. Much art is not necessary, and the invention of it is not so ingenious as that of weaving stockings.*

The oldest kind of lace is that worked with the needle (now exclusively named *point-lace*), and which was by far the dearest.

Needles, Stow writes, were sold in Cheapside in the reign of Queen Mary, and were made by a Spanish negro by a secret art.

Beckman asserts that the knitting of lace is a German invention before 1561, due to Barbara, wife of Christopher Ultman, at St. Annaberg, in Saxony. About that period the mines were less productive, and the making of veils, followed by the families of the miners, had declined, as there was little demand for them. The new invention, therefore, was soon known to the wives and daughters of the miners; and the lace, on account of the low price of labour, soon became fashionable, in opposition to the Italian lace worked with the needle, and even supplanted it in commerce. Beckman could find no mention of the art of knitting lace, nor any of the terms that belong to it, before the middle of the 16th century, therefore he concludes that Barbara Ultman originated the invention, and did not introduce it.

Beckman refers to the history of St. Annaberg, written after the fashion of the day, in Latin†: —

"Hoc anno, 1561, filum album retortum in varias formas Phrygio opere ‡ duci cœpit, quod ut ad mediocrem ornatum adhibitum reprehendi minime potest, præsertim re metallicâ vehementer attritâ, ita cavendum tamen, ne vanitati et luxuriæ serviat."

This year, 1561, white thread, twisted into various patterns, began to be wove into a kind of Phrygian work, which, as it is

* Beckman, Hist. of Inventions, ii. 32.

† Annabergæ urbis Historia, auctore Paulo Jenisio. Dresdæ, 1605, 4to. ii. p. 33.

‡ Phrygian work is embroidery, borders ingeniously worked, and sown upon tapestry.

made use of for an inexpensive set-off of dress, cannot at all be the object of censure provided that due care be taken that this be not rendered subservient to vanity and luxury.*

In the reign of Queen Elizabeth we have evidence that lace was well known, although regarded as sufficiently rare to be deemed a worthy offering to royalty itself. "In the manifold account of gifts accepted by this acquisitive monarch from various grades of her subjects, lace finds honourable mention. It is on record that Sir Philip Sidney presented her Majesty with a 'smock' of cambric, the sleeves and collar wrought with black silk, and edged with a small *bone lace;* whilst Mrs. Twist, the Court laundress, contributed to the regal wardrobe three handkerchiefs of black Spanish work similarly adorned."†

The circumstances and date of the first introduction of lace-making — doubtless from Flanders — are not known. In the east of the north porch in Honiton churchyard is a brass plate to the memory of James Ridge, bone-lace seller, who died in 1617, aged 50, leaving 100*l.* to the poor of that town.

Westcot, in his MS. Survey of Devon (1630), writes, fol. 169., of Honiton: here is made abundance of bone lace, a pretty toy, now greatly in request, and therefore Honiton may say, with merry Martial, "Ille ego sum nulli nugarum laude secundus:"

"In praise for toys such as this
Honiton to none second is."

Some Flemish refugees brought the art of making lace into the western borders of Bedfordshire.

A free school was endowed at Great Marlow, in Buckinghamshire, in 1626, to teach twenty-four boys to read, and twenty-four girls to knit, spin, and make bone lace.

The Count de Marsan brought his former nurse, named

* Thread has been spun by hand in Hainault, worth 400*l.* per lb.

† See in a number of Chambers's Edinburgh publication an admirable account of lace-making, in 32 pages.

Du Mont, from Brussels to Paris, and obtained from Colbert an exclusive right for her to carry on the lace manufactory in that capital in 1666.

During the Protectorate, when every action was made the subject of petty legislation by corporations and the assembled members of dissenting congregations, we may well expect that a new article of ornamental dress would excite attention and be forbidden, or find sanction under some restriction couched in the inimitable phraseology of that time. *Points* (the early French word for our lace) are not absolutely forbidden; but "points, or ribbons, and more laces than are required on garments," furnished matter for a letter from the members of the Baptist churches assembled at Bridgewater, 1655. The "beleeven men" fully believed how careful it was necessary to be in the treatment of brethren and sisters refusing to reform in the wearing of "gold, pearls, and costly array." They desired that these might be proceeded against with all sweetness, and tenderness, and long-suffering, it being not so clearly and generally understood as other things that are more contrary to the light of nature.*

Lace-making went on in several little country places of South-east Devon towards the close of the seventeenth century. After the suppression of Monmouth's rebellion, in 1686, the dragoons of Lord Cornbury and Lord Churchill, afterwards the great Duke of Marlborough, who was born at Ashe House close by, were quartered at Colyton. Soldiers were then a terror to the peaceable. They broke into the house of William Bird, a dealer in bone lace, and stole goods to the value of 325*l.* 17*s.* 9*d.*

Before Lyme Regis began to rise as a watering place, from a state of great decay, about the year 1750, lace-makers occupied almost every house in Broad Street. They worked a dress for Queen Charlotte of Lyme lace, as the Honiton lace-makers have since done for Queen Adelaide. Her present Majesty's order of a bridal dress of *Honiton* lace was

* Church Book of the Baptist Chapel of Lyme Regis.

executed at Beer. The distress of the lace-makers at Honiton, after two great fires in 1756 and 1767, is spoken of.

Lovers used to have their initials entwined, worked on a piece of ornamental lace. Old Catherine Power, the last of the lace-makers at Lyme, and likewise a fortune-teller, begged, some time before her death, a copy of certain initials to be worked in lace. She would, on taking home the order, just "cut the cards"—a modified term for telling a fortune.

A splendid work upon the Great Exhibition* contains some valuable addition to the early history of the lace trade, communicated by Mrs. Treadwin of Exeter.

Although the lace trade was extensive a century ago, it must then and for a long time after have principally consisted in producing the nett or Honiton ground (a nett much like the present machine nett), in which the sprigs first separately made were worked in on the pillow. This kind of nett was very expensive, and one of the old people formerly in the trade showed Mrs. Treadwin a piece about eighteen inches square, which she had had made just previous to the machine netts coming into use, and which then cost her in making 15*l.*, although it was plain nett only. The surprising machinery for the making of nett was introduced when the same size piece of nett was sold for about as many shillings, and now for fewer pence. So effectually did this destroy the trade of hand-made nett, that only two persons are known by Mrs. Treadwin who can make it. Chard, in South Somerset, has two large factories for the manufacture of machine-nett. One employs about 300 hands; another 180 hands, both exclusive of menders; Tiverton, in Devon, has noted factories. The introduction of the new article was the occasion of much suffering, while the unfortunate lace-makers tried to compete—a hopeless effort—with machinery. They could not earn sufficient to maintain life. Young women

* The Industrial Arts of the 19th Century: a series of illustrations of the choicest specimens produced by every nation at the Great Exhibition of Works of Industry, 1851, by M. Digby Wyatt, Architect. Day and Son, 1853.

went out to service; few children were trained to the use of the pillow, and the trade was greatly depressed for twenty years, when Queen Adelaide ordered a Honiton lace dress to be made of Honiton lace sprigs sewn on machine nett. This compromise or union of the two interests found but few followers. Her present gracious Majesty's bridal dress was of Honiton sprigs, connected together by a variety of open works, &c., and all worked on the pillow.

Her Majesty's order found only a few hands employed about the country, none in Lyme or in Dorset, but in Devon over a tract that might be enclosed by a line from Seaton to Exmouth, up the river Exe to Exeter, back the London road to Honiton, thence to Seaton. The trade revived, and affords a good livelihood to many thousand hands, the majority of the female labouring population.

Sidmouth, Beer, Branscombe, Colyton, and Honiton, are the residences of many workers and dealers, some of whom travel through England; but of late, at one time, the demand has far exceeded the supply. Some years ago poverty and lace-making were associated. Such is not now the case.

The West of England has lost the woollen trade. Is it that the genius for manufacturing is wanting? Mrs. Treadwin's skilled remarks would make us believe this is the case. The great majority of the hands are careless and indifferent as to the beauty of their work, and as a body disliking regular work and hours, preferring to work at home by the piece, generally fond of dress, and careless of the future. Finding no one effort made to improve in the art by the village lace-makers, though they were generally able to read and write, the same lady tried to work out some reformation of the old. This has failed, so she is labouring to improve the young lace-makers, in which we trust she may succeed. She affirms that there is not one lace-designer in Devonshire. Her designs used to be, till last summer, from Paris, now from Somerset House and Nottingham, which fact furnishes subject for congratulation. May the future historian be able to enrol Mrs. Treadwin as the person who has added dignity to an art hitherto pursued with very little ability.

Lille lace differs but little from Buckinghamshire lace; Brussels plait from the best Honiton.

Honiton, or west country lace, must now be classed under two heads: —

I. Honiton appliqué, the original lace.

II. Honiton guipure, lace invented about twenty years.

I. The Honiton appliqué, the original description of lace, consists of the finest net, sprigged and edged with a border more or less handsome, used for veils, mantles, dresses, and large articles of ladies' attire. The hand-labour bestowed upon this kind of lace is much smaller than that demanded by the other kind, and the price is proportionably lower.

II. The Honiton guipure, invented within the last twenty years, is not dissimilar in style from the old point lace, although very much lighter in texture. The separate sections of the pattern are united by delicate fibres, which in the best qualities of the lace are made on the pillow, forming, in fact, part of the pattern; but in the less expensive specimens they are made afterwards with a needle and thread. A flounce at the Great Exhibition was five yards long, on which forty women were employed for eight months.* The western lace manufactories are fully employed, in 1855, in the fabric of silk lace.

Travellers have not had to dread coming into the western lace district, as they had to a few stages on the great north road from London. The box of lace there regularly succeeded the dinner. The waiter brought round a box of beautiful specimens of lace for sale, and so levied contributions on the purses of the travellers.

It will be interesting to learn that lace-making has been introduced of late into Nagercoil, in Southern India, by the missionaries.

* See Messrs. Chambers's publication, p. 27

A Postscript about Silk-throwing.

So early as the year 1463 a petition was presented by the "silk women" of this country against the Lombards, who imported thrown silks. We learn by it how extensively silk-throwing and weaving was practised by ladies, so that the nunneries were not the only schools of elegant occupation.

The petition states, "of silk throwing, whereby many a worshipful woman within the same city (London) has lived full honourably, and therewith many good households kept; and many gentlewomen and others in great number like as there be now more than 1000 have been drawn under them in learning the same crafts and occupation, full virtuously unto the pleasance of God, whereby afterwards they have grown to great worship," &c.

Private Lotteries for Houses and Estates.

THE spirit of gambling, unless repressed by law, will be found to break out under various phases to the great detriment of society, which, when it rages, becomes demoralised by its pernicious effects upon the human mind. The excitement grows, as some novel form becomes established from time to time, till a perfect mania reigns.

It has been elsewhere shown how, in the time of Queen Elizabeth, butchers' shops were the scenes of gambling adventure. A particular form of gambling had obtained — that of raffling, or engaging in a game of chance for meat — the prize.

When the havens of England were in a state of great decay, the mode adopted for their restoration was that pernicious one of public lotteries; the first of which took place in the year 1569.

Lotteries, or raffles, were the rage at the close of the

seventeeth century; — not for objects of trifling value, but for whole estates, sometimes for houses and fields.

What a cause for the disturbing the even tenor of private life where the fair chance of the lottery was alone thought of. As might be anticipated where dishonesty came into play, all kinds of fraud were ready.

A notable instance of a private lottery in Dorset, with an episode that grew out of it, has been recorded by the much revered Hutchins, the historian of Dorset. In accounting for the transmission of property, he turned aside to relate a trait of domestic history that occasioned the alienation of an estate.

The estate of Winford Eagle was the property of the Sydenham family.

William Sydenham, Esq., was the son of William, brother of Thomas Sydenham, M.D., the celebrated physician, who adopted the cool treatment in small-pox, used bark in agues, and laudanum.

This Dorsetshire squire, being embarrassed, determined to put up his ancestral estate to the chance of private lottery, intending unfairly to make the prize fall to a poor female relative, whom he depended on being able to prevail upon to let him have it back again for a small consideration.

The young lady had a lover who visited her by stealth, to whom she communicated the news of her being about to have a chance given her. As was previously arranged, the poor relative won the estate, and soon found means to inform her lover, who was waiting to hear the result of her success. Perhaps, suspecting some such manœuvre, the lover advised her not to return the estate to Mr. Sydenham — advice which made her proof against the charms or terrors of persuasion.

The fortunate lady married Doily Michel, Esq., who sold the estate to G. Richards, Esq., of Longbredy. Upon Mr. Sydenham and his two daughters refusing to make a formal surrender of the estate to the vendor, they were committed to Dorchester gaol about the year 1709, where they ended their days.

Much good resulted from this memorable lottery; for owing to the exposure of this case, the system of private lotteries was condemned by an Act of the 10 and 11 William and Mary, which finally put an end to them.

There existed a rage for lotteries, or "sales," as they were called. Every conceivable thing was put up to raffle. There were advertisements for "A Sixpenny sale of Lace," "A Hundred pounds for Half-a-Crown," "A Penny Adventure for a Great Pie," "A Quarter's Rent," "A Freehold Estate," "Threepenny sales of Houses," "A fashionable Coach;" gloves, looking-glasses, chocolate, Hungary water, Indian goods, lacquered ware, fans, &c., were notified to be disposed of in this manner, and the fair mob were called together to draw their tickets by the same means. This fever produced in the end the South Sea bubble.*

Joy at hailing the Return of Spring.

"When that Aprille with his schowres swoote
The drought of Marche hath perced to the roote,
And bathed every veyne in swich licour,
Of which vertue engendered is the flour."

A Domestic Winter Scene. (From Worcester Cathedral.)

* Quarterly Review, June, 1854.

The carver has displayed the curious chimney, the man wrapped up though by the fire, and still, like the cat, suffering from the cold. The two-fingered gloves and two flitches of bacon are deserving of attention. See Stanley's Worcester and Malvern Guide Book, with designs by the Misses Eginton.

To read of keeping May-day, or Whitsuntide, merely as a commemoration, and not from feeling of deep joy at the coming of a genial season and escape from the miseries of a comfortless (coal-less) winter, is a misunderstanding of the matter. Our ancestors suffered from a long dreary winter, when many of our present comforts were unknown; and they rejoiced in the return of genial weather, as many now-a-day do who have partaken of every luxury of the winter season, and have participated in no hardships or exclusion from fresh meat and absence of vegetables.

To secure a sufficient stock of winter food was often a subject of care and difficulty. The merry hunting in the Plantagenet reigns partook of a matter of business, for deer were salted in for winter use. The whole of the winter store of meat was not salted, but a part was larded, or preserved with pig's lard; hence the name of the room in which it was kept, the *larder*. Cattle could not be fattened till Midsummer.

May-day scarcely saw the end of salted and larded meat, and much that was trying to the human frame, when the possessor was not rich. Fish was dear and scarce. Viewing the change of season in this light, our ancestors gave way to joyful manifestations, and had recourse to the following mode of expressing their joy: —

Wm. Tudbold, Mayor of Lyme, 1551.

Item, paid to Robert Willyms to chute the gones on May-day, iiij*d*.

Horace, having no ordnance to fire, called for a vernal dance of joy; if better provided with means, the poet may have had recourse to a noisier demonstration.

The Western Rebellion in the Reign of Edward VI.

AN entry made by John Hassard, mayor of Lyme 5th Edward VI., will serve to introduce some mention of an historical transaction:—

Paid to Thomas Battyn for the hire of a horse in the *Commocion* time, 1*s.* 6*d.*

The Reformation was not introduced in the quiet manner that obtained in other countries. The Rebellion in the reign of Edward VI., of the people of Cornwall and Devon, was one of great violence and bloodshed, as our annals confirm. These west countrymen spurned the Book of Common Prayer as being in *New English,* which *so many* could not understand, as they could neither read nor follow the service in English; Cornish, a dialect of the Celtic, being their language. The insurgents grew more daring, in proportion as mercy was offered to them; and in their 10th article expressed their determination to have nothing to do with the *English* tongue, as follows:—

"We will have the Bible and all books of Scripture in English to be called in again. For we are informed that otherwise the clergy shall not of long time confound the heretics."*

Lord Russel, in this rebellion, from not having received the expected supplies for suppressing it from the Court, at that time so far distant, three merchants of Exeter, Prestwood, Bodlie, and Periam, assisted him with such a sum of money, borrowed on their credit from the merchants of LYME and Taunton, as quite dispelled his worship's heaviness.† Lord Russel defeated the rebels at Exeter, 19th Aug. 1549, with the loss of 1000 men.

* Proclamation of King Henry VIII., A.D. 1526, forbade the buying, receiving, or keeping the New Testament or the Old, in the English, French, or Dutch tongue. Notes and Queries.

† Savage's Edit. of Toulmin's Hist. of Taunton. Hist. of Exeter, Fuller, &c.

Cranmer answered the articles sent forth, some of which had wholly reference to secular objects. One of the grievances was to be redressed by not allowing a person of one hundred mark land to keep more than one servant. The Archbishop inquired what was to be done by the master if he sent the servant to ride to London, and had no other to wait upon him?

Profitable Use made of the Ore or Sea-Weed.

A HISTORY might be written upon the changes that the world has seen in the relative value of the substances with which the vegetable and mineral kingdoms abound. Some products of the earth and sea, once valueless, are now an endless source of wealth; while others, that for centuries furnished riches to the fortunate possessors, have ceased to rank in the list of valuable substances. Modern discoveries in chemical science have opened new sources for man's industry. Our subject leads to an account of the neglect of what was once very valuable, SEA-WEED or ORE-weed. Wherever this grew upon the rocky ledges or shelves upon our sea-coast, it was a useful product. Lyme borough accounts in Edward VI.'s reign show that a regular income was made by letting the right to cut and harvest the ore or sea-weed growing upon the ledges, which are dry at low water to the extent of 500 acres.

The sea-weed was burnt into ashes: Roger Garland, mayor, enters, that he has "received of the man that burns the ower, that was due unto the town, 27*s*." In 1569, "an arrearage of oare" is entered 20*s*. The oar-burning let in 1589, for three years, at 40*s*. a year.

The renters of the ore-weed at Lyme were subject to loss by depredations. They were protected by local municipal laws made for the special occasion on the spot, and those, too, of some severity: in 1569, "a fine for oare" is entered as being 40*s*. This in the margin is marked thus: "For a fyne for burning of oare."

In 1580, an order of the Court of Hustings was made: —

It is ordered that none do burn ore within the parish and liberty without Mr. Mayor's license, upon pain of 10*s*.

This was not a dead letter, for a jury soon after presented an offender for having burnt ore-weed in the parish, and he was fined 2*s*.

Item, presentant quod Thomas Wood cremavit seu comburit vevas, anglice (weeds of the sea, or oare) infra parochiam citra Licenc' Maioris.

Ideo ip̄ in mia̅, 2*s*.

Some persisted in this dishonest practice, so another order was framed in 1596. An entry in 1621 demands some explanation: —

Item, paid Mr. John Roze for the charges of the oar ashes, 1*l*. 12*s*. 8*d*.

This closes the accompts about burning the sea-weed. No renter could be found; the sea-weed was in hand which a useful helper of the corporation managed for the body without success, it would appear.

The sea-weed thrown up after a storm is carted away for manure, for which nothing is paid. Except to a few invalids, to whom the pounded pods of the *Fucus vesiculosus* are beneficial from the iodine they contain, as an application to glandular swellings, the growing sea-weed is now worthless. All soda was formerly derived from kelp, the sea-weed, which contains 6 per cent. of alkali, and sold for 200*l*. a ton before Le Blanc's method came into use.* Proprietors of land on the shores of Scotland were enriched by letting out portions for the preparing of kelp. This harvest has ceased there, as well as on the coast of England. The reduction of the duty on foreign alkali, in 1823, gave the first blow to the kelp manufacture; and the discovery of a process by which a cheaper alkali might be extracted from common salt, the heavy duty on which had been reduced, made both kelp and barilla unsaleable.

* Alum sold for 100*l*. a ton; it is now 10*l*.

Le Blanc, by means of sulphuric acid, converted salt into *sulphate of soda*. Eighty pounds are required for every hundred pounds of salt. Hence the creating a very large demand for sulphuric acid. This is made of sulphur and saltpetre, or nitrate of soda. Some houses in England produce 1000 tons of sulphuric acid annually.

Kelp is now only manufactured for the sake of the iodine it contains; and as this element is most abundant in the sea-weed that grows at such a depth as not to be accessible *in situ*, the kelp for iodine is made from the weed cast ashore after storms. Even in the most favourable places it hardly pays the cost of making it. Thirty tons of kelp produce one ton only of alkali, worth now only about 3*l.* 10*s.*, instead of 200*l.*

As a set-off to the above picture, we may add that a once comparatively worthless material from the same locality,—blue lias limestone,—brings in quite a revenue in the present day; and some strata of the same formation, worthless, as was thought, even among the disregarded layers of that stone, now fetch a high price as a rapidly setting cement.*

Inability to read or write.

How striking the circumstance of our meeting with the epitaphs of men much lauded for their worth, and even ability, who could not read or write! Before learning was general many individuals were unlettered, ignorant in book learning, who were still, considering the age, cultivated men, clever by comparison with others. They proved what oral teaching could do. In Tudor reigns numbers could sign their name, who could do no more in the way of writing. They may have carried their philosophy about with them, and propagated it in the walking place, under the pentice, and in the market.

At a Court of Hustings at Lyme Regis, 2nd November, 1584, "It was agreed at a Court held in the Moot Hall,

* Quart. Rev. CLXXIX., p. 157.

that as well the burgesses and freemen, as well inhabitant as not inhabitant, as all other inhabitants, shall be contributory to the payment of taxes and impositions to be levied towards the charge of the burgesses for the Parliament." And it is added the burgesses chose two assessors on their parts, the mayor and his brethren two on their parts.

The town was not incorporated when this important decision was come to, after having been duly mooted in the Guild hall. After the entry in the Hustings' Book, and some few signatures, appear sundry hieroglyphics, marks, and initial letters, eleven in number, of those who could not write — the legislators who had just determined so wisely on the floor of their little house of assembly.

The following hieroglyphics are placed in laughable juxtaposition with the pedantic Latin of the learned Town Clerk :—

 Signum : Jacobi Hackwell.

 Roberti Tyneham.

 Richardi Stansby.

 Roberti Myco.

 Henrici Palmer.

 Johannis Sanford.

 Roberti Davy.

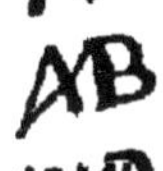 Wm. Bagster.*

 Marci Barens.

 Johannis Ley.

* William Bagster was the ancestor of the members of an honourable London firm, who have a motto expressive of the many *tongues* introduced into their Polyglot editions of the Scriptures. "Πολλαι μεν θνητοις Γλωτται, μια δ' Αθανατοισιν." "Multæ terricolis linguæ, cœlestibus una."

Of ninety inhabitants of Brighton who signed some orders as sanctioning them in 1580, only seven wrote their own autographs. After their names, written for them, the others added marks, such as the anchor, the axe, the wheel, the anvil, and the plough, with other professional instruments and utensils.

The marks remind one of the Paraph of the Spanish, and other merchants of the Continent. This is the name given to a tortuous specimen of caligraphy, in common phrase, a flourish or strike after and below the signature, to render a counterfeit difficult or impossible. The Paraphs of correspondents, kept by houses of business for reference, have an odd effect, and resemble so many reptiles of the Nile twisting and twining in all kinds of shapes.

Lest unfairness may be thought to be dealt to our provincial tradesmen, the writing faculty of an ambassador a century earlier is here given.

Shassek, secretary to the mission of Leo, Baron of Rosmital and Blatna, ambassador from Bohemia to the court of Edward IV., mentions what power in the way of writing the head of that mission displayed at Windsor in 1466. After dining with the Knights of the Garter, he was requested to write his autograph in their mess book or album, a feat which he accomplished with such dubious success that when he had departed an application was sent after him to return and read it. Perhaps this great man could have simply written his name; but the name with his titles added made the performance a difficult task. We here detect an early desire to collect autographs, which has long been an established mania.

The framework of society was, at the period under consideration, differently constructed. The far greater number could not read and write. If a man now-a-days addresses one who is in the latter predicament, he is apt at once to treat him as an inferior in every particular, as a matter of course. It was not so in Elizabeth's reign. In the present age schooling or book learning is necessarily indispensable. Still some who have missed this valuable acquirement are cultivated, and possess great powers of mind, or what is styled ability, as they did in the Tudor reigns. A living Impresario, who labours under these disadvantages, is supposed to be the best judge of music in Europe. I have accidentally had working for me one who could not read or write, and another who was highly accomplished in algebra. The master of these two was the untaught!

Learning was honoured in Elizabeth's and James the First's reigns: a want of ability to read and write was not always treated as a disgrace, though it disqualified for some situations.

Daniel Morfiun, or Murefin, of Leicester, in the next reign, "for that he cannot write, was by most voices discharged from being chamberlain hereafter," and another person was treated in like manner. There was no disgrace attending this exclusion; for this Mr. Morfiun was chosen alderman, and died after having served the office of mayor in 1660.*

It is becoming very rare to meet with a person in the situation of a master who can neither read nor write. A few years since the occurrence was more frequent, and the deficient party wrapped up the circumstance in this expression, "I'm no scholard."

Sir Fowell Buxton's account of Abraham Plaistow, the gamekeeper, who could neither read nor write, is illustrative of the merits of an unlettered man, and of the fact that mentally gifted individuals may be greatly pleased with one who is without school learning.

"My guide, philosopher, and friend, was Abraham Plaistow, the gamekeeper; a man for whom I have ever felt, and still feel, very great affection. He was a singular character: in the first place, this tutor of mine could neither read nor write, but his memory was stored with various rustic knowledge. He had more of natural good sense, and what is called mother-wit, than almost any person I have met with since: a knack which he had of putting everything into new and singular lights made him,

* Nichol's Hist. of Leicester.

and still makes him, a most entertaining, and even intellectual companion. He was the most undaunted of men: I remember my youthful admiration of his exploits on horseback. For a time he hunted my uncle's hounds, and his fearlessness was proverbial. But what made him particularly valuable were his principles of integrity and honour. He never said or did a thing in the absence of my mother of which she would have disapproved. He always held up the highest standard of integrity, and filled our youthful minds with sentiments as pure and as generous as could be found in the writings of Seneca or Cicero. Such was my first instructor, and, I must add, my best; for I think I have profited more by the recollection of his remarks and admonition than by the more learned and elaborate discourses of all my other tutors He was our playfellow and tutor; he rode with us, fished with us, shot with us, upon all occasions."

In a loyal petition from Bridgewater, in 1680, not one half of those who subscribed could write their names. The petition wore in consequence a very extraordinary appearance. The marks resembled hieroglyphics, or, as was satirically expressed, were like so many "reptiles of the Nile."

Persons who had the ability, or "gift," as it was called, to write, had rarely the accomplishment of being able to write well and clearly. Their caligraphy was at fault; hence a scrivener was applied to. This accounts for the excellent writing that is displayed in archives. A clever scrivener was also versed in the language suited to each station, — could deal out the *Suum cuique,* and besides the "writing," often undertook or assisted in "making," — by which is meant inditing a letter. Such is the *Ecrivain et redacteur* of French towns.

The accounts of churchwardens in the fifteenth century were "made" in Latin, so the scrivener was educated in grammar learning. The church official had only to make some mark or nick till the scrivener came, who, learning that two bell ropes had been furnished for the bells, entered: —

> *Item,* pro duos ropys pro campanis, xiiij*d.*
> *Item,* solvere pro faciende de cleper de campanis, xij*d.*

When at a loss for any Latin phrase, as of a single word, the man of letters assumed the vernacular, — could not perhaps, for the pay he received, afford time to turn the matter before him into a dead language. The entries therefore exhibit an example of churchwardens' Latin, a kind of Lingua Franca, *e. g.*: —

> *Item*, pro lavare de sorplyss & vestments, iiij*d.*
> *Item*, pro faciende de cere & coste de vetell, xiij*d.**

Parish clerks in the country, about the year 1600, could not write, and some could scarce read or sing.† The practice of reading each verse of a hymn to be sung was necessary, for the majority could not have benefited by a psalter.

A comparison of anecdotes referring to distant and recent epochs is often striking.

A jury had to make an inventory and valuation of armour, arms, &c. at Sompting, in the reign of Edward I. The jurors duly priced the weapons, which were too often used in everyday life, but were unable to put a price upon two MS. books, "Liber Regum," and "Liber Bestiarum."‡

The time of Horn Books had not then arrived. And it may be asked, who has seen a Horn Book, except as a curiosity in a museum? Thousands were annually manufactured only a few years ago. Some do not know what this earliest school implement really was. The alphabet was inserted in a wooden frame, to be held in the hand, and was covered over with *horn* to protect the paper, hence the whole was called a Horn Book.

Utility or necessity, not the whim of fashion, made tradesmen adopt a sign like the landlords of inns in the present day. "The Two Storks" and "Half Moon" over the window directed many a servant and customer who could not have made out the name or business in letters.

* Account of Cowfold, temp. Edward IV. Sussex Archæol. Coll.

† Nelson's Rights of the Clergy.

‡ W. H. Blauw, Esq, Com. to Sussex Archæol. Soc.

When London was paved or pitched with Scotch stone in 1764, all sign-posts and other posts to divide the foot-way from the roadway were removed.* This altered much the appearance of the streets.

Painting, writes Professor Hart, was the book of the ignorant, who knew not how to read in any other. The Curé of Troyes caused three windows to be painted, to serve as a catechism and instruction book to the people.

With the spread of knowledge of reading and writing, tallies, or nicked sticks, gradually disappeared. The memorandum book, price 2*d.*, and now 1*d.*, superseded the nick-stick for many purposes, as the parish and domestic clocks and watches caused the hour-glass to fall into disuse. Tallies were used long after writing was a common acquirement, the object being to prevent forgery.

Numeral letters were used to express the sums till about 1613, from which time the Arabic figures are employed. From about 1595, though the items are in letters, the totals are in Arabic figures.

Till about the year 1810, and later, type rejected from a printer's cases, because of being broken and worn, was sold to print cheap books for children†, a class of readers which requires distinctness and perfection in each letter.

As we sit in our pew we can see the par son
in the pul pit, and he can see us.

The general extension throughout our country towns of the faculty of reading, among even the lowest class, has proved fatal to the success of a character who now only proclaims his wares with nasal twang and peculiar emphasis in villages and hamlets.

Need I say the "last dying speech and confession man" is here designated,— one who early set off from the county town, at the close of the assize, with a "right true and particular

* Notes and Queries, Oct. 27. 1855, p. 323.

† A B C books sold, in 1583, at 1*d.* each.

account of all those prisoners that had been tried before my Lord Judge," printed on a broad sheet for a penny or half-penny, according to its length.

For many assizes no "last dying speech man" has come to Lyme. The one who visited West Dorset on the latest occasion traversed the Broad Street, Lyme, and the servant-maids, who were wont to flock to the windows and doors to buy, plied their work unmoved. The orator looked back upon the street and entered upon a soliloquy, in which the inhabitants were denounced, and he announced aloud that he would come no more to such a place.

The servants who could read the trials of the prisoners, and the civil cases heard at the assize as well in the county newspapers taken in by their masters, were unwilling to pay for a dry list of names.

Reading is a matter lightly estimated where all the appliances are at hand; master first, then, books. Only take to the secluded valleys of a remote county, there it becomes a difficult matter even yet to obtain instruction. In a deep comb of Devonshire a master was found for a Sunday school. He proved to be a bad character, who was there for concealment. A parishioner took the directions of a class. His services were such as we might suppose to have been like those rendered in the fifteenth century. First boy reads a verse in the New Testament. A pause ensues. The master finds no fault. First boy says to his master, "Reuben dw'unt seem to I that's fitty." Reuben is in doubt whether it is so or not. Thereupon master and scholars, teacher (?) and learners (?) commune together and comment upon the subject matter upon an almost equal amount or modicum of the reading faculty. This state of things obtained in higher branches of learning before this blessing was generally diffused. It can now only be tolerated in a sequestered valley, but must have been so over the whole breadth of the land.

No Mention made of Paintings. — Chained Books.

No mention of any money having been paid for a painting is made in any archives that I have examined. No "limner's" name appears. The fine arts could not have been at all patronised in the country towns under the Tudor sovereigns. A century after the estate of the compounder, Philip Palmer, of Dorney, Bucks, consisted almost entirely of paintings. Where can any mention of an earlier instance of a private gallery be found?

There are no entries for payment for books for private individuals. How long was it after the introduction of printing and printed books that the burgesses of our towns possessed so valuable a property, one justly deemed so precious?

Books printed in black letter were given to churches for the use of the parishioners. They rested upon a large table, and each was chained in a secure manner. One dictionary was placed chained in a school for the use of the scholars, "tyed in a cheyne."

Little could the donor have imagined that a beautiful bound copy of the Holy Scriptures could be purchased for a mere trifling sum of a few pence.

Book chains are happily unknown.

One Adam de Oxenforth made his appearance at York as the first practiser of the art of bookbinding in the reign of Edward III.

Berthelet, the first royal printer, charged one penny a leaf for his work in 1531. At this rate a book would cost a good sum, much more than is charged in the present day.

Particulars respecting the Board and Education of Young Persons of either Sex.

Much attention has been called in the present century to the school system carried on in Yorkshire, which a popular writer has exposed, and so powerfully, that it can be continued no longer.

The great fraud consisted in taking in boys for board and education, as if the usual conditions of such establishments were to be observed. The cultivation of a farm by the master and his numerous pupils was quite kept out of view. The students were partly labourers; school, literally, as the word implies, a place of leisure, was indeed for them a place of toil.

After all the odium which has been thrown upon these northern tricksters, the parents were really as much to blame. They knew the sum paid was no remuneration for clothes, the very meanest food, and any teaching at all. So they expected little under these heads, and surmised the labour element, which entered largely into the affair.

The taking in children to instruct them, and then to employ them for services conducive to the advantage of the keeper of "Dotheboys Hall," is not a modern idea. The terms for schooling were often too low; but it had been fair to have stipulated for services to be rendered to eke out. The modern agricultural schools for the poor have a morning for instruction in books, an afternoon for work, with payment accordingly — all duly set forth in the public notices. There are such for a higher class in Canada.

In James I.'s reign, Sir John Bramston refers, in his Diary, to his going out in the morning, the day on which some particular occurrence took place, with his books to study (?) at a distance of three or four miles, while he watched his master's cows. What season did not afford some object of a boy's pursuit — eggs, apples, and nuts?

A case at the Blandford Jan. Session, in 1626, no doubt excited great interest.

John Dibsdale, late of Langton, in Dorset, clothier, deceased, had placed his daughter Dorothy, two years before this event, with Mrs. Roche, the wife of Mr. Roche, parson of Helton, for the term of five years from thence, to be by her bred up and taught her needle, and gave Mrs. Roche 15*l.*

for his said daughter's teaching and diet, and was to provide apparel for her during the term.

Mr. Thomas White, of Langton, clerk, uncle to the said Dorothy, detained her from Mrs. Roche, who applied to the Court to order Mr. White to send back Dorothy for her term, or else to give her some compensation.

The Court, judging that the contract between Mr. John Dibsdale and Mrs. Roche was for the placing of Dorothy to be taught as a scholar, and not to be employed as a servant, did not think fit to make any order for the relief of Mrs. Roche.*

What could generally be expected from such a commencement of schooling, we will not dignify it by the name of education, as obtained about the middle and close of the seventeenth century at Winchester?

A child six years old was sent, not to the school in the college, but to the care of a Mr. May, a fellow of the college, who boarded the child. The little boy had no master, but was taught at his boarding-house, for it virtually was such, with other gentlemen's sons, by a SELECT NUMBER OF THE SENIOR BOYS, who were to give an account to Dr. Burt, the master of the school, by turns, how these children behaved themselves, and what progress they made in learning. This system was followed for two years, when the boy of eight entered the school, and removed to college between the age of sixteen and seventeen.

This early school, and subsequently college career, furnish matter for much comment by any one who has made the science of education his study.†

The scholars at our large schools had regular cockfights. John Richards, Esq. went, in the year 1700, to see the scholars at Wimborne cock-fight.‡

Cock-fighting would appear to have been an affair of the school, recognised by the masters, and the charges for which

* Mr. T. Hearn, "Qui Quondam."

† Private Memoirs of John Potenger, Esq. Edited by the Rev. C. W. Bingham, &c.

‡ Diary in the New Retrospective Review.

were defrayed by them, to be hereafter paid by the parents, just as some innocent excursions and festivities are managed now-a-days. The credit of the school was without doubt often involved in the proper issue of the fight.

Sir James Mackintosh, when at school at Fortrose in 1776–7, had this entry in his account, in which books were charged 3*s.* 6*d.*: —

To cocks'-fight dues for 2 years, 2*s.* 6*d.* each, 5*s.*

Associated are three months' fees at the dancing-school, minuet, country-dances, and hornpipe, &c.*

At some of our western endowed grammar schools the charges for board were, a century ago, very, indeed surprisingly low. Parents who wonder at this need to be told that the morning and evening draught, two meals of the day, had ceased, and no tea morning or evening had been substituted in their place, except at an extra charge. The fare was mean and scanty. Old women cake-sellers in the neighbourhood of the school house prepared tea and coffee, boiled eggs, and fryed rashers of bacon from a flitch which they kept hung up, and which had been sent by the parents from home. Dinner was the single meal taken at the master's table, who really furnished only partial board, in accordance with the practice of the day.

Firing was charged to a young lady, a boarder in a school at Richmond, from September to April, in 1646, the sum of 19*s.* 6*d.*

In 1697 the board and education at our western grammar schools was 12*l.* a year. Everything was just one-third the price it now bears, and the fare is now excellent and abundant.

Dancing was charged at the rate of a guinea the quarter, and a guinea entrance.

The beginning dinner at some schools with pudding has been supposed to be the invention of some stingy schoolmaster. The same custom is found among the natives of

* Notes and Queries, No. 271.

Suffolk and neighbouring counties to this day. In Tudor reigns dinners commenced with pudding; hence *pudding-time* means the nick of time, or just at the right time.*

Presents of articles of food were customarily made by the parents to the master, and at female schools to the mistress. In the latter-mentioned establishments scanty fare was complained of with great reason, but not the same amount of justice; for the terms were not adequate to enable a wholesome set of meals to be furnished throughout the year without a loss.

Cheap board for pupils was not a too scanty supply of *good* food, but an abundance of food that the young could not eat. The same plan is followed now-a-day in cheap schools.

Sir Symonds D'Ewes experienced this scanty fare at Wambrook, near Chard, which occasioned his not returning to continue his studies in the west.

The late Rev. Sydney Smith said of Winchester school, when presided over by Dr. Joseph Warton, that it was one system of abuse, neglect, and vice. The food was coarse and insufficient, so that he often suffered from absolute hunger. His younger brother Courtenay twice ran away to escape the miseries of the place.

Running away, now hardly known, was once present to the mind of every school boy, and numbers had recourse to it on the first grievance.

The practice of the colleges or grammar schools in France in this century may in one particular be found illustrative of this subject. At the college of Valognes, in the year 1816, there was in the refectory ordinary room a long table, in the centre of which sat the masters on either side. Above them sat the boarders, or full boarders, who had every meal found them in the establishment. Below sat a class of boys who paid very little, and who had partial board. At dinner a basin of soup or broth was set before the latter as before the full boarders, but this was all. They tasted neither fish,

* See Withal's Dictionarie, 1608.

meat, nor fruit, but sat at table eycing the busy scene till the full boarders had finished their dinner or supper; for these two meals, the one at half-past twelve, the other at seven, strictly resembled each other.

This mode of living probably resembled that in practice in England. The partial boarders made up for the scantiness of their food at table by recourse to supplies from home, and those to be purchased at shops, articles of food privately dressed by the cook, &c.

That corporal chastisement was practised at school is not to be wondered at, as it was in vogue everywhere. Parental authority was maintained in the same manner; children of both sexes were subjected to corporal chastisement so long as they continued under the paternal roof.

The making birch rods for great schools is an occupation that requires but little time. *Horsing* is no longer the subject of daily conversation.

Till very recently, and possibly even now in some scholastic establishments belonging to the Catholics in this country, the ferula was administered in a manner likely to correct false grammar and false quantities, and at the same time to inspire a hatred of Saints' names, if not of more. Each blow was given accompanied by the name of some Saint of the Romish calendar, as if he required to be propitiated for an offence specially offered.

A "breeching boy" was the customary member of every royal establishment where a young scion of royalty or nobility was receiving education. This was the scape-goat, the sufferer of the punishment merited by his noble co-student whom he stimulated to exertion, and for whose short-comings he smarted. The reigns of Charles I. of England, and of Louis XV. of France, saw a termination of this practice. Each royal or noble offender may go unpunished, but injustice no longer prevails; vicarious whippings are no more. The royal parent vindicates authority, and corrects incipient error.

Could youth but know the advantages they possess beyond what boys could once command, how deep should their gratitude be! Each boy in a class now possesses a beautiful printed book, his dictionary, his treasure and store-house. Was this always so? No, assuredly not so. In the records of the Boston corporation, A.D. 1578, is an entry of the agreement, "That a dictionary should be bought for the scollers of the Free Scole; and the same boke to be tyed in a cheyne, and set upon a deske in the scoole, whereunto any scollar may have accesse as occasion shall serve." *

How must the little and weak have been impeded in their search into the "ample page" of knowledge, when it pleased the big, and perchance the brutal, to keep the front place! The labour about the dictionary must have been galling and too often fruitless, unless under vigilant inspection one boy was made to turn out for the class.

The relation between master and pupils was very different from what now so happily obtains. The master was a ruler, whose rules and government were disputed by his subjects. Faction engaged their thoughts too often more than study. Affection between the parties was rare, mutual hatred was common; hostility too often was unintermitted. The history of too many schools would be one of rebellious conduct, tyranny, and riotous outbreak.

In the days of corporation exclusiveness in some schools, none but the sons of freemen were admitted to the higher school; the sons of foreigners or aliens — meaning those not free of the borough — were doomed to an inferior position. The fine mind was checked in its aspirations. What must have been the bitter regret of genius thus arrested in a career that was full of hope?

The schoolmaster, half a century ago, figured in an unamiable light compared with his successors. He knew, and was paid to transmit. What he knew he deemed to be honourable, gentlemanlike, patrician, and in no one particular plebeian or vulgar. What came under this designation included in general terms no physical science, which he branded as philosophy; no arithmetic in any shape or form,

* Notes and Queries P. Thompson.

no geometry, no geography, no English history, no English reading, poetry, or prose, spelling, and many other subjects. These were treated as utterly vulgar, and unworthy of a master who was a gentleman. An usher called the writing-master did really teach some of these despised matters, for want of which thousands made shipwreck of life; but as he knew nothing of Latin, and was essentially a plebeian, both the man and his subjects were held in ineffable contempt.

The master never condescended to converse with those confided to his care. He ruled them for Greek and Latin; and his appearance was a prelude to correction and punishment.

The development of character, the encouraging good aspirations, the correction of erroneous views, in a word the man-building, were quite impossible. A baronet found tears gushing from his eyes upon seeing some pupils running up to a master and familiarly conversing with him. He said he had been eight years under the master of a great public school, and had never exchanged one syllable with his well-paid instructor in Greek, Latin, and versification. Eight years' falsely styled education! What might not have been effected in that time for the improvement or the correction of each pupil?

The neglect of writing and arithmetic in the grammar schools was compensated in the writing and more mixed schools by pieces setting forth the marvels of penmanship with flourishes and strikes. Maps were worked up that had occupied a quarter of the year, to the exclusion or nearly so of study or mental exercises by those who never had to do with a map the rest of their lives. These were deceptions practised upon ignorant parents.

The writing schoolmaster, in his prospectus of terms, generally contrived to include as many branches of knowledge or accomplishments as were known.

The relation between masters and boys at our great public schools involved, generally speaking, as was understood, no religious responsibilities. When Dr. Butler, of Shrewsbury School, was addressed by a parent who complained of the deterioration of his son's morals, he replied, "My business is to teach him Greek, and not morality." Chapels have lately been built, and sermons preached and published, some of which the Quarterly Review calls mere advertising puffs of the schools from which they emanate.

Viewing the other side of the picture, the gentle treatment followed in so many schools of the present day, it cannot be concealed that the ordinary difficulties of learning arrest the progress of the majority; an effeminacy of mind is the result; discipline is notoriously bad, and very many lose their chance of success in life, and sink into a bad state of mental inactivity and irreclaimable inefficiency and insignificance, perhaps of vice, all from the want of some slight personal correction.

There is much interesting matter in the following expenses of a young lady's school at Richmond, in 1646, found among some papers by Ev. Ph. Shirley, Esq.* : —

The Account for Peggy's Disbursements since her going to Schoole at Richmond, being in Sept. 1646.

	s.	*d.*
Payd for a louehood - - - - -	2	6
For cariing the truncke to Queenhithe - - -	0	8
For cariing it to Hammersmith - - - -	1	0
Payd for two pair of shoes - - - -	4	0
Payd for a singing booke - - - -	1	0
Given to Mrs. Jervoise's maid - - - -	1	0
Payd for a hairlace and a pair of showstrings - -	1	0
For an inckhorne - - - - - -	0	4
For faggots, 2*s.* 8*d.*; and cleaving of wood, 12*d.* - -	3	8
For 9 li. of soape, 2*s.* 4*d.*; and starch, 4*d.* - -	2	8
For hookes and a bolt for the door - - -	0	9
For sugar and licorish - - - - -	1	4
For silke and thread - - - - -	0	6
For 3 li. of soape, 11*d.*; and starch, 4*d.*, and carrying letters, 6*d.* - - - - - -	1	9
For 3 li. of soape, 12*d.*, and starch, 4*d.* - - -	1	4
For sugar, licorich, and coultsfoot - - -	1	6

* Notes and Queries, April 14. 1855.

	s.	d.
For a necklace, 12*d.*, for a m. of pins, 12*d.* - -	2	0
For a pair of cands (candles?), 6*d.*, for muckadine, 4*d.*, for wormsend (worsted), 2*d.* - - - -	1	0
For showstrings, 6*d.*, for going on errrands, 6*d.* - -	1	0
For 3 li. of soape, 12*d.*, for starch, 4*d.*, for thread and silk, 4*d.* - - - - -	1	8
For a bason, 4*d.*, for carrying letters, 6*d.*, for tape, 4*d.* -	1	2
For soap, 12*d.*, for starch, 4*d.*, for goin on errands, 6*d.* -	1	10
For a pair of pattins, 1*s.* 6*d.*, for three pair of shoes, 6*s.* -	7	4
For callico to line her stockins, 2*d.*, for showstrings, 4*d.*	0	6
For 3 li. of soape, 12*d.*, for a pint of white wine, 4*d.* -	1	4
For ale, 3*d.*, for ½ li. of sugar, 8*d.* - - -	0	11
For a m. of pins, 12*d.*, for a corle and one pair of half-handed gloves, 8*d.* - - - - - -	1	8
Given to the writing mr. - - - - -	2	6
For silver for the toothpick case - - - -	1	6
For silke, 12*d.*, for a toothpick case, 4*d.* - - -	1	4
For a sampler, 12*d.*; for thread, needles, paper, pins, and parchment, 30*d.* - - - - - -	3	6
For a pair of shoes, 2*s.* 2*d.*; for ribbon, 3*d.* - -	2	5
For soape, 19*d.*; for starch, 4*d.*; for cariing a letter, 4*d.*	1	8
To the waterman bringing the (box?) to Richmond -	1	0
For shoestrings, 6*d.*; for a purge, 18*d.* - - -	2	0
For bringing the box from Richmond - - -	1	0
For a coach from Fleete Streete - - - -	1	0
For wood to this time - - - - - -	15	10

Totall disbursements to this 15th day of Aprill, 1647, is - - - - - - 3 18 5

In country towns, seventy years ago, music was a rare accomplishment. There were few opportunities for learning. At Lyme there was not a piano in the whole town. There were musicians, and there were the church singers, who valued their musical acquirements at no mean rate, according to the cosmopolitan plan in the ratio of the supply. At length a blind musical teacher came from Martock, who rode, and had behind him a boy as a guide. Who can now remember Mr. Westlake? He was a good teacher, and was in great demand. He would arrive at a country house in the evening, give a lesson that very evening, rise very early and give a second lesson; then mount for another scene of labour and harmonious usefulness.

The crowning labour — the highest step in the ladder, some half a century ago, was the "Battle of Prague." Let no one disparage the ability to perform this fine *melange* of sounds, — the tramp of cavalry, the firing of great guns, and other musical realisations.

We may have fine music, but properly speaking, no finale in which, as in the "Battle of Prague," the force of music could no farther go. That difficult piece was not attained *per saltum.* There was no royal road to the "Battle of Prague;" that culminating point was only won by due gradation and professional sequence.

The sampler, with patterns of letters, long held its place in girls' schools. There was a posy at the end, and its destiny was to be framed and glazed, as a memento of industry and acquirements in the use of the needle. The sampler was, with females, what a "piece" was among boys. It delighted, and too often deceived the parents. The "piece" was a large sheet of paper with ornamental border around a space intended to be filled with fine penmanship, and often with finer sentiment. How much sound learning was sacrificed for the preparing the "piece!" It has fallen into merited disrepute, and deservedly so. Sound learning was made to yield to caligraphy or fanciful penmanship, — an unprofitable acquirement to the ninety-nine of every hundred.

Wearing Arms.

THE change effected when our countrymen disused the habitual wearing of arms was remarkable; and its effect upon society at large cannot well be sufficiently estimated.

Too many of our forefathers drank at times to excess.

When it was the custom to wear arms, upon any affront being offered at a church-ale, a bull-baiting, or at church particularly, men drew upon each other as readily as their faulty descendants now resent any personal indignity by a blow with the fist.

A quarrelsome man, who is "a striker," is now-a-days a nuisance on any public occasion, and causes confusion, till secured by the constables and peaceably disposed. What intolerable annoyance must a brawling, drunken, armed man have proved himself! Constables made such characters the subject of their presentments at the court leets. A furious, passionate man ran a risk of being described like Henry Davy, by the Lyme constables as, periculosum et irregulatum et pronum homines ad eos ledend' et nocend' (a dangerous and unruly character, ready to hurt and injure other men).* These officials were generally pithy in their entries, *e.g.*: — "John Guppy, killing Henry Seymour," "Williams, killing a soldier," "John Way, drawing blood of a stranger." Two men had fought respectively "with sword and staff (that is, quarter-staff), and "intended to prosecute their lewd purpose."

John Brewer killed William Bull at Castle Combe with a sword, A.D. 1524, and then ran to the church. He spoke with the coroner, abjured the realm, chose a port beyond sea by Dover, and forfeited all his goods and chattels to the lord of the manor.†

Such matters were appropriately returned by the constables as "bloodsheds." In 1569 the Mayor of Lyme paid to Wm. Merchant for healing the Fleming's head, and three days his meat and drink, 20*d.*

The evils arising from going about armed were acknowledged. King Henry VII. issued a proclamation upon the subject. Though our countrymen were allowed to be armed when they travelled through the wilds of uncultivated England, still at other times they were not to be so.

* Presentment, A.D. 1601.

† Hist. of that Manor by Hon. P. Scrope.

The king, out of respect to the surety, peace, and restfulness of all his subjects, forbad the wearing any bills, bows, and arrows, swords, long nor short bucklers, nor any other harness nor *weapons invasive,* in any town or city, but at such times as men journey or ride, upon pain of forfeiture of the weapons and imprisonment.

No man, of whatever rank, was to make any affray or quarrel with any other person.

After this proclamation country corporations began to stir to carry out the wishes of the king. At Leicester, in this reign (Henry VII.), making an affray was viewed as a serious matter. Should blood have been shed, the fine was 6*s.* 8*d.*; without blood, 3*s.* 4*d.* No one was to leave his house after the nine o'clock bell had rung, except officers and the watch, or forfeit 12*d.*; 2*s.* for the second offence, and for the third offence to suffer imprisonment. The Mayor of Leicester, Richard Gyllott, made an order in 1467, that no one in town should bear any weapon except in support of the mayor in case of an affray, so that the mayor had in such an event to arm and lead in person against the rioters; a knight or an esquire might have a sword borne after him. Every countryman was to leave his weapon at his inn, before going about his business in fair or market, and every innkeeper was bidden, at Leicester and in other boroughs, to give warning to his customers to do so. If they wore their weapon it was to be forfeited, and the offender's body was to lie in prison as long as the mayor liked. No townsman was to lend a countryman any weapon, except it was to be used in support of the mayor.*

At Marlborough there was a bye-law made for the special subject:—

> "XXV. Every inhabitant shall have in readiness in his shop or other place where he has ready access, a club, bill, or other necessary weapon, that he or his servants may be in readiness to assist the authorities in suppressing any outcry or breach of the peace." †

* Gutch's Coll. Curioso.—Nicholl's Hist of Leicester.

† Waylen's Hist. of Marlborough.

Rabelais gives a minute description of the dresses of this period, and satirises the custom now first introduced of going about armed; every one, he tells us, carrying "la belle épée au coté, la poignée dorée, le fourreau de velours de la couleur des chausses, le bont d'or et d'orfévrerie, le poignard de même." *

Mankind do not usually burden themselves with that which they do not intend to use. The wearing of arms was no exception. Well might citizens be bidden to provide themselves with weapons to put down a fray, for such was what many gloried in, particularly in public places.

When publicity was the object, no place could be so suitable for a fight as the interior of a church, or a churchyard, when parishioners were assembled at the church hatch, or else in city, or at market. The proclamation of 3 & 4 Philip and Mary, 27 March, 1557, complains how certain quarrelsome persons, both naughty and insolent, provided themselves with swords and rapiers of a much greater length than had been accustomed to be used, and wore gauntlets and vambraces as well as bucklers, with long pikes in them, to be ready for a quarrel, riot, or fray, which they sought, as before said, at church, in the churchyard, &c.

Churches were not then covered with pews, and afforded an open space for a fight, or a theatrical performance. There many deaths and wounds had been dealt.

These long rapiers, exceeding a yard and half a quarter at the blade, were to be broken; for they appear to have been worn for duelling. A dagger was not to exceed twelve inches at the blade.

In 1616 James I. prohibited, by proclamation, the wearing of steelets, or pocket daggers—dagges, or pocket pistols, which were used in duelling.†

The being restrained in the use of offensive weapons

* Handbook to Renaissance Court. — Court of the Crystal Palace by J. Waring.

† Nicholl's Leicester, temp. Elizabeth.

was deemed an indignity by the proud and quarrelsome swash-bucklers of that day. They were not all willing to submit to such a degradation.

So late as Oct. 1854, a jury of freemen at Lyme Regis appeared to consider the conduct of a brother freeman. It was solemnly given to them "in charge to inquire if Nicholas Hassard hath made a breach of his liberty for his disobedience, for he being commanded by the mayor to lay down his weapons, and not to wear them in the street, he hath denyed to lay them down."

"Also he thrust or shouldered Mr. Mayor yesterday night, as Mr. Mayor came by the walke," the space under the old custom house, opposite the Assembly Rooms. Nicholas Hassard forfeited his freedom.*

The individual so punished belonged doubtless to a class who viewed novelties with an evil eye, and who feared that degeneracy could result from some recent introductions. The Swiss were enjoined, about the year 1627, not to neglect to gird on the sword when they went to church, nor to effeminate themselves by the use of tea and coffee.†

Local history abounds with episodes of the evils of men wearing arms. An instance is adduced from Lyme.

The year 1592 was rendered memorable by a melancholy occurrence in the open street. Nicholas Ellesdon, one of the serjeants, arrested a merchant residing at Dowlands, named John Seward, at the suit of one Belpit, of Weymouth, which Seward, in his anger, killed the officer, who was only discharging his duty, and who fell a victim to the practice of wearing arms. In the Hustings' Book for the year the affair appears at length, and it is stated, "the which odious act, by all presumption, happened the rather through the want of clubs in the town; for the having of clubs might be an occasion to restrain such lewd attempts by terrifying such blood-thirsty persons." Clubs not less than seven feet in length were ordered to be pro-

* See the Freemen's Book, p. 290.

† Historical Pictures of the Middle Ages in Black and White, by Mrs. R. Moore.

vided, and in skilful hands proved no doubt, as quarter staves, very efficient weapons. A dexterous practiser of the quarter-staff would bid defiance to any man. A western gentleman, with this weapon, fought at Xeres, in Spain, against three rapiers and poniards. Judge Anderson, a well-known character, pronounced that the killing the serjeant in the street was not murder, but manslaughter; because he had not procured a warrant from the mayor.

No pages or lacqueys were to wear swords, as by a proclamation in the year 1661.

The wearing of arms was in general use at the beginning of the eighteenth century. Dissoluteness and the sword had fierceness lent to them by drink. The sword clubs were suppressed by a royal proclamation in 1724. For full particulars of the bravos of the reign of George I., and how Beau Nash exerted himself at Bath, see the Gent's Mag. for Sept. 1852, for an article by Dr. Doran.

Persons in the United States of America going to coloured balls are required to leave their weapons below. Upon a row happening parties hand them up, if called upon to do so.

The Mohocks, about 1720, when they sallied out upon their nightly orgies, wore their weapons, as we learn that one branch of that fraternity — the "Dancing-Masters" — made persons dance about, by running the points of their swords into their legs. Whole parties of these men, very drunk, would rush forward in the streets of London with their swords drawn, which they used against the unoffending.

Haydn, the composer, played at concerts with a tie wig on, and wearing a sword by his side. He died so late as 1809.

Sumptuary Laws of Dress and Expenditure.

In very ancient times men were compelled by law to regulate their expenditure in various ways, and particularly their dress, according to their rank and their means.

The officer who took account of such matters at Rome, that is, the Censor, held the sumptuary rate-book, the Census; and he judged by that roll what display in living or in dress was allowable to each individual. The several classes of the community were distinct from one another; and each had distinct privileges in the eye of the State.

In order to keep separate the several orders of men or classes, rules were prescribed for each, to regulate their expenditure, their dress, the number of funeral piles that might be lighted, and for various purposes. A part of these, when attentively considered, are found to have been social, a part sumptuary, strictly so called, and some political.

When in modern times our soverigns and our local municipal bodies turned their attention to the regulating every action in daily life of their subjects and fellow townsmen, there was scarcely anything that did not become the subject matter of proclamations or municipal orders and precepts. Some of these openly assailed expensive habits, and regulated the value of the materials any one might wear in garments according to his income. Such were true sumptuary laws, and an imitation of those of the times of the Roman history. Other proclamations wear the semblance of having been dictated by the peculiar taste or fancy of the sovereign. Most profess to regard the welfare of the state and the subject.

Now that every one is left to dress in whatever colour or in materials of whatever value the wearer may choose, and the vast population occasions no trouble or concern to any official, but finds ample check in ridicule against bad taste, and in distress against too prodigal a style of dress or living, it seems strange how so many laws about dress, &c. could have been required. It may be remarked that they were deemed to have been necessary three centuries and a half ago.

Henry VII. saw occasion to restrain the nobles. Lord Bacon tells us of that king's visit to the Earl of Oxford. That nobleman had given his livery to an excessive number of retainers to do honour to his royal guest; who, however, determined, when leaving, not to overlook the breach of the sumptuary laws, but referred him to the Attorney-General, and bade him compound for the penalties incurred — a return which Mr. John Bruce deems not to have been that of a king, but of an informer.

Costume of the Reign of James I.

King Henry VIII. and Queen Mary had found it necessary to have recourse to sumptuary laws for the good of the state and the individual. An extract from one of these surprising and important proclamations will throw light upon the subject.

"The excess of apparel, and the superfluity of unnecessary foreign wares thereto belonging, attracted the attention of Queen Elizabeth, who foresaw the decay of the wealth of the realm by sending so much to foreign countries for the purchase of costly articles of attire; but her majesty considered likewise the wasting and undoing of a great number of young gentlemen, otherwise serviceable, and others seeking, by show of apparel, to be esteemed as gentlemen; who, allured by the vain show of those things, did not only consume themselves, their goods and lands which their parents had left unto them, but also run into such debts and shifts, as they cannot live out of danger of laws, without attempting unlawful acts whereby they are not any ways serviceable to their country as otherwise they might be."

In the following reign an aspirant to a lady's favour found that a suitable wardrobe for the occasion cost more than 100*l.*, and this for one not noble. Dogberry modestly boasted that he was a man that had "two gowns." A great personage had gowns of multitudinous colours and materials, and doublets and hose of great value. Clothing was very costly.

We should dislike, in the present day, to have our incomes ascertained in an inquisitorial manner, in order that the authorities might settle whether we might wear or not sarcenet in the lining of our doublet. When the articles used in the making of our garments were to be regulated by the amount of our income, the ascertaining this point was indispensable.

Those who could spend 40*l.* a year might wear sarcenet in the lining of their hose, doublet, hats, or caps.

Apprentices at the law, and utter barristers, and all merchants of any society, and all that keep household in city or town, and such as may dispend 20*l.* a year, might wear a welf of velvet in their gowns, jackets, or coats.*

None were to wear spurs, swords, rapiers, daggers, skaynes, wood knives or hangers, buckles or girdles, silvered or damasked, except knights' and barons' sons, and others of high degree or place, and gentlemen in ordinary attendance upon

* Proclamation of 1579.

the queen's majesty's person, except gilt, silvered, or damasked spurs.*

No husbandman was to wear in his doublet any other thing than that which is wrought within this realm, fustian and canvass *only* excepted.

No serving man or journeyman in handicrafts taking wages might wear in his doublet any other thing than fustian, canvass, leather, or woollen cloth.

If offending, the apparel was to be forfeited, or the value thereof, and 3*s.* 4*d.* a day fine for every day he should have worn the same.†

Excessive long cloaks in common sight monstrous, and great and excessive ruffs insupportable for charges, and indecent to be worn, were to be left off.

These ruffs were not to be more than a nail in depth.

These matters are adduced as examples, but in fact the proclamations about sumptuary regulations would fill pages. From the highest rank to the individual in humble station there was some rule applicable; there was something that might and might not be worn. Attentively studied, the persons that passed might have their rank discovered; each wore what was equivalent to a badge. Twelve persons of various grades might now each wear a badge with a number, and at a glance the most ignorant could appreciate their relative rank, and perhaps income. Such would be a ready mode; formerly the same object was effected by the regulations of dress. Such is no longer the case. Modern views repudiate such a plan. Many possessed of very different means, the rich land and fundholder, the party living by a profession or a business, dress in the same style, use the same materials, but perhaps differ much in taste. No fur, no silk is forbidden. A legacy which improves the income of a family, or many little adventitious circumstances occurring, cause no necessary change of habiliments. Information of the fact spreads, but no visible sign announces to the passer

* Proclamation of 1579. † Ibid.

by that income has improved, some municipal or other office has been undertaken, or any other remarkable personal occurrence supervened. A fusion of the members of society seems to have taken place, still, when we look at it with keen glance, the distinctions exist as of old; but they are not blazoned by sarcenet or welf of velvet. Each individual, in matter of attire and expense, is left to his own self-government, and each member of society is no longer a machine moved at the will of another, but is self guided, and so displays the result of his taste, his judgment, and prudence, or the want of those things. Personal liberty could not have been exercised or enjoyed while sumptuary laws were in force. A change for the better has taken place, though some are occasionally heard to admire a social state of things, under which those who dress to excess would have been checked or altogether restrained. Varieties of dress, ordered to distinguish the classes of society, partake of the continental or even Oriental character; liberty in dress is consonant with Anglo-Saxon or western feelings and sentiment.

The regulations for the dress of the members of our universities were very numerous. Hats, stuffed-out or bombasted breeches, hosen with only a yard and a half of cloth in them — all was laid down or forbidden by rule.

Apprentices were to wear no long or short wigs above 15*s.* in value, and no point lace.

The most pious of men, a learned and witty writer observed, were not above some regard for fashion, even with reference to very small matters.

Men once gave their minds, to create by means of dress and other insignia, a distinction between each class. Whether this was the result of rank or worldly means, they judged such a course to be necessary. It was a principle of action not only followed before the public, but sedulously attended to in hours of privacy. Thus, in the days of Elizabeth and James, no Puritan divine ever went to bed but with his head in a night-cap of black silk tipped with white. Under the same sovereigns doctors of medicine and privy councillors sank to sleep in night-caps wrought with gold silk.*

Sumptuary laws are spoken of as instances of tyranny and oppression on the part of the sovereign upon his unwilling and reluctant subjects. Nothing can be further from the truth. Sumptuary laws only stamped with authority, regulations about distinction of classes, &c., that society demanded of itself, and would have reflected upon a ruler that did not give heed to and enforce them. The juries of townsmen in boroughs clamoured for cucking-stool, pillory, and other implements of punishment. When these were wanting, the juries presented the authorities as "faulty." They judged the use of these things to be salutary, and so they did sumptuary laws, and that without them all society would be confounded in a kind of ancient chaos.

The doctors of medicine and privy councillors might, had legislators continued to pass sumptuary laws, have been called to account, or had a more humble night-cap prescribed for them. Princes wore similar head gear.

Dr. Doran relates that at the marriage of Frederic Prince of Wales, the son of George II., the royal bridegroom was splendid at night in his robe of gold tissue, and a night-cap wrought with gold silk. Thus attired, he glided among the crowd of fashionable people who stood in the bedroom to greet the illustrious pair; and with this marriage went out the unseemly fashion of such public greetings.

A glance at the passers by in a street will no longer suffice to determine who are the exalted among the male sex, and who belong to somewhat inferior grades. This was easily done when the draper sold the cloth and the trimmings to the many, which the country or village tailor made up, or, it may be said, disfigured. Now the expert country tailor is his own draper. The style of dress is much improved, and town and country become more and more assimilated. This is also the case with the several grades; for a great distinction existed between those who had their clothes

* Dr. Doran.

from town, and the unfortunates doomed to have their persons decorated by a rustic artist.

The subject leads to an opinion that visiting a circle and the gaieties of many watering places have been impaired by an equalisation in dress and *appearance* generally. They argue that many rich persons, and those high in station, do not feel the pleasure that formerly arose from intercourse with the less wealthy; that they feel their province wounded, and themselves spoiled of their honours. In society it is true all nearly dress alike. Still there is much that remains to distinguish besides the broad cloth and the hoop.

The difficulty in distinguishing by outward appearance has produced great effects upon society. Genteel families are very slow in doing so, or avoid altogether the making new acquaintances till a master of ceremonies or a friend has been able to certify *who's who?* Without this precaution individuals widely apart in station would be brought into an intimacy that might be unsuitable and even painful.

Oh! what a glorious occasion when the master of the ceremonies led out the beautiful heiress with lappets hanging from her head to dance the *minuet de la cour,* thus heralding to the assembly that the young lady had "come out," or that the matrimonial market had new game for the fortune hunters, who might now advance. Just so in a preceding century, transactions in most markets were forbidden till after the formal ringing of the market bell.

The age is charged with a special want of respect for superiors. We trust this is not altogether so. A middle class has extended itself, so that one man nearly treads upon the heel of his neighbour. Formerly between a certain class and the gentry there was a wide gulph. The country gentry, who came to reside in or frequent towns, have unavoidably perceived the change; to some it has been disagreeable. Let those who affirm that all distinctions have disappeared only remark clearly what passes around them, and they will perceive a whole series of gradations to be observed, though not signalled by this fur or that point lace or broad cloth, which, had all dressed in character, would have made classification a very ready matter.

We trust that exalted rank and highly cultivated mental abilities meet with true respect. We believe they ever will do so. Bad teaching and bringing up, and other adverse circumstances, are so likely to interfere that all mankind cannot be clever and accomplished.

Cock-fighting and Cock-squailing.

COCK-FIGHTING up to the end of the last century was a very general amusement, and an occasion for gambling. It entered into the occupations of the old and young. Schools had their cock-fights. Travellers agreed with coachmen that they were to wait a night if there was a cock-fight in any town through which they passed. A battle between two cocks had five guineas staked upon it. Fifty guineas, about the year 1760, depended upon the main or odd battle. This made the decision of a "long main" at cock-fighting an important matter. The church bells at times announced the winning of a "long main." Matches were sometimes so arranged as to last the week. When country gentlemen had sat long at table, and the conversation had turned upon the relative merits of their several birds, a cock-fight often resulted, as the birds in question were brought for the purpose into the dining-room.

If apprentices on their parts agreed that they should not be obliged to eat salmon more than twice a week, masters, regarding their interests, stipulated that apprentices should not keep fighting cocks or hunting dogs till they had served seven of their ten years' apprenticeship.

A carriage has been constructed to contain some cocks of a Cornish breed, which brought the valiant birds to London, drawn by post-horses, for a great match. The expense was 500*l.*

Cock-squailing was the twin sister of cock-fighting. So early as the time of Thomas à Becket the practice was universal, and school-boys had a half-holyday given them to enjoy the sport.

Cock-squailing was practised in Dorsetshire at Whitsuntide as well as at Shrovetide. As great was the demand for cocks before the day as for gunpowder before the 5th of November. It was dangerous to pass the streets on Shrove Tuesday amidst the throwing of missiles at the poor birds tied with a string by nearly the whole population.

Various reasons have been assigned to account for the origin of cock-squailing, a cruel practice that engaged at Shrovetide our population the whole breadth of the land. What would a New Zealander have thought of this nation when viewing them so engaged. How could he have reconciled this amusement with Christianity? Perhaps it is most probable that the crowing of the cock when St. Peter denied Christ had furnished, in brutal ages, an excuse for the practice. The witty Sir Charles Sedley, in an epigram upon "A Cock at Rochester," implies that the race was to suffer this annual barbarity by way of punishment for St. Peter's crime: —

> "May'st thou be punish'd for St. Peter's crime,
> And on Shrove Tuesday perish in thy prime."

The rising generation were not allowed to grow up ignorant of the rudiments of this vernal display of cruelty.

When a young couple were blessed with offspring, the mother, while early instilling the rudiments of virtuous instruction, did not fail to procure the means for early capability of keeping Shrove Tuesday in an orthodox manner. The village tailor made a cloth representation of a cock, which, being lined with lead, regained an erect position upon being knocked down by the juvenile cock-squailer. To practise upon a living bird was but the next step in the art. Mothers do occasionally employ the tailor, but are ashamed to own the use and design of the gay appendage to the dresser. The ornamental bird, thanks to better feeling, is now a plaything. The lovely groups of children that are seen in our path-fields keep May in as marked a manner as when each bore an impaled cockchafer.*

Cock-pence are still paid in some grammar schools to the master as a perquisite on Shrove Tuesday.

Young people regularly brought their cocks to school on a Shrove Tuesday. When at college in France in 1816, there was some vestige of cock-squailing by way of lottery. Each boy who squailed paid two sous, and he who killed the bird had it to be cooked for his dinner. This was desirable to those who sat at table without partaking of more than soup or pottage; others did not care about entering for the chance, except some who were ambitious of being thought to take a good aim.†

Bowling-Greens.

"Our bows are turned into bowls."
STOW'S *exclamation.*

BOWLING was one of the games proscribed for many years, not from any fault found with the recreation itself, but because, when bowling, the youths of England must have neglected archery. When the Butts stood in compliance with the act, but neglected as to the shooting at them with bows and arrows, Bowling had become odious in the eyes of the Puritans of our boroughs, in common with all other diversions. The Restoration brought forth all mirth and pastimes. Bowling-greens became the rage, and there the gentry of both sexes met together to bowl, to dine, and to dance, to walk, and engage in conversation. When Beau Nash began his reign at Bath in 1748, the only place for assembling was in the Bowling-green. In Charles II.'s reign there

* See an article upon cruelty in the Author's Life of the Duke of Monmouth, 2 vols. 8vo.

† The sport which kings loved, and for which cock-pits were erected, is now illegal.

were two days in the week in the joyous summer season, when there was a club meeting of the "best of the town" of Lyme to dine at the bowling-green in the middle of the day, and recreate themselves with bowls. The Duke of Monmouth, upon arriving at any town where he wanted to show himself, rode with his party round the bowling-green, where the gay folks of both sexes were. At Tunbridge Wells, when the Duke did not hunt, he went to the bowling-green, where the gentry were wont to bowl and dance. A taste for the recreation of bowling, and for assembling and dining in company at a bowling-green, has passed away. In most towns the once gay locality has been applied to its original purpose — pasturage — no one being found to rent it.

The Manner of collecting Information from the Country on Emergencies by the Court, in early Reigns, illustrated.

WHEN local knowledge was requisite for the due administration of public affairs on an emergency, individuals who were presumed to possess that knowledge used to be summoned to appear at the court or at Westminster. Sometimes, as obtains in the present day, magistrates, the representatives of commissioners, visited the parts where the information lay, and interrogated the parties on the spot.

The principle followed in the above particulars is identical. Even varying circumstances caused the parties questioned to be visited or sent for by the magnates, just as was deemed most expedient.

The summoning a great number of men of a particular class or calling to the Parliament from many towns of several counties to be there at once—a kind of second Parliament for the while—was peculiar to our earlier history.

To obtain correct knowledge of what has occurred, as Sir Walter Raleigh's anecdote illustrates, will ever prove a difficult matter. To come to right conclusions upon what course ought to be pursued for the future is a matter in which many have to exercise their judgment, and deliver an opinion; in a word, to encounter ignorance, prejudice, and a zeal to promote the interests of each man's own locality, demands the exercise of great qualities, and the possession of much knowledge.

Did not Aldrovandus find this to be so when he summoned mariners from the coast of Italy singly to come and answer his questions as to the singing of swans? Each man, we are told, thought if he said swans did not sing in his country that he should bring an opprobrium upon his native land, and furnish a triumph to others. An Englishman declared that English swans sung so sweetly that their songs recreated the mariners as they entered the channel, returning from foreign voyages. A parallel with this was too often to be found in the cases to be adduced.

In 1342 each of our ports had to send two of the better and discreeter mariners to the Parliament to bestow their advice and counsel upon important matters. This experiment, for such we may call it, as it is the first summons recorded in "Rymer's Fœdera," had, it may be fairly presumed, satisfactory results. Numbers were probably found to have been inconveniently great. Let us not cast for a moment a doubt upon the grave and suitable conduct of the mariners called from a distance to deliberate. When the business day was over, like what manner of men could a limner portray them, as they vegetated without tobacco, rum, Hollands, or brandy?

In 1344 one mariner had to be sent up from each port; and again, in 1347, a mariner from each port was required to consult upon the safety of the coasts in the king's absence, as the enemy was prepared for invasion with *galeis guerrinis*, Anglicè war galleys.

When the course of the manufacturing trade went ill at home or abroad, the magistrates called those together who were best acquainted with the causes, and selected some to go to town. Thus in 1622, when the clothing trade in the

West of England was so dead that tradesmen (*i. e.* men of that trade) offered to work for meat and drink only, the justices called together all clothiers, from among whom they selected two from each county of the most sufficient. These were to be sent to Londen before certain commissioners appointed to inquire into the causes of the above deadness of trade, and to settle a course to revive the trade of clothing beyond the seas.*

The visiting particular localities by authorised persons in high office to ascertain the truth of returns sent up to court, or to collect information on the spot, was a peculiar feature in ancient polity. A commissioner or two may now be found sitting in a provincial town and taking evidence, but this is different from the cavalcade of illustrious county magistrates, mayors, municipal persons, and numerous attendants.

In the spring of 1587 several magistrates gave notice, dated 12th March, that they intended to lie at Melcomb, and proceed along the sea coast, and call upon the mayors to attend with all in their respective towns that are skilled in fortification, these magistrates having to use their judgments in viewing the dangerous places for the landing of the enemy.†

We hear nothing of professional men, of engineer and artillery officers. The advice of one clever man in this line would have been more valuable than that of all others, provided his theoretical knowledge and experience were combined with a complete insight into the local particulars. The separation of these two things, so indispensably required for important undertakings, has occasioned losses in our borough outlays of money, in very recent days, to a great amount. Local knowledge is apt to be dignified into all importance by Town Councils, who can with justice cite instances where professional exaltation of itself has superseded due regard to local knowledge. The balance of error lies greatly on the

* Walter Yonge's Diary, p. 56. Camden Society.

† Sherren Papers.

other side, and we may with truth affirm that professional excellence is not valued as it should be in the West of England. Considering that this abounds and is procurable at so cheap a rate, to neglect availing themselves of it is virtually to spurn the benefits of high civilisation, and to fall back upon times when a mayor was solicited to bring "all that had skill in fortification."

The Landing of the Pretender in the West expected. — Some Particulars of the Time.

THE now proverbially quiet West of England has largely participated in many great disturbances of an important character.

There have been foreign landings, — pirates, — "commocion time," which ensued after the Reformation, — the expedition of Perkin Warbeck, — an active prosecution of the civil wars, — Monmouth's rebellion, and one expedition more recent was expected, to which these remarks allude.

When we reflect upon the misery which has attended all the foregoing events, that there has been one year of tribulation the less ought to be a subject of thankfulness.

The West was agitated by partisanship in favour of, and adverse to, the Pretender.

William Pitts, of Lyme, barber and periwig-maker, drinking at the Golden Lion in Colyton in 1715, with Mr. Marwood, Captain Bartlett, Mr. Robert Coade, mariner, and others, was invited by the former to drink the health of Dr. Sacheverell, Sir William Windham, and the Duke of Ormond, who said, "Let us kick the TRUMPERY out of door, and have home our King." Pitts deposed to this effect before the Mayor of Lyme, and affirmed that Marwood meant by these words the turning out his MAJESTY, and bringing in the PRETENDER.

James Butler, second Duke of Ormond, Lord-Lieutenant of Somersetshire, Sir William Wyndham, and others, were watching for an opportunity to declare for the Pretender. Ormond crossed over to France; Sir William Wyndham was seized at his house in Somersetshire, but afterwards escaped. The insurrection in the West came to nothing.

Dr. Thomas Burnett, prebendary of Sarum, writing to the Mayor of Lyme Regis, J. Burridge, Esq. (Dec. 27. 1715), adds this piece of information:—

> "I doubt you shall have been under some apprehensions upon your coasts from the *Pretender*. I believe now the danger is over, and I hope we may say, as Moses did by the Egyptians, 'This day ye have seen the Egyptians, ye shall see them again no more for ever.'" *

John Burridge, the loyal mayor in 1715–6, spent 10*s.* on the occasion of the coronation of George I., and gave to the drummers 2*s.* 6*d.*, and to the bonfire 3*s.* 3*d.* On the 19th of November, upon the receipt of news of the defeat of the rebels at Preston, the same outlay took place; and February 13., upon intelligence of a defeat in Scotland on the Thanksgiving Day, 7th of June, the expenses were doubled, and the guns were fired.

In the next reign associations were entered into in the West to support George II. against the rebels led by the young Pretender. Ralph Allen, the post-horse letter carrier from Marlborough, discovered to General Wade an intended importation of arms to Bath for the Pretender.†

Robert Henley, Esq., Mayor of Lyme, enters into his account, Oct. 9. 1645–6, for money expended at the "Three Cups" on the entering into an association to support his Majesty against the rebels, 2*l.*

* Archives of Lyme.

† Waylen's Hist. of Marlborough.

April 28 & 29. Expenses at the Three Cups on the rebels' defeat, 3*l.* 18*s.* 8*d.*

Two hogsheads of cyder supplied for the populace on the association and on the victory obtained over the rebels, 2*l.*

Several Kinds of Beverages used at various Periods of our History in the South-west of England.

"If thou dost observe duly, thou wilt find that not only terms of speech and the fashions of dress and of manners are changed from one age to another, but yet what is more, the tastes and inclinations of our minds; and this diversity is seen, *etiam* at the same point of time, between one country and another, wherein are not only diversities of manners, which may proceed from the diversity of institutions, but also of TASTES IN MEATS, and various appetites of man." —*Maxims of Guicciardini.*

That the kind of meats used for man's daily sustenance has great connection with his state of civilisation, adaptation to climate, and health, is a fact no one can dispute; hence its importance in many inquiries. No less important is the consideration of what man drinks, whether this is for the necessary aliment of his body, or for his bane, in furnishing him with stimulants that drive him to feverish excitement, to mad actions, and to the perpetration, as a matter of course, of crime.

It does not follow that a man born at a particular period of history, and who suits himself to the manners of his cotemporaries, has given any thought to the comparative superiority of any particular beverage. He was the creature of accident as to the use of this or that article of food. To descant upon these may be interesting.

We can say no more of MEAD, or Metheglin, but that it was the fermented drink of the ancient Britons, made from honey.

WINE, known from the remotest period of history, and then characterised as having a divine origin, was some centuries since sold as a cordial medicine by apothecaries and by mercers. The great made use of wine as an article of luxury for the table from early times; to the people at large it was unknown as such. Wine, the "comfortable stuff" now-a-days of the country poor, was principally used for physic and the Communion.

The latter service greatly differed from that of modern times. The sacred elements were placed upon a credence table for a tasting beforehand, as a security against the admixture of poison. This might have proved fatal to the recipients who consumed a quantity of the wine. A communicant drank deep to evince his sincerity. Rare Ben Jonson was twelve years in the church of Rome; and at his reconciliation to the church of England, upon the occasion of his first communion, in token of his true reconciliation, he drank the full cup of wine.

Wine was largely imported from Gascony into our seaports in the reigns of the Plantagenets. The *Pipæ Gardæ* were large fixed tanks to hold the wine in the centre of the vessels that brought home the produce of the English possessions in France. By this plan space was economised. The sailors of the middle ages understood "sucking the monkey," *i. e.*, furtively drawing off some wine from a cask in course of transit.

Gregory Charlemagne, the first mayor of Lyme Regis in the reign of Edward I., was found, by a jury at the assizes held there, to have sold twenty tons of wine contrary to the assize. The magistrates had fixed the price, and this merchant, *Great-Charley* by name, not liking trade to be fettered, ventured to effect a sale at the price his merchandise would really fetch.

Under the head of "Presents to Great Men," in this volume, there is mention of wine of various kinds given to them, and partaken of in company with them, but only as a luxury, a treat, and not as an article in general use.

If the relative value of money be taken into account, wine was not a cheap commodity. There were fifty-six small wines, and thirty Italian, Grecian, and Spanish wines imported.

The south-west coast of England was the most favoured locality for cheap wine, as compared with inland parts distant from any port. The cost of carriage over roads at times impassable, must have been very great, so as to greatly enhance the value of a pottle of claret. Royal and exalted personages were formerly elevated to a much greater height by comparison above the great mass of society than is now the case. Too often have their manners and mode of life been adduced as examples of the general manners of the time; whereas the two classes were separated by a wide boundary. Frugality in many shapes abode with one class, and left luxury and prodigal expenditure to their fated residence in courts and lordly halls.

Wine, before the introduction of bottles such as are now used, between the years 1760 and 1790, was kept in flask bottles or flasks.

Thus runs the verse of a song: —

"Then for your pottles with handles three,
I'm sure they'll get no praise from me,
For when a man and his wife shall fall to strife,
As they often may do in the course of a life,
The one does lug, and the other does tug,
And betwixt them both they break the jug;
But if it had only been a leather bottel
They might have tugg'd away, yet all had been well.
So let us hope, &c.*

Corks were sold, about 1712, at 18*d.* a gross.

In the reign of Henry IV. every butt of Malmsey and of Tyre obliged the importer to bring with it ten bow-staves.

There was in the household of Edward IV. "a pitcher-

* Notes and Queries, Oct. 14. 1854.

house." There were new ashen cups for the ale, and "pots to serve men of worship."

In the Earl of Northumberland's house, in 1512, there were earthen pots in common use, and also leathern pots.

At an election feast of the Drapers' Company in 1522, earthen pots were used for ale and wine; gilt cups "for red wine and ipocras."

Drinking stone pots were imported from Cologne in the reign of Queen Elizabeth; there was no such manufactures in England. Frequent mention occurs of breaking the stone pots at beer-houses. The reason for doing this was because these pots were not of full measure.

Vins de liqueur were displayed at bed time, when, in conducting strangers to their chambers, these were offered, accompanied by sweetmeats, comfits, &c.

Wine and beer have been placed in antagonism in an anacreontic ascribed to a noble writer * as the prime movers in man. The question is begged that great affairs demand the stimulus of drink; for without it, as is alleged, no important results from the exercise of intellect have been obtained. Wine is made to bear away the palm, and is the real specific for searching out man, and through the corporeal substance, sublimating his mental ability. The writer, perhaps, thought of his order when he dignified wine and made it supersede genius, study, and the *dry* virtues:—

> " The drinkers of beer
> Did ne'er yet appear.
> In matters of any weight
> 'Tis he whose design
> Is quicken'd by wine
> That raises wit to its height."

Even so has it proved in ancient times with respect to the attributing courage, by a graduated scale, to those who habituated themselves to the several beverages.

* Lord Broghill, afterwards the Earl of Orrery.

Æschylus accounted for the superiority of the Greeks in conflict over the Egyptians from their drink *:—

> ἀλλ' ἄρσενάς τοι τῆσδε γῆς οἰκήτορας
> εὑρήσετ', οὐ πίνοντας ἐκ κριθῶν μέθυ.

> Here may you look to meet a race of men,
> Not such as drink your sodden barley mead.

Shakspeare put a sentiment into the mouths of the conquering Normans, that their superiority over the brave but sluggish Saxons was due to the nobler beverage which they drank: —

> "Can sodden water,
> A drench for sur-reigned jades, their barley-broth
> Decoct their cold blood to such valiant heat,
> And shall our quick blood, spirited with wine,
> Seem frosty?" †

The quantity of wine made by the monks in their gardens or vineyards may have been considerable. Wine made of pearmains we should now call perry. A tenure in Norfolk was held by petty serjeanty, and the payment of 200 pearmains and four hogsheads of cider, or wine made of pearmains.‡

At the first mention of BEER let us not forget that, if we are to believe Diodorus, that liquor had a divine origin like wine, Bacchus having taught mankind how to make both.

ALE is mentioned in England as early as the laws of Ina, King of Wessex. Though cider may have been used, ale was the favourite liquor of the Anglo-Saxons and Danes, as it had been of their ancestors in Germany. "In the Edda the drinking large and frequent draughts of this beverage is placed among the chief delights of the Hall of Odin, by which we may estimate the value that was set upon such draughts by those who were waiting for that promotion."§

* Suppl. 957.

† Gent.'s Mag. 1854.

‡ Blomfield's Hist.

§ Smedley, in Encyclo. Metrop.

Beer was an important article, constituting a principal part of two meals when tea, coffee, and spirits were not in use. The mayor and magistrates of most boroughs held an assize of bread and beer. At this *sitting* or assize they settled the price of those articles till the next assize should be held. Petty legislation left nothing to the free action of individuals; hence much injustice was often done, and great discontent prevailed, as in beer-drinking Germany in the present day. Beer riots are described as being still very violent outbreaks.

We will consider beer to have been the principal drink of the great mass of Englishmen as an article of food. Ale was the equivalent of strong beer — the *October* of this century.

Various descriptions of grain were employed in the manufacture of beer — barley, wheat, and oats were used almost indiscriminately, and even sometimes mixed together. Before the introduction of hops, this liquor was flavoured with spices, pepper, and other condiments.

At Hinton House, the seat of Earl Poulett, are preserved some decanters that held the strong beer set on table, marked with the oat. The ale or strong beer was drunk out of long glasses after dinner, as wine now is.

At a Somersetshire hunt dinner, seventy years since, thirteen toasts used to be drunk in strong beer; then every one did as he liked. Some members of the hunt occasionally drank a glass of wine at the wind up, who were not themselves previously wound up.* In country towns, after a dinner at one o'clock P.M., friends used to meet to discuss the local news over their glasses of strong beer, the merits of which furnished a daily theme. At Bampton one knot of gentlemen took four times the duration of the Trojan war, and even then failed to settle which of the party brewed the best beer.

A new liquor gratified, in Charles the Second's reign, the lovers of novelty. This was a strong beer, introduced

* Authority, Major Nath. Knot, of the 2nd Somerset Militia.

to the public from Brunswick, called Mum. So great was the rage for this intoxicating liquor, that ten persons sold it at Lyme without a license, and were made the subject of a presentment. The word was derived from the German *mummeln,* to mumble, or from *mum,* the sign of silence; that is, either drink that will make a cat speak, or drink that will take away the power of speech.

Thus writes Pope: —

> "The clamorous crowd is hush'd with mugs of *mum,*
> Till all, tuned equal, send a general hum."

This foreign drink was rivalled by Dorchester beer, or, as it was named in London, Dorset beer. One who had foolishly indulged calls the drink *foolish.* He writes thus: —

> "May 18. 1725. I found the effect of last night's drinking that foolish Dorset, which was pleasant enough, but did not at all agree with me, for it made me very stupid all day." *

The great Manchester philosopher, who indulged in the above excess, could not have made a west countryman's distinction in his favour. The poor man in question, when seen to be engaged in taking some beer, observed, "I d'wunt drinky for drunky; I do drinky for dry."

In many houses where an aged gentleman is the master, strong beer (now rarely called ale, which latter term is appropriated to a weaker beverage intended to be used at table) is still brewed; but after dinner, at public and private tables, foreign wine, mostly from the peninsula, has supplanted beer, and, we may add, pipes and tobacco.

Whether Cider has been for years the exclusive drink of the men of the cider counties, is proposed for our consideration.

Many speak of cider as having been always in use in the West of England, where men chose between it and

* Byrom's MS. Journal, Chetham Society.

beer or ale; whereas in other parts malt liquor alone could be procured. A distinction must be made between the depths of the country and borough towns.

Cider is now grown, to use a common expression, in great quantities in what is known as the cider country or cider counties. There the great part of the population drink nothing else. Devonshire, parts of Somersetshire, Worcestershire, and Herefordshire, are pre-eminently cider counties.

The early use of a drink called cider, and the production of such immense quantities of that beverage, such as that of ten thousand hogsheads in one parish, viz., Martock in Somersetshire, are two distinct matters.

Cider without doubt is of early origin, and is supposed to have been first known in Africa, as it is mentioned by Tertullian and Augustine, the two fathers. St. Jerome speaks of an inebriating liquor made of the juice of apples.

Biscay, long famed for its cider, received it, as is believed, from the Carthaginians. A full description of this beverage is given by Navagerus, in the journal of his embassy to the Emperor Charles V.

The ancient Britons, like other northern nations, may have made an intoxicating liquor from the *Sorbus*, or service tree; and though hardly from the indigenous crab-apple, yet some perhaps from the better kind of apples introduced by the Romans. The Anglo-Saxons distinguished their "Æppelwin" from wine and mead.

The Normans probably obtained their cider-apple trees from Biscay; the climate and soil there both favoured their growth. To the abbeys of that country we must look for the improvement of apples and cider-making.

Near Valognes, in the department of La Manche, stood the famous abbey of Montebourg. The possessions of this abbey extended to Dorset and Devon. Besides lands in Axmouth parish in South-east Devon, the manor and church given in the reign of Henry II., there were also other lands, and a priory in Loders, near Bridport, Dorsetshire.

Cider was made on the Montebourg lands before the year 1286. The monks, who possessed nearly all the knowledge that prevailed at that era, had introduced upon their estates on this side the channel apple-trees, for the growth of apples for cider-making. They had also taught their tenants how to make cider, according to the approved plan of Normandy, which is still preserved in that part of France, in the Norman islands of Guernsey and Jersey, and in Herefordshire.

W. Villata, of Loders and Bothenhampton, near Bridport, held land of the Abbot of Montebourg, upon payment of six shillings a year, and upon his finding a horse (*ad molendum poma*, &c.), to grind the apples in what is now called a horse-mill.*

The skilful monks may have done much towards the improvement of their estates by the introduction of better fruit trees. Probably others were not disposed to adopt novelties any more than their descendants in the present day.

The Quarantine apple is supposed to be a corruption of Carentan apple. Many other names are old names corrupted in the course of years. A perriwinkle shell-fish is termed a *gobbet.* It is the Norman *gobet,* a mouthful, as the famous cherries of the valley of Montmorency are now called *les bons gobets.*

That cider was made, as before related, in the twelfth century, cannot be denied; but not to any great extent, if we institute a comparison with the great doings now-a-days of cider-making Devon and Somerset.

The Vicar of Dawlish, in the South Hams (now a watering place), received, in 1280, one half the crop of apples, doubtless grown for making cider.†

The word Orchard, or, as it is now pronounced, Orchat, perhaps a name given by the monks from ὄρχατος, has been a fruitful source of error. It was not in any sense the orchard of modern times. The latter is a space planted with

* The late M. de Gerville, the learned antiquary of Valognes, possessed the cartulary of Montebourg. He communicated this information to the Author in 1841. His death took place in 1853.

† See a Manorial Visitation in the possession of the Rev. George Oliver, D.D.

apple trees of greater or less extent, unlike the practice of Normandy and Brittany, where pasture and arable land is crossed by rows of apple trees, and where the English practice of planting the trees in one spot with grass under them does not obtain.

The orchard of early reigns was a place laid out with trees as a pleasure garden for walking, recreation, and sports, having arbours and similar appropriate places. Such a spot, if apple trees prevailed, was called an apple garden, or apple orchard.

An apple garden is spoken of in Domesday Book as existing at Nottingham. Horti and Hortuli are frequent in the same record.

The monks of Lewes Priory, Sussex, had in their inclosure, of thirty-two and a half acres within walls, a paradise (park), a garden, and an APPLE ORCHARD, which felt the effects of a gale, A. D. 1267.*

Some apples were valued in an *orchard* in Norfolk, A. D. 1289, at 6*s.* 8*d.*; the mill, at 9*s.* The apple, like the vine, has been tried in climates and soils quite unsuited to it.†

There were ardent lovers of horticulture among the clergy. Upon the extension of a part of Wells Cathedral about the year 1326, there was a special provision made for the careful preservation of a certain *medlar tree.*‡ Quinces sold, in 1292, at 4*s.* the hundred.

Wycliffe knew of the strength of cider, for he translated the passage, Luke i. 15., "He shal be gret bifore the Lord, and he schal not drynke wyne ne sider."

One Cottingham, of Seaford, gave a bond, 26 Elizabeth, that while he should continue a tippler, he and his household should be orderly, and keep no unlawful games nor evil rule within his house, GARDEN, or ORCHARDS, during the said time of his tippling, *i. e.*, dealing in liquor. In the orchard was doubtless the skittle-alley for summer days.

* Horsfield's Sussex. † Blomfield's Norfolk.
‡ Archæolog. Institute.

Butler, in his "Hudibras," gives, among other requirements of Sidrophel that he knew, —

> "And in what sign best sider's made."

So that in the reign of Charles II., not only was attention paid to the growth of the apple, but to the making this fruit into cider — an operation of importance enough to be referred to an astrologer, then a common practice.

Apple trees and pear trees also began to be much cultivated about the middle of the 17th century. In a pamphlet addressed to the well-known Samuel Hartlib, Esq., A. D. 1657, entitled "Herefordshire Orchards, a Pattern for all England," it is asserted that gennet-moyles bear every other year, and make the best cider. Mordicant, or sharp cider, pleased the peasant or working man, as was the case in France.

In Herefordshire, few cottagers, and even few of the wealthiest yeomen, taste any other drink in the family but cider, except at some special festivals twice or thrice in a year, and that for variety rather than for choice.

The credit of cider had of late years much advanced in the estimation of the best gentry, who had sought out the right method of ripening and hoarding the choicest fruits, and some also of bottling it.

"But I am confident," the writer adds, "that much more may be added to the perfection of it, when they shall also apply to it the due subtleties of the mysterious art of fermentation." *

Each cultivator bestowed greater attention, having proved that —

> "Else false hopes
> He cherishes, nor will his fruit expect
> Th' autumnal season, but in summer's pride,
> When other orchats smile abortive fail."
>
> PHILIPS, *Cider*, book i.

* The late eccentric, A. Cross, Esq., of Bromfield, near Taunton, famous for his experiments in electricity and galvanism, believed he should be able to master fermentation in cider. He did not succeed.

Wassailing the orchards on New Year's Eve is called, in Sussex and those parts, "Apple Howling," from the words used:—

> "Stand fast root, bear well top,
> Pray the God send us a good howling crop, &c."

Hence the entries in former centuries of money given to the "howling boys" may be understood.

Hooker, in his MS. survey, records that the apple was cultivated in Devonshire so early as 1520. He must mean begun to be grown for the purposes of cider. He continues, "but in the beginning of the following century it received more attention."

So long as the narrow lanes served to keep up the communication between the principal towns, and pack-horses did all the work, there being no carts, how could cider in hogsheads have been sent about the country? It could not have been sent to any great distance.

Before the *attention* Hooker speaks of was given to the APPLE, that fruit, and the cider made from it, were very indifferent in quality. Rough, and fit only for working men, the cider of that day was consumed by country people, and the inhabitants of villages and small towns. Fashion alone did not exclude cider from boroughs. The beer laws, we believe, excluded that beverage; these would have been interfered with by the introduction of cider. The importation from another town of beer brewed there, which, according to the language of borough legislation, was called "foreign beer," disturbed the due operation of the beer laws at Weymouth. The "foolish Dorset," or Dorchester beer, and "Mum," so captivated the people of Weymouth, that they spurned the decoction from malt made in their own borough, whatever its strength or flavour might be. A compromise was effected; the men of the borough were indulged; and an impost upon the *imported* beer was levied. Liberty was little understood in the Tudor and early Stuart reigns. As it began to dawn, which we conclude from the alteration in the stringency of borough legislation, individuals exercised the right of buying what commodities suited them, or pleased them, wherever made or produced. Halsers might be made in England at other places than Bridport; good beer might be brought from any other town to gratify the palates of the people of a borough who loathed that brewed in their own locality; cider might be purchased and sent to a townsman's cellar, though not recognised as a beverage by the borough legislators. They had provided no cider-taster, nor clogged the buying and selling it by any bye-laws. There was no assize of cider. It was, very probably before the close of Charles II.'s reign, a beverage held in contempt in towns from its utter inferiority, and if excluded from its interfering with the regulations for the sale of beer, creating no great amount of dissatisfaction and complaint against the worshipful local magnates.

The absence of the mention of cider up to a certain period, in borough archives, is very remarkable. In accompts, where every halfpenny is carefully set down; in dinners of the most homely kind, and feasts, such as the Cobb Ale at Lyme, and the feast at Ford House in a dinner to Charles I., altogether (for the country) very sumptuous up to this period referred to, and which requires to be specified, there is no mention of cider; then cider takes its place with ale and beer, and furnishes an item in every accompt for refreshment or festive enjoyment at table of the inhabitants of boroughs.

In the detailed presentments of the Hustings' Book for Lyme for the year 1597, of the stealers of wood and pollers of trees for fuel, appears this entry:—

Item, they present George Browne's son, Hoode's son, and Thomas Sampford's boy to break into men's orchards and steal apples.

Whether these were apples for the table or for cider matters little, after what has been written above, as no *cider* is mentioned in the archives for one hundred and ten years.

In 1629 apples were cultivated in Massachusetts from

seed imported from England by order of the governor and company of the colony. Governor's Island, in Boston harbour, was given to Governor Winthrop in 1632, on condition that he should plant an orchard upon it.*

A hogshead of Somersetshire cider was brought to Mr. Richards, near Dorchester, A.D. 1699 †, upon the occasion of England and Scotland being united into one kingdom; a hogshead of cider was given by the corporation of Lyme to the soldiers, at a cost of 25*s.*

Wine, beer, and cider were given away at Minchinhampton upon the accession of King George in 1714.

In 1745-6 the accompt of Robert Henley, Esq., Mayor of Lyme, exhibits: —

April 28. Two hogsheads of cider supplied for the populace on the association (to support his majesty George II.), and on the victory obtained over the rebels, 2*l.*

The mayor purchased this cider at Pinney Farm, of Walter Oke, a country gentleman, who farmed his own land, and had planted some of the now far-famed Cleeveland, late Pinney-under-Cliff, with apple trees.

The farmers of the Somersetshire parishes near Sedgemoor, so soon as they heard that the king's forces had won the battle, and defeated the Monmouth men, sent hogsheads of cider to the victors. The price of a hogshead of cider given away at Axminster in 1689 was 17*s.* 6*d.*‡

This beverage was doubtless much improved, so as to be very acceptable to the lower orders of the west country, and also strangers. It had to rise to the dignity of being admitted to civic feasts on equal terms with beer and more potent ale. This point was gained in 1737, when this entry is to be found at Lyme, in a dinner bill: —

Beer, cider, and ale, 8*s.* 10*d.*

In short, as in 1746-7, "Beer, ale, and cider, 10*s.* 4*d.*"

* Notes and Queries, from New York Sun, 1854.

† See his Diary, Retrospective Review.

‡ Pulman's Book of the Axe. N.B. The cask had to be returned.

became an example of a common entry. We may conclude that, as is now the case in cider countries, the civic authorities were divided upon the merits, or in the choice of beer or cider at meals, so both beverages were provided.

The excellence of the cider made throughout the breadth of the cider-growing West is very great; the quantity is enormous. Some localities, which have a good name for their cider, send out much more cider than is produced therein, like in wine countries, so much does man resemble man in all countries and ages. The growers in the localities in question buy Norman apples at a cheap rate, and mix them with their own fruit.

Could the monks of Montebourg have dreamt of cider selling at ten guineas a hogshead for bottling? A wide field for improvement of the fruit trees for orchards still lies before the negligent cultivator. The cockygee, or any other famous apple tree, covers no more space than a worthless tree. Fine cider, properly bottled, is a drink that may compete with much of the sparkling German wine. Those who have met with the following statement will excuse its introduction here.

Some gentlemen, travelling from Strasbourg to Freybury, stopped at the village of Altenheim, in Baden, at an inn kept by a respectable man who farmed his own estate of 100 acres. Perceiving how loaded the trees of his orchard were, the English gentleman spoke of the great crop of apples, and of cider. The German informed them that no *cider* was made in that country; the juice was mixed with the juice of grapes, and made into wine!

In 1854, some growers of cider in Devon and Somerset make much more than a thousand hogsheads in one year when the crop is good.

In many parts of this realm cider is spoken of as a sweet, luscious drink made to please the palate, and with that intent only. Great is the disappointment often felt upon arriving in the cider country, in tasting so much that is rough — at all events, not sweet. The strength and potency of the drink is likewise little suspected. All these things numbers are surprisingly ignorant of. The cider drinker's passions are roused by that beverage, and vice has its full sway. Crime results as from indulgence in other fermented liquors. The Rev. Giles Moore, in his Diary, records in Latin how he had underrated the strength of perry.*

Poor working men drink cider when good food is more requisite for them. The strength of the liquor is injurious, and causes feverish excitement.

Any account of cider would be incomplete without some mention of the imposition of a tax of two shillings, afterwards of four shillings per hogshead.

Sir Francis Dashwood, the Chancellor of the Exchequer in 1763, proposed a new tax on cider and perry, amounting to ten shillings on the hogshead, and to be paid by the first buyer. Earl Stanhope, in his history, vol. v., mentions that the complaints were so loud that a modification of the scheme was allowed, and four shillings were to be paid by the grower, though some cider sold for five shillings, other for fifty shillings a hogshead. The change made the grower liable to the regulations of the excise. The tax was estimated at 75,000*l.*

Worcestershire and Devonshire, "the cyder land," were eager and loud in their complaints. The loyalty of those districts, like that of the cider land of Brittany, was coupled with the growth of cider: —

> "Oh, Charles! oh, best of kings!
>
> . . . . .
>
> Yet was the cyder-land unstained with guilt;
> The cyder-land, obsequious still to thrones,
> Abhorred such base, disloyal deeds, and all
> Her pruning-hooks extended into swords!"
>
> JOHN PHILIPS, *Cider*, book ii.

Lord North married Lady Drake's daughter, of Ashe House. It was in 1765 that his lordship was so frightened

* Sussex Archæol.

when visiting at Ashe, at the shouts of the reapers, and their cry after finishing cutting the wheat on the estate, "We have'n — we have'n!" The cider tax occurred to him. Lord North is said to have looked upon himself as a dead man, and Sir Robert Hamilton, the husband of Lady Drake's sister, seized a sword for defence, till the steward explained the local custom.* In conclusion of cider — just as the Breton, in whatever quarter of the world he may be placed, amidst the choicest luxuries and *cuisine* sighs for his *galette*, even so does the man of the cider counties remember and regret his native liquor. Nothing is to him equal to the beverage of his boyhood.

Spirits used to be called "comfortable waters," and "strong waters," in the reign of James I. When a poor country person begs for spirit now-a-day at the rich man's door, for some one who is sick, he asks by a general term for some "comfortable stuff."

Spirits are not mentioned any more than cider at the great feast at Lyme, the Cobb ale, the dinner at Ford House to King Charles I., nor in any accompt of corporation dinners in the seventeenth century. When Sir George Summers, of Lyme, in 1609, was driven before a hurricane, which led to his discovery of the Bermudas or Summer Islands, there appeared no hope of saving the ship, so water-logged was she at last. In this extremity we learn those who had "comfortable waters" drank to one another as taking their last leaves. Beer was shipped at Lyme when a party were about to sail against the pirates.

The invention of this or that kind of drink is not a subject to be here discussed. It is the coming into general use, and its effect upon society of each beverage, that we wish to describe.

Rum could only have been made after that molasses or treacle became abundant, from the great growth of the sugar-cane about the middle of the seventeenth century.

* See Pulman's Book of the Axe.

When the Duke of Monmouth was being conducted to London in 1685 as a prisoner, having a bad cold, he took at Romsey, while remaining in the saddle, a hot glass of rum and eggs. This "Jamaica" was a fashionable spirit in James the Second's and following reign. In 1856 there is no demand for rum even by spirit drinkers.

Punch, which has rum for its chief ingredient, was all the rage when its due proportions began to be discovered. This compound was adopted at the corporation dinners at Lyme.

We find that the novelty was the rage at its introduction. When Coade was mayor, in 1737, at a feast of the corporation, sixteen bowls of punch were drunk, at a charge of one shilling each. Brandy was sold for many years at one shilling a gallon.

Rum, brandy, Hollands, and wine now being subject to a heavy duty, the smuggling trade began to be brisk. These commodities were brought across from the Channel Islands in small barrels or tubs, and landed at once or sunk in rafts to be taken up when an opportunity offered. The custom house establishments were large, and provided with long boats, in which the officers sailed after smugglers, and crept for sunk rafts.

This smuggling trade during the reigns of the first King Georges threw into the country, at the back of the south coast of England, a great quantity of spirit. The drinking of spirits and water became a common practice, where ale or strong beer was indulged in before. Either in excess is bad. Very generally does an opinion prevail that strong beer drinking, even in excess, could hurt no one. This is incorrect, as is a sweeping charge against the moderate use of spirit, as if any use of it must be hurtful.

The introduction of cheap foreign spirit created a very pernicious habit — that of dram drinking. At Lyme, in 1774, the vestry determined "to afford no relief to those who frequent houses where drams are sold." Dram drinking created private drunkards, who were a rare class in former ages. Drunkenness and conviviality were before that closely allied.

Old women fell under the imputation of liking raw spirits. When the Isle of Man was sold by the Duke of Atholl to the Crown, that it might no longer continue to be a nest of smugglers, the song containing these lines was composed: —

> "There's not an old wife loves a dram,
> But must lament for the Isle of Man."

The use of wine, beer, and cider for a meal — the morning and evening draught — has given way to the decoctions made from foreign products.

The far-famed Sir Anthony Shirley, when he arrived at Aleppo in 1598, first tasted a drink that he described as being "made of a seed which will soon intoxicate the brain," and which, though "nothing toothsome, was wholesome." This was coffee.

I detected the first entry in a mayor's account, in 1686, of that functionary having at the Dorchester assizes taken coffee. Coffee-houses became quite the rage in the metropolis. There was a floating coffee-house opposite Somerset House, called the "Folly." The borough towns of the country soon emulated London in being provided with *coffee-houses*, where every one was admitted who laid down a penny at the bar. Though coffee was only introduced from Turkey in 1650, it became fashionable in the reign of Charles II., and is thus spoken of by Pope in his "Rape of the Lock:" —

> "Coffee, which makes the politician wise,
> And see through all things with his half-shut eyes."

The "Kingdom's Intelligencer" contains these prices: —

In 1662, at a new coffee-house, the "Great Turk," right coffee powder sold at from 4*s.* to 6*s.* 8*d.* per lb.; that pounded in a mortar at 2*s.* a lb.

Chocolate, an Indian drink, was charged 2*s.* 6*d.* a lb.

Tea was to be had from 6*s.* to 60*s.* a lb.

All gentlemen that were customers were invited the next New Year's Day to partake of coffee there "on free cost." See Burn's account of the Tokens in the collection of Mr. Beaufoy. When made, the drink paid 4*d.* a gallon to the excise.

Tea began to be mentioned in the diaries of gentlemen residing in the country after the year 1700; so slowly was the new beverage introduced in parts remote from the great cities.

Drinking when transacting Business.

THE principal men of boroughs, in the Tudor reigns, drank when transacting business of every kind; and this at a tavern, just as the lower orders do in the present day. The sober only complied with a general practice; the intemperate, doubtless, as their modern representatives, seized an opportunity thus offered for inordinate indulgence. The practice once admitted, it was better that the pottle of sack should be drank at a tavern than at the house of business, over which was the family residence. For instance, Mr. William Tudbold, Mayor of Lyme, 1551, enters: —

Item, paid at Robert Davy's when we new agreed with Whytte the mason, vi*d.*

We may in fairness add, that the parties transacting business felt more independent at a tavern than they would in the private residence of either party, and were bound to make some return to the landlord for the use of his house. At home, when wine was produced, many of the family might have been expected to partake. Thus an injurious and expensive habit may have been acquired, or the foundation laid at all events.

Regulations for the Baking and Sale of Bread.

Bread occupies much less space than beer in our borough archives. Few are found faulty in respect of their making the former; and scarcely any regulations have come down to us, while the latter article occasioned many local legislative enactments, deemed, no doubt, to be no more necessary than important. We early read of *horse bread* and *sale bread.* These were, perhaps, much the same, the latter being bread not baked for home consumption, but for *sale*, and the former *sale* bread carried about the country on *horse*-back. A horse-loaf weighed 18 oz. troy, and sold, in 1588, for 1*d.* Nearly every one used to bake for his own use. There was in the 18th century no white bread baker at Lyme, as lately, perhaps still, at Penrith, a town of 8000 inhabitants. There was a great distinction made between the white and black bread bakers in by-gone years. In the archives of Canterbury it appears, that if the white bread and black bread bakers interfered with each other before the Reformation, the fine was 40*s.*; a very considerable sum.*

Henry Palmer and Joan Sampford, widow, were ordered at Lyme, in 1592, from that time to bake no more *sale* bread; *subpœnâ, 5s.*

The entry runs thus: *quod deinceps non pincernant panem vocatum* SALE-BREAD.

There is in some archives mention made of *ranged bread.*

Why these worthies were debarred from carrying on their particular, perhaps newly taken up trade or line of business, nowhere appears. So, in 1610, there is a presentment of Widow Dare and John Sprake's wife, dwelling in Dolman's house, as being common hedge tearers, and that they doth bake *buns* contrary to the statute.

Very probably these individuals were not regular bakers who could be under the eye of authority with respect to keeping the assize, or selling at the price or in the form assigned by the magistrates.

* Archæological Society, Report, 1844.

Every baker of Castle Combe was to bake penny, half-penny, and farthing bread. At the same place, in 1594, two bakers were named to the jury of the Manorial Court as common bakers *panis humani,* and as such they had each to pay 3*d.* for the exercise of their art.*

Just as classical learning was called *human* learning, and in Scotland is now styled *humanities,* so a finer bread was dignified by the learned scrivener of the Court as *panis humanus,* to be rendered WHITE BREAD. Some of the black bread furnished those in the *dark house* fell not under this *human* term.

The book in which the assize of bread was entered was handed over from mayor to mayor, as one of the articles forming a part of the town stuff. The baker of King Henry VIII. was enjoined not to put alum in the bread, nor to mix rye, oaten or bean flour with the same, under pain of the stocks.

The advantage of a public bakehouse was enjoyed at Lyme in 1669, as we learn from a presentment of the oven as endangering the setting the town on fire.

In another place will be found mention of the discipline of the cucking-stool, for bakers selling short weight at Vienna, so late as 1775.

Beer, curious Local Orders, Laws, and Particulars respecting.

WHEN we consider the importance that attached to beer, as furnishing two meals of the four that mortals call their daily portion, viz. the morning and evening draught, before tea and coffee were introduced, or spirits were in common use, we may expect that the good mayors and juries at court leets and courts of hustings had much to engage their attention in reference to this beverage.

The assize of bread and beer, which dates from an early period, is not the subject that has now to be treated of.

* G. P. Scrope, Hist. of Castle Combe.

This was held in our western boroughs with due observance. Some of our interesting accounts of presentments of brewers, and the causes which drew upon them the animadversion of juries, fall more within the province of these pages.

The residents of the manor of Bleadon, Somerset, in the 14th century, who brewed beer for sale, paid to the lord four gallons by way of toll.

The invaluable entries in the archives of the Scrope family, lords of the manor of Castle Combe, Wiltshire, enable us to add much to our previous knowledge. These entries of orders about beer date from so early as 1456, the reign of Henry VI.*

The ale-tasters presented Thomas Cokesale for refusing to sell ale to his neighbours, while he had some on sale, and even while the sign [the Ale-stake] was out. He was fined 4*d.*

In 1461, one Lautroppe was presented for having, contrary to the order, brewed three times under one display of the sign or ale-stake. For this he had to pay 6*d.* We understand, that upon setting out the sign, that beer was on sale, the ale-tasters (*tastatores cerevisiæ*) proceeded to perform their office. This man offended by brewing three times, and only making the usual signal for one brewing. This, had it not been detected, would have enabled him to sell two brewings without the liquor having been tasted by the proper officers, and the public might have had ale sold to them "not sufficiently mighty of the corn, or wholesome for man's body."

To meet this perhaps growing evil practice in 1590 (22 Eliz.), it was ordered, That no innkeeper, common brewer, or typler shall keep in their houses any fewel, as straw or verne, which shall not be thought requisite, and being warned of the constable to rid the same within one day, *sub-pœnâ*, xxs. †

This order was made against the danger of fire, and to

* G. P. Scrope, Esq., M.P., History of Castle Combe, for Private Circulation.

† History of Castle Combe.

prevent tipplers from having the means of conducting these furtive brewings. Here the public good was aimed at.

No one was to brew, in 1461, at the same time as the churchwardens were brewing the church-ale for the profit of the church, under pain of 13*s.* 4*d.*; nor (A.D. 1464) to brew or sell till all the ale brewed for the church was entirely sold. This was brewed for the benefit of the common fund for the relief of the poor, A.D. 1590.*

When the Archbishop of Canterbury should visit his land at Tarring (near Worthing), in Sussex, in 1277, four gallons of the best beer were to be charged only 1*d.* If bad it was to be staved, and a halfpenny or penny charged for the vessel.†

The price of beer at Castle Combe in 1464 was, for

	d.
Best beer, per gallon - - -	2
Second - - - - -	1
Third - - - - -	0½

In 1557, the price had advanced as follows: —

	d.
Best ale under the hair sieve, per gallon	3
Stale - - - - -	4
Second ale - - - -	1½
And when it is stale - - -	2
Smallest ale - - - -	0½
Best ale in their houses, a wine quart -	1
Without the door - - -	0½

They are to sell out of their houses as long as there is three gallons in the house.

No brewer there, in 1590, was allowed to sell his grains out of the town if the town dwellers will buy them at 2*d.* the bushel. This was very high; the same is now sold at 4*d.* the bushel.

It was ordered at Marlborough, A.D. 1524, by the mayor and council, that the brewers should sell of the —

* History of Castle Combe.

† Cartwright's Rape of Bramber.—WARTER.

	d.
Best ale, 12 gallons - - -	16
This rose to 20*d.* in 1532.	
One thurindole - - - -	$0\frac{1}{2}$
2 gallons of small ale - - -	1*

In the reign of Henry VIII. (35th year) Isabella Stansby and another, common brewers at Lyme, were presented for brewing ale not "mighty of the corn," but, on the contrary, too thin and unwholesome, and for selling the same in unlawful measures, for which each was fined 6*d.* (serevis' brassicav' nimis tenue et insalubre et vend' per mens' illicit.')

The orders for brewers are not a few†, no less than for tipplers, or those who sold *tipple* or drink.‡ The ale tasters had an important duty to perform.

In 1572, it was ordered that none of the ale brusters do from henceforth brue but with fewell, and not with hard wood or faggot-wood, upon pain for every time of so doing of 5*s.*§ It is curious that in London the dread of fire caused a law to be made at an assize of beer in 1212, that no baker should bake, or ale-wife brew by night, or with reed, straw, or stubble, only of wood.‖

Six common brewers only, and retailers of ale and beer, were appointed in 1578 at Lyme, besides the brewer "who doth and shall keep the Beer House." There is some doubt as to what we are to understand by this house; it is perhaps the same as is mentioned elsewhere as the brewhouse.

Had only the laws enacted upon this subject been fully carried out, the moral condition of boroughs would have been perfect. No tippler or retailer of beer was to sell to any craftsman or servant of the town, except he was in company with a stranger.¶ Such laws or town orders as this

* Waylen's Marlborough.

† Single Sheet MS., Archives of Lyme.

‡ See Court of Hustings' Book, 1592—1602, p. 567.

§ Fuel had become scarce in the West.

‖ MS. Add. Brit. Mus. 14,252.

¶ Court of Hustings' Book for Lyme.

never were or could have been carried out, and so became a dead letter. In 1612 an order was made that no one should tipple any one day above one hour in any house.

Fifteen tipplers were presented, in 1582, as having made default in the orders. None were to sell beer except in *hooped pots.* Jugs and cups were expressly forbidden in 1614, all beer was to be sold by ale quarts; none henceforth *adores in* cornes, *i. e.* drinking-horns.*

The ale sellers, in 1584, were to sell three pints for 1*d.*† At Castle Combe the price was 1*d.* a quart; second kind, ½*d.* a quart.

In 1594 and 1596, some of the tipplers at Lyme, and vintners also, were fined 40*s.* each for allowing unlawful games in their houses.

There was in Elizabeth's reign a BREW HOUSE which, in 1616, was rented by Steven Chick at 5*l.* a year, and there is an entry of payment for coal, 22*l.* 10*s.*

In 1658 appears an explanatory entry in the Corporation Order Book, "Agreed to take a lease of a house from H. Henley, Esq., for a public BREW HOUSE for the benefit of the poor inhabitants."

The renter was under agreement to brew beer at a certain price, and to be regulated by the authorities.

Before tea and coffee were in use a family consumed more beer, what with the morning and evening draught, than in the present day; hence the saving which constituted the benefit.

Solomon Andrew, Mayor of Lyme, paid, in 1658–9, Thomas Parsons and William Phillips 2*s.*, for their advice about a brew house. In after years there were ring-houses where a small holder of an orchard could have his apples made into cider.

In 1600 the ale and beer sellers had to find sureties in 10*l.* each to keep the orders and conditions. These "Articles

* Hist. Castle Combe as to the Cornes in 1569.

† In 1587 the price of the best ale at Leicester was 1½*d.*; of the second ale, 1*d.*; and of third ale, ½*d.* per gallon.

for the Observance of the Alehouse-Keepers" and beer sellers bear a great resemblance. Those in force at Weymouth, in 1642, were eleven in number.

Drunkenness was punished by a fine of 5*s.*; but this sum was worth more than three times the same amount imposed in the present day for the ultimate and perfect end of drinking — intoxication. The approach towards this state, the voluntary preparation for it,—tippling, the being found on the high way to intoxication,—is now neglected. In Charles I.'s reign the fine imposed was 3*s.* 4*d.* What would be the aggregate of prices in this country if every one found sitting about at public houses was fined 10*s.*?

No less than twenty-six persons of sundry trades were fined each 3*s.* 4*d.* for being common frequenters of alehouses in Sherborne and Castleton, in 1636.

So much has appeared about the unlicensed alehouses, that the form of proceeding in granting a license, while new to many, may prove interesting. The magistrates having been informed that a certain ancient house in Coleman Lane, near the market place, Shaftesbury, the property of Albinus Muston, of Shaston, gent., had been a house of entertainment of travellers, men and horses, for seventy years, and being now re-edified could receive one hundred horses, they agreed that this house should henceforth be reputed, taken and used for and as a common inn, and have all the privileges belonging to an inn.*

A great quantity of beer was sent to Guernsey and Jersey from Poole, in Elizabeth and James I.'s reign. This exportation led to litigation, as the corporation demanded from the common brewer an impost of 4*s.* per brewlock of three tuns, or about 1*d.* per kilderkin. Such an imposition might appear an exaction in the present day; but we should consider what onerous duties corporations were formerly called upon to fulfil. The defence of the coast near fell upon these sea-port boroughs, and not upon the powers who ruled over the kingdom at large.

* Mr T. Hearn, "Qui Quondam."

In Charles the First's reign, the borough authorities very generally (if not universally) forbade ale-wives to brew. When these worthies, the mayors, were despotic, they not only forbade as they could do, but dictated the course they would have pursued. At Weymouth the ale-wives were ordered not to brew, but to buy of the common brewers, while the latter had the price to be charged fixed by authority.

No innkeeper or tippler that might conveniently be served by any *common brewer,* admitted or to be admitted within the town of Lyme, was to brew in their houses, but buy of the common brewers, and such drink only, and of such reasonable size as should be fit for travellers and passengers, and such as the mayor and his brethren should set down as fit, and of such a price. The price settled for the ale-wife in two towns was as follows: —

	Lyme.	Weymouth.
	d.	*d.*
The better sort of ale under the range	3	3
Middle - - - -	0	2
Small - - - - -	1	1

The brewer was to sell the best ale at 6*d.* the barrel, the smallest at 3*d.* At Lyme, if the tippler brewed himself, the ale was to be such as might be sold at the above rate.

From some cause apprehension of a great scarcity was entertained in 1630. The Lords of the Council addressed letters to the magistrates for the suppression of the superfluous number of maltsters, who were judged to be one main cause of the scarcity of corn, and likely to be the means of a dearth, which it was feared would ensue. Agricultural statistics were not more understood than general ones. The Court ordered that no person whatever in the county of Dorset from henceforth do presume, by any ways or means, to convert any grain into malt, except such as are farmers of grounds, and have corn sufficient growing on their own demesne fit for that purpose, until such time as their license shall be renewed again by public authority.*

The grand jury of Dorset at Easter, 1636, complain of neglect respecting the laws regulating the sale of beer. There had been no assize set on beer and ale sold to alehouse-keepers by the common brewers at Sherborne, or elsewhere in the county of Dorset [we suppose for the year].

The system appears in a transition state. The public began to like that beer should be sold according to its value, and that some beer should be brewed of greater strength than could be sold without loss at the price set at assize.

The magistrates, after due consideration, did not choose that the public should have the choice of buying strong beer, but that this beverage should be sold at 12*s.* the hogshead, and the smaller sort at 9*s.* the hogshead.

The sellers had offended by selling out of jugs and cups, and not by ale quarts, contrary to the statute. The magistrates in the midst of their arrangements, full of respect for a great man, relax the stringency of every rule, order, or regulation, whether enjoined by law or not, if it was prejudicial to any of the liberties of John, Earl of Bristol, within his manor of Sherborne, which the Earl was to use as he had been anciently accustomed.

The magistrates had learned how the alehouse-keepers humoured the taste of the day, by brewing their own beer of extraordinary strength, so as to please the public, and sell the more, owing to the superior excellency of the liquor. This was done, too, by small measures; so that, though the price was the same, the quantity was diminished, to meet the improved quality. The authorities forbade all these innovations.†

The constables of Weymouth reported at court day, in 1617, that out of every alehouse the stoning-pots were broken by them.

How were borough authorities to act upon the exclusive

* Mr. T. Hearn, "Qui Quondam," Book of the Dorset Sessions in MS.

† Mr. T. Hearn, "Qui Quondam," from MS. Book of the Proceedings at Dorset Sessions.

system in respect to beer? This was as difficult a point as the introduction of steamers on the Swiss lakes with regard to the boatmen. About the year 1650, foreign beer, which means beer brewed out of the borough, was brought into Weymouth to be sold by innkeepers, to the prejudice of many, *i. e.* the town brewers. The corporation decreed that twelvepence a hogshead should be paid, and this sum to go to the poor. How clearly did the legislators benefit by this bye law! In Switzerland, steamers have to pay something each trip for the benefit of the boatmen, whose employment is greatly diminished.

No flesh was to be dressed or suffered to be dressed within any victualler's house at Lyme on any forbidden day, saving in case of necessity arising from sickness; while at Castle Combe no innkeeper was to dress any flesh on Fridays and Saturdays under pain of 5*s.*, and the eater of the same, 2*s.* 6*d.* Thus both parties, obnoxious to a charge of a breach of the orders, were punished. At Lyme alehouse-keepers were fined, in 1609, 1*l.* 3*s.* 6*d.*, as an entry shows; and alehouse haunters were taught to their cost that they were not dwelling in a borough without laws. Another entry shows that two of the latter had paid a fine of two shillings each.

How the private tradesman was liable to be interfered with will be learnt in respect of the brewer, or common brewer.

No *innkeeper* or *tippler* that might conveniently be served by any *common brewer,* admitted or to be admitted within this town, was to brew in their houses, but buy of the common brewer, and such drink only and of such reasonable size as should be fit for travellers and passengers, and such as the mayor and his brethren should set down as fit and of such price. The best ale was to be sold at 3*d.* a gallon, the worst at 2*d.* If the tippler brewed himself, he was to brew such ale as might be sold at this rate.

No flesh was to be dressed or suffered to be dressed within any victualler's house on any forbidden day, saving in case of necessity arising from sickness.

The Commons, in May 1641, declared that the decree made in the Star Chamber, prohibiting retailing vintners from dressing meat to sell in their own houses, is illegal, and against the liberty of the subject.*

Mr. Robert Bragg, mayor, 1609-18, entered 1*l.* 3*s.* 6*d.* for fines paid by the alehouse-keepers, and 4*s.* for fines of two alehouse haunters.

"The rigid restrictions of the republican rule were also manifested in the strict surveillance maintained over the people, with the view of securing temperance in drinking. Convictions for drunkenness are almost of daily occurrence. And it was frequently the practice to remove all doubt as to the sufficiency of testimony by producing the delinquent in court whilst under bacchanalian influence. Many are the instances in which it is recorded by the convicting justice that some unhappy offender was "drunk in my view." They appear, moreover, to have been in the habit of making nice distinctions as to the various gradations of intoxication. Thus, whilst the earlier stages were taken cognizance of as "tippling," there was an intermediate stage minutely described in the following extract from the information of Alice Wire, March 30, 1655:—

"'Who saith that John Keech was soe distempered with beere that hee was not at that tyme as hee is wont to bee at other tymes, for that hee slept by the ffire about an houre.'

"And on another occasion we are furnished with some criteria of intoxication by an informant, who deposes, that

"'As his conscience tells him the said Gardner was drunke, for he could neither goe well but staggered, nor did he speake plaine.'

"Numberless entries shew that a party of four or five could not sit together in the tap-room of a public house without incurring the risk of being informed against and punished for tippling, that punishment being, in many instances, a public exhibition in the stocks."

The ale-wives of Castle Combe had broken all the orders (A. D. 1568). The Court received the presentment in silence.

The Quarterly Reviewer writes, "One cannot help seeing them in high-crowned hats, with arms akimbo, making

* Verney Papers.

† Mr. Hearn, from the MS. Book of Dorset Sessions.

mouths at the court and jury sworn, and laughing outright at the tithing-man and the rest of creation." This they might have done in Queen Elizabeth's reign. Another state of things was approaching. Ale-wives were influential in a little borough. How many took two meals a day at the ale-wife's! The traveller saluted mine hostess on arriving and departing.

1584. The widow Brooke, ale brewer of Lyme, was dismissed from brewing and selling of ale for divers disorders used in her house.

The Commonwealth men found the ale-wives, or women tipplers, very disobedient to their orders, and did not hesitate to have recourse to bodily punishment for the correction of offenders in this particular.

In 1653, at the general sessions of the peace, when Richard Alford was Mayor of Lyme, and Edmund Prideaux, Esq., Attorney-General to the Commonwealth, recorder, the jury presented Mary Somers, widow, for selling beer without a license; and having been formerly convicted of the same offence, it was ordered by the Court that she shall be whipt according to the statute.

Winifred Somers, widow, Abel Thomas, &c., were ordered to pay 20*s.* for the use of the poor, not having kept the assize; in other words, having disregarded the price fixed by magistrates when they held an assize, or set for that purpose. Those who dealt in any article of consumption fancied they knew better than the authorities at what price it could be rendered to the public.

Winifred Summers, or Somers, widow, was no less a person than the widow of the brother of the celebrated Sir George Summers, the admiral.

In 1656, the licensed beer sellers were presented for selling less than a quart of the best beer for a penny, contrary to the statute. Each was to forfeit 20*s.**

April 20, 1657, the constables presented Abell Thomas,

* Rules about beer at Southampton; see Archæological Journal:—

In 1606, as malt was 2*s.* 6*d.* per bushel, and not above, the mayor and justices order that after Easter Day the beer drawers shall not make or sell but two sorts of beer, and shall sell the double beer at 3*s.* 4*d.* the

John Tucker, Mary Davy, widow, John Collyer, George Alford, Mary Somers, widow, Thomas Templeman, *Wynifrie Somers*, widow, Elizabeth Low, widow, Philip Sandford, and Joseph Sprake, for selling beer without a license, for which they have severally forfeited the several pains in the statute in that behalf incurred, viz., 20*s.* a-piece.*

On the 3rd Jan. 1658, Winifrie Somers, widow, appears first on the list of those tipplers licensed to sell ale and beer, and was bound under a penalty of 20*l.* not to transgress the five laws. These were —

1. Unlawful games.
2. Unnecessary occasion for drinking.
3. Drinking on the Lord's Day.†
4. Unreasonable hours of the night.
5. Disorder and misrule in their houses.

In 1675, seventeen persons were licensed to sell beer (*ad beria vendenda*), each to keep good order, and to have his corn ground at the town mill.

During the troubles, victuallers and alehouse keepers dispensed with the common brewer and baker, and brewed and baked for themselves. This practice was decried by the authorities, as the assize of bread, beer, and ale could not be observed. But the obsolete bye-laws could not be again acted upon. At Marlborough, after the regulation of the borough in 1663, one of the first acts of the council was to endeavour, but ineffectually, to revive the obsolete laws.

The stopping well-known Foot-paths.

FROM the first year when any human being could call a rod of land his own, a path was probably straitened, or an

barrel; the ordinary at 2*s.* A few years later, when malt was at 2*s.* and hops at 8*l.* the hundred, the double beer was sold at 4*s.*, and the ordinary at 2*s.* 6*d.*

In 1631, the vintners were not to sell their Gascoigne wine at more than 6*d.* a quart.

* Court of Hustings' Book, p. 221.

† Hist. of Castle Combe. Beer not to be sold during divine service, nor after nine o'clock at night.

attempt made to stop it, if the doing so brought greater advantage than leaving it untouched. When land became very valuable, then the practice was confirmed. Were it not for some watch-dogs, who look out for the encroachments of the selfish and unjust, the rights and conveniences of the many would be sacrificed to the wary few. No one being specially commissioned to undertake this office, opportunities are embraced from time to time to make some inroad upon the rights of the public. The matter in complaint may not lie concealed; but the difficulty of inducing the only partially interested to come forward,—the difficulty about the expense to be incurred, indecision, the public mind being engrossed at the time by some grand topic,—all conspire to render the accomplishment possible, if not easy.

It is honourable to the discernment and justice of men of past generations that they were sensible of the value and importance of foot-paths. King Edward the First caused an inquisition to be made by the Sheriff of Sussex as to any damage or nuisance that would happen to the king, or others, by the diverting a pathway in the town of Chichester by the Master of St. Mary in that city. The king allowed the path to be stopped up only upon the making another competent pathway, reserving the rights of every one.*

That the population of our great cities should be unable to reach the beautiful country, and enjoy with their children the lovely paths through the corn and hay-fields, is the inevitable result of their inhabiting so widely spread a Babel. It is, however, really distressing to those who view the environs of small country towns to observe, that many old paths have been stopped, and that the population are in some localities becoming no better off than the road-confined inhabitants of cities. Some official should be charged with this matter; and private encroachment should be assailed as a matter of course by him at the public charge. What pleasure can be more pure, more health-inspiring,

* Sussex Archæol. Coll.

than a walk through the open fields? Let us preserve every old right of way around our beautiful country. What is lost in such a case only adds a mere trifle to the means of one whose heirs will not perceive the advantage gained to the detriment of the comfort, the health, and pure enjoyment. Many, however, can exclaim in the words of the poet: —

> "I have trod
> That path from child to man times beyond count,
> And followed through it the still varying year
> From spring to summer. Had it led to heaven
> I could not love it more — and all the folk
> That owned our parish church, aged and young,
> Loved it no less; the child for its own sake,
> And for his pleasant use of it — the old,
> For that 't was once to them a lover's walk,
> And now in darkness and decline of age
> A tender memory — but what was this,
> And all the soul of gentleness beside,
> To the cold spirit that only loves itself,
> And hates whate'er may baulk it in self-love?" *

An early presentment made at Castle Combe introduces an offender who was fined: —

1389, Oct. 21. Decena præsentat quod Thomas Touker, ii*d.*, appropria vit sibi de communi viâ vocatâ Halpenejwey arando de dictâ viâ ad nocumentum, ideo ipse in misericordia.†

Near Axminster is the manor of Weycroft, where stood a mansion house in the castellated style, erected soon after the year 1400, by Sir Thomas Brooke, the ancestor of Lord Cobham. In 1416, the heir to the estate obtained a royal license to crenellate the mansion, and enclose a park of 800 acres. In the course of the formation of this park, Joan, the widow of Sir Thomas Brooke, obstructed several public roads and paths.

The state of society did not allow, perhaps, of an association of humble individuals to resist the powerful lady of

* "Ernest," a poem privately circulated by Capel Loft.

† Scrope's Hist. of Castle Combe.

Holditch, Lyme Regis, and Weycroft. The battle for the restoring the public rights had to be waged by the head of a neighbouring family of great distinction, Sir William Bonville, of Shute House. Avoiding lengthy details, we will only state that Nicholas Wysebeach, the Abbot of Newenham, and five of the abbot's neighbours, were appointed mediators. They decided every point in favour of the public champion, Sir William Bonville, and directed that all the ways should be thrown open. The good abbot had been nominated by the Lady Brooke out of respect to his justice and hospitality. Abbot Wysebeach ought to have been canonized as the prince of arbitrators. Such an office was not to him, hearty soul! a dull matter of statistics, or humdrum matter of business. He would not send the defeated party to pine over disappointed hopes, and the victor to inordinate display of triumph. That monk must have been born with an eye for a *tableau.* By his award a procession that a Watteau should have depicted was formed. After the paths were reopened — business over first — the knight and the lady were to ride together about a mile and a half to Newenham Abbey, below Axminster, on a day appointed, where they were to exchange a kiss in token of peace and friendship, and dine together at the abbot's table! A blessing on all such ending of strife. Should a painter want a subject, here is one ready at hand. The scene lies in South-east Devon; but the meadows by the river Axe, the red earth and the scenery, should render this unmistakeable.*

The warmest admirers of Queen Elizabeth's reign must acknowledge that if it exceeded in advantages the present day, it closely resembled, and was on a par with the latter, in a disposition manifested by many to encroach in various ways upon the rights of the public to paths and common places. The antiquity of path-stopping will surprise those

* The deed in the possession of the devisees of the late Mr. Frampton has been quoted by J. Davidson, Esq., of Seektor, the historian of Newenham Abbey.

who view such a propensity as a growth of very recent times.

The examples given of path-stopping are, with one exception, purposely confined to one locality — Lyme Regis.

In 1584, it was ordered at the Lyme Court of Hustings, that Richard Davidge do leave open the way, according to the old custom, that leadeth into the Great Field before the Feast of St. John the Baptist, upon pain of 20*s.*

At Leicester, about this time, it was ordered that all the common lanes and common places taken in within the remembrance of man shall be laid open again.*

Some of the principal inhabitants of Lyme, in 1594, made a presentment that Silvester Jurden hath showed himself disobedient, in that he hath refused to remove his gate set upon the way going out from the churchyard to the eastern cleeves, and also hath refused to pay the amerciament laid upon the law day for setting up the said gate to the annoyance of the Queen's people.†

In 1596 the jury found that Mr. Robert Hassard hath enclosed a plot of ground which hath been in common time out of mind, and sithence the way is foundred. In another presentment the way was said to be strayted.

This was by St. Andrew's chapel on the way towards Uplyme. St. Andrew's Lane, Cross and Wells, are localities now not known by these names.

Mr. Robert Hassard, in 1598, furnished matter for a presentment, by taking into his ground some part of a lane beyond John Calley's house, and taking the bond-stones (boundary) leading down the way to the Cobb. He was ordered to make it as before, under pain of 20*s.*

A view was taken of the locality, and the measurement entered into the Court of Hustings Book.

Mr. Robert Hassard was amerced, in 1599, the sum of fourpence for having locked a gate, and stopped people from going to the Cobb.

Mr. Walter Harvey was presented, in 1597, for having

* Nichol's History.

† Freeman's Book, p. 291.

enclosed the way upon the down, called Colway down, by the crooked oak, which ought not to be.

John Collier was fined 6*s.* 8*d.* in 1612, for encroaching upon the highway at Shells going up to Lanchycraft.

In 1665 the widow Stone was presented for altering the footpath in Barre Close, leading to Colway Bridge. Would that parties had been found to present every one who has wilfully closed for ever paths of the greatest utility to the town.

In 1647, Mr. John Parrat enclosed a lane leading from Pound Street to the Stile, — also another lane leading to a spring of water which served for the use of the inhabitants adjoining, and also straightening the highway a little below the pound. Robert Reed stopped a passage through his entry down the cleeves towards the Cobb being a common passage in 1677.

A great path case respecting the right of way through the Pinney Undercliff, west of Lyme, which had been litigated for four years, was decided in favour of the public and reopened Sept. 28th, 1843.

The desire to close paths has, we see, existed from early reigns, and many of them, could we only learn the fact, have been preserved by the exercise of public spirit. Be on the alert my countrymen. A duty is owed to posterity.

Merchant Adventurers' petition to be allowed to continue to trade and kidnap on the Coast of Africa.

Should the question be asked, Was the worst feature of slavery — kidnapping — ever tolerated in conversation, or deliberately committed to writing by one engaged in it? We answer in the affirmative.

So late as the year 1700, the merchants of the ports of South-western England found kidnapping profitable, and openly petitioned for liberty to continue that horrible traffic.

All sorts of frauds were practised in order to procure white labour. The Monmouth men had been liberated from their ten years' banishment to the West Indies at the revolution; which made the demand greater. The procuring persons to go out to the West Indies used to be spoken of in odious terms by the old people, at the beginning of this century. If they were correct, all sorts of unfair practices were resorted to.

The following important petition from some of the last of our foreign merchants does not require the aid of an interpreter: it speaks in plain language and with our present humane views upon the subject draws forth deep reprobation.

Slave Trade.*

"Petition of the Merchant Adventurers of the Town of Lyme Regis to Parliament, humbly sheweth,

"That the trade of this port and your petitioners' livelihoods very much depends on the western navigation and plantations, whose productions are chiefly raised by negroes brought from Africa.

"That by encouragement of the late Act of Parliament (9 & 10 William III. c. 26.) for opening of the African trade, divers of the merchants and inhabitants of this town became adventurers therein.

"The petitioners hear that the African Company have been trying to obtain a monopoly of the said trade in a joint stock company exclusive of all the outports, therefore they pray to be allowed to continue to trade to the plantations and kidnap on the coast of Africa."

Who at this date judged there was anything at all wrong in buying, keeping, or selling slaves? If any one did so he must have been before his age or have been deemed to be eccentric. Kidnapping was, however, a branch of commerce in slaves that is not to be often found described or alluded to by the parties engaged in it. At the beginning of this century we may conclude that every branch of slavery was

* See Corporation Papers: Sketch of Petition about 1699 or 1700.

deemed allowable and as having nothing wrong in it. Negro boys had been, in the time of the Commonwealth, in the service of fashionable persons. These had been imported from the Portuguese settlements. The Puritans polled their negro servants like themselves.

In the "Tatler" of 1709, a black boy, twelve years of age, fit to wait upon a gentleman, was offered for sale.* How negroes were purchased and instructed on board a frigate is elsewhere narrated.

The payment of the burgesses of Parliament formerly; their travelling expenses, &c.

WHEN the first parliaments were called, the frame-work of society was in perfect contrast with that of the present day. In no particular will a comparison prove more interesting than in that of circumstances respecting what pertains to the "Burgesses for the Parliament."

The borough tradesmen courted no honour in being chosen for burgesses: therefore they were not disposed to pay anything. On the contrary they travelled, more properly, rode at the cost of those who had chosen them; and were paid by the day while absent in the discharge of their duty. There was very probably some slight honour reflected upon the parties chosen in the eyes of their townsmen. Perhaps the more discreet were selected, the more bold or hardy.

The burgesses sat apart from both barons and knights, who disdained to mix with such mean personages as the burgesses were then regarded. They had no voice in deliberative proceedings, and their consent being given to the taxes required of their boroughs, they separated, though the parliament continued sitting. The burgesses of parliament were chosen, temp. Henry V., at the county court.

* Quarterly Review, June, 1855.

The first representatives of Lyme Regis, at the Parliament holden at Canterbury, in 1295, William Tuluse and Geoffry le Keu, had to furnish each of them two sureties (*manucaptores*), and each received 2*s.* a day. This was not bad pay, considering the relative value of money.

Glanville Sharp states there were only 145 places that sent members to this Parliament.* The burgesses from Lyme Regis went to perform an office they could not refuse, being tenants of the king. Robbers, a want of bridges, distance, no stated regular communication with their homes, and neglect of their private business, made the performance of the duty an onerous one. Those burgesses afforded the greatest amount of satisfaction to themselves and their fellow-townsmen — we would hardly use the word constituents — who stayed the shortest possible time.

When they returned they brought their bill of daily charges and travelling expenses, both for going and returning, which was addressed as a Writ *de expensis* to the mayor and bailiffs.† The Dorset burgesses from Lyme never made their appearance at the Parliaments holden in the north, — a distant and dreaded unknown region, — from 1295 till 1306.

Chard only sent burgesses to Parliament from 1300 to 1329. The town grudged the expense of sending members, and so disused and lost the privilege. The knights of Cornwall about this time charged 2*s.* 6*d.* for each day's expenses and took seven days to make the journey. In Blomefield's Norfolk we find that in the year 1403, 5th Henry IV., the king's writ came to Norwich by which four citizens were to be returned to Parliament instead of two. This additional expense to the city in wages was considered such a burden that 3*l.* were paid to John de Alderford to get the matter altered, which was effected.

In 1323, however clever the burgesses of Lyme may have been, their services could not have been very valuable as they only stayed *p. iiii. dies*, four days! This delay was perhaps

* Report of Committee, temp. James I.

† See William Atte Gate, and Geoffrey le Cok's writ, tested at Westminster in 1311, in the Close Rolls, *m.* 16. *d.*

only what their horses required by way of rest. Here, as in so many other cases, we may well reflect upon the altered features of society, and contrast the riding away on horseback of our ancient burgesses with the railway travelling of their successors. To fairly chronicle these matters is the object of these pages.

The Lyme archives furnish nothing for about two centuries, as Hustings books are wanting. The entries under the Tudor sovereigns are illustrative of the state of society. Mr. Richard Hunt, mayor in 1554, had provided some money in advance towards the burgess, or member of Parliament.

	s.	*d.*
Item, y[t] I have layd howtte for y[e] towne to Mr. Mallocke (of Rusedon) for hys charges to be borges of Plement - - - - - - -	liii	iiij

To be levied at the Comenes hands and no others.

This sum was most probably paid to Mr. Mallocke on starting for the place of the meeting of the Parliament, wherever that locality happened to be. This portion was to be raised from the *inhabitants generally*, and not from the brethren, merchants of the guild, from the burgesses and free men, who were to be assessed, and bear their share of the burden in some other way.* Doubtless the memorandum refers to a clerical arrangement in the levying the sum, and does not dictate a partial and therefore unfair assessment.

The mayor, John Holcombe, in 1559, acknowledges the receipt of *5l.* 6*s.* 6*d.* from William Follet and another for such money as was gathered for the burgesses of Parliament; and more is to be gathered of Robert Moore, John Hassard, and Richard Haiball.

We have seen how nearly three centuries from this date, 1571, the burgesses were paid two shillings a day and their expenses. What change had such a long course of

* A free burgess possessed a freehold, and was made free by a fine and by an oath: a freeman had no freehold.

years effected? Can this be ascertained with certainty?—are questions that readily present themselves, and will find at once a satisfactory answer.

William Ellesdon, when mayor of Lyme in 1571, made up his account for parliamentary service as follows:—

"For the tyme I was burgess of the parliament for 65 days, at 2*s.* the day, viz. 6*l.* 12*s.* from the 29th March to the 2nd of June. And further, that I spent the same time over and above 2*s.* the day for me and my man and two horses the sum of 5*l.* 3*s.* 6*d.*, in all amounting to the sum of 12*l.* 17*s.*"

The daily pay and travelling charges of the burgesses of the parliaments were borne by the borough that consigned these worthies to distant journeying, and in many cases ill-suited and uncongenial duties. At the very first our western boroughs deemed this a burden, which some relieved themselves from by not obeying the writs, as in the case of Chard. The burgesses sent to the early parliaments were tradesmen of their respective boroughs, the Commons of the realm, not holden in much repute. In 1295 they are alluded to as *alii de regno,* "others of the realm," as if not worthy to be specified or designated—a slighting phrase.*

In the course of years a higher class of persons felt a desire to be in Parliament. Some of these could do good service. They were active, influential, and repaid their hire by their useful exertions; other individuals, perhaps, not finding themselves likely to render much service, while the townsmen were unaware of any great work to be performed. There are appearances of mutual concessions, and the making of terms for attaining an honourable post and relieving themselves of a considerable burden.

The paid burgess of the Parliament worked for his employers, and learned for them, before he perilled his life in a long journey by dangers to be encountered by "flood

* Parry's Parliaments and Councils of England.

and field," how he could be useful. "To instruct our burgess" meant very differently from anything similarly worded in the present day. The employers and employed stood in a very different light to the voters, and the rich, perhaps illustrious, member of the present day. During the whole of the session the burgess was ready to be employed in advancing the interests of his borough at court by the tortuous processes so often recorded.

It was agreed in Parliament, A.D. 1580, that any burgess departing without a license should forfeit his wages. About the year 1604 a motion was made in the House that absentees should pay 20*s.*, but which fine was reduced to 6*s.* 8*d.*

In the third year of Edward the Fourth's reign, John Sackvylle, Esq. agreed to be one of the burgesses for Weymouth, at the Parliament to be holden at Westminster, "if holden long time or short, or what it fortune to be, taking for his wages there a cade of mackerel (500 mackerel) though two been delivered, by Christmas next coming." * "Though two been delivered," I read "though two cades have been customarily delivered."

John Wadham the younger, 4th February, 1558, in the reign of Edward VI., captain of Sandsfoot Castle, came to terms with the neighbouring electors, whose borough he helped to guard. He agreed by a paper to serve Melcombe Regis in Parliament as a burgess, without pay, whatever the law might give him.†

It may be fairly said that these two adjoining boroughs laid themselves out to bargain for a burgess that would not be a burden to them. A letter is inserted to show the open treating to secure this object.‡

"(3 Jan. 1558-9.)

"To my loving frendes the maior and his brethren of the town of Melcombe Regis.

"After my hartie commendacons, understanding by the return of your gentill answere your readynesse and good will to accom-

* Ellis's Hist. of Weymouth. † Sherren Papers. ‡ Ibid.

plyshe my request for the nomination and appointment of one of the Burgesses for your town of Melcombe Regis against the next Parliament already summoned and shortly to be assembled, lyke as for the same I have thought good to nominate John Moynes of Bruteport, and to notify in like manner the same unto you, so presuming you accordingly to admit him, I hereby promise unto you to discharge you of such *ordenary* and *dayly stypende* for him whom I name and appoint, as in the like case you and others have heretofore been accustomed to gyve to the burgesses for their attendance in your affaires, there giving you and every of you my hartie thanks for your gentilnes, which I will not forget, with the pleasure I may do you at any tyme to recompense. And so I byd you hartily farewell, from the Court, this iij of January, 1558.

"Your loving frende,

"F. BEDFORD.

"Maior of Melcombe."

So early as the year 1640, voices were unduly procured by inviting to alehouses. Hobby, a candidate, struck one who procured voices against him.*

Human nature remains only what it has appeared in all historical time. The ready spoken in Elizabeth's reign were apt at elections to promise too freely; the recipients of favours and the expectants of benefits often doubtless looked for too much. Hence disputes arose between the contracting parties as to the performance of the conditional agreements.

At the passing of the town accounts at Leicester in 1582, some did mislike that Mr. Stanford, the burgess, had been allowed his charge for the Parliament last past, for that they declared he said when he was chosen burgess, he would not crave his charge except he *did good to the town.* It was thereupon agreed, that if he do at any time good to the town, then his charge to be allowed; otherwise he is to repay again that which he hath received for his charge for the two Parliaments past.†

* Verney Papers, by J. Bruce, Esq.

† Nichol's Hist. of Leicester.

No sooner was a seat in Parliament generally spoken of as a distinction, an honour, an object of the ambition of the great men of the day, than the former reluctance to take the office was changed into a readiness to embrace any opportunity for obtaining a seat in the House. As the burgesses now sat with the knights, and debated with them, some higher qualification than before was necessary; education had been received by all, at least to a certain extent. The imperfections of an uneducated man would be strikingly apparent.

This was the case with the burgess sent from Westbury, Wiltshire, in 1571. He appeared to be unsuitable to the office he had assumed, and we learn from the following very naive account how the matter ended. This has been named the first case of BRIBERY in which mere money supplied the place of family and education. We learn that Thomas Long, a very simple man, and unfit to serve, is questioned how he came to be elected. He confesses that he gave the Mayor of Westbury and another FOUR POUNDS for his place in Parliament. They are ordered to repay this sum, to appear to answer such things as should be objected against them in that house, and a fine of twenty pounds is to be assessed on the corporation and inhabitants of Westbury for their scandalous attempt.*

Not only were gentlemen found very anxious to sit in Parliament, but so early as the beginning of the seventeenth century that species of fraud, since classed as election trickery, was well understood and practised. A remarkable instance of successful deception practised to win an election is here given, which proves the before-named proposition; the narrative contains some mention of the practice of wearing a great man's livery, and the interference and great influence of lord-lieutenants with corporations to secure the return of their favourite.

Mr. George Belgrave, of Belgrave, had offended the Earl

* Parry's Parliaments and Councils of England. See Notes and Queries, May 12, 1854.

of Huntington, Lord-lieutenant of Leicestershire, 1601, who recommended two candidates, and in strong language warned the corporation against electing one so displeasing to him. The earl had learned that Belgrave "still contineweth his great practising in labouring to be chosen."

The above gentleman appeared at the election of the burgesses in a blue coat with a bull head, affirming and protesting that he was the Earl of Huntington's servant, and so wore his lordship's livery, having obtained that favour late the night before through the intervention of Sir Henry Harrington. The artful candidate bemoaned his undutifulness to the earl; and when asked if he brought any letter, he excused the circumstance owing to the lateness of the hour the preceding night when his peace had been made, but pointed to his coat and cognizance as a sufficient proof of the earl's favour, and offered to take a corporal oath to the truth of his statement. The mayor and his brethren were deceived by this "cunning practisore," and elected him. The earl exhibited an information in the Star Chamber against Mr. Belgrave.*

Some burgesses of the Parliament had multifarious duties to perform for their constituents, who sometimes furnished occasion to be reminded that mean matters were not suitable to men of high breeding. Their borough correspondents were at times reminded that council business alone would be attended to by them.†

The burgesses of Poole gave power to the Earl of Bedford, at his special suit and request, 13 Elizabeth, to nominate one of their two burgesses. 26 Elizabeth, the same burgesses allowed the Earl of Leicester to nominate a representative. Giles Estcourt, Recorder of Poole, 27 Eliz. A.D. 1585, wrote to the mayor and burgesses to desire that he might have the nomination of one of the burgesses, either for his own son, or some other person that he would

* See Notes and Queries, for an article by William Kelly, Dec. 10. 1853.

† See Gentleman's Magazine, Sept. 1852, for an account of the Sherren Papers containing such a letter.

undertake should be a fit one, and should discharge the place without any charge to them, while the applicant, the recorder, engaged to be thankful for the favour.

The Earl of Warwick, in 1586, requested (through two friends) the mayor and burgesses of Poole, that they would nominate the young Earl of Bedford, his lordship's ward, for the sake of his grandfather. Like others who ask favours, Thomas Horsey and George Trenchard, who sent the earl's letter, took care to lessen the estimate of the service to be rendered in these words, "we hope there shall not neede much speach or great entreatie, yor selves knowinge how small the courtesie is, and how thankfull it will be taken."

At Leicester, H. Skipwith, Esq., and Thomas Johnson, one of her Majesty's serjeants-at-arms, were appointed burgesses of the Parliament in 1584, and either of them promised to bear their own charges.* It was agreed that Sir Ralph Sadler, Knt., Chancellor of the Duchy of Lancaster, should nominate one.† So at Lyme Regis, Zachary Bethel was chosen, 29 Jan. 1593-4, a burgess of the Parliament by the Marquess of Winchester, while the mayor, burgesses, and freemen elected Robert Hassard. In some counties the lord-lieutenants pretended to have a control over the elections.

John Hassard, burgess of Parliament, worked for the town with great diligence in 1584.‡ There is entered,

	£	s.	d.
Paid for expences of the burgess the first Parliament, 1584, before Xmas - - - - -	8	15	0
Second Parliament after Xmas, all that Parliament time him and his man, and for riding, charge up and down - - - - - -	12	8	0
Expenses of the Lower House for passing a bill -	8	10	0
" Higher " " -	16	9	0
His charge the first Parliament, 57 days, and riding up and down, and fees to the house and serjeant -	12	13	4

* Nichol's Hist. of Leicester. † Ibid.

‡ Town Accompt Book, p. 53., and four following pages.

Additional evidence can be produced to show that seats in Parliament were often much coveted. This was a matter of notoriety in Charles the First's reign.

The interest exerted to secure a vacant burgesses place for Liverpool in 1670 was remarkable. The Duke of Monmouth and Lady Southampton wrote in favour of Mr. Ross, his grace's early tutor, and the whole affair as recently displayed is very interesting.* The Duke of Monmouth appears to have made a practice of writing to corporations in favour of some partisan.

We will adduce an instance of spiteful treatment of those individual voters of a town that did not support a great man's candidate, as a punishment for their preference of another great county man.

Soldiers being billeted in Taunton, Sir John Stawell, of Cotheleston Lodge, near that town, earnestly canvassed the inhabitants to have all their votes for the two burgesses of the Parliament. He was told by them they had reserved a vote for Sir Robert Phillipps, of Montacute House, but that he should have the other. Sir John Stawell took offence at this; and removed some soldiers that were already billeted out, and billeted them upon the mayor and others.

Mr. John Mohun had interfered, as was reported, in some election in Cornwall, and was, like Sir John Stawell, believed in the west to have been sent for by the Parliament and honoured by the court.†

A highly interesting account of travelling to London, stay there, and sundry charges for searches of charters, fees of office, &c., exists, on a single foolscap sheet, among the archives. If this be not the account of John Hassard, the burgess of the Parliament, when paving the way for the incorporation of the town, which I fully believe it to have been, it was that of some other worthy, whose style of living, expenses of travelling, &c., were the same. I

* Historic Society of Lancashire and Cheshire, 1853–54.

† Diary of Walter Yonge, Esq., M.P.

extract the entries illustrative of this part of the subject: —

1586.

For my charges to London and from London, and during my being in London, and for divers other charges for the town.

	s.	d.
First for my charges to London (144 miles) - -	11	6
Item, riding to the Court at Windsor at divers times, and once with a man to attend me - - - -	18	6
Item, paid for horse meat during my being in London -	33	11
Item, paid Mrs. Beymes for my table (*i.e.* board) during my being in London - - - - - -	50	0
Item, paid for boat hire, breakfast, and for wine at my meals, and for fire during my being in London -	21	7
Item, paid for washing of my shirts - - -		20
Item, given to the two maids of the house - -		12
Item, given to Humphrey and to John for dressing of my horse - - - - - - - -		12
Item, paid to Simon Fry for the hire of his mare and shoeing of her to London - - - -	11	0
Item, paid for my charge from London - - -	16	4

The ancient burgesses of the Parliament were paid, as we have recorded, their wages and charges. It is likewise a fact that they applied themselves with great energy and perseverance, just as any agent or attorney now a day would do, to serving the borough. They were no sinecurists. The townsmen furnished duties for them to perform.

Mr. Robert Hassard spent twenty-three weeks in London in 1590 to procure a renewal of the fee-farm rent from the crown. How intimately connected was this burgess of the Parliament with his constituents — his employers and payers! He charges among other matters: —

	£	s.	d.
A large box, and for a lock and key for the charter -		4	0
The hire of a horse from London to Windsor when my horse was lame - - - - -		2	6
Boat hire from London to the court [at Greenwich] at several times - - - - - -	1	0	0

	£	s.	d.
Paid to Forster for carriage up and down of my things for four times - - - - -		19	0
For hire of a horse up and down from London for four times - - - - - -	2	13	4
[13*s.* 4*d.* for hire to London and back, both ways, 288 miles.]			
My expence for myself and my man for twenty-three weeks - - - - - - -	26	18	0
Item, paid for my chamber several to myself - -	1	0	0

A page of the Lyme Regis Court of Hustings' Book for 2 Nov. 1584 possesses, for more reasons than one, unusual interest. Let us consider it in reference to our subject.

It was agreed at a court held in the Moot Hall, that as well the burgesses and freemen, as well inhabitant as not inhabitant, as all other inhabitants, shall be contributory to the payment of taxes and impositions to be levied towards the charge of the burgesses for the Parliament.

The burgesses chose two assessors on their parts; the mayor and his brethren two on their parts.

		£	s.	d.
In 1587.	Mr. Hassard's account for the Parliament was - - - - - -	7	0	0
1593.	Mr. Robert Hassard's charge and fees at the Parliament - - - - -	22	8	0
1604-5.	Sir George Summers, the great admiral, had his allowance of charge at the Parliament	10	0	0
1606.	Ditto ditto	10	0	0
1616.	Mr. John Hassard had the rest of his accompts of Parliament - - - -	2	1	4
1821.	Allowed Mr. Robert Hassard at his going to London to be a burgess in Parliament -	6	13	4

Another instance of money paid in advance.

Entries in the Town Accompt Book in the mayoralty of Wm. Davy, 1623–4: —

	s.	d.
Item, paid Mr. Poulett's man being sent hither about the burgesship, a quart of claret wine - - -	0	6
Item, provided a dyner for Mr. Drake and his company		

	s.	d.
at their being here about choosing a burgess, which cost - - - - - - -	40	0
Item, for provision made for Mr. Robert Hassard, our burgess, when he came from the Parliament - -	10	0

The good townsmen learnt all the news while partaking of refreshment with their burgess just arrived from the distant metropolis.

A few other entries: —

	s.	d.
Item, paid to Mr. Robert Hassard for a box to return up the writ - - - - - -		12
Item, paid for my horse hire and the serjeants when we rode to Mr. Drake upon his return from the Parliament, and for a box of marmalade, and 4lbs. of dry suckett, and a bottle of wine given to his wife - -	11	0
Item, sent to Mr. Drake and to Sir John Drake at several times upon their return from the Parliament, 2 quarts of sack and 2 quarts of claret wine - -	3	0
A collation to Sir John Drake and Mr. Robert Hassard when they returned from the Parliament - -	10	0
Entertaining Mr. John Drake and his company coming to town for a burgess' place upon the death of Mr. Robert Hassard - - - - -	16	9

Members of the corporation of Coblentz and other towns having been chosen to serve as "peers" in the Prussian Chamber, in 1854, refused to accept that honour unless the towns paid their expenses.

Are we destined to revive obsolete customs?

Early travelling in the south-west of England; the manner in which it was performed; the cost of a journey on horseback, and the introduction of stage coaches, &c.

WHAT more probable than that within a few years the writer of facts connected with this subject may be thought to have been creating not recording a past, and that posterity will not yield credit to what is herein recorded? This stamps our time as that proper for submitting incidents to the present generation of which they can certify the truth. Some previous knowledge is required in order to entertain certain subjects.

Three centuries have not rolled by without producing mighty changes in the face of the country, in habits, in prices, and in the relative bearing of the constituent parts of society upon one another. In treating of the expense of sending burgesses to Parliament, mention was necessarily made of the cost of their journeys to the Parliament and back, which is properly a branch of this subject. When great men were expected, the way by which they were to enter the borough was "mended." This, however, in many instances was not the way by which the town is now entered. There is now a road; the former entrance was by a lane, perhaps in quite a different direction. Journeying was once costly, slow, and often, to distant parts, impossible. Communication by letter between distant relatives could not be maintained, except in certain parts. All these things produced immense effects, as the altered circumstances have done in the whole framework of society.

There was no security for the traveller from his fellow men. Hampshire was notorious in the time of the Plantagenets for its bands of freebooters.

It was enacted, in 1285, that the highways leading from one market town to another should be widened, so that there might be no bushes, woods, or dikes within two hundred feet on each side of the road; and those proprietors who refused to cut down underwoods abutting on high roads were to be held responsible for all felonies that might be committed by persons lurking in their covert.*

The last wolf was killed in Scotland in 1680; in Ireland, in 1710.

* H. Turner's Domestic Architecture.

A great authority, Mr. Macaulay, treats of the different appearance of a cockney and a country lord of a manor, and of the unsuitableness of the one to the other, and the incivility that took place when these came in contact.

If country hated town, there was a reciprocity of feeling on the part of town. Insecurity was anticipated in being among our own countrymen far from home. "Cousin John, I've cut a good black-thorn that 'll stand your friend," said an old relative to a young man, sixty years ago, who was about to visit the metropolis. Such a thought would hardly enter the brain of any one at present. Single-stick, when exercised, is so for that particular exercise's sake, and not for self-protection against our own countrymen in our own land. The tailor dresses the man of country and town more and more alike every day, and the fusion will at length be complete.

The same great writer adds, "The chief cause which made the fusion of the different elements of society so imperfect was the extreme difficulty which our ancestors found in passing from place to place. Of all inventions, the alphabet and the printing press alone excepted, those inventions which abridge distance have done most for the civilisation of our species. Every improvement of the means of locomotion benefits mankind morally and intellectually as well as materially, and not only facilitates the interchange of the various productions of nature and art, but tends to remove national and provincial antipathies, and to bind together all the branches of the great human family."

In this century many have been saluted in London with this inquiry, "What, all the way from Dorset?" It was the tailor's fault, that the west countryman was so readily distinguished from a Londoner. The Dorset tailor now visits the metropolis for the fashions. Puttenham, in his "Art of Poesie," lays down as the correct rule for speech or writing, "The usual speech of the Court and that of London, and the shires lying about London within sixty miles, and not much above."

The knights of Cornwall, in the reign of Edward II., claimed their expenses for seven days going to Parliament, and the same time for returning, at 2*s.* 6*d.* a day. Taking into account the relative value of money, they could make the journey cheaper by railroad, and twelve days would be saved each session.

When our mayors and their brethren left the precincts where their supremacy lay, *to ride* into the country at a time when flocks of bustards were to be seen upon our downs, and the population was very inconsiderable, — we mean three centuries ago, — it might be judged that all particulars of their journey are lost. It is not so, however. These worthies entered every penny expended in their official capacity, and little entries give an insight into very interesting matters. Thus, in the archives of Lyme for the year 1552, may be learnt how near to borough towns lay a *terra incognita :* —

	s.	*d.*
Item, paid when Mr. Mayor and Mr. Garland did ride to Mr. Pledges (Pley's ?) to one to teach them the way -		2
Item, for our paynes touching to come home when we might lie out - - - - - - -	1	0

So bad and unknown were cross roads, that guides, shepherds, and persons of a like degree, were usually hired to conduct travellers from one town to another, especially if it were desirable to take a shorter route than the high road. In the absence of bridges it was necessary to have persons well acquainted with the fording places of rivers or streams, or fatal accidents might occur.* King Edward I., in 1299, had seventeen guides when he went from Dover to Chichester, and round to Canterbury.

King Edward III. landed at Rye in May, 1360, and started immediately on horseback for London, where he arrived at 9 o'clock the next morning. This was a royal instance of great dispatch.†

* Hudson Turner's Domestic Architecture.

† Rymer, iii. 490.

Sir W. Springet's lady had great difficulty, in 1643, to hire a coach to Arundel at all, because of the bad road. She did so at last for 12*l.* Her sick husband died, leaving just that sum in his possession. The waters were out; both coach and horses had to be swum in the highways, while the lady was rowed in a boat. Well might King Charles say, when such were the highways, that he wanted dragoons, and that the rebel's foot had no inclination to winter-marches.

Ralph Thoresby, the antiquary, lost his way between Doncaster and York, more than a century later; and Pepys and his wife, travelling in their own coach, lost their way in Charles the Second's reign near Salisbury, and were in danger of having to pass the night on the Plain. The country continued little better than a wilderness till the middle of the seventeenth century.

Charitable good souls left lands and valuables for the making of causeways, such as Maud Heath's Causeway, near Chippenham, in Wiltshire, and the making and mending of feeble bridges and foul ways.

Archbishop Islip, a mediæval prelate, the founder of Canterbury Hall, in Oxford, was not exempt from the sore inconveniences of early travelling. The chronicler tells us how, in riding from Oxford Palace to Mayfield Palace, Kent, in 1362, he fell from his horse in a wet and miry lane, between Sevenoaks and Tunbridge, so that the archbishop was "wet through all over." In that pitiable state he rode on without any change of clothes, and was seized with paralysis.

Mr. John Garland, merchant, Mayor of Lyme in 1569, rode to London on town business. His whole charge for himself and horse in London was 3*l.* 5*s.*; the hire of the horse was 5*s.*

Mr. Roger Keate, who frequently journeyed for the corporation of Weymouth, set out to transact business in London: —

1578-9.

Jan. 21. Reached Blandford at noon. Foul weather, so he remained all night, at a cost of 3*s.* 3*d.* for himself and horse.

22. Salisbury at noon.
    Andover.
23. Basingstoke.
24. London at noon.

His ordinary table for 82 days, two meals a day, were 6*d.* a meal.

Fire, drink in the mornings and other times [equivalent to our breakfast and tea meals], two pence a day.
Horse meat, eight pence a day; occasional shoeing of the horse, eight pence.

The horse was sold away: we may conclude it was his own.

The charge for shoeing a horse, which had been 6*d.*, rose in 1581 to 10*d.* and 12*d.*

Washing his shirts for 79 days, four shillings, or about 4½*d.* per week.
Two pair of shoes for himself, with soleing and mending, 3*s.* 4*d.*
For a pocket, because his pocket was all torn with the carreiage of the money, 6*d.*
Given among the folks, *i. e.* the servants of the house where he lay, 12*d.*
A scrivener for writing letters, 3*s.*

Mr. Keate could write, but not beautifully; could indite, not "make a letter" in its due form and style.

When H. Frances rode to London on the town affairs, there was advanced him, 36*s.*
Roger Keate paid, 1579, for boat hire to and from Avelye in Essex, xv miles, 3*s.* 8*d.*
A dinner at Greenwich, where townsmen from Weymouth happened to meet, 12*d.* a head.

The spirit of clanship waxed strong; and the agent does not blush to enter a meal at double the usual charge upon an occasion when he was expected to do as his fellow-townsmen did at their meeting so far from their home, in a part where the Dorsettians were viewed as "outside barbarians" by those so near the Court.

Sir Anthony Fitzherbert, the judge, under Wolsey, wrote the following, which was very appropriate when long journeys were performed on horseback: —

"An excellent rude lesson, in rude rhyme, for an under serving man to say every time when he taketh horse, for his remembrance, not to forget any implement behind him.

"Purse, dagger, cloak, nightcap, kercheffe, shoeing horn, budget, and shoone (shoes),
Spear, nail, hood, halter, saddle-cloth, spurs, hat, and thy horse comb,
Bow, arrows, sword, buckler, horn, leash, gloves, string, and the braser,
Pen, paper, ink, parchment, red wax, pumise, and books do thou remember,
Penknife, comb, thimble, needle, thread, and point, least that perchance thy girth break.
Bodkin, knife, rubber, give thy horse meat,
See he be shod well, make merry, sing if thou can,
And take heed to thy needments that thou lose none."

A journey in West Dorset and Devon, on horseback, from Weymouth, in the reign of Elizabeth*: —

	d.
Bread for my horse - - - - -	i
Dinner at Borport - - - - - -	vi
[Birport, Burport, since Bridport.]	
Horse meat that same time - - - - - -	ii
Supper at Colliford - - - - - -	vij
[From Charmouth to Colyford by Colway Lane, at the bottom of which was Horn Tavern. The traveller avoided Lyme by leaving it on his left. Leland writes that the bridge was not passable at high water. It is not always possible to follow the road in floods.]	
Horse meat same night - - - - -	vi
Breakfast, Friday - - - - - -	iiij
Supper at Exmouth - - - - - -	vi

* Sherren Papers.

	d.
Horse	vi
Passage at Exmouth	ii
[Over the Exe.]	
Breakfast	iiij
Dinner at Tor	vi
[About two centuries after this four or five houses were built by the sea, at the quay, where a great town, Torquay, has grown up.]	
Horse meat	ii
Passage at Tynemouth	i
[No bridge over the Teign.]	
Supper the same night	vi
At Dartmouth, when with Mr. Mayor, for a quart of wine given him	v
Given him that made the letter	vi
[To the scrivener who was skilled in the due forms of letter writing, and a suitable address of the great.]	
Given him a quart of wine	vi
Supper the same day	viij
Horse meat in Kingswear	xvi
[The horse was left on the east side of the river.]	
Passage at Dartmouth	ii
Horse hire, viii days	viii*s.*
Self at xii*d.* a day as moch	viii*s.*

Abstract.

Expenses of journey, about 164 miles	8	4
Horse hire	8	0
Pay to the traveller	8	0

Fuller saw an ancient lady being drawn to church near Lewes in her own coach, by six oxen. Trees were drawn on Sussex roads by two-and-twenty oxen. A journey from Lewes to London, in the last century, was barely performed in two summer days. The Rev. Giles Moore went in June, 1660:—

	£	s.	d.
His lodging in town cost him, per week		5	6
Beer, sack, and meat	1	1	7

The same gentleman crossed the Solent to the Isle of Wight:—

	s.	d.
Passage for man and horse - - - -	1	10
Passage - - - - - - - -		4
Man and landing - - - - - -		6
Cowes to Portsmouth, two persons and a horse - -	3	0
Boating us - - - - - - -		4

When royal proclamations were sent forth, their echo soon appeared in local municipal bye laws. King James proclaimed that carts and wagons with four wheels, carrying excessive burthens, so galled the high ways and the very foundations of bridges, that the king denounced them to the judges as common nuisances against the weal public, and the use of them an offence. By this proclamation of James I., in the year 1622, no carrier was to travel with a four-wheeled wagon, but only with a cart having two wheels, and only to carry 20 cwt. Any one transgressing this was to be punished.

Queen Elizabeth's State Carriage.

The coach was first introduced in 1564, by William Boonen, a Dutchman, who became coachman to the Queen.

After this expression on the part of the king, we may expect something similar in borough magnates.

In the year 1635, when, perhaps, pack-horses did all the carrying that was required at Weymouth, and probably there was no vehicle in the town besides, the brewers had what are now called brewers' carts to carry out their beer. The authorities passed a bye law that no brewers were to bind the wheels of their carts with iron, as it wore away the pitching of the streets. Precisely similar was the complaint against hackney coaches in 1638, viz. that they broke up the streets.

No one was, by an order, to pass over Gosling's bridge in Lyme, in 1583, with a wain, under a penalty of 20*s.*; a very heavy imposition.*

It having been thought proper to ordain, in the year 1662, that the wheels of each cart or wagon should be four inches in the tyre, this was found to be impracticable, for in some parts the ruts could not receive such wheels, nor could the carriages pass. A proclamation stayed the prosecution of offenders till the further order of Parliament.†

In the time of James I. fish-jobbers rode off with strings of pack-horses, bearing dorsers of fish, received from 25 fishing boats at Lyme, to supply the metropolis.‡

Leland, in the middle of the reign of Henry VIII., praises Salisbury market for flesh, but particularly for fish. He states, "A great part of the principal fish that is taken from Tamar to Hampton (Southampton) resortith to this town." This proves that pack-horses did carry some commodities to a greater distance in a short time.

Hackney coaches were established in London in 1625, and were first licensed in 1660. Sedan chairs were first seen in 1581.

Hackney Coach.

* Archives of Weymouth and Lyme.

† Proclamation, Soc. of Antiquaries.

‡ In 1855, a woman engaged some one in London to send her fish to Lyme for sale! How railroads reverse the order of things.

Cosmo de Medici, Grand Duke of Tuscany, travelled in this country in the spring of the year 1669. He set out from Exeter to Honiton and Axminster in a coach, taking half a day for the journey; and reached Hinton House, the seat of Lord Poulett, the following day. The remark made after leaving Exeter is, "At first we suffered a good deal of inconvenience, because we had to travel a road full of water, and muddy, though not deep."

In bad weather the majority of the highways were impassable. Eight hundred horse were taken prisoners in the civil wars in Lincolnshire while sticking in the mire.*

Sir John Harrington had a neighbour who, being Sheriff of Somerset, listened to a judge who complained of "stonie roads, and feared much the dangers of our western travellinge," and gibed him thus: "In goode trothe, sir, it be but fair playe that you, who so ofte make others feare for their neckes, should in some sorte beginne to thinke of saving your owne." Herewith Judge Minos was not well pleased, but said: "Good maister sheriffe, leave alone my necke, and looke to your owne heeles, for you may one daye be laide by them." This judge afterwards fined the witty sheriff five pounds.

Mr. Robert Jones, Mayor of Lyme, kept an account for the town of his journey to London to surrender the charter. Oct. 1. 1684.

This journey is interesting as belonging to the transition period, partly on horseback, partly by public coach, the return by a hired coach.

To London.	£	s.	d.
Oct. 1. Self and man to Sarum, and two horses [expences arising from inn charges for refreshments, bait of horses] - - - - - -		14	10
Hire of two horses to Sarum, and return home with three horses, wages, and expences - - -	1	12	6
Coach hire from Sarum to London - - -	1	10	0
At several stages to gratify coachmen - -		4	6
Total of expence to London - -	4	1	0

* Waylen's Marlborough.

From London.

	£	s.	d.
Hired coach from London to Lyme [*Vetturino*, like as now-a-day on the Continent] with written agreement	8	0	0
Expended in our journey from London [the time consumed must have been considerable; the halts many] - - - - - - -	3	17	0
Oats and hay at Lyme, and for giving the postillion -		16	0
Total expence of return - - -	12	13	6
A horse kept at the Blue Bear, and paid oastler and tapster, per week - - - - - -		6	7
Charles Sydenham, the servant, allowed him abroad [*i. e.* out of the house] for breakfast, evening draught and Sunday dinner, 2*s.* 6*d.* a week for nine weeks -	1	2	6

This journey, be it remembered, was undertaken after the setting in of winter, and the party returned in the dead of that season. This accounts, probably, for the hiring a coach all the way. It is likely that no public conveyances ran even from London to Salisbury in the winter season. There was advertised, in 1658, travelling as follows: —

Stage coaches from the George Inn, without Aldersgate, London: —

	s.
To Salisbury in two days - - - - - -	xx
To Blandford and Dorchester, two and half days - -	xxx
To Burpurt (Bridport) in three days - - -	xxx
To Exmaster (Axminster), Hunnington (Honiton), and Exeter in four days - - - - - -	xl

There were six regular stage coaches running in England in 1662, some say in 1672. There was a fourday stage to York from London in 1678.

The "Salisbury Journal" advertised, in 1752, that for the better conveyance of travellers, the *Exeter Fast Coach* starts every Monday from the Saracen's Head, Skinner Street, Snow Hill, London.

Monday, dines at Egham.
„ lies at Murrell's Green.
Tuesday, dines at Sutton.
„ lies at Plume of Feathers in Salisbury.
Wednesday, dines at Blandford.
„ lies at King's Arms in Dorchester.
Thursday, at one o'clock, Exeter.

This was accomplished in summer. In winter, six days were required. Fifty miles a day in summer, and thirty in winter, was the distance. The dangers of the road were too great for any one to risk himself on the outside. There were six inside places.

Let us revert to the mayor, Mr. Robert Jones's, return to Lyme. The driver of the hired coach, after having deposited the worshipful the mayor, was open to agree for a job to London again. Persons availing themselves of a return coach were led to speak of "the opportunity" that offered, — so *gelegenheit*, "opportunity," is the name of a return carriage in Germany.

A family about to embark at Falmouth, in 1748, hired a coach and horses in London. A party of young men availed themselves of the opportunity to journey to the metropolis, stipulating that in the event of their reaching a town at any part of the day when cock-fighting should take place in the evening, the coach should lie by for them.*

Travellers deposited their pads or packs, upon their arrival in London, for security, with their goldsmith or banker. The resemblance of one is to be seen sculptured over Child's banking house, Fleet Street.

A person employed to take orders for another rode round to his master's customers, and was, from the saddle-bags he carried behind him, called a *bagman*. See the wonders worked by the figure rhetoricians call Euphemism. The same useful member of society became a *traveller*, or commercial traveller. The figure is expansive; and at length, perhaps not finally, the word *representative* has obtained,

* Davies Gilbert's Hist. of Cornwall.

clashing with a higher appellation, the property of another class.

Foreign journeys might formerly be called foreign rides, for such they of course were. In 1509, Badver, the Venetian ambassador, has proved that in mid winter he had rode, at the age of 62, from Venice to London in twenty-six days.

The very bad roads, and consequent comparative slowness in performing a journey, allowed the use of running footmen; a class of retainers, however admired by the great, doomed to extinction when the state of the roads was improved. Some of the performances of these men were very great. They carried a tall cane or pole with a silver ball at the top, in which was white wine and eggs. The Duke of Marlborough drove his phaeton and four to Windsor, only just beating one of these men, who died soon after. These runners wore no trousers, but only a short silk petticoat with a broad fringe, remind one of the Hemerodromi, or day-runners of the Greeks, one of whom was sent to Sparta from Athens to announce the landing of the Persians.* In some parts these running footmen supported their master's coach when likely to overturn. Without them a journey could not have been undertaken.

Running footmen are among the several particulars that served as a mark to distinguish the very rich from those simply rich. Many such distinctions in daily life existed, which made it a costly matter for those inferior in regard of riches to live with or make the same appearance as their more fortunate neighbours. A greater equality in such respects now prevails; it is the richest persons who make the sacrifice to uniformity. Take as an example the many classifications of dress (enforced by sumptuary proclamations, it is true) which distinguished men into very many classes, according to rank or riches.

If the *Exeter Flying Stage* arrived from London to Dorchester in two days, and at Exeter at the end of the third day, about 1739, the speed must have been considered

* Notes and Queries, No I., 1856

surprising. Those who made use of such a conveyance were doubtless looked upon as presumptuous, neck-or-nothing mortals.

There was a "Devizes chaise" from London at this time which took a route through Reading, Newbury, and Marlborough.

There is a good house at Morcomb-Lake, east of Charmouth, now no longer in the road, owing to this having been diverted. This was a road-side inn, where the judges slept. The FLY COACH from London to Exeter *slept* there the fifth night from town. The coach proceeded the next morning to Axminster, where *it* breakfasted, and there a woman barber *shaved the coach.*

In 1772 the machine or flying machine ran from Bristol to Plymouth in two days, which the rail accomplishes in four hours and a quarter. It would be interesting, if at railway stations ancient times of transport and modern ones were set up for comparison, as was done at the opening of the Mulhausen railway.

The judges rode the circuit on horseback. Sir Nicholas Hyde was censured for being attired in a whitish-blue cloak, that he looked more like a clothier than a judge. He died of fever from riding on circuit fifty miles one hot day. The western gentry rode, and tradesmen rode and walked in company for protection to the metropolis. An instance can be adduced of a journey to London from the neighbourhood of Lyme in a coach, of whatever kind that may have been, in James I.'s reign. Mrs. D'Ewes set out from Coaxden Hall, near Axminster, on her road to London, and arrived in one day at Dorchester, about 27 miles. The shocks sustained owing to the road, and perhaps the particular build of the vehicle, were so great, that the infant son and heir, afterwards the renowned Sir Symonds D'Ewes, cried so violently all the way, that he ruptured himself, and was left behind under the care of Mrs. Margaret Waltham, a female practitioner of the county town of Dorchester.* It may not be improper to state that Mrs. D'Ewes's premature con-

* See MS. Life of Sir Simonds D'Ewes in the Brit. Mus.

finement was afterwards occasioned by a shock in a coach in Bury Street.

Sir Symonds D'Ewes himself afterwards rode to London from Coaxden in 1613, and attributes his safe arrival in the metropolis to God's goodness, for he had *one servant only* with him. Two reigns after this the sheriff of a northern county supplied arms to the retinue of a judge who had not been so prudent as to provide himself with weapons for travelling in England. D'Ewes did not return into the west to school at Wambrook, having felt with dissatisfaction that the fare was very short and hard; a customary fault at this time.

The same year John Clay went from Merryfield, at Ilton near Ilminster, to Oxford, in 1613. The carriage or vehicle was not drawn by horses. He charges thus: —

	s.	*d.*
Laid out for the oxen - -	5	10
Our suppers - - -	4	0
Sope - - - -		4

And this latter article was so charged at every stage nearly.

The travellers, arrested by the waters that were out, often had to claim shelter at some neighbouring farmhouse. Nor was the claim denied. Many old folk had to tell how a night had been spent by the fire. Upon one occasion, where some young ladies were thus delayed in Dorset, returning from a ball, a worthy farmer read some passages from Shakspeare.

Our ancestors had not only to meet with interruption where a flood rendered a ford impassable, there being no bridge, but many bridges were so low that they were not passable at all times. In journeying from Dorset into Devon, the Axe bridge, in Leland's tour, of two arches of stone, served not to pass over at high (spring) tides, otherwise he writes "it doth."* The state of the waters, whether "out or not," and "how long out," was a standing topic with those about to travel and those on the road.

The fears for the safety of a relative who had taken a journey to the distant metropolis were by no means ill

* Pulman's Book of the Axe.

founded. The dangers of the road, both in going and returning, were acknowledged. The travelling over, safety was still out of the case. A great city, upon whose history a whole nation looks with interest, was in the eighteenth century a residence dangerous to the Londoners themselves. Was there not a brutal society, that of the Mohawks, rakes and drunkards who were banded together for violence upon unprotected persons at night? They sallied out to exercise the duties their mad order entailed upon them, and so knocked down, stabbed, cut and carbonadoed people, — honest people about upon their calling — who were so unfortunate as to happen to come in their way. Read Dean Swift's caution to escape the Mohocks, or Mohawks, and his fears. Sir Roger De Coverley went to the playhouse, protected by Captain Sentry. To excel in brutality was the aim of many who, jealous of rivals, emulated their deeds, and laboured to merit a new denomination. While the MOHAWKS flattened noses, gouged out eyes, and slit noses, the TUMBLERS turned females upon their heads, and the DANCING MASTERS kept each unfortunate in motion by pricking his legs with their swords. Space does not allow further mention of the flagrant deeds of the HELLFIRES, or the less atrocities of the NICKERS, about the year 1720. The brutality and blasphemy of these societies were systematic. Their oaths, dictated by the fashion of that mad time, abounded with blasphemies in ridicule of the Trinity. Should it be deemed that Swift and Shenstone, who moved at night with great circumspection, were timid, though the latter says, the pickpockets, armed with couteaus, attacked whole parties at once in the Piazza, Covent Garden, let Dr. Johnson speak how matters stood in 1735: —

> "Prepare for death if here at night you roam,
> And sign your will before you sup from home.
> Some fiery fop with new commission vain,
> Who sleeps on brambles till he kills his man —
> Some frolic drunkard reeling from a feast,
> Provokes a broil, and stabs you for a jest.
> Yet even these heroes mischievously gay,
> Lords of the streets and terrors of the way,

> Flushed as they are with folly, youth, and wine,
> Their prudent insults to the poor confine;
> Afar they mark the flambeaux bright approach,
> And shun the shining train and gilded coach."

Mr. Nuthall, the friend and solicitor of Lord Chatham, returning from Bath to London in 1775, was stopped and fired at near Hounslow, so that he died of the fright.*

When the short peace of Amiens was signed in London Lord Sidmouth, then Mr. Addington, sent an immediate account of the news to his brother-in-law, Capt. Sutton, of New Park, near Devizes. The bells rang the whole of the next day. A waggoner who drove his team from that market to Salisbury told the news in the evening. It was not credited till a London coach arrived with particulars the next day at noon.*

Though the bells rang at Bridgwater upon the news arriving that Cromwell was made Protector nineteen days after the event — so slow was the spread of news, — still some would fain argue that communications were quite rapid enough for all purposes.

The Taunton stage took four days to reach London. Many finding this convenience prepared for them ceased to keep horses, which set going the croakers, who prophesied great evils from the setting up of stage coaches. They said no good hackneys would be bred, and that the agricultural interest would suffer.

When the passengers arrived at night at an inn they clubbed together for a dish or two of meat, and spent not above 12*d.* or 16*d.* at a place.

Acquaintances were made and antipathies created for life between people who sat together for six live-long days in succession, and who took many meals in company. Journeys were unequal in expense. Some gallant, generous fellow-travellers treated the ladies, which some could well afford to

* See the New Monthly, Oct. 1855, an article by A. Andrews.

† J. Waylen, Private Communication.

do; others, less rich, found this a burden. Occasionally male travellers were too prompt in proposing such liberality when their own relatives were those to be treated. In a word, a journey to London from Devon and Dorset was a memorable event never to be effaced from memory, — a serious undertaking, not to be too hastily compared with a journey to London or to Edinburgh in the present day, which may be looked upon as a mere act of locomotion, however splendidly performed.

Sir Richard Steele, — a very affectionate husband certainly, — in the course of his journey to Edinburgh about 1717, sent as many as a dozen letters to his loving wife.

When perusing a little work* detailing a journey to London, in 1771, but more particularly the feelings of the traveller, one is struck at the regret expressed at starting that the journey was not on horseback with its peculiar advantages. The writer rails at the arbitrary bashaw, the ferryman whose services were required for an hour. Some sentiment upon morning, a lark, and nature, is interrupted by the contemplation of the highwayman, Hasslet, hanging on a gibbet for robbing the postman carrying the mail in 1770. A detailed description, very off-handed indeed, follows of the six insides, four ladies, a gentleman of the sword, and the writer, a dissenting minister. The latter discuss and allow their tempers to be greatly ruffled by the question of a standing army. The ladies blame the officer for having allowed himself and another to be compelled to quietly surrender their purses to a highwayman between Highgate and London a few months before. The gallant son of Mars laid it down that no honour was to be earned in contending with a footpad or highwayman. The belligerent male insides come to an agreement not to quarrel about their respective lines of life, and peace is proclaimed for the rest of the journey. Upon arriving at a town in the evening the travellers sometimes went to the play, though they had to start again at two in the morning. The swearing a person upon

* The Travels of the Imagination, &c., by the Rev. James Murray.

his first visit to London upon the horns at Highgate is duly detailed.

A squire from the neighbourhood of Glastonbury, journeying to Sarum in his carriage, about 1780, took care that his footman was provided with a good axe to lop off any branches of trees that might obstruct the progress of the vehicle.

Frost was looked forward to in parts not distant from London as the only cause that could make lanes passable. Timber had been felled, but it was known to be impossible to convey it to neighbouring towns till the muddy lanes were frozen hard.

If we have from lapse of time become incredulous to the difficulties, impediments, or complete bar to progress caused by founderous, bottomless roads, the recent horrors of the operations in the Crimea, caused by six miles of impassable roads, will painfully renew our acquaintance with the old inconveniences experienced. Three thousand miles of sea presented no obstacles: six miles of land, with a bad road, proved insurmountable, and produced great horrors!

Trusty servants were sent on journeys with their mistress or daughter riding behind on a pillion upon horses trained to carry double. Upping-stocks were then indispensable to country houses. The jingling of bells worn by horses in teams warned travellers how they entered some narrow lanes, where two vehicles could not pass abreast. These are now rarely used. Some are occasionally met with near Honiton from Broadhembury, &c., and are pleasing and inspiriting sounds to the ears of a Devonian. Travellers upon meeting at cross roads stopped and asked the news.

The first post-chaise that was introduced into Taunton, about the year 1767, ran from the "Sugar Loaf" inn, kept by Wm. Cann, now a humble public-house at the eastern entrance of Cann's field, near the Bishop's Hull road. The driver, Thomas Phippen, died in 1835, at the age of 104.

From London to Exeter 12*l.* a ton was charged for the transmission of goods, fifteen times what is demanded by railway companies. Pack-horses were no longer required the breed is now extinct. They were attended by a class of men who seem to have borne much resemblance to the Spanish muleteers.* The goods were carried upon *dorsers:* panniers were breadbaskets. Some of these men adopted the new plan of transmission of goods by wagon on the new turnpike roads, and were called carriers.

Some teams of the carriers were composed of thirteen horses. An act restricted these to nine. This was evaded by paying an annual sum to the informers. It was impossible, an informer said, to travel the roads without a breach of the law.

In 1745, the Wiltshire people looked upon the proposed government bill for the improvement of the roads as likely to enhance the already ruinous price for the carriage of goods.

Turnpikes were erected so early as the year 1267. There were such between St. Giles-in-the-Fields and Temple Bar, in the reign of Edward III.† An act passed 1. Mary for the making, repairing, and amending of the common highway and causie in the counties of Dorset and Somerset, between the towns of Shaftesbury and Sherborne.‡

I visited, may I say, the last of this class, Judith Long, in 1849, who was about one hundred years old. Her father kept pack-horses, and had become a carrier after the general construction of turnpike roads, and this old person accompanied him, when young, on his journeys. Being introduced to the aged woman, lying in bed, as one desirous of learning about the pack-horses, she looked up and seeing my straw hat, it being hot weather, took me for a carrier, at least one about to enter upon that line of life. She kindly promised to tell me all I wanted to know; begged me to take the road by Honiton if I wished to spare the cattle, but, for shortness, to go by Newton Poppleford. She warmly recommended, as a house where I should find good treatment, "The Rolling Pin, Chopping Knife," Exeter. What a

* See Macaulay. † Waylen's Hist. of Marlborough.

‡ Notes and Queries, May, 1855.

change had one hundred years effected in the place from which this good old soul thought I was to take my departure, and that once western metropolitan city, my destinanation. I ventured to sound her views as to her observations in her earliest journeys and the state of the town and people at that time as compared with now a-days. There I lost my character for any information I might possess or likelihood to get on in my new calling. The old woman opened her eyes, looked upon me with utter astonishment mingled with pity, and exclaimed, "Lord bless ye, 'tis now a vagabond place." What is a railway world without packhorses? Judith Long died in 1852. She was an admirer of the past.

Persons upon their safe return from London were apt to assume ridiculous airs and superiority over their fellows who had not drunk in political chit-chat like themselves in the city coffee-houses. Inns by the road side were amusing places of resort, for the residents of country towns, and even the clergyman of the parish. The travellers who arrived dispensed the latest news to a craving company, who had no other means of learning what then agitated the great Babel, and other parts of the kingdom. Many a "little great man" was taught how to conduct himself, among the strangers at a tavern, who now a-days only remains in his family, or returns a visit in private company, and so passes year after year without those salutary checks and sarcasm which overbearing manners, purse-pride, and folly require for their correction. The bounds of temperance were too often passed, owing to frequenting in public company the coffee-houses—from which the clubs have grown — and taverns; still other moral good effects were derived from them, if we cannot go the length to style them "the academy of civility and free-school of ingenuity." The excitement for news and readiness to ring bells for joy, or take hasty measures in another way upon hearing some idle report from travellers, forcibly recalls to mind the account Cæsar gives in his Commentaries of the volatile Gauls. These compelled travellers to stop and tell them what they had heard or known in the way of news, and, as no doubt often occurred in our south of England, the news furnished by parties so arrested on their journey was in strict consonance with the known feelings and wishes of the inquirers.

When at festive meetings, the heart opened and the tongue would talk, no subject was so ready as the perils of the road. One spoke of his escape from this or that highwayman, of having to wait, and then, at great peril, having crossed some dangerous water.

The two clothiers deputed by their brothers in that trade, in Dorset, to consider the cause of the decline of their trade in 1622, after labouring in what was a kind of clothier's parliament during two months were robbed on their journey home.

Humble tradesmen walked to London and back, having first made their will, but really they depended much upon casual lifts, and the road wagon carried a motley group who nestled aloft upon the top of the luggage. The journey averaged a week each way.

As an incident of distant communication between places, let me adduce an anecdote of a resident of Edinburgh, who sent two daughters to a boarding-school in London where the holidays were of a month's duration. Upon their arrival in Scotland, if the voyage had been longer than usual, it was time for the young ladies in two or three days to return again; so their vacation was occasionally literally passed at sea.

The lanes were in some parts in such a state that, as at Lyme and the country round for miles, one hundred years ago, no vehicle of any kind was kept. Pack-horses did all the carrying that was required. A carriage was a curiosity which was rarely seen. The construction of turnpike roads, under a general Turnpike Act, in 1755, was an important event in the history of the kingdom. Many, however, viewed this as an unjustifiable cutting up of the country, and even quoted Jeremiah vi. 16. The old conservative coachman, the Marlborough one, would not use the new turnpike road, but stuck to the old waggon track. His grandfather had driven in the slush before him, and he would stick to it till death.

The Blandford waggoner said, "Roads had but one object —for waggon driving. He required but five foot width in a lane, and all the rest might go to the devil." He said "The gentry ought to stay at home and be d——d, and not run gossiping up and down the country." *

Journeys of great length performed in inclement weather upon the roof of a coach were frequently the cause of trying fits of illness and of death. And this in spite of great-coats made of double-milled cloth with ponderous capes of the same material. The protection afforded by closed railway carriages has so reduced the call for this thick cloth that it is no longer made in some western cloth factories. Every one used to have a *great-coat*, properly so called: now all have *over*-coats, few possess the former, because no journeys of twenty hours have to be encountered, and a cold summer morning or a bitter winter wind and rain to be defied.

The cost of an outside place on the mail and the kind of protection required are set forth in verse.

"When to York per mail you start,
Four-caped like other men;
To the book-keeper, so smart,
You pay down three pounds in part;
Two pounds ten before you start;
Sum total, five pound ten."

The traveller on his way to Ireland before the introduction of steam took ship, and might be several days on the water, when there was no steward ready to supply all ordinary wants. This traveller had probably arrived at the sea-port after a long journey, and the precise time for sailing depended upon wind and weather. Hence the necessity for being supplied with a BASKET of provisions for the voyage. This was a source of considerable profit to the landlords of the inns of sea ports. The charges were exorbitant. The bottle

* Doran's Account, Gentleman's Mag. 1852.

of brandy — an invariable accompaniment of each basket — was charged one guinea.

A diary is preserved of a journey to Dublin from Grosvenor Square, 12th June, 1787, in a coach-and-four, accompanied by a post-chaise and pair, and five outriders. The party reached Holyhead in four days at a cost of 75*l.* 11*s.* 3*d.* The state of the intercourse between this country and the sister island at this part of the account is strikingly set forth in the following entries: — Ferry at Bangor, 1*l.* 10*s.*; expenses of the yacht hired to carry the party across the channel, 28*l.* 7*s.* 9*d.*; duty on the coach, 7*l.* 13*s.* 4*d.*; boats on shore, 1*l.* 1*s.*—total, 114*l.* 3*s.* 4*d.*

Visitors to the metropolis had much to say about the lions and their keepers, the beefeaters of the Tower. This was the London sight most famed. To show a country person the lions, or to lionise, has become a common form of expression.

At length came the four-horse mails to Bristol in 1784, and the "Quicksilver mail," to be in turn superseded by the railway locomotive. Some see no occasion for any railways, upon which the Exeter people travel or fly to London in six hours, instead of being so many days and nights.

What can ever compare with the well-appointed mail-coaches, the "Quicksilver mail," &c. in outward display? Their speed was thought to be surprising. Was there in the world a prettier sight than the summer procession of the mail-coaches in London — such horses, such neatness?

At mail-speed, if anything untoward happened, an accident occurred, as on the rail; but not to so many individuals, though dangerous to the passengers, and generally fatal to some. A coachman, instituting a comparison between the two modes of travelling, thus summed up: "I know that if anything goes wrong, *there you are,*" making a sign of upsetting; "but by the rail, if you meet with an accident, *where are you?*"

The communication along our coasts with London by signals from stations upon the hills, where signal-posts were erected, and the acceleration of travelling, owing to the

* Illustrated London News, Jan. 16. 1856.

improved construction of the roads upon the plan of Mr. M'Adam, appeared to leave all further improvements as hopeless. The railway and the electric telegraph have shown how incorrect this view was.

The increased facilities for travelling produced effects that were by many much dreaded. The ruin of market towns was predicted from the number of petty shopkeepers who were found to be living in country villages, assisted by persons who had never served any regular apprenticeship, and worst of all, in defiance of all propriety, actually carrying on a flourishing trade.

Hackney-coaches were decried in 1638 as breaking up the streets, and making the price of hay very great.

An argument used against a canal to Bath from London, in the reign of William III., will elucidate the views of the enemies of the free intercourse of goods as well as men.

The opponents argued, that by lessening the number of land carriers the consumption caused by their numerous cattle would be diminished; the arrival of grain from Bath would lower the prices in Wiltshire, and occasion a fall in rents; for corn brought by water to Bristol, and thence conveyed on horseback, did at some seasons of the year, glut the markets as far as Warminster, Devizes, and other places in Wiltshire.*

The landowners of Sussex and neighbouring counties complained against the making of roads, and petitioned against them. They said the roads would interfere with *their* supplying the metropolis, as they had exclusively done.

Among other complaints against railways at their first introduction, as being unnecessary, I remember to have heard a party demonstrating the causes which had given rise to them. He said the gentry could not set up shops, and still wanted to improve their income; so they devised railways, in which they could invest money and engage in business, really so, without appearing to do so. They were, in short, the parties who cut up the country, for what we could all dispense with!

* Waylen's Marlborough.

The Post, and the cost of Messengers to carry letters before it was established — Newspapers.

"Haste, post haste! Haste with all diligence. For thy life, for thy life!" *

Such was the exciting language used upon official letters in the reign of Henry VIII. to stimulate the sluggard to dispatch. However we may be astonished at the rapidity of modern travelling and communication, we have nothing now-a-days so startling.

The word "POST" is possessed of such magical interest that no apology is required for any elucidation of the subject.

It is necessary to distinguish between the early accounts of a "POST" and "POST OFFICE." These have been too often confounded.

There was a POST in the reign of Edward IV. During the Scotch war, the plan was introduced of placing swift couriers at every twentieth mile; so that by their passing letters from hand to hand the king could obtain the news from a distance of two hundred miles within two days. We shall have to speak of two sorts of Post † at the beginning of the seventeenth century, all of which preceded the establishment of a Post Office, in 1635.

It is interesting to trace the steps by which great public benefits have been introduced. We purpose to do this with respect to the POST in Dorsetshire. From the archives of Lyme many curious foreshadowings of the POST have been extracted.

In 1558, the man who brought round the Council's letters to have the peace proclaimed, and that ships should not depart without license, received 2*s.* 6*d.*, is styled "THE POST." Half-a-crown was the sum paid to a poursuivant who brought a proclamation.

* Tytler's Edward VI., &c.

† Chron. Croy, Halsted's Life of Richard III.

Upon the great alarm caused by the reported coming of the Spanish Armada, Sir John Norris was sent into Dorsetshire by the queen's government.

There was an order at this time to the following effect: —*

Item, that there be a *foote post* appointed in every parish within the shire whose dwelling should be chosen near the church, and a *horse post* in every town."

I find in the Lyme Accompt Book: —

Item, the 11th June, 1588, paid the *foote* post for one month's wages from 14th May, at 6*d.* per week, 2*s.*

9th July, John Gosse the younger, from 14th May to 9th July, for a post horse [*i. e.* 1*s.* 4*d.* per week], 10*s.* 8*d.*†

We are not to understand that this *foot post man* and *horse post man* had carried letters as the postmen of the present day do; but that they had hired themselves at a salary to be always ready to do so upon an emergency. If services were required and duly performed, these were paid for in addition to salary; thus —

1st Sept. John Gosse, from 9th July to 1st Sept., for his post [was paid], 10*s.* 8*d.* ‡

When this *horse post man* had to mount, he was paid both for himself and horse.

Item, paid for a post horse and a man to Weymouth for a gent of my lord admiral's, 10*s.* 8*d.*

* Harleian MS., Brit. Mus. 3324.

† "At Leicester, in 1570, it was agreed at a Common Hall that six post horses be kept, and that 33*s.* 4*d.* be allowed for each. The next year the twenty-four principal men paid 2*s.* each, and the forty-eight 1*s.* each; the residue to be gathered of the commons for the keeping six post horses at 26*s.* 8*d* per horse. Four horses only to be kept to serve at an hour's warning." — *Nichols's Hist. of Leicester.*

‡ See Pulman's Book of the Axe. "The foot post for travelling this year, 1*l.* 5*s.* 10*d.*

From the history of Norwich we may learn the interest corporations began to take in a *post*, or in establishing means for postal communication, so early as the year 1568. It may be interesting also to observe, how one class of persons was sentenced by authority to bear half the burden of that which was proved to be a public good, and a benefit to all her Majesty's loving subjects.

1568. Three postmasters had 3*l.* 13*s.* 4*d.* lent them free of interest, and 4*l.* each, a stipend paid by the sheriffs, the half of which was levied on the innkeepers and tipplers, and gathered by the constables of every ward. No man was to take up post-horses in the city unless he was licensed by warrant from the Queen's majesty, the Duke of Norfolk, the Privy Council, or the mayor; nor to use any horse above twelve or fourteen miles together, for which he was to pay 2*d.* the mile, and 6*d.* to his guide, to go and carry back the horse, and the said horses were not to carry any cloakbag of above ten pounds weight.

Hackney-horses were settled at 12*d.* the first day, and 8*d.* the day after, till re-delivery.*

Merchants could not have afforded to send a special messenger with every letter. They must have made use of opportunities to forward business correspondence, — inconsiderable as it was compared with that of the present day. They were directed by a proclamation, issued in the year 1591, not to use "disavowed persons" to convey their letters. The Government of James I. considered the practice to be dangerous!

The commencement of the regular carriage of the people's letters is enveloped in obscurity. The germ of the present system can be traced to the reign of Charles I.

There was a "Master of the King's Posts," and an office held by the same individual, the "Master of the King's Outward Posts."

The royal posts were used for the transmission of private letters. This practice is supposed to have originated in an

* Blomefield's Norfolk.

act of grace, and to have prevailed to a very considerable extent, so as to attain almost the position of a right upon a certain payment being made. The expenses of the postmaster being regularly paid as a part of the royal establishment, and the conveyance of other letters being optional, it is difficult to believe that no advantage could have accrued to that personage by the facilities he afforded the mercantile community. Such, however, is said to have been the case so late as the year 1635.

This has been accounted for as follows: perhaps the old payments, having been fixed at an earlier period, had not been adapted to the increasing prices of the times, and the scale of payments for conveying letters, &c., was not well adjusted; or the deputies had taken too good care of themselves. It could not have been intended to mean that the transmission of letters of private individuals was not paid for by them. The necessity for the transmission of a letter often existed; and a special messenger would have been required to be sent, perhaps to a great distance, at a heavy cost.

About the year 1635, the office of the Master of the King's Posts had come by descent from the patentee of James I., Lord Stanhope of Harrington, the King's Vice-Chamberlain, to Thomas Witherings; and he had also succeeded in obtaining the mastership of the "Outward Posts," *i. e.* for abroad.

In a country which honours men of practical genius, why has this individual been so little known to fame? The plans of Thomas Witherings were intended to place the postal communications upon something like the present footing, having — I. Fixed rates of postage. II. Horse posts, *vice* foot posts. III. And permission for the public generally to use the establishment. The posts cost the state 3400*l.* a year, instead of serving every one and producing a revenue besides.*

In the reign of James I., there were four lines of posts

* See the subsequent history of the Post Office, traced in the Report of the Secret Committee on the Post Office, 1844, and in the appendix of documents supplied by the Public Record and State Paper Office.

throughout the kingdom; viz., from London, I. To Plymouth. II. To Berwick. III. To Holyhead. IV. To Dover.

From the proceedings carried on in the Court of Requests, which exercised so considerable and equitable a jurisdiction in the 16th and part of the 17th century — 9. Charles I., A. D. 1633, much of the preceding and subsequent information has been derived. All was connected with the squabble between the deputy postmaster, Thomas Parkes, and the packet posts, or postmasters on the western line of road.*

A warrant under the Royal Privy Seal, dated 21st March, 8. James I., has this order, which the western people would think very prejudicial to them: — The stages of posts from London to Plymouth are not necessary, but only in time of war; and being then usually maintained, are to be discharged.

This opinion being found to be erroneous, ten years after, another warrant held that "the requirements of the district necessitated the re-establishment of the said stages, for the necessary despatch of letters and packets." The Lords of the Treasury were directed to pay to Lord Stanhope, as Master of the Posts, the rates as set forth, viz., 23*s.* for the entire journey from London to Plymouth.

In the early part of the year 1629, Feb. 24th, there were the following *Packet Posts*, or *Post Masters*, who sent on *Packets* between London and Plymouth, viz.: —

Roger Pymble, -	Packet Post at	Charing Cross.
James Wilkinson,	,,	Staines.
Henry Davis	,,	Hartford Bridge.
Anthony Spittle	,,	Basingstoke.
John Tarrant	,,	Andover.
Richard Myles,	,,	Salisbury.
Nicholas Compton,	,,	Shaftesbury.

* John Bruce, Esq., F.A.S., brought these particulars to light and gave them to the world in the Gentleman's Magazine, July, 1853, p. 59., having previously illustrated the subject in Notes and Queries. The merit is wholly due to that gentleman, whose matter has been occasionally, but slightly, altered. My thanks are here offered to him.

John Smith, -	Packet Post at	Sherborne.
Thomas Huchins,	„	Crewkerne.
Robert Searle	„	Honiton.
Thomas Newman,	„	Exeter.
Thomas Cruse,	„	Ashburton.
Abraham Jennings,	„	Plymouth.

These postmasters were bound, 8th March, 6. Charles I., in *50l.* each for the faithful performance of their engagements — a faithful and speedy conveyance of all letters that should be brought to them. Their horses were directed to be "able and sufficient, and well furnished of saddles, bridles, girts and stirropes, with good guides to looke to them; who for their said horses shall demand and receive of such as shall ride on them, the prices accustomed." The postmaster was also to have ready "two bags of leather, at the least, well lined with bayes or cotton, to carry the packet in." He was also to have ready "hornes to sound and blow so oft as the post meets company, or four times in every mile."

The "Posts" according to the phraseology of the day were of two distinct kinds: —*

I. The "Thorough Post;" when special messengers, or couriers themselves rode through the whole distance "with horn and guide." They were charged in 1603, 2½*d.* a mile (raised in 1609 to three pence) for the hire of each horse, besides the "guide's groats." The hire was to be paid beforehand.

II. The "Post for the Packet" was the second kind of post. Every postmaster was bound to keep horses ready; and on receipt of a "packet," or parcel containing letters, he was to send it on towards the next stage, within a quarter of an hour after its arrival, entering the transaction in "a large and fair ledger paper book."

The "Post for the Packet" was at first used for the

* See Notes and Queries, Jan. 1. 1853, for an able article from John Bruce, Esq., who refers to the collection of Proclamations belonging to the Royal Society of Antiquaries.

carriage of despatches for the Government, or for ambassadors; but a similar mode of conveyance soon began to be taken advantage of by corporations, merchants, and private persons.

In 1621 the corporation of Lyme paid 5*s.* per week for the postage of letters to London: —

Item, paid for sending letters weekly unto London, 5*s.*

This was the last postal arrangement up to the establishment of the first post, or Running Post, between London, through Dorsetshire, Exeter, and Plymouth, in 1635.

A person named Samuel Jude, perhaps considering that there was a good opening for him on the western line of road, and encouraged by many who thought he would perhaps serve them better than the regular postmasters, set up as *Travelling Post.* The former petitioned the Lords of the Council against Jude, for appropriating to himself the sole carriage of all the merchants' letters and dispatches between London and Plymouth, altogether excluding his Majesty's posts and likewise the carriage of packets on horseback in the nature of a post.

These packet posts, or postmasters, set forth in an answer occasioned by their squabble that the Lords of the Council, upon consideration, found the proceedings of Jude to be very prejudicial to his Majesty's service, in disabling and discouraging of his Majesty's posts, by excluding them from the said employment; and thereupon ordered that his Majesty's packet posts should carry the letters and dispatches of all such merchants and others as should employ them, between London and Plymouth, without Jude's pulling down their bills in either place, or giving them any interruption in the said service. The Lord Mayor of London, and magistrates of Salisbury, Exeter, and Plymouth, and all other his Majesty's subjects, were required to govern themselves accordingly.

At the first arranging about the posts, the merchants of the two extreme points of the line interfered, and procured from Mr. Secretary Cocke that security should be taken from the postmasters.

Thomas Parkes, the deputy postmaster, on the 8th of March, 6 Charles I., entered into an agreement with the factors of London and Plymouth for stages between these two places, viz.; that the said deputy postmaster should provide every one who came to him with letters with a horse and furniture to the next stage at the rate of $2\frac{1}{2}d.$ per mile, and 4*d.* to the guide, called the *guide's groat,* for returning with the horse.

Thomas Parkes asserts that Roger Pymble, the postmaster for the packet at Charing Cross, one of the principal parties to the said agreement, agreed with him that he would send a guide horse for the service in question every Tuesday, for which Pymble was to receive 40*l.* a year. Parkes was to get nothing for this, and yet Pymble often neglected to send the guide horse weekly. Parkes had given a bond for 100*l.* to Robert Barker, of Plymouth, for the due performance of his duties, which he asserts he had carefully observed; and now Pymble, having taken offence at complainant, had combined with Barker to sue complainant on his bond for alleged neglect of duty. Parkes further adds, that he is injured to the amount of 40*l.* a year by the disorderly ridings of Pymble's servants.

Process was speedily issued and an answer was made 29th January 9 Charles I., by Roger Pymble, Robert Barker, and John Northcott.

Pymble denies many of Parkes's statements, and asserts that Parkes had for nearly two years utterly refused and neglected to perform these orders and articles agreed upon; and had taken the whole pay for carrying expresses, and had not been accountable for the same. This neglect had damnified the passengers in frustrating their journey and affairs, and prejudiced the postmasters, so that the penalty would not satisfy them.

Pymble makes this statement, which we can now verify, that "The business, *i. e.* the post, is generally taken, and known to be most useful, and a public good and benefit to his Majesty's loving subjects.

In a general denial of Parkes's statements, it is alleged that he had (with a corrupt practice too much in keeping with the time) much abused and wronged the country in locking up the postmaster's horses, and keeping them a day or night, and re-leasing them again for money, and not using them in any service at all, and *abusing the passengers more than beseemeth.*

It will have been perceived by this quarrel, that good plans or schemes for national benefit cannot be fully carried out while general corruption exists, as in Russia now, and in England two centuries ago. Great improvements require time for their development and full growth.

Strange that a penny-post should have been suggested so early as the year 1656; and that too by a reformer named Hill. His publication is entitled, "A Penny-Post; or a Vindication of the Liberty and Birthright of every Englishman in carrying Merchants' or other Men's Letters against any restraint of farmers of such employments. By John Hill."*

In 1679, the projectors for conveying letters to any part of the city or suburbs of London for a penny a letter, opened their offices at which they hung out tables to advertise people of the thing. The porters, not without good reason supposing there would be a great diminution of their employment, took down and tore the tables wherever they met with them.

Dr. Titus Oates said the letter carrying was a project of the Papists. This penny-post was postponed for twenty years.

The blessing of constant intercourse by letter was not enjoyed to any great extent when few could write, and every letter had to be paid for in respect of its being "made" and "written" before it could be dispatched. Hence the importance of a postal communication was not fully appreciated.

* Illustrated London News.

The postboy, Robert Drew, employed by the post-master at Dorchester to convey letters to Weymouth in 1725, sometimes did not find it convenient to go that journey of seven miles till the next day, Friday, and then he did not blow his horn as was prescribed. Occasionally, when his convenience was interfered with, the postboy sent on the letters by some one going to Weymouth. A townsman, Thomas Pomeroy, having remonstrated with him for these things was violently thrust against his own house, and bruised by the public official; who challenged him to fight as a troublesome complainant, who, if he had gone on, might have eventually come out as a postal reformer, anticipating more recent ones who have only had to contend with underlings through the medium of pen and ink.*

So late as about the middle of last century, the London letters were forwarded from Lyme to Axminster upon a mule so remarkably obstinate that the beast that bore "news from all nations" was urged on with great difficulty. The animal daily struggled to continue in Broad Street where the post office was then situated. Now is the time to chronicle such things. Some years hence they may not be comprehended and surely would not be believed.

Little is known about this early post. Besides the delay caused by bad roads, often perhaps falsely cited by postboys as an excuse, the bribery successfully practised towards the postboys is proved from sundry entries in the mayoralty of Robert Coade, 1669–70.

		s.	*d.*
Nov. 9.	To money pd. the postboy for staying for letters -		6
Dec. 8.	" " " -		6
July 2.	To money paid for letters to Capt. Alford, wherein was inclosed a certificate signed by Mr. Floyer and Mr. Ivy concerning the yearly disbursement of the Cobb and sea works, and *gave the post* for the LENT OF HIS HORSE to ride att Charmouth, and for staying till THE LETTERS WERE WRITTEN - - - - -	1	0

* Archives of Weymouth.

The magistrate, Mr. Floyer, lived at Berne, a mile beyond Charmouth, so the delay must have been considerable.

The *lent of the horse* furnishes another instance of the abuse of a useful institution at a period of corruption.

Let us now turn to the expense and inconvenience of sending letters before there was a post.

Does not the following entry of the year 1549 suggest much to every reflecting mind? Can we refrain from contrasting our advantages of cheap communication with the costly intercourse of really remote London in Tudor reigns?

Lyme, 1549.

Item, delivered unto William Dene to ryd to London, 26*s.* 8*d.*

A letter at the cost of one penny put into the post-office at four in the afternoon is delivered in London at nine the following morning. No fear is expressed of highwaymen, loss of the letter and the life of its bearer. An answer comes, perhaps, at an interval of a few hours. The business is transacted, perhaps, in the most complete manner, but the attendant excitement of ancient days is no more.

Just consider another entry:—

1551.

Bread and ale in the Hall when John Stowell came from London, 2*d.*

Fancy the worthy mayor and his brethren hastening to the Town Hall to receive the messenger and his letter. This might be paralleled now-a-day. The messenger has news of all kinds to relate to the assembled worthies, who can gain late intelligence from no other quarter. They hang upon the mouth of the narrator, and when they at length disperse, their families and the whole town have retailed out with a thousand comments what appears to be astounding intelligence.

The tenants of some manors were to carry letters when required.

Some of the tenants of the manor of Castle Combe, in the

14th century, were to carry letters whenever required, so that they could return within the day.*

The Western rebels in the *commotion time*, in the reign of Edward VI., had among other demands for the effecting their reform one that no person who had not more than 100*l.* a-year should keep two servant men. Cranmer answered at length the curious items of that early call for a change. He showed how unreasonable the demand was, as in case of one servant being sent to London, the master would have no one to wait upon him till the other's return.

In the year 1558 we find in the Town Accompt Book: —

	s.	*d.*
Horse hire to Hinton to certify Mr. Poulett of the muster		6
[The distance is about 18 miles.]		
Town clerk riding to Mr. Gibbs the steward at South Petherton - - - - - - -	2	0
[About 21 miles. This in the reign of Elizabeth.]		
John Jurden, the mayor, enters in 1577.		
Item, for William Goldsmith's charge in riding to my Lord Marquis of Winchester, Lord Lieutenant of Dorset, concerning Thomas Wood's servant begotten with child	6	0
[N.B. Thomas Wood's man was sent to Dorchester.]		

Mr. Roger Keate, who frequently went to town on the business of the Weymouth Corporation charged for money

paid to Hendy for the bringing up a letter from Mr. Mayor, vi*d.*
Item, to the carriers to bring down letters at divers times, xviij*d.*

	s.	*d.*
To Stret for the carriage of a letter to the Council -	13	4
Sending the Commissioners' letter to Poole - -	4	0

The bearers of letters did sometimes grievously disappoint their employers, *e. g.*

George Bagge was paid 20*s.* to convey letters to London, the which letters he carried to Wilton and no further, for the which 20*s.* he is to give accompt for.†

* History of Castle Combe, by J. P. Scrope, Esq., M.P.
† Sherren Papers.

Extracts from the Archives of Lyme Regis.

		s.	*d.*
1620.	Paid Bottle for a letter from Lyme to Crewkerne (14 miles) - - - - - -	1	0
	T. Brown for going after him with another letter	1	8
1621.	Gardener for going with a letter to Salisbury to the registrar - - - - -	6	8

Communication by letter was so expensive that little arrangements tending to lessen the charge were often had recourse to by our frugal townsmen: —

Item, paid, 1622–3, unto Mr. Geare [the vicar] for carrying a letter to Sir Francis Ashley, for which a messenger must else have been sent of purpose, to certify the Lord Keeper the cause of committing James Smith to Dorchester gaol, 20*s*.

		s.	*d.*
1625.	To a messenger from Exeter (28 miles) that came from the governor with a letter - -	1	0
	To a messenger from Colyton (7 miles) with a letter sent by Mr. Yonge - - -		6
	To a messenger that brought a letter for a stay of shipping [*i. e.* an embargo] - - -		6
	To a messenger sent to Bridport (8 miles) for a copy of the letter to proclaim King Charles -		8
	Partridge, for carriage of a letter to Sir Richard Strode - - - - - -	1	0
	[A relative of the Yonge family of Colyton.]		
	To a messenger sent hither by Mr. Yonge -		6
1630.	Given to Mr. Napper's man for bringing a letter from the Earl of Suffolk, the Lord Lieutenant of Dorset concerning the peace with Spain * -	2	6

Great men frequently fixed in their letters the sum which the bearer of their letter or messenger was to receive. A poursuivant that brought a proclamation into the west, generally received *by consent*, as it is expressed, 2*s*. 6*d*.

I can find nothing of merchants riding or sending their

* All these from the Town Accompt Book of Lyme.

own horses; but I cannot venture to assert that they kept none for their use or that of their messengers.

A few charges made by the letters-out of horses in West Dorset are here inserted, as being of great interest and appropriate to the subject. Horses were hired to expedite the delivery of a letter.

	£	s.	d.
In 1584, a horse from Lyme to London and back, kept there six weeks, 288 miles, besides being rode to Windsor occasionally ($1\frac{3}{4}$ per mile) - - -		13	4
Hire of a horse to Windsor from London when the hired horse from Lyme was lame - - - -		2	6
In 1619, a horse from Lyme to London and back was charged - - - - - - -	1	0	0
From Lyme to Dorchester (24 miles) - - -		4	0
" Beaminster (14 miles) - - -		3	6
A horse by the day* - - - - - -		2	0

N.B.—Persons at Southampton who let out horses in 1577, were not allowed to take for a journey of eight days or under, to London or Bristol, above 6*s.* 8*d.*, and for every day after 10*d.*†

The state of the post in France in 1816 resembled ours of former years. At Valognes a carrier left twice a week for Cherbourg. Officers watched the carrier's house. Numerous persons who had letters for that worthy skulked about to avoid being fined for sending letters by such a channel, and so defrauding the revenue. In the end, letters were smuggled in numbers.

Parties travelling by coach from the country to London used to carry a number of letters for the twopenny-post box. To deposit them therein was one of the first duties upon arriving in the metropolis.

It is a trite observation that whatever occurs regularly and without interruption ceases in course of time to excite our surprise, indeed often even appears commonplace and falls short of admiration. Such was the case with that surprising

* Archives of Lyme. † Archæol. Journal, vol. iii. p. 232.

engine of power the NEWSPAPER, which form small beginnings, and producing only small effects, went on to what we now know it, though all its workings are too vast to be measured.

The "Weekly Newes" published in London was the first newspaper. There was a quarto pamphlet of a few leaves entitled "The Diurnal Occurrences or Daily Proceedings of both Houses in this great and happy Parliament, from 3rd Nov. 1640, &c."

Heading of an Early Newspaper.

The writers of *news-letters* formed a numerous class. They sent accounts of remarkable transactions. Some newspapers had blank spaces for the additional matter which the purchaser might choose to insert with his own pen.

Advertising began in earnest with the Restoration. Quack doctors were the first who had recourse to this mode of giving publicity to their panaceas and specifics. The first advertisement in a newspaper was in 1652. It was for a book in praise of Cromwell.

The "Daily Courant" was the first marvel of its kind a newspaper issued daily, which came out in the year 1702.

The provincial towns, Salisbury and Sherborne, the former in 1738, had the distinguished honour of possessing a newspaper establishment. Each distributed their impressions by newsmen whose coming was hailed in town and country-houses. Before the paper had been set up rumour only brought news; now a week elapsed, and each country family was in communication with the world at large. No one need wonder that when deep snow lay or floods were out, the delay of the newsmen created great disappointment. In some parts of Cornwall, the newsman having been seen to approach, parties took that moment for going to the rich man's house who had the paper read out for the benefit of all. Nothing could have been a greater treat. The newsmongers sat in the hall, for no other room would have held them, and servants made *fittens, i. e.* excuses for coming in at the time.

When Glasgow was a fortnight from London the firing of a gun announced the coming in of the post. The members of the Clubs who heard it tumbled out of bed and rushed down to the club room, where a tankard of hot herb ale, or a beverage which was a mixture of rum and sugar, was ready for them before breakfast.*

Early newspapers gave a list of the couples married during the week. This was not a dry announcement of names, but was enlivened by much highly interesting matter.

For example, take a batch of marriages in 1730:—

Mr. Baskett to Miss Pell, with 5000*l.*
Mr. Davis to Mrs. Wylde, with 400*l.* per annum.
The Lord Bishop of St. Asaph to Miss Orell, with 30,000*l.*
J. Whitcombe, Esq., to Miss Allen, with 40,000*l.*
Mr. Will Hurfer to Miss Sally Mitchiner, with 3000*l.*†

Let us take at a venture "The Salisbury Journal," Monday, Jan. 29. 1738-9. No. 53. If just, we must own

* Dr. Strange.

† Notes and Queries: R. W. Hackwood.

that the matrimonial annals, as now recorded, yield the palm of interest to the entries of such matters in early provincial papers. It is something to hear about the person of the bride, her figure, and her fortune.

"Married, at St. George's, Hanover Square, —— Ayres, of the county of Northampton, Esq., to Miss Ann Sampson, only daughter of John Sampson, of the county of Leicester, Esq., a young lady of *10,000l.* fortune.—The Henry Murray, Esq., a young gentleman possessed of a plentiful estate in the county of Wilts, at St. George's, Bloomsbury, to Mrs. Wicks, relict of Simon Wicks, Esq., a fortune of 12,000*l.* and 400*l.* per annum. —Lieutenant Cotton Dent, of the Royal Navy, son of Digby Dent, Esq., late Commodore in the West Indies, to Miss Kitty Bowerbank, daughter of Thomas Bowerbank, Esq., barrack-master of Portsmouth, a lady of merit and fortune.—Villiers Fitz-Gerald, Esq., to Miss Newcomen, eldest daughter to Col. Newcomen, in Ireland, a most agreeable young lady, with a large fortune."

When upon the subject of marriage we may mention a feature of the time which is often alluded to, as the Fleet marriages.

At Keiths Chapel in May Fair, and at the chapel in the Fleet, children could get married in the reign of the two first Georges for a couple of crowns at any time of the day or night. Six thousand persons were said at the time to have been married annually at the former chapel.

Witchcraft and Superstitions Past and Present.

To record the wonderful delusion that all classes laboured under for centuries with respect to witchcraft, and a small part of the follies and atrocities that resulted, would require a volume. Let it be premised that the firm helief in this subject was by no means the opprobrium of the lower classes of society. High and low for a long period equally figure in the path of this superstitution.

It was believed, and that universally, that a malevolent spirit took possession of some human being; and through this agent worked out cruel, wicked, and devilish purposes. Oddly enough, this bad spirit chose for his abode a female advanced in years, and by choice one upon whom age had exerted its greatest power.

King James I. gravely questioned Sir John Harrington, why the devil did work more with ancient women than others. Sir John, ever ready with a jest, said: "We are taught thereof in scripture, where it is told that the devil walketh in dry places."

The ill effects were produced through the agency of the eyes. The old and ugly female was believed to have the power of destroying health, causing dreadful and incurable disease, inducing misfortune in the most uncommon way, and quite blighting the most flourishing crops, by a glance of her evil eye.

It may be asked whether the aged female was a consenting party, or a simply passive object, without help or means of rescue. The answer clearly is, that the woman was considered to be a willing, wicked partner in the diabolical acts, and in no sense the pitiful victim of stern necessity and spiritual superiority.

Municipal archives three centuries ago exhibit the working of the fears of the burgesses.

The juries took up the investigation, and, we shall see, admitted a merchant's widow, the party interested, to give evidence as to the witch that had dealt harm to her: *e. g.* in 1569, an entry was made at Lyme—

Item, we do find that Johane Ellesdon, widow, upon her othe, hathe declared before us that Ellen Walker is a wytche, and that she will approve, and also that James Lugbase, uppon his othe hathe declared before us, that the said Ellen Walker did saie unto the saide Johane Elsdon, that she could witche her no more.

meaning that she had exerted all her power against her. Some old persons finding themselves to be incessantly persecuted raged against the members of society at large, and adopted the odious name assigned them, and no doubt, though with danger to themselves, inspired fear in those who were objects of especial hate.

Where did the mania against witches begin? Among the ignorant and low in station? The question may not be important, as nearly all were ignorant. The language of Bishop Jewell's sermon before Queen Elizabeth, in 1598, was enough to throw a whole country into confusion:—"It may please your grace to understand that witches and sorcerers, within the last four years, are marvellously increased within this your Grace's realm. Your Grace's subjects pine away even unto the death; their colour fadeth—their flesh rotteth—their speech is benumbed—their senses are bereft! I pray God they may never practise further than upon the *subject!*"

For a woman to be old and ugly was, during many reigns, to live in positive danger. Any one might expose her life to imminent peril upon the idlest imputation. We know what numbers perished at the gallows up to 1682, when three poor women from Bideford were sentenced to death at Exeter assize for "bewitching several persons, destroying ships at sea, and cattle by land." These women are said to have been the last that suffered.

Whenever any remarkable disaster befel a member of a family, no difficulty was generally felt in ascribing it to some old person. Epilepsy was universally treated as proceeding from witchcraft. Neighbouring gossips assembled; they pitied the patient, and railed at the wicked author of so much suffering. The patient heard what passed, and adopted all the charges and suggestions of the assembled gossips.

A real case of suspicion of witchcraft here given will present an ordinary type of the class, and serve to convey a clear understanding of the sort of proceedings by which such numbers perished.

Deanes, the wife of Michael Grimmerton, was sent to gaol in 1687 to be tried as a witch.

Richard Storch gave evidence that his son, Nathaniel Storch, was eighteen years of age. When in a (clearly epileptic) fit that lasted two hours, during which time he required six persons to hold him, the son declared he saw the apparition of Deanes Grimmerton, and he had fits every day for a week after, and during the fits he saw the apparition of the before-mentioned. Several persons struck at the place where the afflicted lad pointed without effect. Nathaniel said "she was too cunning for them" and desired them not to strike at it any more, for when they did so it did increase his torture.

PINS.—After several of the fits there have been several *pins* taken out of different parts of his body, and one *iron* nail.

He declared partly what clothes Deanes Grimmerton wore, although sometime she changed some garment.

The father finally attested that he verily thought his son was the worse for the said Deanes Grimmerton, he crying out so against her.

Pins taken out of the body.—Elizabeth Storch, the mother, gave her evidence at length to the same effect. She added that the pins were of brass, and were taken out of various parts of her son's body without *drawing any blood* after them.

How the witch acted.—Nathaniel Storch crowns the evidence with an account of how he was practised upon.

Being at work as a tailor, 9th April, in the house of a townswoman, Deanes Grimmerton came in about one o'clock with a pipe filled with tobacco in her hand, and having lighted the same handed it to the witness, who having smoked a part handed it to another, and so the pipe went round till it was smoked out. He was ill immediately after, and so had continued.

How the witch was dressed.— He had seen the apparition of Deanes Grimmerton last night upon the middle beam of the chamber window, clothed with a long crowned hat, a long red whittle, a red coat, a green apron, and a white cloak about her neck under her whittle, and afterwards go out at the upper part of the window.

Imprisonment takes from the power of the witch.— Nathaniel believed Deanes Grimmerton is the cause of his fits. Since her imprisonment his fits and pain have abated.

Mary Tillman deposed to having a daughter about eighteen years of age. She had been subject to fits, in which eight men could hardly hold her, for three years.

Brass pins extracted. — About a year after her illness began several brass pins were taken from her daughter's shoulders, breast, arms, knees, legs, and feet.

When the witch appears the pains are increased. — At this time her daughter saw the apparition of Deanes Grimmerton, and then was in greater pains than before.

About fourteen weeks before her daughter's death she met Deanes Grimmerton, who abused her in words, saying, "Now thou hast no fits; now art not bewitched." Immediately after, the young woman fell into a pining condition, and so continued until her death. During the said fourteen weeks she was frequently molested by the apparition of the said Deanes Grimmerton.

Burning the pins taken from the body. — At a certain time when the pins were put into a heap of coals to be burned, the young woman was more in torture and pain than before.

The bewitched is fastened to a stool. — After a fit of three hours her daughter being desired to rise from the stool to go to bed, she answered that she could not, for Deanes Grimmerton kept her down. Two women went to move her from the stool but could not till they had pulled Elizabeth and the stool all along the house.

The witch lies upon the afflicted girl. — Tuesday night before Elizabeth's death a neighbour came to see her, when she complained that she could not presently make an answer, and said afterwards the reason was that Deanes Grimmerton was upon her on the bed.

Upon which matters Mary Tillman had suspicion that Deanes Grimmerton was the cause of her daughter's death.

This evidence doomed Deanes Grimmerton to trial by a mittimus from Mr. Standerwick, Mayor of Lyme Regis, June 1st, 1687.

We find no mention of recourse being had to test whether the accused was a witch or not. The church Bible was not used as a counterpoise, nor was Deanes Grimmerton, who smoked the social pipe, thrown into deep water to prove her innocence or guilt. The kind of evidence adduced was deemed sufficient. Where there was a doubt, the witch finder, or witch prover's services, would have been called in if procurable. These professionals went round in some parts, and dreadful is it to contemplate the horrors that ensued after the visits to towns of the arch witch finder. The authorities countenanced these impostors. The bellman sometimes went round to announce the arrival of the witch-finder. It is almost incredible that the same bellman gave out that any one having a complaint against any woman as being a witch, should give in her name, and she should be brought to undergo the ordeal by having a pin run into her by this itinerant. One is led to exclaim, what a time for aged matrons! Without proofs of guilt to be led at once to torture!

In this case the young persons in their fits had *pins* and a *nail* taken from them without any blood following, as the evidence shows. There is no pin-vomiting in this instance such as was sometimes exhibited. Pins were in some way or another deemed a necessary accompaniment to a case of bewitchment. The parents, gossips, or patient, took care that what they believed to be a clear case should not break down for want of a due display of pins, which we see were by some parties burnt, according, no doubt, to prescribed mystic rites. We might laugh at such scenes were it not that a human life often depended upon the result. At last the exhibition of the pins took place in open court. A woman said to be bewitched had placed pins in her stomacher, and by a dexterous dropping of her head in her pretended fits, picked up the supply for each successive ejection. Chief Justice North threw into disrepute this exhibition, which he witnessed, and detected the fraud.

Let us turn from the time when all believed in the existence and malevolent acts of witches to that in which the punishment of death being no longer imposed, and it being futile to bring charges against any one, the age when people believed in witchcraft was supposed to be past. True it is that the upper and middle classes have shaken off this belief in a heathenish superstition; but in every county of the south of England the power of witches is acknowledged, and the belief influences too largely human actions, stands in the way of the real progress of knowledge, while the dictates of Christianity are rendered nugatory as to being an absolute guide and rule of conduct.

A brief narrative of a tale of witchcraft, in the year 1840, drawn from the author's own observation, will illustrate the current of present opinion.

William Way, a little boy, the son of a shoemaker of West Dorset, was, like Nathaniel Storch, attacked with epilepsy, which medical men could only alleviate, for cure was not in their power. The boy's fits were frequent, and painful to the beholders, as all such epileptic paroxysms are. Spectators were many. From the first, when the ailment was too stubborn for doctors, and the contortions of a long fit were hideous, all agreed that the boy had been *overlooked*, or *looked upon*, that is, *bewitched*.

The poor boy heard nothing from the assembled relatives and gossips but about his special enemy, a tall aged female, good Betty Trayte, whose advanced age had implanted a sternness upon her countenance which had caused some to judge her to be a witch. In his fits he screamed out and exclaimed against poor old Betty Trayte, just as Storch did against Deanes Grimmerton. Gossips in numbers looked in and bore away incorrect and wonderful accounts of what they saw and heard. Some Dissenting ministers were applied to in order to counteract by prayer the effects of the bewitchment. A collection was made from thirty young women, virgins, of a penny each. With the money a conspicuous silver ring was purchased, having, it was believed, the power of averting all harm that the witch had or might meditate against the lad, especially if made from the sacrament money.

A mother, about the same time, stood at the west door of Exeter cathedral to beg pence from young women for the same object.

The "virgins'" ring and other charms were judged to have had a good effect. After a time the fits ceased, and the boy grew to be a stout lad, and hired himself to clean boots and shoes. Being one morning absent from his duties, it was announced that he had been afflicted with a dreadful fit, which would incapacitate him for his situation; that he was the worse for some evil person; that it was too bad of *her;* that she ought to be made to suffer, for the poor boy had done *her* no harm. Some wonderful, indeed quite impossible feats performed by the boy in his fits, were reported; how he worked himself like an eel through the bars of his common chair, and what he said against his tormenter.

It was deliberately recommended that the lad's sufferings should be put an end to by drawing blood from the witch by means of a rusty nail. This had been done in numerous instances of late years, with punishment to the operators. The old woman in question applied to the authorities for protection. She needed it; great numbers, though they meddled not in the matter, fully believed that the old woman was a witch, and that drawing blood from her would take away her power of doing mischief.

One century and a half had worked a change. Deanes Grimmerton was no more guilty than Betty Trayte. When the former lay under an imputation, all the classes of the country town, her place of residence, firmly believed in witchcraft: in 1840 the upper and middle classes, with only a few exceptions, were too enlightened to entertain any such superstition. Betty Trayte had the protection of the law administered as it is by those who disbelieve the existence of witches, who gave her their countenance.

Other incidents — the nature of the disease, the sufferings, the inability to cure on the part of the medical practitioners, the calling out when in pain against the malicious woman who had caused his agony, and other matters — furnish a complete parallel.

Many, though they were exasperated against the witch, did not like to own their belief in any such matter, but talked with reserve. Like many who nail up an old shoe in our vessels and houses, though not liking to own their belief, yet consider it would be a pity to receive harm from neglecting so easy a precaution. A piece of bacon stuck with pins used to be suspended in chimneys to interrupt witches in their descent, and so avert their visit. Toads that gained access to a cellar or house were ejected, and with the greatest care; and no injury was offered, because these were regarded, from being used as *familiars* by witches, with veneration or awe.

In both cases a cunning man, conjuror, or white witch, had probably been often consulted. By this we mean a clever, wonderful, beneficent being, who for a money consideration interposes, and by magical arts, charms, and spells, averts the evil eye of the witch from human beings or cattle, and renders innocuous the devilish art and practice of wicked old crones. A famous practitioner lived at West Leigh, co. Devon, near Wellington, who was succeeded by his son. Persons came from three counties to consult this white witch. They paid for consultation, charms, medicine, and directions how to find out the stealers of property. Prayers repeated backwards, and particular verses of the Psalms, to be recited upon swallowing certain nostrums, connected religion with superstition, and that for mammon: being more imposing, the charge was higher. Some of these fortune-tellers and dealers in nostrums, who point out how the witch's designs may be frustrated, are very low in the scale, are prodigiously crafty, and full of bombastic tricking language. Still they drive their trade; and while they do so we have proofs that there yet exists a large amount of ignorance and superstition.

It is believed that a seventh son can cure diseases, but that a seventh son of a seventh son, and no female child born between, can cure the king's evil. Such a favoured individual is really looked on with veneration. When at a farmhouse in Axminster parish, in 1828, engaged in taking a view, though other children were made to stand off, one little urchin was allowed to lay hold of my pencils, &c. I saw that there was something particular in this child, and addressed his mother as follows: — "This little man appears to be a favourite; I presume he is your little Benjamin." "He's a seventh son, sir," said the mother. Affecting an air of surprise, I expressed myself at the instant as being one very anxious to know what a *seventh* son could do? The mother, a very civil woman, told me that "she did think, to cure all diseases, should be the seventh son of a seventh son; but *many folk do come to touch my son*." In April, 1826, a respectable looking woman was engaged in collecting a penny from each of thirty young women, unmarried; the money to be laid out in purchasing a silver ring, to cure her son of epileptic fits. The money was to be freely given, without any consideration, or else the charm would have been destroyed. The young women gave their pence, because it would have been a *pity* for the lad to continue afflicted *if* the charm would cure him.

Some houses are spoken of as being "troublesome" or "haunted." Noises — the crowing of the cock by night, and the death-watch — are fancied to have been heard before the death of any person.

Thus writes Dr. Oliver: — "Such and so various are the superstitions with which a short and precarious life is embittered; and by such empty practices do timid mortals amuse and terrify themselves. They serve, however, to remind us of the imperfection of our nature, unable, by its own unassisted exertions, to disentangle itself from the grovelling weaknesses of matter, to avert the evils of a probationary state, or to govern or control effectually the passions and affections of the mind."

Was not the ancient chronicler, Higden, premature in

his assertions respecting a change in superstitious practices when he thus sings in his "Polychronicon"? —

> "Hos consuevit fallere
> Et ad bella impingere
> Merlini vaticinium,
> Et frequens sortilegium;
> Jam ex convictu Saxonum
> Commutantur in melius
> Ut patet luce clarius."

The discovery of a thief by divination by the sieve and shears, a superstition once greatly practised, is recorded in Dorset in 1660.

One Cockeney lost a gold ring. Edward Hill caused a sieve to turn round three times upon naming the party that was suspected to have the ring, and made use of a pair of shears in his discovery.

Mr. Thomas Hearn adds these remarks: — "This is one of the most ancient modes of divination of which we have any record. It was practised among the early Greeks, and is mentioned by Theocritus, whose words, as translated by Creech, are: —

> "To Agrio, too, I made the same demand;
> A cunning woman she, I crossed her hand:
> She turned the sieve and shears, and told me true,
> That I should love and not be loved by you."

But it was resorted to by that people, not only in questions of love, but for similar purposes to that which Master Cockeney had in view. Potter, Antiq. Græc., vol. i. p. 352., says, "This Koskinomanteia was generally practised to discover thieves, or others suspected of any crime, in this manner: — they tied a thread to the sieve, by which it was upheld, or else placed a pair of shears, which they held up by two fingers, then prayed to the gods to direct and assist them; after that, they repeated the names of the persons under suspicion, and he at whose name the sieve whirled round, or moved, was thought to have committed the fact."

The practice in this county was very similar. Grose tells us, that to discover a thief by the sieve and shears, you must stick the points of the shears in the wood of the sieve, and let two persons support it balanced upright with their two fingers; then read a certain chapter in the Bible, and afterwards ask St. Peter and St. Paul if A. or B. is the thief, naming all the persons you suspect. On naming the real thief, the sieve will turn suddenly round about.

This superstition is mentioned in several old works treating on such subjects; and Hudibras, p. II. c. iii., speaks of

> "the oracle of sieve and shears,
> That turns as certain as the spheres." *

The Ordeal by touching a Corpse.

A LOVE affair, with its attendant murder and incidents arising from the same, may be used to introduce some peculiarities of the era.

In the year 1613, there lived in the country, on the southern border of Somerset, near Wambrook, a Master Babb, who advanced his suit to marry a widow near Taunton. She gave him a refusal; but he afterwards secreted himself in her brewhouse, in order to have an opportunity of again preferring his suit.

The widow, when she heard his offer, exclaimed, in the emphatic language of the time, "Have thee, base rascal? No!" and struck him on the head with a pewter candlestick. Babb killed her with sixteen wounds, and put the knife in a wound, and in her hand, to make it be believed it was a case of self-destruction.

Mr. Warre, an influential magistrate of Hestercombe House, a seat near Taunton, believed the common opinion of

* Mr. T. Hearn, "Qui Quondam."

the time, that if the murderer touched the corpse of his victim the blood would immediately flow from the wound, and discover the guilty. This active magistrate caused the body to be disinterred, that all the inhabitants living within a circle of three miles might assemble to touch the body, and go through this painful ordeal. Babb ran away to escape this dreadful mode of testing each neighbouring inhabitant's innocence. His racking conscience left him no repose: he returned and yielded himself up to justice.

The Assizes for Somerset were held at Chard in 1613, where Babb was tried, and received sentence. He was hanged near Wambrook. Sir Symonds D'Ewes went to see the execution from his school, or from Coaxden Hall, which is at a short distance only from the former place. To that noted writer we are indebted for this account of the episode before narrated.

Skimmington Riding.

THIS celebration, public visitation, saturnalia, punishment administered under the powerful form of ridicule in the midst of a civilisation directed by law, yet entirely lawless, in fact a kind of *Lynching*, — still holds its ground, and so far as my observation extends is not likely to become obsolete.

It is too marked a feature in an account of the customs of several counties to be omitted. The following epitome of the Skimmington is from a communication I made to the late Sir Walter Scott.* Brand says none of the commentators on "Hudibras" have attempted an elucidation of the ceremony, which, however, Hogarth has illustrated.

Skimmington riding is, to a certain extent, a moral agent, not perhaps so much in restraining the vicious as in causing them to shun public observation, thereby not holding out bad examples to the rising youth of both sexes; — in a word, it

* In 1828 It has since appeared in my History of Lyme Regis.

checks those instances of openly profligate and licentious conduct which might else become too prevalent among the lower orders, who cannot, like their superiors, have recourse to legal proceedings against the person who has injured them, or divorce; it brands with infamy all gross instances of licentiousness; and exposes to lasting ridicule those couples who by their dissensions disturb the quiet and order of their neighbourhood, and so set a bad example, either by struggles for domestic ascendancy, or arising from quarrelsome dispositions. A Skimmington riding makes many laugh; but the parties for whom they ride never lose the ridicule and disgrace which it attaches. So far it is a punishment, like the visit of Mumbo Jumbo in Africa. The following are the principal causes for riding the Skimmington:—

1. When a man and his wife quarrel, and he gives up to her. 2. When a woman is unfaithful to her husband, and he patiently submits without resenting her conduct. 3. Any grossly licentious conduct on the part of married persons.

The first cause appears to answer that recorded in "Hudibras," canto ii. line 685. The knight, having mistaken a Skimmington for some other procession, is undeceived as follows:—

> "Quoth Ralpho, "You mistake the matter;
> For all th' antiquity you smatter
> Is but *a riding used of course,*
> *When the grey mare's the better horse.*
> When o'er the breeches greedy women
> Fight to extend their vast dominion,
> And in the cause impatient Grizzle
> Has drubbed her husband with ——
> And brought him under covert-baron
> To turn her vassal with a murrain;
> * * * *
> * * * *
> And they, in mortal battle vanquished,
> Are of their charter disenfranchised.' "

About dusk two individuals, one armed with a skimmer, the other with a ladle, come out of some obscure street, attended by a crowd, whose laughter, huzzas, &c., emulate the well-known *charivari* of the French. The two performers are sometimes in a cart, at other times on a donkey; one personating the wife, the other the husband. They beat each other furiously with the culinary weapons above described, and, warmed by the applause and presence of so many spectators (for all turn out to see a Skimmington), their dialogue attains a freedom, except in using surnames, only comparable with their gestures. On arriving at the house of the parties represented in this moving drama, animation is at its height: the crowd usually stay at that spot some minutes, and then traverse the town. The performers are remunerated by the spectators: the parties that parade the streets with the performers sweep with besoms the doors of those who are likely to require a similar visitation. See Dr. King's "Miscellany": —

> "When the young people ride the Skimmington,
> There is a general trembling in the town;
> Not only he for whom the party rides
> Suffers, but they sweep other doors besides;
> And by that hieroglyphic does appear
> That the good woman is the master there."

Mr. Douce derives *Skimmington* from the *skimming-ladle* used in the procession.

The following letter from Sir Walter Scott will prove, I doubt not, highly interesting: —

To Mr. George Roberts.

"Sir, — I am obliged by your curious letter upon the subject of the Skimmington. We had, or perhaps I might say still have, a simular ritual of popular interference in Scotland, in case of gross scandal, or nuptial transgressions and public quarrels in a household. It is called "riding the stang," the peccant party being seated across a pole (or stang) in no very comfortable position. You will find some notice of the custom in Jamieson's Scottish Dictionary, *voce* Stang. I think the Doctor does not mention that men and women also were sometimes exposed to ride the stang on account of incontinence. Burns made some clever verses (not in his collected works) on a comrade of his who had been accessory to such a saturnalian scene of punishment, in which the exposed female had suffered bodily injury, upon which account the regular police had looked out after the parties who had interfered with their vocation. I have read in Brand's "Popular Antiquities," or some such authority, that scholars in the English universities were subjected to the stang when they neglect prayers. You will find a poem on the Skimmington among Prior's poems — not the folio edition, where it is omitted, but in the large collection. When they ride the Skimmington, it would seem they swept the doors of those whom they threatened with similar discipline. * * * *

"I am, Sir, your much obliged servant,

"WALTER SCOTT.

"Abbotsford, Melrose,
August 2nd, 1828."

As must happen in all popular demonstrations, the truth of the charge rests with some irresponsible party — some one who is to perform in the moving revelry it may be, or an interested person.

In many celebrations of Skimmington riding I never knew the justice of the affair called in question but once: a charge of immorality had been brought by a degraded witness whose false testimony occasioned the Skimmington.

To prove how this matter clings to a man or woman for life, we will adduce an episode at a late Dorchester assize, where a barrister addressed a witness with "I believe you have had a Skimmington for you?" The fact could not be denied. The witness was abashed and damaged by the ridicule of the circumstance.

Natural Phenomena attributed, through Superstition and Ignorance of Physical Science, to Mysterious and Supernatural Causes.

OUR ancestors, before the diffusion of that mass of scientific knowledge which the greatest and wisest of all enlightened nations are labouring to accumulate, never dreamt of attributing great phenomena to natural causes; to account for them upon true reasoning of the physical causes was out of their power. They had recourse to the mighty, unexplained, invisible, latent workings of the Almighty, and would have shrunk from, as impious, the expounder of those beauteous laws which are established throughout creation.

When the belief had firmly rooted itself that the affairs of mankind, whether troubled or smooth, the deliberate wickedness of courts, and the flagrant crimes of the turbulent, were all foreshadowed and portended by extraordinary appearances of earth, sea, and heaven, it follows that we must expect men to be intensely interested at the manifestation of all these, and at the reports of them. In the absence of mysterious phenomena, humble politicians and venders of broad sheets forged rumours of them, and Scripture was wrested to serve the purpose of the mystics.

Earthquakes, to a reader of history, appear to have been very frequent. England would scarcely win its title to be *terra firma* if we received as literal the statements of "convulsions" and "swallowings up," of "hills removed," and such disturbances. Dean Conybeare writes that there has not been a shock of an earthquake in this country sufficient to throw down a church tower.

The lower orders in the country have not yet received their share, some no part, of the generally diffused natural sciences. They, as well as the classes immediately above them, as too often happens, are disposed to attribute many phenomena to the agency of earthquakes.

The great landslip of Dowlands and Bindon, S. E. Devon, Dec. 25th, 1839, took place after a wet season. Great slips were caused on the Jura, and other places. Such had resulted from well known causes in the same locality. Deans Buckland and Conybeare happened to be near at the time. Their explanations were without much effect upon the assembled wonderers. Their science was ridiculed; local history was treated as a fable. About the year 1646, a similar event at Pinney, near that spot, drew good Bishop

Hall, who went to the synod of Dort from Exeter, whose meditations upon the earthquake savour of his age. Men of education, if they feel that much and accurate knowledge of a particular branch of natural science is required on any particular occasion, have recourse to those who have made such their study. This could not be done in Charles the First's reign.

Eclipses continued to be viewed with awe to within a century and half ago. Sunday, 25th Feb., 1589, was called Dark Sunday before Shrove tide, owing to the eclipse on that sabbath day, "fearful to all people's sight to behold." The appearance of a parhelion was deemed sufficiently wonderful to be entered in parish registers.

In a storm which Sir Symonds D'Ewes calls the "great tempest" of 17th of June, 1611, the poor of Wambrook, near Chard, came to the school where he was to beg the scholars to come home and read prayers to them. An ancient man said there was a prophesy touching this tempest before it came, as if the world should then have ended.

The Rev. Andrew Paschall, inducted, in 1662, rector of Chedzoy in Sedgemoor, near Bridgewater, was accounted a learned man of his day. He possessed a turn of mind characteristic of the period. His attention was directed to those curious and rare phenomena which were supposed to augur and foreshadow portentous occurrences. Before the Duke of Monmouth's rebellion he wrote to a great person to represent to the king his apprehensions arising from what he had lately observed, and to entreat the king to cast an eye that way.

The phenomena which disturbed the worthy rector shall be described in his own language: —

"Before our troubles came on, we had such signs as used to be deemed forerunners of such things. In May, 1680, there was that monstrous birth at Isle Brewers, a parish in Somerset, which at that time was much taken notice of — two female children joined in their bodies from the breast downwards. They were born May the 19th, and christened by the names of Aquila and Priscilla. May the 29th I saw them well and likely to live. About at the same time, reports went of divers others in the inferior sorts of animals, both the oviparous and the viviparous kinds. But perhaps many of these, and other odd things then talked of, owed, if not their being, yet their dress, to superstition and fancy. In the January following, Monday the 3rd, about seven in the morning, we had an earthquake, which I myself felt here. It came with a whizzing gust of wind from the west end of my house, which shook it. This motion was observed in Bridgewater, Taunton, Wells, and other places, and near some caverns in Mendip Hills, and was said to be accompanied with thundering noises. In the end of the year 1684, December the 21st, were seen from this place, at sunrising, parhelii, and this when, in a clear, sharp, frosty morning, there were no clouds to make the reflection. It was probably from the thickness of the atmosphere. The place of the fight, which was in the following summer, was near a line drawn from the eyes of the spectator to these mock suns."

There is a letter from the same gentleman to John Aubrey, Esq., 1683, respecting "many prodigious things performed by some discontented demon."

In one case cited none but nonconforming ministers were called to their assistance by the poor afflicted people.

The Decay of old Mercantile Coast Towns, and their Revival as Watering Places.—Altered Manners.—Fossils and early Indications of Geology.

OUR subject leads to the singular fate that attended many of our south coast towns in the course of the last century. They died out as mercantile coast towns; and when near to a point of extinction, they rose, phœnix-like, under a metamorphosed appearance, and enabled a large and new class in society to gratify their wishes and a novel taste.

The decline of these towns was nearly simultaneous, and was due to the same causes. Their rise was cotemporaneous, and is attributable to a novel phase which society took on, to new habits, and to the effects of new medical prescriptive directions.

Many of our coast towns had been the residence of merchants for several centuries, who traded in very small vessels, as was then the custom, to foreign parts. Some towns had manufactures of woollen goods carried on in addition to fishing, and a little trade in shipping.

The war with France, after the revolution and expulsion of James II., put an end to the trade with that country, which has never been re-established. As the old families, the honoured merchants, died off, there were no successors. Their sons withdrew altogether; or if they remained, there was no longer any commerce to occupy their attention. The vessels used in foreign trade gave way to ships which were unsuited to small ports, and large and populous towns drew away and retained all the foreign trade.

Some of our towns straightway declined in a rapid manner, and were in a very low condition.

Weymouth and Lyme, old coast towns, are remarkable instances of this decline.

The Cobb dues at Lyme, in 1708–9, only amounted to 13*l.* 12*s.* 10*d.*

In 1718 the shambles were presented as being in danger of falling. Juries had a special duty to perform, which was, to present the dangerous buildings. There were numerous presentments about the year 1724. Mr. Tatchell, agent to Henry Fane, Esq., wrote his employer, in 1743, of the poverty of the butchers who had rent to pay in the shambles, of the Cobb collector, and of the difficulty of collecting any money.

In 1747 the roads and ways were out of repair. The old names of families who had lived many years in the town no longer appear. The state of the streets, from the account of them furnished by the old people, was truly pitiable. The constables present, in 1762, things "as well as usual."

There was little shipping, and very few respectable inhabitants about the year 1750. Houses were of little value: purchasers could scarcely be procured on any terms, and some were literally given away; while others are known to have been offered, but refused! About this time a weaver's four large rooms, and weaving room besides, let for one shilling a week. The weavers wove the serges at their own houses: the cloth was not dyed. The lower street had large high buildings, some of which projected at each story, which had been the abode in the former century of rich families, but from the effects of time, and neglect of the poorer occupiers, were in a state of extreme decay. The population had dwindled to less than a thousand inhabitants, so that a great many houses remained unoccupied, and were so neglected, that it is an incontestable fact, that no one could walk with safety in the streets during a high wind, which frequently blew down parts of the most tottering buildings. From the year 1692 to 1772 above 118 houses had fallen to ruin, besides many burnt down and never rebuilt and washed away by the sea. A petition to parliament set forth the inability of the town to pay the land tax, which had increased to 6*s.* in the pound, and had been returned *in-super.*

As the old houses fell down, or, having become dangerous, were removed, poor people built themselves with the materials tenements of little value. Some old buildings were repaired in such an excessively clumsy manner as to destroy all vestiges of former proportions.

There were no houses in the environs; there was then a *town's end* in reality, where a century before posts had been driven in to keep out the Cavaliers. Broad Street was inhabited by lace-makers, who worked at their Lyme-lace,—an elegant material, which, however, did not enrich the poor people engaged in that trade.

Most of the serges wove were shipped from Exeter to Ancona. This source of employment ceased as the trade was transferred to the north.

Most of the houses in Broad Street had porches. An old person described, among other things, how ladies in the decline of life used to sit and stand in their porches on summer evenings, to talk to their friends and also to inferiors, in full dress — a white apron instead of a check one, ruffles, &c. Two or three ladies of the principal families were styled "madame." No strangers ever came in the summer. When the members of the Fane family attended elections, &c., they were received by a gentleman named Lisle, at his house in the Butter Market.

The shops were so ill supplied, that, excepting at fairs, very few articles not of ordinary consumption could be procured. The old houses rapidly disappeared, and hovels succeeded in their places. No white bread was sold. The labourers worked for 4*d.* a day.

Smuggling was carried on to a great extent, in spite of the check it had sustained twenty years before, when the regular trade being interfered with, informations were laid, and many persons were imprisoned. Smuggling, the colloquial term for the contraband trade, was viewed as a venial offence by all western people of every degree.

And have not varied circumstances produced decline and utter decay in other towns of foreign countries, as well as in our own land? Read what the historian of the Popes, Ranke (Vol. i. p. 480.), records of the second decline of the Eternal city.

During the absence of the Popes in Avignon, this Rome of the middle ages sunk into equal decay with that ancient Rome which had so long lain in ruins: —

"When Eugenius IV. returned to Rome in the year 1443, it was become a city of herdsmen; its inhabitants were not distinguishable from the peasants of the neighbouring country. The hills had long been abandoned, and the only part inhabited was the plain along the windings of the Tiber; there was no pavement in the narrow streets, and these were rendered yet darker by the balconies and buttresses which propped one house against another; the cattle wandered about as in a village. From San Silvestro to the Porta del Popolo, all was garden and marsh, the haunt of flocks of wild ducks. The very memory of antiquity seemed almost effaced; the Capitol was become the Goats' Hill, the Forum Romanum the Cows' field; the strangest legends were associated with the few remaining monuments."

The aged favoured me with many interesting details respecting the state of things when they were young. Many were *laudatores temporis acti,* and saw nothing good in anything recent. Some, however, were dispassionate, and compared with great justice the relative advantages of the two periods. Such were Benj. Bazeley of Lyme, and Mary Bartlett of Exeter, who conversed with Mr. Edwin Chadwick in Jan. 1855.

Bazeley said the town was very poor indeed. Meat sold — beef at 2*d.* and $1\frac{3}{4}$*d.* a lb., sirloin 3*d.*; veal was never sold by weight, but by the joint. Cheese, the best raw milk, sold at 4*d.* Clothing of all kinds was very dear, and people were very ragged. He remembered a man bringing potatoes in panniers; people used to buy three halfpenny worth. He candidly summed up, after a consideration of wages, and the prices of articles, that the humble members of society could do as well now as then, in spite of the cheapness of some things at that time, upon which he dwelt with pleasure.

In respect of diet, Bazeley spoke of the great use of meat broth, and the lending of some one day by a friendly neighbour to another, who made some in return, and repaid the kindness.

Mary Bartlett, like Bazeley, viewed everything as improved. She saw the benefit of the sanitary measures in operation. Two-thirds of the Exeter people were pitted with the small-pox. They were then worse fed. There were only one baker and one butcher in Exeter. She described the struggles she had at times in crowds to get bread from the baker, and bring it away quite hot. Children were not fed then on bread and butter as now-a-day. Though provisions were cheaper, wages were lower in proportion, and the low wages were more frequently spent in drunkenness.

The perambulating the limits of the parish on the Rogation days, that is, the three days before Ascension, was continued from the ancient practice of walking round in solemn religious procession, chanting the Litanies. The path which the crowd took is often referred to as "the procession path." The perambulation was called "beating the bounds." Some refreshment was furnished by the churchwardens.

Instead of chanting Litanies, parish fought with parish with bats, in the presence of the clergy.

Seeing that this was disused, the old woman pointed out the improved state of manners.

There were no carpets, but only rushes on the floors. In coast towns, sand did the work of rushes.

Carpets gained a signal victory over rushes; and cleanliness rejoices at the result of the contest. Brussels carpets were introduced from Tournay in 1745. By the year 1760 the floors of all respectable houses were carpeted.

The shops of Exeter had no windows, but were open like fishmongers' shops in large towns.*

Though the town of Lyme had so declined, the old corporation observances of high days and remarkable occasions were kept up in their pristine state. The old people referred to these celebrations with great delight, and treated the non-lighting up of bonfires as proofs of degeneracy. Let us take as an example of one year's festivities what was done in the mayoralty of Arthur Raymond of Lyme, in 1660-61: —

	£	s.	d.
Expences at the "Lyon" when the King was proclaimed - - - - - - -	7	18	0
To the boys for a bonfire at the same time - -		5	0
To do on the King of Prussia's beating Count Daun		2	6
Expences at the "Three Cups" the 5th of Nov. -	5	19	4
To George Baker for an entertainment on the King of Prussia's beating Count Daun - - -	2	10	6
Paid the gunner's note for firing, &c. - -		8	0
Expences at the "Lion" on taking Bel Isle - -	1	19	0
Carried forward -	£19	2	4

* Western Times, Jan. 13. 1855.

	£	s.	d.
Brought forward - -	19	2	4
To the boys for a bonfire - - - -		2	6
Expences at the "Three Cups" on taking Pondicherry - - - - - -	5	19	4
Expences at the "Three Cups" on the coronation -	13	15	10
Paid Mary Jackson for cards and ribbonds at the coronation - - - - -		7	6
To Charles Roe for looking after the guns and firing	1	5	6
To farmer Partridge for furze for a bonfire at the coronation - - - - -		6	0
	£40	19	0

Lyme has been adduced as a type of the coast town once commercial, but which had lost its foreign trade — even its kidnapping — in every foreign country, then a clothing and lace-making town, with scarce any intercourse with persons abroad or at home. A coach was a novel sight, and drew the inhabitants to view what was so unusual.

Weymouth might equally well have been cited as an example of decline. The same lament would have applied to it as to Lyme and other old maritime towns. Weymouth had fallen very low, and was the residence of fishermen and smugglers. Poverty was great, and tenements fell down from neglect. Certain rents of assize amounted to only 14*l*.

In 1740 the half of Charlotte Row was offered to an individual if he would enclose the remainder, which he declined, considering it as a bad speculation.*

At Brighton a spot of ground was offered to a hairdresser in fee, upon condition of shaving the possessor. The terms were declined. The land soon became very valuable.

Commerce did not revive, and the woollen trade was doomed to decline also, and to be transferred to other localities.

The arrest that took place in the further decline of the seaport towns, — the metamorphose in the habits of society, —

* Ellis's Hist. of Weymouth.

are worthy of consideration. Great effects were produced; manners were altered; old towns revived, and new towns rapidly arose.

The middle of the eighteenth century is the epoch when this remarkable change, that has to be described, became perceptible.

Before the year 1750 the sea on our southern coast had ever been as pure; — the hills and under cliffs as grand and captivating, still no inland residents came to the fairy land. There is in history no record of any summer sea-side pleasure-taking or health-seeking visits; not a word of bathing. There never had been any convenience for sea-bathing, nor any hot baths. In Queen Elizabeth's reign any scholar of Cambridge University who dared to bathe by day or night was set in the stocks all the day; and, for the second offence, to be whipped with rods.

Whether is the more strange? the neglect of the sea-side for bathing, or the change that now obtained?

Persons of either sex living far from the sea deemed it necessary to rush to the coast so soon as the fine weather had set in. Like the anadromous fishes, a furious desire to migrate seized upon them, and they obeyed the instinctive call. Opinion will be found to have set going this movement. The same moving power has been active on subsequent occasions. Medical practice assumes the mania of fashion, and its votaries obey the call. How many forms of fashionable practice have seriously occupied the attention of society, particularly of the easy classes; but none can, it is to be believed, equal the monster movement of the era under consideration.

Man delights to trace great results to certain causes, and to prove them to be the clear emanation of one mind. Shall injustice be imputed if Dr. Richard Russel be set down as the great instigator of the sea-side mania?

This physician was the son of a London bookseller. His acquirements were great, and a great name was the consequence. In 1750 he published in Latin his well-known "Treatise upon Glandular Consumption, and the Use of Sea Water in Diseases of the Glands." This produced a great effect upon the medical faculty; and in 1753 an English translation was sent forth, which increased his fame and the number of his patients. His course of treatment led him, as might reasonably be supposed, to the coast. He chose Brighton for his residence.

Sea water became the panacea for every ailment. Physicians talked of the sea; descanted upon the number of dips, the hour for immersion; the number of times a-week, the particular locality, and the relative strength or saltness of the water. Determination to the sea-side was set up.

Should we say of Dr. Russel that he caused Brighton alone to rise, — that metropolis of the sea coast? The fame of his practice led other medical men to raise the cry, "to the sea-side." Lodging-houses began to be created in a very great number of localities, as at Brighton. Dr. Russel was to sea-side visitors what Peter the Hermit was to the crusades — the instigator, the genius that raised the latent spirit.

This physician, who produced such great results, died in London when on a visit, in 1759, aged seventy-two, and lies interred at South Malling:—

> Clara per omne ævum Russelli fama manebit,
> Dum retinet vires unda marina suas.*

The rush to the coast to procure the benefit arising from the virtues of SEA WATER must be distinguished from the subsequent movement to the coast to secure the curative effects of the balmy SEA AIR. This was a later movement. The first rush was of those who came to *bathe* in sea water; the second, of those who desired to *breathe* sea air.

Medicinal waters became the rage about the close of the eighteenth century. A new chalybeate, or indeed any mineral spring, occasioned a rush of invalids to drink and

* See Horsfield's Sussex

partake of its healing qualities. This fashion for mineral springs prevailed extensively. A spring discovered at Glastonbury brought in one year 10,000 persons; but the fame was not sustained, and the bath or fountain is only an object of curiosity. A spring with some ordinary chalybeate properties in the park of Hinton St. George, the seat of Earl Poulett, counted a numerous company every morning of neighbouring invalids. Ferruginous, sulphureous properties of particular springs or wells were cried up by certain doctors of physic, and were specially patronised, while others were correspondingly depreciated in Charles the First's reign. Physicians could not make roads; so many of these, perhaps as efficacious as "the Wells" of Tunbridge, remain without repute from having been inaccessible, and when they were so the mania had died away.

When the latter practice obtained, it was a matter of course, when a patient showed symptoms of tubercular consumption, to prescribe a sojourn in Italy or the south of France. Italy was unsuspected of cold or frost, though guilty of both, and having houses not comfortable like our own for invalids. At length some physicians bethought themselves of the south-west of England. In a medical sense it became fashionable, and began to compete effectually with the Isle of Wight. A member of Oriel College thus warmly eulogises the south-west of England: —

"Mild is the clime, though sullen winter reign,
Though frost, with iron grasp, extend his chain;
Some secret charm soon bursts the crystal band,
And strikes the sceptre from his livid hand.
The piercing winds, whose ice-flaked tempest blows
From hills deep buried in a waste of snows,
Soon as they touch this bland, enchanted ground,
Confess the spell, and feel their rigours bound."

Some towns were especially marked out and lauded by physicians for their curative influence in cases of consumption. This was so in a remarkable degree with Sidmouth, when Torquay, Bournemouth, &c., did not exist as towns, or even as villages. There were by the quay at Tor three cottages, which many old persons remembered as the first signs of that large watering-place and winter residence. Ryde had only a few fishermen's houses. Brighton was a small place. Weston super Mare, Clevedon, Burnham, Teignmouth, Budleigh, Salterton, Bournemouth, Dawlish, Bagnor, Worthing, &c., either did not exist, or were insignificant villages.

During the summer months a few invalids occasionally came to enjoy the sea air at Lyme from Bath, Bristol, and Somersetshire; but as machines were unknown, any one wishing to court the embraces of Neptune was obliged to undress on the beach: the accommodations in other respects were equally bad. Till after the construction of the turnpike road from Charmouth through Lyme to Exeter, in 1758, strangers in their journey westward had no opportunity of viewing it. The innkeeper first procured a bathing-machine for the accommodation of travellers, who were enabled to take a dip in a comfortable manner, before proceeding on their journey. It is a curious fact that he placed it at the mouth of the river, where it remained for several years. Many a lovely creature, whose tender frame was shaken by an insidious malady beyond hope of cure, shivered at each plunge; and those in robust health were daily seen in numbers playing mermaids and tritons. Nearly every visitor of the coast was a bather; now comparatively few take the cold bath, excepting as a luxury. The warm baths are in greater request. May-day saw the first immersion; now bathing begins later, and late autumn bathing has its admirers.

A gentleman of Bath, being sent to Weymouth to bathe, had a machine constructed. These conveniences are now universally made use of. While referring to Weymouth, it may be remarked that royalty partook of the coast-ward movement. King George III. and court visited Weymouth for the first time in 1789, when in the annals of that town commences a memorable era known as "the king days."

Much had to be done before the decayed towns could be made to shake off, serpent-like, their old skin, and assume their new character or metamorphose — that of WATERING-PLACES. The demand was steady and marked; that an adequate supply followed we need not feel surprised at.

Housekeepers near the sea began to fit up two or three front rooms in a homely manner, which is the first indication at Lyme of the lodging-house system, now so generally pursued on the whole line of coast: they met with encouragement; others were procured, and it soon happened, as it is somewhere expressed, that the invalids who came in search of health "found the goddess propitious to their prayers, and returning to pay their vows, brought beauty and elegance" in their train. Houses devoted to the reception of visitors were not at first to be procured. The old ruinous towns required much preparation. Lyme had rows of crumbling falling houses, narrow drang ways* leading to the weaving shops, where pack-horses could be led to be loaded. Cottages were so miserable that without their being pulled down nothing could be done to make the town a fitting place of reception for summer visitors.

Mr. Thomas Hollis, a gentleman of well-known repute, mentioned at one time as the probable writer of the letters of "Junius," who travelled abroad in company with Thomas Brand, Esq., of the Hyde, Essex, became possessed of lands at Corscomb in Dorsetshire.

This gentleman had purchased the Three Cups Inn, where he retained apartments for himself, called "Liberty Hall." He purchased a whole row of poor houses in Pound Street, and pulled them down for the improvement of the town. His influence in the metamorphose of Lyme Regis was generally acknowledged. The great Lord Chatham's visits to that town were ascribed by the scandal mongers to his desire to ingratiate himself with the bachelor Mr. Hollis. Toplady, the Calvinistic writer, believed that the Earl hoped this gentleman would have proved a second Sir William Pinsent, who had left his lordship a large estate. Mr. Hollis

* Anglo-Saxon *dringen*, "to press;" a very narrow passage or alley.

died in 1774, and was buried, at his request, in the middle of a field in a grave ten feet deep, when ploughs were set to work immediately that no traces of his burial-place might remain.

In the summer months an agreeable society was formed. The visitors and respectable inhabitants occasionally met at six o'clock to dance in the alcove on the square, now forming a part of the walk. The front was glazed. The whole extent of window was lined with spectators, who took their station to "gaze on the fair" and see the strangers.

Families of good fortune regularly came for the season, and many of the first visitors built houses near the sea, in spots which till then had been entirely neglected. In the course of a few years great changes took place. There were two prices for articles, one for inhabitants, another for visitors. Persons of county family put a sum of money into their trunk, and went to the sea to spend it. Some "land sharks" followed; and amusing adventures might be recorded. Some persons in business, keepers of hotels, libraries, and assembly rooms, made themselves particularly useful to the strangers. Possessed of tact, a few attained a pitch of influence that caused them to be privileged persons, while their senses directed them to use with judgment and effect the advantages of their position — a novel one to themselves and their fellow-townsmen. Houses began to be wholly appropriated to strangers, though none of those pretty cottages which now grace the environs had been erected, and few buildings in a more elevated situation were in existence. A boarding house was opened. The terms for board and lodging were 10*s.* 6*d.* per week. Butter was then 3*d.* a lb.; beef, 4*d.*; a large loaf, 4½*d.*

Mr. Hollis had paved the way for the building of the Assembly Rooms.

This may appear to involve only the outlay of a sum of money; but the effect upon the town at large was deeply felt.

Nearly all the townspeople were Dissenters, and eighty years since that class entertained very strong opinions against cards and dancing. Mr. James Bagster, the builder, a Dissenter, having contracted to build the ball-room, ran home to be the first to announce to his wife that he was going to build *Satan's house;* but he added a saving clause, —"I shall get a hundred pounds by it."

The Assembly Rooms were the great source of delight. Persons penned up in uncomfortable lodgings spent the evening regularly twice a week in society, played at cards, and on Fridays danced. Many took their tea and coffee there every night, for which the charge was only 6*d*.

The principal inhabitants anticipated the coming interference with their habits, having been already waited upon by the minister of the great chapel, and one and all left and became churchmen.

The season began in May, and ended in October. For many years there were no strangers in the winter. In the course of time, fifty houses in the suburbs having been erected, some of the visitors became residents.

Of these some were county families whose object was to save; many were officers on half pay, and individuals possessed of a fair income. The first visitors had to rough it to a certain extent. The people of the little towns were not accustomed to gentry, and had not learnt to suit their habits to the new comers. The grandmother of a baronet lodged by the sea at a village in Dorset, at a homely cottage. She told me that from her bed-room window appeared one morning an object which at first puzzled her. This was a horse's carcase which had been hauled up to the top of a boat's mast by one leg and flayed. This was allowed to hang there for the convenience of the fishermen coming to cut off pieces for bait for their lobster pots and shrimp nets. What would please the strangers in some towns afterwards became quite a study; in others was comparatively neglected.

A boarding-house life was deemed to be very agreeable, and so many had recourse to it that well-frequented houses were to be found everywhere. The English at one time bid fair to emulate the Americans, who are stimulated by necessities, and, guided by taste, a boarding-house people. After a certain experience our countrymen appear to have preferred the privacy of lodgings to the public life of a boarding-table and association. Such establishments to be found in many towns for several years are now given up, not being found to answer. Reading does not thrive in public establishments. They did for summer visiting, but each family prefers their own *ménage*—their own "Home." The fact is now established that the British are essentially a domestic — a home-loving people.

At the Boarding House kept by Mrs. Peckett the company found their own tea and sugar. Each boarder had his tea-caddy; hence the great number who took their coffee and tea at the "Assembly Rooms." There was no expense in this enjoyment of an evening in society and a meal.

The class that moved to the sea-side had, for its marking character, gentle breeding. Officers of both services, and persons of good family, had been bred in habits of self-restraint and self-respect.

This new importation brought a high standard of manners and habits. A decree went out virtually against the common public room or bar of the inn — a very general place of resort in many, if not most towns.

Pride has been charged upon the new comers, and that of being exclusive. In many towns the highest, and many grades below in the scale, associated at the bar, the fives-court, the belfry, and at cock-fights, and badger-baitings. Persons admitted to the new circle gave up the mixed society of such places, and associated only with "presentable people." The effect of this alone upon the social system was very great. The inhabitants of some country towns viewed the operation of this in neighbouring places with great ill-will — nevertheless the separation has continued.

The strangers who came knew nothing of the old natives of the place, moving in humble life; they formed an entirely new class. The inhabitants, who had no connection with them, did not like them. "When they strangers comed," said an old woman upwards of ninety, "then the town was a-spoiled." There was a familiarity amongst the townspeople, engendered by a long residence in the same place, which ought not to have been expected to be shared with new comers. The habits of a country town were not in accordance with those of persons of good income.

The dinner hour at the mayor's feast was two o'clock. The viands were plain, but substantial: pipes and punch were introduced immediately after the cloth was removed. Most of the company departed about midnight. The hospitality of this period is described in a number of the "Edinburgh Review:" a gentleman is spoken of as returning late over bad roads; footman drunk, coachman more drunk, master most drunk! The ringers and singers spent Christmas eve at the clergyman's house with the vicar. The sisters and friends of some of the most respectable inhabitants had stalls in the shambles at the fair; and the young ladies "of the best of the town" raffled there for ribbons.

Among the motives for so many choosing a sea-coast residence may be mentioned:—1. Sea-bathing. 2. Curative influence of climate in consumption and ill-health. 3. A circle of visiting in society. 4. Economy. 5. A compliance with the fashion of the time,—the Continent being closed against the British. 6. Fortune-hunting and match-making.

The polished strangers gave the *ton* to the principal townspeople, who soon became more refined in their manners, and stylish in their mode of living. Card-playing,—principally whist and loo,—was the rage. Circulating libraries contained scarce anything but novels. To purchase books was not customary; there were none offered for sale, but could be procured by an order through the proprietor of the "Sherborne Mercury" newspaper. Company assembled at seven, and retired at eleven,—only a little later than the present hour for commencing the first quadrille.

Weymouth, like Brighton when royalty was present, became crowded, and extremely gay and expensive. Persons of high distinction put up with lodgings that, in spite of the charge per week, were very mean. Many new watering-places sprang into note, where no good houses had ever been erected. The supply was not greater than the demand till the peace of 1815, when the Continent drew away numbers which some towns felt, and have ever since been in a state of vegetation merely, or positive decline. Before the French Revolution of 1830, there were 150,000 English residing in France; soon after that political event the numbers were reduced to 75,000.

Rusticity of manners, confined views of men and things, yielded to intercourse with persons who had travelled, and inspired some desire for seeing the world into the inhabitants of the country town.

It is highly entertaining to listen to octogenarians who have spent their life in some town by the sea-side. They give an interesting account of the *first* visitors to the coast, of a race of perambulators that, swallow-like, set out in settled weather, to enjoy the sea-breezes, and ramble along the shore, till, fatigued with their toilsome and rough walk over the pebbles and ledges, they returned to recruit their strength, and arrange specimens of sea-weed and shells in the homely parlour of some sea-faring man, whose thrifty wife added to his little gain by letting out three rooms to "summer visitors." Persons who came in halcyon days expected little more than cleanliness and attention. Much taste was displayed in the arrangement of shells, pebbles, and sea-weed,—much energy in the search after them. In every sitting-room might be seen some tasteful and fantastic nick-nack of the marine school, a pebble painted to represent the head of a Chinese, with a polished limpet shell for a hat—baskets made of shells, containing different kinds of sea-weed, and all such trifles, which ladies of great taste so well know how to arrange.

The following lines appeared under a bouquet of sea-weed, in an album, and were written by a lady, long a resident of Lyme:—

"Oh call us not weeds, but flowers of the sea,
For lovely, and gay, and bright-tinted are we;
Our blush is as deep as the rose of thy bowers,
Then call us not weeds,—we are ocean's gay flow'rs,

Not nurs'd like the plants of the summer parterre,
Whose gales are but sighs of an evening air ;
Our exquisite, fragile, and delicate forms
Are the prey of the ocean when vex'd with his storms."

About the time that watering-places arose out of the old towns, fossils, called curiosities, became an object that attracted the visitors. One Lock, whom Dr. Maton calls *curi-man*, used to offer to the coach passengers at Charmouth specimens of *verterberries, mushrooms, ladies' fingers, John Dories,* and *cornumomuses.* Richard Anning sold similar objects at Lyme, having learnt how to find such things by accompanying a Mr. South, who is believed to have been employed by the Duchess of Portland.

From this beginning, Mary Anning, his famous daughter, proceeded to great discoveries, and geology became established as a science. The celebrated Dr. William Buckland, Dean of Westminster, was born at Axminster, and the late Sir Henry De la Beche became a resident at Lyme.

The time of heroic geology abounded with great men, as did that of the Argonauts. The discovery of the Ichthyosaurus, the Plesiosaurus, and other wonderful remains, gave dignity to the science.

The exhibition of pretty sea-side objects, — a fairy purse, an ammonite, or belemnite, with sparkling nodules of iron pyrites coming under the denomination of curiosities, — was deemed to be harmless; but fossils, properly so called, led to questions respecting the Mosaic account of the Creation. Fossilisers, in later years called geologists, — those who found fossils, and talked about what creatures they had once been, — were almost universally viewed in a bad light, as infidels and perverters of the Scripture. Every phenomenon visible on the earth's surface, or at the greatest depth to which man has descended, every vestige of early creation, each example of stratification or deposit, all fossil remains of lizard, fish, or mammal, were set down to the Deluge. Persons of an infidel turn of mind used openly to speak of those who came to seek after fossils as being of their own stamp. The clergy denounced the philosophers.

Can any such an episode in the history of our coast be ever gone over again? Certainly not. The Continent may return its self-banished and ever-grumbling British, who have helped to raise prices nearly to an equality with those of our own country. In that case how many large towns of recent origin or recent extension are ready to receive them, — towns which did not exist or were not revived in the last century? Supposing this to happen, there would be only a repetition, but no novelty. The founding new watering-places and revival of old towns under a new guise — so extensively at least, and so generally — as in the last century, cannot in all its features be repeated. The effects of such a novelty might be traced through many ramifications with important results, if our subject demanded it. The wide spread of refinement has eminently arisen from the watering-place system.

How interesting was it to listen to old persons who were among the early visitors in the infancy of watering-places. The gay and novel scenes that charmed their youth were reproduced, and they grew warm in the praise of early visiting, and the gaieties of the sea-side towns. An octogenarian would break into a lament for the decrease of numbers at the evening assembly, and speak of a revival when numbers should be greater. The truth is, that domestic habits have undergone a change. The mode of life of the first frequenter of our sea-side haunts would be unsuitable to those who live in their own houses, or in those rented by the year. Such persons have their own fireside; they read and take in a newspaper at home. Many do not play either at whist or at a round game. If they require a game at chess, there is a board at home, and more than all, there is a piano to gratify the lover of music.

Hours are changed: in a word, society has appeared under a new phase, and while thus constituted, a return to a former state, when the elements were so different, cannot take place. We are irresistibly carried on to experience new results; to return to old combinations, without the old elements is forbidden. New scenes await us in human life. Such is our destiny.

Watering-places may be divided into two classes: 1., those in which is a circle of visiting, to which presentable people find access; 2., those without any general circle of visiting or society whatever.

This is an important distinction, and great effects result from the operation of either condition. Certain members of the community generally find the one class of watering-place suited; the other unsuited to them. Some desire to be private, some are inadmissible. Both these classes choose a town without a circle: to others, visiting and morning calls, added to a sojourn by the sea-side, render the place very desirable.

This subject might be pursued to some length.

Miscellaneous Reminiscences.

OBSERVE those groups of rustics approaching the church-hatch just as the service is beginning. They walk on and enter the porch. Is not this after the good old plan, as their forefathers did before them? Each is guilty of a great omission was the reply: the former generation, as they approached the fabric all sooner or later, were seen to stoop to untie the strings of their knee-breeches, for without having done so, they could not have knelt during the service. This was a necessary preparation for a seemly performance of the form adopted in the act of public worship, and a manifestation of their readiness to be reverential and observant of the duly-prescribed attitude.

During the service those who carried round the plate for subscriptions to a charity punctiliously avoided handing it to a lady. What is not gained now-a-day by a departure from this partial presentation of the plate? Still, oh ye praisers of the past, was he not an innovator? and what new evil did not the novelty introduce or occasion?

Seventy years ago our countrymen had to endure the pelting of the pitiless storm, whether this was considered to be an evil or not, for there was no *umbrella* in use. Tom Coryat spoke well of this implement a century and a half before its introduction into this country. Continental nations used the umbrella, and Jonas Hanway, the philanthropist, dared ridicule by publicly carrying one. In many country towns the introduction of the first umbrella was long remembered: the occasion was a memorable one. Many never would shelter themselves under so coxcombical, so unmanly a novelty, but streamed with rain, to the injury of their health, as they were accustomed of old. All now embrace an opportunity of sheltering themselves under what the croakers prognosticated a hurtful thing, which would stop the circulation of air through the streets. Dr. Jamieson first used an umbrella in Glasgow in 1782. Sangster has made an interesting little book upon the history of this article.

Forty years ago, when daylight was about to be succeeded by darkness, on occasions of any alarm or expected danger the first care of housewives was to look well to their flint and steel, so as to have the means of striking light readily if wanted in the night season. Now Lucifer matches, and various contrivances for producing instantaneous light, have superseded the flint and steel. The trampers' occupation at the "lodging house" in making matches, by cutting up deal wood and dipping the thin slips in brimstone, is gone. The beggar's appeal began with, "Please to buy a penny'th of matches."

Who now hears mention made of a Double Horse — a strong, steady animal, with a pillion behind the saddle for ladies?

Upping stocks and horse blocks were necessary when double horses were in use.

Etiquette required, so late as the year 1773, that fashion

ables should put on a new pair of gloves at every new dance. This made it convenient to have a table covered with gloves for sale in a ball-room. See what Burke says in his "Anecdotes of the Aristocracy" respecting W. M'Clellan, Lord Kircudbright.

The inclosure and cultivation of the Black Down range of hills, on the greensand formation of the geologist, causes the dark fruit, the Whortleberry (*Vaccinium*) to be brought about in less abundance than formerly. The fruit is now used for dyeing in the north of England. During the *Whort-season* children used to assemble to partake of *Whort-pies* made by the landlord of the Black Dog public house, Uplyme. Whort-pies made with a brown crust, and eaten with clouted cream, are a west country delicacy. Pies, pilchard, and various other kinds, are almost a characteristic of Cornwall.

Poachers always abounded. Severe laws were framed against them by kings and nobles; bishops excommunicated them by the greater excommunication by bell, book, and candle.

Setting dogs, for the taking partridges with nets, were cried down by proclamation in 1634, as that game was nearly destroyed. Our ancestors eat game at all seasons of the year.

When persons visited remarkable spots, such as the leads of great buildings, they followed an absurd custom of leaving an imprint of their foot there. Great men were, like the Duke of Buckingham at King's College Chapel, Cambridge, solicited to leave an imprint behind them.

When heralds went round the country boroughs in the reign of James I., they required corporations to show their charters and liberties. These and both seals were to be shown to the heralds at Wells, August 23rd, 1622, and 40*s.* to be paid to them.*

Great coats are no longer necessary for great numbers of persons, not that the seasons are less severe, but that per-

* Corporate Records of Wells City. Notes and Queries, No. 284.

sons travel by rail under cover. Whole factories are closed in the west that made double milled or great coat cloth.

The Roman amphitheatre Mambury, near the railway station at Dorchester, was the scene of a dreadful execution, March 21. 1705.

A person named Channing had murdered her husband; for which she was, according to her sentence, burnt in the middle of the area, having been first strangled. It has been said that 10,000 persons were present, like the ancient Romans seated round the slope of the earthwork.

Tradition reports that a woman named Hall was burnt there Dec. 31. 1660.*

Long flaxen hair was bought from the head at 10*s.* the ounce, and any other fine hair at 5*s.* or 7*s.* the ounce in 1662.

Within the present century the heads of hair of whole families in Devonshire were let out by the year at so much rent per poll. An Exeter perriwig maker went round periodically, cut the locks, and oiled the numskull of each thus left in stubble.

Rook shooting is, in the southern counties, followed by rook pie, which is esteemed as a delicacy. In some parts of England the rook is looked upon much as the Germans call it, "the crow with the white bill;" and who would eat a "carrion crow?"

A north country judge having, at a southern assize, heard several witnesses speak to a conversation at table, where the principal party, an old man, partook of rook-pie, which was intended to be conclusive as to the season of the year, he conceived that this pie was improper and unusual food given to the old person by way of sport. The learned judge, in his address to the jury, commented, in warm terms, upon the disgusting food that had been set before the old man; and was surprised at being informed that rook pie, composed of the wings, legs, and breast, with a beef steak at the bottom

* See Hutchins's Dorset

of the dish, was partaken of with great delight in the south of England as a delicacy of the month of May.

Apropos of delicacies, the wardon pie was not filled with venison, as is so often said, but with wardon pears.

Those infected with the poultry mania will be interested in learning that ducks used to be marked as swans now are. A man was presented at Seaford, by a jury, for marking three ducks with his own mark and cutting out the owner's marks.*

The comparative profit of employing horses or oxen in agriculture has been the subject of discussion of late years, though now settled in favour of the former. The Cistercian monks were large farmers. In the reign of Henry III. A. D. 1216, about fifteen times as many oxen were kept for ploughing as there were of horses.

Peat grew where there is now some of the best land.

There were tide mills when Doomsday-book was compiled. Windmills were first mentioned by Joceline de Brakelonde in his Chronicle, about the year 1190. Fulling mills were erected about the 14th century.

We have alluded to insurance, the provident union of the many to provide against a casualty falling upon one of their number, which is a proof of society having greatly advanced.

The first life assurance company was established by the Mercers' Company in 1698.

* 25 Eliz.

INDEX.

A.

B.

C.

D.

E.

F.

G.

N.

O.

P.

Q.

R.

S.

T.

U.

V.

W.

Y.

Lightning Source UK Ltd.
Milton Keynes UK
UKHW031831161120
373493UK00009B/2001